ECONOMICS TODAY

First Canadian Edition

THE MACRO VIEW

Roger LeRoy Miller

Institute for University Studies, Arlington, Texas

Nancy W. Clegg

Kwantlen University College, B.C.

Addison-Wesley

An imprint of Addison Wesley Longman Ltd.

Don Mills, Ontario • Reading, Massachusetts • Harlow, England
Melbourne, Australia • Amsterdam, The Netherlands • Bonn, Germany

To David, Chris, Gillian, and Alex,
for their support and endless patience over my 'booking.'

N.W.C.

Photo Credits
Page 3, J. L. Pelaez/First Light; page 20, First Light; page 50, L.Redkoles/B. Bennett Studios; page 81, Jean-Marc Biboux/Gamma Liaison; page 105, courtesy of H&R Block Inc.; page 135, Martin Rogers/Stock, Boston; page 163, First Light; page 189, © Mark Antman/The Image Works; page 216, Reuters/Bobby Yip/Archives; page 239, Reuters/Bettmann; page 263, G. Merillon/Gamma; page 283, Barry Brooks/Image Network Inc.; page 317, © Corel Corporation; page 342, Jim Young/Reuters; page 367, *The Hamilton Spectator*; page 384, Ian Lindsay/*Vancouver Sun*; page 410, © Corel Corporation; page 437, courtesy of the Bank of Canada; page 465, © Corel Corporation; page 486, © Jeff Greenberg/The Picture Cube; page 511, Sanguinetti/Monkmeyer.

The publishers will gladly receive information enabling them to rectify any errors in references or credits.

Publisher: Ron Doleman
Managing Editor: Linda Scott
Editor: Muriel Fiona Napier
Proofreader: Gail Copeland
Cover Design: Anthony Leung
Page Design and Layout: Anthony Leung
Production Coordinator: Alexandra Odulak
Manufacturing Coordinator: Sharon Latta Paterson
Printing and Binding: Bryant Press

Canadian Cataloguing in Publication Data

Miller, Roger LeRoy
        Economics today: the macro view

1st Canadian ed.
Includes index.
ISBN 0-201-38934-7

1. Macroeconomics. 2. Economics. I. Clegg, Nancy W., 1949- . II. Title.

HB172.5.M54 1999   339   C99-930526-3

ISBN 0-201-38934-7

Printed and bound in Canada.

B C D E -BP - 03 02 01 00

CONTENTS IN BRIEF

CONTENTS IN DETAIL

PREFACE

FROM THE AUTHOR

When Addison-Wesley asked if I would be interested in adapting Roger LeRoy Miller's *Economics Today* for use in Canada, I was hesitant. I thought, "Why add another principles book to a market that already has several suitable texts?" But when I looked through Miller's ninth edition, I saw immediately why it had survived so long, and been so popular in the American market. *Economics Today* presents economic principles in a straightforward, intuitive manner which is both relevant to, and readily accessible by, introductory economics students.

In this first Canadian edition of *Economics Today*, I have combined the proven approach of the US text with a thorough Canadianization of the material. Issues and applications are the strength of this text. Each chapter begins with an issue that requires a knowledge of certain economic principles to understand; those principles are presented throughout the chapter, and at the end of the chapter an "Issues and Applications" section appears. Two "For Critical Analysis" questions follow, which help reinforce the theory at hand and encourage students to reflect on economics in the "real" world—their world. In addition, each chapter contains several examples, or "mini-issues," which illustrate the points being made in the text. And I have not ignored the effect of the media on our thinking. "Thinking Critically About the Media" boxes in each chapter look carefully at media reports, and what the real economics of the reportage suggest.

At the same time, I have been mindful of Canada's reliance on global events for our economic well-being. I have therefore used many examples and issues which connect Canada with the rest of the world. In keeping with today's "wired world" I have incorporated Internet applications into many of the chapters, and have provided problems for students to solve using the Internet.

Over the years I have found that more of my principles students are heading for degrees in business than in economics. In recognition of this trend, the accompanying Study Guide includes a "Business Section" in each chapter, providing Business Applications and problems that apply economic theory to accounting, marketing, finance, management, small business, and entrepreneurship.

The complete *Economics Today* package makes economics interesting and relevant to principles students. Whether those students are headed for the more academic world of economics or the practical world of business, or are just interested in the way our economy works, *Economics Today* helps them to see today's economics as a part of their lives.

ECONOMIC PRINCIPLES IN PRACTICE

Chapter Opening Issues. Each opening issue motivates student interest in the key chapter concepts. The issue presented is revisited in the "Issues and Applications" section at the culmination of the chapter.

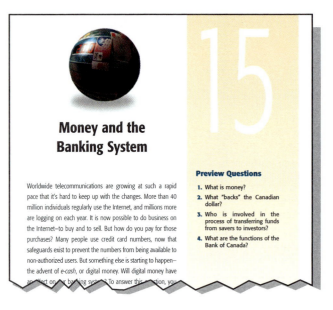

Money and the Banking System

Worldwide telecommunications are growing at such a rapid pace that it's hard to keep up with the changes. More than 40 million individuals regularly use the Internet, and millions more are logging on each year. It is now possible to do business on the Internet—to buy and to sell. But how do you pay for those purchases? Many people use credit card numbers, now that safeguards exist to prevent the numbers from being available to non-authorized users. But something else is starting to happen—the advent of *e-cash*, or digital money. Will digital money have an effect on our banking system? To answer this question, you

Preview Questions

1. What is money?
2. What "backs" the Canadian dollar?
3. Who is involved in the process of transferring funds from savers to investors?
4. What are the functions of the Bank of Canada?

Issues and Applications. The "Issues and Applications" feature is designed to encourage students not just to apply economic concepts, but also to think critically about them. Each begins with the concepts being applied in this instance, and is followed by two "For Critical Analysis" questions that could be used to prompt in-class discussions. Suggested answers to these questions are given at the back of the text (p. 543), as

well as in the Instructor's Manual along with the relevant chapter.

Thinking Critically About the Media.
These boxed items keep students abreast of recent newsmaking issues, while at the same time offering a "twist" on typical media coverage. They encourage students to think critically about, rather than simply accept, what they hear and read in the news.

Policy Examples.
Many of the economic debates reported in the media involve important policy issues. Here, students are presented with various key policy questions on both the domestic and international fronts. Each "Policy Example" and "International Policy Example" is followed by a "For Critical Analysis" question that encourages students to consider exactly what is involved in the discussion, and what the further ramifi-

cations might be. Suggested solutions to these questions are provided in the Instructor's Manual, at the end of the appropriate chapter. In addition, students will find hints and suggested answers with each chapter in the Study Guide.

A World of Global Examples.
International examples emphasize today's global economy. The issues presented in them, and the "For Critical Analysis" question which follows each, help students to understand the worldwide economy and Canada's place in it. Suggested answers to the questions are given in the Instructor's Manual and in the Study Guide.

Examples Closer to Home.
Many thought-provoking and relevant examples highlight Canadian events and demonstrate economic principles. "For Critical Analysis" questions with each encourage students to apply the knowledge and information gained from the example. Possible answers to the questions are provided in the Instructor's Manual and in the Study Guide.

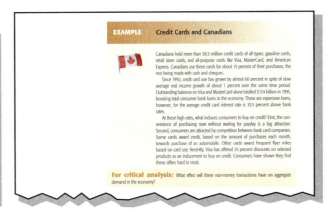

Interacting with the Internet.
At the end of many chapters, World Wide Web sites where students can find further information are given.

As well, an Internet-related exercise is included in the end-of-chapter problem set, requiring students to use the Internet to find economic information.

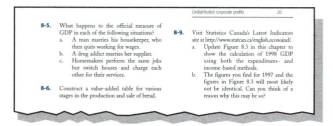

www.econtoday.com. The *Economics Today* Web site provides on-line access to innovative teaching and learning tools.

PEDAGOGY WITH A PURPOSE

This first Canadian edition of *Economics Today* is loaded with the same time-tested pedagogy of Roger LeRoy Miller's successful US text. It helps students *apply* what they learn.

For Critical Analysis. At the end of each example, students are asked to reflect on real-world problems by answering "For Critical Analysis" questions. The answers to the questions are found as follows:
- Issues and Applications—at the end of the student text (p. 543)
- Examples, International Examples, Policy Examples, International Policy Examples—in the student Study Guide, at the end of the relevant chapter
- All "For Critical Analysis" questions (i.e., all of the above)—in the Instructor's Manual, along with the appropriate chapter

Did You Know That ...? Each chapter starts with a provocative question to engage students' interest and lead them into the content of the chapter.

Preview Questions. On the first page of each chapter, several questions are posed, giving purpose and focus for the chapter. These are then fully answered at the end of the chapter. Students are also directed to try answering the preview questions as the topic of each is covered in the text.

Graphs. Articulate and precise, the four-colour graphs illustrate key concepts.

Key Terms. Key terms are printed in bold type, and are defined in the margin of the text the first time they appear. These terms are also reproduced alphabetically in the Glossary at the end of the text (p. 549).

Concepts in Brief. At the end of each major section in each chapter, "Concepts in Brief" summarizes the main points, thus reinforcing students' knowledge as well as testing their learning.

Chapter Summary. Every chapter ends with a concise but thorough summary of the important ideas of the chapter.

Problems. A variety of problems support each chapter, and answers for all odd-numbered problems are provided at the back of the textbook. The complete set of problem answers (both even- and odd-numbered) appears in the Instructor's Manual.

TEACHING/LEARNING PACKAGE

For the Instructor

Instructor's Manual. The Instructor's Manual has been adapted by author Nancy Clegg for this first Canadian edition of *Economics Today*. Features include:
- Chapter overviews, objectives, and outlines
- Points to emphasize, including more theoretical issues for those who wish to stress theory
- Suggested questions for further class discussion

- Answers to the "For Critical Analysis" questions that follow each example in the chapter
- Answers, with detailed step-by-step solutions, to all end-of-chapter problems
- Selected references

www.econtoday.com. The *Economics Today* Web site provides on-line access to innovative teaching and learning tools.

Test Bank. The test bank contains over 1300 multiple-choice questions with answers. The test bank has been adapted by Brenda Abbott.

For the Student

Study Guide. Available in Micro and Macro versions, the Study Guides have been adapted by Sam Fefferman and Brenda Abbott of the Northern Alberta Institute of Technology in Edmonton. Each includes the following:
- Putting the chapter into perspective

- Learning objectives
- Chapter outlines
- Key terms
- Key concepts
- Completion questions
- True-or-false questions
- Multiple-choice questions
- Matching questions
- Problems
- A Business Section, giving applications and problems that relate to economic theory in accounting, marketing, finance, management, small business, and entrepreneurship
- Answers to the problems and questions that are included in the Study Guide
- Hints or answers to the "For Critical Analysis" questions that follow examples in the textbook
- Glossary of terms, defined exactly as in the textbook

www.econtoday.com. The *Economics Today* Web site is designed for the US edition of the text, but contains many features that are of interest and use to Canadian students.

ACKNOWLEDGEMENTS

No author can adapt a principles text without the assistance of others. I have been helped by a hard-working and supportive group at Addison-Wesley. Linda Scott, my Managing Editor, provided assistance in all aspects of this project. My Publisher, Ron Doleman, helped me make decisions about the direction the text should take and provided unending encouragement and confidence in my abilities throughout. My Copy Editor, Muriel Fiona Napier, kept me on task and worked miracles with my prose, and became a good friend in the process. To all these Addison-Wesley team members—including Brian Henderson who initiated the project originally—thank you, and I look forward to working with you again.

I would also like to thank the following professors who helped with the development of this text by offering me their insightful comments and constructive criticisms.

Terri Anderson, *Fanshawe College*
Walter Behnke, *Vancouver Community College*
Tom Chambers, *Canadore College*
Wendy Cornwall, *Mount St. Vincent University*
Victoria Digby, *Fanshawe College*
Peter Fortura, *Algonquin College*

Bill Gallivan, *University College of Cape Breton*
Kevin Gillis, *Mount Royal College*
Carl Graham, *Assiniboine Community College*
James Hnatchuk, *Champlain-Ste. Lambert College*
Lionel Ifill, *Algonquin College*
Ernie Jacobson, *Northern Alberta Institute of Technology*
Robert L. Jeacock, *Malaspina University College*
Cheryl Jenkins, *John Abbott College*
Susan Kamp, *University of Alberta*
Joe Luchetti, *Sault College*
Bill Luxton, *Southern Alberta Institute of Technology*
John Newark, *Athabasca University*
Victor Olshevski, *University of Winnipeg*
David R. Sabiston, *Laurentian University*
Lance Shandler, *Kwantlen University College*
William Sinkevitch, *St. Clair College*
Judith Skuce, *Georgian College*
Campion Swartout, *SIAST-Palliser Institute*

In keeping with the cyberage, and because I would appreciate suggestions about what to do in future editions, you and your students can contact me via the *Economics Today* Web site at: **www.econtoday.com**.

Nancy W. Clegg

PART 1
Introduction

Chapter 1

The Nature of Economics

Chapter 2

Scarcity and the World of Trade-Offs

Appendix A

Reading and Working with Graphs

Chapter 3

Demand and Supply

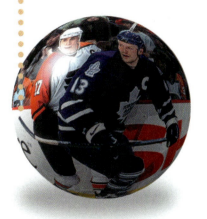

Chapter 4

Extensions of Demand and Supply Analysis

Chapter 5

The Public Sector

Chapter 6

Economies in Transition

The Nature of Economics

For most people, choosing a spouse has never been an inexpensive or easy activity. Not long ago, some people were arguing that the institution of marriage was dying. Nevertheless, over 85 percent of Canadians making up family units are legally married. Spouse selection is clearly an activity that most people eventually choose to engage in. A variety of considerations are involved. For example, the ease or difficulty of obtaining a divorce may have an effect on how spouses are chosen; so may the factor called love. Is there a rational, economic reason why individuals prefer a marriage in which there is mutual love? To answer this question, you need to know about the nature of economics.

Preview Questions

1. What is the difference between microeconomics and macroeconomics?

2. What role does rational self-interest play in economic analysis?

3. Why is the study of economics a science?

4. What is the difference between positive and normative economics?

Did You Know That... between 1987 and 1997, the number of fax machines in Canadian offices and homes increased by over 10,000 percent? During the same time period, the number of bike messengers in downtown Toronto *decreased* by over 50 percent. The world around us is definitely changing. Much of that change is due to the dramatically falling cost of communications and information technology. In the late 1990s, the computers inside video games cost only a few hundred dollars, yet had 50 times the processing power that a US$10 million IBM mainframe had in 1975. It's not surprising that since the start of the 1990s, Canadian firms have been spending more on communications equipment and computers than on new construction and heavy machinery.

Cyberspace, the information superhighway—call it what you want, but your next home (if not your current one) will almost certainly have an electronic address on it. Close to 100 percent of Canadian households have at least one telephone, and more than 80 percent have video recorders. Almost 30 percent of homes have personal computers, and about half of those machines are set up to send and receive information via phone lines. Your decisions about such things as when and what type of computer to buy, whether to accept a collect call from a friend travelling in Europe, and how much time you should invest in learning to use a new multimedia system involve an untold number of variables: where you live, the work your parents do, what your friends think, and so on. But, as you will see, there are economic underpinnings for nearly all the decisions you make.

THE POWER OF ECONOMIC ANALYSIS

Knowing that an economic problem exists every time you make a decision is not enough. You also have to develop a framework that will allow you to analyse solutions to each economic problem—whether you are trying to decide how much to study, which courses to take, if you should finish school, or if Canada should send peacekeeping troops abroad or raise tariffs. The framework that you will learn in this text is based on the *economic way of thinking*.

This framework gives you power—the power to reach informed conclusions about what is happening in the world. You can, of course, live your life without the power of economic analysis as part of your analytical framework. Indeed, many people do. But economists believe that economic analysis can help you make better decisions concerning your career, your education, financing your home, and other important issues. In the business world, the power of economic analysis can help you increase your competitive edge as an employee or as the owner of a business. As a voter, for the rest of your life you will be asked to make judgments about the policies advocated by a particular political party. Many of these policies will deal with questions related to international economics, such as whether the Canadian government should encourage or discourage immigration, prevent foreigners from investing in domestic TV stations and newspapers, or restrict other countries from selling their goods here. Finally, just as taking an art, music, or literature appreciation class increases the pleasure you receive when you view paintings, listen to concerts, or read novels, taking an economics course will increase your understanding when watching the news on TV, listening to it on radio, or reading the newspapers.

DEFINING ECONOMICS

What is economics exactly? Some cynics have defined *economics* as "common sense made difficult." But common sense, by definition, is within everyone's grasp. In the following pages you will encounter numerous examples which show that economics is, in fact, pure and simple common sense.

▶ **Economics**
The study of how people allocate their limited resources to satisfy their unlimited wants.

Economics is one of the social sciences, and as such seeks explanations of real events. All social sciences analyse human behaviour. The physical sciences, on the other hand, generally analyse the behaviour of electrons, atoms, and other nonhuman phenomena.

Economics is the study of how people allocate their limited resources in an attempt to satisfy their unlimited wants. As such, economics is the study of how people make choices.

▶ **Resources**
Things used to produce other things to satisfy people's wants.

▶ **Wants**
What people would buy if their incomes were unlimited.

To understand this definition fully, two other words need explaining: *resources* and *wants*. **Resources** are things that have value and, more specifically, are used to produce other things that satisfy people's wants. **Wants** are all of the things that people would consume if they had unlimited income.

Whenever an individual, a business, or a nation faces alternatives, a choice must be made, and economics helps us study how those choices are made. For example, you have to choose how to spend your limited income. You also have to choose how to spend your limited time. You may have to choose how much of your company's limited funds to spend on advertising and how much to spend on new-product research. In economics, we examine situations in which individuals choose how to do things, when to do things, and with whom to do them. Ultimately, the purpose of economics is to explain choices.

MICROECONOMICS VERSUS MACROECONOMICS

Economics is typically divided into two types of analysis: **microeconomics** and **macroeconomics**.

▶ **Microeconomics**
The study of decision making undertaken by individuals (or households) and by firms.

Microeconomics is the part of economic analysis that studies decision making undertaken by individuals (or households) and by firms. It is like looking through a microscope to focus on the small parts of our economy.

▶ **Macroeconomics**
The study of the behaviour of the economy as a whole, including such economy-wide phenomena as changes in unemployment, the general price level, and national income.

Macroeconomics is the part of economic analysis that studies the behaviour of the economy as a whole. It deals with economy-wide phenomena such as changes in unemployment, the general price level, and national income.

Try Preview Question 1:

What is the difference between microeconomics and macroeconomics?

Microeconomic analysis, for example, is concerned with the effects of changes in the price of gasoline relative to that of other energy sources. It examines the effects of new taxes on a specific product or industry. If price controls were to be re-instituted in Canada, how individual firms and consumers would react to them would be in the realm of microeconomics. The raising of wages by an effective union strike would also be analysed using the tools of microeconomics.

By contrast, issues such as the rate of inflation, the amount of economy-wide unemployment, and the yearly growth in the output of goods and services in the nation all fall into the domain of macroeconomic analysis. In other words, macroeconomics deals with **aggregates**, or totals—such as total output in an economy.

▶ **Aggregates**

Total amounts or quantities; aggregate demand, for example, is total planned expenditures throughout a nation.

Be aware, however, of the blending of microeconomics and macroeconomics in modern economic theory. Modern economists are increasingly using microeconomic analysis—the study of decision making by individuals and by firms—as the basis of macroeconomic analysis. They do this because even though in macroeconomic analysis aggregates are being examined, those aggregates are made up of individuals and firms.

THE ECONOMIC PERSON: RATIONAL SELF-INTEREST

Economists assume that individuals act as *if* motivated by self-interest and respond predictably to opportunities for gain. This central insight of economics was first clearly articulated by Adam Smith in 1776. Smith wrote in his most famous book, *An Inquiry into the Nature and Causes of the Wealth of Nations*, that "it is not from the benevolence of the butcher, the brewer, or the baker that we expect our dinner, but from their regard to their own interest." Otherwise stated, the typical person about whom economists make behavioural predictions is assumed to look out for his or her own self-interest in a rational manner. Because monetary benefits and costs of actions are often the most easily measured, economists most often make behavioural predictions about individuals' responses to ways to increase their wealth, measured in money terms. Let's see if we can apply the theory of rational self-interest to explain an anomaly concerning the makeup of a small town in northeastern British Columbia.

Try Preview Question 2:

What role does rational self-interest play in economic analysis?

EXAMPLE	Atlantic Migration to British Columbia

Fort Nelson is a small town in northern British Columbia, near the Alberta border. In recent years the proportion of residents who were born in Atlantic Canada has grown to around 40 percent. Can we use Adam Smith's ideas to understand why so many people from Atlantic Canada have decided to move west? Perhaps.

Consider the economic conditions in Newfoundland and the other Atlantic provinces. Unemployment is high and hopes for a rapid recovery of the cod fishery are low. Look at Figure 1.1 to see the rate of migration to and from Newfoundland since 1972. Notice that the rate of outmigration has increased rapidly since closure of the cod fishery. Now also consider the economic conditions in Fort Nelson. The town is booming with jobs in forestry, mining, and the service sector. While many people from southern British Columbia are reluctant to

Figure 1.1
Net Migration to and from Newfoundland, 1972–1996

Newfoundland has had more people leave than enter in all but four of the past 24 years. This would suggest that there is something pulling people away to other parts of Canada or the world.

Source: CANSIM University Base. Statistics Canada Series C103456

move to the north, the prospect of steady work in a mill at a starting wage of $12 per hour provides a strong incentive for an unemployed Newfoundlander to move 6,000 kilometres west. The drive for economic well-being explains the Atlantic migration to northern British Columbia.

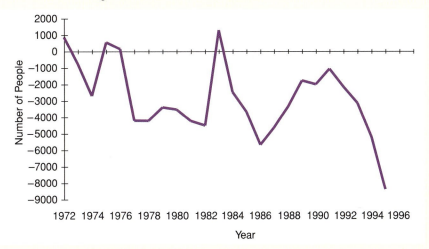

For critical analysis: What nonmonetary reasons are there for people from the Atlantic provinces to move to Fort Nelson?

The Rationality Assumption

▶ **Rationality assumption**
The assumption that people do not intentionally make decisions that would leave them worse off.

The **rationality assumption** of economics, simply stated, is as follows:

> We assume that individuals do not intentionally make decisions that would leave them worse off.

The distinction here is between what people may think—the realm of psychology and psychiatry and perhaps sociology—and what they do. Economics does *not* involve itself in analysing individual or group thought processes. Economics looks at what people actually do in life with their limited resources. It does little good to criticize the rationality assumption by stating, "Nobody thinks that way" or "I never think that way" or "How unrealistic! That's as irrational as anyone can get!"

Take the example of driving. When you consider passing another car on a two-lane highway with oncoming traffic, you have to make very quick decisions: You must estimate the speed of the car you are going to pass, the speed of the oncoming cars, the distance between your car and the oncoming cars, and your car's potential rate of acceleration. If we were to apply a model to your behaviour, we would use the laws of calculus. In actual fact, you and most other drivers in such a situation do not actually think of using the laws of calculus, but we could predict your behaviour *as if* you understood the laws of calculus.

In any event, when you observe behaviour around you, what may seem irrational often has its basis in the rationality assumption, as you can see by the following example.

When It Is Rational *Not* to Learn New Technology

The standard young person's view of older people is that they're reluctant to learn new things. The saying "You can't teach an old dog new tricks" seems to apply. Young people, in contrast, seem eager to learn about new technology–mastering computers and multimedia, playing interactive games, cruising the information superhighway. But there is a rational reason for older people's reduced willingness to learn new technologies. If you are 20 years old and learn a new skill, you will be able to gain returns from your investment in learning over the course of many decades. If you are 60, however, and invest the same amount of time and effort learning the same skill, you will almost certainly not be able to reap those returns for as long a time period. Hence it is perfectly rational for "old dogs" not to want to learn new tricks.

For critical analysis: Some older people do learn to use new technologies as they emerge. What might explain this behaviour?

Responding to Incentives

If it can be assumed that individuals never intentionally make decisions that would leave them worse off, then almost by definition they will respond to different incentives. We define **incentives** as the potential rewards available if a particular activity is undertaken. Indeed, much of human behaviour can be explained in terms of how individuals respond to changing incentives over time.

▶ **Incentives**

Things that encourage us to engage in a particular activity.

School students are motivated to do better by a variety of incentive systems, ranging from gold stars and certificates of achievement when they are young, to bet-

INTERNATIONAL EXAMPLE
Why Are There So Many Brush Fires in Corsica?

Corsica is a Mediterranean French island about 1.5 times the size of Prince Edward Island. Every summer, 10,000 to 40,000 acres of Corsican brush go up in flames. As many as 37 brush fires have been reported on a single day. One might attribute the prevalence of brush fires to the island's physical differences from other European locations, but that is not the explanation. Rather, the European Union (EU) has provided an incentive for some Corsicans to set brush fires deliberately. Most Corsican cattle are left to roam freely on common land, and when brush is burned, more grazing land becomes available. Corsicans who claim that they tend at least 100 head of cattle receive a "suckling cow premium" from the EU, equal to more than US$2,000 a month. The large number of brush fires on the island of Corsica is no accident.

For critical analysis: The average cow in Europe is three years old before she gives birth, whereas in Corsica the average age is a year and a half. Why do you think Corsicans breed their cows earlier than other Europeans?

ter grades with accompanying promises of a "better life" as they get older. There are, of course, negative incentives that affect our behaviour, too. Students who disrupt the class are given after-school detentions or sent to the vice-principal for other punishment.

Implicitly, people react to changing incentives after they have done some sort of rough comparison of the costs and benefits of various courses of action. In fact, making rational choices invariably involves balancing costs and benefits.

The linked concepts of incentive and costs and benefits can be used to explain seeming anomalies in the world around us.

Defining Self-Interest

Self-interest does not always mean increasing one's wealth as measured in dollars and cents. We assume that individuals seek many goals, not just increased monetary wealth. Thus the self-interest part of our economic-person assumption includes goals relating to prestige, friendship, love, power, helping others, creating works of art, and many other matters. We can also think in terms of enlightened self-interest, whereby individuals in the pursuit of what makes them better off also achieve the betterment of others around them. In brief, individuals are assumed to want the right to further their goals by making decisions about how things around them are used.

Otherwise stated, charitable acts are not ruled out by self-interest. The giving of gifts can be considered a form of charity that is nonetheless in the self-interest of the giver. But how efficient is such gift giving?

EXAMPLE *Katimavik*—Combining Self-Interest and Charity

Katimavik, Inuit for "meeting place," is a community service agency which operated from 1977 until 1986, and has recently been revived. The agency sends young people between the ages of 17 and 21 out into communities across Canada to work in locally sponsored jobs. These may take various forms: clearing trails in municipal parks, helping out in daycare centres, assisting seniors as required, and so on. The pay is low: Human Resources Development Canada pays for travel, lodgings, and food, and in addition volunteers are paid $3 per day. At the end of their seven-and-a-half month tour, they receive a further $1,000.

So why did 230 young Canadians choose to volunteer in 1995? Because they wanted to gain practical skills and job experience which would benefit them later. The volunteers, in following their own self-interest, nevertheless gave to the communities in which they worked. Self-interest and charity combine forces in *Katimavik*.

For critical analysis: What do you think would happen to the number of volunteers for *Katimavik* if the daily allowance and final remuneration were eliminated?

Concepts in Brief

- Economics is a social science that involves the study of how individuals choose among alternatives to satisfy their wants.
- Wants are what people would buy if their incomes were unlimited.
- Microeconomics, the study of the decision-making processes of individuals (or households) and firms, and macroeconomics, the study of the performance of the economy as a whole, are the two main branches into which the study of economics is divided.
- In economics, we assume that people do not intentionally make decisions that will leave them worse off. This is known as the rationality assumption.
- Self-interest is not confined to material well-being but also involves any action that makes a person feel better off, such as having more friends, love, power, affection, or providing more help to others.

ECONOMICS AS A SCIENCE

Economics is a social science that makes use of the same kinds of methods used in other sciences such as biology, physics, and chemistry. Similar to these other sciences, economics uses **models**, or **theories**. Economic models, or theories, are simplified representations of the real world that we use to help us understand, explain, and predict economic phenomena in the real world. There are, of course, differences between sciences. The social sciences—especially economics—make little use of laboratory methods in which changes in variables can be explained under controlled conditions. Rather, social scientists, and especially economists, usually have to examine what has already happened in the real world in order to test their models, or theories.

▶ **Models, or theories**

Simplified representations of the real world used as the basis for predictions or explanations.

Models and Realism

At the outset it must be emphasized that no model in *any* science, and therefore no economic model, is complete in the sense that it captures *every* detail or interrelationship that exists. Indeed, a model, by definition, is an abstraction from reality. It is conceptually impossible to construct a perfectly complete realistic model. For example, in physics we cannot account for every molecule and its position, nor for every atom and subparticle. Not only would such a model be prohibitively expensive to build, but also working with it would be impossibly complex.

The nature of scientific model building is such that the model should capture only the essential relationships that are sufficient to analyse the particular problem or answer the particular question with which we are concerned. *An economic model cannot be faulted as unrealistic simply because it does not represent every detail of the real world.* A map of a city that shows only major streets is not necessarily unrealistic if, in fact, all you need to know is how to pass through the city using major streets. As long as a model is realistic in terms of shedding light on the *central* issue at hand or forces at work, it may be useful.

Try Preview Question 3:

Why is the study of economics a science?

A map is the basic model. It is always a simplified representation, always unrealistic. But it is also useful in making (refutable) predictions about the world. If the model—the map—predicts that when you take Campus Avenue to the north, you always reach the campus, that is a (refutable) prediction. If our goal is to explain observed behaviour, the simplicity or complexity of the model we use is irrelevant. If a simple model can explain observed behaviour in repeated settings just as well as a complex one, the simple model has some value and is probably easier to use.

Assumptions

Every model, or theory, must be based on a set of assumptions. Assumptions define the set of circumstances in which our model is most likely to be applicable. When scientists predicted that sailing ships would fall off the edge of the earth, they used the *assumption* that the earth was flat. Columbus did not accept the implications of such a model. He assumed that the world was round. The real-world test of his own model refuted the flat-earth model. Indirectly, then, it was a test of the assumption of the flat-earth model.

Thinking Critically About the Media   Cancer and Smoking

You read it in the newspaper and hear about it on TV—smoking imposes higher costs on all Canadians. The Canadian Cancer Society has convinced the media that smoking is costly due to patients' lengthy hospital stays for treatment of lung cancer and other smoking-related diseases. As a result, life insurance premiums go up. But we also have to look at the other side of the ledger. Premature death due to smoking saves Canadians millions of dollars in pension and medical payments, as well as millions of dollars in nursing home expenses. All things considered, according to economist Jean-Pierre Vidal, smoking does not impose higher costs on all Canadians. (That does not, to be sure, mean that we should encourage more smoking!)

EXAMPLE   Getting Directions

Assumptions are a shorthand for reality. Imagine that you have decided to drive from your home in Windsor to downtown Toronto. Because you have never driven this route, you decide to get directions from the local office of the Canadian Automobile Association (CAA).

When you ask for directions, the travel planner could give you a set of detailed maps showing each city on the way—London, Woodstock, Kitchener, Cambridge, Mississauga, and so on—and then, opening each map, show you exactly how the freeway threads by each of these cities. You would get a nearly complete description of reality because the CAA travel planner will not have used many simplifying assumptions. It is more likely, however, that the travel planner will simply say, "Get on Highway 401 going east. Stay on it for about 400 kilometres. Follow the signs for Toronto. Take any exit marked 'Downtown.'" By omitting all of the trivial details, the travel planner has told you all that you really need and want to know. The models you will be using in this text are similar to the simplified directions on how to drive from Windsor to Toronto—they focus on what is relevant to the problem at hand and omit what is not.

For critical analysis: In what way do small talk and gossip represent the use of simplifying assumptions?

The Ceteris Paribus Assumption: All Other Things Being Equal.

Everything in the world seems to relate in some way to everything else in the world. It would be impossible to isolate the effects of changes in one variable on another variable if we always had to worry about the many additional variables that might also enter the analysis. As in other sciences, economics uses the ***ceteris paribus assumption***. *Ceteris paribus* means "other things constant" or "other things equal."

Consider an example taken from economics. One of the most important determinants of how much of a particular product a family buys is how expensive that product is relative to other products. We know that in addition to relative prices, other factors influence decisions about making purchases. Some of them have to do with income, others with tastes, and yet others with custom and religious beliefs. Whatever these other factors are, we hold them constant when we look at the relationship between changes in prices and changes in how much of a given product people will purchase.

Deciding on the Usefulness of a Model

We generally do not attempt to determine the usefulness, or "goodness," of a model merely by evaluating how realistic its assumptions are. Rather, we consider a model good if it yields usable predictions and implications for the real world. In other words, can we use the model to predict what will happen in the world around us? Does the model provide useful implications as to how things happen in our world?

Once we have determined that the model does predict real-world phenomena, the scientific approach to the analysis of the world around us requires that we consider evidence. Evidence is used to test the usefulness of a model. This is why we call economics an **empirical** science, *empirical* meaning that evidence (data) is looked at to see whether we are right. Economists are often engaged in empirically testing their models.

Consider two competing models for the way students act when doing complicated probability problems to choose the best gambles. One model predicts that, based on the assumption of rational self-interest, students who are paid more for better performance will in fact perform better on average during the experiment. A competing model might be that students whose last names start with the letters A through L will do better than students with last names starting with M through Z, irrespective of how much they are paid. The model that consistently predicts more accurately is the model that we would normally choose. In this example, the "alphabet" model did not work well: The first letter of the last name of the students who actually did the experiment was irrelevant in predicting how well they would perform the mathematical calculations necessary to choose the correct gambles. The model based on rational self-interest predicted well, in contrast.

Models of Behaviour, Not Thought Processes

Take special note of the fact that economists' models do not relate to the way people *think*; they relate to the way people *act*, to what they do in life with their limited resources. Models tend to generalize human behaviour. Normally, the economist does not attempt to predict how people will think about a particular topic, such as a higher price of oil products, accelerated inflation, or higher taxes. Rather, the task at hand is to predict how people will act, which may be quite different from what they say they will do (much to the consternation of poll takers and market researchers). The people involved in examining thought processes are psychologists and psychiatrists, who are not usually economists.

An Economic Model: The Circular Flow of Income

A simple model economists use to explain the workings of the economy is the Circular Flow of Income. Figure 1.2 shows the basic form of the Circular Flow model.

Figure 1.2
The Circular Flow of Income

Firms go to the labour market to hire workers for production. They pay workers a wage, represented by the flow of income from the firms through the labour market to the households. The households spend part of their income purchasing goods and services in the product market. The money they pay for the goods and services flows back to the firms in the form of revenues. If households save any of their income, they put it in the financial market where firms go to borrow money for production purposes. This flow is represented by the arrow from the households through the financial market to the firms.

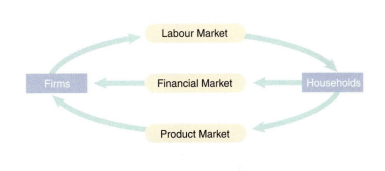

When using the Circular Flow model, we make two main assumptions. The first is that households—people like you and me—produce nothing, but *own* everything in the economy. This makes sense when you think that we own our own labour, and we also own all the firms—whether as shareholders or as entrepreneurs. Firms own nothing, since the shareholders own it all, but they *produce* everything in the economy. As soon as someone produces a good or a service to be sold in the economy, we call that producer a firm.

A good place to start thinking about this model is with the firms. The firms go to the labour market and hire workers to produce their output. In exchange, the firms pay the workers a wage, and income flows *from* the firms *to* the households. Households need food, shelter, and clothing, so they go to the product (or output) market to purchase goods and services. In exchange for the goods and services, the households give the firms a part of their incomes, and income flows *from* the households *to* the firms. So the flow of income in the economy is circular; it flows from firms to households and back to firms again.

We can complicate our model to make it a little more realistic. Most households wish to save part of their income. That part therefore does not flow through the product market, but instead flows to the financial market—to savings accounts with banks, credit unions, and trust companies. These financial institutions hold the households' savings, which they lend to firms that need funds for investment. Thus the income paid out by firms to workers still returns to them via the product market and the financial market.

Whether this is a useful model depends on how well it predicts real-world events. For example, what would happen to the economy if the government decided to put a tax (or an additional tax) on household incomes? Households would have less money to spend and/or save. The Circular Flow model predicts that households would purchase less and save less, and the flows to the firms would diminish. If the flows to the firms diminished, the firms would produce less, and hire fewer workers—thus compounding the problem of shrinking incomes. We could test this prediction by looking at Canada's, and other similar countries', experiences when taxes have risen. We would almost certainly find a slowing in the growth of the economy; our model would represent this as a slowing of the flows between the households and the firms.

If we ask what would happen to our economy if the Americans asked Canadian firms to produce twice as many automobile parts for them than in the past, what will our model predict? We have not included the foreign sector in our simple model, but we could look at the opportunity to increase our sales to the United States as a large injection of income into the firms. The firms would go to the labour market and hire more workers to produce the extra output. Increased income would flow from the firms to the households, and, *ceteris paribus*, back to the firms again. The economy would grow with the increased economic activity.

POSITIVE VERSUS NORMATIVE ECONOMICS

Economics uses *positive analysis*, a value-free approach to inquiry. No subjective or moral judgments enter into the analysis. Positive analysis relates to statements such as "If *A*, then *B*." For example, "If the price of gasoline goes up relative to all other prices, then the amount of it that people will buy will fall." That is a positive economic statement. It is a statement of *what is*. It is not a statement of anyone's value judgment or subjective feelings. For many problems analysed in the hard sciences such as physics and chemistry, the analyses are considered to be virtually value-free. After all, how can someone's values enter into a theory of molecular behaviour? But economists face a different problem. They deal with the behaviour of individuals, not molecules. That makes it more difficult to stick to what we consider to be value-free or **positive economics** without reference to our feelings.

► **Positive economics**

Analysis that is strictly limited to making either purely descriptive statements or scientific predictions; for example, "If *A*, then *B*." A statement of *what is*.

When our values are interjected into the analysis, we enter the realm of **normative economics**, involving *normative analysis*. A positive economic statement is "If the price of gas rises, people will buy less." If we add to that analysis the statement "so we should not allow the price to go up," we have entered the realm of normative economics—we have expressed a value judgment. In fact, any time you see the word *should*, you will know that values are entering into the discussion. Just remember that positive statements are concerned with *what is*, whereas normative statements are concerned with *what ought to be*.

► **Normative economics**

Analysis involving value judgments about economic policies; relates to whether things are good or bad. A statement of *what ought to be*.

Each of us has a desire for different things. This fact means that we have different values. When we express a value judgment, we are simply saying what we prefer, like, or desire. Because individual values are diverse, we expect—and indeed observe—people expressing widely varying value judgments about how the world ought to be.

15

CHAPTER 1 • THE NATURE OF ECONOMICS

Try Preview Question 4:

What is the difference between positive and normative economics?

A Warning: Recognize Normative Analysis

It is easy to define positive economics. It is quite another matter to catch all unlabelled normative statements in a textbook such as this one (or any other), even though authors go over the manuscript many times before it is printed. Therefore, do not get the impression that a textbook's authors will be able to keep all personal values out of the book. They will slip through. In fact, the very choice of which topics to include in an introductory textbook involves normative economics. There is no value-free, or objective, way to decide which topics to use in a textbook. The authors' values ultimately make a difference when choices have to be made. But from your own standpoint, you might want to be able to recognize when you are engaging in normative as opposed to positive economic analysis. Reading this text will help equip you for that task.

Economic Policy

As we noted above, economic models will enhance your ability to understand and predict behaviour. In chapters to come, we'll illustrate how these models prove useful in evaluating, assessing, and reacting to government policies that affect you as a consumer, an employee, an investor, a business owner, and a concerned citizen.

Most government economic policies are action plans designed to achieve commonly accepted socio-economic goals. The major goals are listed here. We discuss them in more detail in Chapter 5.

1. Full Employment: an economy in which people looking for work find jobs reasonably quickly.
2. Efficiency: an economy in which resources are allocated and goods and services are distributed to achieve the maximum benefit for society.
3. Economic Growth: an economy with the ability to increase its rate of production over time to enhance society's well-being.
4. Price Stability: an economy in which prices remain relatively stable over time.
5. Distribution of Income: an economy in which no particular group of people lives below or near the poverty level.

Concepts in Brief

- A model, or theory, uses assumptions and is by nature a simplification of the real world. The usefulness of a model can be evaluated by bringing empirical evidence to bear on its predictions.
- Models are not necessarily deficient simply because they are unrealistic and use simplifying assumptions. Every model in every science requires simplification compared to the real world.
- Most models use the *ceteris paribus* assumption, that all other things are held constant, or equal.
- Positive economics is value-free and relates to statements that can be refuted, such as "If *A*, then *B*." Normative economics involves people's values, and normative statements typically contain the word *should*.

Issues and Applications

How Relevant Is Love in a Marriage Contract?

Concepts Applied:
Rationality assumption, costs, benefits

Economist Gary Becker argues that dating can be understood in terms of the rationality assumption. For instance, the better off an individual thinks he or she may be in a marriage, the more that individual is willing to invest in finding the right mate.

Looking for a mate can be analysed from a sociological, psychological, or anthropological point of view. Here we want to examine this activity in terms of the rationality assumption developed in this chapter. We present an economic analysis based in part on the work of Nobel Prize–winning economist Gary Becker.

Minimizing Costs

According to the rationality assumption, individuals will not knowingly engage in activities that will make them worse off. Consequently, we predict that in choosing a spouse, individuals will naturally want to marry someone with whom they get along. So we predict that likes will attract more often than not: Individuals will tend to marry others with similar values. Dating and "courting" can be viewed as resource-using activities designed to determine with more certainty the values that each potential marriage partner has.

The more benefits one believes can be derived from the marriage contract, the more costs one will incur in searching for a spouse. The longer one searches, the more costs are incurred due to dating and courtship activities. The more durable the marriage contract, the greater the investment people will be willing to make in trying to find the "right" spouse.

Divorce and Wrong Partner Choices

The most durable marriage contract occurs in a legal setting in which divorce is impossible. One benefit is that a spouse cannot later leave because he or she prefers someone else. In many societies, the tendency has been towards fewer restrictions on divorce.

As divorces have become easier (that is to say, less costly), the durability of the marriage contract has seemed to decline. This result follows, at least in part, from economic analysis: As the expected durability of marriage declines, individuals implicitly have less incentive to incur longer searches for the "right" partner. The result: more wrong choices about a partner and hence more frequent divorces.

Why Love Matters

One aspect of love is that the level of happiness of the person loved affects the well-being of the other person. The more one loves another person, the more one is motivated to help that other person. Within a marriage, each spouse is dependent on the other.

When one spouse fails to uphold his or her end of the bargain, this tends to reduce the well-being of the other. Within a marriage, there is no actual iron-clad agreement about who provides what, how, and when. Therefore, it is relatively easy for one spouse not to do what he or she is supposed to do or at least not do it very well. The more love is involved, however, the more each spouse wants to make the other spouse better off. So we predict that marriages work out better the more spouses love each other. Hence individuals generally want to be in a marriage environment in which there is mutual love.

For Critical Analysis

1. Is there any difference between what economics predicts about a "good" marriage and what most people believe anyway?

2. If divorce is impossible, how does this affect spouse selection?

CHAPTER SUMMARY

1. Economics as a social science is the study of how individuals make choices to satisfy wants. Wants are defined as what people would buy if their incomes were unlimited.

2. Economics is usually divided into microeconomic analysis, which is the study of individual decision making by households and firms, and macroeconomics, which is the study of nationwide phenomena, such as inflation and unemployment.

3. The rationality assumption is that individuals never intentionally make decisions that would leave them worse off.

4. We use models, or theories, to explain and predict behaviour. Models, or theories, are never completely realistic because by definition they are simplifications using assumptions that are not directly testable. The usefulness of a theory, or model, is determined not by the realism of its assumptions but by how well it predicts real-world phenomena.

5. An important simplifying assumption is that all other things are held equal, or constant. This is sometimes known as the *ceteris paribus* assumption.

6. No model in economics relates to individuals' thought processes; all models relate to what people do, not to what they think or say they will do.

7. Much economic analysis involves positive economics; that is, it is value-free. Whenever statements embodying values are made, we enter the realm of normative economics, or how individuals and groups think things ought to be.

DISCUSSION OF PREVIEW QUESTIONS

1. What is the difference between microeconomics and macroeconomics?

Microeconomics is concerned with the choice-making processes of individuals, households, and firms, whereas macroeconomics focuses on the performance of the economy as a whole.

2. What role does rational self-interest play in economic analysis?

Rational self-interest is the assumption that individuals behave in a reasonable (rational) way in making choices to further their interests. In other words, we assume that individuals' actions are motivated primarily by their self-interest, keeping in mind that self-interest can relate to monetary and nonmonetary objectives, such as love, prestige, and helping others.

3. Why is the study of economics a science?

Economics is a science in that it uses models, or theories, that are simplified representations of the real world to analyse and make predictions about the real world. These predictions are then subjected to empirical tests in which real-world data are used to decide whether to accept or reject the predictions.

4. What is the difference between positive and normative economics?

Positive economics deals with what is, whereas normative economics deals with what ought to be. Positive economic statements are of the "if ... then" variety; they are descriptive and predictive and are not related to what "should" happen. Normative economics, by contrast, is concerned with what ought to be and is intimately tied to value judgments.

PROBLEMS

(Answers to the odd-numbered problems appear at the back of the book.)

1-1. Construct four separate models to predict the probability that a person will die within the next five years. Include only one determining factor in each of your models.

1-2. Does it matter whether all of a model's assumptions are "realistic"? Why or why not?

1-3. Give a refutable implication (one that can be disproved by evidence from the real world) for each of the following models:

   a. The accident rate of drivers is inversely related to their age.

   b. The rate of inflation is directly related to the rate of change in the nation's money supply.

   c. The wages of professional basketball players are directly related to their high school grade point averages.

   d. The rate at which bank employees are promoted is inversely related to their frequency of absenteeism.

1-4. Is gambling an example of rational or irrational behaviour? What is the difference between gambling and insurance?

1-5. Over the past 20 years, first-class mail rates have increased more than five times over, while prices of long-distance phone calls, televisions, and sound systems have decreased. Over a similar period, it has been reported that there has been a steady decline in the ability of high school graduates to communicate effectively in writing. Do you feel that this increase in the relative price of written communication (first-class mail rates) is related to the alleged decline in writing ability? If so, what do you feel is the direction of causation? Which is causing which?

1-6. If there is no way to test a theory with real-world data, can we determine if it is a good theory? Why is empirical evidence used to validate a theory?

1-7. Identify which of the following statements use positive economic analysis and which use normative economic analysis.

   a. Recent increases in college tuition fees are unfair to students.

   b. The elimination of barriers to the free movement of individuals across European borders has caused wages to become more equal in many industries.

   c. Paying Members of Parliament more provides them with less incentive to commit wrongful acts.

   d. We need more restrictions on companies that pollute because air pollution is destroying our way of life.

1-8. Visit the Mining Co. Web site at http://economics.miningco.com/ and click on "Features." Then select "1998 Features" and click on "Economics and Happiness." Read about the Misery Index and answer the following questions.

   a. Does the Misery Index qualify as an economic model? If yes, how?

   b. What role does positive economics play in devising the Misery Index?

   c. What role does normative economics play in the construction of the Misery Index?

   d. Do you think that the use of normative economics in the construction of the Misery Index invalidates the usefulness of the Index as a model?

INTERACTING WITH THE INTERNET

File Edit View Go Favorites Help
Back Forward Stop Refresh Home Search Favorites History Channels Fullscreen Mail Print Edit

The Internet is a web of educational, corporate, and research computer networks around the world. Today, over 40 million people are using it, and more than 60,000 networks are connected to it. Perhaps the most interesting part of the Internet is the World Wide Web, commonly called the Web, which is a vast interlinked network of computer files all over the world. You can use the Internet to find discussion groups, news groups, and electronic publications. The most common use of the Internet is for electronic mail (e-mail).

At many colleges and universities, you can get an e-mail address and a password. Your address is like a mailbox at which you will receive electronic information. Many of the chapters in this edition of *Economics Today* end with Internet addresses and activities that you will find helpful in your study of the principles of economics. In any event, if you don't already have one you should get an Internet address now. Pick up a copy of the new user's handbook and start using e-mail.

If you want to "surf" (browse) economics resources immediately, go directly to Resources for Economists on the Internet by typing in

http://econwpa.wustl.edu/EconFAQ/EconFAQ.html

This site is maintained by Professor William Goffe of the University of Southern Mississippi. This is his "home page," the table of contents for a particular Web site. On this page you will find a catalogue of "hypertext" pointers, which are highlighted words or phrases that you can click on to connect to places around the Web.

To get in the last laugh, you might want to look up some economist jokes at

http://netec.mcc.ac.uk/JokEc.html

Happy surfing!

2

Scarcity and the World of Trade-Offs

Preview Questions

1. Do affluent people face the problem of scarcity?

2. Fresh air may be consumed at no charge, but is it free of cost to society?

3. Why does the scarcity problem force individuals to consider opportunity costs?

4. Can a "free" college education ever be truly free?

Is there anything more frightening than being the victim of a crime? Most people would say no, though frequently we behave as if we were looking for trouble. We routinely act in ways that increase our chances of becoming crime victims, including leaving valuables in clear view in our cars, or walking to clubs or bars on dark evenings, or wearing expensive clothing and jewellery. Government policymakers pass laws to protect citizens from crime, but they cannot eliminate every risk that exists. They can, however, force society to spend resources to reduce risk to life and property. When they do, a trade-off is involved because risk reduction involves the use of things that are scarce.

▶ **Scarcity**

A situation in which the ingredients for producing the things that people desire are insufficient to satisfy all wants.

Did You Know That... some people make a profit out of standing in line? Prior to a recent *Tragically Hip* concert in Toronto, several "professional line waiters" set up camp at the ticket booth the night before tickets went on sale. When the box office opened the next morning, they bought tickets, not for themselves, but for the many young people who paid them $20 in addition to the price of the ticket to stand in line for them. What were those young people doing? They were working at jobs that paid them more than $20 for the day. They did not want to miss the opportunity to make that income. After all, those young people do not have an unlimited amount of time to work and to stand in line. Time is scarce to them.

SCARCITY

Whenever individuals or communities cannot obtain everything they desire simultaneously, choices occur. Choices occur because of *scarcity*. **Scarcity** is the most basic concept in all of economics. Scarcity means that we do not and cannot have enough income or wealth to satisfy our *every* desire. Scarcity exists because human wants always exceed what can be produced with the limited resources and time that nature makes available.

What Scarcity Is Not

Scarcity is not a shortage. When flooding forced many people in southern Manitoba to leave their homes, TV newscasts showed those evacuated crowding into the local high school gymnasium or community centre common room for the night. A news commentator noted that this crowding was caused by a scarcity of short-term housing. But housing is always scarce—we cannot obtain all we want at a zero price. The flood victims were not facing a scarcity of short-term housing, rather there was a shortage of it. Do not confuse the concept of scarcity, which is general and all-encompassing, with the concept of shortages as evidenced by people standing in line to obtain a particular product.

Scarcity is not the same thing as poverty. Scarcity occurs among the rich as well as the poor. Even the richest person on earth faces scarcity because available time is limited. Low income levels do not create more scarcity. High income levels do not create less scarcity.

Scarcity is a fact of life, like gravity. And just as physicists did not invent gravity, economists did not invent scarcity—it existed well before the first economist ever lived. It exists even when we are not using all of our resources.

Try Preview Question 1:

Do affluent people face the problem of scarcity?

Scarcity and Resources

The scarcity concept arises from the fact that resources are insufficient to satisfy our

▶ **Production**

Any activity that results in the conversion of resources into products that can be used in consumption.

▶ **Land**

The natural resources that are available from nature. Land as a resource includes location, original fertility and mineral deposits, topography, climate, water, and vegetation.

▶ **Labour**

Productive contributions of humans who work, involving both mental and physical activities.

▶ **Physical capital**

All manufactured resources, including buildings, equipment, machines, and improvements to land that is used for production.

▶ **Human capital**

The accumulated training and education of workers.

▶ **Entrepreneurship**

The factor of production involving human resources that perform the functions of raising capital, organizing, managing, assembling other factors of production, and making basic business policy decisions. The entrepreneur is a risk taker.

▶ **Goods**

All things from which individuals derive satisfaction or happiness.

▶ **Economic goods**

Goods that are scarce.

every desire. Resources are the inputs used in the production of the things that we want. **Production** can be defined as virtually any activity that results in the conversion of resources into products that can be used in consumption. Production includes delivering things from one part of the country to another. It includes taking ice from an ice tray to put in your soft-drink glass. The resources used in production are called *factors of production,* and some economists use the terms *resources* and *factors of production* interchangeably. The total quantity of all resources that an economy has at any one time determines what that economy can produce.

Factors of production can be classified in many ways. Here is one such classification:

1. **Land** encompasses all the nonhuman gifts of nature, including timber, water, fish, minerals, and the original fertility of the land. It is often called the *natural resource.*

2. **Labour** is the human resource, which includes all productive contributions made by individuals who work, such as steelworkers, ballet dancers, and professional baseball players.

3. **Physical capital** consists of the factories and equipment used in production. It also includes improvements to natural resources, such as irrigation ditches.

4. **Human capital** is the economic characterization of the education and training of workers. How much the nation produces depends not only on how many hours people work but also on how productive they are, and that, in turn, depends in part on education and training. To become more educated, individuals have to devote time and resources, just as a business has to devote resources if it wants to increase its physical capital. Whenever a worker's skills increase, human capital has been improved.

5. **Entrepreneurship** is actually a subdivision of labour and involves human resources that perform the functions of organizing, managing, and assembling the other factors of production to make business ventures. Entrepreneurship also encompasses taking risks that involve the possibility of losing large sums of wealth on new ventures. It includes new methods of doing common things, and generally experimenting with any type of new thinking that could lead to making more money income. Without entrepreneurship, virtually no business organization could operate.

Goods Versus Economic Goods

Goods are defined as all things from which individuals derive satisfaction or happiness. Goods therefore include air to breathe and the beauty of a sunset, as well as food, cars, and CD players.

Economic goods are a subset of all goods—they are goods derived from scarce resources about which we must constantly make decisions regarding their best use. By definition, the desired quantity of an economic good exceeds the amount that is directly available from nature at a zero price. Virtually every example we use in economics concerns economic goods—cars, CD players, computers, socks, baseball bats, and so on. Weeds are a good example of *bads*—goods for which the desired quantity is much *less* than what nature provides at a zero price.

▶ **Services**
Mental or physical labour or help purchased by consumers. Examples are the assistance of doctors, lawyers, dentists, repair personnel, housecleaners, educators, retailers, and wholesalers; things purchased or used by consumers that do not have physical characteristics.

Sometimes you will see references to "goods and services." **Services** are tasks that are performed for someone else, such as laundry, cleaning, hospital care, restaurant meal preparation, car polishing, psychological counselling, and teaching. One way of looking at services is to think of them as *intangible goods*.

WANTS AND NEEDS

Wants are not the same as needs. Indeed, from the economist's point of view, the term *needs* is objectively indefinable. When someone says, "I need some new clothes," there is no way of knowing whether that person is stating a vague wish, a want, or a life-saving necessity. If the individual making the statement were dying of exposure in northern Quebec during the winter, we might argue that indeed the person does need clothes—perhaps not new ones, but at least some articles of warm clothing. Typically, however, the term *need* is used very casually in most conversations. What people usually mean is that they want something that they do not currently have.

Humans have unlimited wants. Just imagine if every single material want that you might have were satisfied. You can have all of the clothes, cars, houses, CDs, tickets to concerts, and other things that you want. Does that mean that nothing else could add to your total level of happiness? Probably not, because you might think of new goods and services that you could obtain, particularly as they came to market. You would also still be lacking in fulfilling all of your wants for compassion, friendship, love, affection, prestige, musical abilities, sports abilities, and so on.

In reality, every individual has competing wants but cannot satisfy all of them, given limited resources. This is the reality of scarcity. Each person must therefore make choices. Whenever a choice is made to do or buy something, something else that is also desired is not done or not purchased. In other words, in a world of scarcity, every want that ends up being satisfied causes one or more other wants to remain unsatisfied or to be forfeited.

Concepts in Brief

- Scarcity exists because human wants always exceed what can be produced with the limited resources and time that nature makes available.
- We use scarce resources, such as land, labour, physical and human capital, and entrepreneurship, to produce economic goods—goods that are desired but are not directly obtainable from nature to the extent demanded or desired at a zero price.
- Wants are unlimited; they include all material desires and all nonmaterial desires, such as love, affection, power, and prestige.
- The concept of need is difficult to define objectively for every person; consequently, we simply consider that every person's wants are unlimited. In a world of scarcity, satisfaction of one want necessarily means nonsatisfaction of one or more other wants.

SCARCITY, CHOICE, AND OPPORTUNITY COST

The natural fact of scarcity implies that we must make choices. One of the most important results of this fact is that every choice made (or not made, for that matter) means that some opportunity had to be sacrificed. Every choice involves giving up another opportunity to do or use something else.

Consider a practical example. Every choice you make to study one more hour of economics requires that you give up the opportunity to do any of the following activities: study more of another subject, listen to music, sleep, browse at a local store, read a novel, or work out at the gym. Many more opportunities are forgone also if you choose to study economics an additional hour.

Because there were so many alternatives from which to choose, how could you determine the value of what you gave up to engage in that extra hour of studying economics? First of all, no one else can tell you the answer because only you can *subjectively* put a value on each alternative. Only you know the value of another hour of sleep, or of an hour looking for the latest CDs. That means that only you can determine the highest-valued, next-best alternative that you had to sacrifice in order to study economics one more hour. It is you who come up with the *subjective* estimate of the expected value of the next-best alternative.

The value of the next-best alternative is called **opportunity cost**. The opportunity cost of any action is the value of what is given up—the next-highest-ranked alternative—because a choice was made. When you study one more hour, there may be many alternatives available for the use of that hour, but assume that you can do only one thing in that hour—your next-highest-ranked alternative. What is important is the choice that you would have made if you hadn't studied one more hour. Your opportunity cost is the *next-highest-ranked* alternative, not *all* alternatives.

> In economics, cost is always a forgone opportunity.

One way to think about opportunity cost is to understand that when you choose to do something, you lose. What you lose is being able to engage in your next-highest-valued alternative. Thus, the cost of your choice is your next-highest-valued alternative. This is your opportunity cost.

Let's consider the opportunity cost entertainers face when they change bands.

▶ **Opportunity cost**
The highest-valued, next-best alternative that must be sacrificed to attain something or to satisfy a want.

Try Preview Question 2:
Fresh air may be consumed at no charge, but is it free of cost to society?

INTERNATIONAL EXAMPLE
The Costs and Benefits of de-Spicing

In June, 1998, in the middle of the World Spice Tour, Geri Halliwell, better known as "Ginger Spice," announced that she was leaving the pop group Spice Girls. She cited differences with Sporty, Scary, Baby, and Posh (the remaining Spice Girls) as the reason. What was Ginger giving up because of her decision to quit the band?

It is estimated that the Spice Girls earn collectively in excess of 50 million pounds sterling (about $120 million) per year from their CD sales and movie revenues. In addition, the World Spice Tour is estimated to have earned them another $50 million. Ginger's share, after expenses, is about 10 percent of the gross. So her opportunity cost of quitting would be in the range of $17 million during the first year alone.

Why would Ginger elect to quit when the opportunity cost is so great? We know from the last chapter that she will choose to quit when she will make herself better off by doing so. It appears that this is the case: Ginger is not only discussing having her own television show with the British Broadcasting Corporation (BBC), but she will also probably receive a buy-out from the Spice Girls of about $25 million.

For critical analysis: Do you think that by quitting the Spice Girls Ginger is giving up more than the money she would have earned as a member of the group?

THE WORLD OF TRADE-OFFS

Whenever you engage in any activity using any resource, even time, you are *trading off* the use of that resource for one or more alternative uses. The value of the trade-off is represented by the opportunity cost. The opportunity cost of studying economics has already been mentioned—it is the value of the next-best alternative. When you think of any alternative, you are thinking of trade-offs.

Let's consider a hypothetical example of a one-for-one trade-off between the results of spending time studying economics and accounting. For the sake of this argument, we will assume that additional time studying either economics or accounting will lead to a higher grade in the subject studied more. One of the best ways to examine this trade-off is with a graph. (If you would like a refresher on graphical techniques, study Appendix A at the end of this chapter before going on.)

Graphical Analysis

In Figure 2.1, the expected grade in accounting is measured on the vertical axis of the graph, and the expected grade in economics is measured on the horizontal axis. We simplify the world and assume that you have a maximum of 10 hours per week to spend studying these two subjects, and that if you spend all 10 hours on economics, you will get an A in the course. You will, however, fail accounting. Conversely, if you spend all of your 10 hours studying accounting, you will get an A in that subject, but you will flunk economics. Here the trade-off is a special case: one-to-one. A one-to-one trade-off means that the opportunity cost of receiving one grade higher in economics (for example, improving from a C to a B) is one grade lower in accounting (falling from a C to a D).

The Production Possibilities Curve (PPC)

The graph in Figure 2.1 illustrates the relationship between the possible results that can be produced in each of two activities, depending on how much time you choose

Figure 2.1
Production Possibilities Curve for Grades in
Accounting and Economics (Trade-offs)

We assume that only 10 hours can be spent per week on studying. If the student is at point *x*, equal time (5 hours a week) is spent on both courses and equal grades of C will be received. If a higher grade in economics is desired, the student may go to point *y*, thereby receiving a B in economics but a D in accounting. At point *y*, 2.5 hours are spent on accounting and 7.5 hours on economics.

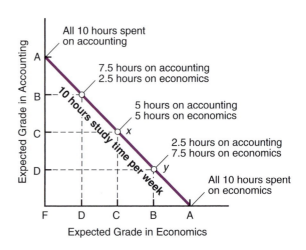

► **Production possibilities**
curve (PPC)

A curve representing all possible combinations of total output that could be produced assuming (1) a fixed amount of productive resources of a given quality, and (2) the efficient use of those resources.

to devote to each. This graph is a representation of a **production possibilities curve (PPC)**.

Consider that you are producing a grade in economics when you study economics and a grade in accounting when you study accounting. Then the graph in Figure 2.1 can be related to the production possibilities you face. The line that goes from A on one axis to A on the other axis therefore becomes a production possibilities curve. It is defined as the maximum quantity of one good or service that can be produced, given that a specific quantity of another is produced. It is a curve that shows the possibilities available for increasing the output of one good or service by reducing the amount of another. In the example in Figure 2.1, your time for studying was limited to 10 hours per week. The two possible outputs were grades in accounting and grades in economics. The particular production possibilities curve presented in Figure 2.1 is a graphical representation of the opportunity cost of studying one more hour in one subject. It is a *straight-line production possibilities curve*, which is a special case. (The more general case is discussed next.) If you decide to be at point *x* in Figure 2.1, five hours of study time will be spent on accounting and five hours will be spent on economics. The expected grade in each course will be a C. If you are more interested in getting a B in economics, you will go to point *y* on the production possibilities curve, spending only two-and-a-half hours on accounting but seven-and-a-half hours on economics. Your expected grade in accounting will then drop from a C to a D.

Note that these trade-offs between expected grades in accounting and economics are the result of *holding constant* total study time as well as all other factors that might influence a student's ability to learn, such as computerized study aids. Quite clearly, if you wished to spend more total time studying, it would be possible to have higher grades in both economics and accounting. In that case, however, we would no longer be on the specific production possibilities curve illustrated in Figure 2.1. We would have to draw a new curve, farther to the right, to show the greater total study time and a different set of possible trade-offs.

Concepts in Brief

- Scarcity requires us to choose. When we choose, we lose the next-highest-valued alternative.
- Cost is always a forgone opportunity.
- Another way to look at opportunity cost is as the trade-off that occurs when one activity is undertaken rather than the next-best alternative activity.
- A production possibilities curve (PPC) graphically shows the trade-off that occurs when more of one output is obtained at the sacrifice of another. The PPC is a graphical representation of, among other things, opportunity cost.

THE CHOICES SOCIETY FACES

The straight-line production possibilities curve presented in Figure 2.1 can be generalized to demonstrate the related concepts of scarcity, choice, and trade-offs that Canada faces. As you will see, the production possibilities curve is a simple but powerful economic model because it can demonstrate these related concepts. The example we will use is the choice between the production of automobiles and newsprint. We assume for the moment that these are the only two goods that can be produced in Canada. Part (a) of Figure 2.2 gives the various possible combinations of automobiles and newsprint. If all resources are devoted to auto production, 3 million per year can be produced. If all resources are devoted to newsprint production, 12 mil-

Figure 2.2

Society's Trade-Off Between Automobiles and Newsprint

The production of automobiles is measured in millions of units per year, while the production of newsprint is measured in millions of tonnes per year. The various combinations are given in part (a) and plotted in part (b). Connecting the points *A–G* with a relatively smooth line gives the production possibilities curve for automobiles and newsprint. Point *R* lies outside the production possibilities curve and is therefore unattainable at the point in time for which the graph is drawn. Point *S* lies inside the production possibilities curve and therefore represents an inefficient use of available resources.

Part (a)

Combination	Automobiles (millions of units per year)	Newsprint (millions of tonnes per year)
A	3.0	0
B	2.9	2
C	2.7	4
D	2.4	6
E	2.0	8
F	1.4	10
G	0	12

Part (b)

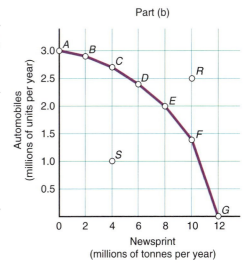

Try Preview Question 3:
Why does the scarcity problem force individuals to consider opportunity costs?

lion tonnes per year can be produced. In between are various possible combinations. These combinations are plotted as points *A*, *B*, *C*, *D*, *E*, *F*, and *G* in part (b) of Figure 2.2. If these points are connected with a smooth curve, Canada's production possibilities curve is shown, demonstrating the trade-off between the production of automobiles and newsprint. These trade-offs occur *on* the production possibilities curve.

Notice the major difference in the shape of the production possibilities curves in Figures 2.1 and 2.2. In Figure 2.1, there is a one-to-one trade-off between grades in economics and in accounting. In Figure 2.2, the trade-off between newsprint production and automobile production is not constant, and therefore the production possibilities curve is a *bowed* line. To understand why the production possibilities curve for a society is typically bowed outward, you must understand the assumptions underlying the PPC.

Assumptions Underlying the Production Possibilities Curve

When we draw the curve that is shown in Figure 2.2, we make the following assumptions:

1. That resources are fully employed.
2. That we are looking at production over a specific time period—for example, one year.
3. That the resource inputs, in both quantity and quality, used to produce automobiles or newsprint are fixed over this time period.
4. That technology does not change over this time period.

▶ **Technology**
Society's pool of applied knowledge concerning how goods and services can be produced.

Technology is defined as society's pool of applied knowledge concerning how goods and services can be produced by managers, workers, engineers, scientists, and craftspeople, using land and capital. You can think of technology as the formula (or recipe) used to combine factors of production. (When better formulas are developed, more production can be obtained from the same amount of resources.) The level of technology sets the limit on the amount and types of goods and services that we can derive from any given amount of resources. The production possibilities curve is drawn under the assumption that we use the best technology that we currently have available, and that this technology doesn't change over the time period under study.

Being off the Production Possibilities Curve

Look again at part (b) of Figure 2.2. Point *R* lies *outside* the production possibilities curve and is *impossible* to achieve during the time period assumed. By definition, the production possibilities curve indicates the *maximum* quantity of one good given some quantity of the other.

It is possible, however, to be at point *S* in Figure 2.2. That point lies beneath the production possibilities curve. If the nation is at point *S*, it means that its resources are not being fully utilized. This occurs, for example, during periods of unemployment. Point *S* and all such points within the production possibilities curve are always attainable but are usually not desirable.

Efficiency

The production possibilities curve can be used to define the notion of efficiency. Whenever the economy is operating on the PPC at points such as *A*, *B*, *C*, or *D*, we say that its production is efficient. Points such as *S* in Figure 2.2, which lie beneath the production possibilities curve, are said to represent production situations that are not efficient.

▶ **Efficiency**

The case in which a given level of inputs is used to produce the maximum output possible. Alternatively, the situation in which a given output is produced at minimum cost.

Efficiency can mean many things to many people. Even within economics, there are different types of efficiency. Here we are discussing efficiency in production, or productive efficiency. An economy is productively efficient whenever it is producing the maximum output with given technology and resources.

A simple commonsense definition of efficiency is getting the most out of what we have as an economy. Clearly, we are not getting the most that we have if we are at point *S* in part (b) of Figure 2.2. We can move from point *S* to, say, point *C*, thereby increasing the total quantity of automobiles produced without any decrease in the total quantity of newsprint produced. We can move from point *S* to point *E*, for example, and have both more automobiles and more newsprint. Point *S* is called an **inefficient point**, which is defined as any point below the production possibilities curve.

▶ **Inefficient point**

Any point below the production possibilities curve at which resources are being used inefficiently.

The concept of economic efficiency relates to how goods are distributed among different individuals and entities. An efficient economy is one in which people who place relatively the most value on specific goods end up with those goods. If you own a vintage electric Fender guitar, but I value it more than you, I can buy it from you. Such trading benefits both of us. In the process, the economy becomes more efficient. The maximum efficiency an economy can reach is when all such mutual benefits through trade have been exhausted.

The Law of Increasing Relative Cost

In the example in Figure 2.1, the trade-off between a grade in accounting and a grade in economics is one-to-one. The trade-off ratio was fixed. That is to say, the production possibilities curve was a straight line. The curve in Figure 2.2 is a more general case. We have re-created the curve in Figure 2.2 as Figure 2.3. Each combination, *A* through *G*, of automobiles and newsprint is represented on the production possibilities curve. Starting with the production of zero newsprint, Canada could produce 3 million automobiles with its available resources and technology. When we increase production of newsprint from zero to 2 million tonnes per year, we have to give up the automobile production represented by that first vertical arrow, *Aa*. From part (a) of Figure 2.2 you can see that this is 0.1 million autos a year (3.0 million − 2.9 million). Again, if we increase production of newsprint by 2 million tonnes per year, we go from *B* to *C*. In order to do so, we have to give up the vertical distance *Bb*, or 0.2 million automobiles a year. By the time we go from 10 million to 12 million tonnes of newsprint, to obtain that 2 million tonne increase we have to forgo the vertical distance *Ff*, or 1.4 million automobiles. In other words, the opportunity cost of the last 2 million tonnes of newsprint is 1.4 million autos, compared with 0.1 million autos, the opportunity cost for the first 2 million tonnes of newsprint (starting at zero production).

Figure 2.3
The Law of Increasing Relative Cost

Consider equal increments of newsprint production, as measured on the horizontal axis. All of the horizontal arrows—*aB*, *bC*, and so on—are of equal length (2 million tonnes). The opportunity cost of going from 10 million tonnes of newsprint per year to 12 million *(Ff)* is much greater than going from zero tonnes to 2 million tonnes *(Aa)*. The opportunity cost of each additional equal increase in newsprint production rises.

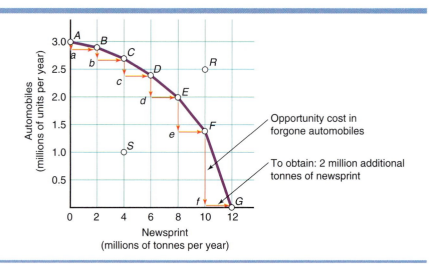

► **Law of increasing relative cost**

The observation that the opportunity cost of additional units of a good generally increases as society attempts to produce more of that good. This accounts for the bowed-out shape of the production possibilities curve.

What we are observing is called the **law of increasing relative cost**. When society takes more resources and applies them to the production of any specific good, the opportunity cost increases for each additional unit produced. The reason that, as a country, we face the law of increasing relative cost (which causes the production possibilities curve to bow outward) is that certain resources are better suited for producing some goods than they are for others. Resources are generally not *perfectly* adaptable for alternative uses. When increasing the output of a particular good, producers must use less efficient resources than those already used in order to produce the additional output. Hence the cost of producing the additional units increases. In our hypothetical example here, at first the mechanical technicians in the automobile industry would shift over to producing newsprint. After a while, though, upholstery specialists and windshield installers would also be asked to help. Clearly, they would be less effective in making newsprint.

As a rule of thumb, the more *specialized the resources, the more bowed the production possibilities curve*. At the other extreme, if all resources are equally suitable for newsprint production or automobile production, the curves in Figures 2.2 and 2.3 would approach the straight line shown in our first example in Figure 2.1.

Concepts in Brief

- Trade-offs are represented graphically by a production possibilities curve (PPC) showing the maximum quantity of one good or service that can be produced, given a specific quantity of another, from a given set of resources over a specified period of time—for example, one year.
- A PPC is drawn holding the quantity and quality of all resources fixed over the time period under study.
- Points outside the production possibilities curve are unattainable; points inside are attainable but represent an inefficient use or under-use of available resources.
- Because many resources are better suited for certain productive tasks than for others, society's production possibilities curve is bowed outward, following the law of increasing relative cost.

ECONOMIC GROWTH AND THE PRODUCTION POSSIBILITIES CURVE

Over any particular time period, a society cannot be outside the production possibilities curve. Over time, however, it is possible to have more of everything. This occurs through economic growth. Figure 2.4 shows the production possibilities curve for automobiles and newsprint shifting outward. The two additional curves represent new choices open to an economy that has experienced economic growth. Such economic growth occurs because of many things, including increases in the number of workers and productive investment in equipment.

Scarcity still exists, however, no matter how much economic growth there is. At any point in time, we will always be on some production possibilities curve; thus we will always face trade-offs. The more we want of one thing, the less we can have of others.

If a nation experiences economic growth, the production possibilities curve between automobiles and newsprint will move outward, as is shown in Figure 2.4. This takes time and does not occur automatically. One reason it will occur involves the choice about how much to consume today.

Figure 2.4

Economic Growth Allows for More of Everything

If the nation experiences economic growth, the production possibilities curve between automobiles and newsprint will shift out, as shown. This takes time, however, and it does not occur automatically. This means, therefore, that we can have more automobiles and more newsprint only after a period of time during which we have experienced economic growth.

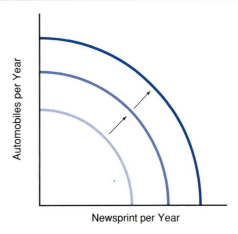

Newsprint per Year

THE TRADE-OFF BETWEEN THE PRESENT AND THE FUTURE

▶ **Consumption**

The use of goods and services for personal satisfaction.

The production possibilities curve and economic growth can be used to examine the trade-off between present **consumption** and future consumption. When we consume today, we are using up what we call consumption or consumer goods—food and clothes, for example. And we have already defined physical capital as the manufactured goods, such as machines and factories, used to make other goods and services.

Why We Make Capital Goods

Why would we be willing to use productive resources to make things—capital goods—that we cannot consume directly? For one thing, capital goods enable us to produce larger quantities of consumer goods or to produce them less expensively than we otherwise could. Before fish are "produced" for the market, equipment such as fishing boats, nets, and poles are produced first. Imagine how expensive it would be to obtain fish for market without using these capital goods. Catching fish with one's hands is not an easy task. The price per fish would be very high if capital goods weren't used.

Forgoing Current Consumption

Whenever we use productive resources to make capital goods, we are implicitly forgoing current consumption. We are waiting until some time in the future to consume the fruits that will be reaped from the use of capital goods. In effect, when we forgo current consumption to invest in capital goods, we are engaging in an economic activity that is forward-looking—we do not get instant utility or satisfaction from our activity. Indeed, if we were to produce only consumer goods now and no capital goods, our capacity to produce consumer goods in the future would suffer. Here we see a trade-off situation.

The Trade-Off Between Consumption Goods and Capital Goods

To have more consumer goods in the future, we must accept fewer consumer goods today. In other words, an opportunity cost is involved here. Every time we make a choice for more goods today, we incur an opportunity cost of fewer goods tomorrow, and every time we make a choice of more goods in the future, we incur an opportunity cost of fewer goods today. With the resources that we don't use to produce consumer goods for today, we invest in capital goods that will produce more consumer goods for us later. The trade-off is shown in Figure 2.5. On the left in part (a), you can see this trade-off depicted as a production possibilities curve between capital goods and consumption goods.

Assume that we are willing to give up $1 billion worth of consumption today. We will be at point A in the left-hand diagram of part (a). This will allow the economy to grow. We will have more future consumption because we invested in more capital goods today. In the right-hand diagram of part (a), we see two goods represented, food and recreation. The production possibilities curve will move outward if we collectively decide to restrict consumption each year and invest in capital goods.

In part (b), we show the results of our willingness to forgo more current consumption. We move to point C, where we have many fewer consumer goods today, but produce a lot more capital goods. This leads to more future growth in this simplified model, and thus the production possibilities curve in the right-hand side of part (b) shifts outward more than it did in the right-hand side of part (a).

Figure 2.5
Capital Goods and Growth

In part (a), the nation chooses not to consume $1 billion, so it invests that amount in capital goods. In part (b), it chooses even more capital goods. The PPC moves even further to the right on the right-hand diagram in part (b) as a result.

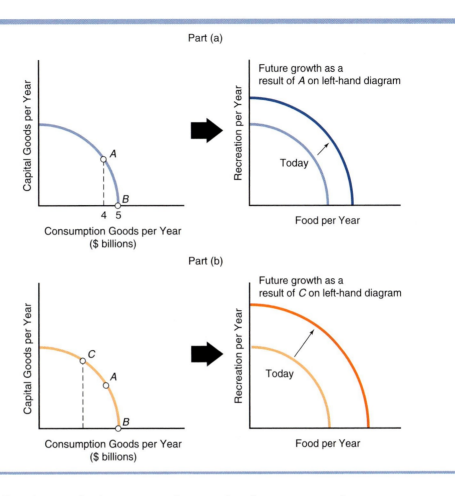

Part (a)

Part (b)

Try Preview Question 4:

Can a "free" college education ever be truly free?

In other words, the more we give up today, the more we can have tomorrow, provided, of course, that the capital goods are productive in future periods and that society desires the consumer goods produced by this additional capital.

INTERNATIONAL EXAMPLE
Consumption Versus Capital Goods in the United States and in Japan

The trade-off of capital versus consumption goods (shown in the production possibilities curves of Figure 2.5) can be observed in real life when we compare different countries. The Japanese, for example, have chosen to devote more than twice the amount of resources each year to the production of capital goods than have the Americans. Not surprisingly, the Japanese have, until recently, experienced a much higher rate of economic growth than the United States. In effect, then, Japan is represented by part (b) in Figure 2.5—choosing more capital goods—and the United States by part (a)—choosing fewer capital goods.

For critical analysis: Does this analysis apply to the trade-off between consumption and human capital for you as an individual? If so, how?

Concepts in Brief

- The use of capital requires using productive resources to produce capital goods that will later be used to produce consumer goods.
- A trade-off is involved between current consumption and capital goods or, alternatively, between current consumption and future consumption. This is because the more we invest in capital goods today, the greater the amount of consumer goods we can produce in the future, and the smaller the amount of consumer goods we can produce today.

SPECIALIZATION AND GREATER PRODUCTIVITY

▶ **Specialization**
The division of productive activities among persons and regions so that no one individual or area is totally self-sufficient. An individual may specialize, for example, in law or medicine. A nation may specialize in the production of lobsters, computers, or cameras.

Specialization involves working at a relatively well-defined, limited endeavour, such as accounting or teaching. It involves a division of labour among different individuals and regions. Most people, in fact, do specialize. For example, you could probably change the oil in your car if you wanted to. Typically, though, you take your car to a garage and let the mechanic do it. You benefit by letting the garage mechanic specialize in changing the oil and in completing other repairs on your car. The specialist has all the proper equipment to do the work, and will likely get the job finished sooner than you could. Specialization usually leads to greater productivity, not only for each individual but also for the country.

Absolute Advantage

▶ **Absolute advantage**
The ability to produce a good or service at an "absolutely" lower cost, usually measured in units of labour or resource input required to produce one unit of the good or service.

Specialization occurs because different individuals and different nations have different skills. Sometimes it seems that some individuals are better at doing everything than anyone else. A president of a large company might be able to type better than any of the typists, file better than any of the file clerks, and wash windows better than any of the window washers. The president has an **absolute advantage** in all of these endeavours— by using fewer labour hours for each task than anyone else in the company. The president does not, however, spend time doing those other activities. Why not? Because a president is paid the most for undertaking managerial duties and specializes in that one particular task despite having an absolute advantage in all tasks. Indeed, absolute advantage is irrelevant in predicting how the president's time is spent; only *comparative advantage* matters.

Comparative Advantage

▶ **Comparative advantage**
The ability to produce a good or service at a lower opportunity cost compared to other producers.

Comparative advantage is the ability to perform an activity at the lowest opportunity cost. You have a comparative advantage in one activity whenever you have the lowest opportunity cost of performing that activity. Comparative advantage is always a *relative* concept. You may be able to change the oil in your car; you might even be able to change it faster than the local mechanic. But if the opportunity cost you face by changing the oil exceeds the mechanic's opportunity cost, the mechanic has a comparative advantage in changing the oil. The mechanic faces a lower opportunity cost for that activity.

You may be convinced that everybody can do everything better than you. In this extreme situation, do you still have a comparative advantage? The answer is yes. To discover your comparative advantage you need to find a job in which your *disadvantage* relative to others is the smallest. You do not have to be a mathematical genius to figure this out. The market tells you very clearly by offering you the highest income for the job for which you have the smallest disadvantage compared to others. Stated differently, to find your comparative advantage no matter how much better everybody else can do the jobs that you want to do, you simply find which job maximizes your income.

The coaches of sports teams are constantly faced with determining each player's comparative advantage. Former Blue Jay Dave Winfield was originally one of the best pitchers in college baseball, winning the most valuable player award for pitching for the University of Minnesota Golden Bears in the 1973 College World Series. After he was drafted by the San Diego Padres, the coach decided to make him an outfielder even though he was one of the best pitchers on the roster. The coach wanted Winfield to concentrate on his hitting. Good pitchers do not bring in as many fans as home-run kings. Dave Winfield's comparative advantage was clearly in hitting homers rather than practising and developing his pitching game.

Scarcity, Self-Interest, and Specialization

In Chapter 1, you learned about the assumption of rational self-interest. It says that for the purposes of our analyses we assume that individuals are rational in that they will do what is in their own self-interest. They will not consciously carry out actions that will make them worse off. In this chapter, you learned that scarcity requires people to make choices. We assume that they make choices based on their self-interest, and attempt to maximize benefits net of opportunity cost. In so doing, individuals choose their comparative advantage and end up specializing. Ultimately, when people specialize, they increase the money income they make and therefore become richer. When all individuals and businesses specialize simultaneously, the gains are seen in greater material well-being. With any given set of resources, specialization will result in higher output.

EXAMPLE How Specialization Can Lead to Career Changes

Most of you will make several career changes during your working lives. Some of these may be forced upon you by circumstance, but others will be because of a comparative advantage you can exploit. Someone who has developed his comparative advantage is William Deverell, author of five novels including *Kill All the Lawyers* and *Platinum Blues*, and the non-fiction work *Fatal Cruise*. He also wrote the pilot for *Street Legal*, a CBC television series.

Deverell started his working life as a journalist in Saskatoon, Montreal, and Vancouver. After attending law school, he began his practice of law in 1964. For 15 years he specialized in criminal law and civil rights, and began writing fiction in his spare time. In 1979 his first novel *Needles*, which won the Seal First Novel award, was published.

In recent years Deverell has not practised law but has specialized in his career as a writer. Fortunately, he recognized his comparative advantage in writing crime fiction, an art few can master.

For critical analysis: What is William Deverell's opportunity cost of choosing to be a full-time writer?

THE DIVISION OF LABOUR

▶ **Division of labour**

The segregation of a resource into different specific tasks; for example, one automobile worker puts on bumpers, another doors, and so on.

In any firm that includes specialized human and nonhuman resources, there is a **division of labour** among those resources. The best-known example of all time comes from one of the earliest and perhaps most famous economists, Adam Smith, who in *The Wealth of Nations* (1776) illustrated the benefits of a division of labour in the making of pins: "One man draws out the wire, another straightens it, a third cuts it, a fourth points it, a fifth grinds it at the top for receiving the head; to make the head requires two or three distinct operations; to put it on is a peculiar business, to whiten the pins is another; it is even a trade by itself to put them into the paper."

Making pins this way allowed 10 workers without very much skill to make almost 48,000 pins "of a middling size" in a day. One worker, toiling alone, could have made perhaps 20 pins a day; therefore, 10 workers could have produced 200. Division of labour allowed for an increase in the daily output of the pin factory from 200 to 48,000! (Smith did not attribute all of the gain to the division of labour according to talent, but credited also the use of machinery and the fact that less time was spent shifting from task to task.)

What we are discussing here involves a division of the resource called labour into different kinds of labour. The different kinds of labour are organized in such a way as to increase the amount of output possible from the fixed resources available. We can therefore talk about an organized division of labour within a firm leading to increased output.

Thinking Critically About the Media   International Trade

If you watch enough news on TV or frequently read the popular press, you get a distinct impression that international trade is somehow different from trade within our borders. At any given time, Canada is either at economic war with the United States over our exports of softwood lumber, or we are fighting with the European Union over whether Canadian furs caught using leg-hold traps should be allowed into the EU. International economics is just like any other type of economics; trade is just another economic activity. Indeed, one can think of international trade as a production process that transforms goods that we sell to other countries (exports) into what we buy from other countries (imports). International trade is a mutually beneficial exchange that occurs across political borders. If you imagine a world that was just one country, trade would still exist worldwide, but it would not be called international trade.

COMPARATIVE ADVANTAGE AND TRADE AMONG NATIONS

Though most of our analysis of absolute advantage, comparative advantage, and specialization has dealt with individuals, it is equally applicable to countries. First consider Canada. The Prairie provinces have a comparative advantage in the production of grains and other agricultural goods. Ontario and Quebec in Central Canada tend to specialize in industrialized production, such as automobiles and newsprint. Not surprisingly, grains are shipped from the Prairies to Central Canada, and automobiles are shipped in the reverse direction. Such specialization and trade allow for higher incomes and standards of living. If both the Prairies and Central Canada were politically defined as separate countries, the same analysis would still hold, but we would call it international trade. Indeed, Europe is smaller than Canada in area, but instead of one nation, Europe has 15. What in Canada we call *interprovincial trade*, in Europe is called *international trade*. There is no difference, however, in the economic results—both yield greater economic efficiency and higher average incomes.

Political problems that do not normally arise within a particular nation often do between nations. For example, if Nova Scotia crab fishers develop a cheaper method of harvesting crabs than fishers in British Columbia, British Columbia fishers will lose out. They cannot do much about the situation except try to lower their own costs of production. If crab fishers in Alaska, however, develop a cheaper method, both Nova Scotia and British Columbia fishers can (and likely will) try to raise political barriers to prevent Alaskan fishers from freely selling their product in Canada. Canadian crab fishers will use such arguments as "unfair" competition and loss of Canadian jobs. In so doing, they are only partly right: Crab-fishing jobs may decline in Canada, but jobs will not necessarily decline overall. If the argument of Canadian crab fishers had any validity, every time a region in Canada developed a better way to produce a product manufactured somewhere else in the country, employment in Canada would decline. That has never happened and never will.

When countries specialize where they have a comparative advantage and then trade with the rest of the world, the average standard of living in the world rises. In effect, international trade allows the world to move from inside the global production possibilities curve towards the curve itself, thereby improving worldwide economic efficiency.

Concepts in Brief

- With a given set of resources, specialization results in higher output; in other words, there are gains to specialization in terms of greater material well-being.
- Individuals and nations specialize in their areas of comparative advantage in order to reap the gains of specialization.
- Comparative advantages are found by determining which activities have the lowest opportunity cost—that is, which activities yield the highest return for the time and resources used.
- A division of labour occurs when different workers are assigned different tasks. Together, the workers produce a desired product.

Issues and Applications

The Cost of Crime

Concepts Applied:
Scarcity, opportunity costs, trade-offs

While the cost of crime is high, the cost of eliminating crime is much higher.

It is impossible today to pick up a newspaper or watch a television newscast without reading or hearing about crime. Reports of murders, assaults, thefts, prostitution, and drug-trafficking are frequent. Not surprisingly, Canadians often express concern about crime rates, and support the notion of increasing the number of police in order to fight crime. But how many more police officers would we require, and what would be the cost?

More than 160,000 automobiles are stolen every year in Canada, many to be sold to eastern European or South American countries. Some studies suggest that each extra police officer hired would reduce automobile thefts by up to seven per year. At that rate, we would have to hire about 23,000 officers to wipe out car theft altogether.

The Cost of Crime

A study by economist Stephen Easton and criminologist Paul Brantingham tried to calculate the cost of crime in Canada for the year 1993. They found that Canada had a relatively low murder rate (53rd out of 83 countries studied) but a relatively high property crime rate (7th out of 83). Property crime includes theft, motor vehicle theft, vandalism, and fraud. This ranking is typical of western developed countries. (The United States is the exception with high rates of both murder and property crime.) Table 2.1 shows a rough breakdown of property crime in Canada for 1993.

Easton and Brantingham estimated the cost to victims of nonviolent property crime to be about $2,000 per incident, for a total of $4 billion per year. When we add to the victims' costs the cost of the courts, the police, and the prisons, the total begins to soar. It continues to climb as we add on the social cost of crime: the emotional trauma and the days of lost or reduced productivity as the victims deal with the shock of being victims.

The Cost of Preventing Crime

Perhaps it would be less costly to prevent crime than to deal with its effects. But how much are we prepared to spend? Currently, one in eight Canadian families owns some sort of burglar alarm, while one in fifty owns a monitored security device. Altogether we spend about $195 million on private security. This amount grew substantially between 1971 and 1991. The number of police officers per capita has also grown since 1971, but more slowly than the number of security guards.

What would it cost to wipe out property crime? We know it would take roughly 23,000 more police officers to stop motor vehicle thefts. At an average salary of $50,000, that would cost taxpayers about $1.15 billion per year. And what about preventing robberies and fraud, to say nothing of violent crime? It is clear that the price tag attached to a "crime-less" society is a high one indeed.

Table 2.1. **Cost to Victims of Property Crime**

Losses	Theft	Vandalism	Break and Enter	Automobile Theft	Robbery	Fraud
Number of reported incidents	888,617	415,645	406,582	156,811	29,961	113,054
Average loss (1993 dollars)	2,054	615	2,225	3,500	2,754	3,403
Total losses (millions of 1993 dollars)	1,821	255	905	549	83	385
Total loss from all sources (millions of 1993 dollars)	3,998					

Source: Paul Brantingham and Stephen T. Easton, *The Crime Bill: Who Pays and How Much?* Vancouver: The Fraser Institute, 1996.

The Trade-Offs That Are Really Involved

Let's assume that the rate of property crime prevention per police officer is the same for the other categories as it is for car theft. We would have to hire about 265,000 more police officers, in addition those mentioned above. The total bill for their salaries would be around $14.5 billion per year, roughly the same amount that Canadians collected in employment insurance in 1997. This sum is $3 billion more than the federal government transferred to the provinces collectively for health, education, and welfare in 1998.

So trade-offs are clearly involved here. With $14.5 billion, Canada could build 20 fixed links like the one between New Brunswick and Prince Edward Island, or 100 new universities like the University of Northern British Columbia. Is the total absence of property crime worth this much to you?

Actually the Risk Is Falling

Violent crime and property crime are everywhere in the news today. Does that mean that Canada is becoming a more dangerous place to live? Fortunately, no. While the property crime rate was three times higher in 1992 than in 1962, it has taken a 20 percent dip in the past six years. So while a larger number of people are the victims of property crime because our population has grown, the proportion of our population that is victimized is falling.

For Critical Analysis

1. Why is opportunity cost such an important concept in analysing government programs to prevent crime?
2. What would happen to the opportunity cost of policing if we allocated more and more of our resources to crime prevention?

CHAPTER SUMMARY

1. All societies at all times face the universal problem of scarcity because we cannot obtain everything we want from nature without sacrifice. Thus scarcity and poverty are not synonymous. Even the richest persons face scarcity because they also have to make choices among alternatives.

2. The resources we use to produce desired goods and services can be classified into land, labour, physical and human capital, and entrepreneurship.

3. Goods are all things from which individuals derive satisfaction. Economic goods are those for which the desired quantity exceeds the amount that is directly available from nature at a zero price. The goods that we want are not necessarily those that we need. The term *need* is indefinable in economics, whereas humans have unlimited *wants*, which are defined as the goods and services on which we place a positive value.

4. We measure the cost of anything by what has to be given up in order to have it. This cost is called opportunity cost.

5. The trade-offs we face as individuals and those we face as a society can be represented graphically by a production possibilities curve (PPC). This curve shows the maximum quantity of one good or service that can be produced, given a specific quantity of another, from a given set of resources over a

specified period of time, usually one year.

6. Because resources are specialized, production possibilities curves bow outward. This means that each additional increment of one good can be obtained only by giving up more and more of the other goods. This is called the law of increasing relative cost.

7. It is impossible to be outside the production possibilities curve, but we can be inside it. When we are, we are in a situation of unemployment, inefficiently organized resources, or some combination of the two.

8. There is a trade-off between consumption goods and capital goods. The more resources we devote to capital goods, the more consumption goods we can normally have in the future (and less currently). This is because more capital goods allow the economy to grow, thereby moving the production possibilities curve outward.

9. You find your comparative advantage by looking at the activity that has the lowest opportunity cost. That is, your comparative advantage lies in the activity that generates the highest income. By specializing in that comparative advantage, you are assured of reaping the gains of specialization.

10. Division of labour occurs when workers are assigned different tasks.

DISCUSSION OF PREVIEW QUESTIONS

1. **Do affluent people face the problem of scarcity?**

   Scarcity is a relative concept and exists because wants are great, relative to the means of satisfying those wants (wealth or income). Even though affluent people have relatively and absolutely high levels of income or wealth, they nevertheless typically want more than they can have (in luxury goods, power, prestige, and so on).

2. **Fresh air may be consumed at no charge, but is it free of cost to society?**

   Individuals are not charged a price for the use of air. Yet truly fresh air is not free to society. If a good were free to society, every person would be able to use all that he or she wanted to use; no one would have to sacrifice anything in order to use that good, and people would not have to compete for it. In Canada, different groups compete for air; for example, environmentalists and concerned citizens compete with automobile drivers and factories for clean air.

3. **Why does the scarcity problem force people to consider opportunity costs?**

   Individuals have limited incomes; as a consequence, an expenditure on an automobile necessarily precludes expenditures on other goods and services. The same is true for society, which also faces the scarcity problem; if society allocates specific resources to the production of a steel mill, those same resources cannot be allocated elsewhere. Because resources are limited, society is forced to decide how to allocate its available resources; scarcity means that the cost of allocating resources to produce specific goods is ultimately assessed in terms of other goods that are necessarily sacrificed. Because there are millions of ways in which the resources allocated to a steel mill might otherwise be allocated, we are forced to consider the *highest-valued* alternative. We define the opportunity cost of a good as its highest-valued alternative; the opportunity cost of the steel mill to society is the highest-valued output that those same resources could otherwise have produced.

4. **Can a "free" college education ever be truly free?**

   Suppose that you were given a college education without having to pay any fees whatsoever. You could say that you were receiving a free education. But someone is paying for your education because you are using scarce resources—buildings, professors' time, electricity for lighting, etc. The opportunity cost of your education is certainly not zero, so in that sense it is not free. Furthermore, by going to college, you are giving up the ability to earn income during that time period. Therefore, there is an opportunity cost to your attending classes and studying. You can approximate that opportunity cost by estimating what your current after-tax income would be if you were working instead of going to school.

PROBLEMS

(Answers to the odd-numbered problems appear at the back of the book.)

2-1. The following sets of numbers represent hypothetical production possibilities for a country in 1998. Plot these points on graph paper.

Cheese	Apples
4	0
3	1.6
2	2.4
1	2.8
0	3.0

Does the law of increasing relative cost seem to hold? Why? On the same graph, plot and draw the production possibilities curve that will represent 10 percent economic growth.

2-2. If, by going to college, you give up the chance to work in your mother's business for 35 hours per week at $7.00 per hour, what would be your opportunity cost of earning a two-year college diploma? What incentives exist to make you incur that opportunity cost? What resources are you giving up today in order to have more in the future?

2-3. Answer the questions using the following information.

Employee	Daily Work Effort	Production
Ann Jones	4 hours	8 jackets
	4 hours	12 ties
Ned Chapman	4 hours	8 jackets
	4 hours	12 ties
		16 jackets
Total daily output		24 ties

a. Who has an absolute advantage in jacket production?
b. Who has a comparative advantage in tie production?
c. Will Jones and Chapman specialize?
d. If they specialize, what will total output equal?

2-4. Two countries, Workland and Playland, have similar populations and identical production possibilities curves but different preferences. The production possibilities combinations are as follows:

Point	Capital Goods	Consumption Goods
A	0	20
B	1	19
C	2	17
D	3	14
E	4	10
F	5	5

Playland is located at point *B* on the PPC, and Workland is located at point *E*. Assume that this situation continues into the future and that all other things remain the same.

a. What is Workland's opportunity cost of capital goods in terms of consumption goods?
b. What is Playland's opportunity cost of capital goods in terms of consumption goods?
c. How would the PPCs of Workland and Playland be expected to compare to each other 50 years in the future?

2-5. Which of the following are part of the opportunity cost of going to a football game in town instead of watching it on TV at home? Explain why.

a. The expense of lunch in a restaurant prior to the football game.
b. The value of one hour of sleep lost because of a traffic jam after the game.
c. The expense of a babysitter for your children if they are too young to go to a football game.

2-6. Assume that your economics and English exams are scheduled for the same day. How would you determine how much time you should spend studying for each exam? Does the grade you are currently receiving in each course affect your decision? Why or why not?

2-7. Some people argue that air is not an economic good. If you agree with this statement, explain why. If you disagree, explain why. (Hint: Is all air the same?)

APPENDIX A

READING AND WORKING WITH GRAPHS

A graph is a visual representation of the relationship between variables. In this appendix, we'll stick to just two variables: an **independent variable,** which can change freely in value, and a **dependent variable,** which changes only as a result of changes in the value of the independent variable. For example, if nothing else is changing in your life, your weight depends on the amount of food you eat. Food is the independent variable and weight the dependent variable.

A table is a list of numerical values showing the relationship between two (or more) variables. Any table can be converted into a graph, which is a visual representation of that list. Once you understand how a table can be converted to a graph, you will understand what graphs are and how to construct and use them.

Consider a practical example. A conservationist may try to convince you that driving at lower highway speeds will help you conserve gas. Table A-1 shows the relationship between speed—the independent variable—and the distance you can go on a litre of gas at that speed—the dependent variable. This table does show a pattern of sorts. As the data in the first column get larger in value, the data in the second column get smaller.

Now let's take a look at the different ways in which variables can be related.

DIRECT AND INVERSE RELATIONSHIPS

Two variables can be related in different ways, some simple, others more complex. For example, a person's weight and height are often related. If we measured the height and weight of thousands of people, we would surely find that taller people tend to weigh more than shorter people. That is, we would discover that there is a **direct relationship** between height and weight. By this we simply mean that an increase in one variable is usually associated with an increase in the related variable. This can easily be seen in part (a) of Figure A-1.

Let's look at another simple way in which two variables can be related. Much evidence indicates that as the price of a specific commodity rises, the amount purchased decreases—there is an **inverse relationship** between the variable's price per unit and quantity purchased. A table listing the data for this relationship would indicate that for higher and higher prices, smaller and smaller quantities would be purchased. We see this relationship in part (b) of Figure A-1.

▶ **Independent variable**

A variable whose value is determined independently of, or outside, the equation under study.

▶ **Dependent variable**

A variable whose value changes according to changes in the value of one or more independent variables.

Table A-1
Gas Consumption as a Function of Driving Speed

Kilometres per Hour	Kilometres per Litre
70	11
80	10
90	9
100	8
110	7
120	6
130	5

▶ **Direct relationship**

A relationship between two variables that is positive, meaning that an increase in one variable is associated with an increase in the other and a decrease in one variable is associated with a decrease in the other.

▶ **Inverse relationship**

A relationship between two variables that is negative, meaning that an increase in one variable is associated with a decrease in the other and a decrease in one variable is associated with an increase in the other.

Figure A-1
Relationships

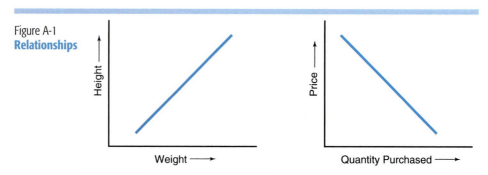

Figure A-2
Horizontal Number Line

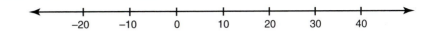

CONSTRUCTING A GRAPH

Let us now examine how to construct a graph to illustrate a relationship between two variables.

▶ **Number line**
A line that can be divided into segments of equal length, each associated with a number.

A Number Line

The first step is to become familiar with what is called a **number line.** One is shown in Figure A-2. There are two things that you should know about it.

1. The points on the line divide the line into equal segments.
2. The numbers associated with the points on the line increase in value from left to right; saying it the other way around, the numbers decrease in value from right to left. However you say it, what we're describing is formally called an *ordered set of points.*

Figure A-3
Vertical Number Line

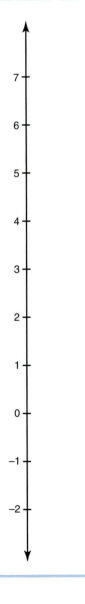

On the number line, we have shown the line segments—that is, the distance from 0 to 10 or the distance between 30 and 40. They all appear to be equal and, indeed, are equal to 13 mm. When we use a distance to represent a quantity, such as barrels of oil, graphically, we are scaling the number line. In the example shown, the distance between 0 and 10 might represent 10 barrels of oil, or the distance from 0 to 40 might represent 40 barrels. Of course, the scale may differ on different number lines. For example, a distance of 1 cm could represent 10 units on one number line but 5,000 units on another. Notice that on our number line, points to the left of 0 correspond to negative numbers and points to the right of 0 correspond to positive numbers.

Of course, we can also construct a vertical number line. Consider the one in Figure A-3. As we move up this vertical number line, the numbers increase in value; conversely, as we descend, they decrease in value. Below 0 the numbers are negative, and above 0 the numbers are positive. And as on the horizontal number line, all the line segments are equal. This line is divided into segments such that the distance between −2 and −1 is the same as the distance between 0 and 1.

Combining Vertical and Horizontal Number Lines

By drawing the horizontal and vertical lines on the same sheet of paper, we are able to express the relationships between variables graphically. We do this in Figure A-4.

We draw them (1) so that they intersect at each other's 0 point and (2) so that they are perpendicular to each other. The result is a set of coordinate axes, where each line is called an axis. When we have two axes, they span a plane.

For one number line, you need only one number to specify any point on the line; equivalently, when you see a point on the line, you know that it represents one number or one value. With a coordinate value system, you need two numbers to specify a single point in the plane; when you see a single point on a graph, you know that it represents two numbers or two values.

Figure A-4
A Set of Coordinate Axes

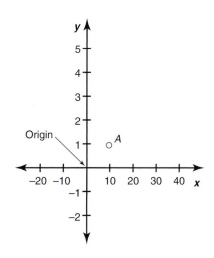

▶ **y axis**

The vertical axis in a graph.

▶ **x axis**

The horizontal axis in a graph.

▶ **Origin**

The intersection of the y axis and the x axis in a graph.

The basic things that you should know about a coordinate number system are that the vertical number line is referred to as the **y axis,** the horizontal number line is referred to as the **x axis,** and the point of intersection of the two lines is referred to as the **origin.**

Any point such as A in Figure A-4 represents two numbers—a value of x and a value of y. But we know more than that; we also know that point A represents a positive value of y because it is above the x axis, and we know that it represents a positive value of x because it is to the right of the y axis.

Point A represents a "paired observation" of the variables x and y; in particular, in Figure A-4, A represents an observation of the pair of values $x = 10$ and $y = 1$. Every point in the coordinate system corresponds to a paired observation of x and y, which can be simply written (x, y)—the x value is always specified first, then the y value. When we give the values associated with the position of point A in the coordinate number system, we are in effect giving the coordinates of that point. A's coordinates are $x = 10$, $y = 1$, or $(10, 1)$.

Table A-2
T-Shirts Purchased

(1) Price of T-Shirts	(2) Number of T-Shirts Purchased per Week
$10	20
9	30
8	40
7	50
6	60
5	70

GRAPHING NUMBERS IN A TABLE

Consider Table A-2. Column 1 shows different prices for T-shirts, and column 2 gives the number of T-shirts purchased per week at these prices. Notice the pattern of these numbers. As the price of T-shirts falls, the number of T-shirts purchased per week increases. Therefore, an inverse relationship exists between these two variables, and as soon as we represent it on a graph, you will be able to see the relationship. We can graph this relationship using a coordinate number system—a vertical and horizontal number line for each of these two variables. Such a graph is shown in part (b) of Figure A-5.

In economics, it is conventional to put dollar values on the y axis. We therefore construct a vertical number line for price and a horizontal number line, the x axis, for quantity of T-shirts purchased per week. The resulting coordinate system allows the

Figure A-5
**Graphing the Relationship
Between T-Shirts
Purchased and Price**

Part (a)

Price per T-Shirt	T-Shirts Purchased per Week	Point on Graph
$10	20	I (20, 10)
9	30	J (30, 9)
8	40	K (40, 8)
7	50	L (50, 7)
6	60	M (60, 6)
5	70	N (70, 5)

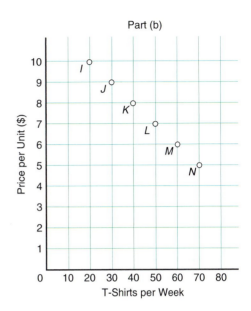

Part (b)

Figure A-6
**Connecting the
Observation Points**

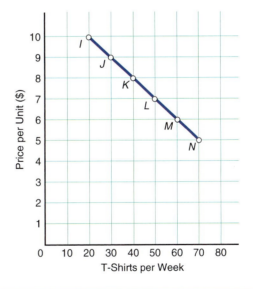

plotting of each of the paired observation points; in part (a), we repeat Table A-2, with a column added expressing these points in paired-data (x, y) form. For example, point J is the paired observation (30, 9). It indicates that when the price of a T-shirt is $9, 30 will be purchased per week.

If it were possible to sell parts of a T-shirt ($\frac{1}{2}$ or $\frac{1}{20}$ shirt), we would have observations at every possible price. That is, we would be able to connect our paired observations, represented as lettered points. Let's assume that we can make T-shirts perfectly divisible. We would then have a line that connects these points, as shown in the graph in Figure A-6.

In short, we have now represented the data from the table in the form of a graph. Note that an inverse relationship between two variables shows up on a graph as a line or curve that slopes downward from left to right. (You might as well get used to the idea that economists call a straight line a "curve" even though it may not curve at all. Much of economists' data turn out to be curves, so they refer to everything represented graphically, even straight lines, as curves.)

THE SLOPE OF A LINE (A LINEAR CURVE)

An important property of a curve represented on a graph is its *slope*. Consider Figure A-7, which represents the quantities of shoes per week that a seller is willing to offer at different prices. Note that in part (a) of Figure A-7, as in Figure A-5, we have expressed the coordinates of the points in parentheses in paired-data form.

The **slope** of a line is defined as the change in the y values divided by the corresponding change in the x values as we move along the line. Let's move from point E to point D in part (b) of Figure A-7. As we move, we note that the change in the y values, which is the change in price, is +\$20, because we have moved from a price of \$20 to a price of \$40 per pair. As we move from E to D, the change in the x values is +80; the number of pairs of shoes willingly offered per week rises from 80 to 160 pairs. The slope calculated as a change in the y values divided by the change in the x values is therefore

$$\frac{20}{80} = \frac{1}{4}$$

It may be helpful for you to think of slope as a "rise" (movement in the vertical direction) over a "run" (movement in the horizontal direction). We show this abstractly in Figure A-8. The slope is measured by the amount of rise divided by the amount of run. In the example in Figure A-8, and of course in Figure A-7, the

Figure A-7
A Positively Sloped Curve

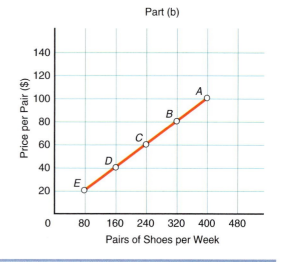

Part (b)

Part (a)

Price per Pair	Pairs of Shoes Offered per Week	Point on Graph
\$100	400	A (400, 100)
80	320	B (320, 80)
60	240	C (240, 60)
40	160	D (160, 40)
20	80	E (80, 20)

Figure A-8
Figuring Positive Slope

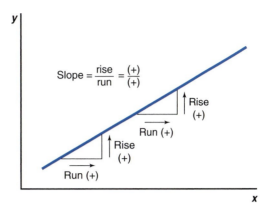

Figure A-9
Figuring Negative Slope

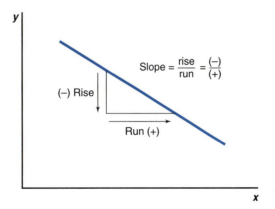

amount of rise is positive and so is the amount of run. That's because it's a direct relationship. We show an inverse relationship in Figure A-9. The slope is still equal to the rise divided by the run, but in this case the rise and the run have opposite signs because the curve slopes downward. That means that the slope will have to be negative and that we are dealing with an inverse relationship.

Now let's calculate the slope for a different part of the curve in part (b) of Figure A-7. We will find the slope as we move from point B to point A. Again, we note that the slope, or rise over run, from B to A equals

$$\frac{20}{80} = \frac{1}{4}$$

A specific property of a straight line is that its slope is the same between any two points; in other words, the slope is constant at all points on a straight line in a graph.

We conclude that for our example in Figure A-7, the relationship between the price of a pair of shoes and the number of pairs of shoes willingly offered per week is linear, which simply means "in a straight line," and our calculations indicate a constant slope. Moreover, we calculate a direct relationship between these two variables, which turns out to be an upward-sloping (from left to right) curve. Upward-sloping curves have positive slopes—in this case, it is $+\frac{1}{4}$.

We know that an inverse relationship between two variables shows up as a downward-sloping curve—rise over run will be a negative slope because the rise and run have opposite signs as shown in Figure A-9. When we see a negative slope, we know that increases in one variable are associated with decreases in the other. Therefore, we say that downward-sloping curves have negative slopes. Can you verify that the slope of the graph representing the relationship between T-shirt prices and the quantity of T-shirts purchased per week in Figure A-6 is $-\frac{1}{10}$?

Slopes of Nonlinear Curves

The graph presented in Figure A-10 indicates a *nonlinear* relationship between two variables, total profits and output per unit of time. Inspection of this graph indicates that at first, increases in output lead to increases in total profits; that is, total profits rise as output increases. But beyond some output level, further increases in output cause decreases in total profits.

Can you see how this curve rises at first, reaches a peak at point *C*, and then falls? This curve relating total profits to output levels appears mountain-shaped.

Considering that this curve is nonlinear (it is obviously not a straight line), should we expect a constant slope when we compute changes in *y* divided by corresponding changes in *x* in moving from one point to another? A quick inspection, even without specific numbers, should lead us to conclude that the slopes of lines joining different points in this curve, such as between *A* and *B*, *B* and *C*, or *C* and *D*, will *not* be the same. The curve slopes upward (in a positive direction) for some values and downward (in a negative direction) for other values. In fact, the slope of the line between any two points on this curve will be different from the slope of the line between any two other points. Each slope will be different as we move along the curve.

Instead of using a line between two points to discuss slope, mathematicians and economists prefer to discuss the slope *at a particular point*. The slope at a point on the curve, such as point *B* in the graph in Figure A-10, is the slope of a line *tangent*

Figure A-10
The Slope of a Nonlinear Curve

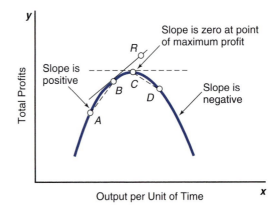

to that point. A tangent line is a straight line that touches a curve at only one point. For example, it might be helpful to think of the tangent at B as the straight line that just "kisses" the curve at point B.

To calculate the slope of a tangent line, you need to have some additional information besides the two values of the point of tangency. For example, in Figure A-10, if we knew that the point R also lay on the tangent line and we knew the two values of that point, we could calculate the slope of the tangent line. We could calculate rise over run between points B and R, and the result would be the slope of the line tangent to the one point B on the curve.

APPENDIX SUMMARY

1. Direct relationships involve a dependent variable changing in the same direction as the change in the independent variable.

2. Inverse relationships involve the dependent variable changing in the opposite direction of the change in the independent variable.

3. When we draw a graph showing the relationship between two economic variables, we are holding all other things constant (the Latin term for which is *ceteris paribus*).

4. We obtain a set of coordinates by putting vertical and horizontal number lines together. The vertical line is called the y axis; the horizontal line, the x axis.

5. The slope of any linear (straight-line) curve is the change in the y values divided by the corresponding change in the x values as we move along the line. Otherwise stated, the slope is calculated as the amount of rise over the amount of run, where rise is movement in the vertical direction and run is movement in the horizontal direction.

6. The slope of a nonlinear curve changes; it is positive when the curve is rising and negative when the curve is falling. At a maximum or minimum point, the slope of the nonlinear curve is zero.

APPENDIX PROBLEMS

(The answer to Problem A-1 appears at the back of the book.)

A-1. Complete the schedule and plot the following function:

$y = 3x$

y	x
	4
	3
	2
	1
	0
	−1
	−2
	−3
	−4

A-2. Complete the schedule and plot the following function:

$y = x^2$

y	x
	4
	3
	2
	1
	0
	−1
	−2
	−3
	−4

3

Demand and Supply

Between 1990 and 1996, the number of suppliers of sports trading cards increased by almost 5,000 percent. You might predict that more suppliers would mean that more cards would be put on the market and the price of cards would fall. In general you would be correct. However, what actually happened was that the prices of some sports cards fell while the prices of others rose. To understand how these seemingly contradictory results are actually quite logical, you will need the tools of supply and demand analysis.

Did You Know That... more than 20 million people worldwide currently own portable cellular phones? Two million Canadians have purchased them since their introduction in 1985. Over the last decade, sales outside Canada have grown between 45 to 50 percent every year. Marketing consultants expect cell phone ownership to increase by 10 to 15 percent per year for the next several years. There are many reasons for the growth in ownership of cellular phones, not least being the dramatic reduction in both price and size thanks to improved and cheaper computer chips used in making them. There is something else at work, though. It has to do with security. In a recent survey, 46 percent of new cellular phone users said that personal safety was the main reason they bought a portable phone. In the case of an automobile breakdown, for example, they would be able to call a garage or tow truck for help.

We could attempt to explain the phenomenon simply by saying that more people like to use portable phones. But that explanation is neither satisfying nor entirely accurate. If we use the economist's primary set of tools, *demand and supply,* we will have a better understanding of the cellular phone's explosion in popularity, as well as many other phenomena in our world. Demand and supply are two ways of categorizing the influences on the price of goods that you buy, and the quantities available. As such, demand and supply form the basis of virtually all economic analysis of the world around us.

As you will see throughout this text, the operation of the forces of demand and supply take place in *markets*. A **market** is an abstract concept referring to all the arrangements individuals have for exchanging with one another. Goods and services are sold in markets, such as the automobile market, the health food market, and the compact disc market. Workers offer their services in the labour market. Companies, or firms, buy workers' labour services in the labour market. Firms also buy other inputs in order to produce the goods and services that you buy as a consumer. They purchase machines, buildings, and land. These markets are in operation at all times. One of the most important activities in them is the setting of the prices of all of the inputs and outputs that are bought and sold in our complicated economy. To understand the determination of prices, you first need to look at the law of demand.

▶ **Market**
All of the arrangements that individuals have for exchanging with one another. Thus we can speak of the labour market, the automobile market, and the credit market.

THE LAW OF DEMAND

Demand has a special meaning in economics. It refers to the quantities of specific goods or services that individuals, either singly or as a group, will purchase at various possible prices, other things being constant. We can therefore talk about the demand for microprocessor chips, French fries, compact disc players, and children.

Associated with the concept of demand is the **law of demand**, which can be stated as follows:

▶ **Demand**
A schedule of how much of a good or service people will purchase at any price during a specified time period, other things being constant.

▶ **Law of demand**
The observation that there is a negative, or inverse, relationship between the price of any good or service and the quantity demanded, holding other factors constant.

> When the price of a good goes up, people buy less of it, other things being equal. When the price of a good goes down, people buy more of it, other things being equal.

The law of demand tells us that the quantity demanded of any commodity is inversely related to its price, other things being equal. In an inverse relationship, one variable moves up in value when the other moves down. The law of demand states that a change in price causes the quantity demanded to change in the *opposite* direction.

Notice that we tacked onto the end of the law of demand the statement "other things being equal." We referred to this in Chapter 1 as the *ceteris paribus* assumption. It means, for example, that when we predict that people will buy fewer CD players if their price goes up, we are holding constant the price of all other goods in the economy as well as people's incomes. Implicitly, therefore, if we are assuming that no other prices change when we examine the price behaviour of CD players, we are looking at the *relative* price of CD players.

The law of demand is supported by millions of observations of how people behave in the marketplace. Theoretically, it can be derived from an economic model based on rational behaviour, as was discussed in Chapter 1. Basically, if nothing else changes and the price of a good falls, the lower price induces us to buy more over a certain period of time. This is because we can enjoy additional net gains that were unavailable at the higher price. For the most part, if you examine your own purchasing behaviour, you will see that it generally follows the law of demand.

Relative Prices Versus Money Prices

▶ **Relative price**
The price of a commodity expressed in terms of another commodity.

▶ **Money price**
The price that we observe today, expressed in today's dollars. Also called the *absolute, nominal,* or *current price.*

The **relative price** of any commodity is its price in terms of another commodity. The actual price that you pay in dollars and cents for any good or service at any point in time is called its **money price**. Consider an example that you might hear quite often around older friends or relatives. "When I bought my first new car, it cost only $1500." The implication, of course, is that the price of cars today is outrageously high because the average new car might cost $20,000. But that is not an accurate comparison. What was the price of the average house during that same year? Perhaps it was only $12,000. By comparison, then, given that houses today average about $150,000, the current price of a new car doesn't sound so far out of line, does it?

The point is that money prices during different time periods don't tell you much. You have to find out relative prices. Consider an example of the price of CDs versus the price of cassettes from last year and this year. In Table 3.1, we show the money price of CDs and cassettes for two years during which both have gone up. That means that we have to pay out more for each in today's dollars and cents. If we look, though, at the relative prices of CDs and cassettes, we find that last year, CDs were twice as expensive as cassettes, whereas this year they are only 1.81 times as expensive. Conversely, if we compare cassettes to CDs, last year they cost only half as much as CDs, but today they cost about 55 percent as much. In the one-year period, while both prices have gone up in money terms, the relative price of CDs has fallen (and, equivalently, the relative price of cassettes has risen).

Try Preview Question 1:
Why are relative prices important in understanding the law of demand?

Table 3.1	Money Price		Relative Price	
Money Price Versus Relative Price	Last Year	This Year	Last Year	This Year
CDs	$18	$20	$18 / $9 = 2.0	$20 / $11 = 1.81
Cassettes	$9	$11	$9 / $18 = 0.5	$11 / $20 = 0.55

The money price of both compact discs (CDs) and cassettes has risen. But the relative price of CDs has fallen (or conversely, the relative price of cassettes has risen).

Thinking Critically About the Media   **The Real Price of Stamps**

The press is fond of pointing out the rise in the price of a particular good, such as a stamp for first-class mail. In the 1940s, a first-class stamp in Canada cost only 4 cents, but by the mid-1990s, it had climbed to 45 cents. That is the absolute price of postage, however. What about the relative price, the price relative to the average of all other prices? The relative price of postage is actually lower today than when it reached its peak in 1975. Many other relative prices have fall-en over the years, ranging from gasoline prices to the prime minister's salary. Indeed, relatively speaking, the prime minister's current $155,000-a-year salary is peanuts compared to what Prime Minister William Lyon Mackenzie King earned in 1946. In relative terms (dollars in 1947), the current prime minister earns only about 78 percent of Mr. King's salary, even though in absolute terms, the current prime minister makes more. Remember, everything is relative.

INTERNATIONAL EXAMPLE
Cross-Border Shopping in Europe

The increase in cross-border shopping is a good example of how individuals respond to relative prices rather than absolute, or money, prices. Several times a week, bargain-conscious Basques from Bilbao, Spain, cross the French border (which is without customs or immigration control because it is part of the European Union) to shop for food. At current exchange rates, similar-quality food costs about 40 percent less on the French side of the border. Similarly, for cost-conscious consumers in Switzerland who live along the border with France, such trips are frequent. Professor Stephen Stearns, of Basel, Switzerland, claims that shopping in France saves a typical family more than 30 percent on its weekly food bill. At current exchange rates, pork and beef cost only half as much in France as they do in Switzerland, and cheese is 40 percent less expensive. Germans and Belgians who live on the border with Luxembourg and the Netherlands often travel to those countries to buy food and consumer products such as shampoo. All this border crossing bears out the fact that relative prices, not absolute (money) prices, determine people's shopping habits.

For critical analysis: How would we calculate the net benefit to cross-border shopping for the people who engage in it? (Hint: What are some of the costs of such shopping?)

Concepts in Brief

- The law of demand states that there is an inverse relationship between the quantity demanded of a good and its price, other things being equal.
- The law of demand applies when other things, such as income and the prices of all other goods and services, are held constant.

THE DEMAND SCHEDULE

Let's take a hypothetical demand situation to see how the inverse relationship between the price and the quantity demanded looks (holding other things equal). We will consider the quantity of computer diskettes demanded *per year* by one person. Without stating the *time dimension*, we could not make sense out of this demand relationship because the numbers would be different if we were talking about the quantity demanded per month, or the quantity demanded per decade.

In addition to implicitly or explicitly stating a time dimension for a demand relationship, we are also implicitly referring to *constant-quality* units of the good or service in question. Prices are always expressed in constant-quality units in order to avoid the problem of comparing commodities that are in fact not truly comparable.

In part (a) of Figure 3.1, we see that if the price were $1 per diskette, 50 of them would be bought each year by our representative individual, but if the price were $5 per diskette, only 10 would be bought each year. This reflects the law of demand. Part (a) is also called simply demand, or a *demand schedule*, because it gives a schedule of alternative quantities demanded per year at different possible prices.

The Demand Curve

Tables expressing relationships between two variables can be represented in graphical terms. To do this, we need only construct a graph that has the price per constant-quality diskette on the vertical axis, and the quantity measured in constant-quality diskettes per year on the horizontal axis. All we have to do is take combinations *A* through *E* from part (a) of Figure 3.1 and plot those points in part (b). Now we connect the points with a smooth line, and *voilà*, we have a **demand curve**[1]. It is downward-sloping (from left to right) to indicate the inverse relationship between the price of diskettes and the quantity demanded per year. Our presentation of demand schedules and curves applies equally well to all commodities, including toothpicks, hamburgers, textbooks, credit, and labour services. Remember, the demand curve is simply a graphical representation of the law of demand.

▶ **Demand curve**

A graphical representation of the demand schedule; a negatively sloped line showing the inverse relationship between the price and the quantity demanded (other things being equal).

---

[1] Even though we call them "curves," for the purposes of exposition we often draw straight lines. In many real-world situations, demand and supply curves will in fact be lines that do curve. To connect the points in part (b) with a line, we assume that for all prices in between the ones shown, the quantities demanded will be found along that line.

Figure 3.1
**The Individual Demand Schedule
and the Individual Demand Curve**

In part (a), we show combinations *A*
through *E* of the quantities of diskettes
demanded, measured in constant-
quality units at prices ranging from $5
down to $1 per disk. In part (b), we plot
combinations *A* through *E* on a grid.
The result is the individual demand
curve for diskettes.

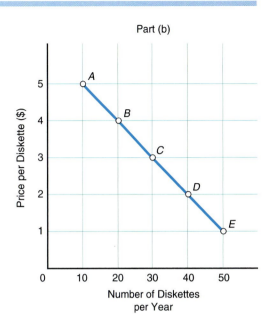

Part (a)

Combination	Price per Constant-Quality Diskette	Quantity of Constant-Quality Diskettes per Year
A	$5	10
B	4	20
C	3	30
D	2	40
E	1	50

Individual Versus Market Demand Curves

The demand schedule shown in part (a) of Figure 3.1 and the resulting demand
curve shown in part (b) are both given for one individual. As we shall see, determining price in the marketplace depends on, among other things, the **market
demand** for a particular commodity. The way in which we measure a market demand
schedule and derive a market demand curve for diskettes or any other commodity is
by adding the individual demand at each price for all those in the market. Suppose
that the market for diskettes consists of only two buyers: buyer 1, for whom we've
already shown the demand schedule in Figure 3.1, and buyer 2, whose demand
schedule is displayed in Figure 3.2, part (a), column 3. Column 1 of Figure 3.2, part
(a) shows the price, and column 2 gives the quantity demanded by buyer 1 (data
taken directly from Figure 3.1). Column 4 states the total quantity demanded at
each price, obtained by adding columns 2 and 3. Graphically, in part (d) of Figure
3.2, we add the demand curves of buyer 1 [part (b)] and buyer 2 [part (c)] to derive
the market demand curve.

There are, of course, literally millions of potential consumers for diskettes. We'll
assume that the summation of all of the consumers in the market results in a demand
schedule, given in part (a) of Figure 3.3, and a demand curve, given in part (b). The
quantity demanded is now measured in millions of units per year. Remember, part
(b) in Figure 3.3 shows the market demand curve for the millions of users of
diskettes. The "market" demand curve that we derived in Figure 3.2 assumed that
there were only two buyers in the entire market. This is why that demand curve is
not a smooth line, whereas the true market demand curve in part (b) of Figure 3.3
is, and has no kinks.

Now consider some special aspects of the market demand curve for new cars.

▶ **Market demand**

The demand of all consumers in
the marketplace for a particular
good or service. The summing at
each price of the quantity
demanded by each individual.

Figure 3.2
The Horizontal Summation of Two Demand Schedules

Part (a) shows how to sum the demand schedule for one buyer with that of another buyer. Column 2 shows the quantity demanded by buyer 1, taken from part (a) of Figure 3.1. Column 4 is the sum of columns 2 and 3. We plot the demand curve for buyer 1 in part (b) and the demand curve for buyer 2 in part (c). When we add those two demand curves horizontally, we get the market demand curve for two buyers, shown in part (d).

Part (a)

(1) Price per Diskette	(2) Buyer 1 Quantity Demanded	(3) Buyer 2 Quantity Demanded	(4) = (2) + (3) Combined Quantity Demanded per Year
$5	10	10	20
4	20	20	40
3	30	40	70
2	40	50	90
1	50	60	110

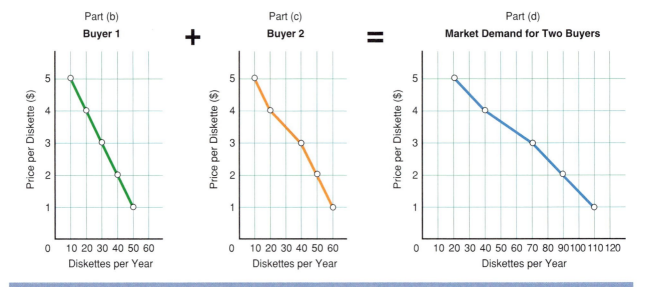

Figure 3.3
The Market Demand Schedule for Diskettes

In part (a), we add up the millions of existing demand schedules for diskettes. In part (b), we plot the quantities from part (a) on a grid; connecting them produces the market demand curve for diskettes

Part (a)

Price per Constant-Quality Diskette	Total Quantity Demanded of Constant-Quality Diskettes per Year (millions)
$5	2
4	4
3	6
2	8
1	10

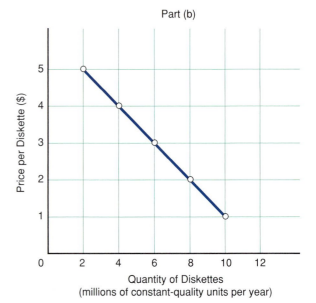

New car prices have risen steadily since the 1960s as increasingly sophisticated consumers demand additional special features in their vehicles. But comprehensive warranties, catalytic converters, air bags, and the like all push up the price of the basic automobile. Monthly car-loan repayments are becoming beyond the means of many Canadian car buyers. In 1996, new car dealers found that sales fell by 10 percent over those in 1995, and they expect further declines over time.

The dealers, however, understand the law of demand. They are offering to lease—rent—new vehicles for monthly payments that are often far below the loan repayments that would be required if the car was actually purchased. As a result, more than 20 percent of all new car deals in Canada in 1996 were leases. Another benefit to the dealers is that the vehicles returned at the end of the lease make a good supply of late-model used cars for those customers still looking to buy an automobile.

For critical analysis: What do you think will happen in the market for used cars over the course of the next five years?

Concepts in Brief

- We measure the demand schedule both in terms of a time dimension and in constant-quality units.
- The market demand curve is derived by summing the quantity demanded by individuals at each price. Graphically, we add the individual demand curves horizontally to derive the total, or market, demand curve.

SHIFTS IN DEMAND

Assume that the federal government gives every student registered in a Canadian college, university, or technical school a personal computer that uses diskettes. The demand curve shown in part (b) of Figure 3.3 is no longer an accurate representation of the total market demand for diskettes. There will now be an increase in the number of diskettes demanded *at each and every possible price*. What we have to do is shift the curve outward, or to the right, to represent the rise in demand. The demand curve in Figure 3.4 will shift from D_1 to D_2. Take any price, say, $3 per diskette. Originally, before the federal government giveaway of personal computers, the amount demanded at $3 was 60 million diskettes per year. After the government giveaway, however, the quantity demanded at $3 is 100 million diskettes per year. What we have seen is a shift in the demand for diskettes.

The shift can also go in the opposite direction. What if colleges uniformly outlawed the use of personal computers by students? Such a regulation would cause a shift inward—to the left—of the demand curve for diskettes. In Figure 3.4, the

Figure 3.4
A Shift in the Demand Curve

If some factor other than price changes, the only way we can show its effect is by moving the entire demand curve, say, from D_1 to D_2. We have assumed in our example that the move was precipitated by the government's giving a free personal computer to every registered college student in Canada. That meant that at all prices, a larger number of diskettes would be demanded than before. Curve D_3 represents reduced demand compared to curve D_1, caused by a law prohibiting computers on campus.

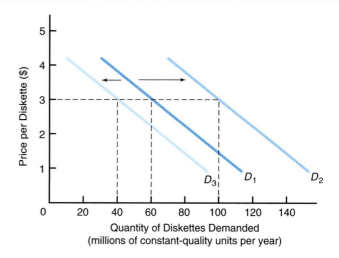

demand curve would shift to D_3; the amount demanded would now be less at each and every possible price.

The Other Determinants of Demand

The demand curve in part (b) of Figure 3.3 is drawn with other things held constant, specifically all of the other factors that determine how much will be bought. There are many such determinants. The major ones are income; tastes and preferences; the prices of related goods; expectations regarding future prices, future incomes, and future product availability; and population (market size). Let's examine each determinant more closely.

Income. For most goods, an increase in income will lead to an increase in demand. The phrase *increase in demand* always refers to a comparison between two different demand curves. Thus for most goods, an increase in income will lead to a rightward shift in the position of the demand curve from, say, D_1 to D_2 in Figure 3.4. You can avoid confusion about shifts in curves by always relating a rise in demand to a rightward shift in the demand curve, and a fall in demand to a leftward shift in the demand curve. Goods for which the demand rises when income rises are called **normal goods**. Most goods, such as shoes, computers, and CDs, are "normal goods." For some goods, however, demand *falls* as income rises. These are called **inferior goods**. Beans might be an example. As households get richer, they tend to spend less and less on beans and more and more on meat. (The terms *normal* and *inferior* are merely part of the economist's terminology; no value judgments are implied by or associated with them.)

Remember, a shift to the left in the demand curve represents a fall in demand, and a shift to the right represents a rise, or increase, in demand.

▶ **Normal goods**

Goods for which demand rises as income rises. Most goods are considered normal.

▶ **Inferior goods**

Goods for which demand falls as income rises.

Tastes and Preferences. A change in consumer tastes in favour of a good can shift its demand curve outward to the right. When Frisbees® became the rage, the demand curve for them shifted outward to the right; when the rage died out, the demand curve shifted inward to the left. Fashions depend to a large extent on people's tastes and preferences. Economists have little to say about the determination of tastes; they have no "good" theories of taste determination or why people buy one brand of a product rather than others. Advertisers, however, do have various theories that they use in trying to make consumers prefer their products to those of competitors.

EXAMPLE   The Boom in Specialty Coffees

Specialty coffee bars are finding out what happens to their demand when there is a shift in consumer tastes for their product. Where less than 5 percent of coffee drinkers drank specialty coffees in 1995, over 10 percent do now, and industry experts predict that by the year 2000, a full 20 percent of coffee served will be specialty coffee.

Does this increase represent an increase in demand for all coffee? No, says the Coffee Association of Canada. About 51 percent of Canadians, as always, drink on average just under three cups of coffee per day. The total amount of coffee served has not changed appreciably since 1995; it remains at about 51 billion cups per year. What has changed is the drinkers' tastes. Instead of ordering plain coffee, more and more coffee drinkers are ordering espressos, lattes, and cappuccinos.

There is no consensus in the coffee industry about why this change is taking place. The Coffee Association of Canada thinks that coffee is replacing alcohol as a social drink because there are fewer health risks associated with drinking coffee. Industry insiders suggest that drinking specialty coffee has become "cool" and imbues the drinkers with a kind of chic and sophistication. What is clear is that no one really knows why Canadian coffee drinkers are changing their minds.

For critical analysis: From the above, what do you think will be happening to the demand for alcohol?

Prices of Related Goods: Substitutes and Complements.   Demand schedules are always drawn with the prices of all other commodities held constant. In other words, when deriving a given demand curve, we assume that only the price of the good under study changes. For example, when we draw the demand curve for butter, we assume that the price of margarine is held constant. When we draw the demand curve for stereo speakers, we assume that the price of stereo amplifiers is held constant. When we refer to *related goods*, we are talking about goods for which demand is interdependent. If a change in the price of one good shifts the demand for another good, those two goods are related. There are two types of related goods: *substitutes* and *complements*. We can define and distinguish between substitutes and complements in terms of how the change in price of one commodity affects the demand for its related commodity.

▶ **Substitutes**

Two goods are substitutes when either one can be used to satisfy a similar want—for example, coffee and tea. The more you buy of one, the less you buy of the other. For substitutes, the change in the price of one causes demand for the other to shift in the same direction as the price change.

Butter and margarine are **substitutes**. Let's assume that each originally cost $4 per kilogram. If the price of butter remains the same and the price of margarine falls from $4 to $2 per kilogram, people will buy more margarine and less butter. The demand curve for butter will shift inward to the left. If, conversely, the price of margarine rises from $4 to $6 per kilogram, people will buy more butter and less margarine. The demand curve for butter will shift outward to the right. An increase in the price of margarine will lead to an increase in the demand for butter, and an increase in the price of butter will lead to an increase in the demand for margarine. For substitutes, a price change in the substitute will cause a change in demand *in the same direction*.

For **complements**, the situation is reversed. Consider stereo speakers and stereo amplifiers. We draw the demand curve for speakers with the price of amplifiers held constant. If the price per constant-quality unit of stereo amplifiers decreases from, say, $500 to $200, that will encourage more people to purchase component stereo systems. They will now buy more speakers than before at any given price. The demand curve for speakers will shift outward to the right. If, by contrast, the price of amplifiers increases from $200 to $500, fewer people will purchase component stereo systems. The demand curve for speakers will shift inward to the left. To summarize, a decrease in the price of amplifiers leads to an increase in the demand for speakers. An increase in the price of amplifiers leads to a decrease in the demand for speakers. Thus for complements, a price change in a product will cause a change in demand *in the opposite direction*.

Are new learning technologies complements or substitutes for college instructors? Read on.

▶**Complements**

Two goods are complements if both are used together for consumption or enjoyment—for example, coffee and cream. The more you buy of one, the more you buy of the other. For complements, a change in the price of one causes an opposite shift in the demand for the other.

EXAMPLE	The Future of College Teaching

In this class and in others, you've probably been exposed to some of the new (and old) instructional technologies such as films and videos, interactive computer software, and interactive CD-ROM learning systems. Your professors have used these as a complement to their teaching, but in the future those technologies may in fact become a substitute for what your professors do in the classroom.

Televised and audio-taped lectures mean that more and more Canadian institutions can offer distance education courses, thus allowing a given number of professors to teach a greater number of students. Athabasca University in Alberta and Simon Fraser University in British Columbia offer enough distance education courses that a student can earn a university degree in business administration, history, or education without ever attending a class. Mount Saint Vincent University in Nova Scotia and CJRT Open College in Ontario offer diplomas entirely through distance education. Now consider interactive CD-ROM learning systems. In theory, virtually every college course could be put on CD-ROM, thereby entirely eliminating the need for instructors. Going one step further, institutions of higher learning are now using the Internet to provide instruction. The University of Western Ontario and Queen's University currently bring their programs to western Canada, offering an executive MBA through a combination of interactive video classroom instruction, high-speed Internet connections, e-mail, and shared application computing.

For critical analysis: What do you predict will happen to the demand curve for college professors in the next decade?

Expectations.   Consumers' expectations regarding future prices, future incomes, and future availability may prompt them to buy more or less of a particular good without a change in its current money price. For example, consumers getting wind of a scheduled 100 percent price increase in diskettes next month may buy more of them today, at today's prices. Today's demand curve for diskettes will shift from D_1 to D_2 in Figure 3.4 on page 58. The opposite would occur if a decrease in the price of diskettes were scheduled for next month.

Expectations of a rise in income may cause consumers to want to purchase more of everything today, at today's prices. Again, such a change in expectations of higher future income will cause a shift in the demand curve from D_1 to D_2 in Figure 3.4. Finally, expectations that goods will not be available at any price will induce consumers to stock up now, increasing current demand.

Population.   An increase in the population in an economy (holding per capita income constant) often shifts the market demand outward for most products. This is because an increase in population means an increase in the number of buyers in the market. Conversely, a reduction in the population will shift most market demand curves inward because of the reduction in the number of buyers in the market.

Changes in Demand Versus Changes in Quantity Demanded

We have made repeated references to demand and to quantity demanded. It is important to realize that there is a difference between a *change in demand* and a *change in quantity demanded*.

Demand refers to a schedule of planned rates of purchase, and depends on a great many nonprice determinants. Whenever there is a change in a nonprice determinant, there will be a change in demand—a shift in the entire demand curve to the right or to the left.

A quantity demanded is a specific quantity at a specific price, represented by a single point on a demand curve. When price changes, quantity demanded changes according to the law of demand, and there will be a movement from one point to another along the same demand curve. Look at Figure 3.5 on page 62. At a price of $3 per diskette, 60 million diskettes per year are demanded. If the price falls to $1, quantity demanded increases to 100 million per year. This movement occurs because the current market price for the product changes. In Figure 3.5, you can see the arrow pointing down the given demand curve D.

When you think of demand, think of the entire curve. Quantity demanded, in contrast, is represented by a single point on the demand curve.

> A change or shift in demand causes the *entire* curve to move. The *only* thing that can cause the entire curve to move is a change in a determinant *other than its own price*.

In economic analysis, we cannot emphasize too much the following distinction that must constantly be made:

Try Preview Question 2:
How can we distinguish between a change in demand and a change in quantity demanded?

A change in a good's own price leads to a change in quantity demanded, for any given demand curve, other things held constant. This is a movement *along* the curve.

A change in any other determinant of demand leads to a change in demand. This causes a shift *of* the curve.

Figure 3.5
Movement Along a Given Demand Curve

A change in price changes the quantity of a good demanded. This can be represented as movement along a given demand schedule. If, in our example, the price of diskettes falls from $3 to $1 apiece, the quantity demanded will increase from 60 million to 100 million units per year.

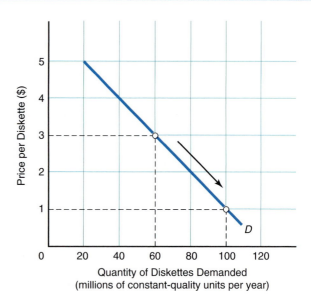

Quantity of Diskettes Demanded
(millions of constant-quality units per year)

Concepts in Brief

- Demand curves are drawn with determinants other than the price of the good held constant. These other determinants are (1) income; (2) tastes and preferences; (3) prices of related goods; (4) expectations about future prices, future incomes, and future availability of goods; and (5) population (number of buyers in the market). If any one of these determinants changes, the demand schedule will shift to the right or to the left.
- A change in demand happens only when there is a change in the other determinants of demand. This change in demand shifts the demand curve to the left or to the right.
- A change in the quantity demanded occurs when there is a change in the price of the good (other things held constant). Such a change in quantity demanded involves a movement along a given demand curve.

THE LAW OF SUPPLY

▶ **Supply**

A schedule showing the relationship between price and quantity supplied for a specified period of time, other things being equal.

The other side of the basic model in economics involves the quantities of goods and services that firms are prepared to *supply* to the market. The **supply** of any good or service is the amount that firms are prepared to sell under certain conditions during a specified time period. The relationship between price and quantity supplied, called the **law of supply**, can be summarized as follows:

▶ **Law of supply**

The observation that the higher the price of a good, the more of that good sellers will make available over a specified time period, other things being equal.

> At higher prices, a larger quantity will generally be supplied than at lower prices, all other things held constant. At lower prices, a smaller quantity will generally be supplied than at higher prices, all other things held constant.

There is generally a direct relationship between quantity supplied and price. For supply, as the price rises, the quantity supplied rises; as the price falls, the quantity supplied also falls. Producers are normally willing to produce and sell more of their product at a higher price than at a lower price, other things being constant. At $5 per diskette, 3M, Sony, Maxell, Fuji, and other manufacturers would almost certainly be willing to supply a larger quantity than at $1 per unit, assuming, of course, that no other prices in the economy had changed.

As with the law of demand, millions of instances in the real world have given us confidence in the law of supply. On a theoretical level, the law of supply is based on a model in which producers and sellers seek to make the most gain possible from their activities. For example, as a diskette manufacturer attempts to produce more and more diskettes over the same time period, it will eventually have to hire more workers and overutilize its machines. Only if offered a higher price per diskette will the manufacturer be willing to incur these extra costs. That is why the law of supply implies a direct relationship between price and quantity supplied.

THE SUPPLY SCHEDULE

Just as we were able to construct a demand schedule, we can construct a *supply schedule*, which is a table relating prices to the quantity supplied at each price. A supply schedule can also be referred to simply as *supply*. It is a set of planned production rates that depends on the price of the product. We show the individual supply schedule for a hypothetical producer in part (a) of Figure 3.6. At $1 per diskette, for example, this producer will supply 200,000 diskettes per year; at $5, it will supply 550,000 diskettes per year.

The Supply Curve

▶ **Supply curve**

The graphical representation of the supply schedule; a line (curve) showing the supply schedule, which generally slopes upward (has a positive slope), other things being equal.

We can convert the supply schedule in part (a) of Figure 3.6 into a **supply curve**, just as we created a demand curve in Figure 3.1. All we do is take the price-quantity combinations from part (a) of Figure 3.6 and plot them in part (b). We have labelled these combinations *F* through *J*. Connecting these points, we obtain an upward-sloping curve that shows the typically direct relationship between price and quantity supplied. Again, we have to remember that we are talking about quantity supplied *per year*, measured in constant-quality units.

Figure 3.6
The Individual Producer's Supply Schedule and Supply Curve for Diskettes

Part (a) shows that at higher prices, a hypothetical supplier will be willing to provide a greater quantity of diskettes. We plot the various price-quantity combinations in part (a) on the grid in part (b). When we connect these points, we find the individual supply curve for diskettes. It is positively sloped.

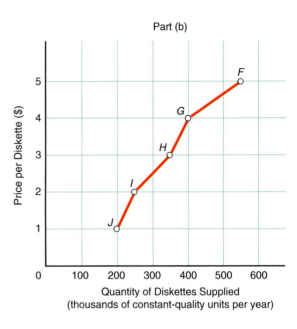

Part (a)

Combination	Price per Constant-Quality Diskette	Quantity of Diskettes Supplied (thousands of constant-quality units per year)
F	$5	550
G	4	400
H	3	350
I	2	250
J	1	200

The Market Supply Curve

Just as we had to add the individual demand curves to get the market demand curve, we need to add the individual producers' supply curves to get the market supply curve. Look at Figure 3.7, in which we horizontally sum two typical diskette manufacturers' supply curves. Supplier 1's data are taken from Figure 3.6; supplier 2 is added. The numbers are presented in part (a). The graphical representation of supplier 1 is in part (b), of supplier 2 in part (c), and of the summation in part (d). The result, then, is the supply curve for diskettes for suppliers 1 and 2. There are many more suppliers of diskettes, however. The total market supply schedule and total market supply curve for diskettes are represented in Figure 3.8, with the curve in part (b) obtained by adding all of the supply curves such as those shown in parts (b) and (c) of Figure 3.7. Notice the difference between the market supply curve with only two suppliers in Figure 3.7 and the one with a large number of suppliers—the entire true market—in part (b) of Figure 3.8. There are no kinks in the true total market supply curve because there are so many suppliers.

Observe what happens at the market level when price changes. If the price is $3, the quantity supplied is 60 million diskettes. If the price goes up to $4, the quantity supplied increases to 80 million per year. If the price falls to $2, the quantity supplied decreases to 40 million diskettes per year. Changes in quantity supplied are represented by movements along the supply curve in part (b) of Figure 3.8.

Try Preview Question 3:

Why is there normally a direct relationship between price and quantity supplied (other things being equal)?

Figure 3.7
Horizontal Summation of Supply Curves

In part (a), we show the data for two individual suppliers of diskettes. Adding how much each is willing to supply at different prices, we arrive at the combined quantities supplied in column 4. When we plot the values in columns 2 and 3 on grids in parts (b) and (c) and add them horizontally, we obtain the combined supply curve for the two suppliers in question, shown in part (d).

Part (a)

(1) Price per Diskette	(2) Supplier 1 Quantity Supplied (thousands)	(3) Supplier 2 Quantity Supplied (thousands)	(4) = (2) + (3) Combined Quantity Supplied per Year (thousands)
$5	550	350	900
4	400	300	700
3	350	200	550
2	250	150	400
1	200	100	300

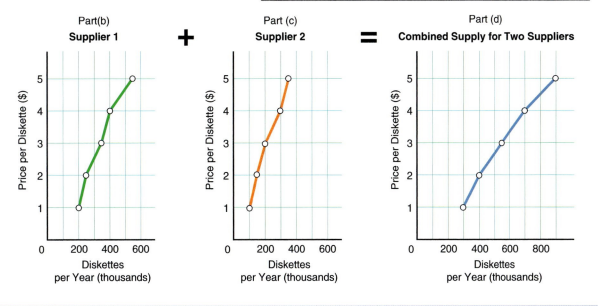

Part(b)
Supplier 1
+
Part (c)
Supplier 2
=
Part (d)
Combined Supply for Two Suppliers

Figure 3.8
The Market Supply Schedule and the Market Supply Curve for Diskettes

In part (a), we show the summation of all the individual producers' supply schedules; in part (b), we graph the resulting supply curve. It represents the market supply curve for diskettes and is upward-sloping.

Part (a)

Price per Constant-Quality Diskette	Quantity of Diskettes Supplied (millions of constant-quality units per year)
$5	100
4	80
3	60
2	40
1	20

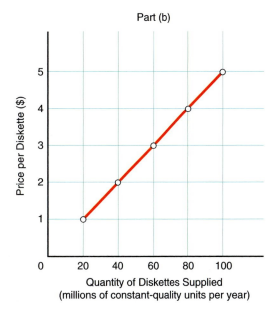

Part (b)

Concepts in Brief

- There is normally a direct, or positive, relationship between price and the quantity of a good supplied, other things held constant.
- The supply curve normally shows a direct relationship between price and quantity supplied. The market supply curve is obtained by horizontally adding individual supply curves in the market.

SHIFTS IN SUPPLY

When we looked at demand, we found out that any change in anything relevant other than the price of the good or service caused the demand curve to shift inward or outward. The same is true for the supply curve. If something relevant changes apart from the price of the product or service being supplied, we will see the entire supply curve shift.

Consider an example. A new method of putting magnetic material on diskettes has been invented. It reduces the cost of producing a diskette by 50 percent. In this situation, diskette producers will supply more product at all prices because their cost of so doing has fallen dramatically. Competition among diskette manufacturers to produce more at every price will shift the supply schedule of diskettes outward to the right from S_1 to S_2 in Figure 3.9. At a price of $3, the quantity supplied was originally 60 million diskettes per year, but now the quantity supplied (after the reduction in the costs of production) at $3 a diskette will be 90 million diskettes a year. (This is similar to what has happened to the supply curve of personal computers and fax machines in recent years as computer memory chip prices have fallen.)

Now consider the opposite case. If the cost of the magnetic material needed for making diskettes doubles, the supply curve in Figure 3.9 will shift from S_1 to S_3. At each price, the number of diskettes supplied will fall due to the increase in the price of raw materials.

Figure 3.9
A Shift in the Supply Schedule

If the cost of producing diskettes were to fall dramatically, the supply schedule would shift rightward from S_1 to S_2 such that at all prices, a larger quantity would be forthcoming from suppliers. Conversely, if the cost of production rose, the supply curve would shift leftward to S_3.

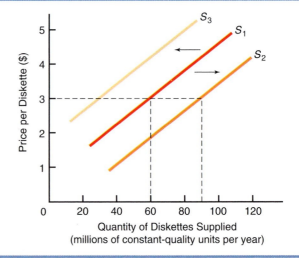

The Other Determinants of Supply

When supply curves are drawn, only the price of the good in question changes, and it is assumed that other things remain constant. The other things assumed constant are the costs of resources (inputs) used to produce the product, technology and productivity, taxes and subsidies, producers' price expectations, and the number of firms in the industry. These are the major nonprice determinants of supply. If any of them changes, there will be a shift in the supply curve.

Cost of Inputs Used to Produce the Product.

If one or more input price falls, the supply curve will shift outward to the right; that is, more will be supplied at each price. The opposite will be true if one or more inputs becomes more expensive. For example, when we draw the supply curve of new cars, we are holding the cost of steel (and other inputs) constant. When we draw the supply curve of blue jeans, we are holding the cost of cotton fixed.

Technology and Productivity.

Supply curves are drawn by assuming a given technology, or "state of the art." When the available production techniques change, the supply curve will shift. For example, when a better, cheaper, production technique for diskettes becomes available, the supply curve will shift to the right. A larger quantity will be forthcoming at every price because the cost of production is lower.

Taxes and Subsidies.

Certain taxes, such as a per-unit tax, are effectively an addition to production costs and therefore reduce the supply. If the supply curve were S_1 in Figure 3.9, a per-unit tax increase would shift it to S_3. A **subsidy** would do the opposite; it would shift the curve to S_2. Every producer would get a "gift" from the government of a few cents for each unit produced.

▶ **Subsidy**

A negative tax; a payment to a producer from the government, usually in the form of a cash grant.

Price Expectations.

A change in the expectation of a future relative price of a product can affect a producer's current willingness to supply, just as price expectations affect a consumer's current willingness to purchase. For example, diskette suppliers may withhold part of their current supply from the market if they anticipate higher prices in the future. The current amount supplied at all prices will decrease.

Number of Firms in the Industry.

In the short run, when firms can only change the number of employees they use, we hold the number of firms in the industry constant. In the long run, the number of firms (or the size of some existing firms) may change. If the number of firms increases, the supply curve will shift outward to the right. If the number of firms decreases, it will shift inward to the left.

Changes in Supply Versus Changes in Quantity Supplied

We cannot overstress the importance of distinguishing between a movement along the supply curve—which occurs only when the price changes for a given supply curve—and a shift in the supply curve—which occurs only with changes in other nonprice factors. A change in price always brings about a change in quantity sup-

INTERNATIONAL EXAMPLE
Changing Technology and the Supply of Salmon

One example of how changes in technology can shift the supply curve out to the right involves salmon. In 1980, the total worldwide catch of salmon (wild and farmed) was just over 10,000 metric tonnes. Since 1980, new technology has been developed in what is called aquaculture, or the farm-raising of fish and related products. Aquaculture currently generates over US$30 billion in worldwide revenues and is one of the world's fastest-growing industries. Farmed salmon from Canada, Chile, Scotland, Norway, and Iceland now exceeds 240,000 metric tonnes a year. Thus it is not surprising that despite a depletion of many wild salmon fishing grounds and a worldwide increase in consumer demand for salmon, the retail price of salmon today (corrected for inflation) is about 50 percent of what it was in 1980.

For critical analysis: What might slow down the growth in salmon farming throughout the world?

plied along a given supply curve. We move to a different coordinate on the existing supply curve. This is specifically called a *change in quantity supplied*. When price changes, quantity supplied changes, and there will be a movement from one point to another along the same supply curve.

When you think of *supply*, think of the entire curve. Quantity supplied is represented by a single point on the curve.

> A change in supply causes the entire curve to shift. The *only* thing that can cause the entire curve to shift is a change in a determinant *other than price*.

Consequently,

> A change in the price leads to a change in the quantity supplied, other things being constant. This is a movement *along* the curve.

> A change in any other determinant of supply leads to a change in supply. This causes a shift *of* the curve.

Concepts in Brief

- If the price changes, we *move along* a curve—there is a change in quantity demanded or supplied. If some other determinant changes, we *shift* a curve—there is a change in demand or supply.
- The supply curve is drawn with other things held constant. If other determinants of supply change, the supply curve will shift. The other major determinants are (1) input costs, (2) technology and productivity, (3) taxes and subsidies, (4) expectations of future relative prices, and (5) the number of firms in the industry.

PUTTING DEMAND AND SUPPLY TOGETHER

In the sections on supply and demand, we tried to confine each discussion to supply or demand only. But you have probably already realized that we can't view the world just from the supply side or just from the demand side. There is an interaction between the two. In this section, we will discuss how they interact and how that interaction determines the prices that prevail in our economy. Understanding how demand and supply interact is essential to understanding how prices are determined in our economy and other economies in which the forces of supply and demand are allowed to work.

Let's first combine the demand and supply schedules and then combine the curves.

Demand and Supply Schedules Combined

Let's place part (a) from Figure 3.3 (the market demand schedule) and part (a) from Figure 3.8 (the market supply schedule) together in part (a) of Figure 3.10. Column 1 shows the price; column 2, the quantity supplied per year at any given price; and column 3, the quantity demanded. Column 4 is merely the difference between columns 2 and 3, or the difference between the quantity supplied and the quantity demanded. In column 5, we label those differences as either excess quantity supplied (a surplus), or excess quantity demanded (a shortage). For example, at a price of $2, only 40 million diskettes would be supplied, but the quantity demanded would be 80 million. The difference is 40 million, which we label as excess quantity demanded (a shortage). At the other end of the scale, a price of $5 per diskette would elicit 100 million in quantity supplied, but quantity demanded would drop to 20 million. This leaves a difference of 80 million units, which we call excess quantity supplied (a surplus).

What do you notice about the price of $3? At that price, the quantity supplied and the quantity demanded per year are both 60 million. The difference, then, is zero. There is neither excess quantity demanded (shortage) nor excess quantity supplied (surplus). Hence the price of $3 is very special. It is called the **market clearing price**—it clears the market of all excess supply or excess demand. There are no willing consumers who want to pay $3 per diskette but are turned away by sellers, and there are no willing suppliers who want to sell diskettes at $3 who cannot sell all they want at that price. Another term for the market clearing price is the **equilibrium price**, the price at which there is no tendency for change. At that price, consumers are able to buy all they want and suppliers are able to sell the quantity that they desire.

Equilibrium

We can define **equilibrium** in general as a point from which there tends to be no movement unless demand or supply changes. Any movement away from this point will set in motion certain forces that will cause movement back to it. Therefore, equilibrium is a stable point. Any point that is not at equilibrium is unstable and cannot be maintained.

▶ **Market clearing, or equilibrium, price**
The price that clears the market, at which quantity demanded equals quantity supplied; the price where the demand curve intersects the supply curve.

▶ **Equilibrium**
The situation when quantity supplied equals quantity demanded at a particular price.

Figure 3.10
Putting Demand and Supply Together

In part (a), we see that at the price of $3, the quantity supplied and the quantity demanded are equal, resulting in neither an excess in the quantity demanded nor an excess in the quantity supplied. We call this price the equilibrium, or market clearing, price. In part (b), the intersection of the supply and demand curves is at E, at a price of $3 per constant-quality diskette and a quantity of 60 million per year. At point E, there is neither an excess in the quantity demanded nor an excess in the quantity supplied. At a price of $2, the quantity supplied will be only 40 million diskettes per year, but the quantity demand-

ed will be 80 million. The difference is excess quantity demanded at a price of $2. The price will rise, so we will move from point A up the supply curve and point B up the demand curve to point E. At the other extreme, $5 elicits a quantity supplied of 100 million but a quantity demanded of only 20 million. The difference is excess quantity supplied at a price of $5. The price will fall, so we will move down the demand curve and the supply curve to the equilibrium price, $3 per diskette.

Part (a)

(1) Price per Constant-Quality Diskette	(2) Quantity Supplied (diskettes per year)	(3) Quantity Demanded (diskettes per year)	(4) Difference (2) – (3) (diskettes per year)	(5) Condition
$5	100 million	20 million	80 million	Excess quantity supplied (surplus)
4	80 million	40 million	40 million	Excess quantity supplied (surplus)
3	60 million	60 million	0	Market clearing price—equilibrium (no surplus, no shortage)
2	40 million	80 million	– 40 million	Excess quantity demanded (shortage)
1	20 million	100 million	– 80 million	Excess quantity demanded (shortage)

Part (b)

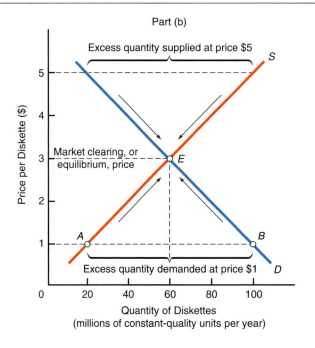

Try Preview Question 4:

Why will the market clearing price occur at the intersection of the supply and demand curves rather than at a higher or lower price?

The equilibrium point occurs where the supply and demand curves intersect. The equilibrium price is given on the vertical axis directly to the left of where the supply and demand curves cross. The equilibrium quantity demanded and supplied is given on the horizontal axis directly underneath the intersection of the demand and supply curves. Equilibrium can change whenever there is a *shock*.

A shock to the supply-and-demand system can be represented by a shift in the supply curve, a shift in the demand curve, or a shift in both. Any shock to the system will result in a new set of supply-and-demand relationships and a new equilibrium; forces will come into play to move the system from the old price-quantity equilibrium (now a disequilibrium situation) to the new equilibrium, where the new demand and supply curves intersect.

Part (b) from Figure 3.3 and part (b) from Figure 3.8 are combined as part (b) in Figure 3.10 on page 70. The only difference now is that the horizontal axis measures both the quantity supplied and the quantity demanded per year. Everything else is the same. The demand curve is labelled *D*, the supply curve *S*. We have labelled the intersection of the two curves as point *E*, for equilibrium. That corresponds to a market clearing price of $3, at which both the quantity supplied and the quantity demanded are 60 million units per year. There is neither a surplus nor a shortage. Point *E*, the equilibrium point, always occurs at the intersection of the supply and demand curves. This is the price towards which the market price will automatically tend to gravitate.

EXAMPLE Dinosaurs and the Price of Amber

When there is a shift in either supply or demand, there is a movement towards equilibrium that usually involves a change in the equilibrium quantity and the equilibrium price. A good example is found in the market for amber, a semi-precious stone in which fossilized insects or plants from millions of years ago are sometimes discovered. In Figure 3.11 (page 72), you see the original supply and demand curves for amber, labelled *S* and D_1. The equilibrium price is P_1, and the equilibrium quantity is Q_1. Then along came a book, and later a movie, called *Jurassic Park*, written by Michael Crichton. In the story mosquitoes that had feasted on dinosaurs a million years ago were trapped in amber. Scientists were able to clone various dinosaurs by removing the DNA from the dinosaur blood inside the fossilized mosquitoes. (The technique remains in the realm of science fiction.) The success of the book and the movie in the early 1990s made amber suddenly popular; in economic terms, the demand curve for amber shifted outward to D_2. Very quickly, the price rose to P_2 and the equilibrium quantity increased to Q_2.

For critical analysis: It has been a few years since the dinosaur craze peaked in Canada. How would you represent what is now occurring in the market in amber, using supply and demand curves?

Figure 3.11
The Changing Price of Amber

With stable supply, a shift in the demand curve for amber from D_1 to D_2 will cause the equilibrium price to rise from P_1 to P_2 and the equilibrium quantity to increase from Q_1 to Q_2.

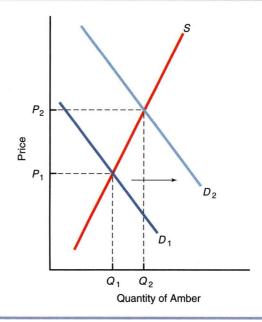

Shortages

The demand and supply curves in Figure 3.10 represent a situation of equilibrium. But a non-market-clearing, or disequilibrium, price will bring into play forces that cause the price to change, and move towards the market clearing price. Then, equilibrium is again sustained. Look once more at part (b) in Figure 3.10 on page 70. Suppose that instead of being at the market clearing price of $3 per diskette, for some reason the market price is $1 per diskette. At this price, the quantity demanded (100 million), exceeds the quantity supplied (20 million). We have a situation of excess quantity demanded at the price of $1. This is usually called a **shortage**. Consumers of diskettes would find that they could not buy all that they wished at $1 apiece. But forces will cause the price to rise: Competing consumers will bid up the price, and suppliers will raise the price and increase output, whether explicitly or implicitly. (Remember, some buyers would pay $5 or more rather than do without diskettes. They do not want to be left out.) We would move from points *A* and *B* towards point *E*. The process would stop when the price again reached $3 per diskette.

At this point, it is important to recall a distinction made in Chapter 2:

▶ **Shortage**

A situation in which quantity demanded is greater than quantity supplied at a price below the market clearing price.

Shortages and scarcity are not the same thing.

A shortage is a situation in which the quantity demanded exceeds the quantity supplied at a price *below* the market clearing price. Our definition of scarcity was much more general and all-encompassing: a situation in which the resources available for producing output are insufficient to satisfy all wants. Any choice necessarily costs an opportunity, and the opportunity is lost. Hence we will always live in a world of scarcity because we must constantly make choices, but we do not necessarily have to live in a world of shortages.

Surpluses

▶ **Surplus**

A situation in which quantity supplied is greater than quantity demanded at a price above the market clearing price.

Now let's repeat the experiment with the market price at $5 per diskette rather than at the market clearing price of $3. Clearly, the quantity supplied will exceed the quantity demanded at that price. The result will be an excess quantity supplied at $5 per unit. This excess quantity supplied is often called a **surplus**. Given the curves in part (b) in Figure 3.10, however, there will be forces pushing the price back down towards $3 per diskette: Competing suppliers will attempt to reduce their inventories by cutting prices and reducing output, and consumers will offer to purchase more at lower prices. Suppliers will want to reduce inventories, which will be above their optimal level; that is, there will be an excess over what each seller believes to be the most profitable stock of diskettes. After all, inventories are costly to hold. But consumers may find out about such excess inventories and see the possibility of obtaining increased quantities of diskettes at a decreased price. It benefits consumers to attempt to obtain a good at a lower price, and they will therefore try to do so. If the two forces of supply and demand are unrestricted, they will bring the price back to $3 per diskette.

Shortages and surpluses are resolved in unfettered markets—markets in which price changes are free to occur. The forces that resolve them are those of competition: In the case of shortages, consumers competing for a limited quantity supplied drive up the price; in the case of surpluses, sellers compete for the limited quantity demanded, thus driving prices down to equilibrium. The equilibrium price is the only stable price, and all (unrestricted) market prices tend to gravitate towards it.

What happens when the price is set below the equilibrium price? Here come the scalpers.

| **EXAMPLE** | **Should Shortages in the Ticket Market Be Solved by Scalpers?** |

If you have ever tried to get tickets to a playoff game in sports, a popular play, or a superstar's rock concert, you know about "shortages." The standard ticket situation for a Stanley Cup hockey game is shown in Figure 3.12 (page 74). At the face-value price of Stanley Cup tickets (P_1), the quantity demanded (Q_2) greatly exceeds the quantity supplied (Q_1). Because shortages last only so long as prices and quantities do not change, markets tend to exhibit a movement out of this disequilibrium towards equilibrium. Obviously, the quantity of Stanley Cup tickets cannot change, but the price can go as high as P_2.

Enter the scalper. This colourful term is used because when you purchase a ticket that is being resold at a price that is higher than face value, the seller is skimming an extra profit off the top. Every time an event sells out, ticket prices by definition have been lower than market clearing prices. Sellouts indicate that the event is very popular, and that there may be people without tickets willing to buy high-priced tickets because they place a greater value on the entertainment event than the actual face value of the ticket. Without scalpers,

Figure 3.12
Shortage of Stanley Cup Tickets

The quantity of tickets for any one Stanley Cup is fixed at Q_1. At the price per ticket of P_1, the quantity demanded is Q_2, which is greater than Q_1. Consequently, there is an excess quantity demanded at the below–market clearing price. Prices can go as high as P_2 in the scalpers' market.

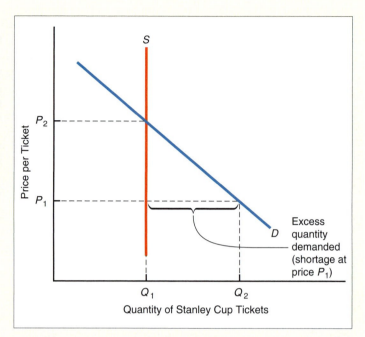

those individuals would not be able to attend the event. In the case of the 1994 Stanley Cup, various forms of scalping occurred nationwide. Tickets have been sold for more than $225 a piece, almost four times their face value. In front of every Stanley Cup game arena, you can find ticket scalpers hawking their wares.

In most provinces, scalping is illegal. In Ontario, convicted scalpers are fined around $500 for each infraction. For an economist, such legislation seems strange. As one Toronto ticket broker said, "I look at scalping like working as a stockbroker, buying low and selling high. If people are willing to pay me the money, what kind of problem is that?"

For critical analysis: What happens to ticket scalpers who are still holding tickets after an event has started?

Concepts in Brief

- The market clearing price occurs at the intersection of the market demand curve and the market supply curve. It is also called the equilibrium price, the price from which there is no tendency to change unless there is a change in demand or supply.
- Whenever the price is greater than the equilibrium price, there is an excess quantity supplied (a surplus).
- Whenever the price is less than the equilibrium price, there is an excess quantity demanded (a shortage).

Issues and Applications

How the Prices of Hockey Cards Have Responded to Changes in Supply and Demand

Concepts Applied: Demand and supply, shifts in demand and supply, relative prices

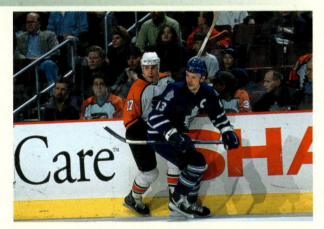

The price of hockey cards depends on their demand and supply. If supply is restricted by acquisitive collectors, prices will rise.

A few years ago, one of the hottest trends in Canada was collecting sporting cards. Baseball cards and hockey cards were no longer sold only as part of chewing gum packs, but were also sold in packages by themselves. The effect of this on the price of sporting cards depends on which card you are talking about: a 1951-52 Maurice Richard card will sell for as much as $2,100 and Gordie Howe's rookie card from the same year now sells for at least $2,800.

However, not all hockey cards have become more valuable over time. For example, the price of a 1979-80 Wayne Gretzky O-Pee-Chee card rose more than 40 percent from $840 to $1,190 between 1990 and 1996, but the price of Gretzky's 1989-90 card fell from $3.50 to $2.10, a change of 40 percent in the opposite direction over the same period. How can the relative prices of these cards change in such different ways?

Increasing Demand for Hockey Cards

The market for hockey cards is shown in parts (a) and (b) of Figure 3.13. Notice that the demand curve, D_1, refers to the year 1990 in both parts, and the demand curve D_2 refers to the year 1996. Part (a), however, is the market for 1979-80 hockey cards, while part (b) is the market for 1989-90 cards.

During the 1979-80 hockey season, only two companies, O-Pee-Chee and Topps, produced trading cards. Therefore the supply

---

Figure 3.13
The Market for Hockey Cards

In part (a), the market for 1970–80 hockey cards is shown. The demand in 1990 is illustrated by D_1, while the demand in 1996 is shown by D_2. The supply in both years is shown by curve S. When demand increases for 1979–80 cards, the price rises from P_1 to P_2. In part (b), both the demand and the supply increases from 1990 to 1996. The price falls from P_3 to P_4 because supply increases more than demand at every price.

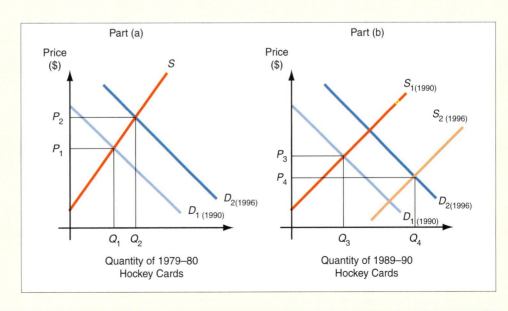

of cards from that year is very limited. This is shown by the supply curve, S, in part (a). When collecting became a fad in North America and the demand for old trading cards increased, something had to give. What happened? The price of Gretzky's 1979-80 trading card rose from P_1 to P_2.

Increasing Supply of Hockey Cards

Over the course of several years, the price rise convinced more firms to supply trading cards. By the 1994-95 hockey season, 106 different companies were listed in the Beckett Hockey Monthly as suppliers! This supply increase is shown in part (b) by the curve S_2. Notice that the price of cards has fallen from P_3 to P_4, since at price P_3 the supply has increased substantially more than demand.

Relatively Rare Cards

If the relative price of hockey cards depends only on supply and demand, why are Maurice Richard's and Gordie Howe's 1951-52

cards worth twice as much as Gretzky's later card? If you said that there must have been an even smaller supply of the earlier cards, you were right. Before 1968, almost all hockey cards were sold in Canada, and Canadians tend to hold onto their valuable collectibles. By contrast, Americans trade their valuables if the market is there, so the supply of post-1968 cards at any given time is relatively greater than that of the earlier years.

For Critical Analysis

1. Some card traders suggest that the hockey players' lockout during the 1994-95 season dampened many collectors' enthusiasm for trading cards. If this is the case, what has happened to the two markets illustrated in parts (a) and (b) of Figure 3.13?

2. What do you think the expansion of the National Hockey League into more American cities is doing to the two markets illustrated in parts (a) and (b) of Figure 3.13?

CHAPTER SUMMARY

1. The law of demand says that at higher prices, individuals will purchase less of a commodity and at lower prices, they will purchase more, other things being equal.

2. Relative prices must be distinguished from absolute, or money, prices. During periods of rising prices, almost all prices go up, but some rise faster than others.

3. All references to the laws of supply and demand refer to constant-quality units of a commodity. A time period for the analysis must also be specified.

4. The demand schedule shows the relationship between various possible prices and their respective quantities purchased per unit time period. Graphically, the demand schedule is a demand

curve and is downward-sloping.

5. The nonprice determinants of demand are (a) income, (b) tastes and preferences, (c) the prices of related goods, (d) expectations, and (e) population, or market, size. Whenever any of these determinants of demand changes, the demand curve shifts.

6. The supply curve is generally upward-sloping such that at higher prices, more will be forthcoming than at lower prices. At higher prices, suppliers are willing to incur the increasing costs of higher rates of production.

7. The nonprice determinants of supply are (a) input costs, (b) technology and productivity, (c) taxes and subsidies, (d) price expectations, and (e) entry and exit of firms.

8. A movement along a demand or supply curve is not the same thing as a shift of the curve. A change in price causes movement along the curve. A change in any other determinant of supply or demand shifts the entire curve.

9. The demand and supply curves intersect at the equilibrium point, marking the market clearing price, where quantity demanded just equals quantity supplied. At that point, the plans of buyers and sellers mesh exactly.

10. When the price of a good is greater than its market clearing price, an excess quantity is supplied at that price; it is called a surplus. When the price is below the market clearing price, an excess quantity is demanded at that price; it is called a shortage.

DISCUSSION OF PREVIEW QUESTIONS

1. **Why are relative prices important in understanding the law of demand?**

   People respond to changes in relative prices rather than changes in absolute prices. If the price of CDs rises by 50 percent next year, while at the same time the prices of everything else, including your wages, also increase by 50 percent, the relative price of CDs has not changed. If nothing else has changed in your life, your normal quantity demanded of CDs will remain about the same. In a world of generally rising prices (inflation), you have to compare the price of one good with the average of all other goods in order to decide whether the relative price of that one good has gone up, gone down, or stayed the same.

2. **How can we distinguish between a change in *demand* and a change in *quantity demanded*?**

   Use the accompanying graphs to aid you. Because demand is a curve, a change in demand is equivalent to a *shift* of the demand curve. Changes in demand result from changes in the other determinants of demand, such as income, tastes and preferences, expectations, prices of related goods, and population. A change in quantity demanded, given demand, is a movement along a demand curve and results only from a change in the price of the commodity in question.

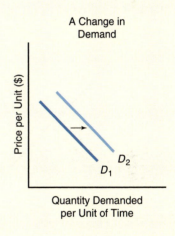

A Change in Demand

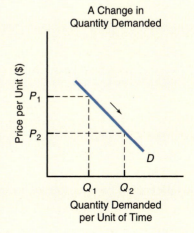

A Change in Quantity Demanded

3. Why is there normally a direct relationship between price and quantity supplied (other things being equal)?

In general, businesses experience increasing *extra* costs as they expand output in the short run. This means that additional units of output, which may be quite similar in physical attributes to initial units of output, actually cost the firm more to produce. Consequently, firms often require a higher and higher price as an incentive to produce more in the short run; this "incentive" effect implies that higher prices, other things being constant, lead to increases in quantity supplied.

4. Why will the market clearing price occur at the intersection of the supply and demand curves rather than at a higher or lower price?

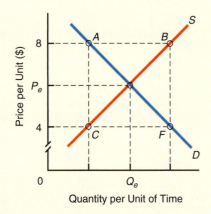

Consider the graph above. To demonstrate that the equilibrium price will be at P_e, we can eliminate all other prices as possibilities. Consider a price above P_e, $8 per unit. By inspection of the graph, we can see that at that price, the quantity supplied exceeds the quantity demanded for this product ($B > A$). Clearly, sellers cannot sell all they wish at $8, and they therefore find it profitable to lower price and decrease output. In fact, this surplus situation exists at *all* prices above P_e. Sellers, competing for sales, will reduce prices if a surplus exists.

Consider a price of $4 per unit, where the quantity demanded exceeds the quantity supplied ($F > C$); a shortage of this commodity exists at a price of $4 per unit. Buyers will not be able to get all they want at that relatively low price. Because buyers are competing for this good, buyers who are willing to give up more of other goods in order to get this one will offer higher and higher prices. By doing so, they eliminate buyers who are not willing to give up more of other goods. An increase in price encourages sellers to produce and sell more. A shortage exists at *any* price below P_e, and therefore price will rise if it is below P_e.

At P_e, the quantity supplied equals the quantity demanded, Q_e, and both buyers and sellers are able to realize their intentions. Because neither group has an incentive to change its behaviour, equilibrium exists at P_e.

(Answers to the odd-numbered problems appear at the back of the book.)

3-1. Construct a demand curve and a supply curve for skateboards, based on the data provided in the following tables.

Price per Skateboard	Quantity Demanded per Year
$75	300,000
50	600,000
35	900,000
25	1,200,000
15	1,500,000
10	1,800,000

Price per Skateboard	Quantity Supplied per Year
$75	1,800,000
50	1,500,000
35	1,200,000
25	900,000
15	600,000
10	300,000

What is the equilibrium price? What is the equilibrium quantity at that price?

3-2. "Hospitals are obviously complementary to physicians' services." Is this statement always correct?

3-3. Five factors, other than price, that affect the demand for a good were discussed in this chapter. Place each of the following events in its proper category, and state how it would shift the demand curve in parentheses.
   a. New information is disclosed that large doses of vitamin C prevent common colds. (Demand for vitamin C)
   b. A drop in the price of educational interactive CD-ROMs occurs. (Demand for teachers)
   c. A fall in the price of pretzels occurs. (Demand for beer)

3-4. Examine the following table, and then answer the questions.

	Price per Unit Last Year	Price per Unit Today
Heating oil	$1.00	$2.00
Natural gas	.80	3.20

What has happened to the absolute price of heating oil? Of natural gas? What has happened to the price of heating oil relative to the price of natural gas? What has happened to the relative price of natural gas? Will consumers, through time, change their relative purchases? If so, how?

3-5. Suppose that the demand for oranges remains constant but a frost occurs in Florida that could potentially destroy one-third of the orange crop. What will happen to the equilibrium price and quantity for Florida oranges?

3-6. "The demand has increased so much in response to our offering of a $75 rebate that our inventory of portable laptop computers is now running very low." What is wrong with this assertion?

3-7. Analyse the following statement: "Federal farm price supports can never achieve their goals because the above-equilibrium price floors that are established by the Ministry of Agriculture invariably create surpluses (quantities supplied in excess of quantities demanded), which in turn drive the price right back down towards equilibrium."

3-8. Suppose that an island economy exists in which there is no money. Suppose further that every Sunday morning, at a certain location, hog farmers and cattle ranchers gather to exchange live pigs for cows. Is this a market, and if so, what do the supply and demand diagrams use as a price? Can you imagine any problems arising at the price at which cows and pigs are exchanged?

3-9. Here is a supply and demand schedule for rain in an Amazon jungle settlement where cloud seeding or other scientific techniques can be used to coax rainfall from the skies.

Price (cruzeriros per yearly centimetre of rain)	Quantity Supplied (centimetres of rain per year)	Quantity Demanded (centimetres of rain per year)
0	200	150
10	225	125
20	250	100
30	275	75
40	300	50
50	325	25
60	350	0
70	375	0
80	400	0

What are the equilibrium price and the equilibrium quantity? Explain.

Extensions of Demand and Supply Analysis

It was billed as the battle of grunge against greed. Eddie Vedder and the other members of Seattle grunge band Pearl Jam decided that the service charges required by Ticketmaster, the biggest distributor of tickets in Canada and the United States, were too high. Pearl Jam took the case to court, claiming that Ticketmaster was extracting its "pound of flesh" from poor fans by exploiting its unique position as an intermediary in the live rock concert business. To understand about intermediaries is to understand about markets and exchange and how the forces of supply and demand can be altered by government actions, all topics discussed in this chapter.

Preview Questions

1. Does an increase in demand always lead to a rise in price?

2. Can there ever be shortages in a market with no restrictions?

3. How are goods rationed?

4. When would you expect to encounter black markets?

Did You Know That... hundreds of thousands of cigarettes are being illegally imported into Manitoba from Ontario every year? Why does a black market in cigarettes exist? Because Ontario, Quebec, and the Atlantic provinces collect substantially less sales tax on each packet of cigarettes than Manitoba, Saskatchewan, and Alberta. Since 1994, over 200 people have been caught smuggling cigarettes for resale into Manitoba, so there must be a continuing demand for these illegal goods. Illegal markets such as the one for cigarettes can be analysed using the supply and demand analysis you learned in Chapter 3. Similarly, you can use this analysis to examine purported shortages of apartments in Toronto, and many other similar phenomena. All of these examples are part of our economy, which we can characterize as a price system.

THE PRICE SYSTEM

▶ **Price system**

An economic system in which relative prices are constantly changing to reflect changes in supply and demand for different commodities. The prices of those commodities are signals to everyone within the system as to what is relatively scarce and what is relatively abundant.

A **price system,** otherwise known as a *market system,* is one in which relative prices are constantly changing to reflect changes in supply and demand for different commodities. The prices of those commodities are the signals to everyone within the system as to what is relatively scarce and what is relatively abundant. Indeed, it is the *signalling* aspect of the price system that provides the information to buyers and sellers about what should be bought and what should be produced. In a price system, there is a clear-cut chain of events in which any changes in demand and supply cause changes in prices. Those price changes in turn affect the opportunities that businesses and individuals have for profit and personal gain. Such changes influence our use of resources.

EXCHANGE AND MARKETS

▶ **Voluntary exchange**

An act of trading, done on a voluntary basis, in which both parties to the trade are subjectively better off after the exchange.

▶ **Terms of exchange**

The terms under which trading takes place. Usually the terms of exchange are equal to the price at which a good is traded.

The price system features **voluntary exchange,** acts of trading between individuals that make both parties to the trade subjectively better off. The **terms of exchange**—the prices we pay for the desired items—are determined by the interaction of the forces underlying supply and demand. In our economy, the majority of exchanges take place voluntarily in markets. A market encompasses the exchange arrangements of both buyers and sellers that underlie the forces of supply and demand. Indeed, one definition of a market is a low-cost institution for facilitating exchange. A market in essence increases incomes by helping resources move to their highest-valued uses by means of prices. Prices are the providers of information.

Transaction Costs

▶ **Transaction costs**

All of the costs associated with exchanging, including the informational costs of finding out price and quality, service record, and durability of a product, plus the cost of contracting and enforcing that contract.

Individuals turn to markets because markets reduce the cost of exchanges. These costs are sometimes referred to as **transaction costs,** which are broadly defined as the costs associated with finding out exactly what is being transacted as well as the cost of enforcing contracts. If you were Robinson Crusoe and lived alone on an island, you would never incur a transaction cost. For everyone else, transaction costs are just as real as the costs of production. High-speed large-scale computers have allowed us to reduce transaction costs by increasing our ability to process information and keep records.

Consider some simple examples of transaction costs. The supermarket reduces transaction costs relative to your having to go to numerous specialty stores to obtain the items you desire. Organized stock exchanges, such as the Toronto Stock Exchange, have reduced transaction costs of buying and selling stocks and bonds. In general, the more organized the market, the lower the transaction costs. One group of individuals who constantly attempt to lower transaction costs are intermediaries.

The Role of the Intermediary

As long as there are costs to bringing together buyers and sellers, there will be an incentive for intermediaries, often called middlemen, to lower those costs. This means that intermediaries specialize in lowering transaction costs. Whenever producers do not sell their products directly to the final consumer, there are, by definition, one or more intermediaries involved. Farmers typically sell their output to distributors, who are usually called wholesalers, who then sell those products to grocery stores.

Recently, technology has reduced the need, and hence the job prospects, for intermediaries.

EXAMPLE	Technology and the Death of Intermediaries

For decades, most airline travellers bought their tickets from a travel agent, not from the airline itself. In 1996, there were more than 2,200 travel agencies in Canada. That year, Air Canada and Canadian Airlines International cut the commissions paid to these intermediaries by capping them at $60 per round-trip domestic flight rather than the 8.25 percent of ticket purchase price which had hitherto been paid. In an effort to reduce the impact of this move on the travel agents, the two carriers raised the base commission rate to 9 percent. Basically, the airlines have realized that there are high-tech alternatives to travel agents for the distribution of their tickets. Each has its own Web site on the World Wide Web and these, along with other on-line services, such as Microsoft's Expedia, allow subscribers to consult airline timetables and to reserve tickets from their homes or office personal computers. As people become more and more familiar with how to use computers, modems, and on-line services, the trend towards cutting out the intermediary, at least in airline travel, will continue.

For critical analysis: How can travel agents more effectively compete with on-line computer services that offer airline reservations?

CHANGES IN DEMAND AND SUPPLY

It is in markets that we see the results of changes in demand and supply. In certain situations, it is possible to predict what will happen to equilibrium price and equilibrium quantity when a change occurs in demand or supply. Specifically, whenever one curve is stable while the other curve shifts, we can tell what will happen to price and quantity. Consider the four possibilities in Figure 4.1. In part (a), the supply curve remains stable but demand increases from D_1 to D_2. Note that the result is both an increase in the market clearing price from P_1 to P_2 and an increase in the equilibrium quantity from Q_1 to Q_2.

In part (b), there is a decrease in demand from D_1 to D_3. This results in a decrease in both the relative price of the good and the equilibrium quantity. Parts (c) and (d) show the effects of a shift in the supply curve while the demand curve is stable. In part (c), the supply curve has shifted to the right. . The relative price of the product falls; the equilibrium quantity increases. In part (d), supply has shifted to the left—there has been a supply decrease. The product's relative price increases; the equilibrium quantity decreases.

Try Preview Question 1:
Does an increase in demand always lead to a rise in price?

Figure 4.1
Shifts in Demand and in Supply: Determinate Results

In part (a), the supply curve is stable at S. The demand curve shifts outward from D_1 to D_2. The equilibrium price and quantity rise from P_1, Q_1 to P_2, Q_2, respectively. In part (b), again the supply curve remains stable at S. The demand curve, however, shifts inward to the left, showing a decrease in demand from D_1 to D_3. Both equilibrium price and equilibrium quantity fall. In part (c), the demand curve now remains stable at D. The supply curve shifts from S_1 to S_2. The equilibrium price falls from P_1 to P_2. The equilibrium quantity increases, however, from Q_1 to Q_2. In part (d), the demand curve is stable at D. Supply decreases as shown by a leftward shift of the supply curve from S_1 to S_3. The market clearing price increases from P_1 to P_3. The equilibrium quantity falls from Q_1 to Q_3.

Part (a)

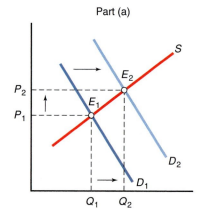

Part (b)

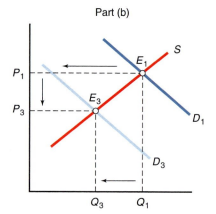

Part (c)

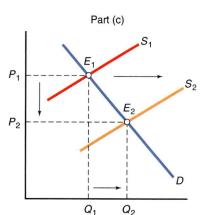

Part (d)

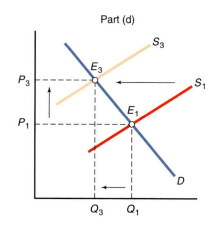

When Both Demand and Supply Shift

The examples given in Figure 4.1 each showed a unique outcome of a shift in either the demand curve holding the supply curve constant, or the supply curve holding the demand curve constant. When both supply and demand curves change, the outcome is indeterminate for either equilibrium price or equilibrium quantity.

When both demand and supply increase, all we can be certain of is that equilibrium quantity will increase. We do not know what will happen to equilibrium price until we determine whether demand increased relative to supply (equilibrium price will rise) or supply increased relative to demand (equilibrium price will fall). The same analysis applies to decreases in both demand and supply, except that in this case equilibrium quantity falls.

We can be certain that when demand decreases and supply increases, the equilibrium price will fall, but we do not know what will happen to the equilibrium quantity unless we actually draw the new curves. If supply decreases and demand increases, we can be sure that equilibrium price will rise, but again we do not know what happens to equilibrium quantity without drawing the curves. In every situation in which both supply and demand change, you should always draw graphs to determine the resulting change in equilibrium price and quantity.

PRICE FLEXIBILITY AND ADJUSTMENT SPEED

We have used a market in which prices are quite flexible as an illustration for our analysis. Some markets are indeed like that. In others, however, price flexibility may take the form of indirect adjustments such as hidden payments or quality changes. For example, although the published price of bouquets of flowers may stay the same, the freshness of the flowers may change, meaning that the price per constant-quality unit changes. The published price of French bread might stay the same, but the quality could go up or down, thereby changing the price per constant-quality unit. There are many ways to change prices without actually changing the published price for a nominal unit of a product or service.

We must also consider the fact that markets do not return to equilibrium immediately. There must be an adjustment time. A shock to the economy in the form of an oil embargo, a drought, or a long strike will not be absorbed overnight. This means that even in free market situations, in which there are no restrictions on changes in prices and quantities, temporary excess quantities supplied and excess quantities demanded may appear. Our analysis simply indicates what the market clearing price ultimately will be, given a demand curve and a supply curve. Nowhere in the analysis is there any indication of the speed with which a market will get to a new equilibrium if there has been a shock. The price may overshoot the equilibrium level. Remember this warning when we examine changes in demand and in supply due to changes in their nonprice determinants.

Now consider how long it takes the world market for gold to adjust to changes in demand and supply.

Try Preview Question 2:
Can there ever be shortages in a market with no restrictions?

INTERNATIONAL EXAMPLE
Keeping Up with World Gold Demand

Gold prices are watched with great interest by miners, jewellers, and speculators alike. These prices are set, like many other goods, by world supply and world demand. But since new gold supplies have to be located before they are mined and subsequently offered on the market, there is almost always an adjustment lag in the market for raw gold.

Throughout the 1950s and 1960s, the price of gold rose slowly, suggesting that supply was pretty well keeping up with demand. However, as the 1970s progressed, people in many western countries started to buy gold as a hedge against inflation. The price began to rise more rapidly, peaking in 1980. Since then, gold prices have varied within a relatively narrow range. Figure 4.2 shows the historical picture of gold prices.

Figure 4.2
Relative Gold Prices, 1956-1996

The relative price of gold is expressed as a price index, where the price in 1986 is set at 100. The price remained quite low and steady until the 1970s, when the demand increased and prices rose. By the 1980s, new deposits of gold were located and were being mined, satisfying some of the world demand for gold.

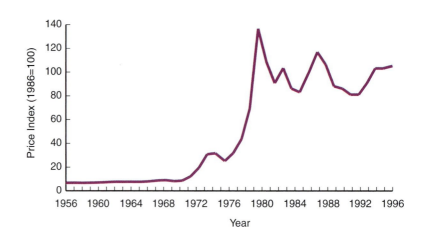

Figure 4.3
Adjustment to Changes in Demand and Supply in the Market for Gold

The world demand for gold in 1960 was D_1 and the supply was S_1. The equilibrium price was P_1. An increase in the demand for gold shifted the demand curve out to D_2; the world price rose to P_2. After some time, new gold deposits were discovered and mined, shifting the supply curve out to S_2. The price fell to P_3, still higher than the original price of P_1.

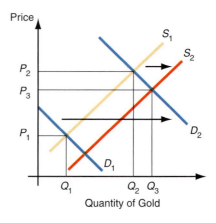

In 1980, 56 percent of world gold production took place in South Africa. China produced 25 percent, North America 6 percent, and Oceania 1 percent. The rising prices of the 1970s induced a search for new reserves of gold, with the result that North America now produces 21 percent and Oceania 12 percent of the world supply. South Africa's share has dropped to 28 percent and China's to 18 percent. However, there was an adjustment lag of almost 10 years while gold supply caught up with demand.

Figure 4.3 illustrates what happened in the market for gold. The demand for gold in 1960, for example, looked like D_1. The supply was S_1 and price at P_1. Through the 1970s, the demand shifted out in response to general inflation, so that by 1980 it was at D_2. However, it took some time for the supply to catch up, and this adjustment lag allowed prices to rise to P_2. Eventually, as new sources of gold were exploited, the supply increased to S_2, resulting in a long-term price of P_3. Notice that P_3 still exceeds P_1 as world demand for gold is still strong.

For critical analysis: Analysts of the world gold market predict that world demand will stay strong, while 100 gold mines will close in the next three to four years. What will this do to the existing demand and supply of gold, and the equilibrium price? How quickly will it happen?

Concepts in Brief

- The terms of exchange in a voluntary exchange are determined by the interaction of the forces underlying demand and supply. These forces take place in markets, which tend to minimize transaction costs.
- When the demand curve shifts outward or inward with a stable supply curve, equilibrium price and quantity increase or decrease, respectively. When the supply curve shifts outward or inward given a stable demand curve, equilibrium price moves in the opposite direction to equilibrium quantity.
- When there is a shift in demand or supply, the new equilibrium price is not obtained instantaneously. Adjustment takes time.

Thinking Critically About the Media   Water "Rationing"

More and more these days, we hear about the lack of water in some city, province, or country. During the summer, most Canadians are allowed to water their lawns only on certain days and at certain times to restrict water usage. A few years ago, Puerto Rico suffered a drought when rainfall dropped to 35 percent below normal; residents of San Juan were subjected to water cutoffs every other day. These stories about "running out of water" always focus on the supply of water, never on the demand. The demand curve for water slopes downward, just like that for any other good or service. When the supply of strawberries increases in the summer, their prices go down; when the supply decreases, their prices go up. When the supply of water falls because of a drought, one way to ration a smaller supply is to increase the price. For some reason, politicians and media announcers reject this possibility, implying that water is different. Beware when you see the word *rationing* in the media; it typically means that the price of a good or service has not been allowed to reach equilibrium.

THE RATIONING FUNCTION OF PRICES

A shortage creates a situation that forces price to rise towards a market clearing, or equilibrium, level. A surplus brings into play forces that cause price to fall towards its market clearing level. The synchronization of decisions by buyers and sellers that creates a situation of equilibrium is called the *rationing function of prices*. Prices are indicators of relative scarcity. An equilibrium price clears the market. The plans of buyers and sellers, given the price, are not frustrated.[1] It is the free interaction of buyers and sellers which sets the price that eventually clears the market. Price, in effect, rations a commodity to demanders who are willing and able to pay the highest price. Whenever the rationing function of prices is frustrated by government-enforced price ceilings that set prices below the market clearing level, a prolonged shortage situation is not allowed to be corrected by the upward adjustment of the price.

You should note that prices which serve rationing functions need not always be stated in dollars and cents. Admission to universities and colleges is often rationed not by tuition (a dollars and cents price) but by grade point average. The highest "bidders" for admission—those with the highest GPAs—are accepted.

There are other ways to ration goods. *First come, first served* is one method. *Political power* is another. *Physical force* is yet another. Cultural, religious, and physical differences have been and are used as rationing devices throughout the world.

Consider "first come, first served" as a rationing device. In countries that do not allow prices to reflect true relative scarcity, first come, first served has become a way of life. We call this *rationing by queues,* where *queue* means "line." Whoever is willing to wait in line the longest obtains meat that is being sold at less than the market clearing price. All who wait in line are paying a higher *total* price than the money price paid for the meat. Personal time has an opportunity cost. To calculate the total price of the meat, we must add up the money price plus the opportunity cost of the time spent waiting.

Lotteries are another way to ration goods. You may have been involved in a rationing-by-lottery scheme during your first year in college when you were assigned a parking pass for campus lots. Selling raffle tickets for popular college sweatshirts is also a method of rationing by lottery.

Rationing by *coupons* has also been used, particularly during wartime. In Canada during World War II, families were allotted coupons that allowed them to purchase specified quantities of rationed goods, such as meat and gasoline. To purchase these goods, you had to pay a specified price *and* give up a coupon.

Rationing by *waiting* may occur in situations in which entrepreneurs are free to change prices to equate quantity demanded with quantity supplied, but choose not to do so. This results in queues of potential buyers. The most obvious conclusion seems to be that the price in the market is being held below equilibrium by some noncompetitive force. That is not true, however.

Try Preview Question 3:
How are goods rationed?

---

[1] There is a difference between frustration and unhappiness. You may be unhappy because you can't buy a Rolls Royce, but if you had sufficient income, you would not be frustrated in your attempt to purchase one at the current market price. By contrast, you would be frustrated if you went to your local supermarket and could get only two cans of your favourite soft-drink when you had wanted to purchase a dozen and had the necessary income.

The reason is that queuing may also arise when the demand characteristics of a market are subject to large or unpredictable fluctuations, and the additional costs to firms (and ultimately to consumers) of constantly changing prices, or of holding sufficient inventories, or providing sufficient excess capacity to cover these peak demands are greater than the costs to consumers of waiting for the good. This is the usual case of waiting in line to purchase a fast-food lunch, or to purchase a movie ticket a few minutes before the next show.

The Essential Role of Rationing

In a world of scarcity, there is, by definition, competition for what is scarce. After all, any resources that are not scarce can be had by everyone at a zero price in as large a quantity as everyone wants, such as air to burn in internal combustion engines. Once scarcity arises, there has to be some method to ration the available resources, goods, and services. The price system is one form of rationing; the others that we mentioned are alternatives. Economists cannot say which system of rationing is best. They can, however, say that rationing via the price system leads to the most efficient use of available resources. This means that generally in a price system, further trades could not occur without making somebody worse off. In other words, in a freely functioning price system, all of the gains from mutually beneficial trade will be exhausted.

Concepts in Brief

- Prices in a market economy perform a rationing function because they reflect relative scarcity, allowing the market to clear. Other ways to ration goods include first come, first served; political power; physical force; lotteries; and coupons.
- Even when businesses can change prices, some rationing by waiting will occur. Such queuing arises when there are large unexpected changes in demand, coupled with high costs of satisfying those changes immediately.

▶ **Price controls**
Government-mandated minimum or maximum prices that may be charged for goods and services.

▶ **Price ceiling**
A legal maximum price that may be charged for a particular good or service.

▶ **Price floor**
A legal minimum price below which a good or service may not be sold. Legal minimum wages are an example.

THE POLICY OF GOVERNMENT-IMPOSED PRICE CONTROLS

The rationing function of prices is often not allowed to operate when governments impose price controls. **Price controls** typically involve setting a **price ceiling**—the maximum price that may be allowed in an exchange. The world has had a long history of price ceilings applied to some goods, wages, rents, and interest rates, among other things. Occasionally a government will set a **price floor**—a minimum price below which a good or service may not be sold. These have most often been applied to wages and agricultural products. Let's consider price controls in terms of price ceilings.

Price Ceilings and Black Markets

As long as a price ceiling is below the market clearing price, imposing a price ceiling creates a shortage, as can be seen in Figure 4.4. At any price below the market clearing, or equilibrium, price of P_e, there will always be a larger quantity demanded than quantity supplied, that is, a shortage. This was discussed initially in Chapter 3. Normally, whenever a shortage exists, there is a tendency for price and output to rise to equilibrium levels. This is exactly what we pointed out when discussing shortages in the market for gold. But with a price ceiling, this tendency cannot be fully realized because everyone is forbidden to trade at the equilibrium price.

The result is fewer exchanges and **nonprice rationing devices**. In Figure 4.4, at an equilibrium price of P_e, the equilibrium quantity demanded and supplied (or traded) is Q_e. But at the price ceiling of P_1, the equilibrium quantity offered is only Q_s. What happens if there is a shortage? The most obvious nonprice rationing device to help clear the market is queuing, or long lines, which we have already discussed.

Typically, an effective price ceiling leads to a **black market**. A black market is a market in which the price-controlled good is sold at an illegally high price through various methods. For example, if the price of gasoline is controlled at lower than the market clearing price, a gas station attendant may take a cash payment on the side in order to fill up a driver's car. If the price of beef is controlled at below its market clearing price, the butcher may give special service to a customer who offers the butcher great seats at an upcoming football game. Indeed, the number of ways in which the true implicit price of a price-controlled good or service can be increased is infinite, limited only by the imagination. (Black markets also occur when goods are made illegal.)

Whenever a nation attempts to freeze all prices, a variety of problems arise. Many of them occurred a few years ago in Mexico.

▶ **Nonprice rationing devices**

All methods used to ration scarce goods that are price-controlled. Whenever the price system is not allowed to work, nonprice rationing devices will evolve to ration the affected goods and services.

▶ **Black market**

A market in which goods are traded at prices above their legal maximum prices or in which illegal goods are sold.

Try **Preview Question 4**:
When would you expect to encounter black markets?

Figure 4.4
Black Markets

The demand curve is D. The supply curve is S. The equilibrium price is P_e. The government, however, steps in and imposes a maximum price of P_1. At that lower price, the quantity demanded will be Q_d, but the quantity supplied will only be Q_s. There is a shortage, and black markets develop. The price at which the restricted quantity could sell on the market (the *implicit* price) rises to P_2.

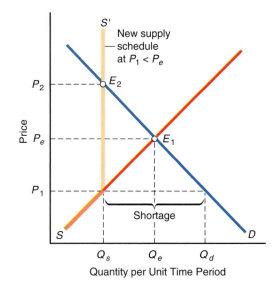

INTERNATIONAL EXAMPLE
Mexico's Price Freeze and the Shopping Cops

The mid-1990s marked a low point for the Mexican economy when its currency, the peso, plunged in value relative to the dollar and other international currencies. In anticipation of rapidly rising domestic prices, the Mexican government imposed a temporary freeze on all prices. Almost immediately, shoppers began complaining about supermarkets, department stores, car dealerships, and mom and pop stores that were illegally raising their prices. In response, the Mexican Consumer Attorney General's Office sent out a small army of "shopping cops" to impose fines as necessary, and temporarily closed hundreds of stores. During one national sample of commercial establishments, 70 percent were found to be cheating on the price freeze.

One way merchants got around government price controls was to place "sold" stickers on merchandise. Consumers then had to agree to pay a higher price in order to obtain the goods. Many automobile dealerships refused to deliver cars bought prior to the dramatic reduction in the value of the Mexican peso. Indeed, the number of ways to evade price controls was limited only by the imagination of buyers and sellers.

For critical analysis: How would you graphically illustrate the situation in Mexico using a supply and demand diagram?

Concepts in Brief

- Government policy can impose price controls in the form of price ceilings and price floors.
- An effective price ceiling is one that sets the legal price below the market clearing price and is enforced. Effective price ceilings lead to nonprice rationing devices and black markets.

THE POLICY OF CONTROLLING RENTS

▶ **Rent control**

The placement of price ceilings on rents.

Most provinces have at some time operated under some form of rent control. **Rent control** is a system under which the provincial government tells building owners how much rent they can charge their tenants. In Canada, rent controls date back to at least World War II. The objective of rent control is to keep rents below levels that would be observed in a freely competitive market.

The Functions of Rental Prices

In any housing market, rental prices serve three functions: (1) to promote the efficient maintenance of existing housing and stimulate the construction of new housing, (2) to allocate existing scarce housing among competing claimants, and (3) to ration the use of existing housing by current demanders.

Rent Controls and Construction.

Rent controls have discouraged the construction of new rental units. Rents are the most important long-term determinant of profitability, and rent controls have artificially depressed them. Consider some examples. Halifax, with less than 15 percent of the population of Toronto, built proportionally more rental units than Toronto in 1995. This, in spite of a 7.2 percent vacancy rate in Halifax, compared to a 1.2 percent vacancy rate in Toronto. The major difference? There were no rent controls in Halifax, while rent increases were strictly controlled in Toronto. In the same year, Vancouver, with 70 percent of the population of Toronto, saw the construction of 11,000 rental units; only 4,000 were built in Toronto. Again, the difference was that there were no rent controls in Vancouver.

Effects on the Existing Supply of Housing.

When rental rates are held below equilibrium levels, property owners cannot use higher rents to recover the cost of maintenance, repairs, and capital improvements. Hence they curtail these activities. In the extreme situation, taxes, utilities, and the expenses of basic repairs exceed rental receipts. The result is abandoned and/or deteriorating buildings. It is estimated that over 15 percent of the rental housing in Toronto will deteriorate so much by the early 2000s that it will be uninhabitable. In the 1970s, when Vancouver did have a system of rent controls, landlords, unable to increase rents, converted thousands of apartments into condominiums. The landlords then sold the condominiums and recouped their investment that way. This had the effect of severely reducing the supply of rental housing, thus making the housing shortage even worse.

Rationing the Current Use of Housing.

Like any other price, rents serve the purpose of rationing output, in this case the allocation of apartments among prospective tenants. When the rent is held at an arbitrarily low level, the number of prospective tenants increases and excess demand develops. Students, for example, who might otherwise live with their families, decide they can afford to live on their own. In this situation, rationing of the available supply of rental housing is achieved through nonprice mechanisms such as queuing or making "under the table" payments to landlords.

Attempts at Evading Rent Controls

The distortions produced by rent controls lead to efforts by both landlords and tenants to evade the rules. This, in turn, leads to the growth of expensive government bureaucracies whose job it is to make sure that those rules are indeed followed. In 1995, the Ontario government spent about $1.8 million administering its *Residential Rent Regulation Act.*

In the 1980s, Ontario landlords had an incentive to speculate on the real estate market. They bought and sold apartment buildings, driving up prices and financing costs. Then they applied for rent increases to cover the rising costs. Tenants, for their part, routinely try to sublet all or part of their rent-controlled apartments at fees substantially above the rent they pay to the owner. They pocket the difference, perhaps to help pay for a more expensive apartment.

Who Gains and Who Loses from Rent Controls?

The big losers from rent controls are clearly landlords. But there is another group of losers—low-income individuals, especially single mothers, trying to find their first apartment. Some observers now believe that rent controls have worsened the problem of homeless people in such cities as Toronto.

Landlords of rent-controlled apartments often charge "key money" before a new tenant is allowed to move in. This is a large up-front cash payment, usually illegal but demanded nonetheless—just one aspect of the black market in rent-controlled apartments. Poor individuals cannot afford a hefty key money payment, nor can they assure the landlord that their rent will be on time or even paid each month. Because controlled rents are usually below market clearing levels, there is little incentive for apartment owners to take any risk on low-income-earning individuals as tenants. This is particularly true when a prospective tenant's chief source of income is a welfare cheque.

INTERNATIONAL EXAMPLE
Rent Controls in Bombay

In the mid-1990s, Bombay, India, had the highest rents of any capital city in the world. The annual rent per square foot for *available* unleased space was estimated at about $200, compared to $30 in downtown Vancouver or Toronto. In addition, most landlords insist on receiving a year's rent in advance, plus an additional security deposit equal to two years' rent. For major businesses, this can add up to millions of dollars, which are usually returned, but in three to five years and without payment of any interest.

One reason Bombay rents are so high is the existence of rent controls and other laws intended to protect tenants. These controls and restrictions have kept out real estate developers, and even scared owners of rentable property out of renting that property, be it commercial or residential. One rent control law makes it almost impossible for a landlord to evict a tenant or to raise rents. Tenants can obtain what is called *statutory tenancy*, which allows them and their descendants to remain without a lease in any property they currently rent. There are situations in Bombay in which renters from 50 years ago still live in the same apartment, paying approximately the same rent as they originally did. Not surprisingly, unleased rental space is hard to find and hence quite expensive.

For critical analysis: What effect do you think Bombay's high rents might have on foreign firms' desire to operate in that city?

Who benefits from rent control? Ample evidence indicates that upper-income professionals benefit the most. These are the people who can use their mastery of the bureaucracy and their large network of friends and connections to exploit the rent control system. These are also the people who can easily afford to pay key money, or to pay an agency to locate an apartment for them.

Because the private sector was unwilling to finance construction of new rental units in an environment of rent controls, the Ontario government has had to spend up to $3.5 billion per year subsidizing the building of non-profit housing. Rents may have been controlled at lower-than-market levels, but renters and homeowners alike paid higher than necessary taxes to fund the government's subsidies.

Concepts in Brief

- Rental prices perform three functions: (1) allocating existing scarce housing among competing claimants, (2) promoting efficient maintenance of existing houses and stimulating new housing construction, and (3) rationing the use of existing houses by current demanders.
- Effective rent controls reduce or alter the three functions of rental prices. Construction of new rental units is discouraged. Rent controls decrease spending on maintenance of existing units and also lead to "housing gridlock."
- There are numerous ways to evade rent controls; key money is one.

PRICE SUPPORTS: THE CASE OF AGRICULTURE

Another way that government can affect markets is by imposing price floors or price supports. In Canada, price supports are most often associated with agricultural products.

Over one-half of Canadian farmers' total sales are regulated by agricultural marketing boards. Chickens, turkeys, eggs, milk, butter, tobacco, and mushrooms are all sold through marketing boards which restrict supply of these products to the marketplace. Consequently, our more than 100 marketing boards are referred to as a *supply-management system*.

In the 1970s, the Canadian government was concerned that farm output prices which fluctuated widely left farmers with good incomes one year, but possibly starvation incomes the next. In an effort to stabilize farm incomes and protect the small family farm, the government legislated marketing boards. The boards then set **quotas** for production for each farm in order to regulate supply. Since the supply was restricted, price rose.

▶ **Quota**

A set amount of output (less than the equilibrium amount) which farmers can supply to marketing boards for sale.

Figure 4.5 shows the effect of a marketing board quota on the market for eggs. The demand curve, D, is the domestic demand for Canadian eggs. The supply curve, S, is the domestic supply of eggs. In the absence of a quota, the equilibrium price and quantity of eggs will be P_e and Q_e. When the marketing board sets a quota on production, it limits the amount that farmers are permitted to produce. A quota which is effective will always be less than the equilibrium quantity, Q_e. The vertical

Figure 4.5
The Regulated Market for Eggs

The market demand and supply curves are D and S, and in an unregulated market equilibrium price and quantity would be P_e and Q_e. The Egg Marketing Board, however, sets a quota at the quantity Q_q. This has the effect of stopping all production past Q_q, and raising the price to P_q where the demand curve meets the regulated supply S_q.

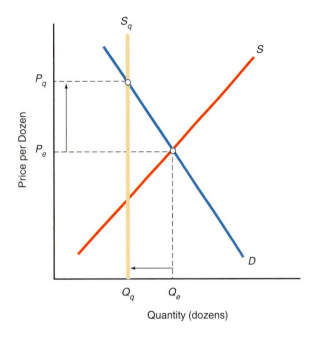

line S_q represents the quota in the egg market. Notice that the quantity traded falls to Q_q while the price rises to P_q. The marketing board, armed with knowledge of consumer demand for its product, can effectively guarantee a price floor simply by setting quotas.

Who Loses When Marketing Boards Regulate Supply?

The consumer pays more for the regulated goods than necessary and is therefore the biggest loser. One estimate suggests that the average Canadian family pays $200 to $400 per year more than it would if all farm produce were sold at unregulated prices.

Prospective farmers lose too. When quotas were first established, they were given to existing producers. New producers, however, have to purchase quotas from other farmers or from the appropriate marketing board. Some quotas have become prohibitively expensive. To buy a minimum-size quota for a chicken farm today would require $1 million; a minimum-size quota for a dairy farm in the Fraser Valley of British Columbia would take $3 million. And that's not counting the cost of the land or the livestock.

Another loser is the foreign farmer who would like to export farm products to Canada. The government restricts entry of foreign produce, because the additional supply would reduce prices. Canada used to keep out foreign produce with import quotas, but the GATT (General Agreement on Tariffs and Trade) in its latest round of talks banned import quotas on agricultural goods. Thus the federal government now uses import duties (i.e., taxes on imported produce) to restrict supply of foreign goods. The tariff on butter from the United States, for example, is 351 percent.

Who Wins When Marketing Boards Regulate Supply?

Existing farmers are clearly the major winners. The boards do stabilize their incomes, so they can plan from one year to the next. Supporters of marketing boards also point out that by guaranteeing a living for Canadian farmers we are providing ourselves with a made-at-home food supply—something much more valuable than the costs associated with supply management. In addition, we are helping to preserve a way of life which is disappearing elsewhere, and that is the family farm.

Some farmers object to being regulated by marketing boards. They believe that they, as entrepreneurs, will be better salespeople for their products than a government bureaucracy. This is happening most clearly in the wheat industry where a special form of marketing board exists.

| **EXAMPLE** | Wheat Farmers and the Canadian Wheat Board |

The Canadian government has been involved in guaranteeing prices for wheat farmers since World War I. In 1917, to regulate the supply of wheat to troops in Europe and to Canadians at home, and to guarantee grain farmers a reasonable living, the government set up the Board of Grain Supervisors. After the war, the Board's name was changed to the Canadian Wheat Board. It still operates today. The Canadian Wheat Board buys all the wheat a farmer produces and sells it on world markets. Farmers cannot sell their wheat independently. The Board advances 75 percent of the expected price to farmers in the spring, and then settles up with them after the wheat is sold in the fall. Farmers never receive less than the expected price, so if the world price is lower than predicted, the Wheat Board suffers a loss. But if the price is higher, farmers are paid more. This has the effect of reducing fluctuations in farm income by putting a floor under the price farmers receive.

Recently, some grain growers have been objecting to being forced to sell to the Wheat Board. They claim that by selling directly to the United States, they would earn $2 to $3 per bushel more, a significant price difference. But other farmers want the Wheat Board to remain. They fear as individual farmers they would not have the leverage to stand up against major wheat buyers and demand a high price. In the end they fear their incomes would fall.

For critical analysis: What do you think would happen to the price of Canadian wheat if half the farmers sold independently, while half sold through the Canadian Wheat Board?

PRICE FLOORS IN THE LABOUR MARKET

▶ **Minimum wage**

A wage floor, legislated by government, setting the lowest hourly rate that firms may legally pay workers.

The **minimum wage** is the lowest hourly wage rate that firms may legally pay their workers. Proponents want higher minimum wages to ensure low-income workers a "decent" standard of living. Opponents claim that higher minimum wages cause increased unemployment, particularly among unskilled teenagers.

Every province in Canada has a minimum wage. Figure 4.6 sets out the hourly minimum wage for each province. For many years the federal government had a minimum wage of $4.00 per hour which applied to federal workers. However, this legislated wage was cancelled some time ago, since all workers were already earning more than the minimum anyway.

What happens when the government passes a floor on wages? The effects can be seen in Figure 4.7. We start off in equilibrium with the equilibrium wage rate of

Figure 4.6
Provincial Minimum Wages

In 1996, every province had a legislated minimum wage. The rate varied from a low of $4.75 to a high of $7.00 per hour. The average minimum wage was $5.67.

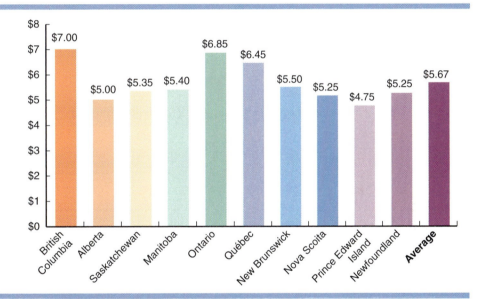

Figure 4.7
The Effect of Minimum Wages

The market clearing wage rate is W_e. The market clearing quantity of employment is Q_e, determined by the intersection of supply and demand at point E. A minimum wage equal to W_m is established. The quantity of labour demanded is reduced to Q_d; the reduction in employment from Q_e to Q_d is equal to the distance between B and A. That distance is smaller than the excess quantity of labour supplied at wage rate W_m. The distance between B and C is the increase in the quantity of labour supplied that results from the higher minimum wage rate.

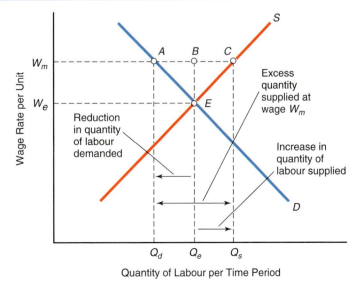

W_e and the equilibrium quantity of labour demanded and supplied equal to Q_e. A minimum wage, W_m, higher than W_e, is imposed. At W_m, the quantity demanded for labour is reduced to Q_d, and some workers now become unemployed. Note that the reduction in employment from Q_e to Q_d, or the distance from B to A, is less than the excess quantity of labour supplied at wage rate W_m. This excess quantity supplied is the distance between A and C, or the distance between Q_d and Q_s. The reason the reduction in employment is smaller than the excess supply of labour at the minimum wage is that the latter also includes a second component, consisting of the additional workers who would like to work more hours at the new, higher minimum wage. Some workers may become unemployed as a result of the minimum wage, but others will move to sectors where minimum wage laws do not apply; wages will be pushed down in these uncovered sectors.

In the long run (a time period that is long enough to allow for adjustment by workers and firms), some of the reduction in labour demanded will result from a reduction in the number of firms, and some will result from changes in the number of workers employed by each firm. Economists estimate that a 10 percent increase in the real minimum wage decreases total employment of those affected by 1 to 2 percent.[2]

QUANTITY RESTRICTIONS

Governments can impose quantity restrictions on a market. The most obvious restriction is an outright ban on the ownership or trading of a good. It is presently illegal to buy and sell human organs. It is also currently illegal to buy and sell certain psychoactive drugs such as cocaine, heroin, and marijuana. It is illegal to open a new chartered bank without obtaining a government charter. This requirement effectively restricts the number of chartered banks in Canada.

Some of the most common quantity restrictions exist in the area of international trade. The Canadian government and many foreign governments impose import quotas on a variety of goods. An **import quota** is a supply restriction that prohibits the importation of more than a specified quantity of a particular good in a one-year period. Canada has had import quotas on cotton textiles, shoes, and immigrant labour. For many years, there were import quotas on dairy products coming into Canada from the United States. These import quotas were recently removed and replaced by tariffs, but the effect is still to limit the amount of dairy products which we import. There are also "voluntary" import quotas on certain goods. Japanese car makers, for example, have agreed since 1981 "voluntarily" to restrict the number of cars they send to Canada.

▶ **Import quota**
A physical supply restriction on imports of a particular good, such as sugar. Foreign exporters are unable to sell in Canada more than the quantity specified in the import quota.

---

[2] Because we are referring to a long-run analysis here, the reduction in labour demanded would be demonstrated by an eventual shift inward to the left of the short-run demand curve, D, in Figure 4.7.

POLICY EXAMPLE

Should the Legal Quantity of Cigarettes Supplied Be Set at Zero?

Nicotine has been used as a psychoactive drug by the Native Peoples of the Americas for approximately 8,000 years. Five hundred years ago, Christopher Columbus introduced tobacco to the Europeans, who discovered that once they overcame the nausea and dizziness produced by chewing, snorting, or smoking the tobacco, they simply could not get along without it. Nicotine quickly joined alcohol and caffeine as one of the world's principal psychoactive drugs of choice. In the century after Columbus returned from the Americas with tobacco, the use of and addiction to nicotine spread quickly around the world. There followed numerous efforts to quash what had become known as the "evil weed." In 1603, the Japanese prohibited the use of tobacco, and repeatedly increased the penalties for violating the ban, which wasn't lifted until 1625. By the middle of the seventeenth century, similar bans on tobacco were in place in Bavaria, Saxony, Zurich, Turkey, and Russia, with punishments ranging from confiscation of property to execution.

What could we predict if tobacco were ever completely prohibited today? Because tobacco is legal, the supply of illegal tobacco is zero. If the use of tobacco were restricted, the supply of illegal tobacco would not remain zero for long. Even if Canadian tobacco growers were forced out of business, the production of tobacco in other countries would increase to meet the demand. Consequently, the supply curve of illegal tobacco products would shift outward to the right as more foreign sources determined they wanted to enter the illegal Canadian tobacco market. The demand curve for illegal tobacco products would emerge almost immediately after the quantity restriction. The price people would pay to satisfy their nicotine addiction would go up.

For critical analysis: What other goods or services follow the same analysis as the one presented here?

Concepts in Brief

- With a price support system, the government sets a quota which limits the amount of output that can be produced. The only way a price support system can survive is for the government to restrict competing imports from adding to domestic supply and thus lowering price.
- When a floor is placed on wages at a rate that is above market equilibrium, the result is an excess quantity of labour supplied at that minimum wage.
- Quantity restrictions may take the form of import quotas, which are limits on the quantity of specific foreign goods that can be brought into Canada for resale purposes.

Issues and Applications

Grunge Meets Greed

Concepts Applied: Markets, exchange, price system, intermediaries, rationing, supply and demand

Pearl Jam's Eddie Vedder refused to sell tickets for the '95–'96 tour through Ticketmaster because the distributor adds on a hefty fee to tickets. Are Ticketmaster's services of convenient ticket purchasing worth the price they charge? Pearl Jam didn't think so.

Arguably, the Seattle grunge band Pearl Jam is one of the most successful rock bands of our time. Not only is it one of the most popular bands in Canada, but it is also the most revolutionary. Pearl Jam refused to make videos for MTV and VH-1 for its second successful album, *Vs.*, and didn't release any singles from that album in Canada. When the band finally decided to tour after an intentionally long hiatus, it demanded a US$20 ceiling on ticket prices, including a top service charge of 10 percent from the leading ticket distributor, Ticketmaster.

Ticketmaster's Position as Intermediary

Ticketmaster uses a highly sophisticated computer system to distribute tickets nationwide for major entertainment events. When asked about Pearl Jam's claims that Ticketmaster was "gouging" fans, a senior company official said that Ticketmaster's investment in that computer system makes it easier for performers to sell large numbers of tickets. Each year, Ticketmaster sells between 50 and 60 million tickets. The official claimed that Ticketmaster has the right to be paid for such services and noted that "if Pearl Jam wants

to play for free, we will be happy to distribute their tickets for free." Ticketmaster currently charges a fee of $5 to $10 per ticket.

The Value That Ticketmaster Adds

Goods have little or no value if consumers cannot obtain them. The value of a good therefore depends on its availability. Intermediaries add value to goods without physically changing them by simply making it easier for consumers to purchase them. As an intermediary, this is what Ticketmaster does. Major entertainment events, such as a Pearl Jam concert, are most profitable and add value to more consumers when they are performed in large venues, such as football stadiums. It would be virtually impossible to service all of the fans desiring to attend a Pearl Jam concert if tickets were sold only at the box office of the venue where the concert was being held. A computerized nationwide system allows popular bands to sell tickets efficiently for concerts at large-capacity venues.

Pearl Jam's Failed Alternative Distribution System

Pearl Jam originally decided to give concerts in the United States without the use of Ticketmaster by distributing tickets through a lottery. Some 175,000 people sent in postcards for the two concerts that were to be held at Constitution Hall in Philadelphia, which seats 3,700 people. Of course, many people who saw those concerts paid extravagant prices by using the services of scalpers. One of the things that Pearl Jam cannot control is the value that fans place on seeing and hearing the band perform live. As long as different fans have different valuations of an activity, there will be some who will willingly give up their tickets at a high enough price, which others will gladly pay.

Neither the lottery nor any other alternatives that Pearl Jam tried to get around the intermediary services of Ticketmaster worked. The band cancelled its 1995–1996 tour. Its spokespersons claimed that "touring without Ticketmaster was too complicated."

Competition for Ticketmaster may be on the horizon, with distributors selling tickets via a high-tech phone system and the Internet.

For Critical Analysis

1. Assume that Ticketmaster distributes 100 percent of all tickets to live entertainment events in Canada. Why wouldn't Ticketmaster charge an even higher service charge per ticket, say, $50?

2. If the government passed a law restricting Ticketmaster to a $2 charge per ticket, what might happen as a result?

CHAPTER SUMMARY

1. A price system, otherwise called a market system, allows prices to respond to changes in supply and demand for different commodities. Consumers' and business managers' decisions on resource use depend on what happens to prices.

2. Exchanges take place in markets. The terms of exchange—prices—are registered in markets that tend to minimize transaction costs.

3. With a stable supply curve, a rise in demand leads to an increase in equilibrium price and quantity; a decrease in demand leads to a reduction in equilibrium price and quantity. With a stable demand curve, a rise in supply leads to a decrease in equilibrium price and an increase in equilibrium quantity; a fall in supply leads to an increase in equilibrium price and a decrease in equilibrium quantity.

4. When both demand and supply shift at the same time, indeterminate results occur. We must know the direction and degree of each shift in order to predict the change in equilibrium price and quantity.

5. When there is a shift in demand or supply, it takes time for markets to adjust to the new equilibrium. During that time, there will be temporary shortages or surpluses.

6. In a market system, prices perform a rationing function—they ration scarce goods and services. Other ways of rationing include first come, first served; political power; physical force; lotteries; and coupons.

7. Government-imposed price controls can take the form of price ceilings, price floors, and quotas. Effective price ceilings—ones that are set below the market clearing price and enforced—lead to nonprice rationing devices and black markets.

8. Rent controls interfere with many of the functions of rental prices. For example, effective rent controls discourage the construction of new rental units. They also encourage "housing gridlock." Landlords lose during effective rent controls. Other losers are typically low-income individuals, especially single mothers, trying to find their first apartments.

9. A quota can take the form of a government-imposed price support for agricultural products. This restricts quantity supplied and drives the price up to the desired level. To maintain that price, the government must restrict competing imports from increasing the domestic supply.

10. A price floor can apply to wages. When the government-imposed minimum wage exceeds the equilibrium wage rate, an excess quantity of labour is supplied. The result is higher unemployment for the affected group of workers.

11. Quantity restrictions can take the form of import quotas, under which there is a limit to the quantity of the affected good that can be brought into Canada and sold.

DISCUSSION OF PREVIEW QUESTIONS

1. Does an increase in demand always lead to a rise in price?

Yes, provided that the supply curve doesn't shift also. If the supply is stable, every rise in demand will cause a shift outward to the right in the demand curve. The new equilibrium price will be higher than the old equilibrium price. If, however, the supply curve shifts at the same time, you have to know in which direction and by how much. If the supply curve shifts outward, indicating a rise in supply, the equilibrium price can rise if the shift is not as great as in demand. If the increase in supply is greater than in demand, the price can actually fall. We can be sure, though, that if demand increases and supply decreases, the equilibrium price will rise. This can be seen in the accompanying graph.

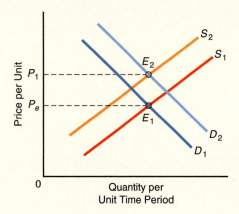

2. Can there ever be shortages in a market with no restrictions?

Yes, there can, because adjustment is never instantaneous. It takes time for the forces of supply and demand to work. In all our graphs, we draw new equilibrium points where a new supply curve meets a new demand curve. That doesn't mean that in the marketplace buyers and sellers will react immediately to a change in supply or demand. Information is not perfect. Moreover, people are often slow to adapt to higher or lower prices. Suppliers may require months or years to respond to an increase in the demand for their product. Consumers take time to respond to new information about changing relative prices.

3. How are goods rationed?

In a pure price system, prices ration goods. Prices are the indicators of relative scarcity. Prices change so that quantity demanded equals quantity supplied. In the absence of a price system, an alternative way to ration goods is first come, first served. In many systems, political power is another method. In certain cultures, physical force is a way to ration goods. Cultural, religious, and physical differences among individuals can be used as rationing devices. The fact is that given a world of scarcity, there has to be some method to ration goods. The price system is only one alternative.

4. When would you expect to encounter black markets?

Black markets occur in two situations. The first is whenever a good or service is made illegal by legislation. Second, there are black markets whenever a price ceiling (one type of price control) is imposed on any good or service. The price ceiling has to be below the market clearing price and enforced for a black market to exist, however. Price ceilings on rents have created black markets for rental units.

PROBLEMS

(Answers to the odd-numbered problems appear at the back of the book.)

4-1. This is a graph of the supply and demand for oranges.

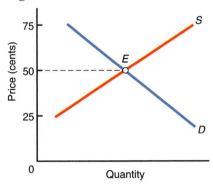

Explain the effect that each of the following events would have on this graph.
a. It is discovered that oranges can cure acne.
b. A new machine is developed that will automatically pick oranges.
c. The government declares a price floor of 25 cents.
d. The government declares a price floor of 75 cents.
e. The price of grapefruits increases.
f. Income decreases.

4-2. What might be the long-run results of price controls that maintained a good's money price below its equilibrium price? Above its equilibrium price?

4-3. Here is a demand schedule and a supply schedule for scientific hand-held calculators.

Price	Quantity Demanded	Quantity Supplied
$10	100,000	0
20	60,000	0
30	20,000	0
40	0	0
50	0	100,000
60	0	300,000
70	0	500,000

What are the equilibrium price and the equilibrium quantity? Explain.

4-4. This is a graph of the supply and demand for raisins.

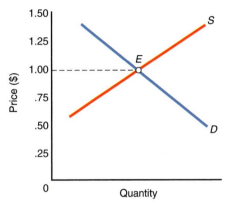

The following series of events occurs. Explain the result of each event.
a. An advertising campaign for raisins is successful.
b. A fungus wipes out half the grape crop (used to make raisins) in California.
c. The price of bran flakes (a complement) increases.
d. The price of dried cranberries (a substitute) increases.
e. The government declares a price floor of 75 cents.
f. The government imposes and enforces a price ceiling of 75 cents.
g. Income increases (assume that raisins are an inferior good).

4-5. Below is a demand schedule and a supply schedule for lettuce.

Price per Crate	Quantity Demanded (crates per year)	Quantity Supplied (crates per year)
$1	10 million	0 million
2	9 million	1 million
3	7 million	3 million
4	5 million	5 million
5	2 million	8 million

What are the equilibrium price and the equilibrium quantity? At a price of $2 per crate, what is the quantity demanded? The quantity supplied? What is this disequilibrium situation called? What is the magnitude of the disequilibrium, expressed in terms of quantities? Now answer the same questions for a price of $5 per crate.

4-6. What is wrong with the following statement? "The demand has increased so much in response to our offering of a $500 rebate that our inventory of cars is now running very low."

4-7. Rent control is a price ceiling. There are also legislated price floors. Assume that the equilibrium price for apples is 10 cents each. Draw the supply and demand diagram to show the effect of a government-imposed price floor, or minimum price, of 15 cents per apple. Be sure to label any shortages or surpluses that result. Then show the effect of a price floor of 5 cents per apple.

The Public Sector

In Canada over the course of a year, thousands of tax lawyers and accountants labour alone or with clients to help those clients reduce their tax liabilities and fill out their tax returns. Canadian taxpayers are each estimated to spend approximately 20 hours a year preparing their taxes. The opportunity cost exceeds $4 billion a year. And that is not the end of the story—many individuals spend a lot of valuable time figuring out ways to change their behaviour so as to reduce the taxes they owe. Although there is never any way to avoid the cost of a tax system completely, there are ways to reduce compliance costs to society. One way is to switch to a more simplified tax system. To understand this issue, you need to know more about government and the public sector.

Preview Questions

1. What problems will you encounter if you refuse to pay a portion of your income tax because you oppose spending on military defence?

2. What is the essence of the public-choice model?

3. In what ways do regressive, proportional, and progressive tax structures differ?

4. Who pays the corporate income tax?

Did You Know That... the average Canadian works from January 1 through June 24 each year to pay for all municipal, provincial, and federal taxes? The average Vancouver resident works approximately one week longer to pay for all of the taxes owed each year. Looked at another way, the average Canadian in a typical eight-hour day works about 3 hours and 50 minutes to pay for government at all levels. The average household with two or more people spends about $26,000 a year in taxes of all kinds. The total amount paid exceeds $270 billion. It would take more than 270,000 millionaires to have as much money as is spent each year by government. So we cannot ignore the presence of government in our society. Government exists, at a minimum, to take care of what the price system does not do well.

WHAT A PRICE SYSTEM CAN AND CANNOT DO

Throughout the book so far, we have alluded to the benefits of a price system. High on that list of benefits is economic efficiency. In its most ideal form, a price system allows resources to move from lower-valued uses to higher-valued uses through voluntary exchange. The supreme point of economic efficiency occurs when all mutually advantageous trades have taken place. In a price system, consumers are sovereign; that is to say, they have the individual freedom to decide what they wish to purchase. Politicians and even business managers do not ultimately decide what is produced; consumers decide. Some supporters of the price system argue that this is its most important characteristic. A market organization of economic activity generally prevents one person from interfering with another in respect to most of that individual's activities. Competition among sellers protects consumers from coercion by one seller, and sellers are protected from coercion by one consumer because other consumers are available.

Sometimes the price system does not generate these results, with too few or too many resources going to specific economic activities. Such situations are called **market failures**. Market failures prevent the price system from attaining economic efficiency and individual freedom, as well as other social goals. Market failures offer one of the strongest arguments in favour of certain economic functions of government, which we now examine.

▶ **Market failure**

A situation in which an unrestrained market economy leads to too few or too many resources going to a specific economic activity.

CORRECTING FOR EXTERNALITIES

In a pure market system, competition generates economic efficiency only when individuals know the true opportunity cost of their actions. In some circumstances, the price that someone actually pays for a resource, good, or service is higher or lower than the opportunity cost that all of society pays for that same resource, good, or service.

Consider a hypothetical world in which there is no government regulation against pollution. You are living in a town that until now has had clean air. A steel

> **Externality**
> A consequence of an economic activity that spills over to affect third parties. Pollution is an externality.

> **Third parties**
> Parties who are not directly involved in a given activity or transaction.

mill moves into town. It produces steel and has paid for the inputs—land, labour, capital, and entrepreneurship. The price it charges for the steel reflects, in this example, only the costs that the steel mill incurred. In the course of production, however, the mill gets one input—clean air—by simply taking it. This is indeed an input because in the making of steel, the furnaces emit smoke. The steel mill doesn't have to pay the cost of using the clean air; rather, it is the people in the community who pay that cost in the form of dirtier clothes, dirtier cars and houses, and more respiratory illnesses. The effect is similar to what would happen if the steel mill could take coal or oil or workers' services free. There has been an **externality**, an external cost. Some of the costs associated with the production of the steel have "spilled over" to affect **third parties**, parties other than the buyer and the seller of the steel.

External Costs in Graphical Form

Look at part (a) in Figure 5.1. Here we show the demand curve for steel to be D. The supply curve is S_1. The supply curve includes only the costs that the firms have to pay. The equilibrium, or market clearing, situation will occur at quantity Q_1. Let us take into account the fact that there are externalities—the external costs that you and your neighbours pay in the form of dirtier clothes, cars, and houses, and

Figure 5.1
External Costs and Benefits

In part (a), we show a situation in which the production of steel generates external costs. If the steel mills ignore pollution, at equilibrium the quantity of steel will be Q_1. If the mills had to pay for the additional cost borne by nearby residents that is caused by the steel mill's production, the supply curve would shift inward to the left to S_2. If consumers were forced to pay a price that reflected the spillover costs, the quantity demanded would fall to Q_2. In part (b), we show the situation in which vaccinations against influenza generate external benefits to those individuals who may not be vaccinated but who will benefit because epidemics will not occur. If each individual ignores the external benefit of the flu shot, the market clearing quantity will be Q_1. If external benefits are taken into account by purchasers of flu shots, however, the demand curve would shift rightward to D_2. The new equilibrium quantity would be Q_2 and the price would be higher, P_2.

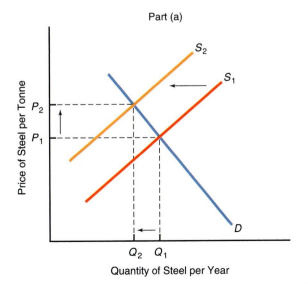

Part (a)

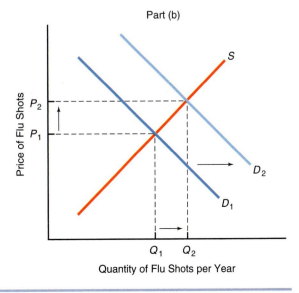

Part (b)

increased respiratory disease due to the air pollution from the steel mill; we also assume that all other suppliers of steel use clean air without having to pay for it. Let's include these external costs in our graph to find out what the full cost of steel production really is. This is equivalent to saying that the price of an input used in steel production increased. Recall from Chapter 3 that an increase in input prices shifts the supply curve inward to the left. Thus in part (a) of the figure, the supply curve shifts from S_1 to S_2. If the external costs were somehow taken into account, the equilibrium quantity would fall to Q_2 and the price would rise to P_2. Otherwise, that price is implicitly being paid, but by two different groups of people. The lower price, P_1, is being explicitly paid for by the purchasers of steel and steel products. The difference between P_2 and P_1 represents the cost that third parties are bearing in the form of dirtier clothes, houses, and cars, and increased respiratory illnesses.

External Benefits in Graphical Form

Externalities can also be positive. To demonstrate external benefits in graphical form, we will use the example of vaccinations against influenza. In part (b) of Figure 5.1, we show the demand curve as D_1 (without taking account of any external benefits) and the supply curve as S. The equilibrium price is P_1, and the equilibrium quantity is Q_1. We assume, however, that flu shots generate external benefits to individuals who may not be vaccinated but will benefit nevertheless because epidemics will not break out. If such external benefits were taken into account, the demand curve would shift outward from D_1 to D_2. The new equilibrium quantity would be Q_2, and the new equilibrium price would be P_2. With no corrective action, this society is not devoting enough resources to flu shots.

When there are external costs, the market will tend to overallocate resources to the production of the good or service in question, for those goods or services will be deceptively low-priced. With the example of steel, too much will be produced because the steel mill owners and managers are not required to take account of the external cost that steel production is imposing on the rest of society. In essence, the full cost of production is unknown to the owners and managers, so the price they charge the public for steel is lower than it would be otherwise. And of course, the lower price means that buyers are willing and able to buy more. More steel is produced and consumed than is socially optimal.

When there are external benefits, the market underallocates resources to the production of that good or service because the good or service is relatively too expensive (because the demand is relatively too low). In a market system, too many of the goods that generate external costs are produced and too few of the goods that generate external benefits are produced.

How the Government Corrects Negative Externalities

The government can in theory correct externality situations in a variety of ways in all cases that warrant such action. In the case of negative externalities, at least two avenues are open to the government: special taxes and legislative regulation or prohibition.

Special Taxes.

In our example of the steel mill, the externality problem originates from the fact that the air as a waste disposal place is costless to the firm but not to society. The government could make the steel mill pay a tax for dumping its pollutants into the air. The government could attempt to tax the steel mill commensurate with the cost to third parties from smoke in the air. This, in effect, would be a pollution tax, or an **effluent fee**. The ultimate effect would be to reduce the supply of steel and raise the price to consumers, ideally making the price equal to the full cost of production to society.

▶ **Effluent fee**
A charge to a polluter that gives the right to discharge into the air or water a certain amount of pollution. Also called a pollution tax.

Regulation.

To correct a negative externality arising from steel production, the government could specify a maximum allowable rate of pollution. This action would require that the steel mill install pollution abatement equipment within its facilities, that it reduce its rate of output, or some combination of the two. Note that the government's job would not be that simple, for it still would have to determine the level of pollution and then actually measure its output from steel production in order to enforce such regulation.

How the Government Corrects Positive Externalities

What can the government do when the production of one good spills benefits over to third parties? It has several policy options: financing the production of the good or producing the good itself, subsidies (negative taxes), and regulation.

Government Financing and Production.

If the positive externalities seem extremely large, the government has the option of financing the desired additional production facilities so that the "right" amount of the good will be produced. Consider again vaccinations against communicable diseases. The government frequently finances campaigns to vaccinate the population. It even operates centres where such vaccinations are free.

Subsidies.

A subsidy is a negative tax; it is a payment made either to a business or to a consumer when the business produces, or the consumer buys, a good or a service. In the case of vaccinations against influenza, the government could subsidize everyone who obtains a flu shot by directly reimbursing those vaccinated or by making payments to doctors who provide the shots. If you are attending a university or college, taxpayers are helping to pay the cost of providing your education; you are being subsidized by as much as 80 percent of the total cost. Subsidies reduce the net price to consumers, thereby causing a larger quantity to be demanded.

Regulation.

In some cases involving positive externalities, the government can require by law that a certain action be undertaken by individuals in the society. For example, regulations require that all school-aged children be vaccinated before entering public and private schools. Some people believe that a basic school education itself generates positive externalities. Perhaps as a result of this belief, we have regulations—laws—that require all school-aged children to be enrolled in a public or private school.

Concepts in Brief

- External costs lead to an overallocation of resources to the specific economic activity. Two possible ways of correcting these spillovers are taxation and regulation.
- External benefits result in an underallocation of resources to the specific activity. Three possible government corrections are financing the production of the activity, subsidizing private firms or consumers to engage in the activity, and regulation.

THE OTHER ECONOMIC FUNCTIONS OF GOVERNMENT

Besides compensating for externalities, the government performs many other functions that affect the way in which exchange is carried out in the economy. In contrast, the political functions of government have to do with deciding how income should be redistributed among households, and selecting which goods and services have special merits and should therefore be treated differently. The economic and political functions of government can and do overlap.

Let's look at four more economic functions of government.

Providing a Legal System

The courts and the police may not at first seem like economic functions of government (although judges and police personnel must be paid). Their activities nonetheless have important consequences on economic activities in any country. You and I enter into contracts constantly, whether they be oral or written, expressed, or implied. When we believe that we have been wronged, we seek redress of our grievances within our legal institutions. Moreover, consider the legal system that is necessary for the smooth functioning of our system. Our system has defined quite explicitly the legal status of businesses, the rights of private ownership, and a method for the enforcement of contracts. All relationships among consumers and businesses are governed by the legal rules of the game. We might consider the government in its judicial function, then, as the referee when there are disputes in the economic arena.

▶ **Property rights**

The rights of an owner to use and to exchange property.

Much of our legal system is involved with defining and protecting **property rights**. Property rights are the rights of an owner to use and to exchange that property. One might say that property rights are really the rules of our economic game. When property rights are well defined, owners of property have an incentive to use the property efficiently. Any mistakes in their decision about the use of property have negative consequences that the owners suffer. Furthermore, when property rights are well defined, owners of property have an incentive to maintain that property so that if those owners ever desire to sell it, it will fetch a better price.

Establishing and maintaining a well-functioning legal system is not a costless activity, as you can see in the following example.

INTERNATIONAL POLICY EXAMPLE
Who Should Pay the High Cost of a Legal System?

When a huge multinational gets into a lengthy and expensive "shouting match" with its detractors, the public ends up footing part of the legal bill. McDonald's operates worldwide, with annual sales of about $50 billion. It has property rights in the goodwill associated with its name. When two unemployed British social activists published a pamphlet with such chapter headings as "McDollar, McGreedy, McCancer, McMurder, McRipoff, McTorture, and McGarbage," McDonald's was not pleased. The pamphlet accused the American company of torturing animals, corrupting children, and exploiting the Third World. So McDonald's went to court in London. When the case began, there were 26 preliminary hearings spread over a four-year time period, and when it went to trial, 180 witnesses were called. McDonald's itself will end up spending many millions of dollars, but British taxpayers will foot the entire bill for the use of the court system. According to the Lord Chancellor's Department, British taxpayers will pay at least £2.5 million (well over $5.5 million).

Should taxpayers continue to pay for all of the court system? No, according to policymakers in Britain. They have a plan to make litigants pay the full cost of court services, specifically judges' salaries. Such a system that forces litigants to pay for the full opportunity cost of the legal system has yet to be instituted in Canada or elsewhere.

For critical analysis: What other costs, besides judges' salaries, do citizens implicitly pay for in their legal system?

Promoting Competition

▶ **Anticombines legislation**
Laws that restrict the formation of monopolies and regulate certain anti-competitive business practices.

▶ **Monopoly**
A firm that has great control over the price of a good. In the extreme case, a monopoly is the only seller of a good or service.

Many people believe that the only way to attain economic efficiency is through competition. One of the roles of government is to serve as the protector of a competitive economic system. The federal and provincial governments have passed **anticombines legislation**. Such legislation makes illegal certain (but not all) economic activities that might, in legal terms, restrain trade—that is, prevent free competition among actual and potential rival firms in the marketplace. The avowed aim of anticombines legislation is to reduce the power of **monopolies**—firms that have great control over the price of the goods they sell. A number of laws have been passed that prohibit specific anti-competitive business behaviour. The Competition Bureau, which is part of Industry Canada, attempts to enforce these anticombines laws. Various provincial judicial agencies also expend efforts at maintaining competition.

Providing Public Goods

The goods used in our examples up to this point have been **private goods**. When I eat a cheeseburger, you cannot eat the same one. So you and I are rivals for that cheeseburger, just as much as rivals for the title of world champion are. When I use a CD player, you cannot use the same player. When I use the services of an auto mechanic, that person cannot work at the same time for you. That is the distinguishing feature of private goods—their use is exclusive to the people who purchase or rent them. The **principle of rival consumption** applies to all private goods by definition. Rival consumption is easy to understand. With private goods, either you use them or I use them.

There is an entire class of goods that are not private goods. These are called **public goods**. The principle of rival consumption does not apply to them. That is, they can be consumed jointly by many individuals simultaneously. Military defence, police protection, and the legal system, for example, are public goods. If you partake of them, you do not necessarily take away from anyone else's share of those goods.

Characteristics of Public Goods.

Several distinguishing characteristics of public goods set them apart from all other goods.[1]

1. **Public goods are often indivisible.** You can't buy or sell $5 worth of the army's ability to protect you from foreign invasion. Public goods cannot usually be produced or sold very easily in small units.
2. **Public goods can be used by more and more people at no additional cost.** Once money has been spent on the armed forces, the defence protection you receive does not reduce the amount of protection bestowed on anyone else. The opportunity cost of your receiving military protection once it is in place is zero.
3. **Additional users of public goods do not deprive others of any of the services of the goods.** If you turn on your television set, your neighbours don't get weaker reception because of your action.
4. **It is difficult to design a collection system for a public good on the basis of how much individuals use it.** It is nearly impossible to determine how much any person uses or values defence. No one can be denied the benefits of military protection for failing to pay for that public good. This is often called the **exclusion principle**.

One of the problems of public goods is that the private sector has a difficult, if not impossible, time in providing them. There is little or no incentive for individuals in the private sector to offer public goods because it is so difficult to make a profit in so doing. Consequently, a true public good must necessarily be provided by government.

▶ Private goods

Goods that can be consumed by only one individual at a time. Private goods are subject to the principle of rival consumption.

▶ Principle of rival consumption

The recognition that individuals are rivals in consuming private goods because one person's consumption reduces the amount available for others to consume.

▶ Public goods

Goods to which the principle of rival consumption does not apply; they can be jointly consumed by many individuals simultaneously at no additional cost and with no reduction in quality or quantity.

▶ Exclusion principle

The principle that no one can be excluded from the benefits of a public good, even if that person hasn't paid for it.

---

[1] Sometimes the distinction is made between pure public goods, which have all the characteristics we have described here, and quasi- or near-public goods, which do not. The major feature of near-public goods is that they are jointly consumed, even though nonpaying customers can be, and often are, excluded—for example, movies, football games, and concerts.

INTERNATIONAL EXAMPLE
Are Lighthouses a Public Good?

One of the most common examples of a public good is a lighthouse. Arguably, it satisfies all the criteria listed in points 1 through 4. In one instance, however, a lighthouse was not a public good in that a collection system was devised and enforced on the basis of how much individuals used it. In the thirteenth century, the city of Aigues-Mortes, a port in southern France, erected a tower, called the King's Tower, designed to assert the will and power of Louis IX (Saint Louis). The 32 metre high tower served as a lighthouse for ships. More importantly, it served as a lookout so that ships sailing on the open sea, but in its view, did not escape paying for use of the lighthouse. Those payments were then used for the construction of the city walls.

For critical analysis: Explain how a lighthouse satisfies the characteristics of public goods described in points 1, 2, and 3.

▶**Free-rider problem**
A problem that arises when individuals presume that others will pay for public goods so that, individually, they can escape paying for their portion without causing a reduction in production.

Free Riders. The nature of public goods leads to the **free-rider problem,** a situation in which some individuals take advantage of the fact that others will shoulder the burden of paying for public goods such as defence. Free riders will argue that they receive no value from such government services as defence and therefore really should not pay for it. Suppose that citizens were taxed directly in proportion to how much they tell an interviewer that they value military protection. Some people will probably say that they are unwilling to pay for it because they don't want any—it is of no value to them. Many of us may end up being free riders when we assume that others will pay for the desired public good. We may all want to be free riders if we believe that someone else will provide the commodity in question that we actually value.

The free-rider problem is a definite issue among nations with respect to the international burden of defence and how it should be shared. A country may choose to belong to a multilateral defence organization, such as the North Atlantic Treaty Organization (NATO), but then consistently attempt not to contribute funds to the organization. The nation knows it would be defended by others in NATO if it were attacked, but would rather not pay for such defence. In short, it seeks a "free ride."

Ensuring Economywide Stability

The government attempts to stabilize the economy by smoothing out the ups and downs in overall business activity. Our economy sometimes faces the problems of unemployment and oscillating prices. The government, especially the federal government, has made an attempt to solve these problems by trying to stabilize the economy. The notion that the federal government should undertake actions to stabilize business activity is a relatively new idea in Canada, encouraged by high unemployment rates during the Great Depression of the 1930s and subsequent theories about possible ways by which government could reduce unemployment. In 1945, the government formally assumed responsibility for economic performance. It established three goals for government accountability: full employment, price stability, and economic growth. These goals have provided the justification for many government economic programs during the post–World War II period.

Concepts in Brief

- The economic activities of government include (1) correcting for externalities, (2) providing a judicial system, (3) promoting competition, (4) producing public goods, and (5) ensuring economywide stability.
- Public goods can be consumed jointly. The principle of rival consumption does not apply as it does with private goods.
- Public goods have the following characteristics: (1) They are indivisible; (2) once they are produced, there is no opportunity cost when additional consumers use them; (3) your use of a public good does not deprive others of its simultaneous use; and (4) consumers cannot conveniently be charged on the basis of use.

THE POLITICAL FUNCTIONS OF GOVERNMENT

At least two areas of government are in the realm of political, or normative, functions rather than that of the economic ones discussed in the first part of this chapter. These two areas are (1) the regulation and/or provision of merit and demerit goods, and (2) income redistribution.

Merit and Demerit Goods

▶ **Merit good**

A good that has been deemed socially desirable through the political process. Museums are an example.

Certain goods are considered to have special merit. A **merit good** is defined as any good that the political process has deemed socially desirable. (Note that nothing inherent in any particular good makes it a merit good. It is a matter of who chooses.) Some examples of merit goods in our society are museums, ballets, and concerts. In these areas, the government's role is the provision of merit goods to the people in society who would not otherwise purchase them at market clearing prices or who would not purchase an amount of them judged to be sufficient. This provision may take the form of government production and distribution of merit goods. It can also take the form of reimbursement for payment on merit goods or subsidies to producers or consumers for part of the cost of merit goods. Governments do indeed subsidize such merit goods as concerts, ballets, and museums. In most cases, such merit goods would rarely be so numerous without subsidization.

▶ **Demerit good**

A good that has been deemed socially undesirable through the political process. Cigarettes are an example.

Demerit goods are the opposite of merit goods. They are goods that, through the political process, are deemed socially undesirable. Cigarettes, gambling, and illegal drugs are examples. The government exercises its role in the area of demerit goods by taxing, regulating, or prohibiting their manufacture, sale, and use. Governments justify the relatively high taxes on alcohol and tobacco by declaring them demerit goods. The best-known example of governmental exercise of power in this area is the stance against certain psychoactive drugs. Most psychoactives (except nicotine, caffeine, and alcohol) are either expressly prohibited, as is the case for heroin, cocaine, and opium, or heavily regulated, as in the case of prescription psychoactives.

Income Redistribution

Another relatively recent political function of government has been the explicit redistribution of income. This redistribution uses two systems: the progressive income tax (described later in this chapter) and **transfer payments**. Transfer payments are payments made to individuals for which no services or goods are concurrently rendered in return. The three key money transfer payments in our system are welfare, old age security payments, and employment insurance benefits. Income redistribution also includes a large amount of income **transfers in kind**, as opposed to money transfers. Two income transfers in kind are health care and low-cost public housing.

The government has also engaged in other activities as a form of redistribution of income. For example, the provision of public education is at least in part an attempt to redistribute income by making sure that the very poor have access to education.

▶ **Transfer payments**

Money payments made by governments to individuals for which no services or goods are concurrently rendered in return. Examples are welfare, old age security payments, and Employment Insurance benefits.

▶ **Transfers in kind**

Payments that are in the form of actual goods and services, such as public education, low-cost public housing, and health care, and for which no goods or services are rendered concurrently in return.

EXAMPLE   **Education Transfer Payments**

The federal government has recently increased its transfers in kind to post-secondary students. The 1998 budget contained a number of incentives to encourage more Canadians to continue their education following secondary school. For example, the government is making available 25,000 Canada Study Grants of $3,000 each for needy students with dependants. In addition, the education credit and child care expense deductions for income tax are extended to part-time as well as full-time students.

The federal government is also providing annual Canada Education Savings Grants of 20 percent of the first $2,000 in contributions to your registered education savings plan. You are also now able to make tax-free withdrawals from your RRSP of up to $10,000 per year to a maximum of $20,000 over four years. However, withdrawals must be paid back within 10 years.

Finally, the government has made a number of improvements to the Canada Student Loan program. For example, interest on student loans is now tax deductible. And for students who have problems repaying their student loans, the government provides up to 30 months of interest relief following graduation.

For critical analysis: Why might a tax deduction for post-secondary education expenses be more beneficial to society than an equivalent dollar tax deduction for home mortgage expenses?

Concepts in Brief

- Political, or normative, activities of the government include the provision and regulation of merit and demerit goods and income redistribution.
- Merit and demerit goods do not have any inherent characteristics that qualify them as such; rather, collectively, through the political process, we make judgments about which goods and services are "good" for society and which are "bad."
- Income redistribution can be carried out by a system of progressive taxation, coupled with transfer payments, which can be made in money or in kind, such as health care and public education.

COLLECTIVE DECISION MAKING: THE THEORY OF PUBLIC CHOICE

The public sector has a vast influence on the Canadian economy. Yet the economic model used until now has applied only to the behaviour of the private sector—firms and households. Such a model does not adequately explain the behaviour of the public sector. We shall attempt to do so now.

Governments consist of individuals. No government actually thinks and acts; rather, government actions are the result of decision making by individuals in their roles as elected representatives, appointed officials, and salaried bureaucrats. Therefore, to understand how government works, we must examine the incentives for the people in government as well as those who would like to be in government— avowed candidates or would-be candidates for elected or appointed positions—and special-interest lobbyists attempting to get government to do something. At issue is the analysis of **collective decision making**. Collective decision making involves the actions of voters, politicians, political parties, interest groups, and many other groups and individuals. The analysis of collective decision making is usually called the **theory of public choice**. It has been given this name because it involves hypotheses about how choices are made in the public sector, as opposed to the private sector. The foundation of public-choice theory is the assumption that individuals will act within the political process to maximize their individual (not collective) well-being. In that sense, the theory is similar to our analysis of the market economy, in which we also assume that individuals are motivated by self-interest.

To understand public-choice theory, it is necessary to point out other similarities between the private market sector and the public, or government, sector; then we will look at the differences.

▶ **Collective decision making**
How voters, politicians, and other interested parties act and how these actions influence nonmarket decisions.

▶ **Theory of public choice**
The study of collective decision making.

Similarities in Market and Public-Sector Decision Making

In addition to the similar assumption of self-interest being the motivating force in both sectors, there are other similarities.

Scarcity.   At any given moment, the amount of resources is fixed. This means that for the private and the public sectors combined, there is a scarcity constraint. Everything that is spent by all levels of government, plus everything that is spent by the private sector, must add up to the total income available at any point in time. Hence every government action has an opportunity cost, just as in the market sector.

Competition.   Although we typically think of competition as a private market phenomenon, it is also present in collective action. Given the scarcity constraint government also faces, bureaucrats, appointed officials, and elected representatives will always be in competition for available government funds. Furthermore, the individuals within any government agency or institution will act as individuals do in the private sector: They will try to obtain higher wages, better working conditions, and higher job-level classifications. They will compete and act in their own, not society's, interest.

Similarity of Individuals.   Contrary to popular belief, there are not two types of individuals, those who work in the private sector and those who work in the public sector; rather, individuals working in similar positions can be considered similar. The difference, as we shall see, is that the individuals in government face a different **incentive structure** than those in the private sector. For example, the costs and benefits of being efficient or inefficient differ when one goes from the private to the public sector.

► **Incentive structure**

The system of rewards and punishments individuals face with respect to their own actions.

One approach to predicting government bureaucratic behaviour is to ask what incentives bureaucrats face. Take Canada Post as an example. The bureaucrats running that Crown Corporation are human beings with qualities similar to those possessed by workers in comparable positions at, say, Northern Telecom or Canadian Airlines. Yet the Post Office does not function like either of these companies. The difference can be explained, at least in part, in terms of the incentives provided for managers in the two types of institutions. When the bureaucratic managers and workers at Northern Telecom make incorrect decisions, work slowly, produce shoddy products, and are generally "inefficient," the profitability of the company declines. The owners—millions of shareholders—express their displeasure by selling some of their shares of company stock. The market value, as tracked on the stock exchange, falls. But what about Canada Post? If a manager, a worker, or a bureaucrat in the Post Office gives shoddy service, there is no straightforward mechanism by which the organization's owners—the taxpayers—can express their dissatisfaction. Despite the Post Office's status as a "government corporation," taxpayers as shareholders do not really own shares of stock in the organization that they can sell.

The key, then, to understanding purported inefficiency in the government bureaucracy is not found in an examination of people and personalities but rather in an examination of incentives and institutional arrangements.

Differences Between Market and Collective Decision Making

There are probably more dissimilarities between the market sector and the public sector than there are similarities.

▶ **Government, or political, goods**

Goods (and services) provided by the public sector; they can be either private or public goods.

Government Goods at Zero Price.

The majority of goods that governments produce are furnished to the ultimate consumers without direct money charge. **Government, or political, goods** can be either private goods or public goods. The fact that they are furnished to the ultimate consumer free of charge does not mean that the cost to society of those goods is zero, however; it only means that the price charged is zero. The full opportunity cost to society is the value of the resources used in the production of goods produced and provided by the government.

For example, none of us pays directly for each unit of consumption of most highways nor for police protection. Rather, we pay for all these things indirectly through the taxes that support our governments—federal, provincial, and municipal. This special feature of government can be looked at in a different way. There is no longer a one-to-one relationship between the consumption of a government-provided good and the payment for that good. Consumers who pay taxes collectively pay for every political good, but the individual consumer may not be able to see the relationship between the taxes paid and the consumption of the good. Indeed, most taxpayers will find that their tax bill is the same whether or not they consume, or even like, government-provided goods.

Use of Force.

All governments are able to engage in the legal use of force in their regulation of economic affairs. For example, governments can exercise the use of expropriation, which means that if you refuse to pay your taxes, your bank account and other assets may be seized by Revenue Canada. In fact, you have no choice in the matter of paying taxes to governments. Collectively, we decide the total size of government through the political process, but individually we cannot determine how much service we pay for just for ourselves during any one year.

Try Preview Question 1:

What problems will you encounter if you refuse to pay a portion of your income tax because you oppose spending on military defence?

Voting Versus Spending.

In the private market sector, a dollar voting system is in effect. This dollar voting system is not equivalent to the voting system in the public sector. There are, at minimum, three differences:

▶ **Majority rule**

A collective decision-making system in which group decisions are made on the basis of 50.1 percent of the vote. In other words, whatever more than half of the electorate votes for, the entire electorate has to accept.

1. In a political system, one person gets one vote, whereas in the market system, the dollars one spends count as votes.
2. The political system is run by **majority rule**, whereas the market system is run by **proportional rule**.
3. The spending of dollars can indicate intensity of want, whereas because of the all-or-nothing nature of political voting, a vote cannot.

Ultimately, the main distinction between political votes and dollar votes here is that political outcomes may differ from economic outcomes. Remember that economic efficiency is a situation in which, given the prevailing distribution of income, consumers get the economic goods they want. There is no corresponding situation using political voting. Thus we can never assume that a political voting process will lead to the same decisions that a dollar voting process will lead to in the marketplace.

▶ **Proportional rule**

A decision-making system in which actions are based on the proportion of the "votes" cast and are in proportion to them. In a market system, if 10 percent of the "dollar votes" are cast for blue cars, 10 percent of the output will be blue cars.

Indeed, consider the dilemma every voter faces. Usually a voter is not asked to decide on a single issue (although this happens); rather, a voter is asked to choose among candidates who present a large number of issues and state a position on each of them. Just consider the average Member of Parliament who has to vote on hundreds of different issues during a five-year term. When you vote for that representative, you are voting for a person who must make hundreds of decisions during the next five years.

Try Preview Question 2:

What is the essence of the public-choice model?

The Role of Bureaucrats

Government programs require people to deliver them. This is manifested today in the form of well-established bureaucracies, in which **bureaucrats** (nonelected officials) work. **Bureaucracies** can exert great influence on matters concerning themselves—the amount of funding granted them and the activities in which they engage. In the political marketplace, well-organized bureaucracies can even influence the expression of public demand itself. In many cases, they organize the clientele (interest groups), coach that clientele on what is appropriate, and stick up for the "rights" of the clientele.

Gauging Bureaucratic Performance

It is tempting, but incorrect, to think of bureaucrats as mere "technocrats," executors of orders and channels of information, in this process. They have at least two incentives to make government programs larger and more resistant to attack than we might otherwise expect. First, society has decided that, in general, government should not be run on a profit-making basis. Measures of performance other than bottom-line profits must be devised. In the private market, successful firms typically expand to serve more customers; although this growth is often incidental to the underlying profitability, the two frequently go hand in hand. In parallel, performance in government is often measured by the number of clients served, and rewards are distributed accordingly. As a result, bureaucrats have an incentive to expand the size of their clientele—not because it is more profitable (beneficial) to society but because that is how bureaucrats' rewards are structured.

In general, performance measures that are not based on long-run profitability are less effective at gauging true performance. This makes it potentially easier for the government bureaucrat to appear to perform well, collect rewards for measured performance, and then leave for greener pastures. To avoid this, a much larger proportion of the rewards given bureaucrats are valuable only as long as they continue being bureaucrats—large staffs, expensive offices, generous pensions, and the like. Instead of getting large current salaries (which can be saved for a rainy day), they get rewards that disappear if their jobs disappear. Naturally, this increases the incentives of bureaucrats to make sure that their jobs don't disappear.

The federal government found recently that non-salary rewards were not sufficient to keep its top bureaucrats in the public service. More and more government executives were being lured away to the private sector with its promise of higher salaries. In 1996 alone, at least six deputy ministers and assistant deputy ministers left for private sector jobs. The government responded early in 1998 with salary increases that ranged from 4 to 19 percent, and implemented a bonus plan for performance that would take salaries even higher. The great majority of public servants were not impressed: they have had a single 3 percent raise between 1991 and 1998 and were not expecting great increases in the foreseeable future.

Rational Ignorance

At this point you may well be wondering why this system still goes on. The answer lies in rational ignorance on the part of voters, ignorance that is carefully cultivated by the members of special interest groups.

On most issues, there is little incentive for the individual voter to expend resources to determine how to vote. Moreover, the ordinary course of living provides most of us with enough knowledge to decide whether we should invest in learning more about a given issue. For example, suppose that Canadian voters were asked to decide if the sign marking the entrance to an obscure national park should be enlarged. Most voters would decide that the potential costs and benefits of this decision are negligible: The new sign is unlikely to be the size of Prince Edward Island, and anybody who has even heard of the national park in question probably already has a pretty good idea of its location. Thus most voters would choose to remain rationally ignorant about the exact costs and benefits of enlarging the sign, implying that (1) many will choose not to vote at all and (2) those who do vote will simply flip a coin or cast their ballot based on some other, perhaps ideological, grounds.

Why Be Rationally Ignorant?   For most political decisions, majority rule prevails. Only a coalition of voters representing slightly more than 50 percent of those who vote is needed. Whenever a vote is taken, the result is going to involve costs and benefits. Voters, then, must evaluate their share of the costs and benefits of any budgetary expenditure. Voters, however, are not perfectly informed. That is one of the crucial characteristics of the real world—information is a resource that is costly to obtain. Rational voters will, in fact, decide to remain at some level of ignorance about government programs because the benefits from obtaining more information may not be worth the cost, given each individual voter's extremely limited impact on the outcome of an election. For the same reason, voters will fail to inform themselves about taxes or other revenue sources to pay for proposed expenditures because they know that for any specific expenditure program, the cost to them individually will be small. At this point it might be useful to contrast this situation with what exists in the nonpolitical private market sector of the economy. In the private market sector, the individual chooses a mix of purchases and bears fully the direct and indirect consequences of this selection (ignoring for the moment the problem of externalities).

PAYING FOR THE PUBLIC SECTOR

Jean-Baptiste Colbert, the seventeenth-century French finance minister, said the art of taxation was in "plucking the goose so as to obtain the largest amount of feathers with the least possible amount of hissing." In Canada, governments have designed a variety of methods of plucking the private-sector goose. To analyse any tax system, we must first understand the distinction between marginal tax rates and average tax rates.

Marginal and Average Tax Rates

If somebody says, "I pay 28 percent in taxes," you cannot really tell what that person means unless you know whether the individual is referring to average taxes paid or

► **Marginal tax rate**

The change in the tax payment divided by the change in income, or the percentage of additional dollars that must be paid in taxes. The marginal tax rate is applied to the highest tax bracket of taxable income reached.

► **Tax bracket**

A specified interval of income to which a specific and unique marginal tax rate is applied.

► **Average tax rate**

The total tax payment divided by total income. It is the proportion of total income paid in taxes.

► **Proportional taxation**

A tax system in which regardless of an individual's income, the tax bill comprises exactly the same proportion. Also called a flat-rate tax.

► **Progressive taxation**

A tax system in which as income increases, a higher percentage of the additional income is taxed. The marginal tax rate exceeds the average tax rate as income rises.

the tax rate on the last dollars earned. The latter concept has to do with the **marginal tax rate**.[2]

The marginal tax rate is expressed as follows:

$$\text{Marginal tax rate} = \frac{\text{change in taxes due}}{\text{change in taxable income}}$$

It is important to understand that the marginal tax rate applies only to the income in the highest **tax bracket** reached, where a tax bracket is defined as a specified level of taxable income to which a specific and unique marginal tax rate is applied.

The **average tax rate** is not the same thing as the marginal tax rate, which is defined as follows:

$$\text{Average tax rate} = \frac{\text{total taxes due}}{\text{total taxable income}}$$

Taxation Systems

No matter how governments raise revenues—from income taxes, sales taxes, or other taxes—all of those taxes can fit into one of three types of taxation systems—proportional, progressive, and regressive, expressing a relationship between the percentage tax, or tax rate, paid and income. To determine whether a tax system is proportional, progressive, or regressive, we simply ask the question, What is the relationship between the average tax rate and the marginal tax rate?

Proportional Taxation.   **Proportional taxation** means that regardless of an individual's income, the taxes comprise exactly the same proportion. In terms of marginal versus average tax rates, in a proportional taxation system, the marginal tax rate is always equal to the average tax rate. If every dollar is taxed at 20 percent, then the average tax rate is 20 percent, as is the marginal tax rate.

A proportional tax system is also called a flat-rate tax. Taxpayers at all income levels end up paying the same percentage of their income in taxes. If the proportional tax rate were 20 percent, an individual with an income of $10,000 would pay $2,000 in taxes, while an individual making $100,000 would pay $20,000, the identical 20 percent rate being levied on both.

Progressive Taxation.   Under **progressive taxation**, as a person's taxable income increases, the percentage of income paid in taxes also increases. In terms of marginal versus average tax rates, in a progressive system, the marginal tax rate is above the average tax rate. If you are taxed 5 percent on the first $10,000 you make, 10 percent on the next $10,000 you make, and 30 percent on the last $10,000 you make, you face a progressive income tax system. Your marginal tax rate is always above your average tax rate.

---

[2] The word *marginal* means "incremental" (or "decremental") here.

INTERNATIONAL EXAMPLE
Marginal Tax Rates Around the World

Table 5.1
Marginal Tax Rates in the Industrialized World, 1994

	Combined Marginal Tax Rate (%) for an Average Production Worker	Marginal Tax Rate (%) for Highest Income Bracket
Australia	35.4	48.4
Canada	49.3	48.1
France	55.3	59.2
Germany	53.4	53.0
Italy	37.0	51.0
Japan	40.8	61.0
New Zealand	33.0	33.0
United Kingdom	35.0	40.0
United States	27.1	44.1

Source: Canadian Tax Foundation

Canadians frequently complain that we pay too much income tax, especially when compared to the United States. While we do pay almost twice what Americans pay in personal income tax, we are not the most highly taxed people in the world.

The Organisation for Economic Co-operation and Development surveyed tax rates in the industrialized world. Table 5.1 shows marginal tax rates for an average production worker, and for workers in the highest income bracket. For a Canadian production worker making about $32,000 per year, the combined marginal tax rate—income taxes plus contributions to the Canada Pension Plan plus Employment Insurance premiums—is about 49.3 percent. Only France and Germany have higher combined rates. Yet, the simple marginal income tax rate for the highest income bracket is 48.1 percent, one of the lowest.

Canada's personal income tax structure is also less progressive than many other countries'. Workers earning only 1.6 times the average production worker's salary fall into the highest income bracket, while in the United States and Japan a worker does not pay the top marginal rate until income is 9.6 times the average production worker's pay.

For critical analysis: Would you expect to see a relationship between the social services provided in a country and the combined marginal tax rate or the simple marginal tax rate? Why?

▶ **Regressive taxation**

A tax system in which as more dollars are earned, the percentage of tax paid on them falls. The marginal tax rate is less than the average tax rate as income rises.

Try Preview Question 3:

In what ways do regressive, proportional, and progressive tax structures differ?

Regressive Taxation. With **regressive taxation**, a smaller percentage of taxable income is taken in taxes as taxable income increases. The marginal rate is below the average rate. As income increases, the marginal tax rate falls, and so does the average tax rate. The Goods and Services Tax (GST) is regressive. Someone earning $10,000 per year pays the same 7 percent sales tax on a tube of toothpaste as someone earning $100,000 per year. But the tube of toothpaste takes up a much larger proportion of the low income earner's budget, so the marginal tax rate for that person is higher. The federal government tries to address this inequity by giving GST rebates to low income earners who apply for them in their income tax returns each year.

Concepts in Brief

- Marginal tax rates are applied to marginal tax brackets, defined as spreads of income over which the tax rate is constant.
- Tax systems can be proportional, progressive, or regressive, depending on whether the marginal tax rate is the same as, greater than, or less than the average tax rate as income rises.

THE MOST IMPORTANT FEDERAL TAXES

The federal government imposes income taxes on both individuals and corporations, and collects sales taxes as well as a variety of other taxes.

The Federal Personal Income Tax

Table 5.2
Federal Marginal Income Tax Rates

These rates became effective in 1992. Taxpayers also pay a surcharge of 3 percent on taxes payable to $12,500 and an additional 5 percent on taxes payable above $12,500.

Marginal Tax Bracket	Marginal Tax Rate
$0–$29,590	17%
$29,590–$59,180	26%
$59,180 and up	29%

Source: Revenue Canada

The most important tax in the Canadian economy is the federal personal income tax, which accounts for about 50 percent of all federal revenues. All Canadian citizens, resident aliens, and most others who earn income in Canada are required to pay federal income tax on all taxable income. The tax rates that are paid depend on the amount of taxable income earned, as can be seen in Table 5.2. Marginal income tax rates at the federal level have varied from as low as 4 percent after the passage of the Income Tax Act in 1917, to as high as 98 percent during World War II. In 1992, the government reduced the top marginal tax rate and cut the number of income tax brackets to three, but broadened the definition of taxable income. The effect of these changes was to make Canada's tax system less progressive.

Advocates of a more progressive income tax system in Canada argue that such a system redistributes income from the rich to the poor, taxes people according to their ability to pay, and taxes people according to the benefits they receive from government. Although there is much controversy over the "redistributional" nature of our progressive tax system, there is no strong evidence that in fact the tax system has ever done much income redistribution in this country. Currently, about 80 percent of all Canadians, rich or poor, pay roughly the same proportion of their income in federal income tax.

The Treatment of Capital Gains

▶ **Capital gain**
The positive difference between the purchase price and the sale price of an asset. If a share of stock is bought for $5 and then sold for $15, the capital gain is $10.

The difference between the buying and selling price of an asset, such as a share of stock or a plot of land, is called a **capital gain** if it is a profit, and a **capital loss** if it is not. Capital gains are taxed at ordinary income marginal tax rates. The taxable part of a capital gain is 75 percent of the net amount of your capital gains minus your capital losses for the year.

Capital gains are not always real. If in one year you pay $100,000 for a house you plan to rent and sell it for 50 percent more 10 years later, your nominal capital gain is $50,000. But what if, during those 10 years, there had been inflation such that average prices had also gone up by 50 percent? Your real capital gain would be zero. But you still have to pay taxes on that $50,000. To counter this problem, many economists have argued that capital gains should be indexed to the rate of inflation.

▶ **Capital loss**
The negative difference between the purchase price and the sale price of an asset.

The Corporate Income Tax

Corporate income taxes account for about 12 percent of all federal taxes collected, and 3.5 percent of all provincial taxes collected. Corporations are generally taxed at a flat rate of 28 percent on the difference between their total revenues (or receipts) and their expenses.

Double Taxation.   Because individual shareholders must pay taxes on the dividends they receive, paid out of after-tax profits by the corporation, corporate profits are taxed twice. If you receive $1,000 in dividends, you have to declare it as income, and you must pay taxes at your marginal tax rate. Before the corporation was able to pay you those dividends, it had to pay taxes on all its profits, including any that it put back into the company or did not distribute in the form of dividends. Eventually the new investment made possible by those **retained earnings**—profits not given out to shareholders—along with borrowed funds will be reflected in the increased value of the stock in that company. When you sell your shares in that company, you will have to pay taxes on the difference between what you paid for them and what you sold them for. In both cases, dividends and retained earnings (corporate profits) are taxed twice.

▶ **Retained earnings**
Earnings that a corporation saves, or retains, for investment in other productive activities; earnings that are not distributed to stockholders.

Who Really Pays the Corporate Income Tax?   Corporations can exist only as long as consumers buy their products, employees make their goods, shareholders (owners) buy their shares, and bondholders buy their bonds. Corporations *per se* do not do anything. We must ask, then, who really pays the tax on corporate income. This is a question of **tax incidence**. (The question of tax incidence applies to all taxes, includ-

▶ **Tax incidence**
The distribution of tax burdens among various groups in society.

ing sales and payroll taxes.) There remains considerable debate about the incidence of corporate taxation. Some economists say that corporations pass their tax burdens on to consumers by charging higher prices. Other economists believe that it is the shareholders who bear most of the tax. Still others believe that employees pay at least part of the tax by receiving lower wages than they would otherwise. Because the debate is not yet settled, we will not hazard a guess here as to what the correct conclusion should be. Suffice to say that you should be cautious when you advocate increasing corporation income taxes. You may be the one who ends up paying the increase, at least in part, if you own shares in a corporation, buy its products, or work for it.

Try Preview Question 4:
Who pays the corporate income tax?

Concepts in Brief

- Because corporations must first pay an income tax on most earnings, the personal income tax shareholders pay on dividends received (or realized capital gains) constitutes double taxation.
- The corporate income tax is paid by one or more of the following groups: shareholder-owners, consumers of corporate-produced products, and employees in corporations.

Unemployment and Pension Taxes

An increasing percentage of federal revenues is accounted for each year by taxes (other than income taxes) levied on payroll. These payroll taxes are for Canada Pension Plan (CPP) benefits and Employment Insurance (EI).

Employment Insurance is a compulsory federal program which provides income assistance in the event of unemployment. EI premiums are paid by employees, and matched by employers. (The employer's contribution is really paid, at least in part, in the form of a reduced wage paid to employees.) Self-employed people must pay both shares. The maximum personal contribution to EI in 1997 was $1,131. EI premiums become part of the government's general revenues; as of 1997, there was a large surplus in the EI account which helped the government balance the budget for the 1998-99 fiscal year.

Thinking Critically About the Media   Employment Insurance

Countless articles have been written about the problem with the Employment Insurance (EI) system in Canada. They all make reference to the employer and employee "contributions" to the EI fund. One gets the impression that EI premiums paid by employees go into a special government account and that employees do not pay for their employers' "contribution" to this account. Both concepts are not merely flawed but grossly misleading. EI premiums are mixed in with the rest of government taxes collected and spent every year. The "contributions" are not contributions at all; they are merely taxes paid to the federal government. The so-called employer contribution, which matches the employee payments, is not in fact paid for by employers but rather by employees because of the lower wages that they are paid. Anybody who quits a job and becomes self-employed finds this out when the time comes to pay one's self-employment taxes (Employment Insurance "contributions"), which effectively double the payments previously being made as an employee.

In 1997, the CPP premium payable on eligible earnings to $32,300 was 3 percent, with employers contributing an equal share on behalf of the employee. CPP premiums do not form part of the government's general revenue, but are managed separately from the government budget. The CPP is a system in which current workers subsidize already retired workers. With the coming retirement of the post-war "baby boomers," the number of retired people will grow much more rapidly than the number of current workers. In anticipation of increased outlays in pension plan benefits, the combined (employer-employee) premium will rise to 9.9 percent of eligible earnings by the year 2003.

The GST

The Goods and Services Tax (GST) is a sales tax which makes up about 14 percent of federal government revenues. Consumers pay a 7 percent tax on virtually all goods and services they purchase in addition to any applicable provincial sales taxes. The GST is a regressive tax since it taxes consumption at the same rate for both the rich and the poor. The federal government tries to mitigate this, however, by giving a rebate of up to $76 four times a year to low income earners. While consumers must pay GST on imports, Canadian exports are exempt. Visitors to Canada may apply for a rebate of the GST they paid on their Canadian purchases when they leave the country.

Some economists argue that in spite of the regressive nature of sales taxes, a tax like the GST is preferable to an income tax. Income taxes tax all income, whether it is spent or saved. Therefore, they argue, saving is discouraged. However, a sales tax taxes only income that is consumed, and so saving is encouraged. The Issues and Applications section at the end of this chapter revisits the pros and cons of this topic.

SPENDING, GOVERNMENT SIZE, AND TAX RECEIPTS

The size of the public sector can be measured in many different ways. One way is to count the number of public employees. Another is to look at total government outlays. Government outlays include all of its expenditures on employees, rent, electricity, and the like. In addition, total government outlays include transfer payments, such as welfare, Employment Insurance benefits, and old age security payments. In Figure 5.2, you see that government outlays prior to World War I did not exceed 8 percent of annual national income. There was a spike during World War I, a significant increase during the Great Depression, and then a huge spike during World War II. Contrary to previous postwar periods, government outlays as a percentage of total national income did not gradually fall, but rather rose fairly regularly until the mid-1970s. Since then, government expenditures have been around 22.5 percent of gross domestic product.

Figure 5.2
Total Government Outlays over Time
Here you see that total government outlays remained small until the 1930s, except during World War I. Since World War II, government outlays have not fallen back to their historical average.

Sources: Statistics Canada, *Canadian Economic Observer,* and M.C. Urquhart and K.A.H. Buckley, *Historical Statistics of Canada.*

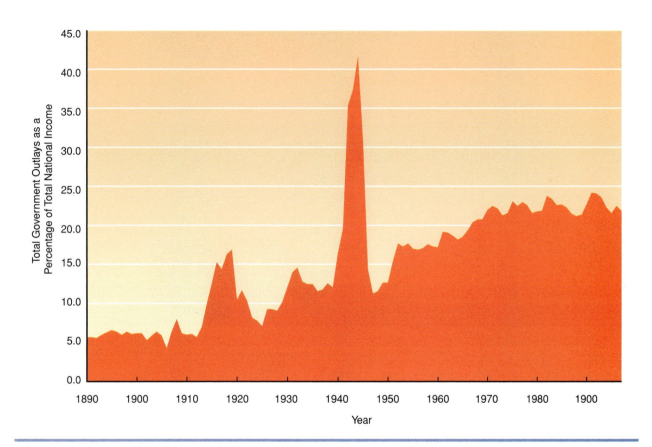

Government Receipts

The main revenue raiser for all levels of government is taxes. We show in the two pie diagrams in Figure 5.3 the percentage of receipts from various taxes obtained by the federal government and by provincial and municipal governments.

The Federal Government.   The largest source of receipts for the federal government is the individual income tax. During the 1997-98 fiscal year, it accounted for 50.3 percent of all federal revenues. After that come Employment Insurance premiums which account for 14.6 percent of total revenues. Next come the GST revenues, corporate income taxes, and a number of other items, such as taxes on imported goods and excise taxes on such things as gasoline and alcoholic beverages.

Provincial and Municipal Governments.   As can be seen in Figure 5.3, there is quite a bit of difference between the origin of receipts for provincial and munici-

Figure 5.3

Sources of Government Tax Receipts

About 65 percent of federal revenues come from income and Employment Insurance taxes, whereas provincial and municipal government revenues are spread more evenly across sources, with less emphasis on taxes based on individual income.

Source: Statistics Canada.

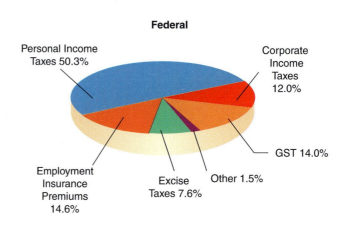

Federal

Personal Income Taxes 50.3%

Corporate Income Taxes 12.0%

GST 14.0%

Employment Insurance Premiums 14.6%

Excise Taxes 7.6%

Other 1.5%

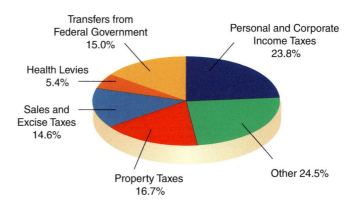

Provincial and Municipal

Transfers from Federal Government 15.0%

Personal and Corporate Income Taxes 23.8%

Health Levies 5.4%

Sales and Excise Taxes 14.6%

Other 24.5%

Property Taxes 16.7%

pal governments and for the federal government. Personal and corporate income taxes account for only 23.8 percent of total provincial and municipal revenues. The next largest source of receipts is from property taxes (used by municipal governments), sales taxes (used mainly by provincial governments), and transfers from the federal government.

Comparing Federal with Provincial and Municipal Spending. A typical federal government budget is given in Figure 5.4. The largest three categories are interest on the debt, elderly benefits, and transfers to the provinces, which together constitute over 60 percent of the total federal budget.

The makeup of provincial and municipal expenditures is quite different. Education and health are the biggest categories, accounting for almost 45 percent of all expenditures.

Figure 5.4

Federal Government Spending Compared to Provincial and Municipal Spending

The federal government's spending habits are quite different from those of the provinces and municipalities. The categories of most importance in the federal budget are interest on the debt, elderly benefits, and transfers to the provinces, which make up over 60 percent. The two most important categories at the provincial and municipal levels are education and health care, which make up almost 45 percent.

Source: Statistics Canada.

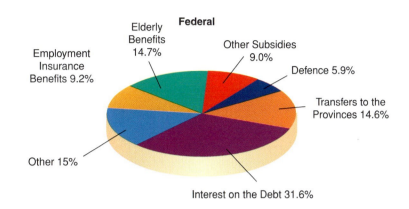

Federal

Elderly Benefits 14.7%
Employment Insurance Benefits 9.2%
Other Subsidies 9.0%
Defence 5.9%
Transfers to the Provinces 14.6%
Other 15%
Interest on the Debt 31.6%

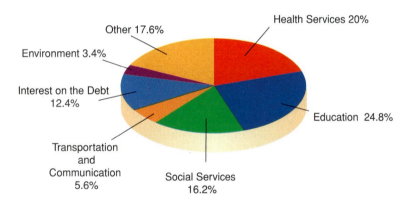

Provincial and Municipal

Health Services 20%
Other 17.6%
Environment 3.4%
Interest on the Debt 12.4%
Education 24.8%
Transportation and Communication 5.6%
Social Services 16.2%

Concepts in Brief

- Total government outlays including transfers have continued to grow since World War II and now account for about 45 percent of yearly total national output.
- Government spending at the federal level is different from that at the provincial and municipal levels. At the federal level, interest on the debt, elderly benefits, and transfers to the provinces account for over 60 percent of the federal budget. At the provincial and municipal levels, education and health comprise almost 45 percent of all expenditures.

Issues and Applications

Should We Switch to a Flat Tax?

Concepts Applied: Average versus marginal tax rates, opportunity cost, progressive income tax system

Each year, Canadian taxpayers spend numerous hours preparing their taxes or hire accountants to do so for them. Switching to a national sales tax, one alternative to our current system, would lead to the downsizing of Revenue Canada and all of the expenses associated with that organization.

Since the enactment of the federal income tax, Canadians have faced a progressive system. The top marginal tax rate soared to 98 percent in 1943, dropped to 80 percent in 1948, dropped again to 60 percent in 1968, and settled at 47 percent starting in 1971. The government reduced the top marginal tax rate to 34 percent in 1983; today it stands at 29 percent. The idea behind a progressive tax system is that the "rich" should pay more. In actuality, what happens is quite a different story. In Figure 5.5 you see that regardless of what the top tax rate is, the federal government obtains around 48 percent of its annual income as tax revenues.

Why? Because people respond to incentives. At high marginal tax rates, the following occurs: (1) rich people hire more tax lawyers and accountants to help them figure out loopholes in the tax system to avoid high marginal tax rates; (2) some people change their investments to take advantage of loopholes that allow them to pay lower marginal tax rates; (3) some people drop out of the labour force, particularly secondary income earners, such as lower-paid working women; and (4) more people engage in off-the-books "underground" activities for cash on which no income taxes are paid.

An Alternative: The Flat Tax

For decades, many economists have argued in favour of scrapping our progressive income tax system and replacing it with a so-called flat tax. The idea behind a flat tax is simple. To calculate what you owe, simply subtract the appropriate exemption from your income and multiply the rest by the flat tax rate, say, 20 percent. For example, a family of four might be able to earn as much as $25,000 or $35,000 a year before it paid any income tax. The major benefits of such a system, according to its advocates, would be the following: (1) fewer resources devoted to figuring out one's taxes; (2) fewer tax lawyers and accountants, who could then be engaged in more productive activities; (3) higher saving and investment; and (4) more economic growth. Opponents of a flat tax argue that (1) federal revenues will fall and a federal budget deficit will occur; and (2) the rich will pay few taxes.

Another Alternative: A National Sales Tax

Alternatively, we could apply some form of a value added tax (VAT) in place of the current income tax. VATs are common throughout Europe. A value-added tax is assessed on the value added by a firm at each stage of production. It is a tax on the value of products that firms sell minus the value of the materials that it bought and used to produce the products. Such a tax is collected by all businesses and remitted directly to the federal government. One of the major benefits of a VAT is that it would significantly downsize Revenue Canada and the expenses associated with that government department. A VAT of, say, 15 to 20 percent in lieu of a federal income tax would be quite similar to a consumption tax.

A Consumption Tax

With a consumption tax, taxpayers pay taxes only on what they consume (spend) out of income, not what they earn. One way to determine such consumption in any year is simply to subtract what is

Figure 5.5
Changing Maximum Marginal Income Tax Rates and Revenues Collected

At the top of the diagram, you can see listed the top marginal tax rates from 1960 to 1995. On the side is the percentage of total annual income collected by the federal government from the income tax system. No matter how high the marginal income tax rate has been, the government has collected about the same percentage of national income in taxes.

Source: W. Irwin Gillespie, *Tax, Borrow & Spend: Financing Federal Spending in Canada 1867-1990.*

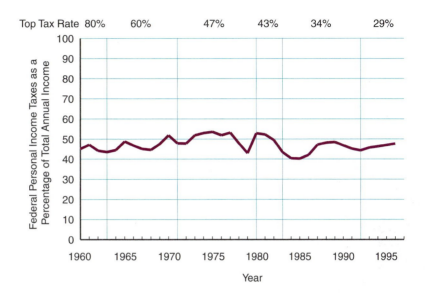

saved from what is earned. The difference is consumption, and that is the base to which a consumption tax would apply. (A consumption tax is actually equivalent to the GST on all goods and services purchased.) In essence, a consumption tax provides an unlimited deduction for saving. As such, it encourages more saving. As you learned in Chapter 2, the less people choose to consume today, the faster the production possibilities curve will shift outward to the right, leading to more economic growth.

What About Fairness?

Every time a new tax system is discussed, the issue of fairness arises. Is it fair, as with a flat federal income tax, that everybody pay the same marginal tax rate, no matter how much each individual earns? Stephen Entin of the Institute for Research on the Economics of Taxation thinks it is: "It is hard to find a definition of 'fairness' more compelling than the idea that every citizen is treated equally." What about a consumption tax, which might be regressive because the poor spend a larger portion of their income than the rich? Is

that a "fair" system? For most economists, these are difficult questions, because they are in the realm of the normative, the value-laden. We can point out that an examination of the evidence shows what reality is. Simply stated, when marginal income tax rates are high, the rich do not, in fact, pay a higher average tax rate than when marginal tax rates are lower. It behooves the rich to find methods to reduce tax liabilities and to expend resources to influence politicians to insert an increasing number of loopholes in the *Tax Act* in order to reduce effective marginal tax rates on those who earn a lot.

For Critical Analysis

1. Do you think employees at Revenue Canada would be for or against the flat-tax system? Explain your choice.

2. Why is a flat-tax system more efficient than a progressive income tax system?

CHAPTER SUMMARY

1. Government can correct external costs through taxation, legislation, and prohibition. It can correct external benefits through financing or production of a good or service, subsidies, and regulation.

2. Government provides a legal system in which the rights of private ownership, the enforcement of contracts, and the legal status of businesses are provided. In other words, government sets the legal rules of the game and enforces them.

3. Public goods, once produced, can be consumed jointly by additional individuals at zero opportunity cost. If users of public goods know that they will be taxed on the basis of their expressed valuation of those public goods, their expressed valuation will be low. They expect to get a free ride.

4. Merit goods (chosen as such, collectively, through the political process) may not be purchased at all or not in sufficient quantities at market clearing prices. Therefore, government subsidizes or provides such merit goods at a subsidized or zero price to specified classes of consumers.

5. When it is collectively decided that something is a demerit good, government taxes, regulates, or prohibits the manufacture, sale, and use of that good.

6. The market sector and the public sector both face scarcity, feature competition, and contain similar individuals. They differ in that many government, or political, goods are provided at zero price, collective action may involve the use of force, and political voting can lead to different results than dollar voting.

7. Bureaucrats often exert great influence on the course of policy because they are in charge of the day-to-day operation of current policy and provide much of the information needed to formulate future policy. Bureaucracies often organize their clientele, coach clients on what is appropriate, and stick up for their rights.

8. Marginal tax rates are those paid on the last dollar of income, whereas average taxes rates are determined by the proportion of income paid in income taxes.

9. With a proportional income tax system, marginal rates are constant. With a regressive system, they go down as income rises, and with a progressive system, they go up as income rises.

10. Government spending at the federal level is different from that at the provincial and municipal levels. Interest on the debt, elderly benefits, and transfers to the provinces account for over 60 percent of the federal budget.

DISCUSSION OF PREVIEW QUESTIONS

1. **What problems will you encounter if you refuse to pay a portion of your income tax because you oppose spending on military defence?**

   You must share in military defence collectively with the rest of the country. Unlike private goods, defence is a public good and must be consumed collectively. You receive benefits from defence whether you choose to or not; the exclusion principle does not work for public goods, such as military defence. The government could make the exclusion principle work better by deporting you to foreign shores if you don't wish to pay for defence. This is typically not done. If you were allowed to forgo taxes allocated to the armed forces, Revenue Canada would be swamped with similar requests. Everyone would have an incentive to claim no benefits from defence (whether true or not) because it must be consumed collectively. So, if you refuse, you may go to jail.

2. What is the essence of the public-choice model?

The essence of the public-choice model is that politicians, bureaucrats, and voters will act so as to maximize their own self-interest (or economic well-being) rather than the community's. In other words, because such people are human, they are subject to the same motivations and drives as the rest of us. They will usually make decisions in terms of what benefits them, not society as a whole. Such an assumption permits economists to apply economic maximization principles to voters, candidates, elected officials, and policymakers.

3. In what ways do regressive, proportional, and progressive tax structures differ?

Under a regressive tax structure, the average tax rate (the percentage of income paid in taxes) falls as income rises. The marginal tax rate is below the average tax rate. Proportional tax structures are those in which the average tax rate remains constant as income rises; the marginal tax rate equals the average tax rate. Under a progressive tax structure, the average tax rate rises as income rises; the marginal tax rate is above the average tax rate. Our federal personal income tax system is an example of a progressive system.

4. Who pays the corporate income tax?

Ultimately, only people can be taxed. As a consequence, corporate taxes are paid by people: corporate owners (in the form of reduced dividends and less stock appreciation for shareholders), consumers of corporate products (in the form of higher prices for goods), and/or employees working for corporations (in the form of lower wages).

PROBLEMS

(Answers to the odd-numbered problems appear at the back of the book.)

5-1. Consider the following system of taxation, which has been labelled *degressive*. The first $5,000 of income is not taxed. After that, all income is assessed at 20 percent (a proportional system). What is the marginal tax rate on $3,000 of taxable income? $10,000? $100,000? What is the average tax rate on $3,000? $10,000? $100,000? What is the maximum average tax rate?

5-2. You are offered two possible bonds to buy as part of your investing program. One is a corporate bond yielding 9 percent. The other is a tax-exempt municipal bond yielding only 6 percent. Assuming that you are certain you will be paid your interest and principal on these two bonds, what marginal tax bracket must you be in to decide in favour of the tax-exempt bond?

5-3. Consider the following tax structure:

Income Bracket	Marginal Tax Rate
$0–$1,500	0%
$1,501–$2,000	14%
$2,001–$3,000	20%

Mr. Smith has an income of $2,500 per annum. Calculate his tax bill for the year. What is his average tax rate? His highest marginal tax rate?

5-4. In 1997, Canada Pension Plan premiums on wages were 3 percent of wages up to $32,300. No further CPP premiums are paid on earnings above this figure. Calculate the average CPP tax rate for annual wages of (a) $4,000, (b) $51,300, (c) $56,000, (d) $100,000. Is the CPP system a progressive, proportional, or regressive tax structure?

5-5. What is meant by the expression "market failure"?

5-6. TV signals have characteristics of public goods, yet TV stations and commercial networks are private businesses. Analyse this situation.

5-7. Assume that you live in a relatively small suburban neighbourhood called Parkwood. The Parkwood Homeowners' Association collects money from homeowners to pay for upkeep of the surrounding stone wall, lighting at the entrances to Parkwood, and mowing the lawn around the perimeter of the area. Each year you are asked to donate $50. No one forces you to do it. There are 100 homeowners in Parkwood.

    a. What percentage of the total yearly revenue of the homeowners' association will you account for?

    b. At what level of participation will the absence of your $50 contribution make a difference?

    c. If you do not contribute your $50, are you really receiving a totally free ride?

5-8. Assume that the only textile firm that exists has created a negative externality by polluting a nearby stream with the wastes associated with production. Assume further that the government can measure the external costs to the community with accuracy and charges the firm for its pollution, based on the social cost of pollution per unit of textile output. Show how such a charge will lead to a higher selling price for textiles and a reduction in the equilibrium quantity of textiles.

5-9. The existence of information and transactions costs has many implications in economics. What are some of these implications in the context of issues discussed in this chapter?

5-10. A favourite political campaign theme in recent years has been to reduce the size, complexity, and bureaucratic nature of the federal government. Nonetheless, the size of the federal government, however measured, continues to increase. Use the theory of public choice to explain why.

5-11. Figures 5.3 and 5.4 give revenues and expenditures for provincial and municipal governments combined. Visit Statistics Canada's Provincial and Territorial General Government Revenue and Expenditure Site at http://www.statcan.ca/english/Pgdb/State/Government/govt08a.htm and locate your province. Calculate what proportion of total revenues and expenditures each category forms. Compare your percentages to Figures 5.3 and 5.4.

    a. Does your government receive relatively more or less of its revenues from any particular source? What characteristics of your provincial economy would account for this?

    b. Does your government spend relatively more or less of its budget in any particular area? What characteristics of your provincial economy would account for this?

File Edit View Go Favorites Help

← Back   → Forward   Stop   Refresh   Home   Search   Favorites   History   Channels   Fullscreen   Mail   Print   Edit

INTERACTING WITH THE INTERNET

For both detailed and summary information on the 1998 Canadian federal budget, see

    http://www.fin.gc.ca/toce/1998/buddoclist98-e.html

    (Future budgets should have a similar name.) At

    http://www.hrdc-drhc.gc.ca/common/income.shtml

you can find material on Old Age Security, the Canada Pension Plan, and Employment Insurance; it is oriented toward both recipients and people interested in how the system works.

    A federal Web site on employment initiatives and employment opportunities for post-secondary students is

    http://canada.gc.ca/programs/pgrind_e.html#opportunities

Economies in Transition

If you visit one of the many thousands of hilly fields in Peru, you will likely meet a peasant family. That family probably has been tilling the soil in the same spot for decades. Most of these families eke out a meagre existence. Very few of them could sell the land they have been cultivating for so many years and pursue an alternative line of work even if they wanted to. To understand why in Peru this is so requires a grasp of the changes that are occurring in the world's economies in transition.

Preview Questions

1. Why does the scarcity problem force all societies to answer the questions *what, how,* and *for whom?*

2. What are the "three *P*s" of pure capitalism?

3. Why do we say that *all* economies are mixed economies?

4. How can economies be classified?

Did You Know That... there used to be a country called the Soviet Union, whose chief of state in 1950 took off his shoe at the United Nations and pounded it on the desk while shouting, "We will bury you"? That person was Nikita Khrushchev; he died in 1971. It took quite a few more years for his country to die, but die it did. The Soviet Union is no more. The 74-year experiment in trying to run an economy without using the price, or market, system will go down in history as one of the greatest social and economic failures of all time. But just because the Soviet Union dissolved itself at the end of 1991 does not mean that the entire world economy automatically became like that of Canada. In particular, the 15 republics of the former Soviet Union, the Soviet "satellite" countries of Eastern Europe, and other nations, including China, are what we call *economies in transition.*

At any point in time, every nation has its own **economic system,** which can be defined as the institutional means through which resources are used to satisfy human wants. No matter what institutional means—marketplace or government—a nation chooses to use, three basic economic questions must always be answered.

▶ **Economic system**
The institutional means through which resources are used to satisfy human wants.

THE THREE BASIC ECONOMIC QUESTIONS

In every country, no matter what the form of government or type of economic system, who is running the government, or how poor or rich the country is, three basic economic questions must be answered. They concern the problem of **resource allocation,** which is simply how resources are to be allocated. As such, resource allocation answers the three basic economic questions of *what, how,* and *for whom* goods and services will be produced.

▶ **Resource allocation**
The assignment of resources to specific uses by determining what will be produced, how it will be produced, and for whom it will be produced.

1. *What and how much will be produced?* Literally billions of different things could be produced with society's scarce resources. Some mechanism must exist that causes some things to be produced and others to remain as either inventors' pipe dreams or individuals' unfulfilled desires.

2. *How will it be produced?* There are many ways to produce a desired item. It is possible to use more labour and less capital or vice versa. It is possible to use more unskilled labour and fewer units of skilled labour. Somehow, in some way, a decision must be made as to the particular mix of inputs, the way they should be organized, and how they are brought together at a particular place.

3. *For whom will it be produced?* Once a commodity is produced, who should get it? In a market economy, individuals and businesses purchase commodities with money income. The question then is what mechanism there is to distribute income, which then determines how commodities are distributed throughout the economy.

Try Preview Question 1:
Why does the scarcity problem force all societies to answer the questions *what, how,* and *for whom?*

THE PRICE SYSTEM AND HOW IT ANSWERS THE THREE ECONOMIC QUESTIONS

As explained in Chapter 4, a price (or market) system is an economic system in which (relative) prices are constantly changing to reflect changes in supply and demand for different commodities. In addition, the prices of those commodities are the signals to everyone within the system as to what is relatively scarce and what is relatively abundant. Indeed, it is the *signalling* aspect of the price system that provides the information to buyers and sellers about what should be bought and what should be produced. The price system, which is characteristic of a market economy, is only one possible way to organize society.

What and How Much Will Be Produced?

In a price system, the interaction of demand and supply for each good determines what and how much to produce. Note, however, that if the highest price that consumers are willing to pay is less than the lowest cost at which a good can be produced, output will be zero. That doesn't mean that the price system has failed. Today consumers do not purchase their own private space shuttles. The demand is not high enough in relation to the supply to create a market. But it may be someday.

How Will It Be Produced?

The question of how output will be produced in a price system relates to the efficient use of scarce inputs. Consider the possibility of using only two types of resources, capital and labour. A firm may have the options given in Table 6.1. It can use various combinations of labour and capital to produce the same amount of output. Two hypothetical combinations are given in the table. How, then, is it decided which combination should be used? In the price system, the **least-cost combination** (technique B in our example) will in fact be chosen because it maximizes profits. We assume that the owners of businesses act as if they are maximizing profits. Recall from Chapter 1 that we assume that individuals act *as if* they are rational.

In a price system, competition *forces* firms to use least-cost production techniques. Any firm that fails to employ the least costly technique will find that other

▶ **Least-cost combination**

The level of input use that produces a given level of output at minimum cost.

Table 6.1

Production Costs for 100 Units of Product X

Technique A or B can be used to produce the same output. Obviously, B will be used because its total cost is less than A's. Using production technique B will generate a $2 savings for every 100 units produced.

Inputs	Input Unit Price	A Production Technique A (input units)	Cost	B Production Technique B (input units)	Cost
Labour	$10	5	$50	4	$40
Capital	8	4	32	5	40
Total cost of 100 units			82		80

companies can undercut its price. In other words, other companies that choose the least-cost production technique will be able to offer the product at a lower price and still make a profit. This lower price will persuade consumers to shift their purchases from the higher-priced firm to the lower-priced one. Inefficient businesses will be forced out of operation.

For Whom Will It Be Produced?

This last question that every economic system must answer involves who gets what. In a market system, the choice about what is purchased is made by individuals, but that choice is determined by the ability to pay. Who gets what is determined by the distribution of money income.

Determination of Money Income.

In a price system, a consumer's ability to pay for consumer products is based on the size of that consumer's money income. That in turn depends on the quantities, qualities, and types of the various human and non-human resources that the individual owns and supplies to the marketplace. It also depends on the prices, or payments, for those resources. When you are selling your human resources as labour services, your money income is based on the wages you can earn in the labour market. If you own nonhuman resources—physical capital and land, for example—the level of interest and rents that you are paid for your physical capital and land will clearly influence the size of your money income and thus your ability to buy consumer products.

Which Consumers Get What?

In a price system, the distribution of finished products to consumers is based on consumers' ability and willingness to pay the market price for the product. If the market price of compact discs is $18, consumers who are able and willing to pay that price will get those CDs. All others won't.

Here we are talking about the *rationing* function of market prices in a price system. Rather than have a central political figure or agency decide which consumers will get which goods, those consumers who are willing and able to pay the market price obtain the goods. That is to say, relative prices ration the available resources, goods, and services at any point in time among those who place the highest value on those items. If scarcity didn't exist, we would not need any system to ration available resources, goods, and services. All of us could have all of everything that we wanted without taking away from what anyone else obtained.

Concepts in Brief

- Any economic system must answer three questions: (1) *What* will be produced? (2) *How* will it be produced? (3) *For whom* will it be produced?
- In a price system, supply and demand determine the prices at which exchanges take place.
- In a price system, firms choose the least-cost combination use of inputs to produce any given output. Competition forces them to do so.
- In a price system, who gets what is determined by consumers' money income and choices about how to use that money income.

TODAY'S INCREASINGLY ALL-CAPITALIST WORLD

Not long ago, textbooks presented a range of economic systems, usually capitalism, socialism, and communism. **Communism** was intended as a system in which the state disappeared and individuals contributed to the economy according to their productivity, receiving income according to their needs. Under **socialism,** the state owned a major share of productive resources except labour. **Capitalism** has been defined as a system under which individuals hold government-protected private property rights to all goods, including those used in production, and their own labour.

▶ **Communism**
In its purest form, an economic system in which the state has disappeared and individuals contribute to the economy according to their productivity and are given income according to their needs.

▶ **Socialism**
An economic system in which the state owns the major share of productive resources except labour. Socialism also usually involves the redistribution of income.

Pure Capitalism in Theory

In its purest theoretical form, market capitalism, or pure capitalism, has the following attributes:

1. Private property rights exist and are upheld by the judicial system.
2. Prices are allowed to seek their own level as determined by the forces of supply and demand. In this sense, pure capitalism is a price system.
3. Resources, including human labour, are free to move in and out of industries and geographic locations. The movement of resources follows the lure of profits— higher expected profits create an incentive for more resources to go where those profits might occur.
4. Risk takers are rewarded by higher profits, but those whose risks turn out to be bad business decisions suffer the consequences directly in terms of reduced wealth.
5. Decisions about what and how much should be produced, how it should be produced, and for whom it should be produced are left to the market. In a pure market capitalist system, all decisions are decentralized and made by individuals in a process of *spontaneous coordination* throughout the economy.

▶ **Capitalism**
An economic system in which individuals own productive resources; these individuals can use the resources in whatever manner they choose, subject to common protective legal restrictions.

Try Preview Question 2:
What are the "three *P*s" of pure capitalism?

One way to remember the attributes of pure capitalism is by thinking of the three Ps: prices, profits, and private property.

The role of government is limited to provision of certain goods, such as defence, police protection, and a legal framework within which property rights and contracts are enforced.

Pure capitalism has also been called a **laissez-faire** system. The French term means "leave [it] alone" or "let [it] be." A pure capitalist system is one in which the government lets the economic actors in the economy make their own decisions without government constraints.

▶ **Laissez-faire**
French for "leave [it] alone"; applied to an economic system in which the government minimizes its interference with the economy.

The Importance of Incentives

It is doubtful that "true" communism ever really existed or could survive in a whole economy. However, various forms of socialism, in which the state owned important parts of the economy, have existed. One can argue that the most important distinguishing feature between capitalist countries and everywhere else is the lack of private property rights. Economics predicts that, for example, when an apartment building is owned by no one (that is, owned by the "state"), there is less incentive for anyone to take care of it. This analysis has predicted well with respect to public housing in Canada. Just imagine an entire country for which all housing is public housing. That is what the former Soviet Union was like. (Note that we are not passing judgment on a system that has few private property rights. Rather, we are simply underscoring the predictions that economists can make regarding how individuals treat such property.)

We pointed out in Chapter 4 that, in a world of scarcity, resources must always be rationed. In economic systems where prices were not allowed to be the rationing device, other methods had to be used. In the former Soviet Union, rationing by queuing (standing in line) was one of the most common. Some economists estimated that the average Russian spent as many hours a week waiting in lines as the average Canadian spends watching television.

Today one might say that the collapse of communism has left the world with one system only, the **mixed economy,** in which decisions about how resources are used are made partly by the private sector and partly by the public sector—capitalism with government. Figure 6.1 represents the size of government relative to annual national output. You can see that even among the traditional capitalist countries of the world, there are great variations. These can be regarded as the different faces of capitalism.

▶ **Mixed economy**

An economic system in which decisions about how resources should be used are made partly by the private sector and partly by the government, or the public sector.

Try Preview Question 3:

Why do we say that *all* economies are mixed economies?

Figure 6.1

Percentage of National Yearly Output Accounted for by Government in Various Countries

Even among countries that have embraced capitalism for a long time, government plays an important, but widely different, role. It constitutes over 60 percent of the economy in Sweden, and about 42 percent in Canada.

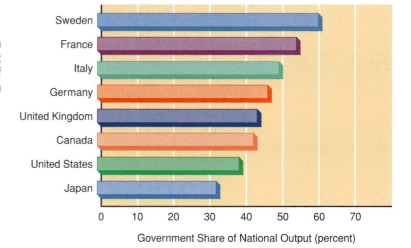

Government Share of National Output (percent)

Try Preview Question 4:
How can economies be classified?

THE DIFFERENT FACES OF CAPITALISM

The world is now left with a single economic system that, thanks to the diversity of human cultures, has a variety of faces. Table 6.2 presents one way to categorize today's economic systems.

Table 6.2
Four Faces of Capitalism

Type of Capitalism	Examples	Characteristics	Problem Areas
Consumer	Canada, United States, New Zealand, Australia, United Kingdom	Borders are relatively open; focus is on profit maximization and laissez-faire.	Low saving and investment rates; income inequality
Producer	Japan, France, Germany	Production is emphasized over consumption; employment is a major policy issue; state controls a relatively large part of the economy.	Consumer dissatisfaction; potential slow future growth rates; inertia within the economy
Family	Indonesia, Malaysia, Thailand, Taiwan	Extended clans dominate business and capital flows.	Lack of modern corporate organizations; lack of money markets
Frontier	Russia, China, Ukraine, Romania, Albania	Many government enterprises pursue for-profit activities; new entrepreneurs emerge every day.	Difficulty of crossing borders; rising criminal activity

Source: Based on, in part, "21st Century Capitalism," *Business Week*, February 23, 1995, p. 19.

Concepts in Brief

- Communism is an economic system under which, in theory, individuals would produce according to their abilities and consume according to their needs. Under socialism, the state owns most major capital goods and attempts to redistribute income.
- Pure capitalism allows for the spontaneous coordination of millions of individuals by allowing the free play of the three *P*s—prices, profits, and property rights. Often, pure capitalism is called a laissez-faire system.
- Incentives matter in any economic system; therefore, in countries that have had few or unenforced property rights, individuals have lacked the incentives to take care of most property that wasn't theirs.
- Most economies today can be viewed as mixed in that they combine private decisions and government controls.

THE TRANSITIONAL PHASE: FRONTIER CAPITALISM

Frontier capitalism describes economies in transition from state ownership and control of most of the factors of production to a system of private property rights in which the price system is used to answer the basic economic questions. Table 6.3 presents theoretical stages in the development of frontier capitalism. Two aspects appear to be the most important: developing the legal system and selling off state-owned businesses.

Table 6.3 **How Frontier Capitalism Develops**	Stage	Characteristics
	I	The central government, as the controller of all economic activities, collapses and starts to disappear. The black market, typically involving government enterprises still owned by the state, expands enormously. Many former state factory managers and other bosses become involved in criminal activities using the state's resources. Government corruption occurs more than before.
	II	Small businesses start to flourish. Families pool funds in order to become entrepreneurs. The rules of commerce are not well understood because there is not yet a well-established commercial law system, nor are property rights well defined or protected by the state.
	III	The economy is growing, but much of its growth is not measured by government statisticians. Small financial markets, such as stock markets, begin to develop. Foreigners cautiously invest in the new stock markets. The government attempts to develop a clear set of commercial laws.
	IV	Foreign corporations are more willing to invest directly in new factories and stores. The state gets serious about selling all businesses that it owns. More resources are devoted to suppressing criminal activity. Commercial law becomes better established and better understood.

Development of the Legal System

In Canada and many other countries, we take a well-established legal system as a given. That does not imply the total absence of a legal system in countries where we are now seeing frontier capitalism. To be sure, the former Soviet Union had a legal system, but virtually none of it had to do with economic transactions, which were carried out by state dictates. Individuals could not own the factors of production, and therefore there were no legal disputes over property rights involving them. Consequently, the legal system in the former Soviet Union and its Eastern European satellites consisted of many volumes of criminal codes—laws against robbery, murder, rape, and theft, as well as so-called economic crimes.

Enter the new world of private property rights and unrestricted exchange of those rights among buyers and sellers. Now what happens when a buyer claims that a seller breached a particular agreement? In Canada, lawyers, courts, and established contract law can be used to settle the dispute. Yet until recently in the frontier economies of the former Soviet Union, there was nothing even vaguely comparable. The rule of law in Canada (and Great Britain—from where much of Canada's law is evolved) has developed over hundreds of years; we cannot expect countries in transition towards full capitalism to create an entire body of law and procedure overnight.

Privatization

▶ **Privatization**

The sale or transfer of state-owned property and businesses to the private sector, in part or in whole. Also refers to contracting out—letting private business take over government-provided services such as garbage collection.

The transition towards capitalism requires that the government reduce its role in the economy. This transition involves what has become known as *privatization.* **Privatization** is the transfer of ownership or responsibility for businesses run by the government, so-called *state enterprises,* to individuals and companies in the private sector. Even in capitalist countries, the government has often owned and run various parts of the economy. During and after World War II, it became the norm for many European governments to "nationalize" different industries. This was particularly true in the United Kingdom, where the steel industry was nationalized, for example. In the early 1980s, France nationalized its banking industry. The opposite

Figure 6.2
The Trend Towards Privatization

Privatization worldwide has been on the upswing since 1985, as shown in part (a). Nationalizations (the opposite of privatizations) reached their peak in about 1970 as is shown in part (b).

Source: OECD and *The Economist,* August 21, 1993, p. 19.

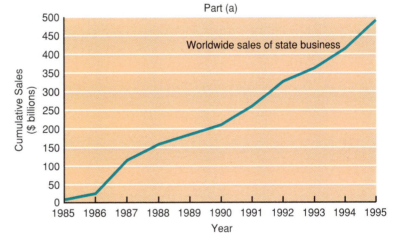

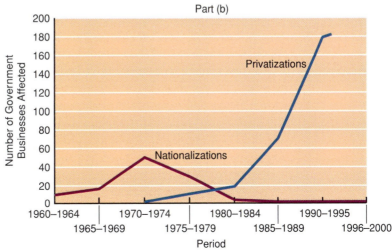

of nationalization is privatization. Late in 1996, Canada privatized air traffic control and sold it to Nav Canada for $1.5 billion.

In the early 1980s, Turkey and Chile were the first capitalist countries to start mass privatization of government-owned businesses. Under Margaret Thatcher, the United Kingdom pioneered the mass privatization of state industry, including the huge road haulage company (NFC), a health care group (Amersham International), telephone services (British Telecom), British Petroleum, and British Aerospace.

A country must employ some method to put government-owned businesses into the hands of the private sector; government-owned businesses are not simply given away to the first party who asks. Imagine if the Canadian government said that it wanted to sell Canada Post. How would it do so? One way is to sell it outright, but there might not be any buyers who would be willing to pay to take over such a giant money-losing corporation. An alternative would involve selling shares of stock to anyone who wanted to buy them at the stated price. This latter technique is indeed the way in which most privatizations have been carried out in established capitalist countries throughout the world over the past 15 or 20 years.

In the former Soviet Union and in Eastern Europe, alternative systems have been devised. For example, citizens, at various times, have been given vouchers granting them the right to purchase a specified number of shares in particular government-owned companies that were being sold off.

The trend in privatization versus nationalization is shown in part (a) of Figure 6.2. The cumulative worldwide sales of state-owned enterprises can be seen in part (b). In Europe, privatization will probably continue into the next century at the rate of over $50 billion a year. Privatization in Latin America will go on for much longer. Finally, privatization in the former Soviet Union and Eastern Europe has in a sense just begun, and may take a long time indeed.

Political Opposition to Privatization

There is often strong political pressure to slow down or even prevent the privatization of state-owned businesses. The political pressure to prevent privatization is derived from simple economics: Managers of state-owned businesses typically have had lifetime job security, better working conditions than they could obtain elsewhere, and little threat of competition. In other words, life for a manager is usually better in a state-owned firm than in that same firm once it has been privatized.

Workers in state-owned firms also believe, often rightly, that their lot in life will not be quite so good if the state-owned firm is sold to the private sector. State-owned firms tend to pay their workers higher wages and give them better fringe benefits, including much better pension plans, than similar firms that are privately owned. For example, an examination of state-owned phone companies in France and Germany shows that they have two to three times as many workers per telephone customer as the private telephone companies in Canada. This comparative overuse of labour in state-owned firms is even more obvious in the republics of the former Soviet Union and in Eastern Europe.

Economists cannot say whether privatization of state-owned firms is good or bad. Rather, economists can simply state that the rigours of a competitive market will generally cause resources to be used more efficiently after privatization occurs. In the process, however, some managers and workers may be made worse off.

Is There a Right Way to Go About the Transition?

Ever since the fall of the Berlin Wall in 1989, economists have debated whether there is a "right" way for former socialist and communist countries to move towards capitalist systems. The once-communist nations have, indeed, embarked on a social experiment in how to move towards a market economy. Basically, they have chosen two methods—a slow one and a fast one. Romania, Russia, and Ukraine have only gradually privatized their economies, whereas the Czech Republic and, to a lesser extent, Poland and Estonia, opted for a "shock treatment."

The rapid move towards a market economy, though not free of problems, has seemed to work better than the go-slow approach. The more slowly the transition occurs, the more the former entrenched bureaucrats in the state-owned businesses have been able to maintain their power over the use of resources. In the meantime, the state-owned businesses continue to use valuable resources inefficiently in these developing countries.

In contrast, a country like the Czech Republic used a voucher system to privatize over 2,000 state-owned enterprises. All citizens were given vouchers—legal rights evidenced on printed certificates—which could be used to purchase shares of stock in state-owned businesses. A stock market quickly developed in which shares of hundreds of companies are now traded every day. After an initial period of transition to a market economy, the Czech Republic has now achieved one of the lowest unemployment rates in Europe.

We will next examine the current situation of two of the largest countries in the world that are in the throes of frontier capitalism. Both are grappling with the problems of the transition from communism to capitalism.

Concepts in Brief

- Today there are four types of capitalism: consumer, producer, family, and frontier. The last begins when a centralized economy starts collapsing and black markets thrive. Eventually small businesses flourish, and then financial markets develop. Finally, foreign investment is attracted, and state-owned businesses are privatized.
- The development of a well-functioning legal system is one of the most difficult problems for an economy in the frontier capitalism stage. Such economies do not have the laws or courts to handle the new system of property right transfers.
- Privatization, or the turning over to the private sector of state-owned businesses, is occurring all over the world in all types of economies. There is much political opposition, however, whenever managers in soon-to-be privatized businesses realize that they may face harder times in a private setting.

RUSSIA AND ITS FORMER SATELLITES, YESTERDAY AND TODAY

Russia was the largest republic in the former Soviet Union. The economic system in place was at times called communism and at other times called command socialism. There is no question that it was a command economy in which there was centralized economic leadership and planning. All economies involve planning, of course; the difference is that in capitalist societies, most of the planning is done by private businesses rather than the government. Leaders in the former Soviet Union believed that its economic planners in Moscow could micromanage an economy that spanned 11 time zones, involved millions of consumers and producers, and affected vast quantities of goods and services.

Imagine trying to run a single business that big! Perhaps more importantly, state ownership in such a large country resulted in unintended consequences throughout the economy. For example, when the government issued production quotas for glass based on the number of panes, the glass produced was almost paper thin and shattered easily. Managers of the glass factories found it took less time to make thin panes of glass which allowed them to produce the required number in the time allotted. In an effort to correct the problem, the government changed its quotas to weight. However, the resulting glass panes were so thick that they were useless. Once again managers found it took less time to meet their quotas if they produced very heavy panes of glass. In short, former Soviet citizens responded rationally to their incentives every time central planners figured out a new way to set production quotas. In the process, untold resources were inefficiently used or completely wasted.

By the time the Soviet Union collapsed in 1991, it consisted of a society in which perhaps one or two percent of the population (the communists, privileged bureaucrats, athletes, and artists) enjoyed a comfortable lifestyle and the rest of the citizens were forced to scrape by. The standard of living of the average citizen prior to the Soviet Union's breakup was at best a quarter, but more realistically one-tenth, of that in Canada. The same was true perhaps to an even greater degree in the former East Germany, Romania, Poland, Hungary, Czechoslovakia (now the Czech Republic and Slovakia), and Albania.

Thinking Critically About the Media | Taking Russia's Pulse

When economists and journalists discuss the transition from the centralized Soviet economy to its current market orientation, they lament the tremendous reduction in national output. Official estimates for the period 1989 to 1995, for example, claim that national output dropped by over 50 percent. True though it may be that output dropped during this time, it is not clear what the actual value of that output was to the population. Much of the reduction was in military hardware, such as missiles. How much did the average citizen lose when that output shrank? Also, fewer television sets and radios were produced during this time period—but the ones produced earlier either never worked properly or tended to explode. Steel mills have been shut down in Russia but they had been using technology that was 45 years old. Further, the official Russian state agency that measures the economy, Goskomstat, has none of the sophistication that Statistics Canada has for measuring a nation's output. Even if Goskomstat had better computers and more refined techniques, it would still miss a vast off-the-books economy that won't be counted by government statisticians for years to come. All in all, Russia's 150 million people earn more and live better than what Goskomstat statistics say.

Privatization During Transition

The fact that a former state-owned business in Russia is now privatized does not mean that shareholders control it the way they do in, say, Canada. In Canada, shareholders elect a board of directors, which then chooses upper management. Shareholders can force out directors who have acted improperly, and can also show their disapproval by selling their shares of stock and purchasing shares in another company. It will be some time before the same system of control operates in all recently privatized Russian businesses. Many such businesses are actually controlled by their managers and workers, not by shareholders. One might use the analogy of a divorced couple still sharing the same house and the children.

In some former Soviet satellite countries, one arm of government sells a state-owned firm and another reappears as its owner. This has happened a lot in Poland, for example, where the government's Industrial Development Agency is managing one of the 15 funds that were set up to take over 440 formerly state-owned enterprises.

In the businesses that are being run by worker cooperatives, there is little incentive to fire the least efficient workers or to seek more highly qualified workers. Manager-owners do not often do much better. Manager-owners of recently privatized firms in Russia clearly do not want to surrender control.

The Persistence of Old Ways

The more an economy tends towards pure market capitalism, the less place there is for a government élite that is able to seize economic power and, more importantly, economic privileges. In Russia today, some of the old Communist Party bases of economic power are being redeveloped. Although newspapers and television stations are now privately owned, their owners are increasingly afraid of angering powerful government interests.

Just a few years ago, President Boris Yeltsin created a new political party named "Our House—Russia." The party was and continues to be backed by wealthy banking and business interests. It consists almost entirely of state bureaucrats and provincial governors and administrators, most of whom are former communists. Prior to the downfall of communism, the political élite were able to use special clinics and hospitals. Today the same persons have the same privileges, although the names of the hospitals have changed. Even a new special food store was built for officials with parliamentary identification cards. Under communism, special food stores served to provide Communist Party élite with low-cost, high-quality food without their having to wait in lines. Why such a special food store has cropped up again in Russia's now more capitalistic system remains something of a mystery.

The Inevitable Crime Wave

The shift to a market economy in Russia has brought with it a major increase in crime, particularly organized crime. Currently, virtually every small business pays protection money to some gang. Moscow boasts at least a million unregistered firearms, and the country as a whole has over 30 million of them. According to former *Toronto Star* Moscow reporter Stephen Handelman, "The second Russian revolution of this century is awash in corruption, opportunism, and crime."

One needs to examine the crime statistics more carefully, though, to get a real feeling for what is happening in this nation in transition. Street crime is certainly greater than it used to be under the Soviet régime. But Moscow is still probably safer than many American cities. With respect to "breaking the law," the legal system is in such a state of flux that probably everyone is breaking the law at one time or another. Because the legal system is in its infancy for facilitating private enterprise, business people have had to resort to extralegal methods to collect debts and enforce contracts. Unfortunately, some of these methods involve firearms and violence.

A good analogy for what is happening in Russia today is the violence associated with the illegal production and sale of alcoholic beverages during the United States' experiment with Prohibition (1920–1933) and what is happening in Russia today. The violence associated with the business of illegal booze disappeared with the repeal of Prohibition. It will not disappear so quickly in Russia, but it certainly will eventually fade out as property rights become better established, the legal system increasingly facilitates trade, and the court system gains enough experience to handle legal problems from the business world.

One must also look at what used to exist under the old system. Because everything belonged to "the people," there was little in the way of communications, credit, banking, and computerization. Money was less important than connections and rank in the Communist Party. People who were adept at thriving in such an environment—the Communist Party élite—have had a comparative advantage in the initial stages of transition to a market economy. They maintain their connections with the state bureaucrats who controlled resources. It is not surprising that many of those in power today are the same communists who were in power a decade ago.

All of this is simply a transition. The incidence of certain crimes in Russia has actually fallen, as can be seen in Figure 6.3.

Figure 6.3
Crime in Russia

While crime increased after the fall of communism in Russia, its rate has recently stabilized or fallen.

Source: Interior Ministry of Russia.

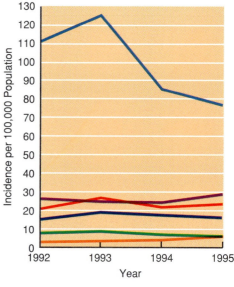

INTERNATIONAL EXAMPLE
A Booming Business in Facelifts by Russian Plastic Surgeons

One of the beneficiaries of Russia's economic system in transition is the facelift industry. There is as yet no legal procedure in Russia for imposing liability on physicians for malpractice. Consequently, a patient who desires a facelift or other cosmetic surgery has no consent forms to sign, and the physician has no malpractice (liability) insurance to purchase. People are travelling from outside Russia to take advantage of the resulting relatively inexpensive plastic surgery. According to one of Russia's best-known plastic surgeons, Igor A. Volf, "Surgeons in the West work in a very rigid frame. They are afraid of being sued by their patients—they fear complications. I do the big, bold operations Western doctors are afraid to do." As word of mouth travels, the demand curve for Russian plastic surgeons is shifting outward to the right.

For critical analysis: What are the costs that a Canadian contemplating a facelift in Moscow would have to include in making a rational decision about going there?

Concepts in Brief

- Russia and its former satellite states in Eastern Europe operated under a system of command socialism with much centralized economic planning. The end result was a declining economy in which a small percentage of the population lived extremely well and the rest very poorly.
- Russia and Eastern Europe are privatizing at varying speeds, depending on the level of political opposition.
- Russia has experienced a crime wave during its transition to capitalism. As property rights and the legal system become more efficient, much of the crime associated with illegal economic activities will probably disappear.

THE PEOPLE'S REPUBLIC OF CHINA

The People's Republic of China remains the largest nation on earth and hence the largest with some form of command socialism. However, a decreasing share of the nation's activity is being guided by government. In fact, China started introducing market reforms in various sectors of the economy well before Russia did.

In 1978, the commune system that had been implemented in the 1950s was replaced by what was known as the *household responsibility system*. Each peasant household became responsible for its own plot of land. Whatever was produced in excess of the minimum obligation to the state remained the property of the household. So the incentives for peasant farmers were quite different from those prior to 1978. Peasants were also encouraged to enrich themselves further by engaging in a

▶ **Incentive structure**

The motivational rewards and costs that individuals face in any given situation. Each economic system has its own incentive structure. The incentive structure is different under a system of private property than under a system of government-owned property, for example.

variety of economic activities. The results were impressive. Between 1979 and 1984, millions of jobs were created in the urban and rural private sector, and farm productivity increased dramatically.

In the 1980s, the highly centralized planning from Beijing, the capital, was relaxed. Decision-making powers were given to state-owned enterprises at the local level. Indeed, China had embarked on a gradual sell-off of state-owned enterprises so that the size of the state-owned sector, which accounted for 70 percent of industrial production in the mid-1980s, dropped to an estimated 40 percent in 1996. The result was an increase in output. The problem with state-owned factories was the **incentive structure.** Managers of those factories never had much incentive to maximize output or minimize cost. Rather, managers of state-owned factories attempted to maximize incomes and benefits for their workers because workers made up a political constituency that was more important than the politicians at the national level.

Thinking Critically About the Media   268 Million Chinese Unemployed?

"China Sees 268 Million Unemployed in 2000." This was the headline a few years ago, reportedly based on statements by mainland Chinese officials in the Labour Ministry. Imagine that— the number of unemployed in China equalling nine times the entire population of men, women, and children in Canada! A frightening prospect, no doubt, but also pure nonsense. Such a large number of unemployed presupposes that there is no way for them to find jobs of any sort. As China shifts towards a market economy, however, many of the unemployed will be able to find jobs in businesses that the current Chinese leadership cannot even conceive of today. That is what happens in a country in transition towards market capitalism. Of course, during the transition, there will be social and human costs associated with higher-than-normal unemployment rates, but that is statistically a temporary blip, not a long-term trend.

Two Decades of Economic Reform

Another major economic reform in China began in 1979, when the central government created a special economic zone in Guangdong province, bordering the nation of Hong Kong. In that special zone, the three Ps of pure capitalism—prices, profits, and private property—have now prevailed for nearly two decades. The result has been economic growth rates that have exceeded those in virtually any other part of the world. Within an area housing less than 1.5 percent of the population, Guangdong province now accounts for about 7 percent of the entire country's industrial output.

Transition Problems in Farming

Even though the Chinese central government was able to increase agricultural production dramatically when it gave peasants the household responsibility system, the agricultural sector has been lagging well behind the industrial sector in recent years. In effect, China has been undergoing an industrial revolution but not an agricultural one. One of the major problems is that peasants do not have legal title to their land. In other words, farmers cannot obtain legal property rights. As a result, the techniques used by agribusiness companies elsewhere in the world cannot be used by most of China's farmers. Peasants, in effect, have their land on loan from the state. The average size of a peasant farm is less than an acre (0.4 hectare) for a family of six. It takes this family about 60 workdays to cultivate this amount of land, whereas a single Canadian farmer can cultivate the same amount of land in about two hours.

Further, there is every incentive for peasant farmers to leave their rural lands and move to the city, where they can earn approximately four times as much income.

A Major Problem: The Rule of Law

As with virtually all countries experiencing frontier capitalism, China faces the perennial issue of how to establish the rule of law. When no specific property rights exist because resources are owned by "the people," the inevitable result is corruption. As with Russia, there is an atmosphere of lawlessness and unpredictability for anyone doing business. Both the government and the army continue to seek bribes and other favours because those two institutions still control many of the resources and influence the way business is conducted in China.

Only very slowly is the institution of a strong legal system being built up in China. The idea of property rights is slow to take hold in a nation where the communist dogma has long denied the concept. A good example is the state-supported bootleg compact disc factories that were first shut down because of international pressure and then reopened a few years ago. That Western singers and musicians are being denied royalties seems not to bother some mainland Chinese government officials.

INTERNATIONAL EXAMPLE
A Tale of Two Countries

Approximately 6 million Chinese, most of whom are directly from or descended from those on mainland China, live in the state of Hong Kong. This colony was leased to the British in the nineteenth century and reverted to Chinese ownership in mid-1997. During its years as a British colony covering a mere 1034 square kilometres (399 square miles), Hong Kong became the world's eighth-largest trading nation, with a higher per capita income than the United Kingdom or France. Total annual output from its 6 million residents exceeded 20 percent of the output of 1.2 billion mainland Chinese. Hong Kong has long been the favourite example of economists who wish to show the efficiency of a system that follows the three *P*s—prices, profits, and private property.

Perhaps more importantly, Hong Kong demonstrates the benefits of a strong legal system. A *Fortune* magazine survey of 500 corporate executives in 32 countries rated Hong Kong above London and New York as the best city for doing business in 1996. Commentators have argued that mainland China does not need Hong Kong's money but rather its rule of law. For decades, these laws have provided businesses with predictable rules governing civil and criminal disputes. Hong Kong has had an independent judicial system, contrary to the one almost completely dominated by the Communist Party on the mainland. Whether the mainland's takeover of Hong Kong results in China's learning from Hong Kong remains to be seen.

For critical analysis: Reread the discussion of comparative versus absolute advantage in Chapter 2. Hong Kong is basically a barren land with no natural resources. What does this say about absolute versus comparative advantage?

The Slow Pace of Privatization

Virtually all state-owned companies in China have provided cradle-to-grave social welfare benefits to their workers. The process of privatization, which started gradually years ago, first requires that these companies slowly eliminate many of these social welfare programs. Such programs are one of the reasons that over 50 percent of state-owned enterprises are losing money every year. You can see from Figure 6.4 which industrial enterprises have the greatest amount of state involvement. It clearly will be many years before the Chinese government is completely (if ever) out of the petroleum and tobacco businesses. But as Figure 6.5 shows, a growing percentage of firms are escaping from state control.

Figure 6.4
Relative Importance of Government in China's Industry

The government in China owns most of the oil, tobacco, and power industries, but is reducing its holdings of other industries.

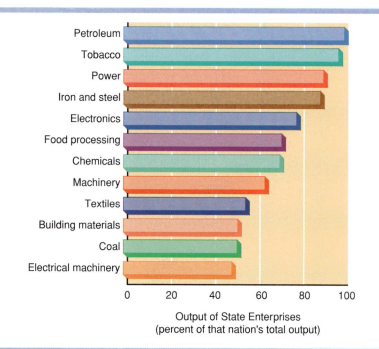

Figure 6.5
The Changing Face of China's Business Ownership

State ownership of all industries in China has fallen from 78 percent in 1978 to only 41 percent in 1996.

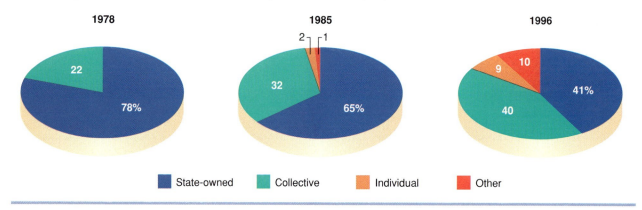

The trend towards privatization in China is inevitably leading to labour dislocations. As state-owned enterprises become privatized, new technology will be introduced that will require fewer labour hours per unit of output. Workers have been, and will continue to be, laid off in recently privatized firms. Laid-off workers will have to seek employment elsewhere, and in the process unemployment rates will rise, at least temporarily.

INTERNATIONAL EXAMPLE
China Eliminates Saturday Work

 In 1995, the Chinese government granted its 450 million urban labourers and students Saturdays off. That adds up to about 1.4 billion extra hours of leisure time every week (labourers and students had been putting in a four-hour Saturday workday). The major beneficiaries of this government edict, besides urban labourers and students, seem to be travel agents. They counted the change in work rules as a windfall.

For critical analysis: What happened to the demand curve for leisure travel after the five-day workweek was instituted?

Concepts in Brief

- China started instituting market reforms in 1979 when it created special economic zones in which the three *P*s of capitalism were allowed to work. Problems remain in agriculture because peasant farmers cannot obtain property rights in land.
- The rule of law as capitalist countries know it is coming slowly to China. Government officials sometimes break contract agreements with foreign investors.
- The process of privatization started years ago but is proceeding slowly. The state still owns most of the businesses in oil, tobacco, power, and iron and steel.

Thinking Critically About the Media   Rich Industrial Nations—Really?

Virtually all news commentators and research organizations continue to classify countries such as Canada, the United States, the United Kingdom, and France as industrial economies. Such an appellation today is a misnomer. In the industrial economies of today, less than one-third of the output is from "industry." Two-thirds of the jobs in so-called industrial economies are from services—doctors, lawyers, computer programmers, and Internet facilitators. Indeed, it might be more appropriate to call the richer countries *knowledge economies* because that is where the primary source of growth will lie—the storage, processing, and distribution of knowledge.

FUTURE ECONOMIC POWER SHIFTS

The fact that there are so many economies in transition today is not just a momentary curiosity. It has implications for the future with respect to which nations will become economic powerhouses. Look at the three parts of Figure 6.6. You see in part (a) that in the mid-1990s, the United States was clearly the world's largest economy. Japan and China were not even half its size. Now look at part (b), which shows

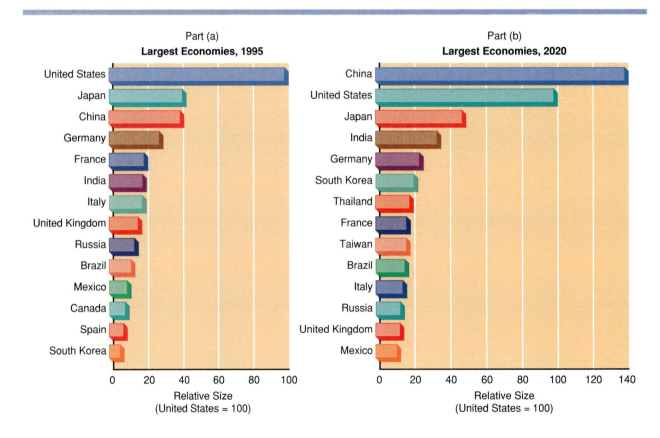

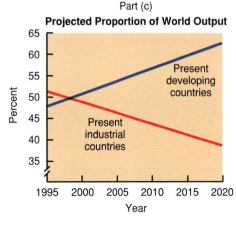

Figure 6.6

World Economic Powerhouses, 1995–2020

While the United States is the largest economy today, by 2020, China may be the world's greatest economic power. In any event, the share of world output from developing countries will increase steadily during that same time period.

Source: World Bank, *Global Economic Prospects.*

the World Bank's prediction of the largest economies in the year 2020. The leading economic powerhouse then is predicted to be China, with the United States a distant second. (These numbers reflect the total size of the economy, not how rich the average citizen is.) Japan will still be among the top three, but India and Indonesia will have expanded dramatically relative to 1995. Indeed, Asia, including India, will be a major economic power in the year 2020. These developments are reflected in part (c) of Figure 6.6, where we show the projected shares of world output of today's industrial countries relative to today's developing countries. Realize, however, that the fact that developing Asian countries will dramatically increase the size of their economies does not mean that westerners will be worse off. Rather, the incomes of most westerners will also increase, but not as rapidly. Given that per-person incomes are generally higher in the West than in Asia, westerners will still remain rich by historical standards. The rest of the world is simply catching up with us.

Issues and Applications

The Peruvian Transition from No Ownership to Clear Title

Concepts Applied: Property rights, incentives, markets, economies in transition

Formal markets do not easily develop where private ownership does not exist. This is the case in Peru, where farmers till family land for generations without a clear title for that land.

By at least one estimate, more than 75 percent of the population of Peru is involved in the "informal society." This term was coined by Peruvian economist Hernando de Soto to emphasize the fact that Peru's official economy is quite small.

Only 20 percent of Peru's land is legally owned. On the remaining 80 percent, which has no true legal ownership, peasant families till the soil as they have done for generations.

Constructing *Pueblos Jovenes*

Cities are actually constructed on the unowned land. They are called *pueblos jovenes*, which means "young cities." Sometimes people who have been living there for a long time or who have tilled the land surrounding them try to register the land in their names. The process can take anywhere from six months to two years, though, and costs thousands of dollars in fees, much more than any peasant family is normally able to pay.

No Ownership, No Market, No Incentive

It is difficult, if not impossible, to create markets when ownership is nonexistent. Informal markets do evolve, and that is what has happened throughout Peru. But without specifically defined property rights, individuals cannot exchange land, for example. Consequently, in Peru, for generations, no large-scale farming has occurred, nor have peasant families experienced much incentive to improve the value of the property on which they farm. It is also not surprising that in the *pueblos jovenes*, construction has been of the flimsiest nature, even by families who have inherited substantial sums of money. If a peasant family doesn't know if it can keep its land, the incentive to invest in it is understandably low.

"Suitcase" Farming

The lack of property rights has created a culture of so-called suitcase farmers in the Upper Huallaga and Rio Apurimac valleys. What the farmers produce, though, is not for normal consumption. It is coca bushes, which provide the raw ingredients for cocaine. Peruvian suitcase farmers plant these bushes, cultivate them, quickly sell them to Colombian buyers, and move off the land.

Enter a New System

Since the beginning of the 1990s, Peru's parliament has passed a number of new property laws. Today, for a nominal cost, it is possible to register ownership of property in a month or so. So far, at least 150,000 families have obtained title to their land for $15 to $20 per parcel.

For a family to establish title to land, the local leaders in the "informal" neighbourhoods have to attest that a family has indeed been using the parcel for generations. If no other family contests ownership of that property, it becomes possible for the family to register ownership.

One group objects to providing well-defined property rights to land: the drug dealers who buy coca plants. They are worried that establishing private property rights to land will discourage the suitcase farmers, leading to a smaller supply of the raw ingredient for cocaine. Not surprisingly, the main office of the Peruvian Institute for Liberty and Democracy, a group that is helping peasants register their land, has been bombed several times.

For Critical Analysis

1. What alternatives would suitcase farmers have if they were given clear ownership rights to the land that they farm?
2. Is it possible to have wealth without legal property rights?

CHAPTER SUMMARY

1. The price system answers the resource allocation and distribution questions relating to what and how much will be produced, how it will be produced, and for whom it will be produced. The question of what to produce is answered by the value people place on a good—the highest price they are willing to pay for it. How goods are produced is determined by competition, which inevitably results in least-cost production techniques. Finally, goods and services are distributed to the individuals who are willing and able to pay for them. This answers the question about for whom goods are produced.

2. Pure capitalism can be defined by the three Ps: prices, profits, and private property.

3. Communism is an economic system in which, theoretically, individuals would produce according to their abilities and consume according to their needs. Under socialism, the state owns most major capital goods and attempts to redistribute income. Most economies today can be viewed as mixed, in that they rely on a combination of private decisions and government controls.

4. Incentives matter in any economic system; consequently, in countries that have had few or unenforced property rights, individuals have lacked the incentives to take care of property that wasn't theirs.

5. Today there are four types of capitalism: consumer, producer, family, and frontier. The last emerges when a centralized economy starts collapsing and black markets thrive. Eventually, small businesses flourish and financial markets develop. Finally, foreign investment is attracted, and state-owned businesses are privatized.

6. The development of a well-functioning legal system is one of the most difficult problems for an economy in the frontier capitalism stage. Such economies do not have the laws or courts to handle property right protection and transfers.

7. Privatization, or turning over state-owned businesses to the private sector, is occurring all over the world in all types of economies. There is much political opposition, however, whenever managers in soon-to-be-privatized businesses realize that they may face harder times in a private setting.

8. Russia and its former satellite states in Eastern Europe operated under a system of command socialism with much centralized economic planning. The end result was a declining economy in which a small percentage of the population lived extremely well and the rest very poorly.

9. Russia has experienced a crime wave during its transition to capitalism. As property rights and the legal system become more efficient, much of the crime associated with illegal economic activities will probably disappear.

10. China started instituting true market reforms in 1979, when it created special economic zones in which the three *P*s of capitalism—prices, profits, and private property—were allowed to work. Problems remain in agriculture because peasant farmers cannot obtain property rights to land.

11. The process of privatization in China started years ago but is proceeding slowly. The state still owns most of the businesses in oil, tobacco, power, and iron and steel.

12. The United States and Japan will remain economic powerhouses, but China could take the lead over the next 25 years. Other Asian countries, including Indonesia, India, Taiwan, South Korea, and Thailand, will become economically much stronger than they are today. Canada will become relatively less powerful, but will still be wealthy compared to the rest of the world.

DISCUSSION OF PREVIEW QUESTIONS

1. **Why does the scarcity problem force all societies to answer the questions *what, how,* and *for whom?***

   Scarcity exists for a society because people want more than their resources will allow them to have. Society must decide *what* to produce because of scarcity. But if wants are severely restricted and resources are relatively superabundant, the question of *what* to produce is trivial—society simply produces *everything* that everyone wants. Superabundant resources relative to restricted wants also make the question of *how* to produce trivial. If scarcity doesn't exist, superabundant resources can be combined in *any* manner; waste and efficiency have no meaning without scarcity. Similarly, without scarcity, *for whom* is meaningless; *all* people can consume *all* they want.

2. **What are the "three *P*s" of pure capitalism?**

   They are prices, profits, and property rights. In a pure capitalist economic system, prices are allowed to change when supply or demand changes. Prices are the signals to all about the relative scarcity of different resources. Profits are not constrained. When profits are relatively great in an industry, more resources flow to it. The converse is also true. Finally, property rights exist and are supported by the legal system.

3. **Why do we say that *all* economies are mixed economies?**

   No economy in the real world is purely capitalistic. Resource allocation decisions in all economies are made by some combination of private individuals and governments. Even under an idealized capitalistic economy, important roles are played by the government; it is generally agreed that government is required for some income redistribution, national defence, protection of property rights, and so on.

4. **How can economies be classified?**

   All societies must resolve the three fundamental economic problems: what, how, and for whom? One way to classify economies is according to the manner in which they answer these questions. In particular, we can classify them according to the degree to which *individuals* privately are allowed to make these decisions. Under pure command socialism, practically all economic decisions are made by a central authority; under pure capitalism, practically all economic decisions are made by private individuals pursuing their own economic self-interest.

PROBLEMS

(Answers to the odd-numbered problems appear at the back of the book.)

6-1. Suppose that you are an economic planner and you have been told by your country's political leaders that they want to increase automobile production by 10 percent over last year. What other industries will be affected by this decision?

6-2. Some argue that prices and profits automatically follow from well-established property rights. Explain how this might occur.

6-3. A business has found that it makes the most profits when it produces $172 worth of output of a particular product. It can choose from three possible techniques, A, B, and C, to produce the desired level of output. The table gives the amount of inputs these techniques use along with each input price.

   a. Which technique will the firm choose, and why?

   b. What would the firm's maximum profit be?

   c. If the price of labour increases to $4 per unit, which technique will be chosen, and why? What will happen to profits?

		Production Technique		
	Input			
	Unit	A	B	C
Input	Price	(units)	(units)	(units)
Land	$10	7	4	1
Labour	2	6	7	18
Capital	15	2	6	3
Entrepreneurship	8	1	3	2

6-4. Answer the questions on the basis of the accompanying graph.

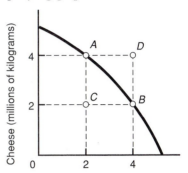

   a. A switch to a decentralized, more market-oriented economy might do what to the production possibilities curve, and why?

   b. What point on the graph represents an economy with unemployment?

6-5. The table gives the production techniques and input prices for 100 units of product X.

		Production Technique		
	Input			
	Unit	A	B	C
Input	Price	(units)	(units)	(units)
Labour	$10	6	5	4
Capital	8	5	6	7

   a. In a market system, which techniques will be used to produce 100 units of product X?

   b. If the market price of a unit of X is $1, which technique will lead to the greatest profit?

   c. The output of X is still $1, but the price of labour and capital changes so that labour is $8 and capital is $10. Which production technique will be used?

   d. Using the information in (c), what is the potential profit of producing 100 units of X?

6-6. The table gives the production techniques and input prices for one unit of product Y.

Input	Input Unit Price	Production Technique A (units)	B (units)	C (units)
Labour	$10	1	3	2
Capital	5	2	2	4
Land	4	3	1	1

a. If the market price of a unit of product Y is $50, which technique generates the greatest potential profit?

b. If input unit prices change so that labour is $10, capital is $10, and land is $10, which technique will be chosen?

c. Assuming that the unit cost of each input is $10 and the price of a unit of Y is $50, which technique generates the greatest profit?

6-7. Visit the World Bank's Selected World Development Indicators website at http://www.worldbank.org/html/iecdd/wdipdf.htm. Open Table 1, Basic Indicators. Notice that the countries are arranged by the size of their economies (GNP per capita) from small to large.

a. Find Canada. What income level group of countries is Canada in?

b. Select one of the low-income economies. Compare its per person GNP with that of Canada. How much larger, in percentage terms, is Canada than your low-income country?

c. Compare the life expectancy at birth in your low-income country with that of a middle-income country and with that of Canada. What conclusions can you draw about health as a country develops? Why do you think this happens?

File Edit View Go Favorites Help

INTERACTING WITH THE INTERNET

Back   Forward   Stop   Refresh   Home   Search   Favorites   History   Channels   Fullscreen   Mail   Print   Edit

Extensive information on Eastern European economic conditions, with an emphasis on financial matters, can be found (for a fee) at

http://www.securities.com/

An excellent source for general information on these and other countries is the CIA's *World Factbook*,

http://www.odci.gov/cia/publications/pubs.html

Information on Canada's relationship with developing countries can be found at the Web site of the Canadian International Development Agency (CIDA) at

http://w3.acdi-cida.gc.ca/

The Organisation for Economic Co-operation and Development (OECD) has extensive information on its Web site about its 29 member countries which include many Eastern European countries as well as the developed western countries. Most of the information is free. You can access the OECD Web site at

http://www.oecd.org/

PART 2

Introduction to Macroeconomics and Economic Growth

Chapter 7

The Macroeconomy:
Unemployment and
Inflation

Chapter 8

Measuring the
Economy's Performance

Chapter 9

Economic Growth:
Technology, Research
and Development, and
Knowledge

The Macroeconomy: Unemployment and Inflation

As a consumer, you certainly worry about changes in the prices of the things you buy. You might even get angry when the prices of your favourite products go up. Government statisticians try to measure what happens to the average of all prices each month by estimating various indexes of price levels. Recently, there have been complaints that government statisticians are not measuring price changes correctly. If the way they measure price level changes ends up reducing the official rate of inflation, how will that affect the economy? To understand this issue, you need to know more about inflation and how it is measured. You will learn more about these topics, as well as unemployment, in this chapter.

Preview Questions

1. Why is frictional unemployment not necessarily harmful?

2. Does it matter whether inflation is anticipated or not?

3. Who is hurt by inflation?

4. How do we describe the phases of national business fluctuations?

CHAPTER OUTLINE

- Unemployment
- Inflation
- Changing Inflation and Unemployment: Business Fluctuations

Did You Know That... although Canada is considered a highly advanced industrialized nation, less and less of its employment is involved in manufacturing? The same is true of the United States, Japan, Germany, France, Italy, and the United Kingdom, where the number of manufacturing workers has been dropping steadily since 1970, despite significant increases in total adult population. Yet the result has *not* been workers permanently out of jobs. Even so, work is a major policy issue facing many countries today. At the core of macroeconomics—the study of the performance and structure of the national economy—are the issues of employment and, more importantly, unemployment.

UNEMPLOYMENT

▶ **Unemployment**

The total number of adults aged 15 years or older who are willing and able to work, and who are actively looking for work but have not found a job.

Unemployment is normally defined as adults actively looking for work, but without a job. Unemployment creates a cost to the entire economy in terms of loss of output. One researcher estimated that at the beginning of the 1990s when unemployment was about 10.5 percent and factories were running at 72 percent of their capacity, the amount of output that the economy lost due to idle resources was almost 6 percent of the total production throughout Canada. (In other words, we were somewhere inside the production possibilities curve that we talked about in Chapter 2.) That was the equivalent of almost $36 billion of schools, houses, restaurant meals, cars, and movies that *could have been* produced. It is no wonder that policymakers closely watch the unemployment figures published by Statistics Canada.

On a more personal level, being unemployed often results in hardship and failed opportunities as well as a lack of self-respect. Psychological researchers believe that being fired creates at least as much stress as the death of a close friend. The numbers that we present about unemployment can never fully convey its true cost to this or any other country.

INTERNATIONAL EXAMPLE
Rising Joblessness Worldwide

Several studies have recently predicted increasing worldwide unemployment until at least the beginning of the twenty-first century. Table 7.1, on page 165, shows that the Canadian unemployment rate in 1996 was not as high as in Italy, France, Belgium, or Spain but was higher than in the United States, Australia, and several European countries. In the year 2000, Canada's relative position will have remained almost the same, but much of Europe will see higher rates of unemployment.

Table 7.1 **Unemployment Rates Around the World**	Country	Projected Unemployment Rate (percent)	
		1996	2000
	Australia	9.5	11.7
	Belgium	12.7	11.8
	Canada	9.4	11.5
	France	12.2	14.0
	Germany	10.0	8.2
	Italy	11.9	13.2
	Japan	2.8	2.8
	Netherlands	9.5	6.8
	Spain	24.4	23.7
	Sweden	7.8	8.3
	Switzerland	3.8	1.3
	United Kingdom	8.2	9.4
	United States	5.8	5.8

Source: International Labor Organization.

For critical analysis: Does the *relative* unemployment rate in Canada have anything to do with the well-being of Canadian workers?

Historical Unemployment Rates

▶ **Labour force**
Individuals aged 15 years or older who either have jobs or are looking and available for jobs; the number of employed plus the number of unemployed.

The unemployment rate, defined as a proportion of the measured **labour force** that is unemployed, dropped to a low of 2.4 percent of the Canadian labour force at the end of World War II, after having reached almost 20 percent during the Great Depression in the 1930s. You can see in Figure 7.1 what happened to unemployment in Canada over the past century. The highest level ever was reached in the Great Depression, but unemployment was also very high during the 1981–86 recession. Unemployment has generally been increasing since World War II.

Employment, Unemployment, and the Labour Force

Figure 7.2, on page 166, presents the population of individuals 15 years of age or older broken into three segments: (1) employed, (2) unemployed, and (3) not in the labour force (a category that includes homemakers, full-time students, and retired persons). Those who are employed and those who are unemployed, added together, make up the labour force. In 1996, the labour force amounted to 13.69 million + 1.42 million = 15.11 million Canadians. To calculate the unemployment rate, we simply divide the number of unemployed by the number of people in the labour force and multiply by 100: 1.42 million ÷ 15.11 million × 100 = 9.4 percent.

$$\text{Unemployment rate} = \frac{\text{number of unemployed workers}}{\text{number of workers in labour force}} \times 100$$

Figure 7.1
Seventy-Five Years of Unemployment

Unemployment reached a low of less than 2 percent during World War II, and a high of almost 20 percent during the Great Depression.

Source: M.C. Urquhart and K.A.H. Buckley, *Historical Statistics of Canada*, and CANSIM University Base, Statistics Canada, Series D76783.

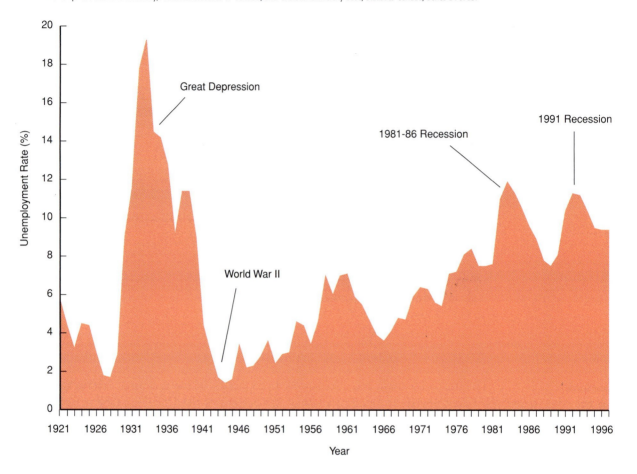

Figure 7.2
Adult Population, 1996

The population aged 15 and older can be broken down into three groups: people who are employed, those who are unemployed, and those not in the labour force.

Source: Statistics Canada, *Canadian Economic Observer.*

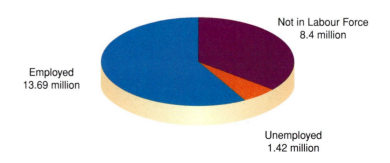

The Arithmetic Determination of Unemployment

▶ **Stock**

The quantity of something, measured at a given point in time—for example, an inventory of goods or a bank account. Stocks are defined independently of time, although they are assessed at a point in time.

▶ **Flow**

A quantity measured per unit of time; something that occurs over time, such as the income you make per week or per year, or the number of individuals who are fired every month.

Because there is a transition between employment and unemployment at any point in time—people are leaving jobs and others are finding jobs—there is a simple relationship between the employed and the unemployed, as can be seen in Figure 7.3. People departing jobs are shown at the top of the diagram, and people taking new jobs are shown at the bottom. If job leavers and job finders are equal, the unemployment rate stays the same. If departures exceed new hires, the unemployment rate rises.

The number of unemployed is some number at any point in time. It is a **stock** of individuals who do not have a job but are actively looking for one. The same is true for the number of employed. The number of people departing jobs, whether voluntarily or involuntarily, is a **flow**, as is the number of people finding jobs. Picturing a bathtub, as illustrated in Figure 7.4, is a good way of remembering how stocks and flows work.

Figure 7.3
The Logic of the Unemployment Rate

Job leavers are individuals who are no longer employed and add to the unemployed (except for those who permanently leave the labour force such as new retirees). When the unemployed find a job, they add to the employed. When both flows are equal, the unemployment rate is stable. If more people leave jobs than find them, the unemployment rate increases, and vice versa.

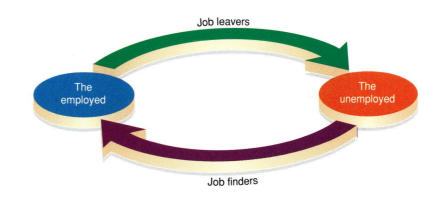

Figure 7.4
Visualizing Stocks and Flows

Unemployment at any point in time is some number that represents a stock, such as the amount of water in a bathtub. People who lose their job constitute a new flow into the bathtub. Those who find a job can be thought of as the water that flows out by the drain.

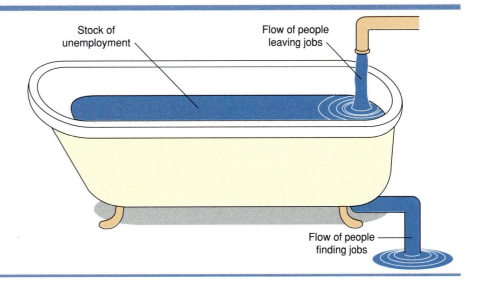

Unemployment Categories. According to Statistics Canada, an individual is considered unemployed if available for work and in any of three categories:

1. Not working, but making specific efforts within the previous four weeks to find a job.
2. Laid off from a job within the previous 26 weeks and waiting for recall.
3. Waiting to begin a new job within the next four weeks.

If the unemployed person is not available for work, then that individual is not considered to be part of the labour force.

Duration of Unemployment. If you are out of a job for a week, your situation is typically much less serious than if you are out of a job for 14 weeks. An increase in the duration of unemployment can increase the unemployment rate because workers stay unemployed longer, thereby creating a greater number of them at any given time. The most recent information on duration of unemployment paints the following picture: 25.1 percent of those who become unemployed find a new job by the end of one month, 27.6 percent find a job within three months, and 27.5 percent are still unemployed after six months. Over the past decade the average duration of unemployment for all unemployed has been 21 weeks. When overall business activity goes into a downturn, the duration of unemployment tends to rise, thereby causing much of the increase in the estimated unemployment rate. In a sense, then, it is the increase in the duration of unemployment during a downturn in national economic activity which generates the bad news that concerns policymakers in Ottawa. Furthermore, the 27.5 percent who stay unemployed longer than six months are the ones who create the pressure on the federal government to "do something." What the government has typically done in the past is extend and supplement unemployment benefits. However, with the Employment Insurance plan implemented in mid-1996, unemployment insurance benefits are more difficult to get. The government hopes this will act as an incentive to the unemployed to look harder for work.

The Discouraged Worker Phenomenon. Critics of the published unemployment rate calculated by the federal government believe that there exist numerous **discouraged workers** and "hidden unemployed." Though there is no exact definition or way to measure discouraged workers, Statistics Canada defines them as people who have dropped out of the labour force and are no longer looking for a job because they believe that the job market has little to offer them. To what extent do we want to include in the measured labour force individuals who voluntarily choose not to look for work, or those who take only two minutes a day to scan the want ads and then decide that there are no jobs?

Some economists argue that people who work part time but are willing to work full time should be classified as "semi-hidden" unemployed. Estimates range as high as 2.5 million workers at any one time fall into this category. Offsetting this factor, though, is *overemployment*. An individual working 50 or 60 hours a week is still counted as only one full-time worker.

▶ **Discouraged workers**
Individuals who have stopped looking for a job because they are convinced that they will not find a suitable one. Typically, they become convinced after unsuccessfully searching for a job.

Thinking Critically About the Media   Declining Job Security?

The decade of the 1990s has been labelled by the media as the one during which millions of workers lost job security. We have been told that corporate downsizing and global competition have resulted in Canadian workers having to accept job changes as a regular part of their lives. Between 1981 and 1985, 46 percent of new jobs created lasted 6 months or less. In 1996, that number had risen to 54 percent. Between 1981 and 1985, 34 percent of new jobs created lasted from 6 months to 5 years. Now only 27 percent last that long. Nevertheless, once a job has lasted for 1 year it is more likely to last longer than 5 years today (56 percent) than in 1991 (48 percent).

▶ **Labour force participation rate**

The percentage of working-age individuals who are not living on a reservation, or in the military, or resident in an institution for the incapacitated, and who are employed or seeking employment.

Labour Force Participation. The way in which we define unemployment and membership in the labour force will affect what is known as the **labour force participation rate.** It is defined as the proportion of working-age individuals who are employed or seeking employment. (If there are discouraged, or hidden, unemployed within any particular group, the labour force participation rate for that particular group will drop.)

Figure 7.5 illustrates the labour force participation rates since 1946. The major change has been the increase in female labour force participation. From a low of 23.2 percent in 1950, the female labour force participation rate climbed steadily to a high of 58.7 percent in 1990. Since then it has dropped slightly to 57.5 percent. Is there an economic explanation for this decrease?

Figure 7.5
Labour Force Participation Rates by Sex

The combined labour force participation rate has increased in recent years. However, over the same period, the male participation rate has fallen, and the female rate has risen markedly.

Source: M.C. Urquhart and K.A.H. Buckley, *Historical Statistics of Canada*, and CANSIM University Base, Statistics Canada, Series D767860, D767895, D768005.

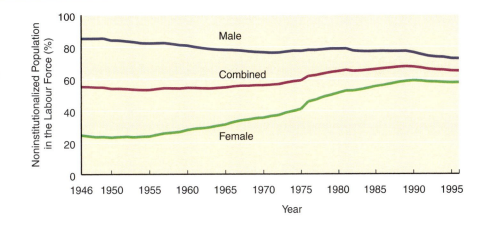

Thinking Critically About the Media   Passive Job Hunters

Frequent reports in the media point out that Canada's 8.5 percent unemployment rate is about 4 percentage points higher than that in the United States. The implication is that Canada is not as competitive, or perhaps as economically buoyant, as our neighbour to the south. However, a recent study reveals another reason for such a large difference. In the United States, the unemployed who only look at newspaper ads for their job search are not included in the definition of "actively looking for work." In Canada, they are. Since 1981, when the two countries' unemployment rates were roughly the same, the proportion of unemployed Canadians who limited their job search to the want ads has risen from 2.4 percent to 7 percent. Removing these "passive job hunters" from the official count of unemployed would reduce the Canadian unemployment rate and bring it closer to that in the United States.

EXAMPLE	Changing Economic Conditions and Female Labour Force Participation

From the end of World War II until the early 1990s, the proportion of women in the labour force steadily increased. But this trend has been reversed in recent years, with more and more women choosing to be homemakers. While this effect is not yet dramatic—the labour force participation rate for women with children under age 16 dropped from 63.2 percent in 1990 to 62.9 percent in 1994—analysts estimate that by the year 2005, 44 percent of Canadian households will have a husband who works and a wife who stays home full-time. While this turnaround is so recent that observers do not yet fully understand it, there are some insights that economics can offer.

Queen's University economist Tanis Day studied the increase in female labour force participation up to the 1980s. She offered many explanations for this trend. Increasingly inexpensive technology such as washing machines and electric stoves and vacuum cleaners reduced the time it took women to do their work inside the home. At the same time, the rise of consumerism aided by ever more radio and television advertising created preferences for market-produced goods over home-produced goods. To purchase these goods, households required more income; women started to bring this extra income home. Finally, over the period following World War II until the 1960s, the female wage was rising relatively quickly, which increased a woman's opportunity cost of remaining at home. Day suggests that the interaction of these forces led increasing numbers of women to choose work outside the home.

What has changed in the 1990s to turn this trend around? Some analysts suggest that consumerism has peaked, with glossy advertisements and television advertising finally overwhelming people's ability to consume. The result is a change in preferences, a return to traditional values where home-produced products are deemed to be more prestigious than mass-produced market-based products. Another reason may be that in the recession-plagued 1990s female wages have not kept up with inflation—that is, real wages (the purchasing power of money wages) have been falling. So too, then, has the opportunity cost of choosing to be a homemaker. Finally, the job market has been changing rapidly in recent years, with many jobs offered only on a part-time or temporary basis. Perhaps the cost of working—childcare, quick meals, stress—has become greater than the benefit of the additional income earned.

For critical analysis: What will happen to women's wages as more women drop out of the labour market? Will this have an effect on their decision?

Concepts in Brief

- Unemployed persons are those 15 years of age and older who are willing and able to work and are actively looking for a job but have not found one.

- The unemployment rate is calculated by dividing the number of unemployed by the total labour force—those who are employed plus those who are unemployed—and multiplying the result by 100. The flow of people leaving jobs and people finding jobs determines the stock of unemployed as well as the stock of employed.
- The duration of unemployment affects the unemployment rate. The number of unemployed workers can remain the same, but if the duration of unemployment increases, the measured unemployment rate will go up.
- While overall labour force participation has risen only a bit since World War II, there has been a major increase in female labour force participation, particularly among married women between the ages of 25 and 34.

The Major Types of Unemployment

Unemployment has been categorized into four basic types: frictional, seasonal, structural, and cyclical.

Frictional Unemployment. Of the almost 15 million Canadians in the labour force, more than 1.3 million will have either changed jobs or taken new jobs during the year; every single month about 1 in 20 workers will have quit, been laid off (told that they will be rehired later), or been permanently fired; another 6 percent will have gone to new jobs or returned to old ones. In the process, more than 3 million persons will have reported themselves unemployed at one time or another. What we call **frictional unemployment** is the continuous flow of individuals from job to job and in and out of employment. There will always be some frictional unemployment as resources are redirected in the market because transaction costs are never zero. To eliminate frictional unemployment, we would have to prevent workers from leaving their present jobs until they had already lined up other jobs at which they would start working immediately, and we would have to guarantee first-time job seekers a job *before* they started looking.

▶ **Frictional unemployment**
Unemployment due to the fact that workers must search for appropriate job offers. This takes time, and so they remain temporarily ("frictionally") unemployed.

▶ **Seasonal unemployment**
Unemployment resulting from the seasonal pattern of work in specific industries. It is usually due to seasonal fluctuations in demand or to changing weather conditions, rendering work difficult, if not impossible, as in the agriculture, construction, and tourist industries.

Seasonal Unemployment. **Seasonal unemployment** comes and goes with seasons of the year in which the demand for particular jobs rises and falls. For example, construction workers can often work only during the warmer months; they are seasonally unemployed during the winter. Summer resort workers can usually get jobs in resorts only during the summer season. They, too, become seasonally unemployed during the winter; the opposite is true for ski resort workers.

▶ **Structural unemployment**
Unemployment resulting from fundamental changes in the structure of the economy. It occurs, for example, when the demand for a product falls drastically so that workers specializing in the production of that product find themselves out of work.

Structural Unemployment. Structural changes in our economy cause some workers to become unemployed permanently or for very long periods of time because they cannot find jobs that use their particular skills. This is called **structural unemployment**. Structural unemployment is not caused by general business fluctuations, although business fluctuations may affect it. And unlike frictional unemployment, structural unemployment is not related to the movement of workers from low-paying to high-paying jobs. Structural unemployment occurs when there is a mismatch of available jobs and available skills. For example, a shipbuilding company in Nova Scotia may have job openings for qualified shipwrights, but all the qualified shipwrights live in British Columbia. Or a printing firm may update its technology, making the skills of its existing workforce obsolete. The firm hires new workers and lays off the old, who are now structurally unemployed.

Cyclical Unemployment. **Cyclical unemployment** is related to business fluctuations. It is defined as unemployment associated with changes in business conditions—primarily recessions and depressions. The way to lessen cyclical unemployment would be to reduce the intensity, duration, and frequency of ups and downs of business activity. Economic policymakers attempt, through their policies, to reduce cyclical unemployment by keeping business activity on an even keel.

▶ **Cyclical unemployment**
Unemployment resulting from business recessions that occur when aggregate (total) demand is insufficient to create full employment.

Full Employment

Does full employment mean that everybody has a job? No, because not everyone is looking for a job—full-time students and full-time homemakers, for example, are not. Is it possible for everyone who is looking for a job always to find one? No, because transaction costs in the labour market are not zero. Transaction costs include any activity whose goal is to enter into, carry out, or terminate contracts. In the labour market, these costs involve time spent looking for a job, being interviewed, negotiating the pay, and so on.

We will always have some frictional unemployment as individuals move in and out of the labour force, seek higher-paying jobs, and move to different parts of the country. **Full employment** is therefore a vague concept implying some sort of balance or equilibrium in an ever-shifting labour market. Of course, this general notion of full employment must somehow be put into numbers so that economists and others can determine whether the economy has reached the full-employment point. Some economists believe that full employment in Canada exists when around 8 percent of the labour force is unemployed. If this is so, then Canada is currently operating at almost full employment. Other observers believe that the real (unofficial) unemployment rate is closer to 13 percent. Because of dismal employment prospects, thousands of discouraged workers have dropped out of the labour market. Thus they are no longer looking for work.

▶ **Full employment**
An arbitrary level of unemployment that corresponds to "normal" friction in the labour market. Today, it is estimated to be around 8 percent.

Try Preview Question 1:
Why is frictional unemployment not necessarily harmful?

Full Employment, Wage Rigidity, and Wait Unemployment

Although the official definition of full employment has changed over the years, there is no question that it occurs at a higher rate of unemployment than it did, say, 40 years ago. Put another way, the apparently unavoidable amount of unemployment in the Canadian economy is growing. In the 1960s it was about 3 percent, whereas today it is at least 8 percent.

There are many explanations for this increase in the full-employment rate of unemployment. One relates to female labour force participation, which has risen dramatically, bringing with it the possibility of additional frictional unemployment due to the fact that women tend more than men to leave and re-enter the labour force because of family responsibilities.

Nonetheless, the rise in the full-employment rate of unemployment seems at odds with the standard supply and demand analysis presented in Chapters 3 and 4. There we showed that if prices are allowed to adjust, there will be neither surpluses nor shortages. A certain portion of unemployment can be defined as a surplus of workers at a particular wage rate that is clearly above equilibrium. It must be, then, that there are wage rigidities (because wages are the price of labour) in the labour market. These result in a situation in which workers are waiting. Workers are unemployed because, at the going wage rate, the quantity of labour supplied exceeds the quantity demanded. This is called **wait unemployment**, and it is due to firms' inability to reduce wages in the face of an excess quantity of labour supplied—by wage rigidities. You already examined one cause of wait unemployment in Chapter 4—minimum wage laws. There are others, including the setting of minimum wages for a firm or an industry because of union power, and a variety of other reasons, some of which you will examine in other chapters.

▶ **Wait unemployment**
Unemployment that is caused by wage rigidities resulting from minimum wages, unions, and other factors.

Concepts in Brief

- Frictional unemployment occurs because of transaction costs in the labour market. For example, workers do not have all the information necessary about vacancies. Structural unemployment occurs when there is a mismatch for geographical or technological reasons of available jobs and available skills.
- The level of frictional unemployment is used in part to determine our (somewhat arbitrary) definition of full employment.
- When wage rigidities exist because of minimum wage laws, union contracts, and other reasons, wait unemployment may result.

INFLATION

▶ **Inflation**
The situation in which the average of all prices of goods and services in an economy is rising.

▶ **Deflation**
The situation in which the average of all prices of goods and services in an economy is falling.

During World War II, you could buy bread for 10 to 15 cents a loaf and have milk delivered fresh to your door for about 25 cents a half gallon (2.25 litres). The average price of a new car was less than $1,000, and the average house cost less than $5,000. Today bread, milk, cars, and houses all cost more—a lot more. Prices in the late 1990s are 10 times what they were in 1940. Clearly, this country has experienced quite a bit of *inflation* since then. We define **inflation** as an upward movement in the average level of prices. The opposite of inflation is **deflation**, defined as a downward movement in the *average* level of prices. Notice that these definitions depend on the average level of prices. This means that even during a period of inflation, some prices can be falling if other prices are rising at a faster rate. The price of computers and computer-related equipment has dropped dramatically since the 1960s, even though there has been general inflation.

To discuss what has happened to inflation in this and other countries, we have to know how to measure it.

Inflation and the Purchasing Power of Money

▶ **Purchasing power**

The value of money for buying goods and services. If your money income stays the same but the price of one good that you are buying goes up, your effective purchasing power falls, and vice versa.

A rose may be a rose may be a rose, but a dollar is not always a dollar. The value of a dollar does not stay constant when there is inflation. The value of money is usually talked about in terms of the **purchasing power** of money. A dollar's purchasing power is the real goods and services that it can buy. Consequently, another way of defining inflation is as a decline in the purchasing power of money. The faster the rate of inflation, the greater the drop in the purchasing power of money.

One way to think about inflation and the purchasing power of money is to discuss dollar values in terms of nominal versus real values. The nominal value of anything is simply its price expressed in today's dollars. In contrast, the real value of anything is its value expressed in purchasing power, which varies with the rate of inflation. Let's say that you received a $100 bill as a gift for your birthday this year. One year from now, the nominal value of that bill will still be $100. The real value will depend on what the purchasing power of money is after one year's worth of inflation. Obviously, if there has been a lot of inflation in one year, the real value of that $100 bill will have dropped.

Measuring the Rate of Inflation

How do we come up with a measure of the rate of inflation? This is indeed a thorny problem for government statisticians. It is easy to determine how much the price of an individual commodity has risen: If last year a light bulb cost 50 cents and this year it costs 75 cents, there has been a 50 percent rise in the price of that light bulb over a one-year period. We can express the change in the individual light bulb price in one of several ways: The price has gone up 25 cents; the price is one and a half (1.5) times as high; the price has risen by 50 percent. An *index number* of this price rise is simply the second way (1.5) multiplied by 100, meaning that the index number would be 150. We multiply by 100 to eliminate decimals because it is easier to think in terms of percentage changes using integers (whole numbers). This is the standard convention adopted for convenience in dealing with index numbers or price levels.

Thinking Critically About the Media   Gasoline Prices

We frequently read in the popular press about Canadian gasoline prices being so much higher than those in the United States because of the extra taxes we pay per litre. This cry grew in volume in March 1996 when there was a temporary shortage of crude oil and gas prices rose sharply. However, before we feel too sorry for ourselves, we should look at gasoline prices elsewhere. The table at the right gives price per litre for unleaded gasoline in Canadian currency for seven countries.

While the American price is about two-thirds the Canadian price, the Canadian price is low relative to those in Europe and Japan. Perhaps we are better off than the media would have us think!

Country	Price per Litre
France	$1.20
Italy	1.17
Germany	1.06
Japan	.98
United Kingdom	.88
Canada	.52
United States	.33

Computing a Price Index. The measurement problem becomes more complicated when it involves a large number of goods, some of whose prices have risen faster than others and some with prices that have fallen. What we have to do is pick a representative bundle, a so-called market basket, of goods and compare the cost of that market basket of goods over time. When we do this, we obtain a **price index**, which is defined as the cost of a market basket of goods today, expressed as a percentage of the cost of that identical market basket of goods in some starting year, known as the **base year**.

▶ **Price index**

The cost of today's market basket of goods expressed as a percentage of the cost of the same market basket during a base year.

▶ **Base year**

The year that is chosen as the point of reference for comparison of prices in other years.

$$\text{Price index} = \frac{\text{cost today of market basket}}{\text{cost of market basket in base year}} \times 100$$

In the base year the price index will always be 100, because the year in the numerator and in the denominator of the above fraction is the same; therefore, the fraction equals 1, and when we multiply it by 100, we get 100. A simple numerical example is given in Table 7.2. In the table there are only two goods in the market basket—corn and microcomputers. The *quantities* in the basket remain the same between the base year, 1992, and the current year, 1998; only the *prices* change. Such a *fixed-quantity* price index is the easiest to compute because the statistician need only look at prices of goods and services sold every year rather than actually observing how much of these goods and services consumers actually purchase each year.

You can use the CPI to calculate the annual rate of inflation. If the CPI rose from 100 to 103 between 1995 and 1996, you could say that the annual rate of inflation was 3 percent. And you would be correct. Putting this into a formula, we have

$$\text{Annual rate of inflation} = \frac{\text{current price index} - \text{previous year's price index}}{\text{previous year's price index}} \times 100$$

Using our example from above, we could calculate the rate of inflation to be

$$\text{Rate of inflation} = \frac{103 - 100}{100} \times 100 = 3\%$$

Table 7.2

Calculating a Price Index for a Two-Good Market Basket

In this simplified example, there are only two goods—corn and microcomputers. The quantities and base-year prices are given in columns 2 and 3. The cost of the 1992 market basket, calculated in column 4, comes to $1,400. The 1998 prices are given in column 5. The cost of the market basket in 1998, calculated in column 6, is $1,700. The price index for 1998 compared with 1992 is 121.43.

(1) Commodity	(2) Market Basket Quantity	(3) 1992 Price per Unit	(4) Cost of Market Basket in 1992	(5) 1998 Price per Unit	(6) Cost of Market Basket at 1998 Prices
Corn	100 bushels	$ 4	$ 400	$ 8	$ 800
Microcomputers	2	500	1,000	450	900
Totals			$1,400		$1,700

$$\text{Price index} = \frac{\text{cost of market basket in 1998}}{\text{cost of market basket in base year 1992}} \times 100 = \frac{\$1,700}{\$1,400} \times 100 = 121.43$$

▶ **Consumer Price Index (CPI)**

A statistical measure of a weighted average of prices of a specified set of goods and services purchased by wage earners in urban areas.

▶ **Producer Price Index (PPI)**

A statistical measure of a weighted average of prices of commodities that firms purchase from other firms.

▶ **GDP deflator**

A price index measuring the changes in prices of all new goods and services produced in the economy.

Real-World Price Indexes. Government statisticians calculate a number of price indexes. The most often quoted are the **Consumer Price Index (CPI)**, the **Producer Price Index (PPI)**, and the **GDP deflator**. The CPI attempts to measure changes only in the level of prices of goods and services purchased by wage earners. The PPI attempts to show what has happened to the price level for commodities that firms purchase from other firms. The GDP deflator attempts to show changes in the level of prices of all new goods and services produced in the economy. The most general indicator of inflation is the GDP deflator because it measures the changes in the prices of everything produced in the economy.

The CPI. Statistics Canada has the task of identifying a market basket of goods and services of the typical consumer. Every so often (usually every 5 to 10 years), the prices of almost 500 goods and services are recorded and used to formulate the base year price level. The current base year is 1996.

Economists have known for years that the way Statistics Canada measures changes in the Consumer Price Index is flawed. Specifically, StatCan has been unable to account for the way consumers substitute less expensive items for higher-priced items. The reason is that the CPI is a fixed-quantity price index, meaning that each month StatCan samples only prices, rather than relative quantities purchased by consumers. In addition, Statistics Canada has been unable to take account of quality changes as they occur. Even if it captures the dramatically falling price of personal computers, it has been unable to reflect the dramatic improvement in quality. Finally, the CPI ignores the introduction of new products.

The PPI. There are a number of Producer Price Indexes, including one for food materials, another for intermediate goods (goods used in the production of other

---

INTERNATIONAL EXAMPLE
The CPI, New Products, and Breakfast Cereals

By definition, a new product that is successful makes the people who buy it better off. The value that consumers place on a new product is greater than the money price. Hence successful new products should reduce the cost of maintaining a given standard of living and therefore reduce the CPI. Economist Jerry Hausman did a study of Apple-Cinnamon Cheerios, introduced by General Mills in 1989. Within three years, that cereal had attained a market share in the United States of 1.6 percent, thus implying a higher value received by 1.6 percent of American breakfast cereal consumers. According to Hausman's calculations, Apple-Cinnamon Cheerios implied a 1.7 percent *reduction* in the average price of cereal (per constant-quality unit). Using the same methodology, Hausman estimated that the CPI overestimates the price of cereals by 20 percent. This so-called new-goods bias in the Canadian CPI has been estimated by Canadian researchers to be as high as 1 percent per year.

For critical analysis: Why do new successful products make consumers better off?

goods), and one for finished goods. Most of the producer prices included are in mining, manufacturing, and agriculture. The PPIs can be considered general-purpose indexes for nonretail markets.

Although in the long run the various PPIs and the CPI generally show the same rate of inflation, such is not the case in the short run. Most often the PPIs increase before the CPI because it takes time for producer price increases to show up in the prices that consumers pay for final products. Often changes in the PPIs are watched closely as a hint that inflation is going to increase or decrease.

The GDP Deflator. The broadest price index reported in Canada is the GDP deflator, where GDP stands for gross domestic product, or annual total national income. Unlike the CPI and the PPIs, the GDP deflator is not based on a fixed market basket of goods and services. The basket is allowed to change with people's consumption and investment patterns. In this sense, the changes in the GDP deflator reflect both price changes and the public's market responses to those price changes. Why? Because new expenditure patterns are allowed to show up in the GDP deflator as people respond to changing prices.

Historical Changes in the CPI. The Consumer Price Index has shown a fairly dramatic trend upward since about World War II. Figure 7.6, on page 178, shows the annual rate of change in the Consumer Price Index since 1867. Prior to World War II, there were numerous periods of deflation along with periods of inflation. Persistent year-in and year-out inflation seems to be a post-World War II phenomenon, at least in this country. As far back as before Confederation, prices used to rise during war periods but then would fall back to more normal levels afterward. This occurred during the War of 1812 and World War I. Consequently, the overall price level in 1940 wasn't much different from 150 years earlier.

INTERNATIONAL EXAMPLE
Hyperinflation

▶ **Hyperinflation**
Extremely rapid rise of the average of all prices in an economy.

Referring to Figure 7.6, look at the highest rates of inflation that Canada has experienced. At the start of the 1981 recession, the estimated inflation rate was over 10 percent. Rarely have we experienced such high inflation rates. Consider, in contrast, the rest of the world. Many countries have experienced and continue to experience **hyperinflation**, an extreme form of inflation during which average prices rise very rapidly. In 1989, Argentina had an inflation rate of 4,923 percent; the following year, in Peru, the rate was 7,481 percent. Russia's 1995 inflation of 340 percent seems almost modest in comparison. The most extreme hyperinflation ever to occur was in Germany in 1923, when prices increased by *700 billion* percent.

For critical analysis: As a consumer, how would your behaviour change during a period of hyperinflation?

Figure 7.6

Inflationary Periods in Canadian History

Since Confederation, there have been numerous periods of inflation in Canada. Here we show them as reflected by changes in the Consumer Price Index. Since World War II, the periods of inflation have not been followed by periods of deflation; that is, even during

peacetime, the price index has continued to rise. The yellow areas represent wartime.

Source: M.C. Urquhart and K.A.H. Buckley, *Historical Statistics of Canada,* and CANSIM University Base, Statistics Canada, Series D490000.

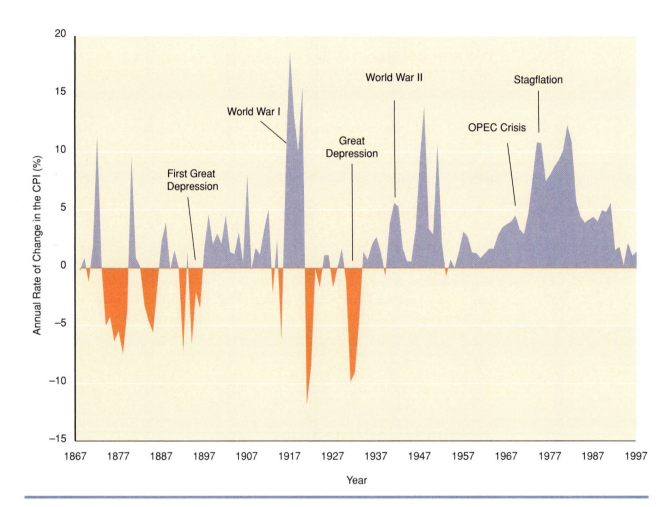

Concepts in Brief

- Once we pick a market basket of goods, we can construct a price index that compares the cost of that market basket today with the cost of the same market basket in a base year.
- The Consumer Price Index (CPI) is the most often used price index in Canada. The Producer Price Index (PPI) is the second most mentioned.
- The GDP deflator measures what is happening to the average price level of *all* new, domestically produced final goods and services in our economy.

Anticipated Versus Unanticipated Inflation

Before examining who is hurt by inflation and what the effects of inflation are in general, we have to distinguish between anticipated and unanticipated inflation. We will see that the effects on individuals and the economy are vastly different, depending on which type of inflation exists.

Anticipated inflation is the rate of inflation that the majority of individuals believe will occur. If the rate of inflation this year turns out to be 10 percent, and that's about what most people thought it was going to be, we are in a situation of fully anticipated inflation.

Unanticipated inflation is inflation that comes as a surprise to individuals in the economy. For example, if the inflation rate in a particular year turns out to be 10 percent when on average people thought it was going to be 5 percent, there will have been unanticipated inflation—inflation greater than anticipated.

Some of the problems caused by inflation arise when it is unanticipated, for when it is anticipated, many people are able to protect themselves from its ravages. With the distinction in mind between anticipated and unanticipated inflation, we can easily see the relationship between inflation and interest rates.

Inflation and Interest Rates

Let's start in a hypothetical world in which there is no inflation and anticipated inflation is zero. In that world, you may be able to borrow money—to buy a computer or a car, for example—at a **nominal rate of interest** of, say, 10 percent. If you borrow the money to purchase a computer or a car and your anticipation of inflation turns out to be accurate, neither you nor the lender will have been fooled. The dollars you pay back in the years to come will be just as valuable in terms of purchasing power as the dollars that you borrowed.

What you ordinarily need to know when you borrow money is the *real rate of interest* that you will have to pay. The **real rate of interest** is defined as the nominal rate of interest minus the anticipated rate of inflation. If you are able to borrow money at 10 percent and you anticipated an inflation rate of 10 percent, your real rate of interest would be zero—lucky you, particularly if the actual rate of inflation turned out to be 10 percent. In effect, we can say that the nominal rate of interest is equal to the real rate of interest plus an *inflationary premium* to take account of anticipated inflation. That inflationary premium covers depreciation in the purchasing power of the dollars repaid by borrowers.[1] Consider the purchase of a home. In 1982, mortgage rates for the purchase of new homes were around 18 percent. By 1996, they had fallen to around 7 percent. Why would anyone have paid 18 percent in 1982 to borrow money to buy a home? Well, home prices in some parts of the country had been rising for several years at 25 percent per year, so at 18 percent, mortgage rates seemed like a good deal. By the mid- to late-1990s, home prices in most places were holding steady.

► **Anticipated inflation**
The inflation rate that we believe will occur; when it does, we are in a situation of fully anticipated inflation.

► **Unanticipated inflation**
Inflation at a rate that comes as a surprise, either higher or lower than the rate anticipated.

► **Nominal rate of interest**
The market rate of interest expressed in today's dollars.

► **Real rate of interest**
The nominal rate of interest minus the anticipated rate of inflation.

Try Preview Question 2:
Does it matter whether inflation is anticipated or not?

---

[1] Whenever there are relatively high rates of anticipated inflation, we must add an additional factor to the inflationary premium—the product of the real rate of interest times the anticipated rate of inflation. Usually this last term is omitted because the anticipated rate of inflation is not high enough to make much of a difference.

There is fairly strong evidence that inflation rates and nominal interest rates move in parallel fashion. Periods of rapid inflation create periods of high interest rates. In the early 1970s, when the inflation rate was between 4 and 5 percent, average interest rates were around 9 percent. At the beginning of the 1980s, when the inflation rate was near 10 percent, interest rates had risen to between 14 and 16 percent. By the early 1990s, when the inflation rate was about 4 percent, nominal interest rates had again fallen to between 7 and 9 percent.

INTERNATIONAL EXAMPLE
Deflation and Real Interest Rates in Japan

Wholesale prices in Japan have been falling for several years. In the past few years, consumer prices also have been falling, which means that Japan has been experiencing *deflation*. What does this have to do with real interest rates in Japan? Real interest rates are roughly equivalent to nominal, or market, rates minus the expected rate of inflation. Market interest rates are rarely negative. If the nominal interest rate a Japanese person has to pay for a mortgage is 4 percent and the expected rate of *deflation* is 3 percent, then the expected real rate of interest is 7 percent, which is extremely high by historical standards. (In Canada, for example, real interest rates have hovered around 4 percent for most of its history.) The point is that in Canada, where we have learned to expect some inflation, we subtract that anticipated inflation from nominal interest rates to obtain real interest rates. In Japan, with expectations of deflation, the Japanese end up adding the expected deflationary rate to the nominal rate of interest to get real rates of interest.

For critical analysis: Why can't nominal interest rates be negative?

Does Inflation Necessarily Hurt Everyone?

Most people think that inflation is bad. After all, inflation means higher prices, and when we have to pay higher prices, are we not necessarily worse off? The truth is that inflation affects different people in different ways. Its effects also depend on whether it is anticipated or unanticipated.

Unanticipated Positive Inflation: Creditor Loses, Debtor Gains.

Creditors lose and debtors gain with unanticipated positive inflation. In most situations, unanticipated inflation benefits borrowers because they are not charged a nominal interest rate that fully covers the rate of inflation that actually occurred. Why? Because the lender did not anticipate inflation correctly. The past several decades have known periods of considerable unanticipated (higher than anticipated) inflation—the late 1960s, the early 1970s, and the late 1970s. During those years, creditors lost and debtors gained.

Protecting Against Inflation.   Banks attempt to protect themselves against inflation by raising nominal interest rates to reflect anticipated inflation. Adjustable-rate mortgages in fact do just that: The interest rate varies according to what happens to interest rates in the economy. Workers can protect themselves by **cost-of-living adjustments (COLAs)**, which are automatic increases in wage rates to take account of increases in the price level.

You can tell if you have been hurt by inflation by calculating the change in your **real income**. Your real income measures how much you can purchase with a given amount of money. If you could purchase two loaves of bread with money earned during one hour of work last year, and you can still purchase that bread with the same number of hours of work this year, then your purchasing power, or your real income, has not changed. If you cannot purchase two loaves of bread with one hour of work, but can only afford one and one-half loaves, then your real income has declined. Conversely, if you can purchase more than two loaves of bread, your real income has increased. To determine the effect of inflation on your real income, calculate the percentage increase (or decrease) in your income in dollars and subtract the annual rate of inflation. Returning to our earlier example, assume that the change in the CPI is 3 percent. Assume also that your money income has risen from $75 per week to $78 per week, giving you an increase in your money income of 4 percent. What effect have these two changes had on your real income?

$$\% \text{ change in real income} = 4\% - 3\% = 1\%$$

In other words, inflation has not hurt you because your money income has risen faster than the rate of inflation.

To the extent that you hold non-interest-bearing cash, you will lose because of inflation. If you have hidden $100 under your mattress and the inflation rate is 10 percent for the year, you will have lost 10 percent of the purchasing power of that $100. If you have your funds in a non-interest-bearing chequing account, you will suffer the same fate. Individuals attempt to reduce the cost of holding cash by putting it into interest-bearing accounts, a wide variety of which often pay nominal rates of interest that reflect anticipated inflation.

The Resource Cost of Inflation.   Some economists believe that the main cost of unanticipated inflation is the opportunity cost of resources used to protect against inflation and the distortions introduced as firms attempt to plan for the long run. Individuals have to spend time and resources to figure out ways to cover themselves in case inflation is different from what it has been in the past. That may mean spending a longer time working out more complicated contracts for employment, for purchases of goods in the future, and for purchases of raw materials.

Inflation requires that price lists be changed. This is called the **repricing**, or **menu**, **cost of inflation**. The higher the rate of inflation, the higher the repricing cost of inflation. Imagine the repricing cost of Argentina's rapid inflation in 1989 compared to that in Canada, where the average inflation rate rarely reaches double digits.

Another major problem with inflation is that usually it does not proceed perfectly evenly. Consequently, the rate of inflation is not exactly what people anticipate. When this is so, the purchasing power of money changes in unanticipated

▶ **Cost-of-living adjustments (COLAs)**
Clauses in contracts that allow for increases in specified nominal values to take account of changes in the cost of living.

▶ **Real income**
The purchasing power of money after the effects of inflation have been taken into account.

▶ **Repricing, or menu, cost of inflation**
The cost associated with recalculating prices and printing new price lists when there is inflation.

ways. Because money is what we use as the measuring rod of the value of transactions we undertake, we have a more difficult time figuring out what we have really paid for things. As a result, resources tend to be misallocated in such situations because people have not really valued them accurately.

Think of any period during which you have to pay a higher price for something that was cheaper before. You are annoyed. But every time you pay a higher price, that represents the receipt of higher income for someone else. Therefore, it is impossible for all of us to be worse off because of rising prices. There are numerous costs to inflation, but they aren't the ones commonly associated with inflation. One way to think of inflation is that it is simply a *change in the accounting system*. One year the price of fast-food hamburgers averages $1; 10 years later the price of fast-food hamburgers averages $2. Clearly, $1 doesn't mean the same thing 10 years later. If we changed the name of our unit of account each year so that one year we paid $1 for fast-food hamburgers and 10 years later we paid, say, 1 peso, this lesson would be driven home.

Try Preview Question 3:
Who is hurt by inflation?

Concepts in Brief

- Whenever inflation is greater than anticipated, creditors lose and debtors gain. Whenever the rate of inflation is less than anticipated, creditors gain and debtors lose.
- Holders of cash lose during periods of inflation because the purchasing power of their cash depreciates at the rate of inflation.
- Households and businesses spend resources in attempting to protect themselves against unanticipated inflation, thus imposing a resource cost on the economy whenever there is unanticipated inflation.

▶ **Business fluctuations**
The ups and downs in overall business activity, as evidenced by changes in national income, employment, and the price level.

▶ **Expansion**
A business fluctuation in which overall business activity is rising at a more rapid rate than previously, or at a more rapid rate than the overall historical trend for the nation.

▶ **Contraction**
A business fluctuation during which the pace of national economic activity is slowing down.

CHANGING INFLATION AND UNEMPLOYMENT: BUSINESS FLUCTUATIONS

Some years unemployment goes up, others it goes down. Some years there is a lot of inflation, other years there isn't. We have fluctuations in all aspects of our macroeconomy. The ups and downs in economywide economic activity are sometimes called **business fluctuations**. When business fluctuations are positive, they are called **expansions**—speedups in the pace of national economic activity. The opposite of an expansion is a **contraction**, which is a slowdown in the pace of national economic activity. The top of an expansion is usually called its *peak*, and the bottom of a contraction is usually called its *trough*. Business fluctuations used to be called *business cycles*, but that term no longer seems appropriate because *cycle* implies predetermined or automatic recurrence, and we certainly haven't had automatic recurrent fluctuations in general business and economic activity. What we have had are contractions and expansions that vary greatly in length. Looking back at Figure 7.6, you can see

Figure 7.7

The Typical Course of Business Fluctuations

An idealized business cycle would go from peak to trough and back again in a regular cycle.

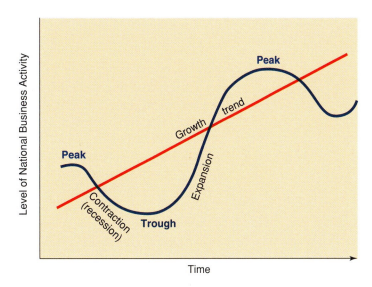

that recessions (deflations) and expansions (inflations) varied in length. The inflation beginning with the OPEC crisis and continuing to the 1981 recession was a period of "stagflation" where both prices and unemployment increased.

If the contractionary phase of business fluctuations becomes severe enough, we call it a **recession**. An extremely severe recession is called a **depression**. Typically, at the beginning of a recession, interest rates rise, and as the recession gets worse, they fall. At the same time, people's income starts to fall and the duration of unemployment increases, so that the unemployment rate increases. In times of expansion, the opposite occurs.

In Figure 7.7, you see that typical business fluctuations occur around a growth trend in overall national business activity shown as a straight upward-sloping line. Starting out at a peak, the economy goes into a contraction (recession). Then an expansion starts that moves up to its peak, higher than the last one, and the sequence starts over again.

Explaining Business Fluctuations: External Shocks

As you might imagine, because changes in national business activity affect everyone, economists for decades have attempted to understand and explain business fluctuations. For years, one of the most obvious explanations has been external events that tend to disrupt the economy. In many of the graphs in this chapter, you have seen that World War I and World War II were critical points in this country's economic history. A war is certainly an external shock—something that originates outside our economy.

Other examples of external shocks, particularly for an agrarian nation, have to do with abrupt changes in the weather. Long-term drought tended to create downturns in national business activity when the majority of Canadians worked on farms. Today,

▶ **Recession**

A period of time during which the rate of growth of business activity is consistently less than its long-term trend, or is negative.

▶ **Depression**

An extremely severe recession.

Try Preview Question 4:

How do we describe the phases of national business fluctuations?

major droughts or floods usually affect specific regions of the Canadian economy. Even if a drought dramatically affected one area, it would rarely cause a national economic downturn.

In the 1970s, due to actions on the part of certain countries in the Middle East, Canada received an "oil shock." The price of oil increased dramatically then, and some economists argue that this had a major effect on national economic activity.

It is not enough for us to say simply that business downturns are caused by external shocks. In the first place, if that were the only determinant of recessions, there would be little reason to study macroeconomics. Second, we know that historically we have had business recessions in the absence of any external shocks. We therefore need a theory of why national economic activity changes. This book develops a series of models that will help you understand the ups and downs of our business fluctuations.

Concepts in Brief

- The ups and downs in economywide business activity are called business fluctuations, which consist of expansions and contractions in overall business activity.
- The lowest point of a contraction is called the trough; the highest point of an expansion is called the peak.
- A recession is a downturn in business activity that lasts for some length of time.
- One possible explanation for business fluctuations relates to external shocks, such as wars, dramatic increases in the price of oil, floods, and droughts.

Issues and Applications

The Policy Effects of Changes in the CPI

Concepts Applied: CPI, cost-of-living indexes, COLAs

Old age security benefits increase quarterly using the CPI to adjust for inflation. Changes in the CPI would have a real effect on the amount recipients receive in their monthly cheques.

In the past, it seemed as if only economists and government statisticians were worried about whether the government accurately measured the consumer price index (CPI). There have always been theoretical arguments about the inability of Statistics Canada to take account of product quality changes as well as the changing mix of products and services purchased by the average Canadian family. If, in response to these and other arguments, changes are made in the way the CPI is measured, it is likely the CPI will show inflation to be somewhat less than would otherwise have been shown. Is this just a theoretical issue? The answer is a resounding no.

What Is Based on the CPI

Union and other contracts that relate to wages are often tied to changes in the CPI. Therefore, if the measured rate of inflation—the annual change in the CPI—turns out to be lower because of the new measurement techniques, such cost-of-living clauses will mean lower wage increases to union employees covered by them.

Old Age Security and the Income Tax Act

Old age pension payments would also be affected. Because pension benefits are often tied to changes in the CPI, a smaller increase in the CPI would reduce automatic increases in old age benefits. Our federal tax system is also in some small part a function of changes in the CPI. An increase in your income due to an increase in the CPI could put you in a higher tax bracket where you would pay more taxes. This is often referred to as "bracket creep."

In the End What Would It Mean?

If the average increase in the CPI were reduced by just 0.5 percent per year, the average old age pension recipient would receive about $3,000 less over the next 10 years. When all pension recipients are factored in, this would amount to a savings to the federal government of hundreds of millions of dollars over that same period. Similar calculations for other federal benefits like Employment Insurance tied to the CPI would yield an additional saving of perhaps a billion dollars.

For Critical Analysis

1. Does an incorrect measure of the CPI affect the way people lose or gain from unanticipated inflation?

2. Who would benefit from an improvement in the measurement of the CPI?

CHAPTER SUMMARY

1. The labour force consists of all persons who are employed plus those who are unemployed. Those over age 15 who are not in the labour force are full-time students, homemakers, and retired persons. The rate of unemployment is obtained by dividing the number of unemployed by the size of the labour force. If the duration of unemployment increases, the rate of unemployment also increases. Labour force participation rates have increased dramatically for women since World War II.

2. There are four types of unemployment in Canada: frictional, seasonal, structural, and cyclical. There is also wait unemployment, which is caused by wage rigidities, such as minimum wage laws and union contracts.

3. Frictional unemployment is caused by the temporary inability of workers to match their skills and talents with available jobs.

4. Structural unemployment occurs when there is a long-term mismatch, due to technological or geographical reasons, of available jobs and available skills.

5. Inflation occurs when the average of all prices of goods and services is rising; deflation occurs when the average of all prices is falling. During periods of inflation, the purchasing power of money falls (by definition).

6. The most commonly used measures of changes in general prices are the Consumer Price Index (CPI), the Producer Price Index (PPI), and the GDP deflator.

7. The nominal rate of interest includes the anticipated rate of inflation. Therefore, when anticipated inflation increases, nominal rates of interest will rise.

8. Whenever the actual rate of inflation turns out to exceed the anticipated rate of inflation, creditors lose and debtors gain because the latter are able to repay debts in cheaper dollars. Of course, if everybody anticipates rising prices, nominal interest rates will rise to take account of this future expected reduction in the purchasing power of the dollar.

9. Workers can protect themselves against inflation by having cost-of-living adjustment (COLA) clauses in their employment contracts.

10. Business fluctuations consist of expansions and contractions. Long contractions are called recessions, and a severe recession is called a depression. One explanation for changes in national economic activity relates to external shocks, such as earthquakes, droughts, floods, wars, and dramatic increases in the price of oil.

DISCUSSION OF PREVIEW QUESTIONS

1. Why is frictional unemployment not necessarily harmful?

Because imperfect information exists in the real world, at any given time some people seeking jobs won't be matched with job vacancies. Given imperfect information, frictional unemployment indicates that the economy is reacting to changes in relative demands and supplies in different sectors. Moreover, frictional unemployment occurs when people climb up the occupational ladder. Thus frictional unemployment is not necessarily harmful to society (or to the individuals involved), and hence the overall unemployment percentage may be a misleading statistic.

2. Does it matter whether inflation is anticipated or not?

Whether inflation is anticipated or not is important to households and firms. When everyone fully and correctly anticipates the rate of future inflation, all contracts will take account of the declining purchasing power of the dollar. Debtors will not be able to gain at the expense of creditors, and employers will not be able to fool employees into agreeing to accept wage increases that do not have an inflationary factor built in. Only when inflation is not anticipated can it have unexpected negative effects on households and firms.

3. Who is hurt by inflation?

In periods of inflation, fixed-income groups are obviously hurt; however, because most retired people collect old age security payments that have increased more rapidly than the price level for the past quarter century, this point is easily overstressed. In periods of unanticipated inflation (or when the rate of inflation is more than that anticipated), creditors are hurt at the expense of borrowers, who gain. Also, people locked into long-term contracts to receive fixed nominal-money amounts (bondholders and other moneylenders, and some pensioners) are hurt if the rate of inflation is greater than they had anticipated. People who hold cash are also hurt by inflation; as prices rise, a given amount of cash buys less.

4. How do we describe the phases of national business fluctuations?

When business fluctuations are positive, they are called expansions, and when they are negative, they are called contractions. The top of the expansion is the peak, and the bottom is the trough. A long-lasting trough is called a recession. If a recession gets very serious, it is called a depression.

PROBLEMS

(Answers to the odd-numbered problems appear at the back of the book.)

7-1. Assume that your taxable income is $30,000 per year. Assume further that you are in the 17 percent tax bracket applied to all income from $0 to $30,000. If your taxable income increases to $30,001 per year, you will move into the 26 percent marginal tax bracket. Your boss gives you a raise equal to 4 percent. How much better off are you?

7-2. Assume that you are receiving employment benefits of $100 a week. You are offered a job that will pay you $150 a week before taxes. Assume further that you would have to pay 7 percent Employment Insurance, plus pension plan premiums, plus federal income taxes equal to 17 percent of your salary. What is the opportunity cost of remaining unemployed—that is, how much will it cost you to refuse the job offer?

7-3. Assume that the labour force consists of 100 people, and that every month five individuals become unemployed while five others who were unemployed find jobs.
a. What is the frictional unemployment rate?
b. What is the average duration of unemployment?

Now assume that the only type of unemployment in this economy is frictional.

c. What is the unemployment rate?

Suppose that a system of unemployment compensation is instituted, and the average duration of unemployment rises to two months.

d. What will the unemployment rate for this economy be now?

e. Does a higher unemployment rate necessarily mean that the economy is weaker or that labourers are worse off?

7-4. Suppose that a country has a labour force of 100 people. In January, Miller, Pulsinelli, and Hooper are unemployed; in February, those three find jobs but Stevenson, Conn, and Lee become unemployed. Suppose further that every month the previous three that were unemployed find jobs and three different people become unemployed.
a. What is this country's unemployment rate?
b. What is its frictional unemployment rate?
c. What is the average duration of unemployment?

7-5. a. Suppose that the nominal interest rate is currently 12 percent. If the anticipated inflation rate is zero, what is the real interest rate?
b. The anticipated inflation rate rises to 13 percent, while the nominal interest rate remains at 12 percent. Does it make sense to lend money under these circumstances?

7-6. An economic slump occurs and two things happen:
a. Many people stop looking for work because they know that the probability of finding a job is low.
b. Many people who become laid off start doing such work at home as growing food and painting and repairing their houses and autos.

Which of these events implies that the official unemployment rate overstates unemployment, and which implies the opposite?

7-7. Columns 1 and 3 in the table show employment and the price level in the economy.

(1) Employment (millions of workers)	(2) Unemployment Rate (%)	(3) Price Level	(4) Rate of Inflation (%)
9.0		1.00	N.A.
9.1		1.08	
9.2		1.17	
9.3		1.28	
9.4		1.42	
9.5		1.59	
9.6		1.81	
9.7		2.10	

a. Assume that the labour force in the economy is 10 million. Compute and enter in column 2 the unemployment rate at each level of employment. (Hint: Divide the number of workers unemployed by the labour force.)

b. For each row (except the first), compute and enter in column 4 the rate of inflation.

7-8. Visit Statistics Canada's economic statistics Web site at http://www.statcan.ca/english/Pgdb/Economy/econom.htm and answer the following questions.

a. Under Labour market, choose "Labour force, employment and unemployment." Calculate the employment rate (not the unemployment rate) for the most recent year. Use the same formula we used to calculate the unemployment rate, but substitute the number of people employed for the number of people unemployed.

b. Under Prices, choose "Consumer price index, 1996 classification, annual average all-items indexes, Canada, historical summary." What was the rate of inflation between 1995 and 1997? (Note: This calculation spans two years so it is not an *annual* rate of inflation.)

INTERACTING WITH THE INTERNET

It can be confusing to access Canadian macroeconomic data because they are published and placed on the Internet by several different agencies. However, many of them place each other's data on the Internet, so you can often run across summary and press releases by chance. One major site is Statistics Canada,

http://www.statcan.ca/

its "The Economy,"

http://www.statcan.ca/Documents/English/Pgdb/economy.htm

and "The Daily,"

http://www.statcan.ca/Daily/English/today/daily.htm

are likely to be of most interest. The Daily covers the CPI and Labour Force Survey as well as selected additional topics in each issue. It also has on-line archives.

Measuring the Economy's Performance

It is referred to as "underground," "grey," "subterranean," "informal," "off-the-books," or "unofficial." Whatever it is called, the underground economy exists in a big way in Canada, and in an even bigger way in Latin America, Europe, and elsewhere. Have you ever bought a cheap umbrella or a pair of earrings from a street vendor? If so, both you and the vendor were partaking in the underground economy. If you have ever done odd jobs and been paid in cash or paid someone else in cash to do odd jobs for you, you have participated in the underground economy. How big is this part of the nation's total economic activity? How distorted are official statistics that measure our nation's performance? To understand and answer these questions, you need to know about how the government officially measures the economy's performance each year.

Preview Questions

1. What is gross domestic product (GDP), and what does it measure?

2. Why are only *final* goods and services evaluated in deriving GDP?

3. Why must depreciation and indirect business taxes less subsidies be added to national income at factor cost in order to derive GDP via the income approach?

4. How does correcting GDP for changes in the price level and population improve the usefulness of GDP estimates?

▶**National income accounting**

A measurement system used to estimate national income and its components; one approach to measuring an economy's aggregate performance.

Did You Know That... whenever a single person who is currently paying a housekeeper marries that housekeeper, government statistics show that the economy's performance has declined? The reason for this seeming anomaly is that government statisticians do not yet consider unpaid housework as contributing to the total annual national income of the country (even though the same services would have to be purchased if not provided free of charge). In spite of such measurement problems, the statistics about the nation's economic performance are watched closely throughout the year by investors, bankers, businesspeople, and macroeconomic policymakers. After all, most people like to know where they stand financially at the end of each month or year. Why shouldn't we have similar information about the economy as a whole? The way we do this is by using what has become known as **national income accounting,** the main focus of this chapter.

But first we need to revisit the flow of income within an economy, for it is the flow of goods and services from businesses to consumers and payments from consumers to businesses that constitute economic activity.

THE SIMPLE CIRCULAR FLOW

The concept of a circular flow of income (ignoring taxes) involves two principles:

1. In every economic exchange, the seller receives exactly the same amount that the buyer spends.
2. Goods and services flow in one direction and money payments flow in the other.

In the simple economy shown in Figure 8.1, there are only businesses and households. It is assumed that businesses sell their *entire* output *immediately* to households, and that households spend their *entire* income *immediately* on consumer products. Households receive their income by selling the use of whatever factors of production they own, such as labour services.

Profits Explained

We have indicated in Figure 8.1 that profit is a cost of production. You might be under the impression that profits are not part of the cost of producing goods and services; but profits are indeed a part of this cost because entrepreneurs must be rewarded for providing their services or they won't provide them. Their reward, if any, is profit. The reward—the profit—is included in the cost of the factors of production. If there were no expectations of profit, entrepreneurs would not incur the risk associated with the organization of productive activities. That is why we consider profits a cost of doing business.

Total Income or Total Output

▶ **Total income**

The yearly amount earned by the nation's resources (factors of production). Total income therefore includes wages, rents, interest and profits that are received, respectively, by workers, land-owners, capital owners, and entrepreneurs.

▶ **Final goods and services**

Goods and services that are at their final stage of production and will not be transformed into yet other goods or services. For example, wheat is normally not a final good because usually it is used to make bread, which is a final good.

The arrow that goes from businesses to households at the bottom of Figure 8.1 is labelled "Total income." What would be a good definition of **total income?** If you answered "the total of all individuals' income," you would be right. But all income is actually a payment for something, whether it be wages paid for labour services, rent paid for the use of land, interest paid for the use of capital, or profits paid to entrepreneurs. It is the amount paid to the resource suppliers. Therefore, total income is also defined as the annual *cost* of producing the entire output of **final goods and services.**

The arrow at the top of the figure, going from households to businesses, represents the dollar value of output in the economy. This is equal to the total monetary value of all final goods and services for this simple economy. In essence, it represents the total business receipts from the sale of all final goods and services produced by businesses and consumed by households. Business receipts are the opposite side of household expenditures. When households purchase goods and services with money, that money becomes a *business receipt*. Every transaction, therefore, simultaneously involves an expenditure as well as a receipt.

Figure 8.1
The Circular Flow of Income and Product

Businesses provide final goods and services to households (upper clockwise loop), who in turn pay for them with money (upper counterclockwise loop). Money flows in a counterclockwise direction and can be thought of as a circular flow. The dollar value of output is identical to total income because profits are defined as being equal to total business receipts minus business outlays for wages, rents, and interest.

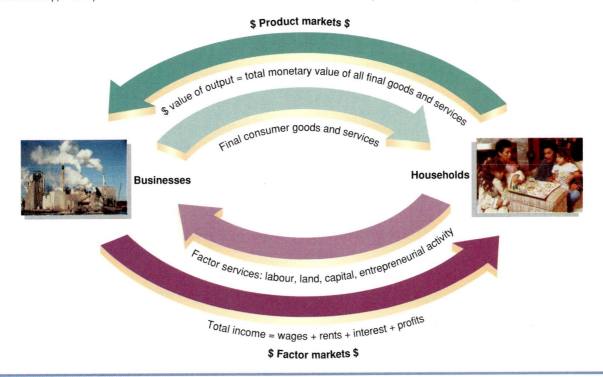

Product Markets. Transactions in which households buy goods take place in the product markets—that's where households are the buyers and businesses are the sellers of consumer goods. *Product market* transactions are represented in the upper loops in Figure 8.1. Note that consumer goods and services flow to household demanders, while money flows in the opposite direction to business suppliers.

Factor Markets. *Factor market* transactions are represented by the lower loops in Figure 8.1. In the factor market, households are the sellers; they sell resources such as labour, land, capital, and entrepreneurial ability. Businesses are the buyers in factor markets; business expenditures represent receipts or, more simply, income for households. Also, in the lower loops of Figure 8.1, factor services flow from households to businesses, while the money paid for these services flows in the opposite direction from businesses to households. Observe also the circular flow of money (counterclockwise) from households to businesses and back again from businesses to households; it is an endless circular flow.

Why the Dollar Value of Total Output Must Equal Total Income

Total income represents the income received by households in payment for the production of goods and services. Why must total income be identical to the dollar value of total output? First, as Figure 8.1 shows, spending by one group is income to another. Second, it is a matter of simple accounting and the economic definition of profit as a cost of production. Profit is defined as what is *left over* from total business receipts after all other costs—wages, rents, interest—have been paid. If the dollar value of total output is $1,000 and the total of wages, rent, and interest for producing that output is $900, profit is $100. Profit is always the *residual* item that makes total income equal to the dollar value of total output.

Concepts in Brief

- In the circular flow model of income and output, households sell factor services to businesses that pay for those factor services. The receipt of payments is total income. Businesses sell goods and services to households that pay for them.
- The dollar value of total output is equal to the total monetary value of all final goods and services produced.
- The dollar value of final output must always equal total income.

NATIONAL INCOME ACCOUNTING

We have already mentioned that policymakers need information about the state of the national economy. Historical statistical records on the performance of the national economy aid economists in testing their theories about how the economy really works. National income accounting is therefore important. Let's start with the most commonly presented statistic on the national economy.

Gross Domestic Product

▶ **Gross domestic product (GDP)**

The total market value of all final goods and services produced by factors of production located within a country's borders.

Gross domestic product (GDP) represents the total market value of the country's annual final product, or output, produced per year by factors of production located within national borders. We therefore formally define GDP as the total market value of all final goods and services produced in an economy during a year. We are referring here to a *flow of production*. A country produces at a certain rate, just as you receive income at a certain rate. Your income flow might be at a rate of $5,000 per year or $50,000 per year. Suppose you are told that someone earns $500. Would you consider this a good salary? There is no way to answer that question unless you know whether the person is earning $500 per month or per week or per day. Thus you have to specify a time period for all flows. Income received is a flow. You must contrast this with, for example, your total accumulated savings, which is a stock measured at a point in time, not across time. Implicit in just about everything we deal with in this chapter is a time period—usually one year. All the measures of domestic product and income are specified as rates measured in dollars per year.

Try Preview Question 1:

What is gross domestic product (GDP), and what does it measure?

Stress on Final Output

▶ **Intermediate goods**

Goods used up entirely in the production of final goods.

GDP does not count **intermediate goods** (goods used up entirely in the production of final goods) because to do so would be to count them twice. For example, even though grain that a farmer produces may be that farmer's final product, it is not the final product for the nation. It is sold to make bread. Bread is the final product.

We can use a numerical example to clarify this point further. Our example will involve determining the **value added** at each stage of production. Value added is the amount of dollar value contributed to a product at each stage of its production. In Table 8.1 (page 194) we see the difference between total value of all sales and value added in the production of a donut. We also see that the sum of the values added is equal to the sale price to the final consumer. It is the 15 cents that is used to measure GDP, not the 32 cents. If we used the 32 cents, we would be double-counting from stages 2 through 5, for each intermediate good would be counted at least twice—once when it was produced and again when the good it was used in making was sold. Such double-counting would grossly exaggerate GDP.

▶ **Value added**

The dollar value of an industry's sales minus the value of intermediate goods (for example, raw materials and parts) used in production.

Try Preview Question 2:

Why are only *final* goods and services evaluated in deriving GDP?

Exclusion of Financial Transactions, Transfer Payments, and Secondhand Goods

Remember that GDP is the measure of the value of all final goods and services produced in one year. Many more transactions occur that have nothing to do with final goods and services produced. There are financial transactions, transfers of the ownership of pre-existing goods, and other transactions that should not and do not get included in our measure of GDP.

Table 8.1
Sales Value and Value Added at Each Stage of Donut Production

(1) Stage of Production	(2) Dollar Value of Sales	(3) Value Added
Stage 1: Fertilizer and seed	$.01] _____	$.01
Stage 2: Growing	.02] _____	.01
Stage 3: Milling	.04] _____	.02
Stage 4: Baking	.10] _____	.06
Stage 5: Retailing	.15] _____	.05
Total dollar value of all sales $.32		Total value added $.15

Stage 1: A farmer purchases a penny's worth of fertilizer and seed, which are used as factors of production in growing wheat.

Stage 2: The farmer grows the wheat, harvests it, and sells it to a miller for 2 cents. Thus we see that the farmer has added 1 cent's worth of value. That 1 cent represents income paid to the farmer.

Stage 3: The miller purchases the wheat for 2 cents and adds 2 cents as the value added; that is, there is 2 cents for the miller as income. The miller sells the ground wheat flour to a donut-baking company.

Stage 4: The donut-baking company buys the flour for 4 cents and adds 6 cents as the value added. It then sells the donut to the final retailer.

Stage 5: The donut retailer sells fresh hot donuts at 15 cents apiece, thus creating an additional value of 5 cents.

We see that the total value of sales resulting from the production of one donut was 32 cents, but the total value added was 15 cents, which is exactly equal to the retail price. The total value added is equal to the sum of all income payments.

Financial Transactions. There are three general categories of purely financial transactions: (1) the buying and selling of securities, (2) government transfer payments, and (3) private transfer payments.

1. **Securities.** When you purchase a share of existing stock in the Bank of Nova Scotia, someone else has sold it to you. In essence, there was merely a *transfer* of ownership rights. You paid $100 to obtain the share certificate. Someone else received the $100 and gave up the share certificate. No producing activity took place at that time. Hence the $100 transaction is not included when we measure gross domestic product.

2. **Government transfer payments.** Transfer payments are payments for which no productive services are provided in exchange at the same time. The most obvious government transfer payments are old age security benefits, veterans' payments, and unemployment compensation. The recipients make no contribution to current production in return for such transfer payments (although they may have made contributions in the past to receive them). Government transfer payments are not included in GDP.

3. **Private transfer payments.** Are you receiving money from your parents in order to live at school? Has a wealthy relative ever given you a gift of money? If so, you have been the recipient of a private transfer payment. This is merely a transfer of funds from one individual to another. As such, it does not constitute productive activity and is not included in gross domestic product.

Transfer of Secondhand Goods. If I sell you my two-year-old minivan, no current production is involved. I transfer to you the ownership of a vehicle that was produced two years ago; in exchange, you transfer to me $10,000. The original purchase price of the minivan was included in GDP in the year I purchased it. To include it again when I sell it to you would be counting the value of the van a second time.

Other Excluded Transactions. Many other transactions are not included in GDP for practical reasons:

1. Household production—home cleaning, child care, and other tasks performed by people within their own households and for which they are not paid through the marketplace
2. Otherwise legal underground transactions—those that are legal but not reported and hence not taxed, such as paying housekeepers in cash that is not declared as income
3. Illegal underground activities—these include prostitution, illegal gambling, and the sale of illicit drugs

You will learn more about the size of the underground economy in this and other countries in the Issues and Applications section at the end of this chapter. Right now, let's consider some suggestions for measuring unpaid household production.

POLICY EXAMPLE Measuring Household Production

In the 1980s, the Decade for Women World Conference passed a resolution calling for all nations to include the unpaid contributions of women in GDP calculations. At least two countries, France and Norway, have started to release "satellite" GDP figures that incorporate estimates of unpaid household production. Australia and Germany are studying a similar procedure, as is Canada.

Of course, any estimate of unremunerated household work has serious problems. For instance, parents do housework, raise children, and cook meals while others volunteer to look after seniors and help the disadvantaged. All of these tasks could be accomplished through market forces, which would then make them part of GDP. But the puzzle has been—how can this work be valued? Is housework a minimum wage job, in which case we could just count up the number of hours spent doing housework and multiply them by the minimum wage? Or should we look at the opportunity cost of housework? If someone who would make $20 per hour working at an "outside" job does housework instead, should that housework be valued at the $20 per hour rate, or at the minimum wage rate?

Another problem concerns the quality of household work. Some homemakers serve fabulous gourmet meals while others warm up canned and frozen foods. Should they be valued equally? Yet another difficulty lies in knowing where to stop counting: A person can hire a valet to help him or her get dressed in the morning. Should we therefore count the time spent getting dressed as part of unpaid household work? Both men and women perform services around the house every day of the year. Should all of these unpaid services be included in a new measurement of GDP?

In 1995, Statistics Canada published a study called *Households' Unpaid Work: Measurement and Valuation*, in which it estimated that Canadians of working age performed up to 25 billion hours of unpaid work in 1992. This figure is 23 percent more than the number of paid hours worked that same year. Convert this figure to 40 hours-per-week, 49 weeks-per-year jobs, and you'll find that Canadians are collectively doing the unpaid work of 730,000 people!

The dollar estimates of the value of this unpaid work vary greatly, largely because of the measuring problems we discuss above. The lowest estimate of its value in 1992 was $235 billion; the highest was $374 billion. If this amount were added to GDP, nominal GDP would be 34 percent to 54 percent larger.

The Canadian government is not yet ready to include a measure of unpaid work in GDP. But it did include questions in the 1996 Census about the amount of non-market work done by women. This may be a first step towards putting a dollar value on this recognized but uncounted source of labour in the Canadian economy.

For critical analysis: In general, which countries would have the smallest amount of unpaid household production? (Hint: Think about labour force participation rates.)

Concepts in Brief

- GDP is the total market value of final goods and services produced in an economy during a one-year period by factors of production within the country's borders. It represents the flow of production over that one-year period.
- To avoid double-counting, we look only at final goods and services produced or, alternatively, at value added.
- In measuring GDP, we must exclude (1) purely financial transactions, such as the buying and selling of securities; (2) government transfer payments and private transfer payments; and (3) the transfer of secondhand goods.
- Many other transactions are excluded from GDP, among them household services rendered by homemakers, underground economy transactions, and illegal economic activities.

TWO MAIN METHODS OF MEASURING GDP

If the definition of GDP is the total value of all final goods and services produced during a year, then to measure GDP we could add up the prices times the quantities of every individual commodity produced. But this would involve a monumental, if not impossible, task for government statisticians.

▶ **Expenditure approach**
A way of computing national income by adding up the dollar value at current market prices of all final goods and services.

The circular flow diagram presented in Figure 8.1 gives us a shortcut method for calculating GDP. We can look at the *flow of expenditures*, which consists of consumption, investment, government purchases of goods and services, and net expenditures in the foreign sector (net exports). This is called the **expenditure approach**

▶ **Income approach**
A way of measuring national income by adding up all components of national income, including wages, interest, rent, and profits.

▶ **Durable consumer goods**
Consumer goods that have a life span of more than three years.

▶ **Nondurable consumer goods**
Consumer goods that are used up within three years.

▶ **Services**
Mental or physical labour or help purchased by consumers. Examples are the assistance of doctors, lawyers, dentists, repair personnel, housecleaners, educators, retailers, and wholesalers; things purchased or used by consumers that do not have physical characteristics.

▶ **Gross private domestic investment**
The creation of capital goods, such as factories and machines, that can yield production and hence consumption in the future. Also included in this definition are changes in business inventories and repairs made to machines or buildings.

▶ **Investment**
Any use of today's resources to expand tomorrow's production or consumption.

▶ **Producer durables, or capital goods**
Durable goods having an expected service life of more than three years that are used by businesses to produce other goods and services.

▶ **Fixed investment**
Purchases by businesses of newly produced producer durables, or capital goods, such as production machinery and office equipment.

to measuring GDP, in which we add the dollar value of all final goods and services. We could also use the *flow of income*, looking at the income received by everybody producing goods and services. This is called the **income approach**, in which we add the income received by all factors of production.

Deriving GDP by the Expenditure Approach

To derive GDP using the expenditure approach, we must look at each of the separate components of expenditures and then add them together. These components are: consumption expenditures, investment, government expenditures, and net exports.

Consumption Expenditures. How do we spend our income? As households or as individuals, we spend our income through consumption expenditure *(C)*, which falls into three categories: **durable consumer goods, nondurable consumer goods**, and **services**. Durable goods are *arbitrarily* defined as items that last more than three years; they include automobiles, furniture, and household appliances. Nondurable goods are all the rest, such as food and gasoline. Services are intangible commodities: medical care, education, and so on.

Housing expenditures constitute a major proportion of anybody's annual expenditures. Rental payments on apartments are automatically included in consumption expenditure estimates. People who own their homes, however, do not make rental payments. Consequently, government statisticians estimate what is called the *implicit rental value* of owner-occupied homes. It is equal to the amount of rent you would have to pay if you did not own the home but were renting it from someone else.

Gross Private Domestic Investment. We now turn our attention to **gross private domestic investment** *(I)* undertaken by businesses. When economists refer to investment, they are referring to additions to productive capacity. **Investment** may be thought of as an activity that uses resources today in such a way that they allow for greater production in the future and hence greater consumption in the future. When a business buys new equipment or puts up a new factory, it is investing; it is increasing its capacity to produce in the future.

The layperson's notion of investment often relates to the purchase of stocks and bonds. For our purposes, such transactions simply represent the *transfer of ownership* of assets called stocks and bonds. Thus you must keep in mind the fact that in economics, investment refers *only* to additions to productive capacity, not to transfers of assets.

In our analysis, we will consider the basic components of investment. We have already mentioned the first one, which involves a firm buying equipment or putting up a new factory. These are called **producer durables**, or **capital goods**. A producer durable, or a capital good, is simply a good that is purchased not to be consumed in its current form but to be used to make other goods and services. The purchase of equipment and factories—capital goods—is called **fixed investment**.

The other type of investment has to do with the change in inventories of raw materials and finished goods. Firms do not immediately sell off all their products to consumers. Some of this final product is usually held in inventory waiting to be sold. Firms hold inventories to meet future expected orders for their products. When a firm

▶ **Inventory investment**
Changes in the stocks of finished goods and goods in process, as well as changes in the raw materials that businesses keep on hand. Whenever inventories are decreasing, inventory investment is negative; whenever they are increasing, inventory investment is positive.

increases its inventories of finished products, it is engaging in **inventory investment**. Inventories consist of all finished goods on hand, goods in process, and raw materials.

The reason that we can think of a change in inventories as being a type of investment is that an increase in such inventories provides for future increased consumption possibilities. When inventory investment is zero, the firm is neither adding to nor subtracting from the total stock of goods or raw materials on hand. Thus if the firm keeps the same amount of inventories throughout the year, inventory *investment* has been zero.

In estimating gross private domestic investment, government statisticians also add consumer expenditures on *new* residential structures because new housing represents an addition to our future productive capacity in the sense that a new house can generate housing services in the future.

Government Expenditures.

In addition to personal consumption expenditures, there are government purchases of goods and services *(G)*. The government buys goods and services from private firms and pays wages and salaries to government employees. Generally, we value goods and services at the prices at which they are sold. But many government goods and services are not sold in the market. Therefore, we cannot use their market value when computing GDP. The value of these goods is considered equal to their cost. For example, the value of a newly built road is considered equal to its construction cost and is included in the GDP for the year it was built.

Net Exports (Foreign Expenditures).

To get an accurate representation of gross domestic product, we must include the foreign sector. As Canadians, we purchase foreign goods called *imports*. The goods that foreigners purchase from us are our *exports*. To get an idea of the *net* expenditures from the foreign sector, we subtract the value of imports from the value of exports to get net exports (*X*) for a year:

$$\text{Net exports }(X) = \text{total exports} - \text{total imports}$$

To understand why we subtract imports rather than ignoring them altogether, consider that we are using the expenditures approach. If we want to estimate *domestic* output, we have to subtract Canadian expenditures on the goods of other nations.

Thinking Critically About the Media   Avoiding GDP Mania

Every quarter, the federal government publishes its estimates of the rate of growth of real GDP for the previous quarter on an annualized basis. If, for example, GDP corrected for inflation was estimated to increase by one-half of 1 percent, the government would announce a first-quarter growth rate of 2 percent per year. Once these statistics are announced, journalists have a field day analysing whether the economy is growing, not growing, slowing down, head-

ing for a soft landing, overheating, and so on. The problem with these initial quarterly statistics is that they are often wrong. On occasion, quarterly annualized GDP growth rates have been corrected a month later by as much as 75 percent! Consequently, it is a good idea to wait a few months and to examine only revised GDP statistics from Statistics Canada.

Mathematical Representation Using the Expenditure Approach

We have just defined the components of GDP using the expenditure approach. When we add them all together, we get a definition for GDP, which is as follows:

$$GDP = C + I + G + X$$

where

C = consumption expenditures
I = investment expenditures
G = government expenditures
X = net exports

The Historical Picture. To get an idea of the relationship among C, I, G, and X, look at Figure 8.2, which shows gross domestic product, personal consumption expenditures, government purchases, and gross private domestic investment plus net exports from 1926 to 1997. When we add up the expenditures of the household, business, government, and foreign sectors, we get GDP.

Figure 8.2
Seventy Years of GDP and Its Components

Here we see a display of gross domestic product, personal consumption expenditures, government purchases, gross private domestic investment and net exports for the years 1926–1997. Actually, during the Great Depression of the 1930s, gross private domestic investment decreased dramatically, pulling down GDP with it. Because of the scale of the figure the huge drop in investment spending is not immediately obvious.

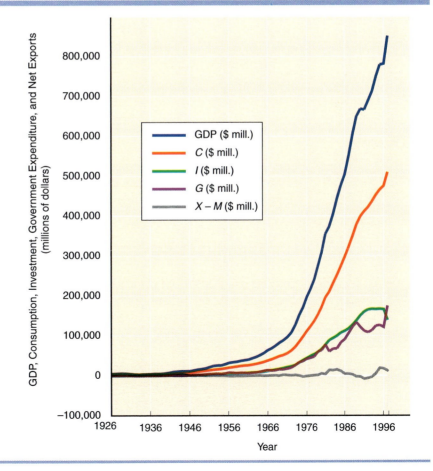

▶ **Depreciation**

Reduction in the value of capital goods over a one-year period due to physical wear and tear and also to obsolescence; also called *capital consumption allowance.*

▶ **Net domestic product (NDP)**

GDP minus depreciation.

▶ **Capital consumption allowance**

Another name for depreciation, the amount that businesses would have to save in order to take care of the deterioration of machines and other equipment.

Depreciation and Net Domestic Product.   We have used the terms *gross domestic product* and *gross private domestic investment* without really indicating what *gross* means. The dictionary defines it as "without deductions," as opposed to *net.* Deductions for what, you might ask. The deductions are for something we call **depreciation**. In the course of a year, machines and structures wear out or are used up in the production of domestic product. For example, houses deteriorate as they are occupied, and machines need repairs or they will fall apart and stop working. Most capital, or durable, goods depreciate. An estimate of this is subtracted from gross domestic product to arrive at a figure called **net domestic product (NDP)**, which we define as follows:

$$NDP = GDP - depreciation$$

Depreciation is also called **capital consumption allowance** because it is the amount of the capital stock that has been consumed over a one-year period. In essence, it equals the amount a business would have to put aside to repair and replace deteriorating machines. Because we know that

$$GDP = C + I + G + X$$

we know that the formula for NDP is

$$NDP = C + I + G + X - depreciation$$

Alternatively, because net $I = I -$ depreciation,

$$NDP = C + net\ I + G + X$$

▶ **Net investment**

Gross private domestic investment minus an estimate of the wear and tear on the existing capital stock. Net investment therefore measures the change in capital stock over a one-year period.

Net investment measures *changes* in our capital stock over time and is positive nearly every year. Because depreciation does not vary greatly from year to year as a percentage of GDP, we get a similar picture of what is happening to our national economy by looking at either NDP or GDP data.

Concepts in Brief

- The expenditure approach to measuring GDP requires that we add up consumption expenditures, gross private investment, government purchases, and net exports. Consumption expenditures include consumer durables, consumer nondurables, and services.
- Gross private domestic investment *excludes* transfers of asset ownership. It includes only additions to the productive capacity of a nation, repairs on existing capital goods, and changes in business inventories.
- We value government expenditures at their cost because we do not usually have market prices at which to value government goods and services.
- To obtain net domestic product (NDP), we subtract from GDP the year's depreciation of the existing capital stock.

Deriving GDP by the Income Approach

If you go back to the circular flow diagram in Figure 8.1, you see that product markets are at the top of the diagram and factor markets are at the bottom. We can calculate the value of the circular flow of income and product by looking at expenditures—which we just did—or by looking at total factor payments. Factor payments are called income. We calculate **gross domestic income (GDI)**, which we will see is identical to gross domestic product (GDP). Using the income approach, we calculate five categories of payments to individuals: wages, corporate profits before taxes, interest and investment income, farm and non-incorporated nonfarm business income, and an inventory valuation adjustment.

▶ **Gross domestic income (GDI)**

The sum of all income—wages, corporate profits before taxes, interest, farm and non-incorporated nonfarm income, and inventory valuation adjustment—paid to the four factors of production.

1. *Wages.* The most important category is, of course, wages, including salaries and other forms of labour income, such as income in kind, and incentive payments. We also count payroll deductions for Employment Insurance and pension plans (both the employees' and the employers' contributions), and other fringe benefits.
2. *Corporate Profits Before Taxes.* Businesses either pay out their profits before taxes to their shareholders, the households, or reinvest them in the business. Regardless of the distribution, these corporate profits are counted as income.
3. *Interest and investment income.* Here, interest payments do not equal the sum of all payments for the use of funds in a year. Instead, interest is expressed in net rather than in gross terms. Net interest received by households is the difference between the interest they receive (from savings accounts, certificates of deposit, and the like) and the interest they pay (to banks for mortgages, credit cards, and other loans).
4. *Farm and Non-incorporated Nonfarm Business Income.* This category includes income earned by owners of businesses who supply their own labour and capital to their businesses. It could also be referred to as "proprietors' income." Rent and imputed rents are also included here.
5. *Inventory Valuation Adjustment.* Our final category allows for an adjustment to corporate profits to account for price changes. If a business is holding inventory and inflation increases the market price of the business's output, the value of that output will not reflect its value when it was produced. This category is subtracted (in the case of inflation) from corporate profits to get a more accurate measure of new production.

All of the payments listed are *actual* factor payments made to owners of the factors of production. When we add them together, though, we do not yet have gross domestic income. We have to take account of two other components: **indirect business taxes less subsidies**, such as sales and business property taxes, and depreciation, which we have already discussed.

▶ **Indirect business taxes less subsidies**

All business taxes except the tax on corporate profits. Indirect business taxes include sales and business property taxes. Subsidies to business from government are subtracted because they represent a flow of taxes back to business.

Indirect Business Taxes Less Subsidies.

Indirect taxes are the (nonincome) taxes paid by consumers when they buy goods and services. When you buy a book, you pay the price of the book plus GST (or HST in the Atlantic provinces). The business is actually acting as the government's agent in collecting the sales tax, which it in turn passes on to the government. Such taxes therefore represent a business expense and are included in gross domestic income.

The government sometimes subsidizes a business by giving it money to help reduce its production costs. Since a subsidy returns to the business some of the taxes paid, we need to subtract the value of subsidies from indirect business taxes.

Depreciation.   Just as we had to deduct depreciation to get from GDP to NDP, so we must *add* depreciation to go from net domestic income to gross domestic income. Depreciation can be thought of as the portion of the current year's GDP that is used to replace physical capital consumed in the process of production. Because somebody has paid for the replacement, depreciation must be added as a component of gross domestic income.

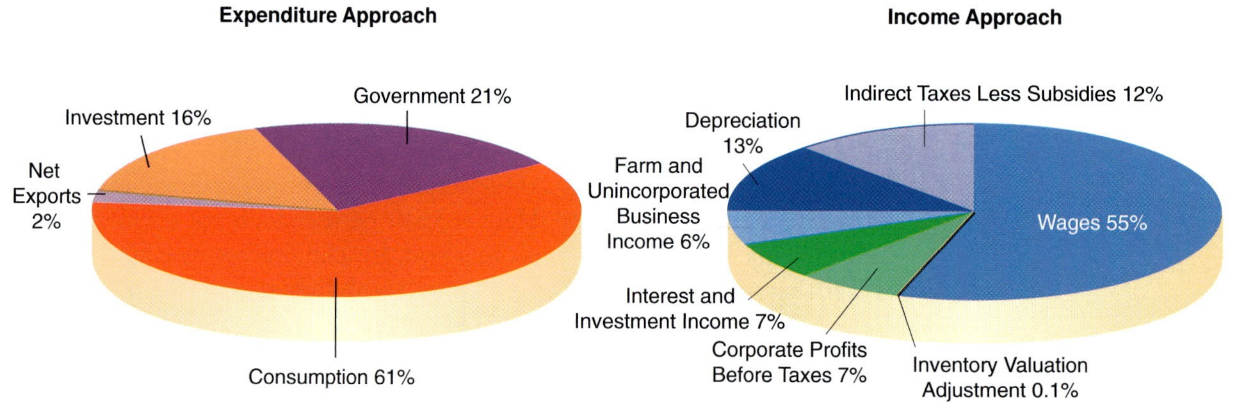

Try Preview Question 3:

Why must depreciation and indirect business taxes less subsidies be added to national income at factor cost in order to derive GDP via the income approach?

Expenditure Approach

Government 21%
Investment 16%
Net Exports 2%
Consumption 61%

Income Approach

Indirect Taxes Less Subsidies 12%
Depreciation 13%
Farm and Unincorporated Business Income 6%
Wages 55%
Interest and Investment Income 7%
Corporate Profits Before Taxes 7%
Inventory Valuation Adjustment 0.1%

Figure 8.3
Gross Domestic Product and Gross Domestic Income, 1997 (in millions of 1997 dollars per year)

By using the two different methods of computing the output of the economy, we come up with gross domestic product and gross domestic income, which are by definition equal. One approach focuses on expenditures, or the flow of product; the other approach concentrates on income, or the flow of costs.

Source: Statistics Canada.

Expenditure Point of View—Product Flow		Income Point of View—Cost Flow	
Expenditures by Different Sectors:		**Domestic Income (at Factor Cost):**	
Household sector		*Wages*	
Personal consumption expenses	$505,896	All wages, salaries, and supplemental employee compensation	$445,804
Government sector		*Corporate profits before taxes*	
Purchase of goods and services	186,705	All business profits earned prior to payment of taxes	85,695
Business sector		*Interest and investment income*	
Gross private domestic investment (including depreciation)	147,576	Payments on deposits and on loans	46,187
Foreign sector		*Farm and non-incorporated nonfarm business income*	
Net exports of goods and services	14,343	Income earned by small business owners and farmers	54,400
Statistical discrepancy	583	*Inventory valuation adjustment*	
		Change in value of inventory due to inflation during the year	−1,622
		Nonincome expense items	
		Indirect business taxes less subsidies	114,501
		Capital consumption allowance	110,722
		Statistical discrepancy	−584
Gross domestic product	$855,103	Gross domestic income	$855,103

▶ **Nonincome expense items**

The total of indirect business taxes less subsidies and depreciation.

The last two components of GDP—indirect business taxes less subsidies and depreciation—are called **nonincome expense items**.

Figure 8.3 shows a comparison between gross domestic product and gross domestic income for 1997. Whether you decide to use the expenditure approach or the income approach, you will come out with the same number. There are usually statistical discrepancies, but they are normally relatively small.

Concepts in Brief

- To derive GDP using the income approach, we add up all factor payments, including wages, corporate profits, interest and investment income, farm and non-incorporated nonfarm business income, and inventory valuation adjustment.
- To get an accurate estimate of GDP with this method, we must also add indirect business taxes less subsidies and depreciation to those total factor payments.

OTHER COMPONENTS OF NATIONAL INCOME ACCOUNTING

Gross domestic income or product does not really tell how much income people have access to for spending purposes. To get to those kinds of data, we must make some adjustments, which we now do.

National Income at Factor Cost (NI)

We know that net domestic product (NDP) represents the total market value of goods and services available for both consumption, used in a broader sense here to mean "resource exhaustion," and net additions to the economy's stock of capital. NDP does not, however, represent the income available to individuals within that economy because it includes indirect business taxes, such as sales taxes. We therefore deduct these indirect business taxes less subsidies from NDP to arrive at the figure for all factor income of resource owners. The result is what we define as **national income at factor cost (NI)**—income *earned* by the factors of production.

▶ **National income (NI)**

The total of all factor payments to resource owners. It can be obtained by subtracting indirect business taxes less subsidies from NDP.

Personal Income (PI)

National income does not actually represent what is available to individuals to spend—because some people obtain income for which they have provided no concurrent good or service, and others earn income but do not receive it. In the former category are mainly recipients of transfer payments from the government, such as old age security, welfare, and Employment Insurance benefits. These payments represent shifts of funds within the economy by way of the government, where no good or service is concurrently rendered in exchange. The other category, income earned but not received, consists primarily of corporate retained earnings. When transfer payments

▶ **Personal income (PI)**

The amount of income that households actually receive before they pay personal income taxes.

▶ **Disposable personal income (DPI)**

Personal income after personal income taxes have been paid.

are added and when income earned but not received is subtracted, we end up with **personal income (PI)**—income *received* by the factors of production prior to the payment of personal income taxes.

Disposable Personal Income (DPI)

Everybody knows that you do not get to take home all your salary. To get **disposable personal income (DPI),** we subtract all personal income taxes from personal income. This is the income that individuals have left for consumption and saving.

Deriving the Components of GDP

Table 8.2 takes you through the steps necessary to derive the various components of GDP. It shows how you go from gross domestic product to net domestic product, to national income at factor cost, to personal income, and then to disposable personal income.

We have completed our rundown of the different ways that GDP can be computed and of the different variants of national income and product. What we have not yet touched on is the difference between national income measured in this year's dollars, and national income representing real goods and services.

Table 8.2
Going from GDP to Disposable Income, 1997

	Millions of Dollars
Gross domestic product (GDP)	855,103
Minus depreciation	−110,722
Net domestic product (NDP)	744,381
Minus indirect business taxes less subsidies	−114,501
National income at factor cost (NI)	629,880
Minus corporate retained earnings	−44,926
Plus government transfer payments	+107,016
Personal income (PI)	691,970
Minus personal income tax and nontax payments	168,259
Disposable personal income (DPI)	523,711

Source: Statistics Canada.

Concepts in Brief

- To obtain national income, we subtract indirect business taxes less subsidies from net domestic product. National income gives us a measure of all factor payments to resource owners.
- To obtain personal income, we must add government transfer payments, such as old age security benefits and veterans' allowances. We must subtract income earned but not received by factor owners, such as corporate retained earnings, Employment Insurance premiums, and corporate income taxes.
- To obtain disposable personal income, we subtract all personal income taxes from personal income. Disposable personal income is income that individuals actually have for consumption or saving.

DISTINGUISHING BETWEEN NOMINAL AND REAL VALUES

So far we have shown how to measure nominal income and product. When we say "nominal," we are referring to income and product expressed in the current "face value" of today's dollar. Given the existence of inflation or deflation in the economy, we must also be able to distinguish between the **nominal values** that we will be looking at and the **real values** underlying them. Nominal values are expressed in current dollars. Real income involves our command over goods and services—purchasing power—and therefore depends on money income and a set of prices. Thus real income refers to nominal income corrected for changes in the weighted average of all prices. In other words, we must make an adjustment for changes in the price level. Consider an example. Nominal income per person in 1960 was only about $1,700 per year. In 1997, nominal income per person was just over $23,000. Were people really that badly off in 1960? No, for nominal income in 1960 is expressed in 1960 prices, not in the prices of today. In today's dollars, the per-person income of 1960 would be closer to $9,250, or almost 40 percent of today's income per person. This is a meaningful comparison between income in 1960 and income today. (The uncorrected 1960 data show per-person income to be only 8 percent of today's income.) Next we will show how we can translate nominal measures of income into real measures by using an appropriate price index, such as the CPI or the GDP deflator discussed in Chapter 7.

> ▶ **Nominal values**
> The values of variables such as GDP and investment expressed in current dollars, also called *money values;* measurement in terms of the actual market prices at which goods are sold.

> ▶ **Real values**
> Measurement of economic values after adjustments have been made for changes in the average of prices between years.

Correcting GDP for Price Changes

If a compact disc (CD) costs $15 this year, 10 CDs have a market value of $150. If next year a CD costs $20, the same 10 CDs will have a market value of $200. In this case, there is no increase in the total quantity of CDs, but the market value will have increased by one-third. Apply this to every single good and service produced and sold in Canada and you realize that changes in GDP, measured in *current* dollars, may not be a very useful indication of economic activity. If we are really interested in variations in the *real* output of the economy, we must correct GDP (and just about everything else we look at) for changes in the average of overall prices from year to year. Basically, we need first to generate an index that approximates the changes in average prices. We then must divide that estimate into the value of output in current dollars to adjust the value of output to what is called **constant dollars**, or dollars corrected for general price level changes. This price-corrected GDP is called *real GDP*.

> ▶ **Constant dollars**
> Dollars expressed in terms of real purchasing power using a particular year as the base or standard of comparison, in contrast to current dollars.

EXAMPLE   Correcting GDP for Price Level Changes, 1990–1997

Let's take a numerical example to see how we can adjust GDP for changes in prices. We must pick an appropriate price index in order to adjust for these price level changes. We mentioned the Consumer Price Index, the Producer Price Index, and the GDP deflator in Chapter 7. Let's use the GDP deflator to adjust our figures. Table 8.3 gives 8 years of GDP figures. Nominal GDP figures are shown in column 2. The price level index (GDP deflator) is in column 3, with base year of 1992 when the GDP deflator equals 100. Column 4 shows real (inflation-adjusted) GDP in 1992 dollars.

The formula for real GDP is

$$\text{Real GDP} = \frac{\text{nominal GDP}}{\text{price level}} \times 100$$

Table 8.3
Correcting GDP for Price Changes

To correct GDP for price changes, we first have to pick a price level index (the GDP deflator) with a specific year as its base. In our example, the base year is 1992; the price level index for that year is 100% = 1.00. To obtain 1992 constant-dollar GDP, we divide the price level index into nominal GDP. In other words, we divide column 3 into column 2 (and multiply by 100). This gives us column 4, which is a measure of real GDP expressed in 1992 purchasing power.

(1) Year	(2) Nominal GDP (billions of dollars per year)	(3) Price Level Index (base year 1992 = 100)	(4) = [(2)÷(3)] × 100 Real GDP (billions of dollars per year in constant 1992 dollars)
1990	669.5	96.0	697.4
1991	667.5	98.8	675.6
1992	690.1	100.0	690.1
1993	724.9	101.2	716.3
1994	762.3	102.4	744.4
1995	799.1	105.1	760.3
1996	820.3	106.6	769.5
1997	855.1	107.1	798.4

Source: Statistics Canada.

The step-by-step derivation of real (constant-dollar) GDP is as follows: The base year is 1992, so the price index must equal 100. In 1992, nominal GDP was $690.1 billion, and so too was real GDP expressed in 1992 dollars. In 1993, the price level increased to 101.2. Thus to correct 1993's nominal GDP for inflation, we divide the price index, 101.2, into the nominal GDP figure of $724.9 billion and then multiply it by 100. The result is $716.3 billion, which is 1993 GDP expressed in terms of the purchasing power of dollars in 1992. What about a situation when the price level is lower than in 1992? Look at 1991. Here the price index shown in column 3 is 98.8. That means that in 1991, the average of all prices was about 99 percent of prices in 1992. To obtain 1991 GDP expressed in terms of 1992 purchasing power, we divide nominal GDP, $667.5 billion, by 98.8 and then multiply by 100. The result is a larger number –$675.6 billion. Column 4 in Table 8.3 is a better measure of how the economy has performed than column 2, which shows nominal GDP changes.

For critical analysis: A few years ago, the base year for the GDP deflator was 1986. What does a change in the base year for the price level index affect?

Plotting Nominal and Real GDP

Nominal GDP and real GDP from 1970 to 1996 are plotted in Figure 8.4. Notice that there is quite a big gap between the two GDP figures, reflecting the amount of inflation that has occurred. Note further that the choice of a base year is arbitrary. We have chosen 1986 as the base year in our example. This happens to be a base year recently used by the government.

Per Capita GDP

Looking at changes in real gross domestic product may be deceiving, particularly if the population size has changed significantly. If real GDP over a 10-year period went up 100 percent, you might jump to the conclusion that the material well-being of the economy had increased by that amount. But what if during the same period population increased by 200 percent? Then what would you say? Certainly, the amount of real GDP per person, or *per capita real GDP*, would have fallen, even though total deflated (or real) GDP had risen. What we must do to account not only for price changes but also for population changes is first deflate GDP and then divide by the total population, doing this for each year. If we were to look at certain less developed countries, we would find that in many cases, even though real GDP has risen over the past several decades, per capita real GDP has remained constant or fallen because the population has grown just as rapidly or more quickly.

Figure 8.4
Nominal and Real GDP

Here we plot both nominal and real GDP. Real GDP is expressed in the purchasing power of 1986 dollars. The gap between the two represents price level changes.

Source: Statistics Canada.

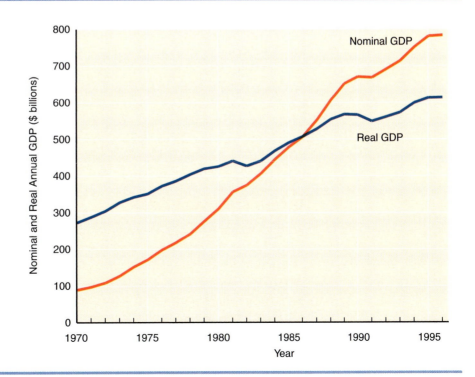

Try Preview Question 4:
How does correcting GDP for changes in the price level and population improve the usefulness of GDP estimates?

The difficulties of using GDP as an indicator of social well-being do not end here. In fact, there has been a running battle over the use of GDP statistics because, according to its critics, such numbers do not capture the true overall well-being of a nation. How do we take account of changes in leisure time? How do our national income accounts recognize increased traffic congestion, air pollution in our cities, crime in the streets, and so on? And housework, which constitutes a major amount of the labour performed in Canada, isn't even counted in GDP.

Concepts in Brief

- To correct nominal GDP for price changes, we first use a base year for our price index and assign it the number 100 percent (or 1.00). Then we construct an index based on how a weighted average of the price level has changed relative to that base year. For example, if in the next year a weighted average of the price level indicates that prices have increased by 10 percent, we would assign it the number 110 (or 1.10). We then divide each year's price index, so constructed, into its respective nominal GDP figure (and multiply by 100).
- We can divide the population into real GDP to obtain per capita real GDP.

COMPARING LIVING STANDARDS THROUGHOUT THE WORLD

It is relatively easy to compare the standard of living of a family in Montreal with that of one living in Saskatoon. Both families get paid in dollars, and can buy the same goods and services at Canadian Tire, McDonald's, and Safeway. It is not so easy, however, to make a similar comparison between a family living in Canada and one in, say, India. The first problem concerns money. Indians get paid in rupees, their national currency, and buy goods and services with those rupees. That means that just as we can compare families in Montreal and Saskatoon, we can compare the living standards of a family in Delhi with one in Bombay. But how do we compare the average standard of living in India with that in Canada?

Foreign Exchange Rates

▶ **Foreign exchange rate**
The price of one currency in terms of another.

In earlier chapters, you have encountered international examples that involved local currencies, but the dollar equivalent always has been given. The dollar equivalent is calculated by looking up the **foreign exchange rate** that is published daily in major newspapers throughout the world. If you know that you can exchange $1 for 6 francs, the exchange rate is 6 to 1 (in other words , a franc is worth about 17 cents). So if French incomes per capita are, say, 100,000 francs, that translates to $17,000 at an exchange rate of 6 francs to $1. For years, statisticians calculated relative GDP by simply adding up each country's GDP in its local currency and dividing by each respective dollar exchange rate.

True Purchasing Power

The problem with simply using foreign exchange rates to convert other countries' GDP and per capita GDP into dollars is that not all goods and services are bought and sold in a world market. Restaurant food, housecleaning services, and home repairs do not get exchanged across countries. In countries that have very low wages, those kinds of services are much cheaper than foreign exchange rate computations would imply. Government statistics claiming that per capita income in some poor country is only $300 a year seems shocking. But such a statistic does not tell you the true standard of living of people in that country. Only by looking at what is called **purchasing power parity** can you determine other countries' true standards of living compared to ours.

▶ **Purchasing power parity**

Adjustment in exchange rate conversions that takes into account differences in the true cost of living across countries.

But even purchasing power does not tell the whole story of the relative well-being of countries. We need to look beyond incomes to other factors such as life expectancy and literacy levels to get a truer picture of living standards. In the following example you'll see that the United Nations has done just that.

INTERNATIONAL EXAMPLE
Comparing Standards of Living

In 1990, the United Nations Development Programme (UNDP) declared that comparing per capita incomes across nations did not provide a balanced picture of relative standards of living. Therefore, the UNDP created a Human Development Index (HDI) which takes into account both the real GDP of each country, and the life expectancy at birth, as well as educational attainment of its citizens. By combining these factors, the UNDP hoped to illustrate that the size of an economy measured by its GDP does not necessarily indicate the state of human well-being.

The 1995 HDI declared Canada amongst 174 countries studied as the best place in the world to live, although our per capita income ranked third behind the United States and Hong Kong. Second overall was the United States, and third was Japan. The Netherlands and Norway placed fourth and fifth. The top five developing nations on the HDI were Cyprus, Barbados, Bahamas, Korea, and Argentina.

To illustrate the difficulty of using real GDP as a measure of human well-being, the UNDP pointed out that while New Zealand and Switzerland ranked 14th and 15th on the HDI, New Zealand's real per capita income was US$12,600 compared to Switzerland's US$35,760. Both Ecuador and Morocco had per capita incomes of about US$1,000, but Ecuador placed 64th while Morocco placed 123rd.

After the release of the 1995 HDI, Informetrica, a Canadian think tank, applied the same criteria to the Canadian provinces. The result? Saskatchewan is the best province in the best country in which to live.

For critical analysis: Which country's citizens enjoy a greater well-being? New Zealand's or Switzerland's? Ecuador's or Morocco's?

Concepts in Brief

- The foreign exchange rate is the price of one currency in terms of another.
- Statisticians often calculate relative GDP by adding up each country's GDP in its local currency and dividing by the dollar exchange rate.
- Because not all goods and services are bought and sold in the world market, we must correct exchange rate conversions of other countries' GDP figures in order to take into account differences in the true cost of living across countries.

Issues and Applications

The Worldwide Underground Economy

Concepts Applied: GDP, unemployment rate, incentives, marginal tax rate

GDP statistics do not include "informal" market activities that occur in countries because it is impossible to track these activities. While Canada has a large underground economy, it is much larger in Spain and other European countries. Here in Spain, street vendors entice shoppers with their goods.

Beyond the difficulties of obtaining accurate measurements of GDP and NDP and the like, government statisticians have to face the reality that a certain amount of economic activity can never be captured by official statistics. Why? Because each year, a variety of economic transactions take place completely outside the system. Ordinarily, when one thinks about unofficial or underground activities, one's thoughts immediately turn to drug trafficking, illegal gambling, and prostitution. To be sure, these underground activities are significant. But tens of millions of otherwise law-abiding citizens participate frequently in the "informal" economy. Anybody who buys, sells, or works for cash or an equivalent payment for which no record is kept and on which no taxes are paid is participating in the underground economy.

Incentives Lead the Way

At the heart of the underground economy are the incentives for individuals and businesses. With respect to criminal activity, the incentives are clear: Fines and jail time are enough of an incentive to cause criminals to make sure that none of their activities are reported. For people engaged in noncriminal off-the-books activities, there is one major incentive: to reduce or avoid income and sales taxes. The greater the marginal income tax rate, the greater the incentive to be paid in cash without declaring it. Hence the underground economy was presumably much smaller in Canada prior to 1917, when Canada started collecting federal income taxes. With respect to sales taxes, one would surmise that the amount of unreported retail sales is lower in Alberta, which has no provincial

Figure 8.5
The Underground Economy in Selected Countries

Source: Organisation for Economic Cooperation and Development.

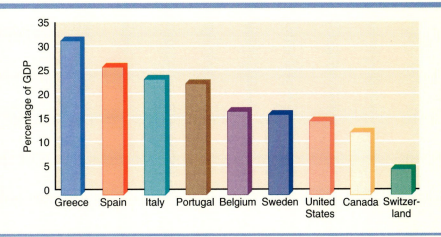

sales taxes, than in provinces such as Nova Scotia and Newfoundland, which have relatively high combined GST and provincial sales taxes.

Unemployment and Welfare Benefits Count Too

An additional incentive for some individuals to work in the underground economy is to avoid losing unemployment benefits or welfare benefits. Consequently, measured unemployment rates are typically biased upward because a certain percentage of the people receiving unemployment benefits are actually working "off-the-books." In some countries, such as Spain, at least 35 percent of the recipients of unemployment benefits now have jobs.

How Big Is the Underground Economy?

By definition, the underground economy is not measured. Therefore, its size is even harder to assess than the size of the "aboveground" economy. Nonetheless, we do have estimates. At an international conference in 1994, estimates of the size of Canada's underground economy ranged from 3 percent to 21 percent of GDP. In dollar terms this would translate into $37.5 billion

to $158 billion of underground transactions each year. Eventually, analysts narrowed the estimates down to between 10 percent and 15 percent of reported economic activity.

The Global Underground Economy

The underground economy may seem large in Canada, but in Spain and Greece it is much larger, as can be seen in Figure 8.5. We can conclude on the basis of this figure that official GDP statistics for Greece, Spain, Italy, and Portugal significantly underestimate actual GDP in those countries.

For Critical Analysis

1. Revenue Canada periodically makes estimates of tax revenues lost because of the underground economy. It simply multiplies current tax rates by estimated "off-the-books" income to come up with the figures. Why is Revenue Canada overestimating tax revenues lost due to the underground economy?

2. What change in government policy would reduce the size of the underground economy in Canada?

CHAPTER SUMMARY

1. Households provide labour services, land, capital, and entrepreneurship, for which they are paid wages, rent, interest, and profits. Profits are considered a factor cost—they are the reward for entrepreneurship or risk taking. Profits are a residual payment.

2. In the simplest representation of our economy, there are only households and businesses. The circular flow goes from households to factor markets to businesses and from businesses to product markets to households.

3. National income accounting is the method by which economists attempt to measure statistically the variables with which they are concerned in their study of macroeconomics.

4. One of the concepts most often used in national income accounting is gross domestic product (GDP), which is defined as the total market value of all *final* goods and services produced annually by domestic factors of production. The stress on *final* is important to avoid the double-counting of intermediate goods used in the production of other goods.

5. We can compute GDP using the expenditure approach or the income approach. In the former, we merely add up the dollar value of all final goods and services; in the latter, we add up the payments generated in producing all those goods and services, or wages, corporate profits before taxes, interest, farm and non-incorporated non-farm income, and inventory valuation adjustment, plus indirect business taxes less subsidies and depreciation.

6. It is difficult to measure the market value of government expenditures because generally government-provided goods are not sold at a market clearing price. We therefore value government expenditures at their cost for inclusion in our measure of GDP.

7. Investment does not occur when there is merely a transfer of assets among individuals; rather, it occurs only when new productive capacity, such as a machine tool, is built.

8. Part of our capital stock is worn out or becomes obsolete every year. To take account of the expenditures made merely to replace such capital equipment, we subtract depreciation from GDP to yield net domestic product (NDP).

9. To correct for price changes, we deflate GDP with a price index to come up with real GDP. To take account of rising population, we divide by population to arrive at per capita real GDP.

10. To compare GDP across countries, we must first apply the foreign exchange rate to GDP expressed in the local currency and then adjust the exchange rate to take account of the purchasing power of that income. This is called the purchasing power parity approach.

DISCUSSION OF PREVIEW QUESTIONS

1. **What is gross domestic product (GDP), and what does it measure?**

   Gross domestic product is defined as the market value of all final goods and services produced during one year by domestic factors of production. Because GDP is measured per unit of time, it is a flow concept. Economists try to estimate GDP in order to evaluate the productive performance of an economy during the year; economists also use GDP estimates to aid them in judging overall economic well-being.

2. **Why are only *final* goods and services evaluated in deriving GDP?**

   Because GDP estimates are an attempt to evaluate an economy's performance and to generalize about group well-being, we must be careful to evaluate only final goods and services; other-wise GDP would be exaggerated. For example, because an automobile uses plastic, steel, coke, rubber, coal, and other products in its manufacture, to count each of these and the value of the automobile would be double counting. Thus to count steel *and* the automobile when it is sold is to count steel twice and hence to exaggerate the economy's performance and the group's economic well-being. Steel in this instance would not be a final good; it would be an intermediate good.

3. **Why must depreciation and indirect business taxes less subsidies be added to national income at factor cost in order to derive GDP via the income approach?**

   The expenditure approach to GDP counts expenditures on *all* final goods and services; in particular, expenditures on all investment goods amount to gross investment. The income approach to GDP estimation, by contrast, sums the wages, profits, interest, and other receipts of income earners. Because depreciation is not a wage, profit, interest, or other income, the expenditure approach would yield a higher number. In order to compare correctly, we must add depreciation to national income at factor cost to calculate GDP via the income approach. Similarly, indirect business taxes (excise, sales, and property taxes) less subsidies are automatically reflected in the expenditure approach, whereas this category is not included in wages, profit, interest, or other receipts to factors of production.

4. How does correcting GDP for changes in the price level and population improve the usefulness of GDP estimates?

When the price level is rising (during periods of inflation), GDP estimates would overstate true productive activity and group economic well-being. Similarly, when the general price level is falling (during periods of deflation), GDP estimates would understate productive activity and group economic well-being. If population is rising more rapidly than real output, real GDP estimates would rise, but living standards might well fall. Dividing by population corrects for such cases. Per capita real GDP is a better clue to productive activity and overall economic well-being than nominal GDP.

PROBLEMS

(Answers to the odd-numbered problems appear at the back of the book.)

8-1. The following are a year's data for a hypothetical economy.

	Billions of Dollars
Consumption	400
Government spending	350
Gross private domestic investment	150
Exports	150
Imports	100
Depreciation	50
Indirect business taxes less subsidies	25

a. Based on the data, what is the value of GDP? NDP? NI?

b. Suppose that in the next year exports increase to $175 billion, imports increase to $200 billion, and consumption falls to $350 billion. What will GDP be in that year?

c. If the value of depreciation (capital consumption allowance) should ever exceed that of gross private domestic investment, how would this affect the future productivity of the nation?

8-2. Look back at Table 8.3, which explains how to correct GDP for price level changes. Column 4 of that table gives real GDP in terms of 1992 constant dollars. Change the base year to 1994. Recalculate the price level index and then recalculate real GDP—that is, express column 4 in terms of 1994 dollars instead of 1992 dollars.

8-3. Study the following table; then answer the questions.

Stage of Production	Sales Receipts	Intermediate Costs	Value Added
Coal	$2	$0	$2
Steel	5	2	3
Manufactured autos	8	5	3
Sold autos	9	8	1

a. What is the intermediate good for steel production? How much did it cost?
b. What is the value added resulting from auto manufacturing?
c. If automobiles are the only final goods produced in this economy, what would be the GDP via the expenditures approach?
d. If automobiles are the only final goods produced in this economy, what would be the GDP via the income approach?

8-4. At the top of a piece of paper, write the headings "Production Activity" and "Nonproduction Activity." List each of the following under one of these headings by determining which would go into our measure of GDP.
a. Mr. X sells his used car to Mr. Y.
b. Joe's used car lot sells a car to Mr. Z and receives a $50 profit for doing so.
c. Merrill Lynch receives a brokerage commission for selling stocks.
d. Ms. Arianas buys 100 shares of Dofasco stock.
e. Mrs. LeMaistre cooks and keeps house for her family.
f. Mr. Singh mows his own lawn.
g. Mr. Singh mows lawns for a living.
h. Mr. Smith receives a welfare payment.
i. Mrs. Johnson sends her daughter $500 for a semester of studies at College U.

8-5. What happens to the official measure of GDP in each of the following situations?
a. A man marries his housekeeper, who then quits working for wages.
b. A drug addict marries her supplier.
c. Homemakers perform the same jobs but switch houses and charge each other for their services.

8-6. Construct a value-added table for various stages in the production and sale of bread.

8-7. Consider the following table for an economy that produces only four goods.

Good	1992 Price	1992 Quantity	1997 Price	1997 Quantity
Pizza	$ 4	10	$ 8	12
Cola	12	20	36	15
T-shirts	6	5	10	15
Business equipment	25	10	30	12

Assuming a 1992 base year:
a. What is nominal GDP for 1992 and 1997?
b. What is real GDP for 1992? For 1997?

8-8. Examine the following figures for a hypothetical year; then calculate GDP, NDP, NI, PI, and DPI.

	Billions of Dollars
Consumption	400
Net exports	−20
Transfer payments	20
Gross investment	100
E.I. and C.P.P. contributions	10
Government purchases	120
Net investment	50
Dividends	20
Indirect business taxes less subsidies	10
Corporate income taxes	30
Personal income taxes	60
Undistributed corporate profits	20

8-9. Visit Statistics Canada's Latest Indicators site at http://www.statcan.ca/english.econoind/.
a. Update Figure 8.3 in this chapter to show the calculation of 1998 GDP using both the expenditures- and income-based methods.
b. The figures you find for 1997 and the figures in Figure 8.3 will most likely not be identical. Can you think of a reason why this may be so?

INTERACTING WITH THE INTERNET

Current GDP press releases and other related material, such as historical data, can be found at Statistics Canada's Web site:

http://www.statcan.ca/Daily/English/today/daily.htm

Statistics Canada also maintains an extensive database, CANSIM, which you can access on the Internet. However, you will have to pay a nominal fee for retrieval of much of the information.

http://www.statcan.ca/Documents/English/CANSIM/index.html

9

Economic Growth: Technology, Research and Development, and Knowledge

Preview Questions

1. What is economic growth?

2. What does economic growth measure?

3. What are some of the ways in which you can experience economic growth for yourself or for your family?

4. What are the determinants of economic growth?

The "Canadian way of life" involves a political system that can be loosely defined as representative democracy. Canadians for the most part are certain that democracy is good, and that our foreign policy should therefore be to foster democracy throughout the world. Political freedom exists in various degrees in the 200 or so nations of the world, yet many of those nations have become democratic only in this decade. Do we have evidence to demonstrate that increased political freedom and more democracy lead to higher standards of living? To answer this question, you need to know how we define economic growth and what its determinants are.

Did You Know That...at the beginning of the twentieth century, Argentina had the sixth highest per capita income in the world, but now at the end of the century it is around fortieth, somewhat below Iran? Consider also that 100 years ago, Hong Kong was basically a barren rock, but today its per capita income exceeds that of France and the United Kingdom. How can we explain such dramatic changes in relative living standards? From an arithmetic point of view, the answer is simple: Argentina experienced little, and in some cases negative, economic growth over the past century, whereas Hong Kong had significant economic growth. That answer, though, does not tell us *why* economic growth rates differed in these two countries. That is the task of this chapter. Should you care about the rate of economic growth in Canada? The answer is yes, if you care about your future standard of living and that of your children and grandchildren. You have already demonstrated that you care about your future standard of living; otherwise, you would not be bothering to obtain a higher education. Obviously, you want to make sure that you experience economic growth as an individual. Now it is time to consider the country as a whole.

HOW DO WE DEFINE ECONOMIC GROWTH?

Remember from Chapter 2 that we can show economic growth graphically as an outward shift of a production possibilities curve, as is seen in Figure 9.1. If there is economic growth between 1998 and 2025, the production possibilities curve will shift outward. The distance that it shifts represents the amount of economic growth,

Figure 9.1
Economic Growth

If there is growth between 1998 and 2025, the production possibilities curve for the entire economy will shift outward from the line labelled 1998 to the line labelled 2025. The distance that it shifts represents an increase in the productive capacity of the nation.

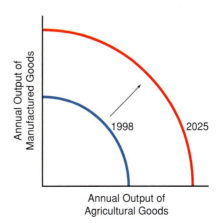

defined as the increase in the productive capacity of a nation. Although it is possible to come up with a measure of a nation's increased productive capacity, it would not be easy. Therefore, we turn to a more readily obtainable definition of economic growth.

Most people have a general idea of what economic growth means. When a nation grows economically, its citizens must be better off in some ways, usually in terms of their material well-being. Typically, though, we do not measure the well-being of any country solely in terms of its total output of real goods and services, or in terms of real GDP without making some adjustments. After all, India has a GDP about three times as large as that of Switzerland. The population of India, though, is about 125 times greater than that of Switzerland. Consequently, we view India as a relatively poor country and Switzerland as a relatively rich one. Thus to measure how much a country is growing in terms of annual increases in real GDP, we have to adjust for population growth. Our formal definition becomes this: **Economic growth** occurs when there are increases in per capita real GDP; it is measured by the rate of change in per capita real GDP per year. Figure 9.2 presents the historical record of real GDP per person in Canada.

▶ **Economic growth**
Increases in per capita real GDP measured by its rate of change per year.

Try Preview Question 1:
What is economic growth?

Figure 9.2
The Historical Record of Canadian Economic Growth
The graph traces per capita real GDP in Canada since 1900. Data are given in 1986 dollars.

Source: Statistics Canada.

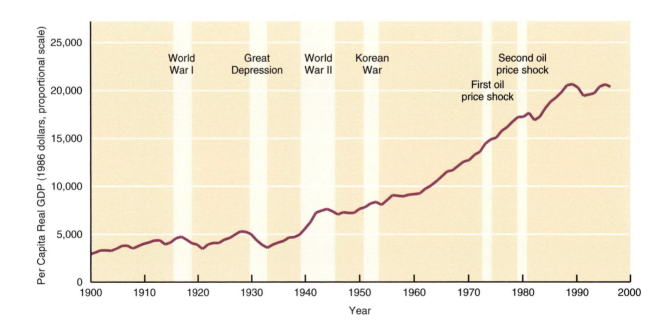

INTERNATIONAL EXAMPLE
Growth Rates Around the World

Table 9.1
Per Capita Growth Rates in Various Countries

Table 9.1 shows the annual average rate of growth of income per person in selected countries. Notice that Canada during the time period under study is positioned about midway in the pack. In other words, even though we are one of the world's richest countries, our recent rate of economic growth is not particularly high.

Sources: World Bank; International Monetary Fund.

Country	Average Annual Rate of Growth of Income per Capita, 1970–1995 (%)
Switzerland	1.8
Sweden	1.9
Netherlands	2.2
United Kingdom	2.3
Germany	2.4
France	2.7
United States	2.8
Italy	2.8
Canada	3.0
Spain	3.1
Japan	4.8
Turkey	5.3
China	6.1

For critical analysis: "The largest change is from zero to one." Does this statement have anything to do with relative growth rates in poorer versus richer countries?

Problems in Definition

Our definition of economic growth says nothing about the *distribution* of output and income. A nation might grow very rapidly in terms of increases in per capita real output, while at the same time its poor people remain poor or become even poorer. Therefore, in assessing the economic growth record of any nation, we must be careful to pinpoint which income groups have benefited the most from such growth.

Real standards of living can go up without any positive economic growth. This can occur if individuals are, on average, enjoying more leisure by working fewer hours but producing as much as they did before. For example, if per capita real GDP in Canada remained at $20,000 a year for a decade, we could not automatically jump to the conclusion that Canadians were, on average, no better off. What if, during that same 10-year period, average hours worked fell from 37 per week to 33 per week? That would mean that during the 10 years under study, individuals in the labour force were "earning" four hours more leisure a week. Actually, nothing so extreme has occurred in this country, but something similar has. Average hours worked per week fell steadily until the 1960s, at which time they levelled off. That means that during much of the history of this country, the increase in per capita real GDP *understated* the actual economic growth that we were experiencing because we were enjoying more and more leisure time as things progressed.

Is Economic Growth Bad?

Some commentators on our current economic situation believe that the definition of economic growth ignores its negative effects. Some psychologists even contend that we are made worse off because of economic growth. They say that the more we grow, the more "needs" are created so that we feel worse off as we become richer. Our expectations are rising faster than reality, so we presumably always suffer from a sense of disappointment. Clearly, the measurement of economic growth cannot take into account the spiritual and cultural aspects of the "good life." As with all activities, there are costs and benefits. You can see some of those listed in Table 9.2.

Try Preview Question 2:
What does economic growth measure?

In any event, any measure of economic growth that we use will be imperfect. Nonetheless, the measures that we do have allow us to make comparisons across countries and over time and, if used judiciously, can enable us to gain important insights. Per capita real GDP, used so often, is not always an accurate measure of economic well-being, but it is a serviceable measure of productive activity.

Table 9.2
Costs and Benefits of Economic Growth

Benefits	Costs
Reduction in illiteracy	Environmental pollution
Reduction in poverty	Breakdown of the family
Improved health	Isolation and alienation
Longer lives	Urban congestion
Political stability	

The Importance of Growth Rates

Notice back in Table 9.1 that the growth rates in real per capita income for most countries differ by very little—generally, only a few percentage points. You might want to know why such small differences in growth rates are important. What would it matter if we grew at 3 percent rather than at 4 percent per year?

It matters a lot—not for next year or the year after but for the more distant future. The power of compound interest is impressive. Let's see what happens with three different annual rates of growth: 3 percent, 4 percent, and 5 percent. We start with $100 billion per year, which is approximately equal to the gross domestic product of Canada in 1971. We then compound this $100 billion, or allow it to grow, into the future at these three different growth rates. The difference is huge. In 50 years, $100 billion per year becomes $438 billion per year if compounded at 3 percent per year. Just one percentage point more in the growth rate, 4 percent, results in a real GDP of $711 billion per year in 50 years, almost double the previous amount. Two percentage points difference in the growth rate—5 percent per year—results in a real GDP of $1.15 trillion per year in 50 years, or nearly three times as much. Obviously, there is a great difference in the results of economic growth for very small differences in annual growth rates. That is why nations are concerned if the growth rate falls even a little in absolute percentage terms.

Table 9.3
One Dollar Compounded Annually at Different Interest Rates

Here we show the value of a dollar at the end of a specified period during which it has been compounded annually at a specified interest rate. For example, if you took $1 today and invested it at 5 percent per year, it would yield $1.05 at the end of one year. At the end of 10 years, it would equal $1.63, and at the end of 50 years, it would equal $11.50.

Number of Years	Interest Rate						
	3%	4%	5%	6%	8%	10%	20%
1	1.03	1.04	1.05	1.06	1.08	1.10	1.20
2	1.06	1.08	1.10	1.12	1.17	1.21	1.44
3	1.09	1.12	1.16	1.19	1.26	1.33	1.73
4	1.13	1.17	1.22	1.26	1.36	1.46	2.07
5	1.16	1.22	1.28	1.34	1.47	1.61	2.49
6	1.19	1.27	1.34	1.41	1.59	1.77	2.99
7	1.23	1.32	1.41	1.50	1.71	1.94	3.58
8	1.27	1.37	1.48	1.59	1.85	2.14	4.30
9	1.30	1.42	1.55	1.68	2.00	2.35	5.16
10	1.34	1.48	1.63	1.79	2.16	2.59	6.19
20	1.81	2.19	2.65	3.20	4.66	6.72	38.30
30	2.43	3.24	4.32	5.74	10.00	17.40	237.00
40	3.26	4.80	7.04	10.30	21.70	45.30	1,470.00
50	4.38	7.11	11.50	18.40	46.90	117.00	9,100.00

Compound Interest. When we talk about growth rates, we are basically talking about compound interest. In Table 9.3, we show how $1 compounded annually grows at different interest rates. We see in the 3 percent column that $1 in 50 years grows to $4.38. We merely multiplied $100 billion times 4.38 to get the growth figure in our earlier example. In the 5 percent column, $1 grows to $11.50 after 50 years. Again, we multiplied $100 billion times 11.50 to get the growth figure for 5 percent in the preceding example.

EXAMPLE | **What If Canada Had Grown a Little Bit Less or More Each Year?**

In 1870, the per-person real GDP expressed in 1997 dollars was $2,330. That figure had grown to $29,225 by the end of 1997. The average economic growth rate was therefore about 1.75 percent per year. What if the Canadian growth rate over the same century and a quarter had been simply 1 percent less—only 0.75 percent per year? Per capita real GDP in 1997 would have been only 30 percent of what it actually was. Canada would have ranked somewhere around thirty-eighth on the scale of per capita income throughout the world. We would be poorer than Greece or Portugal.

Consider a rosier scenario: What if the Canadian economic rate of growth had been one point higher, or 2.75 percent per year? Today's per capita real GDP would be more than three times its actual value, or about $90,000!

For critical analysis: Can you relate this example to anything in your own life? (Hint: Use the compound interest rates in Table 9.3 to make various predictions about your future standard of living.)

Concepts in Brief

- Economic growth can be defined as the increase in real per capita output measured by its rate of change per year.
- The benefits of economic growth are reductions in illiteracy, poverty, and illness, as well as increases in life spans, and political stability. The costs of economic growth may include environmental pollution, alienation, and urban congestion.
- Small percentage-point differences in growth rates lead to large differences in real GDP over time. These differences can be seen by examining a compound interest table such as the one in Table 9.3.

PRODUCTIVITY INCREASES: THE HEART OF ECONOMIC GROWTH

Let's say that you are required to type 10 term papers and homework assignments a year. You have a word processor to do so, but you do not know how to touch-type. You end up spending an average of two hours per typing job. The next summer, you buy a touch-typing tutorial to use on your word processor and spend a few minutes a day improving your typing speed. The following term, you spend only one hour per typing assignment, thereby saving 10 hours a semester. You have become more productive. This concept of productivity relates to your ability (and everyone else's) to

Figure 9.3

Nonfarm Canadian Productivity Growth

Whereas productivity growth in the services sector was relatively robust until the early 1980s, productivity in the manufacturing sector has been increasing almost consistently since the 1960s. The recessions of the 1980s and 1990s slowed productivity growth in both sectors.

Source: Statistics Canada, CANSIM University Base, Series I700600 and I700606.

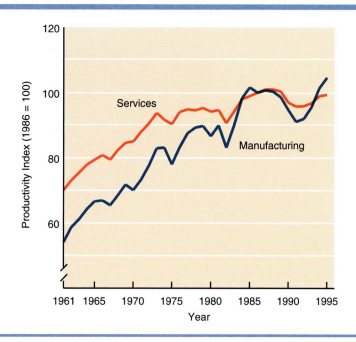

▶ **Labour productivity**
Total real domestic output (real GDP) divided by the number of workers (output per worker).

produce the same output with fewer labour hours. Thus **labour productivity** is normally measured by dividing the total real domestic output (real GDP) by the number of workers or the number of labour hours. Labour productivity increases whenever average output produced per worker during a specified time period increases. Clearly, there is a relationship between economic growth and increases in labour productivity. If you divide all resources into just capital and labour, economic growth can be defined simply as follows:

Economic growth = rate of growth of capital + rate of growth of labour +
rate of growth in the productivity of capital and of labour

If everything else remains constant, improvements in labour productivity ultimately lead to economic growth and higher living standards.

Although productivity growth seemed to lag in Canada from the mid-1970s through the mid-1980s, there is quite a bit of evidence that it has been on the rise since then. Figure 9.3 on the previous page traces productivity growth in the manufacturing and service sectors of the economy.

INTERNATIONAL EXAMPLE
How Does Canadian Productivity Compare to the Rest of the World?

One way economists use productivity is as a rough measure of competitiveness: the more productive the resources, all else held constant, the lower the cost of the product. However, in measures of productivity and competitiveness, all else is not held constant. For example, some countries have governments which encourage high productivity by making access to education or new technology easy. Other countries have governments which discourage growth of productivity by enforcing regulations which make labour market changes in response to technology changes difficult.

Table 9.4
Relative Competitiveness of Countries

Source: "The C-word Strikes Back," *The Economist,* June 1, 1996, p. 76.

Country	Rank	Country	Rank
Singapore	1	Thailand	14
Hong Kong	2	Britain	15
New Zealand	3	Finland	16
United States	4	Netherlands	17
Luxembourg	5	Chile	18
Switzerland	6	Austria	19
Norway	7	South Korea	20
Canada	8	Sweden	21
Taiwan	9	Germany	22
Malaysia	10	France	23
Denmark	11	Israel	24
Australia	12	Belgium	25
Japan	13		

The World Economic Forum is one body which tries to measure relative productivity among 49 countries. It ranks countries in order of their ability "to achieve sustained high rates of growth in GDP per capita." In Table 9.4, you will note that Canada is ranked 8th out of the top 25 countries. Notice that some countries which we usually point to as being very productive are indeed ahead of Canada: Singapore, Hong Kong, the United States. But notice too that some countries we do not usually think of as being less productive than Canada have a lower rank: Taiwan, Japan, South Korea.

The World Economic Forum cannot guarantee that Canada will grow faster than the lower ranked countries in the years to come. Perhaps the better measure of improvement would be to see Canada move up in the list.

For critical analysis: Could Canada move up in the list because of events in other countries? Would that mark an improvement in Canada's competitiveness?

ONE FUNDAMENTAL DETERMINANT OF THE RATE OF ECONOMIC GROWTH: THE RATE OF SAVING

Economic growth does not occur in a vacuum. It is not some predetermined fate of a nation. Rather, economic growth depends on certain fundamental factors. One of the most important factors that affect the rate of economic growth and hence long-term living standards is the rate of saving.

A basic proposition in economics is that if you want more tomorrow, you have to take less today.

> To have more consumption in the future, you have to consume less today and save the difference between your consumption and your income.

Try Preview Question 3:
What are some of the ways in which you can experience economic growth for yourself or for your family?

On a national basis, this implies that higher saving rates eventually mean higher living standards in the long run, all other things held constant. Concern has been growing in Canada that we are not saving enough, which means that our rate of sav-

---

Thinking Critically About the Media | **Productivity as a Prerequisite for International Competitiveness**

The recurring major story about the Canadian economy relates to the rate of growth of productivity–or more generally, the lack thereof. The claim in the media is that if Canada fails to sustain high productivity, it will lose out in the competitive race among nations. The fallacy in such media stories is that the benefit of high productivity is somehow related to allowing Canada to compete with other countries. The reality is that with the benefit of high productivity, *any* country can produce more with the same amount of resources. That means that all its residents can consume more, which in turn means a higher standard of living because of higher productivity. As a nation, we would want higher productivity even if no other country in the world existed!

ing may be too low. Saving is important for economic growth because without saving, we cannot have investment. If all income is consumed each year, there is nothing left over for saving, which could be used by business for investment. If there is no investment in our capital stock, there could be little hope of much economic growth.

The relationship between the rate of savings and per capita real GDP is shown in Figure 9.4. A nation with one of the highest rates of saving is Japan. Why?

Figure 9.4

Relationship Between Rate of Saving and per Capita Real GDP

This diagram shows the combination of per capita real GDP and the rate of saving expressed as the average percentage of annual real GDP for many nations since 1960. Centrally planned economies and major oil-producing countries are not shown.

Source: After Robert Summers and Alan Heston, "A New Set of International Comparisons of Real Product and Price Level," *Review of Income and Wealth,* March 1988.

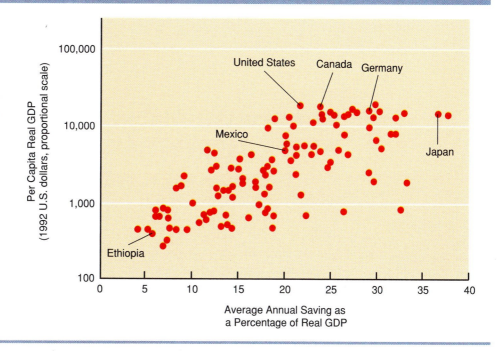

INTERNATIONAL EXAMPLE

Why Do the Japanese Save So Much?

The rate of saving in Japan is roughly one-third more than what it has been in Canada, expressed as a percentage of income. One possible reason is that the Japanese have been unable to borrow as freely as their Canadian counterparts. The typical down payment for a Japanese family wishing to buy a house is 40 percent, compared with only 15 percent in Canada. The average house price in Japan is more than twice what it is in Canada. Consequently, to purchase a home, a typical Japanese family has to save more than a typical Canadian family. In addition, the Japanese have for many years been rewarded more for saving than in Canada because their tax system has taxed the rate of return to saving relatively less than in Canada.

For critical analysis: Explain why you might consider paying off a mortgage on your home as a form of saving.

Concepts in Brief

- Economic growth is numerically equal to the rate of growth of capital plus the rate of growth of labour plus the rate of growth in the productivity of capital and of labour. Improvements in labour productivity, all other things being equal, lead to greater economic growth and higher living standards.
- One fundamental determinant of the rate of growth is the rate of saving. To have more consumption in the future, we have to save rather than consume. In general, countries that have had higher rates of saving have had higher rates of growth in real GDP.

NEW GROWTH THEORY AND WHAT DETERMINES GROWTH

▶ **New growth theory**
A relatively modern theory of economic growth which examines the factors that determine why technology, research, innovation, and the like are undertaken and how they interact.

A simple arithmetic definition of economic growth has already been given. Growth rates of capital and labour plus the growth rate in their productivity are simply defined as the components of economic growth. Economists have had good data on the growth of the labour force as well as the growth of the physical capital stock in Canada. But when you add those two growth rates together, you still do not get the total economic growth rate in Canada. The difference has to be due to improvements in productivity. Economists typically labelled this "improvements in technology," and that was that. More recently, proponents of what is now called the **new growth theory** argue that technology cannot simply be looked at as an outside factor without explanation. Technology must be examined from the point of view of what drives it. What are the forces that make productivity grow in Canada and elsewhere?

Thinking Critically About the Media   Do New Technologies Signal the End of Work?

Throughout the world, the media as well as numerous "experts" have painted a gloomy picture for the average working person. They point out that the newest technologies have led to a reduction in the percentage of workers who devote their time to manufacturing. Efficient production lines certainly do require fewer workers, and sophisticated telecommunications have reduced the need for physical offices. During one recent talk show in England, the commentator stated that "the rich no longer need the poor. More and more goods can be produced with fewer and fewer workers. Therefore, permanent unemployment will grow." Such commentaries have been popular since the weaving machine and its single operator replaced the work that 10 people did before. The idea is that the other 9 workers were unemployed forever. Both theory and data render such media analyses basically meaningless.

In Canada, in spite of dramatic increases in technology, the population increased over 7 million between 1975 and 1998 while the number of unemployed has increased by only 800,000. And theoretically, there is no limit to employment. Labour employment is a function of the supply and demand for labour. Demand is not a fixed constant somehow based on a mechanical relationship between the number of widgets produced and the number of workers needed to produce them. Workers released from industries that are more productive because of new technologies must—and do—find employment elsewhere, often in other industries that are expanding. (After all, wants *are* unlimited.)

Growth in Technology

Consider some startling statistics about the growth in technology. Look at Figure 9.5 to learn what may happen to computers in the future. Microprocessor speeds may increase from 350 megahertz to 800 megahertz by the year 2011. By that same year, the size of the thinnest circuit line within a transistor will decrease by 77 percent. The typical memory capacity of computers will jump from 64 megabytes, or about the equivalent text in the *Encyclopaedia Britannica*, to 64 gigabytes—a thousandfold increase.

Figure 9.5

Growth in Computer Capacity

In 1997, the typical computer might have 64 megabytes of dynamic random access memory (RAM). By the year 2002, that will increase to over 1,000 megabytes, or a gigabyte. By 2011, it will be 64 gigabytes. Similarly dramatic increases in microprocessor speed and reductions in transistor circuit thinness will also occur.

Source: Semiconductor Industry Association.

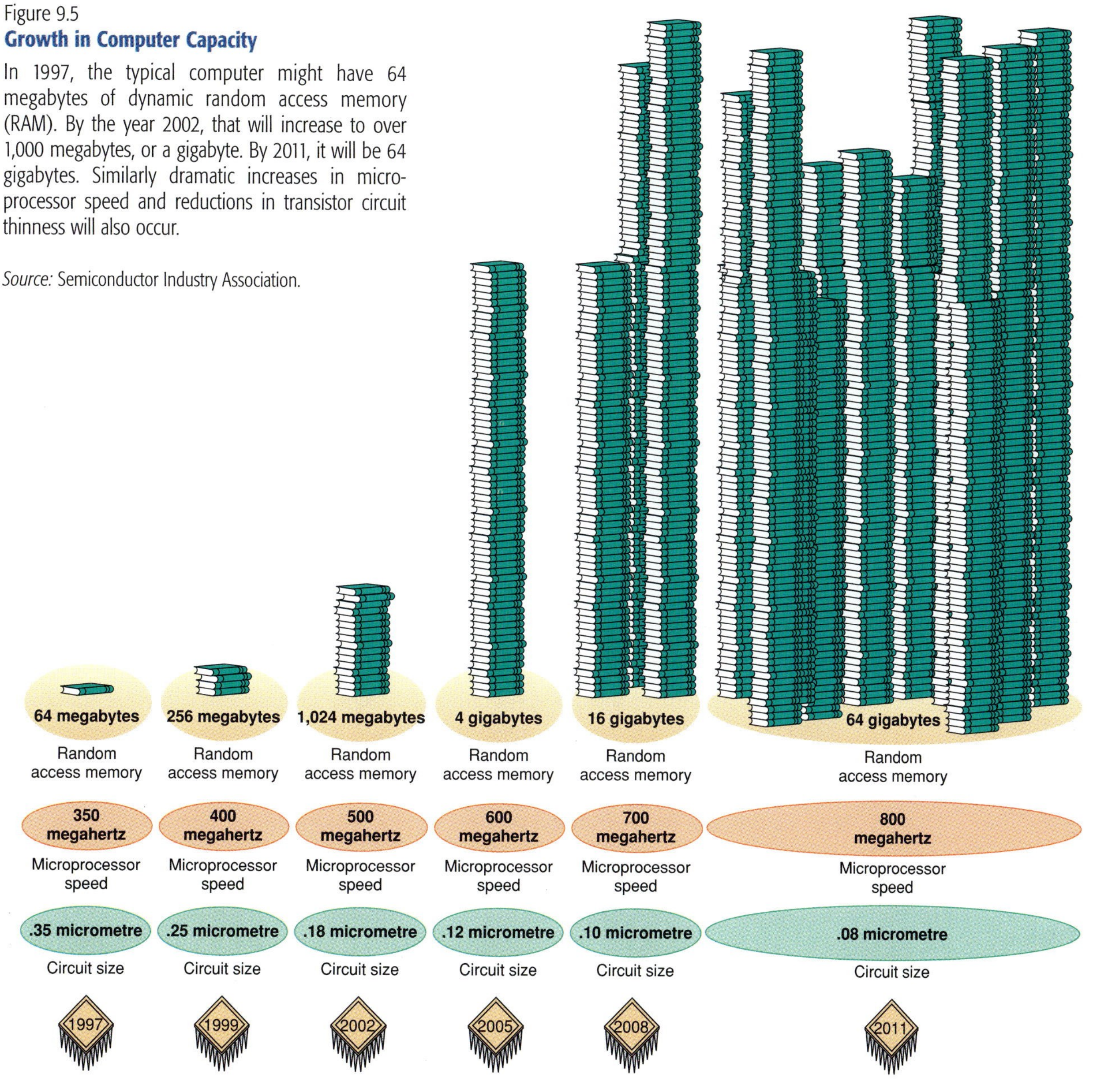

64 megabytes	256 megabytes	1,024 megabytes	4 gigabytes	16 gigabytes	64 gigabytes
Random access memory	Random access memory	Random access memory	Random access memory	Random access memory	Random access memory
350 megahertz	400 megahertz	500 megahertz	600 megahertz	700 megahertz	800 megahertz
Microprocessor speed	Microprocessor speed	Microprocessor speed	Microprocessor speed	Microprocessor speed	Microprocessor speed
.35 micrometre	.25 micrometre	.18 micrometre	.12 micrometre	.10 micrometre	.08 micrometre
Circuit size	Circuit size	Circuit size	Circuit size	Circuit size	Circuit size
1997	1999	2002	2005	2008	2011

By 2005, new microchip plants will produce 1,000 transistors a week for every person on earth. Predictions are that computers may become as powerful as the human brain by 2020.

Technology: A Separate Factor of Production

We now recognize that technology must be viewed as a separate factor of production which is sensitive to rewards. In other words, one of the major foundations of new growth theory is this:

The greater the rewards, the more technological advances we will get.

Let's consider several aspects of technology here, starting with research and development.

INTERNATIONAL EXAMPLE
Technology and Light

For an even more impressive example of how technology has worked, consider what it has done to the true price of light. Economist William Nordhaus examined the price of 1,000 lumen-hours of light from 1880 to today. Even without correcting for inflation, the price has fallen from 40 cents to about 1/10 cent. After Nordhaus took account of true changes in other prices, he came up with a startling conclusion: Light in 1880 was about 1,000 times more expensive than it is today. Now that's progress.

For critical analysis: Why do we relate the falling price of artificial light to technological progress?

Research and Development

A certain amount of technological advance results from research and development (R&D) activities that have as their goal the development of specific new materials, new products, and new machines. How much spending a nation devotes to R&D can have an impact on its long-term economic growth. Part of how much a nation spends depends on what businesses decide is worth spending. That, in turn, depends on their expected rewards from successful R&D. If your company develops a new way to produce computer memory chips, how much will it be rewarded? The answer depends on whether others can freely copy the new technique.

Patents. To protect new techniques developed through R&D, we have a system of **patents**, protections whereby the federal government gives the patent holder the exclusive right to make, use, and sell an invention for a period of 20 years. One can argue that this special position given to owners of patents increases expenditures on R&D and therefore adds to long-term economic growth.

▶ **Patent**

A government protection that gives an inventor the exclusive right to make, use, or sell an invention for a limited period of time (currently, 20 years in Canada).

Positive Externalities and R&D.   Positive externalities are benefits from an activity that do not spill over to the instigator of the activity. In the case of R&D spending, a certain amount of the benefits go to other companies that do not have to pay for them. In particular, according to economists David Coe and Elhanan Helpman, about a quarter of the global benefits of R&D investment in the top seven industrialized countries goes to foreigners. For every 1 percent rise in the stock of research and development in North America alone, for example, productivity in the rest of the world increases by about 0.04 percent. One country's R&D expenditures benefit foreigners because foreigners are able to import goods from technologically advanced countries and then use them as inputs in making their own industries more efficient. In addition, countries that import high-tech goods are able to imitate the technology.

The Open Economy and Economic Growth

People who study economic growth today tend to emphasize the importance of the openness of the economy. Free trade encourages a more rapid spread of technology and industrial ideas. Moreover, open economies may experience higher rates of economic growth because their own industries have access to a bigger market. When trade barriers are erected in the form of tariffs and the like, domestic industries become isolated from global technological progress. This occurred for many years in former communist countries and in many developing countries in Latin America and elsewhere. Figure 9.6 shows the relationship between economic growth and the openness as measured by the level of protectionism of a given economy.

Figure 9.6
The Relationship Between Protectionism and Economic Growth

Closed economies are ones in which the government prevents imports from entering the country and, sometimes, exports from leaving the country. Such protectionism closes off the economy to new technologies. Here you see the relationship between the level of protectionism and economic growth rates measured on a per capita basis. The data seem to indicate that the more closed an economy, the lower its rate of growth, all other things held constant.

Source: Economic Review, Fourth Quarter 1993, p. 3.

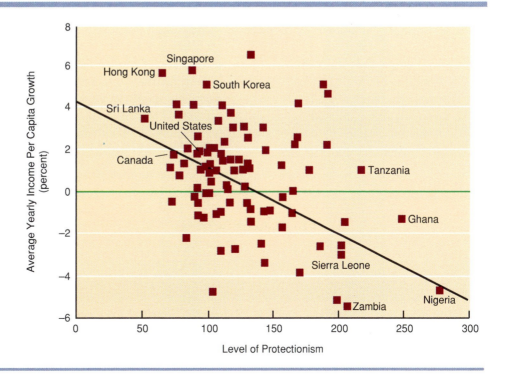

Innovation and Knowledge

▶ **Innovation**

Transforming an invention into something that is useful to humans.

We tend to think of technological progress as, say, the invention of the transistor. But invention means nothing by itself; **innovation** is required. Innovation involves the transformation of something new, such as an invention, into something that benefits the economy either by lowering production costs or providing new goods and services. Indeed, the new growth theorists believe that real wealth creation comes from innovation and that invention is but one aspect of innovation.

Historically, technologies have moved relatively slowly from invention to innovation to widespread use, and the dispersion of new technology remains for the most part slow and uncertain. The inventor of the transistor thought it might be used to make better hearing aids. At the time it was invented, the only reference to it in the *New York Times* was in a small weekly column called "News of Radio." When the laser was invented, no one really knew what it could be used for. It was initially used to help in navigation, measurement, and chemical research. Today, it is used in the reproduction of music, printing, surgery, and telecommunications. Tomorrow, who knows?

Much innovation involves small improvements in the use of an existing technology. Such improvements develop from experimentation and discovery, which have been fostered in the Japanese automobile market, for example.

INTERNATIONAL EXAMPLE
Innovation in the Japanese Auto Industry

The automobile has been around for a century. By the 1950s, American automobile manufacturers were fairly well convinced that they had developed the best and most efficient assembly-line operation in the world. They did so through what were called time-and-motion studies. A "final" set of directions was given to each worker on the assembly line, and that worker adhered to those directions. The Japanese decided to improve on this through a process of experimentation and discovery. In Japanese automobile plants, workers were encouraged to experiment with small changes in how they assembled a car—should the door moulding go on before or after the door is put on the car? Gradually, Japanese automobile workers became more efficient than their American counterparts. The process came about through small innovative changes, not one great invention.

For critical analysis: How many ways are there to put together a car?

The Importance of Ideas and Knowledge

Economist Paul Romer has added at least one important factor that determines the rate of economic growth. He contends that production and manufacturing knowledge is just as important as the other determinants and perhaps even more so. He considers knowledge a factor of production that, like capital, has to be paid for by forgoing current consumption. Economies must therefore invest in knowledge just as they invest in machines. Because past investment in capital may make it more profitable to acquire more knowledge, there exists the possibility of an investment-knowledge cycle in which investment spurs knowledge and knowledge spurs investment. A once-and-for-all increase in a country's rate of investment may permanently raise that country's growth rate. (According to traditional theory, a once-and-for-all increase in the rate of saving and therefore in the rate of investment simply leads to a new steady-state standard of living but not one that continues to increase.)

Another way of looking at knowledge is that it is a store of ideas. According to Romer, ideas are what drive economic growth. We have become, in fact, an idea economy. Consider Seattle's Microsoft Corporation. A relatively small percentage of that company's labour force is involved in actually producing diskettes. Rather, a majority of Microsoft workers are attempting to discover new ideas that can be translated to computer code that can then be placed on diskettes. The major conclusion that Romer and other new growth theorists draw is this:

> Economic growth can continue as long as we keep coming up with new ideas.

The Importance of Human Capital

Knowledge, ideas, and productivity are all tied together. One of the threads is the quality of the labour force. Increases in the productivity of the labour force are a function of increases in human capital, the fourth factor of production discussed in Chapter 2. Recall that human capital is the knowledge and skills that people in the workforce acquire through education, on-the-job training, and self-teaching. To increase your own human capital, you have to invest by forgoing income-earning activities while you attend school. Society also has to invest in the form of libraries and teachers. According to the new growth theorists, human capital is at least as important as physical capital, particularly when trying to explain international differences in living standards.

As you will see in Chapter 21, one of the most effective ways that developing countries can become developed is by investing in secondary schooling.

One can argue that policy changes that increase human capital will lead to more technological improvements. One of the reasons concerned citizens, policymakers, and politicians are looking for a change in Canada's schooling system is that our educational system seems to be falling behind that of other countries. This lag is greatest in science and mathematics—precisely the areas that are required for developing better technology.

Try Preview Question 4:

What are the determinants of economic growht?

Concepts in Brief

- New growth theory argues that the greater the rewards, the more rapid the pace of technology. And greater rewards spur research and development.
- The openness of an economy seems to correlate with its economic rate of growth.
- Invention and innovation are not the same thing. Inventions are useless until innovation transforms them into things that people find valuable.

- According to the new growth economists, economic growth can continue as long as we keep coming up with new ideas.
- Increases in human capital can lead to greater rates of economic growth. These come about by increased education, on-the-job training, and self-teaching.

POPULATION AND IMMIGRATION AS THEY AFFECT ECONOMIC GROWTH

There are several ways to view population growth as it affects economic growth. On the one hand, population growth means an increase in the amount of labour, which, as we have previously learned, is one component of economic growth. On the other hand, population growth can be seen as a drain on the economy because for any given amount of GDP, more population means lower per capita GDP. Most economists agree that the first view is historically correct. Population growth drives technological progress, which then increases economic growth. The theory is simple: If there are 50 percent more people in Canada, there will be 50 percent more geniuses. And with 50 percent more people, the rewards for creativity are commensurately greater. Otherwise stated, the larger the potential market, the greater the incentive to become ingenious.

Does the same argument apply to immigration? Yes, according to most studies that indicate immigrants have a higher labour force participation rate and lower unemployment rate than other Canadians. This should, in the long run, boost potential output. In addition, on average, immigrants have more education than other Canadians, and call upon our social programs less frequently.

Not all researchers agree with this view, and few studies exist to back up the theories advanced here. The area is currently the focus of much research.

PROPERTY RIGHTS AND ENTREPRENEURSHIP

If you were in a country where bank accounts and businesses were periodically seized by the government, how willing would you be to leave your money in a savings account or to invest in a business? Certainly you would be less willing than if such things never occurred. In general, the more certain private property rights are, the more capital accumulation there will be. People will be willing to invest their savings in endeavours that will increase their wealth in future years. They have property rights in their wealth that are sanctioned and enforced by the government. In fact, some economic historians have attempted to show that it was the development of well-defined private property rights that allowed Western Europe to increase its growth rate after many centuries of stagnation. The ability and certainty with which they can reap the gains from investing also determine the extent to which business owners in other countries will invest capital in developing countries. The threat of nationalization that hangs over some developing nations probably prevents the massive amount of foreign investment that might be necessary to allow these nations to develop more rapidly.

The property rights, or legal structure, in a nation are closely tied to the degree with which individuals use their own entrepreneurial skills. In Chapter 2, we identified entrepreneurship as the fifth factor of production. Entrepreneurs are the risk takers who seek out new ways to do things and create new products. To the extent that entrepreneurs are allowed to capture the rewards from their entrepreneurial activities, they will seek to engage in those activities. In countries where such rewards cannot be captured because of a lack of property rights, there will be less entrepreneurship. Typically, this results in fewer investments and a lower rate of growth.

Concepts in Brief

- While some economists argue that population growth stifles economic growth, others contend that empirically the opposite is true. The latter economists consequently believe that immigration should be encouraged rather than discouraged.
- Well-defined and protected property rights are important for fostering entrepreneurship. In the absence of well-defined property rights, individuals have less incentive to take risks, and economic growth rates usually suffer.

Issues and Applications

Democracy and Prosperity: Cause or Effect?

Concepts Applied: Economic growth, per capita real GDP

Nondemocratic countries that achieve high standards of living through steady economic growth tend to become more democratic over time. Taiwan had its first full democratic election in 1996. Here, election workers count ballots at a polling station in Taipei.

Most Canadians believe that they have the best political system on earth. They support this belief by pointing out the disastrous economic results of the alternative political system called communism that existed in the former Soviet Union and throughout Eastern Europe prior to the 1990s. Does this therefore mean that democracy is good for economic growth? Consistent economic growth in this country seems to imply that the answer is yes (except for the Great Depression, of course). The real question, though, is whether democracy causes economic growth or whether economic growth causes democracy.

Benefits of Democracy

Democracy has the great benefit of reining in government power.

In principle and in theory, it provides a check on the ability of public officials to carry out too many unpopular projects. Further, it normally prevents public officials from stealing from public coffers on a grand scale.

Costs of Democracy

Political freedom in the form of democracy carries with it the ability of special-interest groups to gain personally at the expense of society as a whole. Through the democratic process, special-interest groups can prevent lower-priced goods (and labour) from entering the country, quash new businesses that would compete with existing businesses, and impose other inefficient policies.

What Does the Real World Show?

What does the real world tell us about the relationship between democracy and economic growth rates? Economist Robert Barro studied more than 100 countries over the past three decades. After adjusting for differences in other factors, he concluded that "the overall effect of more democracy on the growth rate is moderately negative." The evidence shows that once a moderate amount of political freedom has been attained, democracy either doesn't help economic growth or renders it slightly less than it would have been otherwise.

Could High Economic Growth Cause Democracy?

According to Barro's research, the link between democracy and

economic growth is probably reversed. That is to say, when non-democratic countries have achieved high standards of living through consistent economic growth, they tend to become more democratic over time. There are a number of important examples today, including Chile, Portugal, South Korea, Spain, and Taiwan. Using this model, Barro predicted that Algeria, Indonesia, Iran, Iraq, Mexico, Peru, Singapore, Sudan, and Syria will all become more democratic by the year 2000.

For Critical Analysis

1. Assume that more democracy (increased political freedom) leads to a lower economic rate of growth in some countries. Are there still reasons to encourage more democracy in those countries? If so, what are these reasons?

2. "Political freedoms tend to erode over time if they are out of line with a country's standard of living." Analyse this statement.

CHAPTER SUMMARY

1. Economic growth is defined as the rate of increase in per capita real GDP. It can be shown graphically as an outward shift in the production possibilities curve. Small changes in rates of growth lead to large differences in GDP over time because of compounding.

2. Economic growth can be defined as being numerically equal to the rate of growth of capital plus the rate of growth of labour plus the rate of growth in the productivity of capital and of labour.

3. To consume more in the future, you have to save —not consume—today. The rate of saving is a key determinant of a nation's rate of economic growth.

4. The new growth theorists argue that advances in technology are a function of the rewards to those advances. In particular, research and develop-

ment will increase the more it is rewarded.

5. The more open an economy, the faster its rate of economic growth.

6. Although inventions are important, they have no value until they are made useful by innovation. Innovations may be slow to occur and may involve small improvements in the use of existing technologies. Economic growth can continue as long as we keep coming up with new ideas.

7. Increases in human capital can occur because of schooling and on-the-job training. Schooling requires a personal investment by the student— giving up consumption that would otherwise be available through paid work—as well as investment by society in teachers and libraries. Differences in standards of living across countries can, to some extent, be explained by differences in the level of human capital investment.

8. Empirically, increased population size has been associated with higher rates of economic growth. Consequently, immigration can be viewed as good rather than bad.

9. Well-defined property rights and resulting entrepreneurship may explain differences in rates of economic growth. Increased certainty about property rights may lead to more capital accumulation and higher rates of economic growth in nations in which property rights have been uncertain in the past.

DISCUSSION OF PREVIEW QUESTIONS

1. **What is economic growth?**

   By economic growth, economists are referring to the rate of increase in an economy's real level of output over time. It is generally agreed that the rate of changes in per capita (corrected for population change) real (corrected for price level changes) GDP is a good measure of an economy's economic growth. The very long-run economic growth rate for Canada is approximately 1.75 percent per year—with much deviation around this trend line, of course.

2. **What does economic growth measure?**

   Many people try to make inferences about changes in economic well-being from a nation's economic growth rate; presumably, higher growth rates imply more rapid increases in living standards. Others have argued that increased income inequality may accompany rapid economic growth, as a relatively small percentage of the population may benefit from economic growth while the majority experiences little economic improvement. Critics also point out that rapid economic growth is not necessarily consistent with increases in the spiritual, cultural, or environmental quality of life. However, because per capita increases in real GDP do not measure the increased leisure that usually accompanies economic growth, this measure may *understate* economic well-being. Economic growth is therefore a rather crude measure of changes in a nation's well-being and is perhaps a better indicator of its productive activity.

3. **What are some of the ways in which you can experience economic growth for yourself or for your family?**

You can experience economic growth only if you are willing to sacrifice something. When you continue to go to school, you are sacrificing your current ability to earn and consume income. But in exchange for that sacrifice, you are developing skills and talents that will allow you to have a higher income in the future. You are investing in yourself (human capital) by sacrificing current consumption now.

If you wish to accumulate much wealth during your lifetime, you must be willing to sacrifice current consumption. You do this by not consuming all of your income—that is, by saving part of it. The more you save, the more you can accumulate. In particular, if you invest your accumulated savings in wise savings outlets, you will be rewarded by a compounded rate of growth so that in the future you will have accumulated larger amounts of wealth.

4. **What are the determinants of economic growth?**

One obvious determinant of economic growth is the quantity and quality of a nation's natural resources—although this determinant can easily be exaggerated. Hence many slowly developing nations have bountiful natural resources, and some rapidly developing areas have very few. The quality and quantity of labour and capital are also important determinants of economic growth, as is a nation's rate of technological progress. A decidedly underrated determinant of economic growth is the industriousness and willingness of people to be productive—which is surely related to personal incentives related to property rights. The certainty of property rights may also affect a nation's growth rate.

PROBLEMS

(Answers to the odd-numbered problems appear at the back of the book.)

9-1. The graph shows the production possibilities frontier for an economy. Which of the labelled points would be associated with the highest feasible growth rate for this economy?

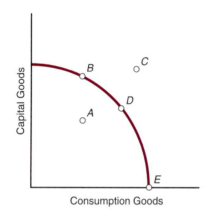

9-2. Why might an economy be operating inside its production possibilities curve?

9-3. Consider the following table, which describes growth rate data for four countries between 1989 and 1998.

	Annual Growth Rate (%)			
Country	J	K	L	M
Nominal GDP	20	15	10	5
Price level	5	3	6	2
Population	5	8	2	1

a. Which country has the largest rate of output growth per capita?
b. Which country has the smallest rate of output growth per capita?

9-4. Use Table 9.3 (p. 221) to answer the following questions.
a. Country A has a growth rate of 3 percent, and country B has a growth rate of 4 percent. Assume that they both start off with equal incomes. How much richer will country A be after 10 years? After 50 years?
b. Assume that country A has twice the income per capita of country B. Country A is growing at 3 percent, and country B is growing at 4 percent. Will country B ever catch up? If so, when?

PART 3

National Income Determination

Micro Foundations: Aggregate Demand and Aggregate Supply

In a matter of minutes on January 17, 1995, fifty-storey office buildings, steel and concrete freeways, and tens of thousands of houses collapsed in the Japanese city of Kobe. The earthquake measured 7.2 on the Richter scale. Thousands of people were killed, and hundreds of thousands left homeless. The estimated cost of rebuilding: $150 billion. To understand what effect this terrible tragedy had on the economy of Japan, you need to understand how aggregate demand and aggregate supply work together to create the equilibrium level of real GDP.

Preview Questions

1. Why does the aggregate demand curve slope downward?

2. Why is the long-run aggregate supply curve vertical?

3. Why does the short-run aggregate supply curve slope upward?

4. How can we show improvements in technology using aggregate demand and aggregate supply analysis?

Did You Know That...when economic analysts forecast how quickly the Canadian economy will grow in future years, they have to estimate how much consumers will spend *and* how much businesses will produce in response *and* how these two events will interact to change the price level across the economy. No wonder it's so difficult to come up with reliable estimates! To make matters worse, unforeseen events—called "shocks" to the economy—occur and often make existing forecasts look way off the mark. In this chapter you will learn about one method economists use to explain changes in output, unemployment, and the price level in our economy.

SPENDING AND TOTAL EXPENDITURES

As explained in Chapter 8, GDP is the dollar value of total expenditures on domestically produced final goods and services. Because all expenditures are made by individuals, firms, or governments, the total value of these expenditures must be what each of these market participants decides it will be. The decisions of individuals, managers of firms, and government officials determine the annual dollar value of total expenditures. You can certainly see this in your role as an individual. You decide what the total value of your expenditures will be in a year. You decide how much you want to spend and how much you want to save. Thus if we want to know what determines the total value of GDP, the answer would be clear: the spending decisions of individuals like you; firms; and municipal, provincial, and federal governments. In an open economy, we must also include foreign individuals, firms, and governments (foreigners, for short) that decide to spend their money income in Canada.

Simply stating that the dollar value of total expenditures in this country depends on what individuals, firms, governments, and foreigners decide to do really doesn't tell us much, though. Two important issues remain:

1. What determines the total amount that individuals, firms, governments, and foreigners want to spend?
2. What determines whether this spending will result in a higher output of goods and services (quantities) or higher prices (inflation)?

▶ **Aggregate demand**
The total of all planned expenditures for the entire economy.

▶ **Aggregate supply**
The total of all planned production for the entire economy.

The way we will answer these questions in this chapter is by developing the concepts of *aggregate demand* and *aggregate supply*. **Aggregate demand** is the total of all planned expenditures in the economy. **Aggregate supply** is the total of all planned production in the economy. Given these definitions, we can now proceed to construct an aggregate demand curve and an aggregate supply curve.

THE AGGREGATE DEMAND CURVE

▶**Aggregate demand curve**
A curve showing planned purchase rates for all goods and services in the economy at various price levels, all other things held constant.

The **aggregate demand curve,** *AD,* gives the various quantities of all final commodities demanded at various price levels, all other things held constant. Recall the components of GDP that you studied in Chapter 8: consumption spending, investment expenditures, government purchases, and net foreign demand for domestic production. They are all components of aggregate demand. Throughout this chapter and the next, whenever you see the aggregate demand curve, realize that it is a shorthand way of talking about the components of GDP that are measured by government statisticians when they calculate total economic activity each year. In Chapter 12 you will look more closely at the relationship between these components, and in particular at how consumption spending depends on income.

Aggregate Demand Curve

The aggregate demand curve gives the total amount of *real* domestic income that will be purchased at each price level. Real domestic income consists of the output of final goods and services in the economy—everything produced for final use by either businesses or households. This includes computer software, socks, shoes, medical and legal services, sailboats, and millions of other goods and services that people buy each year. A graphic representation of the aggregate demand curve is seen in Figure 10.1. The horizontal axis measures real gross domestic output, or real GDP. For our measure of the price level, we use the GDP price deflator on the vertical axis. The aggregate demand curve is labelled *AD.* If the GDP deflator is 100, aggregate quantity demanded is $800 billion per year (point *A*). At price level 120 it is $700 billion per year (point *B*). At price level 140 it is $600 billion per year (point *C*). The higher the price level, the lower will be the total real output demanded by the economy, everything else remaining constant, as shown by the arrow along *AD* in Figure 10.1. Conversely, the lower the price level, the higher will be the total real output demanded by the economy, everything else staying constant.

Figure 10.1
The Aggregate Demand Curve

Because of the real-balance, interest rate, and open economy effects, the aggregate demand curve, *AD,* slopes downward. If the price level is 100, we will be at point *A* with $800 billion of real GDP demanded per year. As the price level increases to 120 and 140, we will move up the aggregate demand curve to points *B* and *C*.

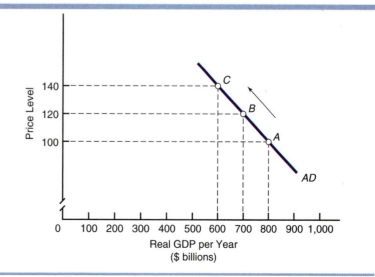

Let's take the year 1997. Looking at Statistics Canada preliminary statistics reveals the following information:

- GDP was $855 billion.
- The price level as measured by the GDP deflator was 107.1 (base year 1992, when the index equals 100).
- Real GDP (output) was $798 billion in 1992 dollars.

What can we say about 1997? Given the dollar cost of buying goods and services and all of the other factors that go into spending decisions by individuals, firms, governments, and foreigners, the total amount of real domestic output demanded by firms, individuals, governments, and foreigners was $798 billion in 1997 (in terms of 1992 dollars).

What Happens When the Price Level Rises?

What if the price level in the economy rose to 120 tomorrow? What would happen to the amount of real goods and services that individuals, firms, governments, and foreigners wish to purchase in Canada? When we asked that question about individual commodities in Chapter 3, the answer was obvious: The quantity demanded would fall if the price went up. Now we are talking about the *price level*—the average price of *all* goods and services in the economy. The answer is still that the total quantities of real goods and services demanded would fall, but the reasons are different. Remember that in Chapter 3, when the price of one good or service went up, the consumer would substitute other goods and services. For the entire economy, when the price level goes up, the consumer doesn't simply substitute one good for another, for now we are dealing with the demand for all goods and services in the entire country. There are *economywide* reasons that cause the aggregate demand curve to slope downward. They involve at least three distinct forces: the *real-balance effect*, the *interest rate effect*, and the *open economy effect*.

The Direct Effect: The Real-Balance Effect.

A rise in the price level will have a direct effect on spending. Individuals, firms, governments, and foreigners carry out transactions using money. Money in this context only consists of currency and coins that you have in your pocket (or stashed away) right now. Because people use money to purchase goods and services, the amount of money that people have influences the amount of goods and services they want to buy. For example, if you found a $10 bill on the sidewalk, the amount of money you had would rise. This would likely have a *direct* effect on the amount of spending in which you would engage. Given your greater level of money balances—currency in this case—you would almost surely increase your spending on goods and services. Similarly, if while on a trip downtown you had your pocket picked, there would be a direct effect on your desired spending. For example, if your wallet had $30 in it when it was stolen, the reduction in your cash balances—in this case currency—would no doubt cause you to reduce your planned expenditures. You would ultimately buy fewer goods and services. This response is sometimes called the **real-balance effect** (or *wealth effect*) because it relates to the real value of your cash balances. While your nominal cash

▶ **Real-balance effect**

The change in the real value of money balances when the price level changes, all other things held constant. Also called the *wealth effect*.

balances may remain the same, any change in the price level will cause a change in the real value of those cash balances—hence the real-balance effect on the quantity of aggregate goods and services demanded.

When you think of the real-balance effect, just think of what happens to your real wealth if you have, say, a $100 bill hidden under your mattress. If the price level increases by 10 percent, the purchasing power of that $100 bill drops by 10 percent, so not only may you feel less wealthy, you actually are. This will reduce your spending on all goods and services by some small amount.

The Indirect Effect: The Interest Rate Effect.

There is a more subtle, but equally important, *indirect* effect on your desire to spend. As we said before, when the price level goes up, the real value of your money balances declines. You end up with too few real money balances relative to other things that you own. After all, we all own a bit of many things—clothes, money balances, bicycles, cars, CD players, and perhaps houses and stocks and bonds. If, because of the price level increase, you find out that you have too few real money balances, you might actually go out and borrow to replenish them. When there are more people going in the front door of lending institutions to borrow money than there are people coming in the back door, as it were, to lend the money, the price of borrowing is going to go up. The price you pay to borrow money is the interest rate you have to pay. Because more people want to borrow now to replenish their real cash balances, interest rates will rise, and this is where the indirect effect—the **interest rate effect**—on total spending comes in.

▶ **Interest rate effect**
One of the reasons that the aggregate demand curve slopes downward is because higher price levels indirectly increase the interest rate, which in turn causes businesses and consumers to reduce desired spending due to the higher cost of borrowing.

Higher interest rates make it less attractive for people to buy houses and cars. Higher interest rates also make it less profitable for firms to install new equipment and to erect new office buildings. Whether we are talking about individuals or firms, the indirect effect of a rise in the price level will cause a higher level of interest rates, which in turn reduces the amount of goods and services that people are willing to purchase when the price level rises. Therefore, an increase in the price level will tend to reduce the quantity of aggregate goods and services demanded. (The opposite occurs if the price level declines.)

The Open Economy Effect: The Substitution of Foreign Goods.

Remember from Chapter 8 that GDP includes net exports—the difference between exports and imports. In an open economy, we buy imports from other countries and ultimately pay for them through the foreign exchange market. The same is true for foreigners who purchase our goods (exports). Given any set of exchange rates between the Canadian dollar and other currencies, an increase in the price level in Canada makes Canadian goods more expensive relative to foreign goods. Foreigners have downward-sloping demand curves for Canadian goods. When the relative price of Canadian goods goes up, foreigners buy fewer Canadian goods and more of their own. In Canada, the cheaper-priced foreign goods now result in Canadians wanting to buy more foreign goods rather than Canadian goods. The result is a fall in exports and a rise in imports when the domestic price level rises. That means that a price level increase tends to reduce net exports, thereby reducing the amount of real goods and services purchased in Canada. This is known as the **open economy effect.**

▶ **Open economy effect**
One of the reasons that the aggregate demand curve slopes downward is because higher price levels result in foreigners desiring to buy fewer Canadian-made goods while Canadians now desire more foreign-made goods, thereby reducing net exports, which is equivalent to a reduction in the amount of real goods and services purchased in Canada.

What Happens When the Price Level Falls?

What about the reverse? Suppose now that the GDP deflator falls to 100 from an initial level of 120. You should be able to trace the three effects on desired purchases of goods and services. Specifically, how do the real-balance, interest rate, and open economy effects cause people to want to buy more? You should come to the conclusion that the lower the price level, the greater the quantity of output of goods and services demanded.

The aggregate demand curve, *AD*, shows the quantity of aggregate output that will be demanded at alternative price levels. It is downward-sloping, as is the demand curve for individual goods. The higher the price level, the lower the quantity of aggregate output demanded, and vice versa.

Aggregate Demand Versus *Individual* Demand

Try Preview Question 1:
Why does the aggregate demand curve slope downward?

Even though the aggregate demand curve, *AD*, in Figure 10.1 on page 241 looks quite similar to the individual demand curve, *D*, to which you were introduced in Chapters 3 and 4, it is not the same. When we derive the aggregate demand curve, we are looking at the entire economic system. The aggregate demand curve, *AD*, differs from an individual demand curve, *D*, because we are looking at the *entire* circular flow of income and product when we construct *AD*.

SHIFTS IN THE AGGREGATE DEMAND CURVE

In Chapter 3 you learned that any time a nonprice determinant of demand changed, the demand curve shifted inward to the left or outward to the right. The same analysis holds for the aggregate demand curve, except we are now talking about the nonprice-level determinants of aggregate demand. So when we ask the question, "What

---

Table 10.1
Determinants of Aggregate Demand

Aggregate demand consists of the demand for domestically produced consumption goods, investment goods, government purchases, and net exports. Consequently, any change in the demand for any one of these components of real GDP will cause a change in aggregate demand. Here are some possibilities.

Changes That Cause an Increase in Aggregate Demand	Changes That Cause a Decrease in Aggregate Demand
A drop in the foreign exchange value of the dollar	A rise in the foreign exchange value of the dollar
Increased security about jobs and future income	Decreased security about jobs and future income
Improvements in economic conditions in other countries	Declines in economic conditions in other countries
A reduction in real interest rates (nominal interest rates corrected for inflation) not due to price level changes	A rise in real interest rates (nominal interest rates corrected for inflation) not due to price level changes
Tax decreases	Tax increases
An increase in the amount of money in circulation	A decrease in the amount of money in circulation

determines the position of the aggregate demand curve?" the fundamental proposition is as follows:

> Any non-price-level change that increases aggregate spending (on domestic goods) shifts *AD* to the right. Any non-price-level change that decreases aggregate spending (on domestic goods) shifts *AD* to the left.

The list of potential determinants of the position of the aggregate demand curve is virtually without limit. Some of the most important "curve shifters" with respect to aggregate demand are presented in Table 10.1.

INTERNATIONAL EXAMPLE
The Effects of the Recession in the European Community

The European Community (EC) became a relatively unified single trading block on December 31, 1992. It represents about 375 million consumers in the 15 countries: France, Greece, Germany, the United Kingdom, Portugal, the Netherlands, Belgium, Spain, Italy, Denmark, Ireland, Austria, Finland, Sweden, and Luxembourg. Consumers in those countries buy some Canadian goods, including jeans, wheat, fish, automobiles, and computer software. A recession in the EC would therefore have an effect on aggregate spending in Canada on domestically produced goods. The way we show this is by shifting the aggregate demand curve, *AD*, in to the left. Look at Figure 10.2. There you see the aggregate demand curve shifting from AD_1 to AD_2. *AD* shifts because a non-price-level determinant of aggregate demand has changed. In this particular example, the non-price-level determinant was foreigners' income.

Figure 10.2
Aggregate Demand Curve Shift

Any non-price-level determinant that causes a decrease in total desired aggregate spending will shift the aggregate demand curve from AD_1 to AD_2.

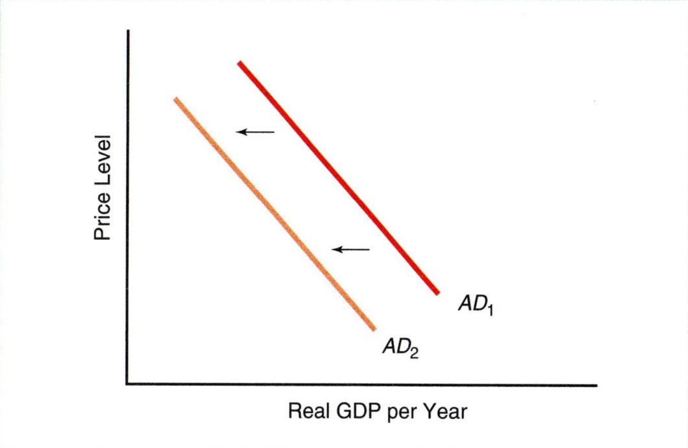

For critical analysis: Can you show how a bumper agricultural crop in the EC would affect the Canadian aggregate demand curve?

Concepts in Brief

- Aggregate demand is the total of all planned expenditures in the economy, and aggregate supply is the total of all planned production in the economy. The aggregate demand curve shows the various quantities of all commodities demanded at various price levels; it is downward-sloping.
- There are three reasons the aggregate demand curve is downward-sloping: the direct effect, the indirect effect, and the open economy effect.
- The direct effect, sometimes called the real-balance effect, occurs because price level changes alter the real value of cash balances, thereby directly causing people to desire to spend more or less, depending on whether the price level decreases or increases.
- The indirect, or interest rate, effect is caused via interest rate changes that mimic price level changes. At higher interest rates, people desire to buy fewer houses and cars, and vice versa.
- The open economy effect occurs because of the substitution towards foreign goods when the domestic price level increases and a shift away from foreign goods when the domestic price level decreases.

THE AGGREGATE SUPPLY CURVE

The aggregate demand curve tells us how much output will be demanded given the price level. It also indicates the point towards which the price level will gravitate for any *given* total output. Knowing the position and shape of the aggregate demand curve does not tell us anything about how the *total* dollar value of spending will ultimately be divided between output—real goods and services—and prices. To determine this and thus the equilibrium level of real GDP, we must introduce supply conditions.

When we talk about aggregate supply, we have to distinguish between the long run, when all adjustments to changes in the price level can be made, and the short run, when all adjustments to changes in the price level cannot be made. Therefore, we must derive two different aggregate supply curves.

▶ **Long-run aggregate supply curve**

A vertical line representing real output of goods and services based on full information and after full adjustment has occurred. Can also be viewed as representing the real output of the economy under conditions of full employment—the full-employment level of real GDP.

Long-Run Aggregate Supply Curve

In Chapter 2 we showed the derivation of the production possibilities curve. At any point in time, the economy can be inside or on the production possibilities curve, but never outside it. The only way we can have more of everything is through economic growth—the production possibilities curve moves outward as shown in part (a) of Figure 10.3. The idea behind the production possibilities curve can be translated into what we call the **long-run aggregate supply curve** (*LRAS*).

Put yourself in a world in which nothing has been changing, year in and year out. The price level has not changed. Technology has not changed. The prices of

Figure 10.3
The Long-Run Aggregate Supply Curve and Shifts in It

In part (a), we repeat a diagram that we used in Chapter 2 to show the meaning of economic growth. Over time, the production possibilities curve shifts outward. In part (b), we demonstrate the same principle by showing the long-run aggregate supply curve as initially a vertical line at *LRAS* at $700 billion of real GDP per year. As our endowments increase, the *LRAS* moves outward to *LRAS*$_{2002}$.

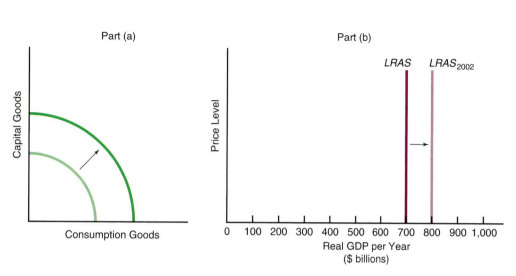

inputs that firms must purchase have not changed. Labour productivity has not changed. This is a world that is fully adjusted and in which people have all the information they are ever going to get about that world. The long-run aggregate supply curve in this world is some amount of output of real goods and services, say, $700 billion of real GDP. We can show long-run aggregate supply simply by a vertical line at $700 billion of real GDP. This is what you see in part (b) of Figure 10.3. That curve, labelled *LRAS*, is a vertical line determined by tastes, technology, and the **endowments** of resources that exist in our economy. It is the full-information and full-adjustment level of real output of goods and services. It is the level of real output that will continue being produced year after year, forever, if nothing changes.

Another way of viewing the *LRAS* is to think of it as the full-employment level of real GDP. When the economy reaches full employment, no further adjustments will occur unless a fundamental change occurs.

To understand why the long-run aggregate supply curve is vertical, think about the long run. The price level has no effect on real output (real GDP per year) because higher output prices will be accompanied by comparable changes in input prices, and suppliers will therefore have no incentive to increase or decrease output. Remember that in the long run, everybody has full information and there is full adjustment to price level changes.

▶ **Endowments**

The various resources in an economy, including both physical resources and such human resources as ingenuity and management skills.

Try Preview Question 2:
Why is the long-run aggregate supply curve vertical?

What If Non-Price-Level Variables Change? Clearly, as the years go by, things do change. Population increases, we discover more resources, and we improve technology. That means that over time, at least in a growing economy such as ours, *LRAS* will shift outward to the right, as in Figure 10.3. We have drawn *LRAS* for the year 2002 to the right of our original *LRAS* of $700 billion of real GDP. The number we attached to *LRAS*$_{2002}$ is $800 billion of real GDP, but that is only a guess; the point is that it is to the right of today's *LRAS*.

Aggregate Demand and Long-Run Output.   Because *LRAS* depends on technology and endowments, aggregate demand in the long run has no bearing on the level of output of real goods and services. Draw any *AD* curve on $LRAS_{2002}$ in part (b) of Figure 10.3, and you will see that the only thing that changes will be the price level. In the long run, the output of real goods and services is supply-side determined. Only shifts in *LRAS* will change long-run levels of output of real goods and services.

Short-Run Aggregate Supply Curve

▶ **Short-run aggregate supply curve**

The relationship between aggregate supply and the price level in the short run, all other things held constant; the curve is normally positively sloped.

The **short-run aggregate supply curve,** *SRAS*, represents the relationship between the price level and the real output of goods and services in the economy *without* full adjustment and full information. Just as we drew the supply curve for an individual good or service in Chapter 3 holding everything constant except the price of the good or service, we will do the same here. The short-run aggregate supply curve is drawn under the assumption that all determinants of aggregate supply other than the price level will be held constant. Most notably, we hold constant the prices of the inputs used in the production of real goods and services. Now, what does this mean? It means that when we hold the prices of the factors of production constant in the short run, as the price level rises, it becomes profitable for all firms to expand production. Otherwise stated, changes in the price level in the short run can affect real output because some production costs might be relatively fixed in nominal terms. Therefore, an increase in the price level increases expected profits.

Why Can Output Be Expanded in the Short Run?   In the short run, if the price level rises, output can be expanded (even beyond the economist's notion of the normal capacity of a firm). That is to say, the overall economy can temporarily produce beyond its normal limits or capacity, for a variety of reasons:

1. In the short run, most labour contracts implicitly or explicitly call for flexibility in hours of work at the given wage rate. Therefore, firms can use existing workers more intensively in a variety of ways: They can get them to work harder. They can get them to work more hours per day. And they can get them to work more days per week. Workers can also be switched from *uncounted* production, such as maintenance, to *counted* production, which generates counted output. The distinction between counted and uncounted is simply what is measured in the marketplace, particularly by government statisticians and accountants. If a worker cleans a machine, there is no measured output. But if that worker is put on the production line and helps increase the number of units produced each day, measured output will go up. That worker's production has then been counted.

2. Existing capital equipment can be used more intensively. Machines can be worked more hours per day. Some can be made to work at a faster speed. Maintenance can be delayed.

3. Finally, and just as important, if wage rates are held constant, a higher price level means that profits go up, which induces firms to hire more workers. The duration of unemployment falls, and thus the unemployment rate falls. And people who were previously not in the labour force (homemakers and younger or older workers) can be induced to enter.

All these adjustments cause national output to rise as the price level increases.

Figure 10.4
The Short-Run Aggregate Supply Curve

The short-run aggregate supply curve, *SRAS*, slopes upward because with fixed input prices, at a higher price level firms make more profits and desire more output. They use workers and capital more intensively. At price level 100, $600 billion of real GDP per year is supplied. If the price level rises to 120, $700 billion of real GDP per year will be supplied.

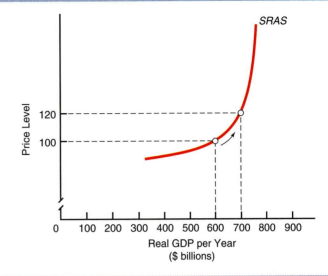

The Shape of the Short-Run Supply Curve.

Even if firms want to continue increasing production because the price level has risen, they cannot do this forever. Which means that when we hold input prices constant, the extra output that will be forthcoming for the three reasons just listed must eventually come to an end. Individual workers get tired. Workers are more willing to work one extra weekend than they are eight extra weekends in a row. Machines cannot go forever without maintenance. Finally, as all firms are hiring more workers from the pool of unemployed, it gets harder (more costly) to find workers at the existing level of wages.

What does all this mean? Simply that the short-run aggregate supply curve at some point must get steeper and steeper.

Graphing the Short-Run Aggregate Supply Curve.

Look at Figure 10.4. There you see the short-run aggregate supply curve, *SRAS*. As we have drawn it, after a real GDP of $700 billion, it starts to become steeper and steeper, and by the time it gets close to $800 billion, it is very steep indeed.[1] If the price index, as represented by the GDP deflator, is 100, the economy will supply $600 billion per year of real GDP in Figure 10.4. If the GDP deflator increases to 120, the economy will move up the *SRAS* to $700 billion of real GDP per year.

The Difference Between Aggregate and Individual Supply.

Although the aggregate supply curve tends to look like the supply curve for an individual commodity, the two curves are not exactly the same. A commodity supply curve reflects a change in the price of an individual commodity *relative* to the prices of other goods, whereas the aggregate supply curve shows the effects of changes in the price *level* for the entire economy.

Try Preview Question 3:
Why does the short-run aggregate supply curve slope upward?

---

[1] If there is a maximum short-run amount of output, at some point the *SRAS* becomes vertical. However, there is always some way to squeeze a little bit more out of an economic system, so the *SRAS* does not necessarily have to become vertical, just extremely steep.

SHIFTS IN THE AGGREGATE SUPPLY CURVE

Just as there were non-price-level factors that could cause a shift in the aggregate demand curve, there are non-price-level factors that can cause a shift in the aggregate supply curve. The analysis here is not quite so simple as the analysis for the non-price-level determinants for aggregate demand, for here we are dealing with both the short run and the long run—*SRAS* and *LRAS*. Still, anything other than the price level that affects supply will shift aggregate supply curves.

Shifts in Both Short- and Long-Run Aggregate Supply

There is a core class of events that causes a shift in both the short-run aggregate supply curve and the long-run aggregate supply curve. These include any change in our endowments of the factors of production.[2] Any change in land, labour, or capital will shift *SRAS* and *LRAS*. Furthermore, any change in the level of our technology or knowledge will also shift *SRAS* and *LRAS*. Look at Figure 10.5. Initially, the two curves are $SRAS_1$ and $LRAS_1$. Now consider a big oil discovery in Manitoba in an area where no one thought oil existed. This shifts $LRAS_1$ to $LRAS_2$ at $750 billion of real GDP. $SRAS_1$ also shifts outward horizontally to $SRAS_2$.

Try Preview Question 4:

How can we show improvements in technology using aggregate demand and aggregate supply analysis?

Figure 10.5

Shifts in Both Short- and Long-Run Aggregate Supply

Initially, the two supply curves are $SRAS_1$ and $LRAS_1$. Now consider a big oil find in Manitoba in an area where no one thought oil existed. This shifts $LRAS_1$ to $LRAS_2$ at $750 billion of real GDP. $SRAS_1$ also shifts outward horizontally to $SRAS_2$.

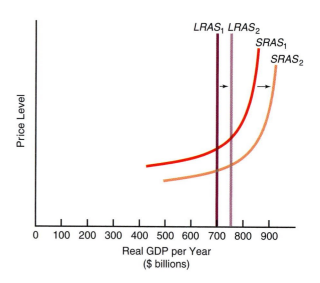

[2] There is a complication here. A big enough increase in natural resources not only shifts aggregate supply outward but also affects aggregate demand. Aggregate demand is a function of people's wealth, among other things. A big oil discovery in Canada will make enough people richer that desired total spending will increase. For the sake of simplicity, we ignore this complication.

Shifts in *SRAS* Only

Some events, particularly those that are short-lived, will temporarily shift *SRAS* but not *LRAS*. One of the most obvious is a temporary shift in input prices, particularly those caused by external events that are not expected to last forever. Consider the possibility of an announced 90-day embargo of oil from the Middle East to Canada. Oil is an important input in many production activities. The 90-day oil embargo will cause at least a temporary increase in the price of this input. You can see what happens in Figure 10.6. *LRAS* remains fixed, but $SRAS_1$ shifts to $SRAS_2$ reflecting the increase in input prices—the higher price of oil. This is because the rise in costs at each level of real GDP per year requires a higher price level to cover those costs.

We summarize the possible determinants of aggregate supply in Table 10.2. These determinants will cause a shift in either the short-run or the long-run aggregate supply curve, or both, depending on whether they are temporary or permanent.

Table 10.2
Determinants of Aggregate Supply

The determinants listed here can affect short-run or long-run aggregate supply (or both), depending on whether they are temporary or permanent.

Changes That Cause an Increase in Aggregate Supply	Changes That Cause a Decrease in Aggregate Supply
Discoveries of new raw materials	Depletion of raw materials
Increased competition	Decreased competition
A reduction in international trade barriers	An increase in international trade barriers
Fewer regulatory impediments to business	More regulatory impediments to business
An increase in labour supplied	A decrease in labour supplied
Increased training and education	Decreased training and education
A decrease in marginal tax rates	An increase in marginal tax rates
A reduction in input prices	An increase in input prices

Figure 10.6
Shifts in *SRAS* Only

A temporary increase in an input price will shift the short-run aggregate supply curve from $SRAS_1$ to $SRAS_2$.

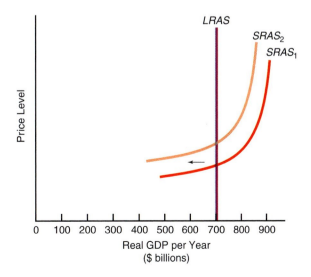

Concepts in Brief

- The long-run aggregate supply curve, *LRAS*, is a vertical line determined by technology and endowments of natural resources in an economy. It is the full-information and full-adjustment level of real output of goods and services.
- If population increases, more resources are discovered, or technology improves, *LRAS* will shift outward to the right.
- The short-run aggregate supply curve, *SRAS*, shows the relationship between the price level and the real output of goods and services in the economy without full adjustment or full information. It is upward-sloping.
- Output can be expanded in the short run because firms can use existing workers and capital equipment more intensively. Also, in the short run, when input prices are fixed, a higher price level means higher profits, which induces firms to hire more workers.
- Any change in land, labour, or capital will shift both *SRAS* and *LRAS*. A temporary shift in input prices, however, will shift only *SRAS*.

EQUILIBRIUM

As you discovered in Chapter 3, equilibrium occurs where demand and supply curves intersect. It is a little more complicated here because we have two types of aggregate

Figure 10.7
Equilibrium

Equilibrium will occur where the aggregate demand curve intersects the short-run aggregate supply curve and the long-run aggregate supply curve. In this diagram it is at price level 120 and a real GDP of $700 billion per year.

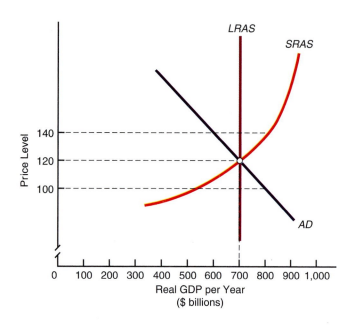

supply curves, long-run and short-run. Let's look first at short-run equilibrium. It occurs at the intersection of aggregate demand, *AD*, and short-run aggregate supply, *SRAS*, as shown in Figure 10.7. The equilibrium price level is 120, and the equilibrium annual level of real GDP is $700 billion. If the price level increased to 140, there would be an excess quantity of real goods and services supplied in the entire economy, and the price level would tend to fall. If the price level were 100, aggregate quantity demanded would be greater than aggregate quantity supplied, and buyers would bid up prices so that the price level would move towards 120.

In Figure 10.7 you see that we have drawn the long-run aggregate supply curve, *LRAS*, so that there is full equilibrium in both the short run and the long run at price level 120. At price level 120 this economy can operate forever at $700 billion without the price level changing.

In the short run, it is possible for us to be on *SRAS* to the right and above the intersection with *AD* and *LRAS*. Why? Because more can be squeezed out of the economy in the short run than would occur in the long-run, full-information, full-adjustment situation. Although in this economy a real GDP greater than $700 billion per year is possible, it is not consistent with long-run aggregate supply. Firms would be operating beyond long-run desired capacity, and inputs would be working too long and too hard for too little money. Input prices would begin to rise. When this happens, we can no longer stay with the same *SRAS*, because it was drawn with input prices held constant.

If the economy finds itself on *SRAS* below and to the left of the intersection of *AD* and *LRAS*, the opposite will occur. Firms are operating well below long-run capacity, and there are too many unemployed inputs. Input prices will begin to fall. We can no longer stay with the same *SRAS*, because it was drawn with constant input prices. *SRAS* will shift down.

Thinking Critically About the Media   **Can Recessions Be Good for the Economy?**

Every time there is a recession, or a period when a contractionary gap exists in the Canadian economy, some business commentators proclaim that it is good for the economy. Why? Because a minor recession, according to them, forces firms to "cut out the fat," to become more efficient and generally make themselves fitter, the better to compete in a competitive world. By definition, though, a recession is a period when the nation's full productive potential is not being used. That means that every time we experience a recession, we permanently give up billions of dollars of output and hence some significant amount of welfare to our society.

CONSEQUENCES OF CHANGES IN AGGREGATE SUPPLY AND DEMAND

We now have a basic model of the entire economy. We can trace the movement of the equilibrium price level and the equilibrium real GDP when there are shocks to the economy. Whenever there is a shift in our economy's curves, the equilibrium

▶ **Aggregate demand shock**

Any shock that causes the aggregate demand curve to shift inward or outward.

▶ **Aggregate supply shock**

Any shock that causes the aggregate supply curve to shift inward or outward.

price level or real GDP level (or both) may change. These shifts are called **aggregate demand shocks** on the demand side and **aggregate supply shocks** on the supply side.

In Chapter 4 you learned what happened to the equilibrium price and quantity when there was a shift in demand, then a shift in supply, and then shifts in both curves. In the analysis that follows, we will be using the same basic analysis, but you should remember that we are now talking about changes in the overall price level and changes in the equilibrium level of real GDP per year.

Aggregate Demand Shifts While Aggregate Supply Is Stable

Now we can show what happens when aggregate supply remains stable but aggregate demand falls. The outcome may be the possible cause of a recession and can, under certain circumstances, explain a rise in the unemployment rate. In Figure 10.8 you see that with AD_1, both long-run and short-run equilibrium are at $700 billion of real GDP per year (because $SRAS$ and $LRAS$ also intersect AD_1 at that level of real GDP). The long-run equilibrium price level is 120. A reduction in aggregate demand shifts the aggregate demand curve to AD_2. The new intersection with $SRAS$ is at $680 billion per year, which is below the economy's long-run aggregate supply. The difference between $700 billion and $680 billion is called the **contractionary gap**, which is defined as the difference between the short-run equilibrium level of real GDP and how much the economy could be producing if it were operating at full employment on its $LRAS$.

▶ **Contractionary gap**

The gap that exists whenever the equilibrium level of real national income per year is less than the full-employment level as shown by the position of the long-run aggregate supply curve.

Figure 10.8

The Effects of Stable Aggregate Supply and a Decrease in Aggregate Demand: The Contractionary Gap

If the economy is at equilibrium at E_1, with price level 120 and real GDP per year of $700 billion, a shift inward of the aggregate demand curve to AD_2 will lead to a new short-run equilibrium at E_2. The equilibrium price level will fall to 115, and the short-run equilibrium level of real GDP per year will fall to $680 billion. There will be a contractionary gap.

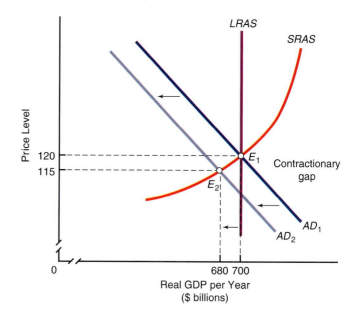

Effect on the Economy of an Increase in Aggregate Demand

▶ **Expansionary gap**
The gap that exists whenever the equilibrium level of real national income per year is greater than the full-employment level as shown by the position of the long-run aggregate supply curve.

We can reverse the situation and have aggregate demand increase to AD_2, as is shown in Figure 10.9. The initial equilibrium conditions are exactly the same as in Figure 10.8. The move to AD_2 increases the short-run equilibrium from E_1 to E_2 such that the economy is operating at $720 billion of real GDP per year, which exceeds *LRAS*. This is a condition of an overheated economy, typically called an **expansionary gap.**

Figure 10.9

The Effects of Stable Aggregate Supply with an Increase in Aggregate Demand: The Expansionary Gap

The economy is at equilibrium at E_1. An increase in aggregate demand to AD_2 leads to a new short-run equilibrium at E_2 with the price level rising from 120 to 125 and the equilibrium level of real GDP per year rising from $700 billion to $720 billion. The difference is called the expansionary gap.

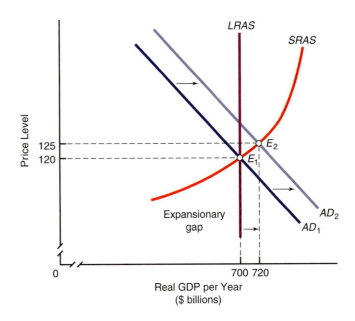

EXAMPLE   **The Effect of World War I**

One way we can show what happens to the equilibrium price level and the equilibrium real GDP level with an aggregate demand shock is to consider the effect on Canada's economy of fighting World War I (1914–18) in Europe. In Figure 10.10 you see the equilibrium price level of 133 (1900=100) and the equilibrium real GDP level of $1.8 billion at the long-run aggregate supply curve. The war effort shifts aggregate demand from AD_{prewar} to $AD_{World War I}$. Equilibrium moves from E_1 to E_2, and the price level moves from 133 to 176. The short-run equilibrium real GDP increases to $2.3 billion per year by 1917. The government's spending for the war caused *AD* to shift outward to the right. Also notice that the war effort temporarily pushed the economy above its long-run aggregate supply curve.

Figure 10.10
The Effects of War on Equilibrium

World War I shifted aggregate demand to $AD_{\text{World War I}}$. Equilibrium moved from E_1 to E_2 temporarily.

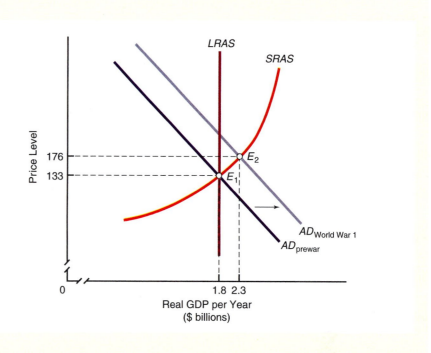

For critical analysis: What would have happened if World War I had lasted for 10 years instead of 4? How would you show it on Figure 10.10?

EXPLAINING INFLATION: DEMAND-PULL OR COST-PUSH?

When you first examined inflation in Chapter 7, no theory was given for why the general level of prices might rise. You can use the *AD-AS* framework to explain inflation. Indeed, Figure 10.9 is what is known as a theory of demand-side inflation, sometimes called *demand-pull inflation*. Whenever the general level of prices rises because of continual increases in aggregate demand, we say that the economy is experiencing **demand-pull inflation**—inflation caused by increases in aggregate demand. (Some economists argue that economywide increases in demand—increased aggregate demand—often occur when the amount of money in circulation increases faster than the growth in the economy. You will read more about this subject in Chapter 17.)

> **Demand-pull inflation**
>
> Inflation caused by increases in aggregate demand not matched by increases in aggregate supply.

An alternative explanation comes from the supply side. Look at Figure 10.11. The initial equilibrium conditions are the same as in Figure 10.9 and Figure 10.10. Now, however, there is a decrease in the aggregate supply curve, from $SRAS_1$ to $SRAS_2$. Equilibrium shifts from E_1 to E_2. The price level has increased from 120 to 125, too, while the equilibrium level of real GDP per year decreased from $700 billion to $680 billion. If there are continual decreases in aggregate supply, the situation is called **cost-push inflation.**

> **Cost-push inflation**
>
> Inflation caused by a continually decreasing short-run aggregate supply curve.

Figure 10.11

The Effects of Stable Aggregate Demand and a Decrease in Aggregate Supply: Supply-Side Inflation

If aggregate demand remains stable but $SRAS_1$ shifts to $SRAS_2$, equilibrium changes from E_1 to E_2. The price level rises from 120 to 125. If there are continual decreases in aggregate supply of this nature, the situation is called cost-push inflation.

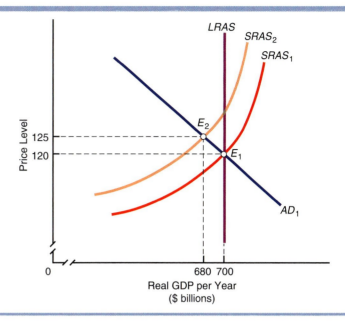

As the example of cost-push inflation shows, if the economy is initially in equilibrium on its *LRAS*, a decrease in *SRAS* will lead to a rise in the price level. Thus any abrupt change in one of the factors that determine aggregate supply will shift the equilibrium level of real GDP and the equilibrium price level. If the economy for some reason is operating to the left of its *LRAS*, an increase in *SRAS* will lead to a simultaneous *increase* in the equilibrium level of real GDP per year and a *decrease* in the price level. You should be able to show this in a graph similar to Figure 10.11.

Thinking Critically About the Media   The Real Price of Gas

Since the 1970s, the media have made references to the "high price of gas." A typical comment by some senior citizens interviewed on TV might be, "When I was a kid, gas cost only the equivalent of 5 cents a litre." The interviewee is obviously referring to the nominal price of gasoline. References to nominal prices during periods of inflation are virtually meaningless. Only after a nominal price is corrected for general price level changes can we make a meaningful comparison to the price of the same product or service today. In the case of gas, the price of a litre in the late 1990s, in real terms, is not much higher than it was a few years after World War II.

EXAMPLE   The Oil Price Shock of the 1970s

One of the best examples of an aggregate supply shock occurred in the 1970s. During several periods, the supply of crude oil to Canada was restricted. These restrictions were the result of actions taken by the Organization of Petroleum Exporting Countries (OPEC). The oil embargo had an almost immediate impact

Figure 10.12
The Effects of Oil Price Shocks on the Economy

In the 1970s, the supply of crude oil to Canada was restricted. Higher oil prices raised the cost of production. $SRAS_1$ shifted to $SRAS_2$, and equilibrium went from E_1 to E_2 with a higher price level and a lower equilibrium real GDP per year.

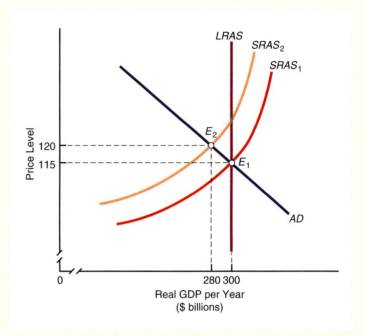

on the price of oil and petroleum products, mainly gasoline and heating oil. Higher oil prices raised the cost of production in many Canadian industries that relied on petroleum. The result was a shift in the aggregate supply curve as shown in Figure 10.12. The equilibrium shifted from E_1–$300 billion of real GDP per year and a price level of 115–to E_2–equilibrium real GDP of $280 billion and a price level of 120.

For critical analysis: If the price of oil had remained permanently high, what would have happened to *LRAS* in Figure 10.12?

Concepts in Brief

- Short-run equilibrium occurs at the intersection of the aggregate demand curve, *AD*, and the short-run aggregate supply curve, *SRAS*. Long-run equilibrium occurs at the intersection of *AD* and the long-run aggregate supply curve, *LRAS*. Any unanticipated shifts in aggregate demand or supply are called aggregate demand shocks or aggregate supply shocks.
- When aggregate demand shifts while aggregate supply is stable, a contractionary gap can occur, defined as the difference between the equilibrium level of real GDP and how much the economy could be producing if it were operating on its *LRAS*. The reverse situation leads to an expansionary gap.
- With stable aggregate supply, an abrupt shift in *AD* may lead to what is called demand-pull inflation. With a stable aggregate demand, an abrupt shift inward in *SRAS* may lead to what is called cost-push inflation.

Issues and Applications

The Ultimate Aggregate Supply Shock: The Kobe Earthquake

Concepts Applied: Aggregate demand, aggregate supply, long-run aggregate supply, aggregate supply shock, equilibrium, real GDP

The Kobe earthquake in Japan was devastating in terms of casualties and property. Property damages were estimated at over $125 billion, roughly 0.8 percent of Japan's total wealth.

When the worst earthquake to hit Japan since 1923 occurred, the Japanese economy had already suffered more than four years of hard times—a recession during which the economy was operating to the left of its LRAS. This situation is similar to the contractionary gap illustrated in Figure 10.8.

Human and Physical Cost of the Kobe Earthquake

The human suffering caused by Japan's most serious earthquake in decades was enormous. More than 6,000 people were killed, and tens of thousands more were injured. Over 115,000 buildings were completely destroyed, and tens of thousands of others were damaged. All in all, the earthquake wiped out 0.8 percent of Japan's

total wealth. The final estimated cost of the destruction was almost 10 trillion yen, or about $125 billion.

At First Blush: Reconstruction Equals Increased Employment

After the Kobe earthquake, a number of economists throughout the world argued that the quake would revive the stagnating Japanese economy. After all, if factory people are unemployed, the reconstruction after the disaster would create income from resources that would otherwise remain unused. The problem with such an analysis, however, is that it ignores what has happened to the wealth of the Japanese economy. A loss of $125 billion in wealth can never be a benefit to a nation. Although it is true that employment may have increased because of reconstruction after the Kobe earthquake, as a nation, Japan has permanently lost $125 billion.

Using Analysis

In Figure 10.13 you see that LRAS before the earthquake was $5 trillion. The economy was operating with the contractionary gap at E_1,

---

Figure 10.13
The Effects of the Kobe Earthquake in Japan

Japan was already operating below its *LRAS* at E_1 when the earthquake hit Kobe. Its $LRAS_{postquake}$ dropped to $4.9 trillion of real GDP per year from $5 trillion. Even if aggregate demand shifted to AD_2, the new equilibrium at E_2 would be below $5 trillion per year.

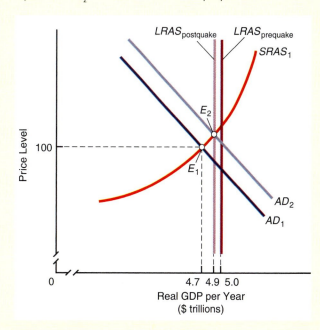

the price level at 100, and the equilibrium level of real GDP at $4.7 trillion per year. The earthquake shifted LRAS to LRAS_{postquake} at $4.9 trillion, which means that even if the contractionary gap were completely eliminated, the Japanese would be worse off in the long run.

What About Aggregate Demand?

Remember that increases in aggregate demand can develop through government spending increases. It is possible, then, that aggregate demand could shift from AD_1 to AD_2. The new equilibrium would shift to E_2, at $4.9 trillion per year. Notice, however, that

it is below the equilibrium level of real GDP per year that could have been achieved prior to the earthquake

For Critical Analysis

1. What would the government of Japan have to do to induce a shift of its *LRAS* supply curve back out to $5 trillion?

2. Are there any circumstances under which a natural disaster could actually be good for an economy?

CHAPTER SUMMARY

1. Aggregate demand is the total of all planned expenditures on final goods and services, and aggregate supply is the total of all planned production.

2. The aggregate demand curve gives the various quantities of all commodities demanded at various price levels. It slopes downward due to the real-balance effect, the interest rate effect, and the open economy effect.

3. Aggregate demand is not the same thing as individual demand, because individual demand curves are drawn holding income, among other things, constant. The aggregate demand curve reflects the entire circular flow of income and product.

4. Any non-price-level change that increases aggregate spending on domestic goods shifts the aggregate demand curve to the right. Any non-price-level change that decreases aggregate spending on domestic goods shifts the aggregate demand curve to the left.

5. There are two aggregate supply curves. The long-run aggregate supply curve is a vertical line, the location of which depends on tastes, technology, and endowments of natural resources; it assumes full information and full adjustment.

The short-run aggregate supply curve is drawn without full information and full adjustment and slopes upward, but it is not vertical.

6. Output can be expanded in the short run because firms can work both capital and labour more intensively and because firms with fixed input prices experience higher profits as the price level increases and therefore desire to hire more workers. The closer to capacity the economy is running, the steeper the short-run aggregate supply curve becomes.

7. There are events that shift both the long-run and short-run aggregate curves simultaneously. These include any change in the endowments of factors of production (land, labour, or capital). A temporary change in an input price, by contrast, shifts only the short-run aggregate supply curve.

8. Equilibrium occurs at the intersection of aggregate demand, short-run aggregate supply, and long-run aggregate supply.

9. The economy may experience shifts in aggregate demand and supply, called aggregate demand shocks and aggregate supply shocks. The impacts of such shocks on the equilibrium level of real output depend on the time period under study and other factors.

DISCUSSION OF PREVIEW QUESTIONS

1. Why does the aggregate demand curve slope downward?

There are three reasons for believing that the quantity demanded for real output rises as the price level falls, and vice versa. A decrease in the price level leads to higher real money balances, all other things held constant. This increased real wealth causes a direct effect on consumers' spending decisions. There is an indirect effect via interest rates, which move with price level changes. As the price level falls, the interest rate will fall, and consumers will want to spend more on houses and cars. Finally, in an open economy, if the price level falls, people will want domestic goods rather than imports, and foreigners will want to buy more of our goods.

2. Why is the long-run aggregate supply curve vertical?

The definition of the long-run aggregate supply curve is the amount of real output of goods and services that will be produced in the long run with full information and full adjustment. With full information and full adjustment, changes in the price level do not affect real output. Real

output in the long run is solely a function of tastes, technology, and endowments of land, labour, and capital. Hence the long-run aggregate supply curve is a vertical line.

3. Why does the short-run aggregate supply curve slope upward?

As the price level increases, firms presumably face fixed input prices in the short run. Their profits go up, and will rise even more if they increase production. They do so by working their labour force and their capital equipment more intensively, thereby generating more output.

4. How can we show improvements in technology using aggregate demand and aggregate supply analysis?

Improvements in technology shift both the long-run aggregate supply curve and the short-run aggregate supply curve outward. Essentially, you can show this using aggregate supply and aggregate demand analysis by drawing the curves that are shown in Figure 10.5.

PROBLEMS

(Answers to the odd-numbered problems appear at the back of the book.)

10-1.

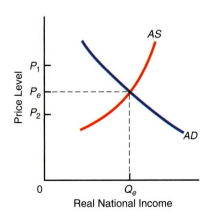

Given the curves in the accompanying graph, discuss why the equilibrium price level will be at P_e and not at P_1 or P_2.

10-2. In the discussion of why the *AD* curve slopes downward from left to right, notice that nothing was said about what happens to the quantity of real output demanded when the price level rises and causes wealth to fall for people in businesses who own mortgages on houses and buildings. Why not? (Hint: What is the *net* effect to the whole economy when the price level rises and causes a wealth loss to lenders who get paid back in fixed nominal dollars?)

10-3. Distinguish between short-run and long-run supply curves.

10-4. How is aggregate demand affected when the price level in *other* economies decreases? What happens to aggregate demand when the price level in *this* economy falls?

10-5. Suppose that aggregate supply decreases while aggregate demand is held constant.
a. What happens to the price level?
b. What happens to national output?

Classical and Keynesian Macro Analyses

Canada suffered from double-digit unemployment rates during the Great Depression of the 1930s, as well as during the 1983-1985 and 1991-1994 recessions. However, by late 1998, Canadians had come to expect slightly lower unemployment rates of about 8 to 9 percent, and Americans, rates that hovered around 5 to 6 percent. In contrast, the 375 million individuals who comprise the European Union (EU) of 15 nations in Western Europe learned to live with average unemployment rates exceeding 11 percent. Even when European countries expand out of a recession, their unemployment rates remain stubbornly in the double digits. To understand why unemployment remains so high in Europe, but not quite as high in Canada, you need to learn about equilibrium in the labour market and how it fits in with classical and Keynesian views of macroeconomics.

Preview Questions

1. What are the assumptions of the classical macro model?

2. What determines the rate of interest in the classical model?

3. Why do Keynesian economists believe that the short-run aggregate supply curve is horizontal?

4. Why is real GDP said to be demand-determined when the short-run aggregate supply curve is horizontal?

Did You Know That... in spite of continuing general inflation, magazine publishers tend to keep the same magazine prices for more than a year? According to one study by economist Stephen G. Cecchetti, the typical magazine publisher lets inflation eat away at a quarter of the magazine's price before a new price is printed on the magazine. This common example of "sticky" prices gives just a hint that our economy may not instantaneously adapt itself to changes in macroeconomic variables such as an increase in the rate of inflation. Economists want to know what causes fluctuations in employment, output, and the price level. The fact that magazine prices are sticky is just one empirical observation that would lead researchers to develop macroeconomic models that somehow reflect the less flexible nature of certain prices. Such was not the case with the classical economists, who had a different view of how the macroeconomy operated. We will start this chapter with a look at the classical model of the economy and then examine a model developed in the twentieth century.

THE CLASSICAL MODEL

The classical model, which traces its origins to the 1770s, was the first systematic attempt to explain the determinants of the price level and the national levels of output, income, employment, consumption, saving, and investment. The term *classical model* was coined by John Maynard Keynes, a Cambridge University economist, who used it to refer to the way in which earlier economists had analysed economic aggregates. Classical economists—Adam Smith, J. B. Say, David Ricardo, John Stuart Mill, Thomas Malthus, and others—wrote from the 1770s to the 1870s. They assumed, among other things, that all wages and prices were flexible and that competitive markets existed throughout the economy. Starting in the 1870s, so-called neoclassical economists, including Alfred Marshall, introduced a mathematical approach that allowed them to refine earlier economists' models.

Say's Law

▶ **Say's law**

A dictum of economist J. B. Say that supply creates its own demand; producing goods and services generates the means and the willingness to purchase other goods and services.

Every time you produce something for which you receive income, you generate the income necessary to make expenditures on other goods and services. That means that an economy producing $700 billion of GDP (final goods and services) simultaneously produces the income with which these goods and services can be supplied. As an accounting identity, *actual* aggregate income always equals *actual* aggregate expenditures. Classical economists took this accounting identity one step further by arguing that total national supply creates its own demand. They asserted what has become known as **Say's law:**

> Supply creates its own demand; hence it follows that *desired* expenditures will equal *actual* expenditures.

Figure 11.1
Say's Law and the Circular Flow
Here we show the circular flow of income and output. The very act of supplying a certain level of goods and services necessarily equals the level of goods and services demanded, in Say's simplified world.

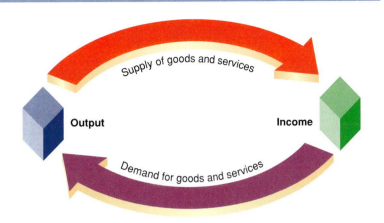

What does Say's law really mean? It states that the very process of producing specific goods (supply) is proof that other goods are desired (demand). People produce more goods than they want for their own use only if they seek to trade them for other goods. Someone offers to supply something only because that person also has a demand for something else. The implication of this, according to Say, is that no general glut, or overproduction, is possible in a market economy. From this reasoning, it seems to follow that full employment of labour and other resources would be the normal state of affairs in such an economy.

Underlying Say's law is the assumption that wants are unlimited and, further, that the primary goal of economic activity is consumption for oneself or one's family, either in the present or in the future. If a more or less self-sufficient family wants to increase its consumption, it can do so by producing more and trading its surplus of one good to get more of another good.

Say indicated that an oversupply of some goods might occur in particular markets. He argued that such surpluses would simply cause prices to fall, thereby decreasing production in the long run. The opposite would occur in markets in which shortages temporarily appeared.

All this seems reasonable enough in a simple barter economy in which households produce most of the goods they need and trade for the rest. This is shown in Figure 11.1, where there is a simple circular flow. But what about a more sophisticated economy in which people work for others and there is no barter but rather the use of money? Can these complications create the possibility of unemployment? And does the fact that labourers receive money income, some of which can be saved, lead to unemployment? No, said the classical economists to these last two questions. They based their reasoning on a number of key assumptions.

Assumptions of the Classical Model

The classical model makes four major assumptions:

1. *Pure competition exists.* No single buyer or seller of a commodity or an input can affect its price.

▶ **Money illusion**

Reacting to changes in money prices rather than relative prices. If workers whose wages double when the price level also doubles think they are better off, the workers are suffering from money illusion.

Try Preview Question 1:

What are the assumptions of the classical macro model?

2. *Wages and prices are flexible.* The assumption of pure competition leads to the notion that prices, wages, interest rates, and the like are free to move to whatever level supply and demand dictate (in the long run). Although no *individual* buyer can set a price, the community of buyers or sellers can cause prices to rise or to fall to an equilibrium level.

3. *People are motivated by self-interest.* Businesses want to maximize their profits, and households want to maximize their economic well-being.

4. *People cannot be fooled by money illusion.* Buyers and sellers react to changes in relative prices. That is to say, they do not suffer from **money illusion.** For example, workers will not be fooled into thinking they are better off by a doubling of wages if the price level has also doubled during the same time period.

The classical economists concluded, after taking account of the four major assumptions, that the role of government in the economy should be minimal. If all prices, wages, and markets are flexible, any problems in the macroeconomy will be temporary. The market will come to the rescue and correct itself.

Thinking Critically About the Media | **What Will Interest Rates Be Tomorrow?**

Interest rates are more than just the prices that cause equilibrium to occur in the saving and investment markets. Changes in the interest rate can determine the profitability of banks and other institutions. They can also determine whether an investment was a smart move or a foolish one. Not surprisingly, the media frequently quote economic forecasters to inform readers and viewers whether interest rates will be high or low in the future. Virtually all such predictions should be taken with a grain of salt. One study of interest rate forecasts at the beginning of the 1990s showed that all major interest rate moves were missed by forecasters. Long-term studies demonstrate that forecasters do no better than someone guessing interest rate changes by flipping a coin.

The Problem of Saving

When income is saved, it is not reflected in product demand. It is a type of *leakage* in the circular flow of income and output because saving withdraws funds from the income stream. Consumption expenditures can fall short of total output now. In such a situation, it does not appear that supply necessarily creates its own demand.

The classical economists did not believe that the complicating factor of saving in the circular flow model of income and output was a problem. They contended that each dollar saved would be invested by businesses so that the leakage of saving would be matched by the injection of business investment. *Investment* here refers only to additions to the nation's capital stock. The classical economists believed that businesses as a group would intend to invest as much as households wanted to save. Equilibrium between the saving plans of consumers and the investment plans of businesses comes about, in the classical economists' world, through the working of the credit market. In the credit market, the *price* of credit is the interest rate. At equilibrium, the price of credit—the interest rate—is such that the quantity of credit demanded equals the quantity of credit supplied. Planned investment just equals planned saving, for saving represents the supply of credit and investment represents the demand for credit.

The Interest Rate: Equating Desired Saving and Investment. In Figure 11.2, the vertical axis measures the rate of interest in percentage terms; on the horizontal axis are the quantities of desired saving and desired investment per unit time period. The desired saving curve is really a supply curve of saving. It shows how much individuals and businesses wish to save at various interest rates. People want to save more at higher interest rates than at lower interest rates.

Investment, primarily desired by businesses, responds in a predictable way. The higher the rate of interest, the more expensive it is to invest and the lower the level of desired investment. The desired investment curve slopes downward. In this simplified model, the equilibrium rate of interest is 5 percent, and the equilibrium quantity of saving and investment is $70 billion per year.

Try Preview Question 2:

What determines the rate of interest in the classical model?

Figure 11.2

Equating Desired Saving and Investment in the Classical Model

The demand curve for investment is labelled "Desired investment." The supply of resources used for investment occurs when individuals do not consume but save instead. The desired saving curve is shown as an upward-sloping supply curve of saving. The equilibrating force here is, of course, the interest rate. At higher interest rates, people desire to save more. But at higher interest rates, businesses demand less investment because it is more expensive to invest. In this model, at an interest rate of 5 percent, the quantity of investment desired just equals the quantity of saving desired (supply), which is $70 billion per year.

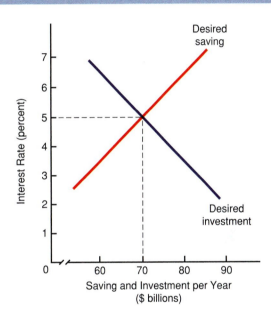

INTERNATIONAL EXAMPLE
High Interest Rates and Loan Sharks in Naples

Although the simple diagram shown in Figure 11.2 reveals an equilibrium rate of interest of 5 percent, people who seek loans often have to pay much more than 5 percent. Someone who wishes to borrow purchasing power from a creditor may not always have access to regular banks and other lending facilities that charge "normal" equilibrium interest rates. In Naples, Italy, more than 20 percent of the citizens lack a regular income. When they go to a bank to borrow, they are often denied. They turn to alternative moneylenders, of which there are about 40,000 today. These so-called loan sharks sometimes charge interest rates as high as 400 percent a year.

The Jesu Nuovo church, under the direction of Father Massimo Rastrelli, decided to fight back against the loan sharks. He founded the St. Joseph Moscati Foundation Anti-usury Solidarity Fund. (Usury means lending at exorbitant interest rates.) Over a four-year period, Father Rastrelli obtained 16 million lire (about $13,000 at the prevailing exchange rate), which he deposited in local banks as collateral (security) for loans. Individuals in the clutches of loan sharks are able to borrow money from the fund at reasonable interest rates to pay off their debts to the loan sharks.

For critical analysis: People in the business world in Canada rarely, if ever, turn to loan sharks to obtain funds to start new businesses or expand existing ones. Why don't they use the services of loan sharks?

Equilibrium in the Labour Market

Now consider the labour market. If an excess quantity of labour is supplied at a particular wage level, the wage level is above equilibrium. By accepting lower wages, unemployed workers will quickly be put back to work. We show equilibrium in the labour market in Figure 11.3.

Figure 11.3
Equilibrium in the Labour Market

The demand for labour is downward-sloping; at higher wage rates, firms will employ fewer workers. The supply of labour is upward-sloping; at higher wage rates, more workers will work longer and more people will be willing to work. The equilibrium wage rate is $12, with an equilibrium employment per year of 13.5 million workers.

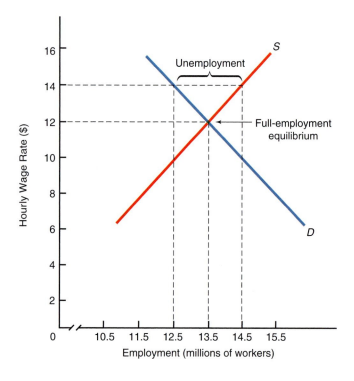

Equilibrium of $12 per hour and 13.5 million workers employed represents full-employment equilibrium. If the wage rate were $14 an hour, there would be unemployment—14.5 million workers would want to work, but businesses would want to hire only 12.5 million. In the classical model, this unemployment is eliminated rather rapidly by wage rates dropping back to $12 per hour. As you will see in the Issues and Applications section at the end of this chapter, there are forces that may prevent workers from offering to work at the lower wage rates that would lead to full employment.

The Relationship Between Employment and Real GDP.   Employment is not simply some isolated figure that government statisticians estimate. Rather, the level of employment in an economy determines its real GDP (output), other things held constant. A hypothetical relationship between input (number of employees) and output (rate of real GDP per year) is shown in Table 11.1. We have highlighted the row that has 13.5 million workers per year as the labour input. That might be considered a hypothetical level of full employment, and it is related to a rate of real GDP of $700 billion per year.

Table 11.1 **The Relationship Between Employment and Real GDP**	Labour Input per Year (millions of workers)	Real GDP per Year ($ billions)
	9.8	400
	10.4	500
	12.0	600
	13.5	700
	14.5	800
	16.0	900

Classical Theory, Vertical Aggregate Supply, and the Price Level

In the classical mould of reasoning, long-term unemployment is impossible. Say's law, coupled with flexible interest rates, prices, and wages, would always tend to keep workers fully employed so that the aggregate supply curve, as shown in Figure 11.4 (page 270), is vertical at Q_0. We have labelled the supply curve *LRAS*, consistent with the long-run aggregate supply curve introduced in Chapter 10. It was defined there as the quantity of output that would be produced in an economy with full information and full adjustment of wages and prices year in and year out. In the classical model, this happens to be the *only* aggregate supply curve that exists in equilibrium. Everything adjusts so fast that we are essentially always on or quickly moving towards *LRAS*. Furthermore, because the labour market is working well, Q_0 is always at, or soon to be at, full employment. Full employment is defined as the amount of employment that would exist year in and year out if all parties in the labour market fully anticipated any inflation or deflation that was occurring. Full employment does not mean zero unemployment because there is always some frictional unemployment (discussed in Chapter 7), even in the classical world.

Figure 11.4

Classical Theory and Increases in Aggregate Demand

The classical theorists believed that Say's law and flexible interest rates, prices, and wages would always lead to full employment at Q_0 along the vertical aggregate supply curve, *LRAS*. With aggregate demand, AD_1, the price level is 100. An increase in aggregate demand shifts AD_1 to AD_2. At price level 100, the quantity of real GDP per year demanded is A on AD_2, or Q_1. But this is greater than at full employment. Prices rise, and the economy quickly moves from E_1 to E_2 at the higher price level of 110.

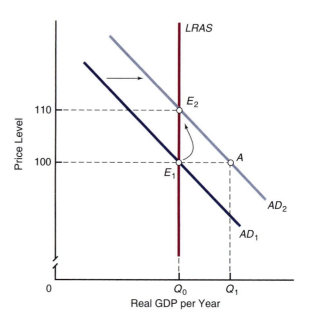

Effect of an Increase in Aggregate Demand in the Classical Model. In this model, any change in aggregate demand will soon cause a change in the price level. Consider starting at E_1, at price level 100. If the aggregate demand shifts to AD_2, at price level 100, output would increase to Q_1. But that is greater than the full-employment level of output of real GDP, Q_0. The economy will attempt to get to point A, but because this is beyond full employment, prices will rise, and the economy will find itself back on the vertical *LRAS* at point E_2 at a higher price level, 110. The price level will increase at output rates in excess of the full-employment level of output because employers will end up bidding up wages for now more relatively scarce workers. In addition, factories will be bidding up the price of other inputs at this greater-than-full-employment rate of output.

The level of real GDP per year clearly does not depend on any changes in aggregate demand. Hence we say that in the classical model, the equilibrium level of real GDP per year is completely *supply-determined*. Changes in aggregate demand affect only the price level, not the output of real goods and services.

Effect of a Decrease in Aggregate Demand in the Classical Model. The effect of a decrease in aggregate demand in the classical model is the converse of the analysis just presented for an increase in aggregate demand. You can simply reverse AD_2 and AD_1 in Figure 11.4. To help you see how this analysis works, consider the flowchart in Figure 11.5.

Figure 11.5
Effect of a Decrease in Aggregate Demand in the Classical Model

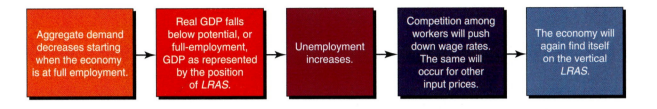

Concepts in Brief

- Say's law states that supply creates its own demand and therefore desired expenditures will equal actual expenditures.
- The classical model assumes that (1) pure competition exists, (2) wages and prices are completely flexible, (3) individuals are motivated by self-interest, and (4) they cannot be fooled by money illusion.
- When saving is introduced into the model, equilibrium occurs in that market through changes in the interest rate such that desired saving equals desired investment at the equilibrium rate of interest.
- In the labour market, full employment occurs at a wage rate at which quantity demanded equals quantity supplied. That particular level of employment is associated with a certain value of real GDP per year.
- In the classical model, because the *LRAS* is vertical, the equilibrium level of real GDP is supply-determined. Any changes in aggregate demand simply change the price level.

KEYNESIAN ECONOMICS AND THE KEYNESIAN SHORT-RUN AGGREGATE SUPPLY CURVE

The classical economists' world was one of fully utilized resources. There would be no unused capacity and no unemployment. However, post–World War I Europe entered a period of long-term economic decline that could not be explained by the classical model. John Maynard Keynes developed an explanation that has since become known as the Keynesian model, which presented an explanation of the Great Depression in the 1930s. Keynes argued that if we are in a world in which there are large amounts of excess capacity and unemployment, a positive aggregate demand shock will not raise prices and a negative aggregate demand shock will not cause firms to lower prices. This situation is depicted in Figure 11.6 (page 272). The short-run aggregate supply curve is labelled as the horizontal line *SRAS*. If we start

Figure 11.6

Demand-Determined Income Equilibrium

If we assume that prices will not fall when aggregate demand falls and that there is excess capacity so that prices will not rise when aggregate demand increases, the short-run aggregate supply curve is simply a horizontal line at the given price level, P_0, represented by *SRAS*. An aggregate demand shock that increases aggregate demand to AD_2 will increase the equilibrium level of real national income per year to Q_2. An aggregate demand shock that decreases aggregate demand to AD_3 will decrease the equilibrium level of real national income to Q_3. The equilibrium price level will not change.

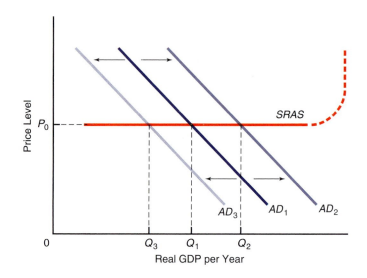

out in equilibrium with aggregate demand at AD_1, the equilibrium level of real GDP per year will be Q_1 and the equilibrium price level will be P_0. If there is an aggregate demand shock such that the aggregate demand curve shifts outward to the right to AD_2, the equilibrium price level will not change; only the equilibrium level of real GDP per year will increase, to Q_2. Conversely, if there is an aggregate demand shock that shifts the aggregate demand curve to AD_3, the equilibrium price level will again remain at P_0, but the equilibrium level of real GDP per year will fall to Q_3.

Under such circumstances, the equilibrium level of real GDP per year is completely *demand-determined*.

The horizontal short-run aggregate supply curve represented in Figure 11.6 is often called the **Keynesian short-run aggregate supply curve.** It is so named because Keynes hypothesized that many prices, especially the price of labour (wages), are "sticky downward." According to Keynes, the existence of unions and of long-term contracts between workers are real-world factors that can explain the downward inflexibility of *nominal* wage rates. Such "stickiness" of wages makes *involuntary* unemployment of labour a distinct possibility. The classical assumption of everlasting full employment no longer holds.

Further, even in situations of excess capacity and large amounts of unemployment, we will not necessarily see the price level falling; rather, all we will see is continuing unemployment and a reduction in the equilibrium level of real GDP per year. Thus general economywide equilibrium can occur and endure even if there is excess capacity. Keynes and his followers argued that capitalism was therefore not necessarily a self-regulating system sustaining full employment. At the time, Keynes was attacking the classical view of the world, which argued that markets would all eventually be in equilibrium—prices and wages would adjust—so that full employment would never be far away.

A pretty good example of a horizontal short-run aggregate supply curve can be seen by examining data from the aftermath of the Great Depression of the 1930s.

▶ **Keynesian short-run aggregate supply curve**

The horizontal portion of the aggregate supply curve in which there is unemployment and unused capacity in the economy.

Figure 11.7
Real GDP and the Price Level, 1931–1939

In a depressed economy, increased aggregate spending can increase output without raising prices. This is what John Maynard Keynes believed, and the data for Canada's recovery from the Great Depression seem to bear this out. In such circumstances, the level of real output is demand-determined.

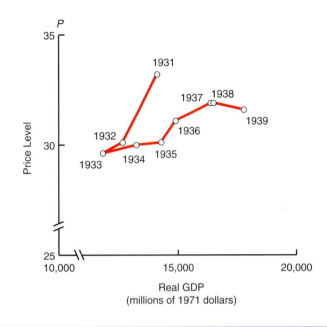

Look at Figure 11.7, where you see real GDP in millions of 1971 dollars on the horizontal axis and the price level index on the vertical axis. From the early days of recovery from the Great Depression through the outbreak of World War II, real GDP increased without much rise in the price level. During this period the economy experienced neither supply constraints nor any dramatic changes in the price level. The most simplified Keynesian model in which prices do not change is essentially an immediate post-Depression model that fits the data very well during this period.

Try Preview Question 3:

Why do Keynesian economists believe that the short-run aggregate supply curve is horizontal?

INCOME DETERMINATION USING AGGREGATE DEMAND AND AGGREGATE SUPPLY: FIXED VERSUS CHANGING PRICE LEVELS

The underlying assumption of the simplified Keynesian model is that the relevant range of the short-run aggregate supply schedule (*SRAS*) is horizontal, as shown in part (a) of Figure 11.8 on page 274. There you see that short-run aggregate supply is fixed at price level 120. If aggregate demand is AD_1, the equilibrium level of real GDP is at $700 billion per year. If aggregate demand increases to AD_2, the equilibrium level of real GDP increases to $800 billion per year. Compare this situation with the standard upward-sloping short-run aggregate supply curve presented in Chapter 10. In part (b) of Figure 11.8, *SRAS* is upward-sloping, with its slope becoming steeper and steeper after it crosses long-run aggregate supply, *LRAS*. Recall that *LRAS* is the level of real GDP that the economy would produce year in and year out with full information and full adjustment. It is sometimes called the

Figure 11.8
Income Determination with Fixed vs. Flexible Prices

In part (a), the price level index is fixed at 120. An increase in aggregate demand from AD_1 to AD_2 moves the equilibrium level of real GDP from $700 billion per year to $800 billion per year. In part (b), *SRAS* is upward-sloping. The same shift in aggregate demand yields an equilibrium level of real GDP of only $750 billion per year and a higher price level index at 130.

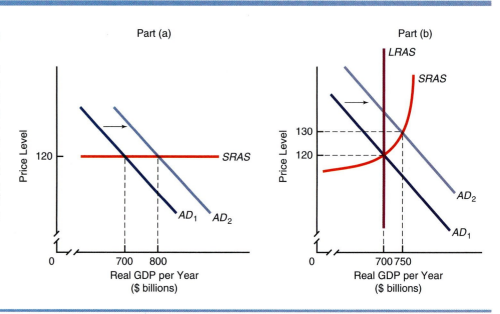

full-employment level of real GDP because, presumably, full employment occurs when there is full information and full adjustment possible in the economy. If aggregate demand is AD_1, the equilibrium level of real GDP in part (b) is also $700 billion per year, also at a price level of 120. A similar increase in aggregate demand to AD_2 as occurred in part (a) produces a different equilibrium, however. Equilibrium real GDP increases to $750 billion per year, which is less than in part (a) because part of the increase in *nominal* GDP has occurred through an increase in the price level to 130.

Try Preview Question 4:

Why is real GDP said to be demand-determined when the short-run aggregate supply curve is horizontal?

EXAMPLE   Keynesian Analysis of the Great Depression

At the beginning of 1929, the Canadian economy was doing quite well, with the unemployment rate hovering around 3 percent. A year later it was over 9 percent, and by 1933 it had climbed to almost 20 percent. The real GDP of 1929 was not reached again until 1937, when another business downturn hit the economy. We can use the Keynesian analysis presented in Figure 11.9 to describe what happened. Aggregate demand to start with is AD_{1929}. According to Keynes and his followers, the economy experienced a dramatic reduction in aggregate demand, represented by a shift to AD_{1933}. To prevent massive unemployment, wages and prices would have to have fallen such that a new equilibrium would have been at point *A* on *LRAS*. Even though many wages and prices did fall, they didn't fall sufficiently. Consequently, a new equilibrium was established at E_2. Real GDP fell from about $52 billion to $37 billion (expressed in 1986 dollars). By 1933, the economy was operating at 20 percent below its potential output represented by *LRAS*.

Figure 11.9
Keynesian Analysis of the Great Depression

Aggregate demand dropped from AD_{1929} to AD_{1933}. The price level would have had to drop to point A on $LRAS$ in order to avoid unemployment. In reality, it did not, so that the new equilibrium shifted from E_1 to E_2. By 1933, the economy was operating at about 20 percent below its potential output.

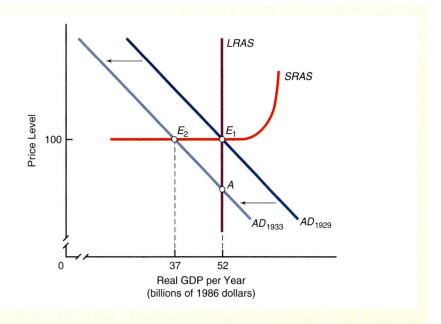

For critical analysis: If the equilibrium stayed at E_2, what do you expect would eventually happen to $LRAS$?

Concepts in Brief

- If we assume that we are operating on a horizontal short-run aggregate supply curve, the equilibrium level of real GDP per year is completely demand-determined.
- The horizontal short-run aggregate supply curve has been called the Keynesian short-run aggregate supply curve because Keynes believed that many prices, especially wages, would not be reduced even when aggregate demand decreased.

AGGREGATE DEMAND AND SUPPLY IN AN OPEN ECONOMY

In many of the international examples in the preceding chapters, we had to translate foreign currencies into dollars when the open economy was discussed. We used the exchange rate, or the price of the dollar relative to other currencies. In Chapter 10 you also discovered that the open economy effect was one of the reasons the aggregate demand curve slopes downward. When the domestic price level rises, Canadians want to buy cheaper-priced foreign goods. The opposite occurs when the Canadian domestic price level falls. Currently, the foreign sector of the Canadian economy constitutes about 33 percent of all economic activities.

How a Stronger Dollar Affects Aggregate Supply

Assume that the dollar becomes stronger in international foreign exchange markets. If last week the dollar could buy 4 francs but this week it now buys 5 francs, it has become stronger. To the extent that Canadian companies import raw and partially processed goods from abroad, a stronger dollar can lead to lower input prices. This will lead to a shift outward to the right in the short-run aggregate supply curve as shown in part (a) of Figure 11.10. In that simplified model, equilibrium GDP would rise and the price level would fall. The result might involve increased employment and lower inflation.

How a Stronger Dollar Affects Aggregate Demand

There is another effect of a stronger dollar that we must consider. Foreigners will find that Canadian goods are now more expensive, expressed in their own currency. After all, a $15 Nova Scotia lobster before the stronger dollar cost a French person 60 francs when the exchange rate was 4 to 1. After the dollar became stronger and the exchange rate increased to 5 to 1, that same $15 lobster would cost 75 francs. Conversely, Canadians will find that the stronger dollar makes imported goods cheaper. The result for Canadians is fewer exports and more imports, or lower net exports (exports minus imports). If net exports fall, employment in export industries will fall: This is

Figure 11.10
The Effects of a Stronger Dollar

When the dollar increases in value in the international currency market, lower prices for imported inputs result, causing a shift outward to the right in the short-run aggregate supply schedule from $SRAS_1$ to $SRAS_2$ in part (a). If nothing else changes, equilibrium shifts from E_1 to E_2 at a lower price level and a higher equilibrium real GDP per year. A stronger dollar can also affect the aggregate demand curve because it will lead to fewer net exports and cause AD_1 to fall to AD_2 in part (b). Equilibrium would move from E_1 to E_2, a lower price level, and a lower equilibrium real GDP per year.

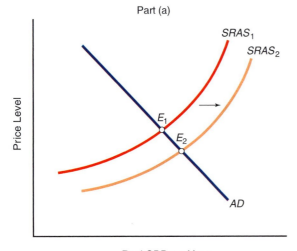

Part (a)

Part (b)

represented in part (b) of Figure 11.10. After the dollar becomes stronger, the aggregate demand curve shifts inward from AD_1 to AD_2. The result is a tendency for equilibrium real GDP and the price level to fall, and unemployment to rise.

The Net Effect

We have learned, then, that a stronger dollar *simultaneously* leads to an increase in *SRAS* and a decrease in *AD*. Remember from Chapter 4 that in such situations, the result depends on which curve shifts more. If the aggregate demand curve shifts more than the short-run aggregate supply curve, equilibrium real GDP will fall. Conversely, if the aggregate supply curve shifts more than the aggregate demand curve, equilibrium real GDP will rise.

You should be able to redo this entire analysis for a weaker dollar.

ECONOMIC GROWTH IN AN AGGREGATE DEMAND AND SUPPLY FRAMEWORK

Much (not all) of the Keynesian macroeconomic analysis to which you have been introduced in this chapter, and which you will examine in the next chapter, relates to short-run fluctuations in unemployment, inflation, and other macroeconomic variables. Whether one uses some variant of classical macroeconomic analysis or the Keynesian analysis, over time, short-term business fluctuations tend to iron out. We are left with economic growth, which can occur with or without inflation.

Figure 11.11

Economic Growth, Aggregate Demand, and Aggregate Supply

Economic growth can be shown using short-run and long-run aggregate demand and supply curves. Aggregate demand, AD_1, intersects short-run aggregate supply, $SRAS_1$, at E_1, yielding $700 billion of real GDP per year at a price level of 100. This yearly real GDP is consistent with full employment. The long-run aggregate supply curve is vertical at $700 billion and is labelled $LRAS_1$. With economic growth, $LRAS_1$ moves outward to $800 billion per year. Short-run aggregate supply shifts to $SRAS_2$, and aggregate demand increases to AD_2. New equilibrium is at E_2, still at a price level of 100. There is no inflation.

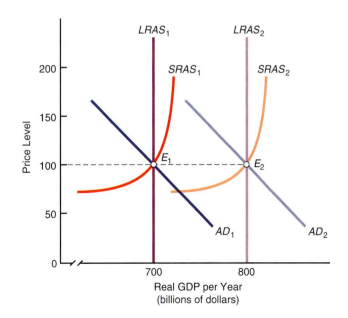

Economic Growth Without Inflation

Look at Figure 11.11 on the previous page. We start in equilibrium with AD_1 and $SRAS_1$ intersecting at the long-run aggregate supply curve, $LRAS_1$, at a price level of 100. Real GDP per year is $700 billion. Economic growth occurs due to labour force expansion, capital investments, and other occurrences. The result is a rightward shift in the long-run aggregate supply curve to $LRAS_2$. As the long-run productive capacity of the nation grows, the economy doesn't stay on its short-run aggregate supply curve, $SRAS$. Rather, $SRAS$ shifts along with shifts in aggregate demand due to population increases and rising per capita income. It is thus possible for us to achieve real GDP of $800 billion without any increase in the price level. The short-run aggregate supply curve moves outward to $SRAS_2$ and intersects AD_2 at E_2 where the new long-run aggregate supply curve, $LRAS_2$, has moved.

EXAMPLE   ## The Canadian Record over the Past Few Decades

Figure 11.12
Economic Growth and Inflation in Canada

This figure shows the points where aggregate demand and aggregate supply have intersected each year from 1969 to the present. Canada has experienced economic growth over this period, but not without inflation.

Sources: Statistics Canada, *Canadian Economic Observer,* and *Canadian Economic Observer Historical Supplement.*

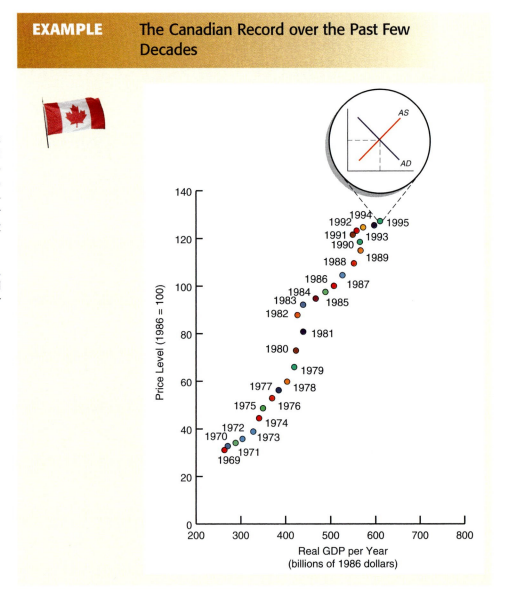

What has been Canada's experience regarding economic growth and the rate of inflation over the past few decades? Has it resembled Figure 11.11? The answer can be seen in Figure 11.12, which reflects the Canadian experience from 1969 to 1995. In essence, each of the points represents the intersection of aggregate supply and aggregate demand for that year. Since 1969, the price level has clearly risen. So, too, has real GDP. Apparently, the Canadian economy has been unable to experience economic growth without inflation.

For critical analysis: As an individual, should you care whether Canada has economic growth with or without inflation? Explain your answer.

In the world just hypothesized, aggregate demand shifts outward so that at the same price level, 100, it intersects the new short-run aggregate supply curve, $SRAS_2$ at the rate of real GDP that is consistent with more or less full employment (on $LRAS_2$). Firms sell all the output produced at the new level without changing prices. In some situations, however, inflation may accompany growth.

Concepts in Brief

- A change in the international value of the dollar can affect both the $SRAS$ and aggregate demand.
- A stronger dollar will reduce the cost of imported inputs, thereby causing the $SRAS$ to shift outward to the right, leading to a lower price level and a higher equilibrium real GDP per year, given no change in aggregate demand.
- In contrast, a stronger dollar will lead to lower net exports, causing the aggregate demand curve to shift inward, leading to a lower price level and a lower equilibrium real GDP per year. The net effect depends on which shift is more important. The opposite analysis applies to a weakening dollar in international currency markets.
- It is possible to have economic growth with and without inflation. If the aggregate demand curve shifts outward to the right at the same speed as the aggregate supply curve, there will be no inflation accompanying economic growth.

Issues and Applications

High European Unemployment, or Keynes Revisited?

Concepts Applied: Employment and unemployment, equilibrium, sticky wages, wait unemployment, unemployment duration, marginal tax rate

The unemployment rate in France and other European countries hovers around 11 percent, compared to about 9 percent in Canada and 6 percent in the United States. One reason for the higher rate of unemployment in the EU is the disincentive to find work, due to social programs that provide generous unemployment benefits.

At the beginning of the 1970s, the Canadian unemployment rate was a little more than 6 percent. The average rate for all of Europe was less than half that—about 2.4 percent. Since then, unemployment rates in Canada have gone up and down, but the average has remained a bit above 8.5 percent. The experience in the EU has been much more dramatic, where the average unemployment rate has risen from about 2.4 percent in 1970 to over 11 percent in the 1990s—more than a fourfold increase!

Keynes Revisited

Remember that at the heart of Keynesian macroeconomic analysis is the concept of persistent unemployment in a deep recession or a great depression. This is because wages tend to be sticky downward. Keynes postulated that because of union and other contracts,

a decrease in aggregate demand would not lead to a reduction in wages and other prices. Consequently, aggregate demand would be insufficient, and unemployment would result. In Europe today, not only are there union contracts that prevent wages from falling, but there are a host of other impediments to the classical economists' view of a freely functioning employment market.

The Duration of Unemployment

First, one must note that part of the reason Europe's high unemployment rate exists is because over half of the unemployed are out of work for a year or more. In Canada, only 12 percent of the unemployed have been out of work for more than a year. Remember from Chapter 7 that an increase in the duration of unemployment, with the same absolute number of people being fired or laid off for any given time period, will necessarily increase the rate of unemployment. Thus one of the major reasons that Europe suffers from such high unemployment is that workers take so long to find other jobs.

The Incentive to Work or Not to Work

The simple supply and demand diagram for employment shown in Figure 11.3 ignores any incentives for remaining unemployed. Otherwise stated, it ignores any disincentive to return to work once unemployed. In general, the EU countries offer generous unemployment benefits. For example, in France one can receive over 60 percent of previous (gross) pay for several years, no matter how much one was earning. In general, EU countries offer minimum income compensation and other benefits to the unemployed. In certain countries, formerly low-income-earning individuals who become unemployed will actually face a marginal tax rate of over 100 percent if they go back to work, because benefits are withdrawn if income is earned. Consequently, the rewards for re-entering the labour market are so minimal that they provide little incentive to look for a job.

Employers' Full Cost of Hiring

On the employers' side of the ledger, there are numerous costs associated with hiring a new worker. These include the so-called social charges, which in some countries equal twice the hourly pay of low-income employees. Also, in many EU countries, employers are required to give severance pay if the employer decides to fire a recently hired employee. This means that employers have diminished incentives to hire new workers, even during an economic expansion.

The only way that workers can effectively offer their services at a lower wage rate, thereby complying with the classical economists' view of the labour market, is by agreeing to work "off-the-books." Of course, as we pointed out in Chapter 7, they still are nonetheless counted as unemployed.

Wait Unemployment

Rather than having a flexible labour market, as the classical economists assumed, Europe now has a relatively inflexible labour market. Much of the unemployment is simply wait unemployment, which we defined in Chapter 7 as unemployment due to workers' inability to offer their services at lower than prevailing wage rates. These prevailing wage rates include the additional "perks" and social charges that employers by law must offer every worker in most EU countries. These charges make the true wage considerably

higher than the apparent money wage.

For Critical Analysis

1. Why might it be difficult for European politicians to dismantle programs that result in large amounts of wait unemployment?
2. What effect will persistent high unemployment in the EU have on its economic growth?

CHAPTER SUMMARY

1. The classical model was developed in the 1770s by such economists as Adam Smith, David Ricardo, John Stuart Mill, and Thomas Malthus. It attempted to explain the determinants of the price level and national income and employment.

2. Say's law holds that supply creates its own demand. A more complete classical model assumes (a) pure competition, (b) wage and price flexibility, (c) self-interest motivation throughout the population, and (d) no money illusion. With the introduction of saving, the classical economists believed, the market economy would still reach full employment of resources because planned saving would be met by planned investment. Saving is the supply of credit, and investment is the demand for credit. The interest rate in the credit market was assumed to be flexible, like all other prices, so equilibrium would always prevail, and therefore planned saving would always equal planned investment.

3. Because the classical model posits a vertical long-run aggregate supply curve, any changes in aggregate demand simply change the equilibrium price level. The equilibrium level of real GDP per year is completely supply-determined.

4. Whenever we are operating on a horizontal short-run aggregate supply curve, the equilibrium level of real GDP is completely demand-determined by the position of the aggregate demand curve. The Keynesian short-run aggregate supply curve is typically given as horizontal

because Keynes assumed that wages and prices would not be reduced even if aggregate demand decreased substantially.

5. If we relax the assumption of a fixed price level, we are then operating on the upward-sloping portion of the short-run aggregate supply curve. Hence an increase in aggregate demand will lead to some increase in the price level. This increase in the price level will have an offsetting effect on equilibrium total planned expenditures because of wealth, interest rate, and foreign goods substitution effects. Under such circumstances, any increase in aggregate demand will lead to both an increase in the price level and an increase in output.

6. A stronger dollar will reduce the cost of imported inputs, thereby causing the *SRAS* to shift outward to the right, leading to a lower price level and a higher equilibrium real GDP per year, given no change in aggregate demand.

7. In contrast, a stronger dollar will lead to lower net exports, causing the aggregate demand curve to shift inward, leading to a lower price level and a lower equilibrium real GDP per year. The net effect depends on which shift is more important. The opposite analysis applies to a weakening dollar in international currency markets.

8. It is possible to have economic growth with or without inflation. If the aggregate demand curve shifts outward to the right at the same speed as the aggregate supply curve, there will be no inflation accompanying economic growth.

DISCUSSION OF PREVIEW QUESTIONS

1. **What are the assumptions of the classical macro model?**

   In the classical model, the following four assumptions are made: (a) the existence of pure competition, (b) complete wage and price flexibility, (c) individuals motivated by self-interest, and (d) individuals not fooled by money illusion.

2. **What determines the rate of interest in the classical model?**

   In the classical model, the interaction between desired investment and desired saving determines the equilibrium rate of interest in the economy. Otherwise stated, the equilibrium rate of interest is determined at the intersection of the desired investment curve and the desired saving curve.

3. **Why do Keynesian economists believe that the short-run aggregate supply curve is horizontal?**

   In the horizontal range of the *SRAS* curve, changes in real GDP (output) occur without changes in the price level. This pure quantity response (no price response) to changes in *AD* reflects Keynes' assumption that during a depression or a very deep recession, businesses have so much excess capacity that *increases* in *AD* will elicit only an increase in output; businesses

that try to increase prices in such a situation discover that they lose sales to competitors. Similarly, a *reduction* in *AD* will lead only to a reduction in output; businesses won't reduce prices. Keynes assumed that in modern economies the existence of unions and contracts to support the unemployed imply that wages are sticky downward—wages aren't likely to fall even during periods of significant unemployment. Businesses have a certain control over prices and, confronting wages that are sticky, prefer to reduce output instead of price.

4. **Why is real GDP said to be demand-determined when the short-run aggregate supply curve is horizontal?**

   When the *SRAS* curve is horizontal, real GDP will change only in response to a change in *AD*. If *AD* increases, real GDP rises; if *AD* decreases, real GDP falls. Therefore, real GDP merely responds to changes in *AD*, which is therefore the primary mover in the economy. According to Keynes, businesses are prepared to produce *any* output level; the output level that they do produce is the most profitable one, and that depends on *AD*. This theory says that if you want to predict what real GDP and national employment will be in the future, discover what is happening to *AD* now.

PROBLEMS

(Answers to the odd-numbered problems appear at the back of the book.)

11-1. The desired investment curve intersects the desired saving curve in the economy at an interest rate of 8 percent. The current market rate of interest is 9 percent. Outline what will now take place in the economy so that the saving and investment market is in equilibrium.

11-2. Look at Figure 11.3 on page 268 again. At a wage rate of $12 per hour, 13.5 million workers are employed. This is called full-employment equilibrium. Does that mean there is no unemployment?

11-3. Show the effects of a decrease in aggregate demand in the classical model.

11-4. On one graph, show economic growth with associated increases in the price level.

Consumption, Income, and the Multiplier

There has been a lot of talk on the television and in the newspapers recently about native land claims settlements and their costs. Some observers say that the cost of settling these claims will be prohibitive, not only in the payout of the claims but also in the negotiating process. Others disagree. To understand how native land claim settlements could hurt or benefit our economy, you need to have a background in the relationship between income, consumption, investment, and the multiplier, the subject of this chapter.

Preview Questions

1. How do we interpret the 45-degree reference line?

2. What does the total planned expenditures curve indicate?

3. What is the concept of the multiplier, how does it work, and what is its main determinant?

4. What might cause shifts in the total planned expenditures curve?

Did You Know That...personal consumption expenditures in Canada have averaged about 60 percent of gross domestic product for decades? Each year, Canadians purchase millions of television sets, millions of pairs of shoes, millions of compact discs, and billions of stress-reducing pills, among other products and services. We are a nation of spenders, and our personal consumption expenditures help to keep the Canadian economic machine moving day in and day out. As it turns out, John Maynard Keynes focused much of his research on what determines how much you and I decide to spend each year. Remember that aggregate demand consists of consumption expenditures, plus expenditures for investment purposes, what the government spends, and what foreigners spend on domestically produced output. As you will learn in this chapter, Keynes focused on the relationship between how much people earn and their willingness to engage in personal consumption expenditures. In this chapter you will learn about that relationship as well as the influence of investment, government, and the foreign sector on the economy's equilibrium level of real output per year.

SOME SIMPLIFYING ASSUMPTIONS IN A KEYNESIAN MODEL

Continuing in the Keynesian tradition, we will assume that the short-run aggregate supply curve within the relevant range is horizontal. That is to say, we assume that it is similar to Figure 11.6 on page 272, meaning that the equilibrium level of real GDP is demand-determined. That is why Keynes wished to examine the elements of desired aggregate expenditures.

Also, for the time being we will not be concerned with the problem of inflation, because by definition, along the Keynesian short-run aggregate supply curve, inflation is impossible. Finally, given that the price level is assumed to be unchanging, all of the variables with which we will be dealing will be expressed in real terms. After all, with no change in the price level, any change in the magnitude of an economic variable, such as income, will be equivalent to a real change in terms of purchasing power. Hence we will be examining Keynes' income-expenditure model of real GDP determination in a world of inflexible prices.

To simplify the income determination model that follows, a number of assumptions are made:

1. Businesses pay no indirect taxes (for example, sales taxes).
2. Businesses distribute all of their profits to shareholders.
3. There is no depreciation (capital consumption allowance), so gross private domestic investment equals net investment.
4. The economy is closed—that is, there is no foreign trade.

▶ **Consumption**
Spending on new goods and services out of a household's current income. Whatever is not consumed is saved. Consumption includes such things as buying food and going to a concert.

▶ **Saving**
The act of not consuming all of one's current income. Whatever is not consumed out of spendable income is, by definition, saved. *Saving* is an action measured over time (a flow), whereas *savings* are a stock, an accumulation resulting from the act of saving in the past.

▶ **Consumption goods**
Goods bought by households to use up, such as food, clothing, and movies.

Given all these simplifying assumptions, real disposable income will be equal to real national income minus taxes.[1]

Definitions and Relationships Revisited

You can do only two things with a dollar of income (in the absence of taxes): consume it or save it. If you consume it, it is gone forever. If you save the entire dollar, however, you will be able to consume it (and perhaps more if it earns interest) at some future time. That is the distinction between **consumption** and **saving.** Consumption is the act of using income for the purchase of consumption goods. **Consumption goods** are goods purchased by households for immediate satisfaction. Consumption goods are such things as food, clothing, and movies. By definition, whatever you do not consume you save and can consume at some time in the future.

Stocks and Flows: The Difference Between Saving and Savings. It is important to distinguish between *saving* and *savings. Saving* is an action that occurs at a particular rate—for example, $10 a week or $520 a year. This rate is a flow. It is expressed per unit of time, usually a year. Implicitly, then, when we talk about saving, we talk about a *flow* or rate of saving. *Savings,* by contrast, is a *stock* concept, measured at a certain point or instant in time. Your current *savings* are the result of past *saving.* You may presently have *savings* of $2,000 that are the result of four years' *saving* at a rate of $500 per year. Consumption, being related to saving, is also a flow concept. You consume from after-tax income at a certain rate per week, per month, or per year.

Relating Income to Saving and Consumption. Obviously, a dollar of take-home income can be either consumed or not consumed. Realizing this, we can see the relationship among saving, consumption, and disposable income:

$$\text{Consumption} + \text{saving} \equiv \text{disposable income}$$

This is called an *accounting identity.* It has to hold true at every moment in time. From it we can derive the definition of saving:

$$\text{Saving} \equiv \text{disposable income} - \text{consumption}$$

Recall that disposable income is what you actually have left to spend after you pay taxes.

▶ **Investment**
The spending by businesses on things such as machines and buildings, which can be used to produce goods and services in the future. The investment part of total income is the portion that will be used in the process of producing goods in the future.

▶ **Capital goods**
Producer durables; nonconsumable goods that firms use to make other goods.

Investment

Investment is also a flow concept. *Investment* as used in economics differs from the common use of the term, as we have already pointed out. In everyday speech, it is often used to describe putting money into the stock market or real estate. In economic analysis, investment is defined as expenditures by firms on new machines and buildings—**capital goods**—that are expected to yield a future stream of income. This we have already called *fixed investment.* We also included changes in business inventories in our definition. This we have already called *inventory investment.*

---

[1] Strictly speaking, we are referring here to net taxes—that is, the difference between taxes paid and transfer payments received. If taxes are $100 billion but individuals receive transfer payments—Old Age Security benefits, unemployment benefits, and so forth—of $30 billion, net taxes are equal to $70 billion.

Concepts in Brief

- If we assume that we are operating on a horizontal short-run aggregate supply curve, the equilibrium level of real GDP per year is completely demand-determined.
- Consumption is a flow which occurs repeatedly over time. It represents the purchase of consumer goods and services such as food, clothing, and restaurant meals.
- *Saving* is also a flow, something that occurs over time. It equals disposable income minus consumption. *Savings* are a stock. They are the accumulated results of saving.
- Investment too is a flow. It includes expenditures on new machines, buildings, and equipment, as well as changes in business inventories.

DETERMINANTS OF PLANNED CONSUMPTION AND PLANNED SAVING

In the classical model, the supply of saving was determined by the rate of interest: The higher the rate of interest, the more people wanted to save and therefore the less

Table 12.1

Real Consumption and Saving Schedules: A Hypothetical Case

Column 1 presents real disposable income from zero up to $20,000 per year; column 2 indicates planned consumption per year; column 3 presents planned saving per year. At levels of disposable income below $10,000, planned saving is negative. In column 4, we see the average propensity to consume, which is merely planned consumption divided by disposable income. Column 5 lists average propensity to save, which is planned saving divided by disposable income. Column 6 is the marginal propensity to consume, which shows the proportion of additional income that will be consumed. Finally, column 7 shows the proportion of additional income that will be saved, or the marginal propensity to save.

Combination	(1) Real Disposable Income per Year (Y_d)	(2) Planned Real Consumption per Year (C)	(3) Planned Real Saving per Year ($S \equiv Y_d - C$) (1) – (2)	(4) Average Propensity to Consume (APC $\equiv C/Y_d$) (2) ÷ (1)	(5) Average Propensity to Save (APS $\equiv S/Y_d$) (3) ÷ (1)	(6) Marginal Propensity to Consume (MPC $\equiv \Delta C/\Delta Y_d$)	(7) Marginal Propensity to Save (MPS $\equiv \Delta S/\Delta Y_d$)
A	$ 0	$ 2,000	$ –2,000	—	—	—	—
B	2,000	3,600	–1,600	1.8	–.8	.8	.2
C	4,000	5,200	–1,200	1.3	–.3	.8	.2
D	6,000	6,800	– 800	1.133	–.133	.8	.2
E	8,000	8,400	– 400	1.05	–.05	.8	.2
F	10,000	10,000	0	1.0	.0	.8	.2
G	12,000	11,600	400	.967	.033	.8	.2
H	14,000	13,200	800	.943	.057	.8	.2
I	16,000	14,800	1,200	.925	.075	.8	.2
J	18,000	16,400	1,600	.911	.089	.8	.2
K	20,000	18,000	2,000	.9	.1	.8	.2

people wanted to consume. According to Keynes, the interest rate is not the primary determinant of an individual's saving and consumption decisions.

Keynes argued that saving and consumption decisions depend primarily on an individual's real current income.

The relationship between planned consumption expenditures of households and their current level of real income has been called the **consumption function.** It shows how much all households plan to consume per year at each level of real disposable income per year. Using for the moment only columns 1, 2, and 3 of Table 12.1, we will present a consumption function for a hypothetical household.

We see from Table 12.1 that as real disposable income rises, planned consumption also rises, but by a smaller amount, as Keynes suggested. Planned saving also increases with disposable income. Notice, however, that below an income of $10,000, the planned saving of this hypothetical family is actually negative. The further that income drops below that level, the more the family engages in **dissaving,** either by going into debt or by using up some of its existing wealth.

▶ **Consumption function**

The relationship between amount consumed and disposable income. A consumption function tells us how much people plan to consume at various levels of disposable income.

▶ **Dissaving**

Negative saving; a situation in which spending exceeds income. Dissaving can occur when a household is able to borrow or use up existing owned assets.

Figure 12.1
The Consumption and Saving Functions

If we plot the combinations of real disposable income and planned real consumption from columns 1 and 2 in Table 12.1, we get the consumption function. At every point on the 45-degree line, a vertical line drawn to the income axis is the same distance from the origin as a horizontal line drawn to the consumption axis. Where the consumption function crosses the 45-degree line at *F*, we know that consumption equals real disposable income and there is zero saving. The vertical distance between the 45-degree line and the consumption function measures the rate of saving or dissaving at any given income level. If we plot the relationship between column 1, real disposable income, and column 3, planned real saving, from Table 12.1, we arrive at the saving function shown in the lower part of this diagram. It is the complement of the consumption function presented above it.

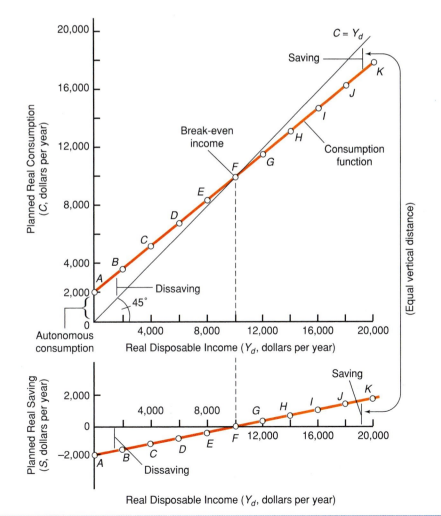

Graphing the Numbers

When we constructed demand and supply curves in Chapter 3, we merely plotted the points from a table showing price-quantity pairs onto a diagram whose axes were labelled "Price" and "Quantity." We will graph the consumption and saving relationships presented in Table 12.1 in the same manner. In the upper part of Figure 12.1, the vertical axis measures the level of planned real consumption per year, and the horizontal axis measures the level of real disposable income per year. In the lower part of the figure, the horizontal axis is again real disposable income per year, but now the vertical axis is planned real saving per year. All of these are on a dollars-per-year basis, which emphasizes the point that we are measuring flows, not stocks.

As you can see, we have taken income-consumption and income-saving combinations *A* through *K* and plotted them. In the upper part of Figure 12.1, the result is called the *consumption function*. In the lower part, the result is called the *saving function*. Mathematically, the saving function is the *complement* of the consumption function because consumption plus saving always equals disposable income. What is not consumed is, by definition, saved. The difference between actual disposable income and the planned level of consumption per year *must* be the planned level of saving per year.

How can we find the rate of saving or dissaving in the upper part of Figure 12.1? We draw a line that is equidistant from both the horizontal and the vertical axes. This line is 45 degrees from either axis and is often called the **45-degree reference line.** At every point on the 45-degree reference line, a vertical line drawn to the income axis is the same distance from the origin as a horizontal line drawn to the consumption axis. Thus at point *F*, where the consumption function intersects the 45-degree line, real disposable income equals planned consumption. Point *F* is sometimes called the *break-even income point* because there is neither positive nor negative saving. This can be seen in the lower part of Figure 12.1 as well. The planned annual rate of saving at a real disposable income level of $10,000 is indeed zero.

▶ **45-degree reference line**
The line along which planned real expenditures equal real national income per year.

Dissaving and Autonomous Consumption

To the left of point *F* in either part of Figure 12.1, this hypothetical family engages in dissaving, either by going into debt or by consuming existing assets, including savings. The amount of saving or dissaving in the upper part of the figure can be found by measuring the vertical distance between the 45-degree line and the consumption function. This simply tells us that if our hypothetical family starts above $10,000 of real disposable income per year and then temporarily finds its real disposable income below $10,000, it will not cut back its consumption by the full amount of the reduction. It will instead go into debt or consume existing assets in some way to compensate for part of the loss.

Now look at the point on the diagram where real disposable income is zero but planned consumption per year is $2,000. This amount of planned consumption, which does not depend at all on actual disposable income, is called **autonomous**

▶ **Autonomous consumption**
The part of consumption that is independent of (does not depend on) the level of disposable income. Changes in autonomous consumption shift the consumption function.

consumption. The autonomous consumption of $2,000 is *independent* of the level of disposable income. That means that no matter how low the level of income of our hypothetical family falls, the family will always attempt to consume at least $2,000 per year. (We are, of course, assuming here that the family's real disposable income does not equal zero year in and year out. There is certainly a limit to how long our hypothetical family could finance autonomous consumption without any income.) That $2,000 of yearly consumption is determined by things other than the level of income. We don't need to specify what determines autonomous consumption; we merely state that it exists and that in our example it is $2,000 per year. Just remember that the word *autonomous* means "existing independently." In our model, autonomous consumption exists independently of the hypothetical family's level of real disposable income. (Later we will review some of the non-real-disposable-income determinants of consumption.) There are many possible types of autonomous expenditures. Hypothetically, we can consider that investment is autonomous—independent of income. We can assume that government expenditures are autonomous. We will do just that at various times in our discussions to simplify our analysis of income determination.

Average Propensity to Consume and to Save

▶ **Average propensity to consume (APC)**

Consumption divided by disposable income; for any given level of income, the proportion of total disposable income that is consumed.

▶ **Average propensity to save (APS)**

Saving divided by disposable income; for any given level of income, the proportion of total disposable income that is saved.

Let's now go back to Table 12.1, and this time look at columns 4 and 5: **average propensity to consume (APC)** and **average propensity to save (APS).** They are defined as follows:

$$APC \equiv \frac{\text{consumption}}{\text{real disposable income}}$$

$$APS \equiv \frac{\text{saving}}{\text{real disposable income}}$$

Notice from column 4 in Table 12.1 that for this hypothetical family, the average propensity to consume decreases as real disposable income increases. This decrease simply means that the fraction of the family's real disposable income going to saving rises as income rises. The same fact can be found in column 5. The average propensity to save (APS), which at first is negative, finally hits zero at an income level of $10,000 and then becomes positive. In this example, the APS reaches a value of 0.1 at income level $20,000. This means that the household saves 10 percent of a $20,000 income.

It's quite easy for you to figure out your own average propensity to consume or to save. Just divide your total real disposable income for the year into what you consumed and what you saved. The result will be your personal APC and APS, respectively, at your current level of income. This gives the proportions of total income that are consumed and saved.

Marginal Propensity to Consume and to Save

▶ **Marginal propensity to consume (MPC)**

The ratio of the change in consumption to the change in disposable income. A marginal propensity to consume of 0.8 tells us that an additional $100 in take-home pay will lead to an additional $80 consumed.

▶ **Marginal propensity to save (MPS)**

The ratio of the change in saving to the change in disposable income. A marginal propensity to save of 0.2 indicates that out of an additional $100 in take-home pay, $20 will be saved. Whatever is not saved is consumed. The marginal propensity to save plus the marginal propensity to consume must always equal 1, by definition.

Now we go to the last two columns in Table 12.1: **marginal propensity to consume (MPC)** and **marginal propensity to save (MPS).** We have used the term *marginal* before. It refers to a small incremental or decremental change (represented by Δ in Table 12.1). The marginal propensity to consume, then, is defined as:

$$MPC \equiv \frac{\text{change in consumption}}{\text{change in real disposable income}}$$

The marginal propensity to save is defined similarly as:

$$MPS \equiv \frac{\text{change in saving}}{\text{change in real disposable income}}$$

What do MPC and MPS tell you? They tell you what percentage of a given increase or decrease in income will go towards consumption and saving, respectively. The emphasis here is on the word *change*. The marginal propensity to consume indicates how much you will change your planned rate of consumption if there is a change in your real disposable income. If your marginal propensity to consume is 0.8, that does not mean that you consume 80 percent of *all* disposable income. The percentage of your real disposable income that you consume is given by the average propensity to consume, or APC, which is not, in Table 12.1, equal to 0.8. In contrast, an MPC of 0.8 means that you will consume 80 percent of any *increase* in your disposable income. In general, we assume that the marginal propensity to consume is between zero and 1. We assume that individuals increase their planned consumption by more than zero and less than 100 percent of any increase in real disposable income that they receive.

Consider a simple example in which we show the difference between the average propensity to consume and the marginal propensity to consume. Assume that your consumption behaviour is exactly the same as our hypothetical family's behaviour depicted in Table 12.1. You have an annual real disposable income of $18,000. Your planned consumption rate, then, from column 2 of Table 12.1 is $16,400. So your average propensity to consume is $16,400 ÷ $18,000 = 0.911. Now suppose that at the end of the year your boss gives you an after-tax bonus of $2,000. What would you do with that additional $2,000 in real disposable income? According to the table, you would consume $1,600 of it and save $400. In that case, your *marginal* propensity to consume would be $1,600 ÷ $2,000 = 0.8, and your marginal propensity to save would be $400 ÷ $2,000 = 0.2. What would happen to your *average* propensity to consume? To find out, we add $1,600 to $16,400 of planned consumption, which gives us a new consumption rate of $18,000. The average propensity to consume is then $18,000 divided by the new higher salary of $20,000. Your APC drops from 0.911 to 0.9. By contrast, your MPC remains in our simplified example 0.8 all the time. Look at column 6 in Table 12.1. The MPC is 0.8 at every level of income. (Therefore, the MPS is always equal to 0.2 at every level of income.) Underlying the constancy of MPC is the assumption that the amount that you are willing to consume out of additional income will remain the same in percentage terms no matter what level of real disposable income is your starting point.

Some Relationships

Consumption plus saving must equal income. Both your total real disposable income and the change in total real disposable income are either consumed or saved. The proportions of either measure must equal 1, or 100 percent. This allows us to make the following statements:

$$APC + APS = 1 \ (= 100 \text{ percent of total income})$$

$$MPC + MPS = 1 \ (= 100 \text{ percent of the } \textit{change} \text{ in income})$$

The average propensities as well as the marginal propensities to consume and save must total 1, or 100 percent. Check the two statements by adding the figures in columns 4 and 5 for each level of real disposable income in Table 12.1. Do the same for columns 6 and 7.

Causes of Shifts in the Consumption Function

A change in any other relevant economic variable besides real disposable income will cause the consumption function to shift. There is a virtually unlimited number of such nonincome determinants of the position of the consumption function. When population increases or decreases, for example, the consumption function will shift up or down, respectively. Changes in expectations can also shift the consumption function. If the average household believes that the rate of inflation is going to fall dramatically in the years to come, the current consumption function will probably shift down: Planned consumption would be less at every level of real disposable income than before this change in expectations. Real household **wealth** is also a determinant of the position of the consumption function. An increase in real wealth of the average household will cause the consumption function to shift upward. A decrease in real wealth will cause it to shift downward.

▶ **Wealth**
The stock of assets owned by a person, household, firm, or country. For a household, wealth can consist of a house, cars, personal belongings, bank accounts, and cash.

Concepts in Brief

- The consumption function shows the relationship between planned rates of consumption and real disposable income per year. The saving function is the complement of the consumption function because saving plus consumption must equal real disposable income.
- The average propensity to consume (APC) is equal to consumption divided by real disposable income. The average propensity to save (APS) is equal to saving divided by real disposable income.
- The marginal propensity to consume (MPC) is equal to the change in planned consumption divided by the change in real disposable income. The marginal propensity to save (MPS) is equal to the change in planned saving divided by the change in real disposable income.
- Any change in real disposable income will cause the planned rate of consumption to change; this is represented by a movement along the consumption function. Any change in a nonincome determinant of consumption will shift the consumption function.

DETERMINANTS OF INVESTMENT

Investment, you will remember, is defined as expenditures on new buildings and equipment and changes in business inventories. Real gross private domestic investment in Canada has been extremely volatile over the years relative to real consumption. If we were to look at net private domestic investment (investment after depreciation has been deducted), we would see that in the depths of the Great Depression and at the peak of the World War II effort, the figure was negative. In other words, we were eating away at our capital stock—we weren't even maintaining it by completely replacing depreciated equipment.

If we compare real investment expenditures historically with real consumption expenditures, we find that the latter are relatively less variable over time than the former. Why is this so? The answer is that the real investment decisions of businesspeople are based on highly variable, subjective estimates of how the economic future looks. We just discussed the role of expectations in determining the position of the consumption function. Expectations play an even greater role in determining the position of the investment function. This could account for much of the instability of investment over time.

The Planned Investment Function

Consider that at all times, businesses perceive an array of investment opportunities. These investment opportunities have rates of return ranging from zero to very high, with the number (or dollar value) of all such projects inversely related to the rate of return. Because a project is profitable only if its rate of return exceeds the opportunity cost of the investment—the rate of interest—it follows that as the interest rate falls, planned investment spending increases, and vice versa. Even if firms use retained earnings (internal financing) to fund an investment, the higher the market rate of interest, the greater the *opportunity cost* of using those retained earnings. Thus it does not matter in our analysis whether the firm must seek financing from external sources or can obtain such financing by using retained earnings. Just consider that as the interest rate falls, more investment opportunities will be profitable, and planned investment will be higher.

It should be no surprise, therefore, that the investment function is represented as an inverse relationship between the rate of interest and the value of planned investment. A hypothetical investment schedule is given in part (a) of Figure 12.2, and plotted in part (b). We see from this schedule that if, for example, the rate of interest is 5.5 percent, the dollar value of planned investment will be $60 billion per year. Notice, by the way, that planned investment is also given on a per-year basis, showing that it represents a flow, not a stock. (The stock counterpart of investment is the stock of capital in the economy measured in dollars at a point in time.)

What Causes the Investment Function to Shift?

Because planned investment is assumed to be a function of the rate of interest, any non-interest-rate variable that changes can have the potential of shifting the investment function. Expectations of businesspeople is one of those variables. If higher

Figure 12.2
Planned Investment

In the hypothetical planned investment schedule in part (a), the rate of planned investment is asserted to be inversely related to the rate of interest. If we plot the data pairs from part (a), we obtain the investment function, *I*, in part (b). It is negatively sloped.

Part (a)

Rate of Interest (percent per year)	Planned Investment per Year ($ billions)
7.5	20
7	30
6.5	40
6	50
5.5	60
5	70
4.5	80
4	90
3.5	100
3	110

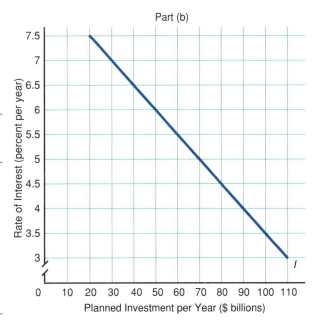

Part (b)

future sales are expected, more machines and bigger plants will be planned for the future. More investment will be undertaken because of the expectation of higher future profits. In this case the investment schedule, *I*, would shift outward to the right, meaning that more investment would be desired at all rates of interest. Any change in productive technology can potentially shift the investment function. A positive change in productive technology would stimulate demand for additional capital goods and shift the investment schedule, *I*, outward to the right. Changes in business taxes can also shift the investment schedule. If they increase, we predict a leftward shift in the planned investment function.

Concepts in Brief

- The planned investment schedule shows the relationship between investment and the rate of interest; it slopes downward.
- The non-interest-rate determinants of planned investment are expectations, innovation and technological changes, and business taxes.
- Any change in the non-interest-rate determinants of planned investment will cause the planned investment function to shift so that at each and every rate of interest a different amount of planned investment will be obtained.

CONSUMPTION AS A FUNCTION OF REAL NATIONAL INCOME

We are interested in determining the equilibrium level of real national income per year. But when we examined the consumption function earlier in this chapter, it related planned consumption expenditures to the level of real disposable income per year. We have already shown where adjustments must be made to GDP in order to get real disposable income (see Table 8.2 in Chapter 8). Real disposable income turns out to be less than real national income because net taxes (taxes minus government transfer payments) are usually about 16 to 24 percent of national income. A representative average in the 1990s is about 20 percent, so disposable income, on average, has in recent years been around 80 percent of national income.

If we are willing to assume that real disposable income, Y_d, differs from real national income by an amount T every year, we can relatively easily substitute real national income for real disposable income in the consumption function.

We can now plot any consumption function on a diagram in which the horizontal axis is no longer real disposable income but rather real national income, as in Figure 12.3. Notice that there is an autonomous part of consumption that is so labelled. The difference between this graph and the graphs presented earlier in this chapter is the change in the horizontal axis from real disposable income to real national income per year. For the rest of this chapter, assume that this calculation has been made, and the result is that the MPC out of real national income equals 0.8, suggesting that 20 percent of changes in real national income are either saved or paid in taxes: In other words, of an additional $100 earned, an additional $80 will be consumed.

Figure 12.3

Consumption as a Function of Real National Income

This consumption function shows the rate of planned expenditures for each level of real national income per year. There is an autonomous component in consumption equal to $30 billion. Along the 45-degree reference line, planned consumption expenditures per year, C, are identical to real national income per year, Y. The consumption curve intersects the 45-degree reference line at a value of $150 billion per year.

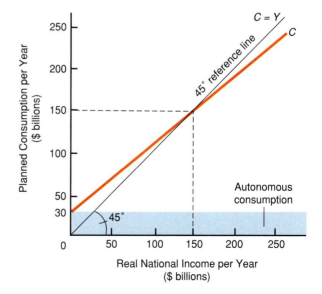

The 45-Degree Reference Line

Like the earlier graphs, Figure 12.3 shows a 45-degree reference line. The 45-degree line bisects the quadrant into two equal spaces. Thus along the 45-degree reference line, planned consumption expenditures, *C*, equal real national income per year, *Y*. One can see, then, that at any point where the consumption function intersects the 45-degree reference line, planned consumption expenditures will be exactly equal to real national income per year, or *C* = *Y*. Note that in this graph, because we are looking only at planned consumption on the vertical axis, the 45-degree reference line is where planned consumption, *C*, is always equal to real national income per year, *Y*. Later, when we add investment, government spending, and net exports to the graph, the 45-degree reference line with respect to *all* planned expenditures will be labelled as such on the vertical axis. In any event, consumption and real national income are equal at $150 billion per year. That is where the consumption curve, *C*, intersects the 45-degree reference line. At that income level, all income is consumed.

Try Preview Question 1:

How do we interpret the 45-degree reference line?

Adding the Investment Function

Another component of private aggregate demand is, of course, investment spending, *I*. We have already looked at the planned investment function, which related investment to the rate of interest. You see that as the downward-sloping curve in part (a) of Figure 12.4. Recall from Figure 11.2 that the equilibrium rate of interest is determined at the intersection of the desired savings schedule, which is labelled *S* and is

---

Figure 12.4 **Combining Consumption and Investment**
In part (a), we show the determination of real investment in billions of dollars per year. It occurs where the investment schedule intersects the saving schedule at an interest rate of 5 percent and is equal to $70 billion per year. In part (b), investment is a constant $70 billion per year. When we add this amount to the consumption line, we obtain in part

(c) the *C* + *I* line, which is vertically higher than the *C* line by exactly $70 billion. Real national income is equal to *C* + *I* at $500 billion per year where total planned expenditure, *C* + *I*, is equal to actual real national income, for this is where the *C* + *I* line intersects the 45-degree reference line, on which *C* + *I* is equal to *Y* at every point.

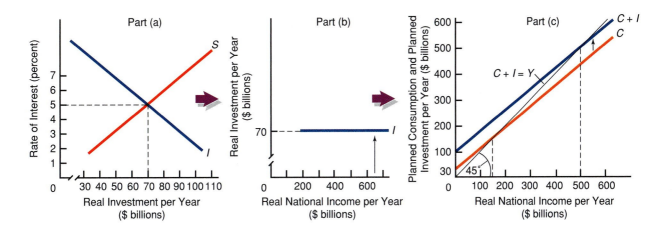

upward-sloping. The equilibrium rate of interest is 5 percent, and the equilibrium rate of investment is $70 billion per year. The $70 billion of real investment per year is *autonomous* with respect to real national income—that is, it is independent of real national income. In other words, given that we have a determinant investment level of $70 billion at a 5 percent rate of interest, we can treat this level of investment as constant, regardless of the level of national income. This is shown in part (b) of Figure 12.4. The vertical distance of investment spending is $70 billion. Businesses plan on investing a particular amount—$70 billion per year—and will do so no matter what the level of real national income.

How do we add this amount of investment spending to our consumption function? We simply add a line above the *C* line that we drew in Figure 12.3 that is higher by the vertical distance equal to $70 billion of autonomous investment spending. This is shown by the arrow in part (c) of Figure 12.4. Our new line, now labelled *C + I*, is called the *consumption plus investment line*. In our simple economy without government expenditures and net exports, the *C + I* curve represents total planned expenditures as they relate to different levels of real national income per year. Because the 45-degree reference line shows all the points where planned expenditures (now *C + I*) equal real national income, we label it *C + I = Y*. Equilibrium *Y* equals $500 billion per year. Equilibrium occurs when total planned expenditures equal total planned production (given that any amount of production in this model in the short run can occur without a change in the price level).

Try Preview Question 2:

What does the total planned expenditures curve indicate?

EXAMPLE   The Cost of Separation

In the referendum of October 30, 1995, 50.6 percent of Quebeckers voted "No" to separation from the rest of Canada. There was much economic and political uncertainty leading up to the referendum, and this was seen in the form of higher interest rates. As we know, when interest rates are relatively high, both consumption and investment fall. What might happen to the Canadian economy if Quebec does vote in the future to separate? While predictions vary from optimistic low-cost to pessimistic high-cost , a middle-of-the-road estimate was given by the Chair of the Bank of Montreal, Matthew Barrett, at the Bank's 1996 annual general meeting. He suggested that the political uncertainty that would follow a "Yes" vote would cause interest rates to rise, possibly to 13 percent. In response, consumption and investment would fall, eventually costing the rest of Canada $150 billion to $200 billion in forgone GDP over the following 5 years. This translates to about $20,000 for every family of four in Canada.

How could we portray this information in terms of Figure 12.4? The rise in interest rates would shift the *C* curve down (the interest rate effect), thus also shifting the *C + I* curve down. But the higher interest rates would also lead to reduced investment, shifting the *C + I* curve down closer to the *C* curve. This double effect would reduce real national GDP by a significant amount.

For critical analysis: What would happen to consumption and investment in the new independent Quebec?

SAVING AND INVESTMENT: PLANNED VERSUS ACTUAL

Figure 12.5 shows the planned investment curve as a horizontal line at $70 billion per year. Investment is completely autonomous in this simplified model—it does not depend on the level of income.

The planned saving curve is represented by S. Because in our model whatever is not consumed is, by definition, saved, the planned saving schedule is the complement of the planned consumption schedule, represented by the C line in Figure 12.3. For better exposition, we look at only a small part of the saving and investment schedules—real national incomes between $400 and $600 billion per year.

Why does equilibrium have to occur at the intersection of the planned saving and planned investment schedules? If we are at E in Figure 12.5, planned saving equals planned investment. All anticipations are validated by reality. There is no tendency for businesses to alter the rate of production or the level of employment because they are neither increasing nor decreasing their inventories in an unplanned way.

If we are producing at a real national income level of $600 billion instead of $500 billion, planned investment, as usual, is $70 billion per year, but it is exceeded by planned saving, which is $90 billion per year. This means that consumers will purchase less of total output than businesses had anticipated. Unplanned business inventories will now rise at the rate of $20 billion per year, bringing actual investment into line with actual saving because the $20 billion increase in inventories is included in actual investment. But this rate of output cannot continue for long. Businesses will respond to this unplanned increase in inventories by cutting back production and employment, and we will move towards a lower level of real national income.

Conversely, if the real national income is $400 billion per year, planned investment continues annually at $70 billion; but at that output rate, planned saving is only $50 billion. This means that households and businesses are purchasing more of real

Figure 12.5
Planned and Actual Rates of Saving and Investment
Only at the equilibrium level of real national income of $500 billion per year will planned saving equal actual saving, planned investment equal actual investment, and hence planned saving equal planned investment.

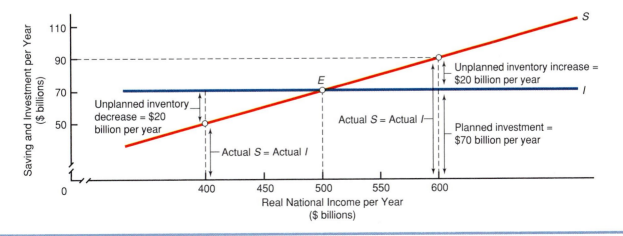

national income than businesses had planned. Businesses will find that they must draw down their inventories below the planned level by $20 billion (business inventories will fall now at the unplanned rate of $20 billion per year), bringing actual investment into equality with actual saving because the $20 billion decline in inventories is included in actual investment (thereby decreasing it). But this situation cannot last forever either. In their attempt to increase inventories to the desired previous level, businesses will increase output and employment, and real national income will rise towards its equilibrium value of $500 billion per year. Figure 12.5 demonstrates the necessary equality between actual saving and actual investment. Inventories adjust so that saving and investment, after the fact, are *always* equal in this simplified model. (Remember that changes in inventories count as part of investment.)

Every time the saving rate planned by households differs from the investment rate planned by businesses, there will be a shrinkage or an expansion in the circular flow of income and output (introduced in Chapter 8) in the form of unplanned inventory changes. Real national income and employment will change until unplanned inventory changes are again zero—that is, until we have attained the equilibrium level of real national income.

Concepts in Brief

- We assume that the consumption function has an autonomous part that is independent of the level of real national income per year. It is labelled "autonomous consumption."
- For simplicity, we assume that investment is autonomous with respect to real national income and therefore unrelated to the level of real national income per year.
- The equilibrium level of real national income can be found where planned saving equals planned investment.
- Whenever planned saving exceeds planned investment, there will be unplanned inventory accumulation, and national income will fall as producers reduce output. Whenever planned saving is less than planned investment, there will be unplanned inventory depletion, and national income will rise as producers increase output.

Thinking Critically About the Media   Small Businesses and New Jobs

One of the darlings of both politicians and the media is small business. According to a common explanation of job creation, small businesses are the source of all new jobs. In recent years, there has been a lot of talk concerning major corporate "restructuring" and the subsequent laying off of thousands of workers. Yet an examination of all of the available data does not support the conclusion that only small firms are hiring. Although it is true that small businesses hire at four times the rate, relative to their total employment, as midsized and big businesses, small businesses also *eliminate* jobs at a far higher rate. In other words, hiring is not the same as job creation because we have to look at the difference between hirings and firings. Indeed, while some big businesses are in the news because of layoffs, others are hiring and are not getting news coverage. For instance, one year, the media reported that CN and General Motors had laid off 18,000 workers; that same year, however, Syncrude Canada Ltd. announced it would be creating 44,000 new jobs in its oil sands project. The moral of the story is that headlines are not always based on the overall economic picture.

KEYNESIAN EQUILIBRIUM WITH GOVERNMENT AND THE FOREIGN SECTOR ADDED

Government

We have to add government spending, G, to our macroeconomic model. We assume that the level of resource-using government purchases of goods and services (federal, provincial, and municipal), *not* including transfer payments, is determined by the political process. In other words, G will be considered autonomous, just like investment (and a certain component of consumption). In Canada, resource-using government expenditures are around 20 percent of real national income. The other side of the coin, of course, is that there are taxes, which are used to pay for much of government spending. We will simplify our model greatly by assuming that there is a constant **lump-sum tax** of $100 billion a year to finance $100 billion of government spending. This lump-sum tax will reduce disposable income and consumption by the same amount. We show this in Table 12.2 (column 2) on the next page, where we give the numbers for a complete model.

▶ **Lump-sum tax**

A tax that does not depend on income or the circumstances of the taxpayer. An example is a $1,000 tax that every family must pay, irrespective of its economic situation.

The Foreign Sector

Not a week goes by without a commentary in the media about the size of our foreign trade balance. In some years, our trade balance is positive (the value of exports exceeds the value of imports) while in others it is negative (the value of imports exceeds the value of exports). The difference between exports and imports is *net exports*, which we label X in our graphs. For simplicity, let us assume that exports exceed imports (net exports, X, is positive) and furthermore that the level of net exports is autonomous—independent of national income. Assume a level of X of $10 billion per year. In Table 12.2, net exports is shown in column 8 as $10 billion per year.

In fact, the level of exports depends on international economic conditions, especially in the countries that buy our products. If there is a decline in the foreign exchange value of the Canadian dollar or if our trading partners experience economic growth, they will want to purchase more of our products. If the converse holds true, our exports will fall. We have seen this recently with the economic crisis in Asia. The economies of Japan, South Korea, and several other Asian countries faltered severely, leaving consumers and businesses in those countries less willing to purchase our goods and services. As a result, we saw our own net exports fall. This would be portrayed as a downward shift of our $C + I + G + X$ curve.

The level of imports depends on economic conditions here in Canada. If the foreign exchange value of the Canadian dollar falls, we will purchase fewer of the now more expensive goods and services from other countries. If the federal government raises import taxes or tariffs on imported goods, those goods become more expensive for us to import and we will purchase fewer of them. Since the value of imports is subtracted from the value of exports to find net exports, a *decrease* in the value of imports will *increase* the value of net exports, and vice versa.

Table 12.2 **The Determination of Equilibrium Real National Income with Net Exports**
Figures are billions of dollars.

(1) Real National Income	(2) Taxes	(3) Real Disposable Income	(4) Planned Consumption	(5) Planned Saving	(6) Planned Investment	(7) Government Spending	(8) Net Exports (exports – imports)	(9) Total Planned Expenditures (4)+(6)+(7)+(8)	(10) Unplanned Inventory Changes	(11) Direction of Change in Real National Income
200	100	100	110	−10	70	100	10	290	−90	Increase
250	100	150	150	0	70	100	10	330	−80	Increase
300	100	200	190	10	70	100	10	370	−70	Increase
400	100	300	270	30	70	100	10	450	−50	Increase
500	100	400	350	50	70	100	10	530	−30	Increase
600	100	500	430	70	70	100	10	610	−10	Increase
650	100	550	470	80	70	100	10	650	0	Neither (equilibrium)
700	100	600	510	90	70	100	10	690	+10	Decrease
800	100	700	590	110	70	100	10	770	+30	Decrease

Determining the Equilibrium Level of Real National Income per Year

We are now in a position to determine the equilibrium level of real national income per year under the continuing assumptions that the short-run aggregate supply curve is horizontal; that investment, government, and the foreign sector are autonomous; and that planned consumption expenditures are determined by the level of real national income. As can be seen in Table 12.2, total planned expenditures of $650 billion per year equal real national income of $650 billion per year, and this is where we reach equilibrium.

Remember that equilibrium *always* occurs when total planned expenditures equal total production (given that any amount of production in this model in the short run can occur without a change in the price level).

Now look at Figure 12.6, which shows the equilibrium level of real national income. There are two curves, one showing the consumption function, which is the exact duplicate of the one shown in Figure 12.3, and the other being the $C + I + G + X$ curve, which intersects the 45-degree reference line (representing equilibrium) at $650 billion per year.

Whenever total planned expenditures differ from real national income, there are unplanned inventory changes. When total planned expenditures are greater than real national income, inventory levels drop in an unplanned manner. To get them back up, firms seek to expand their production, which increases real national income. Real national income rises towards its equilibrium level. Whenever total planned expen-

Figure 12.6
The Equilibrium Level of Real National Income

The consumption function, with no government and thus no taxes, is shown as C. When we add autonomous investment, government, taxes, and net exports, we obtain $C + I + G + X$. We move from E_1 to E_2. The equilibrium level of real national income is $650 billion per year.

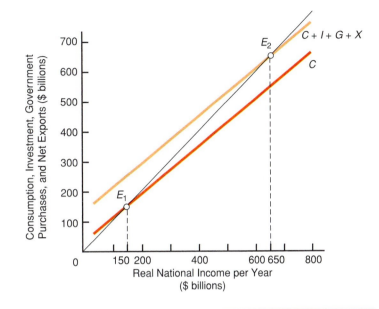

ditures are less than real national income, the opposite occurs. There are unplanned inventory increases, causing firms to cut back on their production. The result is a drop in real national income towards the equilibrium level.

Concepts in Brief

- When we add autonomous investment, I, and autonomous government spending, G, to the consumption function, we obtain the $C + I + G$ curve, which represents total planned expenditures for a closed economy. In an open economy, we add the foreign sector, which consists of exports minus imports, or net exports, X. Total planned expenditures are thus represented by the $C + I + G + X$ curve.
- The equilibrium level of real national income can be found by locating the intersection of the total planned expenditures curve with the 45-degree reference line. At that level of real national income per year, planned consumption plus planned investment plus government expenditures plus net exports will equal real national income.
- Whenever total planned expenditures exceed real national income, there will be unplanned decreases in inventories; the size of the circular flow of income will increase, and a higher level of equilibrium real national income will prevail. Whenever planned expenditures are less than real national income, there will be unplanned increases in inventories; the size of the circular flow will shrink, and a lower equilibrium level of real national income will prevail.

THE MULTIPLIER

Look again at part (c) of Figure 12.4. Assume for the moment that the only expenditures included in real national income are consumption expenditures. Where would the equilibrium level of income be in this case? It would be where the consumption function *(C)* intersects the 45-degree reference line, which is at $150 billion per year. Now we add the autonomous amount of planned investment, or $70 billion, and then determine what the new equilibrium level of income will be. It turns out to be $500 billion per year. Adding $70 billion per year of investment spending increased the equilibrium level of income by *five* times that amount, or by $350 billion per year.

What is operating here is the multiplier effect of changes in autonomous spending. The **multiplier** is the number by which a permanent change in autonomous investment or autonomous consumption is multiplied to get the change in the equilibrium level of real national income. Any permanent increases in autonomous investment or in any autonomous component of consumption will cause an even larger increase in real national income. Any permanent decreases in autonomous spending will cause even larger decreases in the equilibrium level of real national income per year. To understand why this multiple expansion (or contraction) in the equilibrium level of real national income occurs, let's look at a simple numerical example.

We'll use the same figures we used for the marginal propensity to consume and to save. MPC will equal 0.8, or $\frac{4}{5}$, and MPS will equal 0.2, or $\frac{1}{5}$. Now let's run an experiment and say that businesses decide to increase planned investment perma-

▶ **Multiplier**

The ratio of the change in the equilibrium level of real national income to the change in autonomous expenditures; the number by which a change in autonomous investment or autonomous consumption, for example, is multiplied to get the change in the equilibrium level of real national income.

Table 12.3
The Multiplier Process

We trace the effects of a permanent $10 billion increase in autonomous investment spending on the equilibrium level of real national income. If we assume a marginal propensity to consume of 0.8, such an increase will eventually elicit a $50 billion increase in the equilibrium level of real national income per year.

	Assumption: MPC = .8, or $\frac{4}{5}$		
(1)	(2) Annual Increase in Real National Income	(3) Annual Increase in Planned Consumption	(4) Annual Increase in Planned Saving
Round	($ billions per year)	($ billions per year)	($ billions per year)
1 ($10 billion per year increase in *I*)	10.00	8.000	2.000
2	8.00	6.400	1.600
3	6.40	5.120	1.280
4	5.12	4.096	1.024
5	4.09	3.277	0.819
•	•	•	•
•	•	•	•
•	•	•	•
All later rounds	16.38	13.107	3.277
Totals (*C* + *I* + *G*)	50.00	40.000	10.000

nently by $10 billion a year. We see in Table 12.3 that during what we'll call the first round in column 1, investment is increased by $10 billion; this also means an increase in real national income of $10 billion, because the spending by one group represents income for another, shown in column 2. Column 3 gives the resultant increase in consumption by households that received this additional $10 billion in real income. This is found by multiplying the MPC by the increase in real income. Because the MPC equals 0.8, consumption expenditures during the first round will increase by $8 billion.

But that's not the end of the story. This additional household consumption is also spending, and it will provide $8 billion of additional real income for other individuals. Thus during the second round, we see an increase in real income of $8 billion. Now, out of this increased real income, what will be the resultant increase in consumption expenditures? It will be 0.8 times $8 billion, or $6.4 billion. We continue these induced expenditure rounds *ad infinitum* and find that because of an initial increase in autonomous investment expenditures of $10 billion, the equilibrium level of real national income has increased by $50 billion. A permanent $10 billion increase in autonomous investment spending has induced an additional $40 billion increase in consumption spending, for a total increase in real national income of $50 billion. In other words, the equilibrium level of real national income has changed by an amount equal to five times the change in investment.

The Multiplier Formula

It turns out that the autonomous spending multiplier is equal to the reciprocal of the marginal propensity to save. In our example, the MPC was $\frac{4}{5}$; therefore, because MPC + MPS = 1, the MPS was equal to $\frac{1}{5}$. The reciprocal is 5. That was our multiplier. A $10 billion increase in planned investment led to a $50 billion increase in the equilibrium level of real income. Our multiplier will always be the following:

$$\text{Multiplier} \equiv \frac{1}{1-\text{MPC}} \equiv \frac{1}{\text{MPS}}$$

You can always figure out the multiplier if you know either the MPC or the MPS. Let's take some examples. If MPS = $\frac{1}{4}$,

$$\text{Multiplier} = \frac{1}{\frac{1}{4}} = 4$$

Repeating again that MPC + MPS = 1, then MPS = 1 − MPC. Hence we can always figure out the multiplier if we are given the marginal propensity to consume. In this example, if the marginal propensity to consume were given as $\frac{3}{4}$,

$$\text{Multiplier} = \frac{1}{1-\frac{3}{4}} = \frac{1}{\frac{1}{4}} = 4$$

By taking a few numerical examples, you can demonstrate to yourself an important property of the multiplier:

The smaller the marginal propensity to save, the larger the multiplier.

Otherwise stated:

The larger the marginal propensity to consume, the larger the multiplier.

Demonstrate this to yourself by computing the multiplier when the marginal propensities to save equal $\frac{3}{4}$, $\frac{1}{2}$, and $\frac{1}{4}$. What happens to the multiplier as the MPS gets smaller?

When you have the multiplier, the following formula will then give you the change in the equilibrium level of real national income due to a permanent change in autonomous spending:

$$\text{Multiplier} \times \text{change in autonomous spending} =$$
$$\text{change in equilibrium level of real national income}$$

The multiplier, as we have mentioned, works for a permanent increase or permanent decrease in autonomous spending. In our earlier example, if the autonomous component of consumption had fallen by $10 billion, the reduction in the equilibrium level of real national income per year would have been $50 billion per year.

Significance of the Multiplier

Depending on the size of the multiplier, it is possible that a relatively small change in planned investment or autonomous consumption can trigger a much larger change in the equilibrium level of real national income per year. In essence, the multiplier magnifies the fluctuations in the equilibrium level of real national income initiated by changes in autonomous spending.

As was just stated, the larger the marginal propensity to consume, the larger the multiplier. If the marginal propensity to consume is $\frac{1}{2}$, the multiplier is 2. In that case, a $1 billion decrease in (autonomous) investment will elicit a $2 billion decrease in the equilibrium level of real national income per year. Conversely, if the marginal propensity to consume is $\frac{9}{10}$, the multiplier will be 10. That same $1 billion decrease in planned investment expenditures with a multiplier of 10 will lead to a $10 billion decrease in the equilibrium level of real national income per year.

Try Preview Question 3:
What is the concept of the multiplier, how does it work, and what is its main determinant?

EXAMPLE	Changes in Investment and the Great Depression

Changes in autonomous spending lead to shifts in the total expenditures ($C + I + G + X$) curve and, as you have seen, cause a multiplier effect on the equilibrium level of real GDP per year. A classic example apparently occurred during the Great Depression. Indeed, some economists believe that it was an autonomous downward shift (collapse) in the investment function that provoked the Great Depression. Look at part (a) of Figure 12.7. There you see the net investment in

Canada from 1929 to 1941 (expressed in 1986 dollars). Clearly, during business contractions, decision makers in the business world can and do decide to postpone long-range investment plans for buildings and equipment. This causes the business recovery to be weak unless those business plans are revised. If you examine real GDP in part (b) of Figure 12.7, you see that the contraction that started in 1929 reached its trough in 1933. The expansion was relatively strong for the following five years, but then strengthened dramatically as the economy geared up to fight World War II. Some researchers argue that had World War II not occurred when it did, the Canadian economy would have remained weak, since business would have had no reason to revise their investment plans upward.

Figure 12.7
Net Private Domestic Investment and Real GDP During the Great Depression

In part (a), you see how net private investment expressed in billions of 1986 dollars declined starting in 1930 and continued to decline for several years. It started to increase in 1934, although it declined again in 1936. Look at part (b). There you see how changes in GDP seem to mirror changes in net private domestic investment.

Source: Statistics Canada, *Canadian Economic Observer Historical Supplement.*

Part (a)	
Year	**Net Private Domestic Investment (billions of 1986 dollars)**
1929	10.08
1930	8.33
1931	4.43
1932	1.71
1933	1.04
1934	2.82
1935	3.79
1936	3.53
1937	5.93
1938	6.13
1939	7.97
1940	9.40
1941	10.31

Part (b)

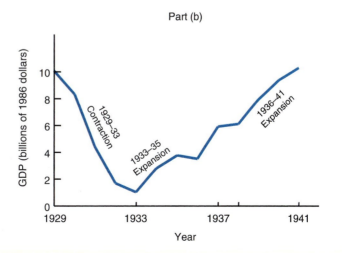

For critical analysis: Relatively speaking, how healthy was the national economy in 1941? (Hint: Look at part (b) of Figure 12.7.)

THE MULTIPLIER EFFECT WHEN THE PRICE LEVEL CAN CHANGE

Clearly, the multiplier effect on the equilibrium overall level of *real* national income will not be as great if part of the increase in *nominal* national income occurs because of increases in the price level. We show this in Figure 12.8. The intersection of AD_1 and *SRAS* is at a price level of 120 with equilibrium real national income of $500 billion per year. An increase in autonomous spending shifts the aggregate demand curve outward to the right to AD_2. If price level remained at 120, the short-run equilibrium level of real GDP would increase to $550 billion per year because, for the $10 billion increase in autonomous spending, the multiplier would be 5, as it was in Table 12.3. But the price level does not stay fixed because ordinarily *SRAS* is positively sloped. In this diagram, the new short-run equilibrium level of real national income is hypothetically $530 billion of real national income per year. Instead of the multiplier being 5, the multiplier with respect to the equilibrium changes in the output of real goods and services—real national income—is only 3. The multiplier is smaller because part of the additional income is used to pay higher prices; not all is spent on increased output, as is the case when the price level is fixed.

If the economy is at an equilibrium level of real national income that is greater than *LRAS*, the implications for the multiplier are even more severe. Look again at Figure 12.8. The *SRAS* curve starts to slope upward more dramatically after $500 billion of real national income per year. Therefore, any increase in aggregate demand will lead to a proportionally greater increase in the price level and a smaller increase in the equilibrium level of real national income per year. The multiplier effect of any increase in autonomous spending will be relatively small because most of the changes will be in the price level. Moreover, any increase in the short-run equilibrium level of real national income will tend to be temporary because the economy is temporarily above *LRAS*—the strain on its productive capacity will raise prices.

Figure 12.8
Multiplier Effect on Equilibrium of Real National Income

A $10 billion increase in autonomous spending (investment, government, or net exports), which moves AD_1 to AD_2, will yield a full multiplier effect only if prices are constant. If the price index increases from 120 to 125, the multiplier effect is less, and the equilibrium level of real national income goes up only to, say, $530 billion per year instead of $550 billion per year.

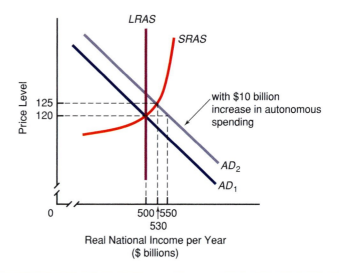

THE RELATIONSHIP BETWEEN AGGREGATE DEMAND AND THE $C + I + G + X$ CURVE

There is clearly a relationship between the aggregate demand curves that you studied in Chapters 10 and 11 and the $C + I + G + X$ curve developed in this chapter. After all, aggregate demand consists of consumption, investment, and government purchases, plus the foreign sector of our economy. There is a major difference, however, between the aggregate demand curve, AD, and the $C + I + G + X$ curve: The latter is drawn with the price level held constant, whereas the former is drawn, by definition, with the price level changing. In other words, the $C + I + G + X$ curve shown in Figure 12.6 on page 301 is drawn with the price level fixed. To derive the aggregate demand curve, we must now allow the price level to change. Look at the upper part of Figure 12.9. Here we show the $C + I + G + X$ curve at a price level equal to 100 and equilibrium at $800 billion of income per year. This gives us point A in the lower graph, for it shows what real income would be at a price level of 100.

Figure 12.9
The Relationship Between AD and the $C + I + G + X$ Curve

In the upper graph, the $C + I + G + X$ curve at a price level equal to 100 intersects the 45-degree reference line at E_1, or $800 billion of real income per year. That gives us point A (price level = 100; real income = $800 billion) in the lower graph. When the price level increases to 200, the $C + I + G + X$ curve shifts downward, and the new equilibrium level of real income is at E_2 at $600 billion per year. This gives us point B in the lower graph. Connecting points A and B, we obtain the aggregate demand curve.

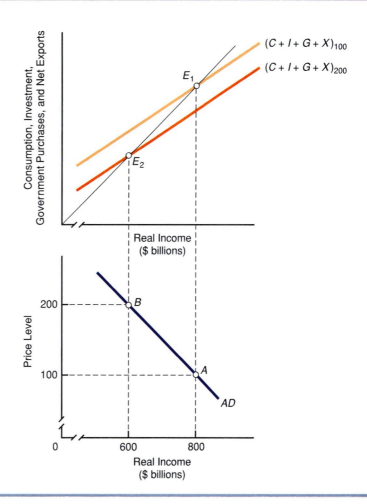

Now let's assume that in the upper graph, the price level doubles to 200. What are the effects?

1. A higher price level can decrease the purchasing power of any cash that people hold (the real-balance effect). This is a decrease in real wealth, and it causes consumption expenditures, C, to fall, thereby putting downward pressure on the $C + I + G + X$ curve.

2. Because individuals attempt to borrow more to replenish their real cash balances, interest rates will rise, which will make it more costly for people to buy houses and cars (the interest rate effect). Higher interest rates make it more costly, for example, to install new equipment and to erect new buildings. Therefore, the rise in the price level indirectly causes a reduction in the quantity of aggregate goods and services demanded.

3. In an open economy, our higher price level causes the foreign demand for our goods to fall (the open economy effect). Simultaneously, it increases our demand for others' goods. If the foreign exchange price of the dollar stays constant for a while, there will be an increase in imports and a decrease in exports, thereby reducing the size of X, again putting downward pressure on the $C + I + G + X$ curve. The result is that a new $C + I + G + X$ curve at a price level equal to 200 generates an equilibrium at E_2 at $600 billion of real income per year. This gives us point B in the lower part of Figure 12.9. When we connect points A and B, we obtain the aggregate demand curve, AD.

Table 12.4 sets out some of the non-price factors which will change total planned expenditure and therefore affect aggregate demand.

Try Preview Question 4:
What might cause shifts in the total planned expenditures curve?

Table 12.4
Non-Price Factors That Affect Aggregate Demand

Changes in consumption, investment, government expenditure, and net exports can increase or decrease aggregate demand.

Increases Aggregate Demand	Decreases Aggregate Demand
Consumption	
• rise in level of personal wealth	• fall in level of personal wealth
• fall in personal taxes	• rise in personal taxes
• fall in personal debt	• rise in personal debt
• more optimistic expectations about the economy	• less optimistic expectations about the economy
Investment	
• fall in real interest rates	• rise in real interest rates
• decrease in business taxes	• increase in business taxes
• more optimistic expectations of profitability	• less optimistic expectations of profitability
Government	
• more spending in the economy	• less spending in the economy
Net Exports	
• decrease in value of the Canadian dollar	• increase in value of the Canadian dollar
• increase in value of our trading partners' currency	• decrease in value of our trading partners' currency
• increase in our trading partners' GDP	• decrease in our trading partners' GDP
• increase in Canadian import taxes	• decrease in Canadian import taxes

Concepts in Brief

- Any change in autonomous spending shifts the expenditure curve and causes a multiplier effect on the equilibrium level of real national income per year.
- The multiplier is equal to the reciprocal of the marginal propensity to save.
- The smaller the marginal propensity to save, the larger the multiplier. Otherwise stated, the larger the marginal propensity to consume, the larger the multiplier.
- The $C + I + G + X$ curve is drawn with the price level held constant, whereas the AD curve allows the price level to change. Each different price level generates a new $C + I + G + X$ curve.

Issues and Applications

Can Native Land Claims Settlements Have a Multiplier Effect?

Concepts Applied: Government transfer payments, investment, the multiplier, equilibrium level of real GDP

Critics claim that Native land claims settlements are costing the government too much. They have overlooked the multiplier effect which will translate spending on the settlements into general increases in GDP which will benefit everyone.

The 1990s marked the decade of land claims settlement in Canada. In November 1994, Manitoba's 61 native bands negotiated a framework agreement which allows for self-rule within 10 years. In January 1996, the Nisga'a of northern British Columbia was the first of 48 bands in that province to settle their land claim. On April 1, 1999, Inuit people of the North West Territories began to govern their own new territory, Nunavut, which means "our land" in Inuktitut, the Inuit language. In each case, the final result will include a monetary payment from some level of government to the Native Peoples. Will this make non-native Canadians poorer? No, not according to the theory we have learned in this chapter.

An Increase in Spending

Take, for example, the 48 land claims to be settled in British Columbia. Analysts believe that negotiations will cost the province $25 million per year, and will take 40 years to complete. Total combined spending to finance the negotiations should reach roughly $1.2 billion. The federal government will pay $330 million, while the British Columbia government will cover the remainder.

Other areas of spending to be done before the land claims are finally settled include $100 million for public information campaigns, $50 million for consultations with interested lobby groups, and $70 million to finance the drawing up of interim agreements. These costs do not include the estimated $6 billion which will be part of the actual land claim settlements.

Spending on Domestic Goods and Services

Where will the $1.2 billion negotiation money go? Into the British Columbia economy. It will pay for meeting facilities for talks, legal services for drafting the proper agreements, clerical help for keeping minutes and producing documents, not to mention travel costs as the parties travel around the province for negotiations. One study estimated that for every $1 the province of British Columbia spends in this way, there will be a ripple (or multiplier) effect of $3.

A Rise in GDP

The majority of the spending will be done by the federal government. This spending will act like an autonomous increase in consumption and investment, depending on the use of the funds, which will yield the multiplier effect. What will be the effect on British Columbia's GDP? If the total provincial spending per year is $40 million, then the increase in GDP should be $120 million per year ($40 million times 3). Over the cost of 40 years of negotiations, this could boost the province's real GDP by $4.8 billion in 1995 terms!

For Critical Analysis

1. What conditions will have to exist for British Columbia's real GDP to benefit from the $6 billion which is settlement of the actual claim?

2. Can you think of a way that the province's real GDP may not benefit? (Hint: Think of the size of the multiplier.)

CHAPTER SUMMARY

1. If we assume that there are large amounts of excess capacity and labour unemployment, we can use the horizontal portion of the short-run aggregate supply curve. Therefore, prices are assumed to be constant, and nominal values are equivalent to real values.

2. A consumption function, in its simplest form, shows that current real consumption is directly related to current real disposable income. The complement of a consumption function is a saving function. A saving function shows the relationship between current real saving and current real disposable income.

3. The marginal propensity to consume shows how much additional income is devoted to consumption. The marginal propensity to save is the difference between 1 and the marginal propensity to consume. Otherwise stated, the marginal propensity to save plus the marginal propensity to consume must equal 1.

4. We must be careful to distinguish between average and marginal propensities. The average propensity to consume is the amount of total real consumption divided by total real disposable income. The average propensity to save is the total amount of real saving divided by total real disposable income. The marginal propensities relate to changes in consumption and saving resulting from changes in income.

5. Some nonincome determinants of planned consumption are wealth, expectations, and population.

6. Investment is made by the business sector of the economy. Investment is the spending by businesses on such things as new machines and buildings that can be used later in the production of goods and services. Investment is the use of resources to provide for future production. There are numerous determinants of investment, including the rate of interest, changes in expectations, innovation and technology, and business taxes.

7. When we add the consumption function, autonomous investment, autonomous government spending, and the autonomous net exports function, we obtain the $C + I + G + X$ curve, which gives us total planned expenditures per year. The equilibrium level of real national income occurs where the $C + I + G + X$ curve intersects the 45-degree reference line, or where total planned expenditures exactly equal real national income (total production).

8. When total planned expenditures exceed real national income, inventories will be drawn down more rapidly than planned. As a result, firms will expand production and, in the process, hire more workers, thus leading to an increase in output and employment. The opposite occurs when total planned expenditures are less than real national income.

9. Planned saving and planned investment must be equal at the equilibrium rate of real national income (ignoring government and foreign transactions). Whenever the actual level of real national income exceeds the equilibrium level, an unplanned inventory increase will trigger production cuts and layoffs. Whenever actual real national income is less than the equilibrium level of real national income, an unplanned inventory decrease will cause increased production and employment.

10. A key aspect of simplified Keynesian analysis is that a change in investment will result in a multi-

ple change in equilibrium income. The size of the multiplier effect of a change in autonomous investment is positively related to the marginal propensity to consume. The higher the marginal propensity to consume, the greater the autonomous investment multiplier. We find the autonomous investment multiplier by first finding the marginal propensity to save (1 minus the marginal propensity to consume), expressed as a fraction, and taking the inverse of that fraction. A marginal propensity to consume of 0.8 means that the marginal propensity to save is 0.2 or $\frac{1}{5}$. The inverse of $\frac{1}{5}$ is 5; thus the investment multiplier is 5.

11. The $C + I + G + X$ function is related to the AD function through price level changes. A shift up in the $C + I + G + X$ function due to a price level decrease represents a movement down along the AD curve. Conversely, a shift down of the $C + I + G + X$ function due to a price level increase represents a movement up along the AD curve.

DISCUSSION OF PREVIEW QUESTIONS

1. How do we interpret the 45-degree reference line?

Because the 45-degree reference line bisects the total planned expenditures/real national income quadrant, total planned expenditures *exactly* equal real national income at all points on this line. Hence equilibrium is possible at any point on the 45-degree reference line.

2. What does the total planned expenditures curve indicate?

The total planned expenditures curve indicates what the community intends to spend at every level of real national income. In a closed (omitting international transactions), private (omitting government transactions) economy, the total planned expenditures curve equals the value of consumption expenditures plus the value of investment expenditures at every level of real national income.

3. What is the concept of the multiplier, how does it work, and what is its main determinant?

The multiplier concept says, simply, that a $1 shift in the total planned expenditures curve will cause the equilibrium level of national income to change by more than $1. In particular, a $1 increase (shift upward) in the total planned expenditures curve will cause the equilibrium level of national income to rise by more than $1; a $1 decrease (shift downward) in the total planned expenditures curve will cause the equilibrium level of national income to fall by more than $1. In a closed, private economy, changes (shifts) in the total planned expenditures curve are caused by changes (shifts) in autonomous consumption and autonomous investment.

Let's take an example. Suppose that we start from an equilibrium position and then autonomous net investment rises by $1 due to an increase in the output and sale of one machine priced at $1. The people who produced this machine receive an extra $1 in income (above last year's income). Thus income already rises by $1 in the first round. The people who produced the machine will spend some of the increase in their income and save some of it. Because one person's expenditure is another's income, income will rise again. Thus if the MPC is $\frac{3}{4}$, the group that produced the machine (and received a $1 increase in income) will spend 75 cents on goods and services and will save 25 cents. The 75 cents spent becomes income for the people who produced the 75 cents' worth of consumer goods. Note that after two rounds, national income has already increased by $1.75 ($1 + $0.75); we already have a multiplier effect. Moreover, there is no reason this process should stop here; the people who just received an increase in income of 75 cents will spend some and save some. The amount they spend becomes income for others. Thus the multiplier effect exists because increases in income lead to increases in consumption expenditures, which in turn lead to further income increases. Because one person's expenditure is another's income, it follows that the higher the MPC, the more the equilibrium level of income will change for given changes in autonomous expenditures.

4. **What might cause shifts in the total planned expenditures curve?**
In our model, total planned expenditures equal consumption (C), investment (I), government purchases of goods and services (G), and net exports (X). For simplicity, we have made the last three components of total planned expenditures autonomous—that is, independent of the level of real disposable income. Consumption also has an autonomous component. Therefore, any change in the nonincome determinants of consumption—for example, changes in expectations—will shift the C + I + G + X curve. Furthermore, because I, G, and X are all considered autonomous, any change in those functions will also shift the C + I + G + X curve.

PROBLEMS

(Answers to the odd-numbered problems appear at the back of the book.)

12-1. Complete the accompanying table.
  a. Plot the consumption and saving schedules on graph paper.
  b. Determine the marginal propensity to consume and the marginal propensity to save.
  c. Determine the average propensity to consume and the average propensity to save for each level of income.

Disposable Income	Consumption	Saving
$ 500	$ 510	$ _____
600	600	_____
700	690	_____
800	780	_____
900	870	_____
1,000	960	_____

12-2. Make a list of determinants, other than income, that might affect your personal MPC.

12-3. List each of the following under the heading "Stock" or "Flow."
  a. The Chens have $100 of savings in the bank.
  b. Smith earns $200 per week.
  c. Labatt's Breweries owns 2,000 trucks.
  d. Inventories rise at 400 units per year.
  e. Brochu consumes $80 per week out of income.
  f. The equilibrium quantity is 1,000 per day.
  g. The corporation spends $1 billion per year on investments.

12-4. The rate of return on an investment on new machinery is 9 percent.
  a. If the market interest rate is 9.5 percent, will the investment be carried out?
  b. If the interest rate is 8 percent, will the machinery be purchased?
  c. If the interest rate is 9 percent, will the machinery be purchased?

12-5.

Real National Income	Consumption Expenditures	Saving	Investment	APC	APS	MPC	MPS
$1,000	$1,100	$ _____	$100	_____	_____	_____	_____
2,000	2,000	_____	_____	_____	_____	_____	_____
3,000		_____	_____	_____	_____	_____	_____
4,000		_____	_____	_____	_____	_____	_____
5,000		_____	_____	_____	_____	_____	_____
6,000		_____	_____	_____	_____	_____	_____

The data in the table above apply to a hypothetical economy. Assume that the marginal propensity to consume is constant at all levels of income. Further assume that investment is autonomous.

a. Draw a graph of the consumption function. Then add the investment function, giving you $C + I$.

b. Right under the first graph, draw in the saving and investment curves. Does the $C + I$ curve intersect the 45-degree line in the upper graph at the same level of real national income as where saving equals investment in the lower graph? (If not, redraw your graphs.)

c. What is the multiplier effect from the inclusion of investment?

d. What is the numerical value of the multiplier?

e. What is the equilibrium level of real national income and output without investment? With investment?

f. What will happen to income if autonomous investment increases by $100?

g. What will the equilibrium level of real national income be if autonomous consumption increases by $100?

12-6. Assume a closed, private economy.

a. If the MPC = 0, what is the multiplier?

b. What is the multiplier if the MPC = $\frac{1}{2}$? If the MPC = $\frac{3}{4}$? If the MPC = $\frac{9}{10}$? If the MPC = 1?

c. What happens to the multiplier as the MPC rises?

d. In what range does the multiplier fall?

12-7. Calculate the multiplier for the following cases.

a. MPC = 0.9

b. MPS = 0.3

c. MPS = 0.15

d. $C = \$100 + 0.65Y$

12-8. What component of the Canadian $C + I + G + X$ curve will the following events affect, and will these events lead to an increase or a decrease in our aggregate demand?

a. Japan recovers from its economic crisis and consumers start to spend again.

b. The federal government pays out $3 million in scholarships to post-secondary students.

c. Because of the low value of the Canadian dollar, Canadians take their summer holidays in Canada instead of in other countries.

d. Low inflation during the last quarter causes the Bank of Canada to reduce its interest rates.

A PPENDIX B

THE KEYNESIAN CROSS AND THE MULTIPLIER

We can see the multiplier effect more clearly if we look at Figure B-1, in which we see only a small section of the graphs that we used in Chapter 12. We start with an equilibrium level of real national income of $650 billion per year. This equilibrium occurs with total planned expenditures represented by $C + I + G + X$. The $C + I + G + X$ curve intersects the 45-degree reference line at $650 billion per year. Now we increase investment, I, by $10 billion. This increase in investment shifts the entire $C + I + G + X$ curve vertically to $C + I' + G + X$. The vertical shift represents that $10 billion increase in autonomous investment. With the higher level of planned expenditures per year, we are no longer in equilibrium at E. Inventories are falling. Production will increase. Eventually, planned production will catch up with total planned expenditures. The new equilibrium level of real national income is established at E' at the intersection of the new $C + I' + G + X$ curve and the 45-degree reference line, along which $C + I + G + X = Y$ (total planned expenditures equal real national income). The new equilibrium level of real national income is $700 billion per year. Thus the increase in equilibrium real national income is equal to five times the permanent increase in planned investment spending.

Figure B-1
Graphing the Multiplier

We can translate Table 12.3 on page 302 into graphic form by looking at each successive round of additional spending induced by an autonomous increase in planned investment of $10 billion. The total planned expenditures curve shifts from $C + I + G + X$, with its associated equilibrium level of real national income of $650 billion, to a new curve labelled $C + I' + G + X$. The new equilibrium level of real national income is $700 billion. Equilibrium is again established.

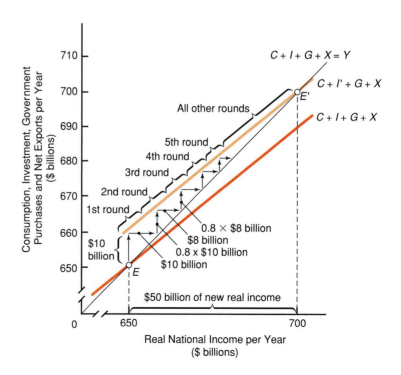

PART 4

Fiscal Policy and Deficit Spending

Fiscal Policy

Lighthouses are a part of Canadian life. With two long, jagged coasts, Canada has invested a lot of resources in keeping seafarers safe. The Coast Guard, an arm of the Canadian government, runs the lighthouses and also carries out rescues of people in distress at sea.

For all but 2 of the past 40 years, however, the federal government has spent more than it has received in tax revenues. Sometimes the expenditures were deliberate—the native land claims discussed in the previous chapter; sometimes they were unplanned—an increase in unemployment insurance benefits during a recessionary period. Recently, the federal government decided to replace the workers in many of the lighthouses with automated lights. Does the government no longer care about the safety of mariners, or is there some other force acting to make the government cut the money spent on staffing lighthouses? To answer this question, you have to understand fiscal policy.

Preview Questions

1. What is fiscal policy?

2. How does the crowding-out effect tend to offset expansionary fiscal policy?

3. What types of time lags exist between the need for fiscal stimulus and the time when such stimulus actually affects the national economy?

4. What is automatic fiscal policy, and how does it lend stability to an economy?

Did You Know That... the first type of income tax was probably established in the 1200s and 1300s during times of war in the Italian city-states? Canada's first income tax, introduced in 1917 to help pay for World War I, ranged from 1 percent on incomes over $2,000 a year to 6.6 percent on incomes over $20,000 per year. Two years later it was raised so that the bottom rate was 1.3 percent on incomes over $1,500, and the top rate was 10.7 percent on incomes over $20,000. At first the government promised the tax would be temporary; hence its name "Dominion Income War Tax." Today, federal income taxes are taken for granted. More important for this chapter, the federal tax system is now viewed as being capable of affecting the equilibrium level of real GDP. On the spending side of the budget, changes in the federal government's expenditures are also viewed as potentially capable of changing the equilibrium level of real GDP.

FISCAL POLICY

► **Fiscal policy**
The discretionary changing of government expenditures and/or taxes in order to achieve national economic goals, such as high employment with price stability.

Deliberate, discretionary changes in government expenditures and/or taxes in order to achieve certain national economic goals is the realm of **fiscal policy.** Some national goals are high employment (low unemployment), price stability, economic growth, and improvement in the nation's international payments balance. Fiscal policy can be thought of as a deliberate attempt to cause the economy to move to full employment and price stability more quickly than it otherwise might.

Fiscal policy has typically been associated with the economic theories of John Maynard Keynes and what is now called *traditional* Keynesian analysis. Recall from Chapter 11 that Keynes' explanation of the Great Depression was that there was insufficient aggregate demand. Because he believed that wages and prices were "sticky downward," he argued that the classical economists' view of the economy automatically moving towards full employment was inaccurate. To Keynes and his followers, government had to step in to increase aggregate demand. In other words, expansionary fiscal policy initiated by the federal government was the way to ward off recessions and depressions.

Traditional Keynesian economics dominated academic and government policy-making debates (and often actions) in the 1960s and 1970s. The federal budget of 1973, for example, was expressly focused on halting rising unemployment. In true Keynesian fashion, taxes were cut and government expenditures increased in the hope of "kickstarting" the economy.

As you will see in Chapter 18, modern-day variants of Keynesian analysis are now taking centre stage in policymaking discussions.

Changes in Government Spending

Recall that in Chapter 10 (Figures 10.8 and 10.9 on pages 254 and 255), we looked at the contractionary gap and the expansionary gap. The former was defined as the

Figure 13.1
Expansionary Fiscal Policy: Two Scenarios

If there is a contractionary gap and equilibrium is at E_1 in part (a), fiscal policy can presumably increase aggregate demand to AD_2. The new equilibrium is at E_2 at higher real GDP per year and a higher price level. If, though, we are already on *LRAS* as in part (b), expansionary fiscal policy will simply lead to a temporary equilibrium at E_2 and a final equilibrium at E_3, again at *LRAS* of \$700 billion of real GDP per year but at a higher price level of 135.

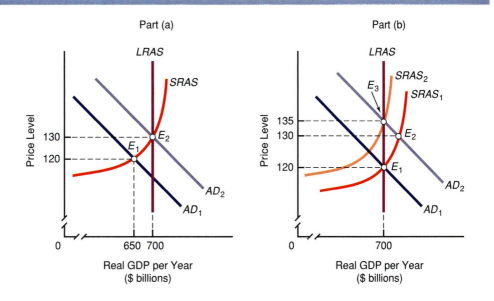

amount by which the current level of real GDP fell short of how much the economy could be producing if it were operating on its *LRAS*. The latter was defined as the amount by which the equilibrium level of real GDP exceeds the long-run equilibrium level as given by *LRAS*. In this section we examine fiscal policy in the context of a contractionary gap.

When There Is a Contractionary Gap. The government, along with firms, individuals, and foreigners, is one of the spending agents in the economy. When the government decides to spend more, all other things held constant, the dollar value of total spending must rise. Look at part (a) of Figure 13.1. We start at short-run equilibrium with AD_1 intersecting *SRAS* at \$650 billion of real GDP per year. There is a contractionary gap of \$50 billion of real GDP per year—the difference between *LRAS* (the economy's long-run potential) and the short-run equilibrium level of real GDP per year. When the government decides to spend more, the aggregate demand curve shifts to the right to AD_2. Here we assume that the government knows exactly how much more to spend so that AD_2 intersects *SRAS* at \$700 billion, or at *LRAS*. Because of the upward-sloping *SRAS*, the price level has risen from 120 to 130. Real GDP has gone to \$700 billion per year. (Nominal GDP has gone up by even more because it consists of the price level index times real GDP. Here the GDP deflator has gone up by 10 ÷ 120 = 8.33 percent.)[1]

When the Economy Is Operating on Its *LRAS*. Suppose that the economy is operating on *LRAS*, as in part (b) of Figure 13.1. An increase in government spending shifts the aggregate demand curve from AD_1 to AD_2. Both prices and real

---

[1] Percent change in price index = change in price index/price index = (130 − 120)/120 = 8.33 percent

output of goods and services begin to rise towards the intersection of E_2. But this rate of real GDP per year is untenable in the long run because it exceeds *LRAS*. In the long run, expectations of input owners—workers, owners of capital and raw materials, and so on—are revised. The short-run aggregate supply curve shifts from $SRAS_1$ to $SRAS_2$ because of higher prices and higher resource costs. Real GDP returns to the *LRAS* level of $700 billion per year. The full impact of the increased government expenditures is on the price level only, which increases to 135. Therefore, an attempt to increase real GDP above its long-run equilibrium can be accomplished only in the short run.

Reductions in Government Spending.

The entire process shown in Figure 13.1 can be reversed. Government can reduce spending, thereby shifting the aggregate demand curve inward. You should be able to show how this affects the equilibrium level of the price index and the real output of goods and services (real GDP) on similar diagrams.

Changes in Taxes

The spending decisions of firms, individuals, and foreigners depend on the taxes levied on them. Individuals in their roles as consumers look to their disposable (after-tax) income when determining their desired rate of consumption. Firms look at their after-tax profits when deciding on the level of investment to undertake. Foreigners look at the tax-inclusive cost of goods when deciding whether to buy in Canada or elsewhere. Therefore, holding all other things constant, a rise in taxes causes a reduction in aggregate demand for three reasons: (1) It reduces consumption, (2) it reduces investment, and (3) it reduces net exports. What actually happens depends, of course, on whom the taxes are levied.

Figure 13.2
Contractionary Fiscal Policy: Two Scenarios

In part (a), the economy is initially at E_1, which exceeds *LRAS*. Contractionary fiscal policy can move aggregate demand to AD_2 so the new equilibrium is at E_2 at a lower price level and now at *LRAS*. In part (b), similar contractionary fiscal policy initially moves equilibrium from E_1 to E_2, but then it goes to E_3 at *LRAS*. The only long-run effect is to lower the price level to 100.

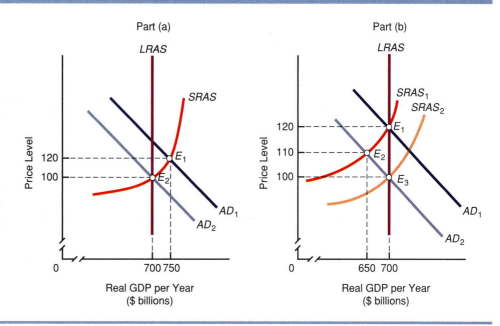

When the Current Short-Run Equilibrium Is Greater than *LRAS.*

Assume that aggregate demand is AD_1 in part (a) of Figure 13.2. It intersects *SRAS* at E_1, which is at a level greater than *LRAS*. In this situation, an increase in taxes shifts the aggregate demand curve inward to the left. For argument's sake, assume that it intersects *SRAS* at E_2, or exactly where *LRAS* intersects AD_2. In this situation, the equilibrium level of real GDP falls from $750 billion per year to $700 billion per year. The price level index falls from 120 to 100.

If the Economy Is in Long-Run Equilibrium.

Assume that the economy is already at short-run and long-run equilibrium as shown in part (b) of Figure 13.2. The aggregate demand curve, AD_1, intersects both *LRAS* and *SRAS* at $700 billion of real GDP per year. If aggregate demand decreases to AD_2, a new temporary equilibrium will occur at E_2 with the price level at 110 and real equilibrium GDP at $650 billion per year. That means that in the short run, prices and the real output of goods and services fall. Input suppliers revise their expectations downward. The short-run aggregate supply curve shifts to $SRAS_2$. The real level of equilibrium GDP returns to the *LRAS* level of $700 billion per year. The full long-run impact of fiscal policy in this situation is solely on the price level, which falls to 100.

Effects of a Reduction in Taxes.

The effects of a reduction in taxes are exactly the reverse of the effects of an increase in taxes. Figure 13.1 and the accompanying discussion of the effects of an increase in government expenditures provide the full analysis.

Try Preview Question 1:
What is fiscal policy?

Thinking Critically About the Media   Tax Rates and Tax Revenues

Every time the federal government–or provincial and municipal governments, for that matter–announces a change in tax rates, the media are quick to pick up on projected increases or decreases in tax revenues. The arithmetic is simple: If Revenue Canada obtains $10 billion from the highest-earning individuals, it will garner $12 billion if their tax rates are increased by 20 percent. But tax revenues received after the tax rate increase are nowhere near those projected. Why? Because individuals and businesses are not static–they respond to higher marginal tax rates by retiring earlier, entering the job market later, engaging in the off-the-books underground economy, quitting second jobs, and compensating in other ways. The rule must be this: Never assume a static economy.

INTERNATIONAL EXAMPLE
Did Roosevelt's New Deal Really Provide a Stimulus?

During the Great Depression, US President Franklin Roosevelt implemented his "New Deal," which was influenced by Keynes' view that government had to increase "effective" aggregate demand to get an economy going again. To be sure, Roosevelt's New Deal included what appeared on the surface to be large federal government expenditures and numerous government jobs programs. We have to look at the total picture of the American economy, however. During the Great Depression, taxes were raised repeatedly. The Revenue Act of 1932, for example, passed during the depths of the Depression, brought the largest percentage increase in federal taxes in the history of the United States in peacetime—it almost doubled total federal tax revenues. Federal government deficits during the Depression years were small. In fact, in 1937 the total government budget—including federal, state, and local levels—was in surplus by $300 million. That means that at the same time that the federal government was increasing expenditures, local and state governments were decreasing them. If we measure the total of federal, state, and local fiscal policies, we find that they were truly expansive only in 1931 and 1936, compared to what the government was doing prior to the Great Depression. No wonder the New Deal failed to kickstart the American economy!

For critical analysis: Did the New Deal have any effect on the Canadian economy?

Concepts in Brief

- Fiscal policy is defined as the discretionary change in government expenditures and/or taxes in order to achieve such national goals as high employment or reduced inflation.
- If there is a contractionary gap and the economy is operating at less than long-run aggregate supply (*LRAS*), an increase in government spending can shift the aggregate demand curve to the right and perhaps lead to a higher equilibrium level of real GDP per year. If the economy is already operating on *LRAS*, in contrast, expansionary fiscal policy in the long run simply leads to a higher price level.
- Changes in taxes can have similar effects on the equilibrium rate of real GDP and the price level. A decrease in taxes can lead to an increase in real GDP, but if the economy is already operating on its *LRAS*, eventually such decreases in taxes will lead only to increases in the price level.

POSSIBLE OFFSETS TO FISCAL POLICY

Fiscal policy does not operate in a vacuum. Important questions have to be answered: If government expenditures increase, how are those expenditures financed, and by whom? If taxes are increased, what does the government do with the taxes? What will happen if individuals worry about increases in *future* taxes because there is more government spending today with no increased taxes? What will happen when provinces and municipalities also exercise their fiscal powers? All of these questions involve *offsets* to the effects of fiscal policy. We will look at each of them and others in detail.

Indirect Crowding Out

Consider an increase in government expenditures. If government expenditures rise and taxes are held constant, something has to give. Our government does not simply take goods and services when it wants them. It has to pay for them. When it pays for them and does not simultaneously collect the same amount in taxes, it must borrow. This means that an increase in government spending without raising taxes creates additional government borrowing from the private sector (or from foreigners).

The Interest Rate Effect.

Holding everything else constant, if the government attempts to borrow more from the private sector to pay for its increased budget deficit, it is not going to have an easy time selling its bonds. If the bond market is in equilibrium, when the government tries to sell more bonds, it is going to have to offer a better deal in order to get rid of them. A better deal means offering a higher interest rate. This is the interest rate effect of expansionary fiscal policy financed by borrowing from the public. In this sense, when the federal government finances increased spending by additional borrowing, it may push interest rates up. When interest rates go up, it is more expensive for firms to finance new construction, equipment, and inventories. It is also more expensive for individuals to finance their cars and homes. Thus a rise in government spending, holding taxes constant (in short, deficit spending), tends to crowd out private spending, dampening the positive effect of increased government spending on aggregate demand. This is called the **crowding-out effect**. In the extreme case, the crowding out may be complete, with the increased government spending having no net effect on aggregate demand. The final result is simply more government spending and less private investment and consumption. Figure 13.3 shows how the crowding-out effect occurs.

Further, as you'll discover in the next chapter, as the government borrows more and more money, its overall debt climbs. As the debt grows large relative to GDP, investors may question the government's ability to use fiscal policy to manage the economy. They perceive an increased risk in buying more bonds. Thus the government has to offer even higher interest rates to continue to finance its spending.

▶ **Crowding-out effect**
The tendency of expansionary fiscal policy to cause a decrease in planned investment or planned consumption in the private sector; this decrease normally results from the rise in interest rates.

Figure 13.3
The Crowding-out Effect in Words

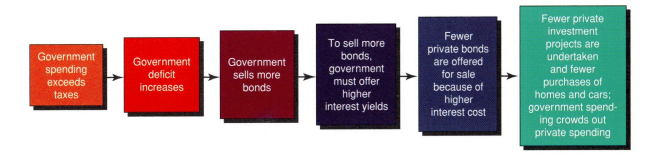

The Firm's Investment Decision.

To understand the interest rate effect better, consider a firm that is contemplating borrowing $100,000 to expand its business. Suppose that the interest rate is 6 percent. The interest payments on the debt will be 6 percent times $100,000, or $6,000 per year ($500 per month). A rise in the interest rate to 9 percent will push the payments to 9 percent of $100,000, or $9,000 per year ($750 per month). The extra $250 per month in interest expenses will discourage some firms from making the investment. Consumers face similar decisions when they purchase houses and cars. An increase in the interest rate causes their monthly payments to go up, thereby discouraging some of them from purchasing cars and houses.

Graphical Analysis.

You see in Figure 13.4 that the initial equilibrium, E_1, is below *LRAS*. But suppose that government expansionary fiscal policy in the form of increased government spending (without increasing taxes) shifts aggregate demand from AD_1 to AD_2. In the absence of the crowding-out effect, the real output of goods and services would increase to $700 billion per year, and the price level would rise to 120 (point E_2). With the (partial) crowding-out effect, however, as investment and consumption decline, partly offsetting the rise in government spending, the aggregate demand curve shifts inward to the left to AD_3. The new equilibrium is now at E_3, with real GDP of $675 billion per year at a price level of 115.

Planning for the Future: The New Classical Economics

Economists have implicitly assumed that people look at changes in taxes or changes in government spending only in the present. What if people actually think about the size of *future* tax payments? Does this have an effect on how they react to an increase in government spending with no tax increases? Some economists, who call them-

---

Figure 13.4
The Crowding-out Effect

Expansionary fiscal policy that causes deficit financing initially shifts AD_1 to AD_2. Equilibrium initially moves towards E_2. But because of crowding out, the aggregate demand curve shifts inward to AD_3, and the new short-run equilibrium is at E_3.

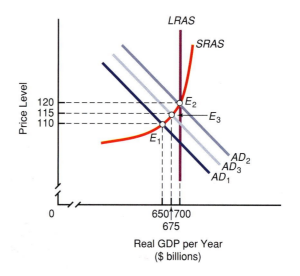

selves the *new classical economists*, believe that the answer is yes. What if people's horizons extend beyond this year? Don't we then have to take into account the effects of today's government policies on the future?

Consider an example. If the government wants to spend $1 today, it can raise tax revenues by $1 and the public's responsibility to the government for that particular dollar has now been met and will never return. Alternatively, the government can borrow $1 today and the public will owe $1 plus interest later. Realizing that $1 today is mathematically equivalent to $1 plus interest next year, people may save the $1 to meet the future tax liabilities. Therefore, whether the $1 spending is financed by taxation or by borrowing, the two methods of finance are equivalent.

Increased government spending without an increase in taxes, according to the new classical economists, will not necessarily have a large impact on aggregate demand. In terms of Figure 13.4, the aggregate demand curve will shift inward from AD_2 to AD_3. In the extreme case, if consumers fully compensate for a higher tax liability in the future by saving more, the aggregate demand curve shifts all the way back to AD_1 in Figure 13.4. This is the case of individuals fully discounting their increased tax liabilities. The result is that an increased budget deficit created entirely by a current tax cut has literally no effect on the economy. This is known as the **Ricardian equivalence theorem**, after the nineteenth-century economist David Ricardo, who first developed the argument publicly.

Though the Ricardian equivalence theorem has generated much theoretical excitement, recent empirical studies cast some doubt on its relevance. Between 1983 and 1997, government spending exceeded government taxes by over $20 billion every year. Private savings rates declined by about one-half over the same period, to the lowest they have ever been.

► **Ricardian equivalence theorem**

The proposition that an increase in the government budget deficit has no effect on aggregate demand.

Direct Crowding Out

Government has a distinct comparative advantage over the private sector in certain activities such as diplomacy and national defence. In other words, certain resource-using activities in which the government engages do not compete with the private sector. In contrast, some of what government does—such as education—competes directly with the private sector. When government competes with the private sector, **direct expenditure offsets** to fiscal policy may occur. For example, if the government starts providing milk at no charge to students who are already purchasing milk, there is a direct expenditure offset. Households spend less directly on milk, but government spends more.

The normal way to analyse the impact of an increase in government spending on aggregate demand is implicitly to assume that government spending is not a substitute for private spending. This is clearly the case for defence spending. Whenever government spending is a substitute for private spending, however, a rise in government spending causes a direct reduction in private spending to offset it.

► **Direct expenditure offsets**

Actions on the part of the private sector in spending money that offset government fiscal policy actions. Any increase in government spending in an area that competes with the private sector will have some direct expenditure offset.

The Extreme Case. In the extreme case, the direct expenditure offset is dollar for dollar, so we merely end up with a re-labelling of spending from private to public. Assume that you have decided to spend $100 on groceries. When you arrive at the checkout counter, you are met by an Agriculture Canada official. She announces that she will pay for your groceries—but only the ones in the cart. Here increased government spending is $100. You leave the store in bliss. But just as you are deciding how to spend the $100, a Revenue Canada inspector meets you. He announces that as a result of the current budgetary crisis, your taxes are going to rise by $100. You have to pay right now. Increases in taxes have now been $100. We have a balanced-budget increase in government spending. Under the assumption of a complete direct expenditure offset, there would be no change in total spending. We simply end up with higher government spending, which directly crowds out exactly the same amount of consumption. Aggregate demand and GDP are unchanged. Otherwise stated, if there is a full direct expenditure offset, the government spending multiplier is zero.

The Less Extreme Case.   Much government spending has a private-sector substitute. When government expenditures increase, there is a tendency for private spending to decline somewhat (but not in proportion), thereby mitigating the upward impact on total aggregate demand. To the extent that there are some direct expenditure offsets to expansionary fiscal policy, predicted changes in aggregate demand will be reduced. Consequently, real output and the price level will be less affected.

Try Preview Question 2:

How does the crowding-out effect tend to offset expansionary fiscal policy?

INTERNATIONAL POLICY EXAMPLE

French Policymakers Ignore Crowding-out Effects

In the past few years, persistent high unemployment rates have been a major campaign topic in virtually every national election in the European Union. It came as no surprise, therefore, that the latest president of France, Jacques Chirac, chose a "pro-employment" prime minister, Alain Juppé. Juppé quickly put into effect the French government's plan to increase jobs. At the heart of the plan was a sum of 50 billion francs (about $14 billion) to create jobs at small and medium-sized companies. This was done by reducing some of the employer taxes owed on low-salaried employees. In addition, the government offered subsidies to companies that hired long-term unemployed persons. The French government projected that 700,000 jobs would be created from mid-1995 through the beginning of 1997. Clearly, French government policymakers do not believe that much, if any, crowding out will occur.

At the same time, though, the French government increased marginal tax rates on corporations, increased the value-added tax on virtually everything sold in France from 18.6 percent to 20.6 percent, and imposed a "temporary" 10 percent tax surcharge on "large fortunes."

For critical analysis: Soon after the new French policy was announced, the head of the forecasting unit of the Paris Chamber of Commerce argued that the government would need to spend as much as 80 billion francs (about $22 billion) if it were "really serious" about fighting unemployment. What does this criticism ignore?

The Open Economy Effect

The open economy effect is a variant of the crowding-out effect, but one that now works its way through changes in net exports. If government spending is increased without a rise in taxes, or if taxes are decreased without a reduction in government spending, the federal government must borrow more. As we pointed out, the government has to offer more attractive interest rates, so overall interest rates go up. When interest rates go up in Canada, foreigners demand more securities such as Canadian government bonds. When they do this, they have to pay for the bonds with dollars. After all, the typical Japanese stock and bond firm cannot buy more Canadian government bonds without getting its hands on more Canadian dollars. This increases the demand for dollars at the same time that it increases the supply of yen. The value of the yen falls relative to the value of the dollar in international transactions. When this occurs, Japanese-made goods become cheaper in Canada, and Canadian-made goods become more expensive in Japan. Canadians want to buy more Japanese goods, and the Japanese want to buy fewer Canadian goods. This causes a reduction in net exports (X) and cuts into any increase in aggregate demand. In sum, to the extent that federal deficit spending reduces net exports, the effect of expansionary fiscal policy will be less.

Combined Government Spending Effect

The federal government is not the only government with the power to tax and spend. We saw in Chapter 5 that provinces collect taxes to spend on highway maintenance, environmental protection, education, and welfare for example. Cities and towns collect taxes to spend on local streets, police, and property development. Because provinces and municipalities have less access to financing through the bond market, they are typically more reluctant to finance their expenditures through debt.

This greater reluctance to deficit finance means that provinces and municipalities usually cut their expenditure during recessions as tax revenues fall, and increase spending as the economy and tax revenues improve. This pro-cyclical behaviour can offset federal government attempts to bolster a foundering economy with deficit spending.

The Supply-Side Effects of Changes in Taxes

We have talked about changing taxes and changing government spending, the traditional tools of fiscal policy. We have not really talked about the possibility of changing marginal tax rates. In our federal tax system, higher incomes are taxed at higher rates. In that sense, Canada has a progressive federal individual income tax system. Expansionary fiscal policy might involve reducing marginal tax rates. Advocates of such changes argue that (1) lower tax rates will lead to an increase in productivity because individuals will work harder and longer, save more, and invest more; and (2) increased productivity will lead to more economic growth, which will lead to higher real GDP. The government, by applying lower marginal tax rates, will not necessarily lose tax revenues, for the lower marginal tax rates will be applied to a growing tax base because of economic growth—after all, tax revenues are the prod-

▶**Supply-side economics**

The notion that creating incentives for individuals and firms to increase productivity will cause the aggregate supply curve to shift outward.

uct of a tax rate times a tax base. People who support this notion are called supply-side economists. **Supply-side economics** involves changing the tax structure to create incentives to increase productivity. Due to a shift outward to the right in the aggregate supply curve, there can be greater output without upward pressure on the price level.

Effect of Changes in Tax Rates on Labour. Consider the supply-side effects of taxes on labour. An increase in tax rates reduces the opportunity cost of leisure, thereby inducing individuals (at least on the margin) to reduce their work effort and to consume more leisure. But an increase in tax rates will also reduce spendable income, thereby shifting the demand for leisure curve inward to the left. Here a reduction in real spendable income shifts the demand curve for all goods and services, including leisure, inward to the left. The outcome of these two effects depends on which of them is stronger. Supply-side economists argue that in the 1970s and 1980s the first effect dominated: increases in marginal tax rates caused workers to work less, and decreases in marginal tax rates caused workers to work more.

INTERNATIONAL EXAMPLE
Supply-Side Economics in History

Supply-side economics has a long history, dating back to at least the fourteenth-century. The greatest of medieval Islamic historians, Abu Zayd Abd-Ar-Rahman Ibn Khaldun (1332–1406) included a view of supply-side economics in his monumental book, *The Muqaddamh* (1377). He pointed out that "When tax assessments... upon the subjects are low, the latter have the energy and desire to do things. Cultural enterprises grow and increase.... [Therefore] the number of individual imposts [taxes] and assessments mounts." If taxes are increased both in size and rates, "the result is that the interest of subjects in cultural enterprises disappears, because when they compare expenditures and taxes with their income and gain and see little profit they make, they lose all hope." Khaldun concluded that "At the beginning of a dynasty, taxation yields a large revenue from small assessments. At the end of a dynasty, taxation yields a small revenue from large assessments."

For critical analysis: How do this scholar's economic theories apply to the modern world?

Concepts in Brief

- Indirect crowding out occurs because of an interest effect in which the government's efforts to finance its deficit spending cause interest rates to rise, thereby crowding out private investment and spending, particularly on cars and houses. This is called the crowding-out effect.
- Many new classical economists believe in the Ricardian equivalence theorem, which argues that an increase in the government budget deficit has no effect on aggregate demand because individuals correctly perceive their

increased future taxes and therefore save more today to pay for them.

- Direct crowding out occurs when government spending competes with the private sector and is increased. Direct expenditure offsets to fiscal policy may occur.
- There is an open economy effect that offsets fiscal policy. Like the crowding-out effect, it occurs because the government's increased deficit causes interest rates to rise. This encourages foreigners to invest more in Canadian securities. When they do so, they demand more dollars, thereby increasing the international value of the dollar. As a result, Canadian-made goods become more expensive abroad and foreign goods cheaper here, so Canada exports fewer goods and imports more.
- Changes in marginal tax rates may cause supply-side effects if a reduction in marginal tax rates induces enough additional work, saving, and investing. Government tax receipts can actually increase. This is called supply-side economics.

DISCRETIONARY FISCAL POLICY IN PRACTICE

We can discuss fiscal policy in a relatively precise way. We draw graphs with aggregate demand and supply curves to show what we are doing. We could even in principle estimate the offsets that were just discussed. However, even if we were able to measure all of these offsets exactly, would-be fiscal policymakers still face problems: which fiscal policy mix to choose, and the various time lags involved in conducting fiscal policy.

Fiscal Policy Mix

Suppose it is agreed that fiscal policy is desirable. What is the proper mix of taxes and government expenditures? Let's say that policymakers decide that a change in taxes is desirable. At least seven options are available:

1. Permanent change in personal income taxes
2. Permanent change in corporate income taxes
3. Temporary change in personal income taxes
4. Temporary change in corporate income taxes
5. Change in payroll taxes such as EI and CPP contributions
6. Change in depreciation allowance on investment expenditures
7. Change in specific consumption tax, such as on oil

Note that all of these are tax changes, but their effects on individual groups will be different, and special-interest groups will be lobbying politicians to protect specific interests.

Alternatively, assume policymakers decide that a change in government expenditures is desirable. There are disadvantages to these changes. Political wrangling will arise over the amount, type, and geographic location of the expenditure change ("spend more in my city or province, less in someone else's"). Furthermore, if the expenditure is to be made on a capital goods project, such as a highway, a dam, or a public transportation system, the problem of timing arises. If started during a recession, should or could such a project be abandoned or delayed if inflation emerges before the project is finished? Are delays or reversals politically feasible, even if they are economically sensible?

Time Lags

▶ **Recognition time lag**
The time required to gather information about the current state of the economy.

▶ **Action time lag**
The time required between recognizing an economic problem and putting policy into effect. The action time lag is short for monetary policy but quite long for fiscal policy, which requires legislative approval.

▶ **Effect time lag**
The time that elapses between the onset of policy and the results of that policy.

Policymakers must be concerned with various time lags. Quite apart from the fact that it is difficult to measure economic variables, it takes time to collect and assimilate such data. Thus policymakers must be concerned with the **recognition time lag**, the period of months that may elapse before economic problems can be identified.[2]

After an economic problem is recognized, a solution must be formulated; thus there will be an **action time lag**, the period between the recognition of a problem and the implementation of policy to solve it. For fiscal policy, the action time lag is particularly long. It must be approved by Parliament, and much political wrangling and infighting accompany legislative fiscal policy decision making. It is not at all unusual for the action time lag to last a year or two. Then it takes time to put the policy into effect. After Parliament enacts a fiscal policy as legislation, it takes time to decide, for example, who gets the new federal construction contract, and so on.

When we add the recognition time lag to the action time lag, we get what is known as the *inside lag*. That is how long it takes to get a policy from inside the institutional structure of our federal government.

Finally, there is the **effect time lag:** After fiscal policy is enacted, it takes time for it to affect the economy. Multiplier effects take more time to work through the economy than it takes an economist to shift a curve on a chalkboard.

Because the various fiscal policy time lags are long, a policy designed to combat a recession might not produce results until the economy is experiencing inflation, in which case the fiscal policy would worsen the situation. Or a fiscal policy designed to eliminate inflation might not produce effects until the economy is in a recession; in that case, too, fiscal policy would make the economic problem worse rather than better.

Furthermore, because fiscal policy time lags tend to be *variable* (anywhere from one to three years), policymakers have a difficult time fine-tuning the economy. Clearly, fiscal policy is more an art than a science.

Try Preview Question 3:

What types of time lags exist between the need for fiscal stimulus and the time when such stimulus actually affects the national economy?

AUTOMATIC STABILIZERS

Not all changes in taxes (or in tax rates) or in government spending (including government transfers) constitute discretionary fiscal policy. There are several types of automatic (or nondiscretionary) fiscal policies. Such policies do not require new leg-

---

[2] Final annual data for GDP, after various revisions, are not forthcoming for three to six months after the year's end.

▶ **Automatic, or built-in, stabilizers**
Special provisions of the tax law that cause changes in the economy without the direct action of the government. Examples are the progressive income tax system and Employment Insurance.

islation. Specific automatic fiscal policies—called **automatic**, or **built-in, stabilizers**—include the progressive federal income tax system itself and the government transfer system; the latter includes Employment Insurance (EI) and Old Age Security benefits (OAS).

The Federal Progressive Income Tax

We have in Canada a progressive income tax that ranges from 17 percent for taxable incomes below $29,590 to 29 percent on incomes above $59,180. (Provincial and municipal taxes are extra.) For an individual, as taxable income rises, the marginal tax rate rises, and as taxable income falls, so does the marginal tax rate. Think about this now in terms of the entire economy. If the nation is at full employment, personal income taxes may yield the government, say, $60 billion per year. Now suppose that, for whatever reason, business activity suddenly starts to slow down. Workers are not allowed to put in as much overtime as before. Some workers are laid off, and some must change to jobs that pay less. Some workers and executives might take voluntary pay cuts. What happens to federal income taxes when wages and salaries go down? Across the economy taxes are still paid, but at a lower marginal rate than before, because the tax schedule is progressive. As a result of these decreased taxes, disposable income—the amount remaining after taxes—doesn't fall by the same percentage as before-tax income. In other words, the individual doesn't feel the pinch of recession as much as we might think if we ignored the progressive nature of our tax schedule. The *average* tax rate falls when less is earned.

Conversely, when the economy suddenly comes into a boom period, people's incomes tend to rise. They can work more overtime and can change to higher-paying jobs. Their *disposable* income does not, however, go up as rapidly as their total income because their average tax rates are rising at the same time. Revenue Canada ends up taking a bigger bite. In this situation, the progressive income tax system tends to stabilize any abrupt changes in economic activity. (Actually, the progressive tax structure simply magnifies any stabilization effect that might exist.)

Employment Insurance

Like the progressive income tax, Employment Insurance stabilizes aggregate demand. Throughout the business cycle, it reduces changes in people's disposable income. When business activity drops, most laid-off workers automatically become eligible for Employment Insurance benefits. Their disposable income therefore remains positive, although certainly it is less than when they were employed. During boom periods there is less unemployment, and consequently fewer Employment Insurance payments are made to the labour force. Less purchasing power is being added to the economy because fewer benefits are paid out. Historically, the relationship between the unemployment rate and unemployment insurance schemes has been strongly positive.

Stabilizing Impact

The key stabilizing impact of the progressive income tax and Employment

Figure 13.5
Automatic Stabilizers

Here we assume that as real national income rises, tax revenues rise and government transfers fall, other things remaining constant. Thus as the economy expands from Y_f to Y_1, a budget surplus automatically arises; as the economy contracts from Y_f to Y_2, a budget deficit automatically arises. Such automatic changes tend to drive the economy back towards its full-employment output level.

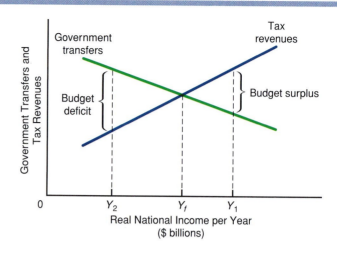

Insurance is their ability to mitigate changes in disposable income, consumption, and the equilibrium level of national income. If disposable income is prevented from falling as much as it would during a recession, the downturn will be moderated. In contrast, if disposable income is prevented from rising as rapidly as it would during a boom, the boom will not get out of hand. The progressive income tax and unemployment benefits thus provide automatic stabilization to the economy. We present the argument graphically in Figure 13.5.

Old Age Security Benefits

Every Canadian is eligible to receive Old Age Security (OAS) benefits on turning 65 years of age. This non-contributory program is aimed at reducing the amount a person's income falls on retirement from the workforce. Because everyone at every economic level receives this benefit, the government "claws back" through increased taxes the OAS paid to wealthier Canadians. This way, those pensioners whose consumption would otherwise drop drastically are able to continue consuming, thus supporting *AD* across the economy.

Try Preview Question 4:

What is automatic fiscal policy, and how does it lend stability to an economy?

WHAT DO WE REALLY KNOW ABOUT FISCAL POLICY?

There are two ways of looking at fiscal policy, one that prevails during normal times and the other during abnormal times.

Fiscal Policy During Normal Times

During normal times (without "excessive" unemployment, inflation, or problems in the national economy), we know that given the time lag between the recognition of the need to increase aggregate demand and the impact of any expansionary fiscal policy, and given the very modest size of any fiscal policy action that the government actually will take, discretionary fiscal policy is probably not very effective. The government ends up doing too little too late to help in a minor recession. Moreover, fiscal policy that generates repeated tax changes (as it has done) creates uncertainty, which may do more harm than good. To the extent that fiscal policy has any effect during normal times, it probably achieves this by way of automatic stabilizers rather than by way of discretionary policy.

Fiscal Policy During Abnormal Times

During abnormal times, fiscal policy can be effective. Consider some classic examples: the Great Depression and times of war.

The Great Depression.   When there is a substantial catastrophic drop in real GDP, as there was during the Great Depression, fiscal policy probably can do something to stimulate aggregate demand. Because so many people are cash-constrained, government spending is a good way during such periods to get cash into their hands.

Wartime.   Wars are in fact reserved for governments. War expenditures are not good substitutes for private expenditures—they have little or no direct expenditure offsets. Consequently, war spending as part of expansionary fiscal policy usually has noteworthy effects, such as during World War II, when real GDP increased dramatically, bringing an end to the Great Depression.

The "Soothing" Effect of Keynesian Fiscal Policy

One view of traditional Keynesian fiscal policy does not relate to its being used on a regular basis. As you have learned in this chapter, there are many problems associated with attempting to use fiscal policy. But if we should encounter a severe downturn, fiscal policy is available. Knowing this may reassure consumers and investors. After all, the ability of the federal government to prevent another Great Depression—given what we know about how to use fiscal policy today—may take some of the large risk out of consumers' and particularly investors' calculations. This may induce more buoyant and stable expectations of the future, thereby smoothing investment spending.

Concepts in Brief

- Time lags of various sorts reduce the effectiveness of fiscal policy. These include the recognition time lag, the action time lag, and the effect time lag.
- Two automatic, or built-in, stabilizers are the progressive income tax and Employment Insurance.
- Built-in stabilizers tend automatically to moderate changes in disposable income resulting from changes in overall business activity.
- Though discretionary fiscal policy may not necessarily be a useful tool in normal times because of time lags and the government debt, it may work well during abnormal times, such as depressions and wartime. In addition, the existence of fiscal policy may have a soothing effect on consumers and investors.

Issues and Applications

The Real-World Political Constraints on Fiscal Policy

Concepts Applied: Fiscal policy, multiplier effect

Cape Spear lighthouse has warned mariners of Newfoundland's rocky coast for over 150 years. Automating it would cut its operating cost, but could result in higher costs for search and rescue operations.

When the government uses discretionary fiscal policy and cuts taxes, no one seems to mind. But when it uses the same authority to cut spending, there is often a strong reaction from those affected. From the early 1970s until 1997, the federal government consistently spent more than its income. However, the tide is starting to turn as policymakers chop spending to balance the budget without increasing taxes.

Where to Cut Spending

Lighthouse-keepers, recent victims of government cuts, have a long history in Canada. The first lighthouse built was at Cape Spear in Newfoundland, the most easterly point of North America. The Cape Spear lighthouse has been kept by the same family—the Cantwells—since 1846. On the other side of the continent, Pachena Point lighthouse, west of Victoria, has been in operation since 1906. It was built the year after 126 people died when the SS Valencia went aground on the cliffs off Pachena Point.

The Multiplier Effect

In 1996, the federal government automated 32 lighthouses on the east coast and 35 on the west coast, for a saving of about $7 million per year. This decision was made to help the Coast Guard balance its budget, which was also cut by about $12 million per year.

This saving will probably hardly reduce aggregate demand nor, through the multiplier, GDP, as the government still spends about $135 billion dollars each year. However, critics say there may be multiplier effects of a different sort as a result of the automation of the lighthouses.

Lighthouses are typically located where the coast is dangerous for mariners. Their keepers maintain the light and repair the electronic fog detector—which some keepers say malfunctions about 25 percent of the time. They also pass weather warnings on to fishers and other seafarers, and watch for environmental problems such as oil slicks. Perhaps most importantly, they watch for and direct mariners in distress to safe havens.

Will This Result in a Real Cost-Saving?

What will happen in the Canadian economy as a result of automating the lighthouses? Proponents say, nothing. There are already over 1,200 unattended beacons on both coasts. Together with the new technology to be installed in the newly automated lighthouses, this warning system will be sufficient to ensure safe navigation. The decrease in the deficit will make Canada a more attractive place for business to invest. Economic growth will be the long-run result.

Critics argue that the marine accident rate has been climbing in recent years, as more people take to the water for recreation. In British Columbia alone, for example, the marine accident rate has increased by 300 percent since 1983. Critics say this rate will continue to climb, and the increase in required Coast Guard rescue operations will put a strain on the economy which will exceed the savings from automation. The federal deficit may not in the end be reduced. And the cost may be too high.

It is still too soon to tell what the long-run effect is: growth, or unacceptable loss. But one thing is for sure. There will be some opportunity cost attached to automating the lighthouses. What that cost is depends on which side of the question you are on.

For Critical Analysis

1. What is the opportunity cost of automating the lighthouses?
2. What would be the effect on the Canadian economy of raising taxes rather than cutting expenditures in order to balance the Coast Guard's budsget?

CHAPTER SUMMARY

1. Fiscal policy involves deliberate discretionary changes in government expenditures and personal income taxes. Typically, policymakers argue in favour of fiscal policy during a contractionary gap.

2. Increased government spending when there is a contractionary gap can lead to a shift outward in the aggregate demand curve such that the equilibrium level of real GDP per year increases. If, however, the economy is already operating on its long-run aggregate supply curve (*LRAS*), the increase in aggregate demand will simply lead in the long run to a rise in the price level, all other things held constant.

3. Individuals respond to changes in after-tax profits, after-tax (disposable) income, and the tax-inclusive cost of foreign goods. Consequently, changes in taxes will change aggregate demand by changing consumption, investment, and net exports.

4. A decrease in taxes can lead to an increase in aggregate demand and in the equilibrium level of real GDP per year, provided that the economy is not already on its long-run aggregate supply curve. If it is, such tax decreases will simply lead to a higher price level.

5. There are numerous possible offsets to any fiscal policy. Indirect crowding out occurs when increased deficit spending requires the government to borrow more and drives interest rates up. Increased interest rates cause private firms to undertake fewer investments. This is called the crowding-out effect.

6. The new classical economists believe in the Ricardian equivalence theorem, a proposition stating that an increase in the government budget deficit has no effect on aggregate demand because individuals properly discount increased future tax liabilities and therefore increase saving when the government engages in new deficit spending.

7. Direct crowding out occurs when the government competes with the private sector and then increases spending in those areas of competition. There is a direct expenditure offset. This occurs, for example, when the government increases direct payments for school lunches that students' parents have been paying for anyway.

8. There is a possible open economy effect offsetting fiscal policy. Deficit spending that leads to increased interest rates causes foreigners to invest more in Canada. To do so, they demand more dollars, thereby increasing the international price of our currency. Our goods become more expensive to foreigners, they buy less, and the result is a reduction in net exports that offsets the fiscal policy stimulus.

9. If marginal tax rates are lowered, individuals and firms may react by increasing work, saving, and investing. People who believe this favour supply-side economics, which involves changing the tax structure to create incentives to increase productivity.

10. Time lags, including the recognition time lag, the action time lag, and the effect time lag, tend to reduce the effectiveness of fiscal policy. When we add the recognition time lag to the action time lag, we get what is known as the inside lag, because this is how long it takes to get a policy from inside the institutional structure of our federal government.

11. Automatic stabilizers include personal income taxes and Employment Insurance. Automatic stabilizers counter ups and downs in fiscal activity without the necessity for legislative action.

DISCUSSION OF PREVIEW QUESTIONS

1. **What is fiscal policy?**

   Fiscal policy refers to the changing of governmental expenditures and/or taxes in order to eliminate expansionary and contractionary gaps. Proponents of fiscal policy make the value judgment that price stability and full employment are worthwhile goals. Proponents also assume that our knowledge of positive economics is sufficient to achieve these normative goals.

2. **How does the crowding-out effect tend to offset expansionary fiscal policy?**

   When the government spends more without increasing taxes or taxes less without reducing spending, it increases the government budget deficit. When the government attempts to sell more bonds to finance the increased deficit, it may end up increasing interest rates. Higher interest rates induce private businesses to reduce investment projects and also cause consumers to reduce their purchases of houses and cars. Therefore, expansionary fiscal policy tends to crowd out private investment and spending.

3. **What types of time lags exist between the need for fiscal stimulus and the time when such stimulus actually affects the national economy?**

   There is a lag between the start of a recession and the availability of relevant data—the recognition time lag. There is a lag between the recognition of a need for a fiscal policy and putting one in motion—the action time lag. And there is a lag between policy implementation and tangible results—the effect time lag.

4. **What is automatic fiscal policy, and how does it lend stability to an economy?**

   With discretionary fiscal policy, government spending and taxing policies are consciously applied to stabilize an economy. Automatic fiscal policy, by contrast, does not require conscious policy or government legislation; automatic fiscal policy results from institutional characteristics in the economy. Thus a progressive tax structure and an unemployment insurance system (which are already in force) automatically change taxes and government outlays as national income changes. In particular, as national income falls in a recession, government outlays for unemployed workers automatically increase, and tax revenues fall as lower incomes push people into lower marginal tax brackets. These automatic stabilizers counteract declining national income. Similarly, in an expansionary period, tax revenues automatically rise (as people are forced into higher marginal tax brackets), and Employment Insurance benefits fall. Thus aggregate demand is automatically counteracted by higher tax revenues and decreased government outlays. Because income increases or decreases are automatically countered to a certain extent by a progressive tax system and an unemployment insurance program, we say that automatic fiscal policy lends stability to the Canadian economy.

PROBLEMS

(Answers to the odd-numbered problems appear at the back of the book.)

13-1. What is discretionary fiscal policy? What are automatic stabilizers? Give examples of each.

13-2. Assume that you are a new Member of Parliament. You believe that expansionary government fiscal policy will pull the country rapidly out of its recession. What are some of the possible tax and spending changes you could recommend? What are the possible mixes?

13-3. Given the existence of automatic stabilizers, a recession is expected to generate a budget deficit, and an expansion is expected to generate a budget surplus. If the generation of such budget deficits or surpluses is to be countercyclical, what assumptions must be made about how consumers react to such budget deficits or surpluses?

13-4. How do economists distinguish between budget deficits or surpluses that occur automatically and those that are the result of discretionary policy?

13-5. Visit Canada's Finance Department at http://www.fin.gc.ca/fedprove/mfte.html. This site sets out the major transfers from the federal to the provincial governments. Scroll through this document until you find your province. You will find a table setting out the amount the federal government has transferred for each of the last three fiscal years. Do you think that these transfers have allowed your province to pursue expansionary or contractionary policy? Explain your answer.

INTERACTING WITH THE INTERNET

File Edit View Go Favorites Help

Back Forward Stop Refresh Home Search Favorites History Channels Fullscreen Mail Print Edit

The Department of Finance publishes information about the federal budget (with both detailed and summary information) at

http://www.fin.gc.ca

Statistics Canada also provides recent information on all levels of government revenues and expenditures at

http://www.statcan.ca/Documents/English/Pgdb/State/govern.htm

A PPENDIX C

FISCAL POLICY: A KEYNESIAN PERSPECTIVE

The traditional Keynesian approach to fiscal policy differs in three ways from that presented in Chapter 13. First, it emphasizes the underpinnings of the components of aggregate demand. Second, it assumes that government expenditures are not substitutes for private expenditures and that current taxes are the only taxes taken into account by consumers and firms. Third, the traditional Keynesian approach focuses on the short run and so assumes that as a first approximation, the price level is constant.

CHANGES IN GOVERNMENT SPENDING

Figure C-1 measures real national income along the horizontal axis and total planned expenditures (aggregate demand) along the vertical axis. The components of aggregate demand are consumption *(C)*, investment *(I)*, government spending *(G)*, and net exports *(X)*. The height of the schedule labelled $C + I + G + X$ shows total planned expenditures (aggregate demand) as a function of income. This schedule slopes upward because consumption depends positively on income. Everywhere along the 45-degree reference line, planned spending equals income. At the point Y^*, where the $C + I + G + X$ line intersects the 45-degree line, planned spending is consistent with real national income. At any income less than Y^*, spending exceeds income, and so income and thus spending will tend to rise. At any level of income greater than Y^*, planned spending is less than income, and so income and thus spending will tend to decline. Given the determinants of $C, I, G,$ and X, total spending (aggregate demand) will be Y^*.

The Keynesian approach assumes that changes in government spending cause no direct offsets in either consumption or investment spending because G is not a substitute for $C, I,$ or X. Hence a rise in government spending from G to G' causes the

Figure C-1
The Impact of Higher Government Spending on Aggregate Demand

Government spending increases, causing $C + I + G + X$ to move to $C + I + G' + X$. Equilibrium increases to Y^{**}.

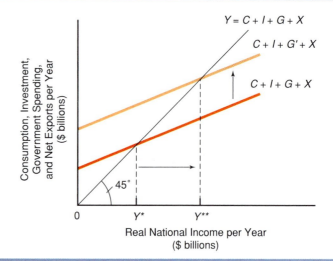

Figure C-2
The Impact of Higher Taxes on Aggregate Demand

Higher taxes cause consumption to fall to C'. Equilibrium decreases to Y^{**}.

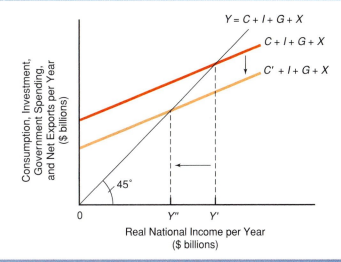

$C + I + G + X$ line to shift upward by the full amount of the rise in government spending, yielding the line $C + I + G' + X$. The rise in government spending causes income to rise, which in turn causes consumption spending to rise, which further increases income. Ultimately, aggregate demand rises to Y^{**}, where spending again equals income. A key conclusion of the Keynesian analysis is that total spending rises by *more* than the original rise in government spending because consumption spending depends positively on income.

CHANGES IN TAXES

According to the Keynesian approach, changes in current taxes affect aggregate demand by changing the amount of disposable (after-tax) income available to consumers. A rise in taxes reduces disposable income and thus reduces consumption; conversely, a tax cut raises disposable income and thus causes a rise in consumption spending. The effects of a tax increase are shown in Figure C-2. Higher taxes cause consumption spending to decline from C to C', causing total spending to shift downward to $C' + I + G + X$. In general, the decline in consumption will be less than the increase in taxes because people will also reduce their saving to help pay the higher taxes. Thus although aggregate demand declines to Y'', the decline is *smaller* than the tax increase.

THE BALANCED-BUDGET MULTIPLIER

One interesting implication of the Keynesian approach concerns the impact of a balanced-budget change in government spending. Suppose that the government increases spending by $100 million and pays for it by raising current taxes by $100 million. Such a policy is called a *balanced–budget increase in spending*. Because the higher spending tends to push aggregate demand *up* by *more* than $100 million while the higher taxes tend to push aggregate demand *down* by *less* than $100 million, a most remarkable thing happens: A balanced-budget increase in *G* causes total spending to rise by *exactly* the amount of the rise in *G*—in this case, $100 million. We say that the *balanced-budget multiplier* is equal to 1. Similarly, a balanced-budget reduction in spending will cause total spending to fall by exactly the amount of the spending cut.

THE FIXED PRICE LEVEL ASSUMPTION

The final key feature of the Keynesian approach is that it typically assumes that as a first approximation, the price level is fixed. Recall that nominal income equals the price level multiplied by real output. If the price level is fixed, an increase in government spending that causes nominal income to rise will show up exclusively as a rise in *real* output. This will in turn be accompanied by a decline in the unemployment rate because the additional output can be produced only if additional factors of production, such as labour, are utilized.

PROBLEMS

C-1. In this problem, equilibrium income is $500 billion and full-employment equilibrium is $640 billion. The marginal propensity to save is $\frac{1}{7}$. Answer the questions using the data in the following graph.

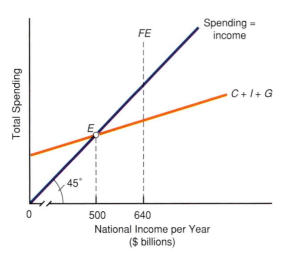

a. What is the marginal propensity to consume?

b. By how much must new investment or government spending increase to bring the economy up to full employment?

c. By how much must government cut personal taxes to stimulate the economy to the full-employment equilibrium?

C-2. Consider the following model; then answer the questions.

If $C = 30 + \frac{3}{4}Y$ and $I_n = 25$, equilibrium $Y = \$220$.

a. If government expenditures equal $5, what will be the new equilibrium level of national income? (Hint: Aggregate spending $\equiv C + I + G$.)

b. What was the government spending multiplier in this example?

C-3. Assume that MPC $= \frac{9}{10}$; then answer the following questions.

a. If government expenditures fall by $500, by how much will the aggregate expenditure curve shift downward? By how much will equilibrium income change?

b. If taxes fall by $500, by how much will the aggregate expenditure curve shift upward? By how much will equilibrium income change?

C-4. Assume that MPC $= \frac{3}{4}$; then answer the following questions.

a. If government expenditures rise by $100 million, by how much will the aggregate expenditure curve shift upward?

b. If taxes rise by $100 million, by how much will the aggregate expenditure curve shift downward?

c. If both taxes and government expenditures rise by $100 million, by how much will the aggregate expenditure curve shift? What will happen to the equilibrium level of income?

d. How does our conclusion in the second part of (c) change if MPC $= \frac{9}{10}$? If MPC $= \frac{1}{2}$?

14

Deficit Spending and the Public Debt

Preview Questions

1. By what methods can the federal government obtain purchasing power?

2. What is the difference between the gross public debt and the net public debt?

3. What is the burden of the public debt?

4. What are some suggested ways to reduce a federal government deficit?

From 1994 to 1998, the federal government made deficit reduction its primary policy objective. While most analysts agree that this course was necessary and the correct one to take, there is some disagreement over the method used. For example, should deficit reduction have come through cutting costs? Or should it have been as a result of tax increases that would increase revenues? Or should deficit reduction have occurred in the longer run by decreasing taxes on businesses to encourage job creation thus developing a larger tax base to pay taxes in the future? To understand the ins and outs of this issue, you will need to learn about fiscal policy and its effect on the deficit and the public debt.

Did You Know That... until 1998 your federal government so consistently spent more than it received that by the time you read this, the total accumulated net public debt will be around $600 billion? Here is what $600 billion could buy: about 1.2 trillion pieces of sushi, or 400 billion cheeseburgers, or 400 textbooks for every man, woman, and child in Canada. Your individual share of what the federal government owes is around $20,000. Should you be worried? The answer is both yes and no, as you will see in this chapter. First, let's examine what the government actually does when it spends more than it receives.

GOVERNMENT FINANCE: FILLING THE GAP

When the government spends more than it receives, its spending exceeds its tax revenues. Life must go on, though, so the government has to finance this shortfall somehow. Barring any resort to money creation (the subject matter of Chapters 15, 16, and 17), the Bank of Canada sells IOUs on behalf of the Canadian government, in the form of securities that are normally called bonds. In effect, the federal government asks Canadians and others to lend money to the government to cover its deficit. For example, if the federal government spends $10 billion more than it receives in revenues, the Bank of Canada will raise that $10 billion by selling $10 billion of new government bonds. The people who buy government bonds (i.e., lend money to the Canadian government) will receive interest payments over the life of the bond. In return, the Canadian government receives immediate purchasing power.

The Historical Record of Deficit Financing

The process of how the government finances the deficit is relatively straightforward. So, too, are the data that show the historical record of deficit financing in Canada. In part (a) of Figure 14.1 (page 344), you can see that while federal government tax revenues have remained less than 20 percent of GDP, from 1981 to 1996 federal government expenditures have consistently been greater than 20 percent. The difference in the two curves in part (a) represents the federal budget deficit expressed as a percentage of GDP. Notice that in 1998 the government recorded a budget surplus—its revenues exceeded its expenditures for the first time since 1977. In part (b), you see the absolute growth in federal government tax revenues and expenditures. The shaded red area represents the actual dollar size of the deficit since World War II.

Try Preview Question 1:
By what methods can the federal government obtain purchasing power?

Deficits Versus Debt: The Distinction Between Stocks and Flows

You have already learned the distinction between stocks and flows. The same analysis can be applied to the difference between the federal budget deficit and the total

Figure 14.1

Two Ways of Viewing the Historical Record of Federal Deficit Financing

In part (a), federal expenditures and revenues are expressed as a percentage of GDP. The difference is the federal deficit, also expressed as a percentage of GDP. Since the mid-1990s expenditures as a percentage of GDP have fallen, and in 1998 they were less than revenues. In part (b), we express federal expenditures and federal revenues in nominal dollar terms. The difference is, of course, the nominal dollar deficit or surplus.

Sources: Statistics Canada, *Canadian Economic Observer* and *Canadian Economic Observer Historical Supplement.*

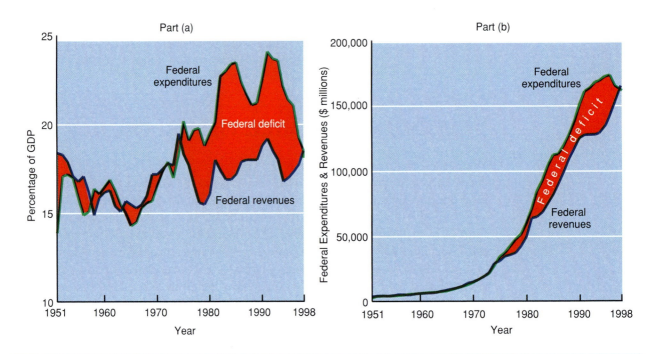

> ▶ **Public debt**
>
> The total value of all outstanding federal government securities.

accumulated **public debt.** The public debt is a stock. At any point in time, it is some number, such as $500 billion. The federal budget deficit, in contrast, is a flow. If it is $20 billion, that means that the federal government is spending at a rate of $20 billion per year more than it is receiving in taxes and other revenues. Hence if this year the public debt is $500 billion and each year the federal government has a deficit of $20 billion, then next year the public debt will be $520 billion, the year after that it will be $540 billion, and so on.

The Relative Size of the Federal Deficit

The problem with looking at part (b) of Figure 14.1 is that the annual deficit is expressed as a current dollar figure. In a growing economy (both through real output increases and inflation), what is perhaps more important is the relative size of the federal budget deficit expressed as a percentage of GDP. This is shown in Figure 14.2. You can see that the federal budget deficit expressed as a percentage of GDP reached its peak during the late 1980s before falling back, again rose until 1993, and has been falling ever since. In 1998, the deficit was negative, that is, the government recorded a budget surplus.

Figure 14.2
The Federal Budget Deficit Expressed as a Percentage of GDP

The budget deficit reached its peak during the late 1980s and hit another peak during early 1994, but has fallen ever since.

Sources: Statistics Canada, *Canadian Economic Observer* and *Canadian Economic Observer Historical Supplement.*

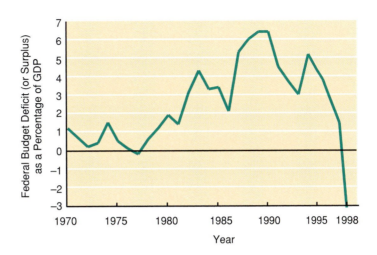

INTERNATIONAL POLICY EXAMPLE
Will the European Union Have Its Way?

Figure 14.3
European Union Budget Deficits

Only 7 of the 15 EU countries have deficits that fall below 3 percent of GDP.

Source: European Commission.

The European Union has outlined a policy strategy that requires all of its 15 members to have government deficits that do not exceed 3 percent of GDP. Each country must reach this goal by the year 1999 in order for all EU countries to adopt a common currency. As shown in Figure 14.3, by 1996, only 7 of the 15 EU countries had met that goal.

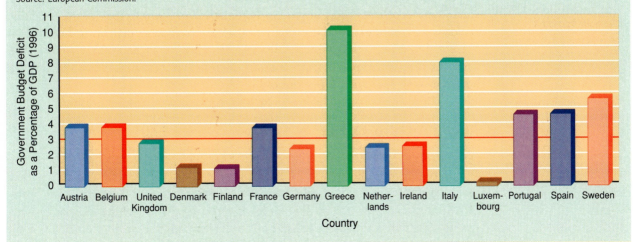

For critical analysis: If Canada were part of the European Union, how would its annual government budget deficit stack up against the deficits of other members?

Concepts in Brief

- Whenever the federal government spends more than it receives, it runs a budget deficit.
- The budget deficit is a flow, whereas the accumulated budget deficits are a stock, called the public debt.
- The federal deficit expressed as a percentage of GDP hit a peak of around 6.5 percent in the late 1980s, fell back, rose to another peak in 1994, and has been falling ever since.

ACCUMULATED DEFICITS: THE PUBLIC DEBT AND INTEREST PAYMENTS ON IT

As you have already learned, every time the federal government runs a deficit, it must borrow from the private sector and foreigners, thereby increasing its debt.

The Public Debt

▶ **Gross public debt**
All federal government debt irrespective of who owns it.

▶ **Net public debt**
Gross public debt minus the value of financial assets held by government agencies.

Try Preview Question 2:
What is the difference between the gross public debt and the net public debt?

All federal public debt, taken together, is called the **gross public debt.** When we subtract from the gross public debt the financial assets held by government agencies, we arrive at the **net public debt.** The net public debt normally increases whenever the federal government runs a budget deficit—that is, whenever total government outlays are greater than total government revenues. Look at column 3 in Table 14.1. The total net public debt has been growing continuously since 1970, although the government may choose to use part of its 1998 budget surplus for debt reduction. Expressed in terms of per capita figures, however, it has not grown so rapidly. (We should also take account of inflation.) Perhaps a better way to look at the Canadian national debt is to examine it as a percentage of GDP, which we do in Figure 14.4. We see that after World War II, this ratio fell steadily until the mid-1970s. Since then, the ratio of net public debt to annual income has more or less continued to rise and now hovers around 70 percent of GDP.

How Did Our Debt Get So Big?

If you look at Figure 14.4 you will see that the net public debt soared during World War II, then declined steadily until 1974. Since then the debt has grown, although recent budget surpluses may be used for debt reduction. How did this second growth get its start?

After the experience of the Great Depression when so many families were poverty-stricken, Canadians decided not to let that happen again. Between the end of the Great Depression and the early 1970s, the federal government legislated programs like the *Unemployment Insurance Act* (1941), the *Family Allowance Act* (1944), the *Old Age Security Act* (1951), and the *National Hospital Insurance Act* (1957) better known as medicare. Over the decades these programs were amended, making

Table 14.1
The Federal Deficit, Our Public Debt, and the Interest We Pay on It

Net public debt in column 3 is defined as total federal debt minus total federal financial assets. Per capita net public debt is obtained by dividing population into the net public debt.

Year	(1)	(2) Federal Budget Deficit (billions of current dollars)	(3) Net Public Debt (billions of current dollars)	(4) Net Public Debt per Capita (current dollars)	(5) Net Interest Costs (billions of current dollars)	(6) Net Interest as a Percentage of GDP
1940		0.1	3.3	290	0.1	1.4
1945		1.8	11.3	936	0.4	3.3
1950		0.7 surplus	11.6	846	0.4	2.1
1955		0.2 surplus	11.3	720	0.5	1.7
1960		0.2	12.1	677	0.8	2.0
1965		0.5 surplus	15.5	789	1.1	2.2
1970		0.4 surplus	17.8	836	1.9	2.1
1975		1.4	24.0	1,057	3.7	2.2
1980		11.6	72.3	2,940	9.9	3.2
1981		14.0	84.7	3,402	13.7	3.8
1982		11.9	97.7	3,877	16.7	4.5
1983		25.7	125.6	4,934	17.4	4.3
1984		31.7	162.3	6,315	20.9	4.7
1985		37.0	202.4	7,802	24.6	5.1
1986		33.9	238.5	9,102	26.1	5.2
1987		30.7	269.6	10,155	27.8	5.0
1988		27.6	297.3	11,054	31.7	5.2
1989		26.8	325.8	11,900	37.4	5.7
1990		28.0	354.3	12,749	41.8	6.2
1991		31.9	385.0	13,693	41.5	6.2
1992		38.0	419.9	14,767	38.8	5.6
1993		39.2	460.8	16,026	38.3	5.4
1994		40.2	508.2	17,374	38.0	5.1
1995		36.1	545.7	18,432	42.0	5.5
1996		31.9	574.3	19,280	46.9	5.9
1997		13.7	583.2	19,256	45.0	5.5
1998		3.2 surplus	583.2	—	41.5	4.8

Sources: Statistics Canada, *Canadian Economic Observer Historical Supplement,* and Department of Finance, *Budget 1998.* Data for 1998 are estimates.

them universal (i.e., available to everyone) and indexing them to inflation. The long economic expansion of the 1950s and 1960s made the government believe these programs would always be affordable.

In 1973 the Organization of Petroleum Exporting Countries (OPEC) cut back on oil production to raise the price and increase their revenues. The price of oil, an

Figure 14.4

Net Canadian Public Debt as a Percentage of GDP

During World War II, the net public debt grew dramatically. It fell until the mid-1970s, then started rising again.

Source: Statistics Canada, *Canadian Economic Observer* and *Canadian Economic Observer Historical Supplement.*

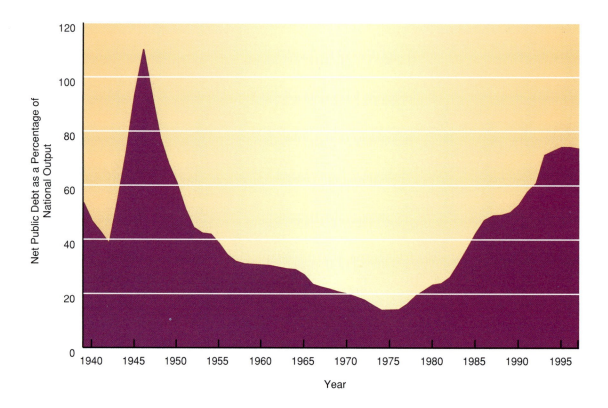

input to virtually everything produced in the West, quadrupled. Prices soared, Canadian firms went bankrupt, thousands of employees lost their jobs, and consumers cut back spending. With universal unemployment insurance indexed to inflation, benefits paid to the unemployed mushroomed, while premiums paid in, as well as personal and corporate taxes, declined. Further, the federal government, to help out struggling firms, reduced oil taxes and provided subsidies to keep firms producing.

As the Canadian economy started to recover from this shock, the entire Western world slipped into the 1981–83 recession. Once again, payments out in social programs rose relative to revenues, and the debt climbed again. In 1994, the federal government declared war on the deficit. The rest of this chapter and the Issues and Applications section deal with this subject.

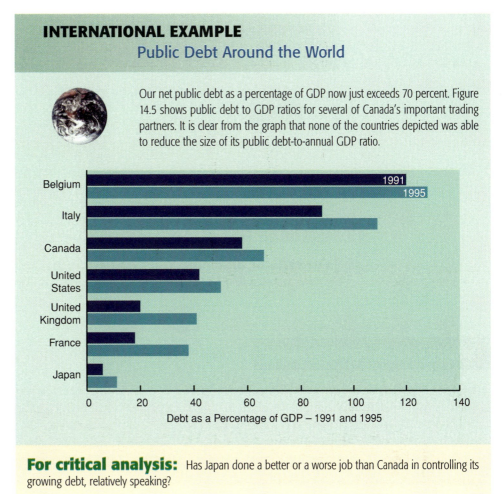

INTERNATIONAL EXAMPLE
Public Debt Around the World

Our net public debt as a percentage of GDP now just exceeds 70 percent. Figure 14.5 shows public debt to GDP ratios for several of Canada's important trading partners. It is clear from the graph that none of the countries depicted was able to reduce the size of its public debt-to-annual GDP ratio.

Figure 14.5
Rising Debt in Canada's Trading Partners
Over the next few years, the public debt of many EU countries is expected to rise.

Source: The Economist, February 3, 1996.

Debt as a Percentage of GDP – 1991 and 1995

For critical analysis: Has Japan done a better or a worse job than Canada in controlling its growing debt, relatively speaking?

Annual Interest Payments on the Public Debt

Consider the size of interest payments on the public debt as shown in column 5 of Table 14.1. Those interest payments started rising dramatically around 1975. Expressed as a percentage of GDP in column 6, today they are more than twice what they were a half century ago. As long as the government borrows from Canadians, the interest payments will be made to Canadians. In other words, we owe the debt to ourselves; some people are taxed so that the government can pay interest to others (or themselves). But we have seen a rising share of the public debt owned by foreigners, reaching its peak in 1993 at 26.6 percent. Foreigners still own around 24 percent of our public debt. So we don't just owe it to ourselves.

INTERNATIONAL POLICY EXAMPLE
Belgium's Diminishing Policy Options

Belgium's public debt is approaching 150 percent of GDP. This figure has little meaning until one examines its effect on the Belgian government's policy options. The interest costs of its public debt have risen to over 40 percent of its government's budget. This increasing net interest cost of the public debt in Belgium is steadily crowding out everything else the government wants to do. Recently, it stopped maintaining its national road system. If Belgium continues to add to its public debt through annual budget deficits the way it has done in the past, the net interest payment on that public debt will eventually crowd out every other government expenditure!

For critical analysis: The government of Canada now pays out about 28 percent of its revenues in interest costs. What actions is our government taking to stall the rise in interest payments?

Thinking Critically About the Media   Canada Pension Plan

During 1996 when the Canada Pension Plan was under review, the media frequently warned that the Plan would go broke in the next 10 to 15 years unless premiums were doubled at once. The media decried the possibility of this hike, claiming Canadians and businesses would not be willing to pay it. But Canada's premiums, then at 4.6 percent of insured earnings, are actually low relative to other countries'. A World Bank study shows the rate of pension premiums in the United States is 12.4 percent, 20 percent in France, 23 percent in Austria, and 26 percent in Italy. Only Iceland, at 2 percent, was lower than Canada of all the OECD countries!

The Burden of the Public Debt

From 1984 to 1997, the net public debt of Canada more than doubled, to about $600 billion. The public debt is the total of all the outstanding debt owed by the federal government to its individual and institutional lenders. Whenever the federal government is in deficit, the public debt rises; for example, in fiscal 1996, the federal government deficit was about $32 billion, so the public debt increased by that amount in that fiscal year. Because of the large deficits incurred by the federal government in the 1980s and 1990s, the public debt rose dramatically—at least in nominal values. We shall now analyse whether federal deficits, and the accompanying increase in the public debt that they generate, impose a burden on future generations or are irrelevant.

As you read the remainder of this chapter, try to keep two things in mind. First, given the level of government expenditures, the main alternative to the deficit is higher taxes; therefore, the costs of a deficit should be compared to the costs of higher taxes, not to zero. Second, it is important to distinguish between the effects of deficits when full employment exists and when substantial unemployment exists.

Federal Budget Deficits: A Burden on Future Generations?

Assume that the federal government decides to increase government expenditures on final goods and services by $10 billion, and that it can finance such expenditures either by raising taxes by $10 billion or by selling $10 billion of bonds. Many economists maintain that the second option, deficit spending, would lead to a higher level of national consumption and a lower level of national private saving than the first option.

The reason this is so, say these economists, is that if people are taxed, they will have to forgo private consumption now as they substitute government goods for private goods. Suppose that taxes are not raised, but instead the public buys bonds to finance the $10 billion in government expenditures. The community's disposable income is the same, and it has increased its assets by $10 billion in the form of bonds. The community will either (1) fail to realize that its liabilities (in the form of future taxes due to an increased public debt that must eventually be paid) have *also* increased by $10 billion or (2) believe that it can consume the governmentally provided goods and simultaneously purchase the same quantity of privately provided consumer goods because the bill for the currently governmentally provided goods will be paid by *future* taxpayers.

If full employment exists, then as people raise their present consumption (the same quantity of private consumption goods, but more public consumption goods), something must be crowded out. In a closed economy, investment (spending on capital goods) is crowded out. The mechanism by which this crowding out occurs is an increase in the interest rate: Deficit spending increases the total demand for credit but leaves the total supply of credit unaltered. The rise in interest rates that causes a reduction in the growth of investment and capital formation in turn slows the growth of productivity and improvement in the community's living standard.

The foregoing analysis suggests that deficit spending can impose a burden on future generations in two ways. First, unless income grows dramatically, future generations will have to be taxed at a higher rate to retire the higher public debt resulting from the present generation's increased consumption of governmentally provided goods. Second, the increased level of consumption by the present generation crowds out investment and reduces the growth of capital goods; this leaves future generations with a smaller capital stock and thereby reduces their wealth.

Paying Off the Public Debt in the Future. Suppose that after 50 years of running deficits, the public debt becomes so large that each adult person's tax liability is $50,000. Suppose further that the government chooses (or is forced) to pay off the debt at that time. Will that generation be burdened with our generation's overspending? The debt is, after all, owed (mostly) to ourselves. It's true that every adult will have to come up with $50,000 in taxes to pay off the debt; but then the government will use that money to pay off bondholders, who are (mostly) the same people. Thus *some* people will be burdened because they owe $50,000 and own less than $50,000 in government bonds. But others will receive more than $50,000 for the bonds they own. As a generation or a community, they will pay and receive about the same amount of money.

Of course, there could be a burden on some low-income adults who will find it difficult or impossible to obtain $50,000 to pay the tax liability. Still, nothing says that taxes to pay off the debt must be assessed equally; it seems likely that a special tax would be levied, based on the ability to pay.

Our Debt to Foreigners.

We have been assuming that most of the debt is owed to ourselves. What about the 24 percent of our public debt that is owned by foreigners?

It is true that if foreigners buy Canadian government bonds, we do not owe that debt to ourselves, and a potential burden on future generations may result. But not necessarily. Foreigners will buy our government's debt if the inflation-adjusted, risk-adjusted, after-tax rate of return on such bonds exceeds what the investors can earn in their own country or some other country. If they buy Canadian bonds voluntarily, they perceive a benefit in doing so.

It is important to realize that not all government expenditures can be viewed as consumption; government expenditures on such things as highways, bridges, dams, research and development, and education might properly be perceived as investments. If the rate of return on such investments exceeds the interest rate paid to foreign investors, both foreigners and future Canadians will be economically better off. What really matters is on what the government spends its money. If government expenditures financed by foreigners are made on wasteful projects, a burden may well be placed on future generations.

We can use the same reasoning to examine the problem of current investment and capital creation being crowded out by current deficits. If deficits lead to slower growth rates, future generations will be poorer. But if the government expenditures are really investments, and if the rate of return on such public investments exceeds the interest rate paid on the bonds, both present and future generations will be economically richer.

The Effect of Unemployment.

If the economy is operating at a level substantially below full-employment real GDP, crowding out need not take place. In such a situation, an expansionary fiscal policy via deficit spending can increase current consumption (of governmentally provided goods) without crowding out investment. Indeed, if some government spending is in the form of high-yielding public investments, both present and future generations can be economically richer; such public investments will provide positive benefits in the future.

Not All Borrowing Is Bad.

Don't get the impression that the government should never borrow. After all, borrowing is not always bad. Consider an example of a student who has a choice of borrowing money for one of two purposes: the purchase of a home entertainment centre or tuition payments to attend college. Borrowing for the first purpose may prove to be burdensome; borrowing for the second purpose—building human capital—may allow the student to reap greater returns in the form of higher income later. The same analysis can be applied to government borrowing. There is a difference between government borrowing to purchase Canada Day fireworks shows, and government borrowing to invest in the

Try Preview Question 3:

What is the burden of the public debt?

Trans-Canada Highway system. One can conclude, therefore, that increased public debt is not necessarily bad if it creates a net investment for the future.

Are Deficits Relevant?

Much of the analysis to this point has assumed that deficit spending increases the demand for credit, while the supply of credit remains constant. Hence the interest rate rises and investment is crowded out. But what if the community realizes that an increase in the public debt also represents an increase in its future tax liabilities—the Ricardian equivalence theorem? Further, what if people wish not to burden their own children with an increased public debt? Because the deficit has increased, they would increase their current saving in order to enable their children to meet future debt obligations. In fact, because their taxes do not rise, their disposable income is higher, and they can save by purchasing the new government bonds. In the process, interest rates will not rise. Deficit spending may not lead to crowding out.

Many people plan to (and do) bestow wealth on others. The latest research shows that from 25 to 50 percent of all saving is undertaken in order to transfer wealth to relatives (usually children) during an individual's lifetime. And most people also bestow wealth on their heirs at death. To illustrate the point, assume that parents intend to leave $200,000 to their descendants and that they have saved sufficiently to achieve that goal. Then suppose that the government engages in deficit spending so that their heirs' future tax liabilities rise by $20,000. Realizing that they no longer have achieved their goal, the parents might increase the amount they save now so as to cover their heirs' additional future $20,000 tax liability.

If both the supply of credit (saving) and the demand for credit rise, there is no theoretical reason for believing that the interest rate will rise. If that is so, crowding out won't occur; the growth of investment and capital production won't be retarded, and future generations need not have lower living standards.

Concepts in Brief

- When we subtract the value of financial assets held by government agencies from the gross public debt, we obtain the net public debt.
- There may be a burden of the public debt on future generations if they have to be taxed at higher rates to pay for the current generation's increased consumption of governmentally provided goods; also there may be a burden if there is crowding out of current investment, resulting in less capital formation and hence a lower economic growth rate.
- If a significant part of our public debt is bought by foreigners, then we no longer "owe it to ourselves." If the rate of return on the borrowed funds is higher than the interest to be paid, future generations can be made better off by government borrowing, but will be worse off if the opposite is true.

FEDERAL BUDGET DEFICITS IN AN OPEN ECONOMY

Many economists believe that the Canadian current account deficit is just as serious a problem as the government budget deficit. The current account balance is the sum of the values of exports minus imports, plus interest payments we receive from other countries minus payments out to other countries, plus net gifts. (We'll spend more time looking at the balance of payments in Chapter 20.) Since our net gifts balance tends to be around zero and our exports usually exceed our imports, this means that a deficit on the current account arises because we are paying out to other countries more interest and dividends on their investments in Canada than we are receiving from the rest of the world. The current account went from a surplus of $2.6 billion in 1984 to a deficit of $27.5 billion in 1991. The balance has improved somewhat since then.

By virtue of this current account deficit, foreigners have accumulated Canadian dollars and have purchased Canadian assets (real estate, corporate stocks, bonds, and so on). If this country continues to incur these deficits, foreigners will continue to purchase assets here. This could eventually present problems. For one, what if foreign investors suddenly decide to sell such assets or take their money out of the country? Another concern is with foreigners gaining political power along with their accumulation of Canadian assets. Here we concentrate on the linkage between federal budget deficits and current account deficits.

What the Evidence Says

Figure 14.6 shows the Canadian current account deficits and surpluses compared to federal budget deficits and surpluses. The year 1986 appears to be a watershed year, for that is when the current account took a marked turn for the worse. Concurrently, the federal budget deficit grew progressively larger.

On the basis of the evidence presented in Figure 14.6, it appears that there is a close relationship between the current account and fiscal deficits: Larger current account deficits follow shortly after larger fiscal deficits.

Why the Two Deficits Are Related

Intuitively, there is a reason we would expect federal budget deficits to lead to current account deficits. You might call this the unpleasant arithmetic of current account and federal budget deficits.

Assume that the federal government runs a budget deficit. Assume further that Canadians use their savings to buy government-issued bonds to finance the deficit. Where, then, does the money come from to finance business investment? The answer is that part of it must come from abroad. That is to say, dollar holders abroad invest in Canadian businesses by buying their stocks, or by investing directly in business operations. In this case, the dividends earned on their stocks, or the interest earned on their investments, flow out of the country. The current account goes into deficit because this outflow of capital exceeds to a large measure the capital flowing

Figure 14.6
Canada's Twin Deficits

Canada current account balance hovered around zero until 1986. Then we started running large deficits, as shown in this diagram. The federal budget has been in deficit for many years, starting in earnest in 1978. The question is, has the federal budget deficit created the current account deficit?

Source: Statistics Canada, *Canadian Economic Observer* and *Canadian Economic Observer Historical Supplement.*

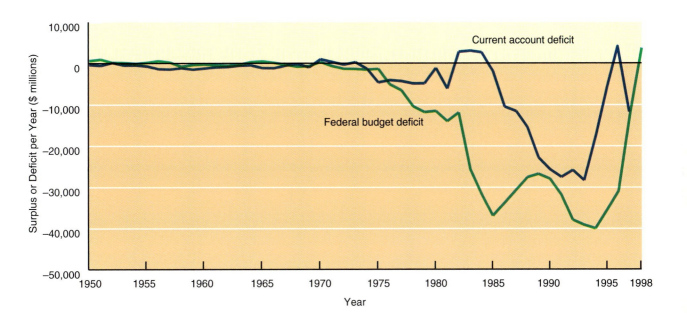

into Canada from similar Canadian investment abroad. In other words, the outflow is large enough to offset the surplus on the trade account.

The reason that foreigners are induced to invest in Canadian business is that domestic Canadian interest rates will normally rise, all other things held constant, whenever there is an increase in government deficits financed by increased borrowing.

HAS THE DEFICIT BEEN MEASURED CORRECTLY?

Part of the problem, according to some economists, is that we are measuring the deficit incorrectly, and that we need to change the government accounting system to come up with a better measure of the deficit.

Capital Budgeting Theory

The federal government has only one budget to guide its spending and taxing each fiscal year. It does not distinguish between current spending for upkeep on the Prime

Minister's residence, for example, and spending for a new park that's going to last for many years to come. By contrast, businesses have two budgets. One, called the *operating budget*, includes expenditures for current operations, such as salaries and interest payments. The other is called a *capital budget*, which includes expenditures on investment items, such as machines and buildings.

Some economists recommend that the government should set up a capital budget, thereby removing investment outlays from its operating budget. Opponents of such a change in the accounting rules for the federal government point out that such an action would allow the government to grow even faster than currently because many new expenditures could be placed in the capital budget, thereby reducing the operating budget deficit and reducing the pressure to cut the growth in federal government spending.

Pick a Deficit, Any Deficit

Even using standard accounting techniques, the federal budget deficit can vary dramatically depending on what is, or is not, included. Three sets of accounts are published each year, each with a different calculation of the federal government deficit. The *public accounts* calculation is the narrowest measure of the federal deficit. It includes only budgets of government departments, and excludes those of government agencies, boards, or business enterprises. The *Financial Management System (FMS)* and the *System of National Accounts (SNA)* include both the budgets of government departments and of government agencies and business but differ in what they exclude. Rather than going into the details to explain each of these deficits, the point to understand is that no one number gives a complete picture of how much the government is spending over and above what it is receiving.

SUGGESTIONS FOR REDUCING THE DEFICIT

There have been many suggestions about how to reduce a government deficit. They include increasing taxes, reducing federal government expenditures, and changing the accounting system. Another suggestion takes a long-term look at deficit reduction: increase the deficit now in order to create jobs so that in the future more people will have jobs and more people will pay taxes, thus reducing the deficit. Let's examine these.

Increasing Personal Taxes

From an arithmetic point of view, a federal budget deficit can be wiped out by simply increasing the amount of taxes collected. Let's see what this would require. The data for 1996 are instructive. The 1996 federal budget deficit was about $32 billion. This is as much as Canadians paid in total individual income taxes to the federal government in all of 1982. That deficit in 1996 shows that for the year, the federal government spent about $1,080 more than it had in tax revenues for every person in the country. To eliminate the deficit by raising taxes, we need $2,300 more in taxes every year from *every worker* in Canada just to balance the budget. In 1996, Canadians paid about $65 billion in personal federal income taxes. Every taxpayer would have to pay 45 percent more in income taxes to balance the budget. Needless to say, reality is such that we will never see a simple tax increase that will wipe out a sizeable annual federal budget deficit.

Taxing the Rich.   Some people suggest that the way to eliminate a deficit is to raise taxes on the rich. Currently, over 50 percent of all federal income taxes are already being paid by the top 30 percent of families. The entire bottom 60 percent of families (those earning below $45,000 per year) pay slightly less than 45 percent of federal income taxes. Families earning below $30,000 pay just less than 20 percent of federal income taxes. What does it mean to tax the rich more? If you talk about taxing "millionaires," you are referring to those who pay taxes on more than $1 million income per year. There are only around 2,300 of them in Canada. Changing marginal tax rates at the upper end will show similarly unimpressive results. An increase in the top marginal tax rate from 29 percent to 35 percent will raise, at best, only about $2.5 billion in additional taxes (assuming that people do not figure out a way to avoid the higher tax rate). This $2.5 billion per year in extra tax revenues represented only 8 percent of the estimated 1996 federal budget deficit.

Increasing Other Taxes.   Other ways to increase government revenues include increasing corporate taxes, increasing "sin" taxes, and instituting user fees.

Some analysts suggest that more revenue could come from corporate taxes which currently make up about 11 percent of revenues. In 1995, 450 corporations, each with more than $500,000 in profits, paid little or no tax because of write-offs and tax credits. A further 244 companies collectively deferred corporate income taxes of $40 billion in 1994 alone, enough to cover the deficit and then some. However, before endorsing this solution, refer back to Chapter 13 and what happens to the economy when business costs are raised.

The government relies on "sin" taxes for about 1.5 percent of its revenue. Cigarettes and alcohol contain large tax components which may vary from province to province. Because these products tend to be somewhat addictive, people will pay the increased taxes and continue consuming

Consider gasoline. Each litre of unleaded gas sold in Canada, for example, contains an 18 percent federal tax (11¢ per litre for a 60¢ per litre price) and 5 percent GST (4¢ per litre). Gasoline tax is another area of frequent increase.

In further search of revenue, the federal government has recently instituted new taxes and fees as well. For example, business travellers who collect frequent flyer miles now have to pay income tax on the value of the personal flights they take using business frequent flyer miles. Also being considered are user fees for things such as rescue costs. Mountaineers in Switzerland and Germany pay for their personal rescue costs with special insurance policies. In Pakistan, mountain climbers must post a $5,500 bond when climbing in war zones, to cover any cost of a forced evacuation. Why not Canada too, say observers.

Excess premiums from Employment Insurance also decrease the deficit. See the Issues and Applications section at the end of this chapter.

Thinking Critically About the Media   **The Flat Tax**

The idea of replacing our progressive income tax system with a flat tax is gaining support in the media. A flat tax would tax incomes at one rate—say 20 percent—after allowing only substantial personal exemptions—say $40,000 for a family of four. One of the attractive aspects of the flat tax is that it is simple: there are no loopholes, and the tax return would probably be one page long. Tax evasion would decline, and the $60 billion per year which now goes to the accoun-tants and tax lawyers of the wealthy could be put to more productive use. However, if the poor don't pay tax because their incomes are less than the allowable personal deductions, and if the wealthy pay less tax on investment and other income, then where will the tax revenues come from? The media seldom dwell on the travails of the middle class, who would pay more under this system than they do under the current one.

Decreasing Expenditure, Especially on Social Services

Almost 25 percent of the federal government's expenditure is in the form of transfers to provinces for social programs including post-secondary education, health, and social services. The Chrétien government in 1995 announced significant cuts to these transfers. In the past, transfer funds were earmarked for specific programs. Under the new plan, the funds may be used however the provinces wish, or in other words, the cuts may be distributed whatever way the provinces choose. The only proviso is that health care continue to conform to the *Canada Health Act* and that no residence requirements be enforced for social assistance claimants. Figure 14.7 shows the amount of cash and tax points that the federal government is transferring to the provinces under the new Canada Health and Social Transfer (CHST) program.

Critics of this program claimed that the federal government was simply offloading its deficit onto the provinces, and that the provinces had to find ways to engineer cuts. Most provinces responded by cutting the size of their civil services, some closed hospitals, some raised tuition fees. New sources of revenue were also

Figure 14.7

Planned Canada Health and Social Transfers (CHST) 1994–2000

The federal government transfers to the provinces cash and tax points to be used for social services, health care, and post-secondary education. In an effort to control its spending, the federal government announced cuts for 1996 and 1997, with no change until the year 2000.

Source: Federal Government Budget 1995 and 1996.

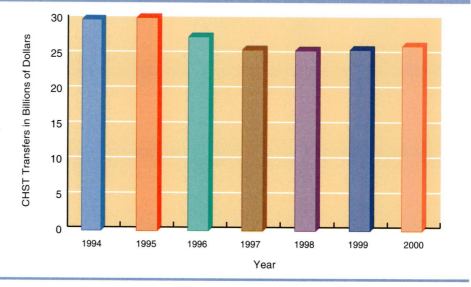

found: legalized casino gambling and video lottery terminals (VLTs), for example, have brought in substantial revenues. Critics were concerned about the possible social costs of gambling, even if run by the government.

Try Preview Question 4:

What are some suggested ways to reduce the federal government deficit?

The federal government, however, pointed to the health of the provincial fiscal situations in its own defence. Table 14.2 shows the provincial government surpluses and deficits for 1997. With the exception of Ontario and Quebec, the provinces were all managing to run either budgetary surpluses or very small budget deficits.

Table 14.2
Provincial Budgets for 1998 (millions of dollars)

The federal government justifies off-loading some of its spending on the provinces by pointing to their sound fiscal situations relative to its own.

Province	Surplus (Deficit) (millions of dollars)
British Columbia	191
Alberta	2,425
Saskatchewan	206
Manitoba	180
Ontario	(3,323)
Quebec	(1,779)
New Brunswick	0
Nova Scotia	22
Prince Edward Island	5
Newfoundland	20

Source: Statistics Canada.

Concepts in Brief

- Some people argue that the federal budget deficit or surplus is measured incorrectly because it lumps together spending on capital and spending on consumption. It is therefore argued that there should be an operating budget and a capital budget.
- Some observers see a close correlation between foreign trade deficits and federal budget deficits.
- Suggested ways to reduce a deficit are to increase taxes, particularly on the rich, and to reduce expenditures, particularly on social programs.

Issues and Applications

Employment Insurance and the Deficit

Concepts Applied: The multiplier, business cycles, payroll taxes, opportunity cost

In 1998, federal Finance Minister Paul Martin brought down the first surplus budget since 1970. Part of the surplus was due to the large excess of Employment Insurance premiums over payments out to claimants.

From 1970 to 1994, the federal government ran ever-increasing deficits which fuelled our burgeoning debt. In 1994, the Chrétien government declared war on the deficit, promising to reduce it to not more than 2 percent of GDP in the future. As we know, there were three ways to do this: the government could increase revenues, decrease expenditures, or do some of both. The major policy tool chosen was decreasing expenditures.

Government Budget

It is easy to see that reducing payments to the provinces would effectively decrease the federal government's financial obligations, but how does making EI harder to get decrease the deficit? Parts (a) and (b) of Figure 14.8 show the breakdown of government revenues and expenditures. Unlike the Canada Pension Plan funds, the premiums paid in and the benefits paid out are treated as part of the government's general revenues. Therefore, if the premiums

don't change while fewer EI claims are made, the deficit decreases. In 1996 and 1997, premiums paid in each year exceeded benefits paid out by $5 billion.

Figure 14.8
Employment Insurance Premiums and Benefits

Part (a) shows Employment Insurance premiums as a proportion of general government revenues. Part (b) shows benefits as a proportion of general expenditures. Fewer people claiming unemployment for a given level of premiums will have the effect of reducing the deficit.

Source: Federal Government Budget 1997.

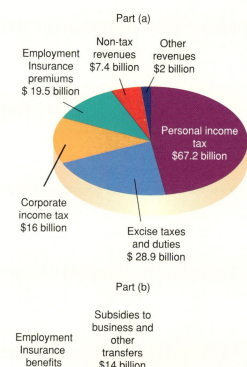

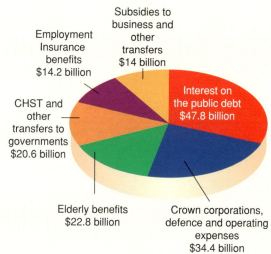

Less Effective Automatic Stabilizer

This plan was not without its detractors. Employment Insurance (which was called Unemployment Insurance until 1996) was designed to keep Canada from again falling into a depression like that of the 1930s. When the economy contracts, workers who are laid off claim Employment Insurance, and are provided with an income. That income allows them to continue consuming, although at reduced levels, and continued consumption acts as an incentive for firms to keep investing and producing. The theory is that eventually the economy, through the multiplier effect, will recover.

Critics of the stricter EI rules claim that lower benefit payments will detract from the plan's force as an automatic stabilizer. Once the economy stalls, workers who lose their jobs will be forced to restrict consumption, and the multiplier effect will work in the negative direction—consumption falls, which leads firms to experience inventory buildup, to slow production, and then to lay off even more workers. The point of Employment Insurance is to halt the natural course of the business cycle, and to kickstart the economy towards recovery.

Enlarge the Tax Base

Private sector employers also criticized the policy of retaining premium levels while cutting benefits. Workers do not carry the whole weight of EI premiums. Employers also pay $2.95 into the plan for each $100 of payroll. This payment and others—for instance a similar payment to the Canada Pension Plan—are referred to as payroll taxes.

A recent University of Toronto study claims that if the EI payroll tax were to be reduced from $2.95 to $2.10 per $100 of payroll, the private sector would be able to create 200,000 jobs over two years. Since business costs would be lower, prices would fall, quantity demanded would rise, and employers would be able to hire more workers. With a given income tax rate, federal government revenues would rise as unemployment fell. More people working, more income tax paid.

Trade-offs

As always, there is an opportunity cost to whatever course the government takes. With its current policy, the deficit has been eliminated. However, unemployment has not gone away. By keeping the payroll taxes at their current level, employers have had no incentive to create jobs. If the government were to reduce payroll taxes, employment would expand and revenues would rise. A surplus might even occur, allowing the government to reinstate some of the cut expenditures and pay down some of the debt.

For Critical Analysis

1. What is the underlying trade-off facing the government?

2. Employees and employers both pay payroll taxes. If the employees' EI payroll tax were reduced as well, what effect would that reduction have on consumers and the deficit?

CHAPTER SUMMARY

1. Whenever government expenditures exceed government revenues, a budget deficit occurs. Federal deficit spending as a share of GDP reached its peak right after World War II. In recent years, it has run at about 3 percent of GDP. In 1998, the federal government even recorded a surplus.

2. The federal government will not go bankrupt just because the public debt is rising, for it has its taxing authority to cover interest payments on the debt, which is constantly rolled over.

3. Government use of resources today must be paid for by people living today, because there is a trade-off between private use of resources and government use of resources in any one year.

4. To the extent that the existence of the federal deficit encourages foreigners to purchase Canadian assets, there is a potential problem that we no longer owe the public debt to ourselves. To the extent that the capital invested by foreigners in Canada has been productively used, however, future generations will be no worse off and in fact may be better off by the fact that foreigners have invested in this country.

5. If all taxpayers perfectly anticipate increased future tax liabilities due to higher deficits, saving will increase to cover those tax liabilities. Future productivity will therefore not be affected, nor will interest rates rise; there will be no crowding-out effect.

6. Some people argue that the federal budget deficit is measured incorrectly because it lumps together spending on capital and spending on consumption. It is therefore argued that there should be an operating budget and a capital budget.

7. Suggested ways to reduce the deficit are to increase taxes, particularly on the rich, and to reduce expenditures, particularly on social programs.

DISCUSSION OF PREVIEW QUESTIONS

1. **By what methods can the federal government obtain purchasing power?**

   In Canada, the federal government is able to obtain purchasing power by selling bonds, taxing, or creating money. Provincial and municipal governments can also obtain purchasing power by selling bonds and by taxing, but only the federal government has the power to create money in Canada. Perhaps surprisingly, regardless of how government expenditures are financed, most of the burden of government expenditures falls on the present generation; the effects of government money creation and bond sales are similar to the effects of taxation. All of the methods of financing government expenditures require the present generation to consume fewer consumer goods now in order to get more governmentally provided goods. Taxation does so in an obvious way; government bond sales compete with private industry bond sales, thereby contracting the private sector.

2. **What is the difference between the gross public debt and the net public debt?**

   The gross public debt is all federal government debt irrespective of who owns it. The net public debt is the gross public debt minus federally owned financial assets.

3. **What is the burden of the public debt?**

   If federal spending that increases the public debt crowds out private investment, future generations will be burdened with a lower capital stock and lower incomes. If the Ricardian equivalence theorem holds—if people in fact increase saving today to pay for higher tax liabilities in the future when there is deficit spending—crowding out is not inevitable, and this burden may not be as great as presumed.

4. **What are some suggested ways to reduce a federal government deficit?**

   The two most obvious ways to reduce a federal budget deficit are increasing taxes and reducing expenditures. Reductions in federal spending face political problems because of the difficulty the provinces have in reducing spending on social programs.

PROBLEMS

(Answers to the odd-numbered problems appear at the back of the book.)

14-1. In 1999, government spending is $800 billion and taxes collected are $770 billion. What is the federal budget deficit in that year?

14-2. Look at the accompanying table showing federal budget spending and federal budget receipts. Calculate the federal budget deficit as a percentage of GDP for each year.

Year	Federal Budget Receipts ($ billions)	Federal Budget Spending ($ billions)	GDP ($ billions)
1988	109.3	127.8	605.9
1989	117.4	137.7	650.7
1990	125.6	150.8	669.5
1991	130.9	161.1	667.5

14-3. It may be argued that the effects of a higher public debt are the same as the effects of higher taxes. Why?

14-4. To reduce the size of the deficit (and reduce the growth in the net public debt), a politician suggests that "we should tax the rich." The politician makes a simple arithmetic calculation in which he applies the increased tax rate to the total income reported by "the rich" in a previous year. He says that this is how much the government could receive from the increased taxes on "the rich." What is the major fallacy in such calculations?

14-5. Proponents of capital budgeting theory argue that whenever the government invests in capital expenditures, such as roads and dams, such government spending should be put in a separate budget called the capital budget. In doing so, the federal government's budget deficit would thereby be reduced by the amount of government capital spending. Would such a change in measuring the government deficit change anything? Explain.

14-6. What is the relationship between the annual federal government budget deficit and the net public debt?

14-7. The Statistics Canada Web site http://www.statcan.ca/english/Pgdb/ contains information which will help you fill out a table similar to Table 14.1 for your province.

   a. Choose "The State" and then "Government." Calculate your province's deficit for the year listed.

   b. How much were the interest charges on your provincial public debt?

   c. From the main page, choose "The Economy in Detail" and "Economic Conditions." Calculate the interest charges as a percentage of your province's GDP.

   d. Compare your answers to Table 14.1. Is your province or Canada as a whole in better fiscal shape (i.e., which has less interest costs as a percentage of GDP)?

INTERACTING WITH THE INTERNET

A breakdown of the federal government's debt into its various components can be found at

http://www.statcan.ca/english/Pgdb/State/Government/govt03.htm

You can get day-by-day updates on the size of the public debt at

http://www.consecol.org/cgi-bin/debt_clock/

Information about the Employment Insurance program is available at

http://canada.gc.ca/programs/pgrind_e.html#insurance

PART 5

Money, Monetary Policy, and Stabilization

Money and the Banking System

Worldwide telecommunications are growing at such a rapid pace that it's hard to keep up with the changes. More than 40 million individuals regularly use the Internet, and millions more are logging on each year. It is now possible to do business on the Internet—to buy and to sell. But how do you pay for those purchases? Many people use credit card numbers, now that safeguards exist to prevent the numbers from being available to non-authorized users. But something else is starting to happen— the advent of *e-cash*, or digital money. Will digital money have an effect on our banking system? To answer this question, you need to know what money is and how it relates to what banks do today.

Preview Questions

1. What is money?
2. What "backs" the Canadian dollar?
3. Who is involved in the process of transferring funds from savers to investors?
4. What are the functions of the Bank of Canada?

Did You Know That... the typical dollar coin changes hands 50 times a year? Cash, of course, is not the only thing we use as money. As you will see in this chapter, our definition of money is much broader. Money has been important to society for thousands of years. In 300 BC Aristotle claimed that everything had to "be accessed in money, for this enables men always to exchange their services, and so makes society possible." Money is indeed a part of our everyday existence. We have to be careful, though, when we talk about money because it means two different things. Most of the time when people say "I wish I had more money," they mean that they want more income. Thus the normal use of the term *money* implies the ability to purchase goods and services. In this chapter, in contrast, you will use the term **money** to mean anything that people generally accept in exchange for goods and services. Most people think of money as the paper bills and coins they carry. But the concept of money is normally more inclusive. Table 15.1 provides a list of the types of money that have been used throughout the history of civilization. The best way to understand money is to examine its functions.

▶ **Money**

Any medium that is universally accepted in an economy both by sellers of goods and services as payment for those goods and services and by creditors as payment for debts.

Table 15.1
Types of Money

This is a partial list of things that have been used as money. Native Canadians used wampum, beads made from shells. Fijians used whale teeth. The early colonists in North America used tobacco. And cigarettes were used in prisoner-of-war camps during World War II and in post–World War II Germany.

Iron	Boar tusk	Playing cards
Copper	Red woodpecker scalps	Leather
Brass	Feathers	Gold
Wine	Glass	Silver
Corn	Polished beads (wampum)	Knives
Salt	Rum	Pots
Horses	Molasses	Boats
Sheep	Tobacco	Pitch
Goats	Agricultural implements	Rice
Tortoise shells	Round stones with centres removed	Cows
Porpoise teeth	Crystal salt bars	Paper
Whale teeth	Snail shells	Cigarettes

Source: Roger LeRoy Miller and David D. VanHoose, *Modern Money and Banking*, 3d ed. (New York: McGraw-Hill, 1993), p. 13.

THE FUNCTIONS OF MONEY

Money traditionally serves three functions. The one that most people are familiar with is money's function as a *medium of exchange*. Money also serves as a *unit of account*, and a *store of value* or *purchasing power*. Anything that serves these three functions is money. Anything that could serve these three functions could be considered money.

Money as a Medium of Exchange

▶ **Medium of exchange**
Any asset that sellers will accept as payment.

When we say that money serves as a **medium of exchange,** what we mean is that sellers will accept it as payment in market transactions. Without some generally accepted medium of exchange, we would have to resort to barter. In fact, before money was used, transactions took place by means of barter. **Barter** is simply a direct exchange—no intermediary good called money is used. In a barter economy, the shoemaker who wants to obtain a dozen water glasses must seek out a glassmaker who at exactly the same time is interested in obtaining a pair of shoes. For this to occur, there has to be a *double coincidence of wants*. If there isn't, the shoemaker must go through several trades in order to obtain the desired dozen glasses—perhaps first trading shoes for jewellery, then jewellery for some pots and pans, and then the pots and pans for the desired glasses.

▶ **Barter**
The direct exchange of goods and services for other goods and services without the use of money.

Money facilitates exchange by reducing the transaction costs associated with means-of-payment uncertainty—that is, with regard to goods that the partners in any exchange are willing to accept. The existence of money means that individuals no longer have to hold a diverse collection of goods as an exchange inventory. As a medium of exchange, money allows individuals to specialize in any area in which they have a comparative advantage and to receive money payments for their labour. Money payments can then be exchanged for the fruits of other people's labour. The use of money as a medium of exchange permits more specialization and the inherent economic efficiencies that come with it (and hence greater economic growth). Money is even more important when used for large amounts of trade.

Thinking Critically About the Media   A Return to Barter

Every few years you read stories about Canadians (or Americans) deciding to "return to bartering." An electrician agrees to rewire a dentist's house in exchange for major dental work; a lawyer agrees to prepare a will in exchange for an annual physical checkup by a doc-tor. Such actions are not really designed to avoid the use of money and return to the "simple life." Rather, such exchanges without the use of money are typically undertaken to avoid the payment of income taxes. Barter is not back.

Money as a Unit of Account

▶ **Unit of account**
A measure by which prices are expressed; the common denominator of the price system; a central property of money.

A **unit of account** is a way of placing a specific price on economic goods and services. Thus as a unit of account, the monetary unit is used to measure the value of goods and services *relative* to other goods and services. It is the common denominator, or measure, the commonly recognized unit of value measurement. The dollar is the monetary unit in Canada. It is the yardstick that allows individuals easily to compare the relative value of goods and services. Accountants at Statistics Canada use dollar prices to measure national income and domestic product, a business uses dollar prices to calculate profits and losses, and a typical household budgets regularly anticipated expenses using dollar prices as its unit of account.

Another way of describing money as a unit of account is to say that it serves as a *standard of value* that allows economic actors to compare the relative worth of various goods and services. It allows for comparison shopping, for example.

Money as a Store of Value

▶ **Store of value**
The ability to hold value over time; a necessary property of money.

One of the most important functions of money is that it serves as a **store of value** or purchasing power. The money you have today can be set aside to purchase things later on. In the meantime, money retains its nominal value, which you can apply to those future purchases. If you have $1,000 in your chequing account, you can either spend it today on goods and services, spend it tomorrow, or spend it a month from now. In this way, money provides a way to transfer value (wealth) into the future.

Liquidity

▶ **Liquidity**
The degree to which an asset can be acquired or disposed of without much danger of any intervening loss in *nominal* value and with small transaction costs. Money is the most liquid asset.

Money is an asset—something of value—that accounts for part of personal wealth. Wealth in the form of money can be exchanged later for some other asset. Although it is not the only form of wealth that can be exchanged for goods and services, it is the one most widely and readily accepted. This attribute of money is called **liquidity**. We say that an asset is liquid when it can easily be acquired or disposed of without high transaction costs and with relative certainty as to its value. Money is by definition the most liquid asset there is. Just compare it, for example, with a share of stock listed on the Toronto Stock Exchange. To buy or sell that share, you usually call a stockbroker, who will place the buy or sell order for you. This generally must be done during normal business hours. You have to pay a commission to the broker. Moreover, there is a distinct probability that you will get more or less for the stock than you originally paid for it. This is not the case with money. Money can be easily converted to other asset forms. Therefore, most individuals hold at least a part of their wealth in the form of the most liquid of assets, money. You can see how assets rank in liquidity relative to one another in Figure 15.1.

Try Preview Question 1:
What is money?

When we hold money, however, we pay a price for this advantage of liquidity. That price is the interest yield that could have been obtained had the asset been held in another form—for example, in the form of stocks and bonds.

The cost of holding money (its opportunity cost) is measured by the alternative interest yield obtainable by holding some other asset.

Figure 15.1
Degrees of Liquidity
The most liquid asset is, of course, cash. Liquidity decreases as you move from right to left.

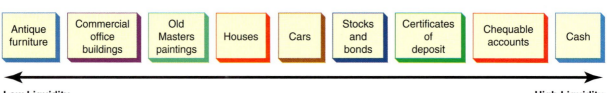

Low Liquidity   High Liquidity

MONETARY STANDARDS, OR WHAT BACKS MONEY

Today in Canada, all of us accept coins, paper currency, and balances in **demand deposits** (chequing accounts with banks and other financial institutions) in exchange for items sold, including labour services. The question remains, why are we willing to accept as payment something that has no intrinsic value? After all, you could not sell cheques to anybody for use as a raw material in manufacturing. The reason is that in this country the payments arise from a **fiduciary monetary system**. This means that the value of the payments rests on the public's confidence that such payments can be exchanged for goods and services. *Fiduciary* comes from the Latin *fiducia*, which means "trust" or "confidence." In our fiduciary monetary system, money, in the form of currency or chequing accounts, is not convertible to a fixed quantity of gold, silver, or some other precious commodity. The paper money that people hold cannot be exchanged for a specified quantity of some specified commodity. The bills are just pieces of paper. Coins have a value stamped on them that is normally greater than the market value of the metal in them. Nevertheless, currency and deposit accounts are money because of their acceptability and predictability of value.

Acceptability

Demand deposits and currency are money because they are accepted in exchange for goods and services. They are accepted because people have confidence that they can later be exchanged for other goods and services. This confidence is based on the knowledge that such exchanges have occurred in the past without problems. Even during a period of relatively rapid inflation, we would still be inclined to accept money in exchange for goods and services because it is so useful. Barter is a costly and time-consuming alternative.

Realize always that money is socially defined. Acceptability is not something that you can necessarily predict. For example, you will probably have trouble spending Canadian currency in most businesses in the United States. Unless they are close to the Canadian border and deal frequently with Canadians, Americans do not have faith in Canadian money and therefore will not accept it in payment for goods and services.

Predictability of Value

The purchasing power of the dollar (its value) varies inversely with the price level. The more rapid the rate of increase of some price level index, such as the Consumer Price Index, the more rapid the decrease in the value, or purchasing power, of a dollar. Money still retains its usefulness even if its value—its purchasing power—is declining year in and year out, as in periods of inflation, because it still retains the characteristic of predictability of value. If you believe that the inflation rate is going to be around 10 percent next year, you know that any dollar you receive a year from now will have a purchasing power equal to 10 percent less than that same dollar this year. Thus you will not necessarily refuse to use money or accept it in exchange simply because you know that its value will decline by the rate of inflation next year.

Try Preview Question 2:

What "backs" the Canadian dollar?

Concepts in Brief

- Money is defined by its functions, which are as a medium of exchange, a unit of account or standard of value, and a store of value or purchasing power.
- Because money is a highly liquid asset, it can be disposed of without high transaction costs and with relative certainty as to its value.
- Canada has a fiduciary monetary system—our money is not convertible into a fixed quantity of a commodity such as gold or silver.
- Money is accepted in exchange for goods and services because people have confidence that it can later be exchanged for other goods and services. Another reason for this is that it has a predictable value.

DEFINING THE CANADIAN MONEY SUPPLY

▶ **Money supply**

The amount of money in circulation.

Money is important. Changes in the total **money supply**—the amount of money in circulation—and changes in the rate at which the money supply increases or decreases affect important economic variables, such as the rate of inflation, interest rates, employment, and the equilibrium level of real national income. Although there is widespread agreement among economists that money is indeed important, they have never agreed on how to define or measure it. Therefore we have several measures of the money supply.

The Narrowest Measure: M1

One measure of the money supply consists of the following:

1. Currency
2. Demand deposits

The narrowest official designation of the money supply, including currency and demand deposits, is **M1**. The two elements of M1 for a typical year are presented in part (a) of Figure 15.2.

▶ **M1**

The money supply, taken as the total value of currency plus demand deposits in chartered banks.

Currency.   Currency includes Canadian coins and paper currency, usually in the form of bank notes, issued by the Bank of Canada. Although not nearly as important as chequable deposits as a percentage of the money supply, currency has increased in significance in Canada. One of the major reasons for the increased use of currency in the Canadian economy is the growing number of illegal transactions, including under-the-table work agreements and the drug trade.

Figure 15.2
Composition of the M1 and M2 Money Supply, 1996

Part (a) shows the M1 money supply, the larger component of which is demand deposits (about 58 percent). M2 consists of M1 plus two other components, the most important of which is personal savings deposits at chartered banks (about 76 percent).

Source: Bank of Canada Review. Data are for 1996.

Part (a)

Currency and coins
$26.8 billion
41.7%

Demand deposits
$37.5 billion
58.3%

M1 = $64.3 billion

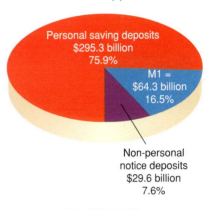

Part (b)

Personal saving deposits
$295.3 billion
75.9%

M1 =
$64.3 billion
16.5%

Non-personal
notice deposits
$29.6 billion
7.6%

M2 = $389.2 billion

POLICY EXAMPLE   Eliminating the $1 and $2 Bills

Since 1990, the federal government has replaced our $1 and $2 bills with coins—the "loonie" and the "toonie." What drove the government to weigh down our pockets and purses with heavy money? There are three reasons, all related to government revenue: coins last longer than bills, coins are quite inexpensive to produce, and the government makes a tidy profit on the replacement of bills with coins.

Coins Are Durable. You've probably been given in change a $5 bill which looks like it is about to fall apart. This is due to the wear and tear on paper currency as it is circulated in the economy. As paper currency wears out, banks and other financial institutions return to the Bank of Canada those bills that are on their last legs. The Bank then arranges for new replacement bills. A coin like the toonie, however, does not wear out quickly and has to be replaced much less frequently. A loonie or a toonie has a 20-year life span, while a paper note will last for just one year. The government saves about $12.5 million per year just on production costs of the $1 and $2 coins.

Coins Are Cheap to Produce. The government buys its coins from the Royal Canadian Mint, located in Winnipeg, at a price which includes the cost of production and a margin of profit for the Mint. While the government doesn't make money purchasing pennies at 1.4¢ each and nickels at 5¢ each, it makes a profit on the other coins. For example, it costs 4¢ to produce a dime, 8¢ to produce a quarter, 13¢ to produce a $1 coin, and only 16¢ to turn out a $2 coin.

Coins Earn a Profit for the Government. In 1996, the Mint turned out about 14 new coins per second, 24 hours per day, to meet the government's target of putting about 300 million $2 coins into circulation by 1997. Each time the Bank of Canada returned a $2 coin to a chartered bank in exchange for a used $2 bill, the Bank earned $1.84 in profit—after all, the chartered bank paid $2 for the coin which cost 16¢ to make. This profit amounted to about $500 million during the first two years of toonie production.

Will we see the replacement of our $5 and $10 bills with coins in the near future? Probably not, as those bills don't circulate as quickly and therefore do not wear out as fast.

For critical analysis: If the government decided to replace the $20 bill with a coin, what would happen to the amount of seigniorage—the profit it makes from producing our currency—it would earn?

> **▶ Chequable deposits**
> Any deposits in a near bank or a chartered bank on which a cheque may be written.

> **▶ Near bank**
> Financial institutions such as trust companies, credit unions and *caisses populaires* that offer most of the same services as chartered banks.

Demand Deposits. Most major transactions today are done with cheques. The convenience and safety of using cheques has made chequing accounts the most important component of the money supply. For example, it is estimated that in 1997 currency transactions accounted for only about 0.5 percent of the *dollar* amount of all transactions. The rest (excluding barter) involved cheques. Cheques are a way of transferring the ownership of deposits in financial institutions. They are normally acceptable as a medium of exchange. The financial institutions that offer **chequable deposits** are numerous and include virtually all **near banks**—trust companies, and credit unions and *caisses populaires*. However, only chequing accounts held in chartered banks are included in the measure of M1.

What About Credit Cards?

Even though a large percentage of transactions are accomplished by using a plastic credit card, we do not consider the credit card itself money. Remember the functions of money. A credit card is not a unit of account or a store of value. The use of your credit card is really a loan to you by the issuer of the card, be it a bank, a retail store, or a gas company. The proceeds of the loan are paid to the business that sold you something. You must pay back the loan to the issuer of the credit card, either when you get your statement or with interest throughout the year if you don't pay off your balance. (We ignore those with credit card debt which they cannot repay.) It is not a store of value. Credit cards *defer*, rather than complete, transactions that ultimately involve the use of money.

A relative newcomer, the *debit card* automatically withdraws money from your bank account. When you use your debit card to purchase something, you are giving an instruction to your bank to transfer money directly from your bank account to the store's bank account. If the store in which you are shopping has a direct electronic link to the bank, that transfer may be made instantaneously. Use of a debit card does not create a loan. A debit card is therefore not a new type of "money."

EXAMPLE Credit Cards and Canadians

Canadians hold more than 58.5 million credit cards of all types: gasoline cards, retail store cards, and all-purpose cards like Visa, MasterCard, and American Express. Canadians use these cards for about 15 percent of their purchases, the rest being made with cash and cheques.

Since 1992, credit card use has grown by almost 60 percent in spite of slow average real income growth of about 1 percent over the same time period. Outstanding balances on Visa and MasterCard alone totalled $17.4 billion in 1995, boosting total consumer bank loans in the economy. These are expensive loans, however, for the average credit card interest rate is 10.5 percent above bank rates.

At these high rates, what induces consumers to buy on credit? First, the convenience of purchasing now without waiting for payday is a big attraction. Second, consumers are attracted by competition between bank card companies. Some cards award credit, based on the amount of purchases each month, towards purchase of an automobile. Other cards award frequent flyer miles based on card use. Recently, Visa has offered 25 percent discounts on selected products as an inducement to buy on credit. Consumers have shown they find these offers hard to resist.

For critical analysis: What effect will these non-money transactions have on aggregate demand in the economy?

A Broader Measure of Money: M2

▶ **M2**
M1 plus (1) personal savings and (2) non-personal notice deposits.

A broader measure the money supply involves taking into account not only the most liquid assets that people use as money, which are already included in the definition of M1, but also other assets that are highly liquid—that is, that can be converted into money quickly without loss of nominal dollar value and without much cost. These assets are personal savings accounts (many of which have chequing privileges) and non-personal notice deposits. Part (b) of Figure 15.2 on page 373 shows the components of **M2**—money as a temporary store of value. We examine each of these components in turn.

▶ **Savings deposits**
Interest-earning funds at chartered banks that can be withdrawn at any time without payment of a penalty.

Savings Deposits.   **Savings deposits** in chartered banks are part of the M2 money supply. A savings deposit is distinguishable from a time deposit because savings funds may be withdrawn without payment of a penalty. Funds are fully protected against loss in their nominal value.

▶ **Non-personal notice deposits**
Interest-earning funds deposited by firms at chartered banks which can in practice be withdrawn at any time without payment of a penalty.

Non-personal Notice Deposits.   **Non-personal notice deposits** are similar to savings deposits, but are funds deposited by firms. Although legally the firms are required to give the bank "notice" of withdrawal, this requirement is rarely observed.

▶ **Central bank**
A banker's bank, usually an official institution that also serves as a country's treasury's bank. Central banks normally regulate commercial banks.

▶ **Bank of Canada**
Canada's central bank.

▶ **Financial intermediation**
The process by which financial institutions accept savings from businesses, households, and governments and lend the savings to other businesses, households, and governments.

▶ **Financial intermediaries**
Institutions that transfer funds between ultimate lenders (savers) and ultimate borrowers.

Other Money Supply Definitions. When all of these assets are added together, the result is M2. The composition of M2 is given in part (b) of Figure 15.2 (page 373).

Economists and researchers have come up with even broader definitions of money than M2.[1] More assets are simply added to the definition.

Just remember that there is no one best definition of the money supply. For different purposes, different definitions are appropriate. If we want to use a definition that seems to correlate best with economic activity on an economy-wide basis, M2 is probably best.

THE CANADIAN BANKING STRUCTURE

Canada's banking system consists of a **central bank** called the **Bank of Canada**. In addition, there are a large number of commercial banks (also called chartered banks), which are privately owned, profit-seeking institutions, and near banks.

Financial Intermediaries: Sources and Uses of Funds

The financial institutions in our banking system are all in the same business—transferring funds from savers to investors. This process has become known as **financial intermediation**, and its participants are called **financial intermediaries**. Savers lend funds through financial intermediaries (banks, credit unions, etc.) to borrowers such as businesses, governments, and home buyers. The process of financial intermediation is illustrated in Figure 15.3.

Figure 15.3
The Process of Financial Intermediation

The process of financial intermediation is depicted here. Note that ultimate lenders and ultimate borrowers are the same economic units–households, businesses, and governments–but not necessarily the same individuals. Whereas individual households can be net lenders or borrowers, households as an economic unit are net lenders. Specific businesses or governments similarly can be net lenders or borrowers; as economic units, both are net borrowers.

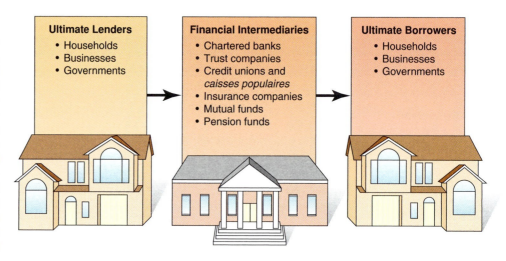

Ultimate Lenders	Financial Intermediaries	Ultimate Borrowers
• Households • Businesses • Governments	• Chartered banks • Trust companies • Credit unions and *caisses populaires* • Insurance companies • Mutual funds • Pension funds	• Households • Businesses • Governments

---

[1] They include M3, which is equal to M2 plus non-personal fixed term deposits and foreign currency held in Canada by Canadian residents. Yet another measure is M2+, which is equal to M2 plus near bank deposits.

▶ **Liabilities**
Amounts owed; the legal claims against a business or household by nonowners.

▶ **Assets**
Amounts owned; all items to which a business or household holds legal claim.

Try Preview Question 3:
Who is involved in the process of transferring funds from savers to investors?

Each financial intermediary has its own primary source of funds, which are called **liabilities**. When you deposit $100 in your chequing account in the bank, the bank creates a liability—it owes you $100—in exchange for the funds deposited. A commercial bank gets its funds from chequing and savings accounts; an insurance company gets its funds from insurance policy premiums.

Each financial intermediary normally has a different primary use of its **assets**. For example, a credit union usually makes small consumer loans, whereas a mortgage loan company makes mainly home mortgage loans. Table 15.2 lists the assets and liabilities of financial intermediaries. Be aware, though, that the distinction between different financial institutions is becoming more and more blurred. As the laws and regulations change, there will be less need to make any distinction. All may ultimately be treated simply as financial intermediaries.

Table 15.2
Financial Intermediaries and Their Assets and Liabilities

Financial Intermediary	Assets	Liabilities
Chartered banks	Bank loans and other consumer debt, business loans, home mortgages	Chequing accounts, savings deposits, currency
Trust and mortgage loan companies	Home mortgages, consumer debt	Chequing accounts, savings deposits
Credit unions and *caisses populaires*	Consumer debt, mortgage loans	Credit union shares, chequing accounts, savings deposits
Insurance companies	Mortgages, bonds, shares	Insurance contracts, annuities, pension plans
Pension and retirement funds	Bonds, time deposits	Pension plans, life insurance
Mutual funds	Short-term credit instruments such as large-bank CDs, Treasury bills, stocks, bonds, currency, and foreign investment	Fund shares

Concepts in Brief

- The money supply can be defined in a variety of ways. M1, which consists of currency and demand deposits in chartered banks, is the most narrowly defined.
- Demand deposits (chequing accounts) are any deposits in financial institutions on which the deposit owner can write cheques.
- Credit cards are not part of the money supply, for they simply defer transactions that ultimately involve the use of money.
- When we add savings deposits and non-personal notice deposits to M1, we obtain the measure known as M2.
- Financial intermediaries transfer funds from ultimate lenders (savers) to ultimate borrowers. This process of financial intermediation is undertaken by chartered banks, trust companies, mortgage loan companies, credit unions and *caisses populaires*, insurance companies, mutual funds, and pension funds.

CANADA'S CENTRAL BANKING SYSTEM

The Bank of Canada is Canada's central bank. It oversees the Canadian monetary system and as such is considered the country's monetary authority. The Bank of Canada was established with the *Bank of Canada Act* of 1934 and opened its doors for business in 1935. At first privately owned, by 1938 the federal government had nationalized it. Basically, the Bank of Canada was set up to create stability in the Canadian banking system, and to provide a mechanism for settling international accounts. It was also set up to act as the federal government's banker and financial adviser.

Organization of the Bank of Canada.

The Bank of Canada is governed by a Board of Directors consisting of the Governor of the Bank of Canada, the Senior Deputy Governor, 12 directors from non-banking occupations, and the Deputy Minister of Finance, who is a non-voting member of the Board. The Governor is appointed by the Board, with Cabinet approval, for a seven-year term. Directors are appointed for three-year terms. Regional representation is a priority when appointing directors.

The Board of Directors must meet at least four times per year, but frequently meets more often. The day-to-day operations of the Bank are directed by an executive committee of the Board, consisting of the Governor, the Senior Deputy Governor, and two to four other directors who meet weekly. While the Bank of Canada is ultimately responsible to the federal government, it is an independent body charged with maintaining price stability and economic growth in Canada. Whether this independence is beneficial is the topic of the Issues and Applications section at the end of Chapter 16.

The Bank of Canada's Customers.

The Bank of Canada accepts deposits from the federal government and the chartered banks only. Almost all federal government transactions pass through the Bank of Canada, although the government also has accounts with the chartered banks. Chapter 16 looks more closely at this relationship.

The chartered banks hold deposits at the Bank of Canada for two reasons. First, the banks hold a large part of their reserve deposits in these accounts. Until 1992, they were required to hold reserves by law; however, the *Bank Act* of 1992 eliminated this requirement. Now they hold reserves at the Bank of Canada as part of prudent banking practice.

The second reason the chartered banks hold reserves at the Bank of Canada is to facilitate cheque clearing. When your employer pays you with a $200 cheque drawn on the Royal Bank and you deposit it in your account at the Bank of Nova Scotia, no money actually changes hands. All across Canada, similar transactions are taking place at financial institutions. At the end of the day, the **Canadian Payments Association** adds up all the money that each bank owes the other—for instance, the Royal Bank would owe the Bank of Nova Scotia $200 for your paycheque—and arrives at a net transfer of funds that should be made between banks. If the Toronto-

▶ **Canadian Payments Association (CPA)**

A regulated organization which operates a national cheque-clearing and settlements system.

Dominion Bank owes the Bank of Montreal $1.5 million, for example, while the Bank of Montreal owes the Toronto-Dominion Bank $1 million, the Canadian Payments Association would ask the Bank of Canada to transfer $500,000 out of the reserve deposits of the Toronto-Dominion Bank and into the deposits of the Bank of Montreal. Near banks maintain deposits with the chartered banks so that they may participate in the cheque clearing process as well.

Functions of the Bank of Canada

The Bank of Canada serves four basic functions. It conducts monetary policy on behalf of the federal government, it acts as a lender of last resort to the financial community, it issues bank notes, and it is fiscal agent and financial advisor to the government. Let's examine each of these functions in more detail.

Monetary Policy. The Bank of Canada is charged with keeping inflation within a target band of 1 to 3 percent to facilitate economic growth. It does this primarily by varying the reserve deposits held by the chartered banks at the Bank of Canada. This and other processes are discussed in more depth in Chapters 17 and 18.

Lender of Last Resort. Occasionally the chartered banks will feel their reserve deposits are lower than they would like. In these situations, the banks can ask the Bank of Canada for short-term loans to ensure that they do not run short of cash to satisfy withdrawals. This practice lends stability to the system. Should a bank not be able to meet demand for withdrawals, it could be forced into bankruptcy.

Issuing Bank Notes. From the opening of Canada's first chartered bank in 1871, the chartered banks issued their own bank notes. This practice declined when the Bank of Canada began issuing Canadian currency, and stopped completely in 1945. The Bank of Canada now is the only body which can issue legal bank notes in Canada.

Fiscal Agent and Financial Advisor. The Bank of Canada acts as the federal government's fiscal agent and financial advisor. In this capacity, it manages the government's debt by arranging payment of interest to debt-holders, and payment in full on maturing debt. It also holds government deposits, and provides advice with respect to issuing government securities. The Bank of Canada frequently intervenes in the foreign exchange market to support the external value of the Canadian dollar and to manage the government's holdings of foreign reserves. Chapter 20 looks at the foreign exchange market in more detail.

Table 15.3 shows a consolidated balance sheet for the Bank of Canada. Its assets consist mainly of Government of Canada securities and Treasury bills. These securities form part of the public debt. The Bank's liabilities are mostly currency in circulation, with chartered bank reserve deposits the next largest component.

Try Preview Question 4:

What are the functions of the Bank of Canada?

Table 15.3	Assets		Liabilities	
Bank of Canada Consolidated Balance Sheet at July 1, 1998 (millions of dollars)	Treasury Bills of Canada	$ 13,067	Currency in circulation	$30,364
	Other Government of Canada securities	16,034	Government of Canada deposits	8
Source: Bank of Canada Review.	Foreign currency	326	Chartered bank deposits	797
	Other assets	2,689	Other deposits	361
			Other liabilities	586
	Total assets	**$ 32,116**	**Total liabilities**	**$ 32,116**

EXAMPLE   Is Canadian Tire Money Real Money?

One of the functions of the Bank of Canada is to issue bank notes. Canadian Tire, however, issues its own "currency," which can be used to purchase goods and services at any Canadian Tire store. Every time you purchase with cash one dollar's worth of merchandise, you receive five cents in Canadian Tire money. Is this note "real" money?

If you said, no, Canadian Tire money is not real money, you would be right. However, in some instances it is used in place of real money. Consider the bartender who is given Canadian Tire notes as part of a tip. If that individual's car happens to need new tires, for example, then those notes are as good as money. If the bartender doesn't want anything from Canadian Tire, then they are worthless.

But what if the bartender had a friend who wanted to buy tires? The two could exchange the Canadian Tire money for Canadian currency, which is real money. However, one of the tests of Canadian legal tender is that it must be accepted in payment of debts in Canada. In this instance Canadian Tire money would not measure up.

For critical analysis: What conditions would have to exist for Canadian Tire money to act as real money in practice, if not in theory?

Concepts in Brief

- The Bank of Canada is Canada's central bank. It is run by a Board of Directors from non-banking occupations, as well as the Governor and Senior Deputy Governor of the Bank.
- The only customers of the Bank of Canada are the federal government and the chartered banks. The chartered banks hold reserve deposits at the Bank of Canada as a precaution in case of heavy withdrawals, and to facilitate cheque clearing.
- The Canadian Payments Association handles cheque clearing for the financial community.
- The Bank of Canada conducts monetary policy on behalf of the federal government, acts as a lender of last resort to the financial community, issues bank notes, and provides financial advice to the federal government.

Issues and Applications

Watch Out for E-Cash

Concepts Applied: Money, money supply, transactions accounts

Mondex cards and e-cash are changing the way we think about money. They may also force us to change our definition of the money supply.

I t began with seashells and beads. Objects that were once used as money were gradually replaced by standardized commodities, such as gold and silver. Then came paper money and, next, chequing accounts. With chequing accounts and new technology have come electronic means of handling money, such as ATMs and debit cards.

Enter Mondex

Two British banks, National Westminster and Midland, started a plastic-and-silicone cash substitute called Mondex cards. They resemble ATM cards but carry a computer chip inside. This is data money. Bank customers can transfer data money onto their cards over the phone if they have a "smart" phone in their house. In Canada, Visa is pioneering a smart card called VisaCash, similar to the Mondex card.

Now there's e-money too. Companies other than banks have started their own forms of electronic money called e-cash. E-cash operates completely outside the network of banks, cheques, and paper currency. In other words, accounts are debited and credited without cash or cheques changing hands (just as banks have begun to do among themselves). Some of the companies in the e-cash game, such as Microsoft and Xerox, are well known; others, such as CyberCash and DigiCash, are less well known. Perhaps e-cash's biggest opportunity for success will be on the Internet, where electronic commerce is growing daily. People will be able to download money to their PC or to palm-sized electronic wallets, or transfer money instantly to Internet merchants.

The Benefits of E-Cash

E-cash may turn out to be more convenient than traditional money, particularly on the Internet. Banks that decide to issue e-cash may find it cheaper than handling cheques and paper records.

The Risks of E-Cash

The traditional definition of money will certainly no longer hold if e-cash becomes the preferred method of carrying out transactions. The Bank of Canada will have less ability to control the money supply. Furthermore, e-cash may present problems if it is stored in computer systems. What if the systems crash? Equally, electronic counterfeiting may turn out to be a serious problem. Computer hackers who break into an e-cash system might be able to steal money from thousands or even hundreds of thousands of individuals all at once. Finally, e-cash may allow for more tax evasion and money laundering.

For Critical Analysis

1. Will there be any way to measure the size of the e-cash element of the money supply in the future?
2. Is e-cash really a form of money?

CHAPTER SUMMARY

1. The functions of money are a medium of exchange, a unit of account (standard of value), and a store of value or purchasing power.

2. We have a fiduciary monetary system in Canada—our money, whether in the form of currency or chequing accounts, is not convertible into a fixed quantity of a commodity, such as gold or silver.

3. Our money is exchangeable for goods and services because it has acceptability: People have confidence that whatever money they receive can be exchanged for other goods and services later. Our money also has a predictable value.

4. There are numerous ways to define the money supply. One method is called M1, which stresses the role of money as a medium of exchange. Another method is M2, which stresses the role of money as a temporary store of value.

5. Our central bank is the Bank of Canada. Its governing body is the Board of Directors.

6. The basic functions of the Bank of Canada are (a) conducting monetary policy, (b) acting as a lender of last resort, (c) issuing bank notes, and (d) advising the federal government on financial matters and acting as its fiscal agent.

DISCUSSION OF PREVIEW QUESTIONS

1. **What is money?**
   Money is defined by its functions. Thus money is whatever is generally accepted for use as a medium of exchange, a unit of account, and a store of value or purchasing power. In various places in the world throughout history, different items have performed these functions: wampum, gold, silver, cows, stones, paper, diamonds, salt, cigarettes, and many others.

2. **What "backs" the Canadian dollar?**
   Some students think that the Canadian dollar is "backed" by gold, but alas (some experts say fortunately), this is not the case. Canada is presently on a fiduciary monetary standard, and as such the Canadian dollar is backed only by faith—the public's confidence that it can be exchanged for goods and services. This confidence comes from the fact that other people will accept the dollar in transactions because our government has declared it legal tender and because, despite inflation, it still retains the characteristic of predictability of value.

3. **Who is involved in the process of transferring funds from savers to investors?**
   Financial intermediation involves the transfer of funds from savers to investors. The ultimate lenders are the savers—households, businesses, and governments, including the federal government and provincial and municipal governments. The ultimate borrowers are also households, businesses, and governments—the same economic units but not necessarily the same individuals. Between ultimate lenders and ultimate borrowers are financial intermediaries, including commercial banks, trust companies, mortgage loan companies, credit unions and *caisses populaires*, insurance companies, mutual funds and pension funds.

4. **What are the functions of the Bank of Canada?**
   The Bank of Canada has four basic functions. It conducts monetary policy on behalf of the federal government. It acts as a lender of last resort to the financial community. It issues bank notes. Finally, the Bank of Canada acts as the fiscal agent and financial advisor to the federal government.

PROBLEMS

(Answers to the odd-numbered problems appear at the back of the book.)

15-1. Consider each type of asset in terms of its potential use as a medium of exchange, a unit of account, and a store of value or purchasing power. Indicate which use is most appropriately associated with each asset.

a. A painting by Renoir
b. A 90-day Canadian Treasury bill
c. A notice deposit account with a trust company in St. John's, Newfoundland
d. One share of IBM stock
e. A $50 Bank of Canada note
f. A MasterCard credit card
g. A chequing account in a credit union in Manitoba
h. A lifetime pass to the Montreal Expos' home baseball games

15-2. The value of a dollar is the reciprocal of the price index. In 1986 the CPI had a value of 1; hence the value of a dollar in 1986 equalled $1. If the price index now is 2, what is the value of the dollar in 1986 prices? If the price index is 2.5?

15-3. What are the components of M2?

15-4. How have technological changes altered the form of money?

15-5. Elsa Lee can make several uses of her money. Indicate for each case whether her money is being used as a medium of exchange (E), a unit of account (A), or a store of value (V).
a. Lee has accumulated $600 in her chequing account at a chartered bank.
b. Lee decides to use this $600 to purchase a new washing machine and goes shopping to compare the prices being charged by different dealers for the machine she wishes to buy.

c. Lee finds that the lowest price at which she can purchase the machine she wants is $498.50. She has the dealer deliver the machine and agrees to pay the dealer in 30 days.
d. Thirty days later, Lee sends the dealer a cheque drawn on her chequing account to pay for the washer.

15-6. Explain why a debit card is not a new form of money.

15-7. Consider a barter economy in which 10 goods and services are produced and exchanged. How many exchange rates exist in that economy, which does not use money?

15-8. Cash and cheques account for nearly 75 percent of the total number of all payments in Canada, and wire transfers account for over 60 percent of the dollar value of all payments in Canada. How can both situations be true simultaneously?

15-9. The Currency Museum of the Bank of Canada at http://www.schoolnet.ca/collections/bank/english/index.htm lists several periods of currency use in Canada's history. Select three periods and describe the types of currencies used at those times. Note that clicking on the picture of the currency will result in a larger photograph of the same thing. How effective do you think those currencies were in terms of fulfilling the medium of exchange, store of value, and unit of account functions? Explain your answer.

INTERACTING WITH THE INTERNET

Extensive Bank of Canada information can be found at

http://www.bank-banque-canada.ca/

It includes current and past monetary statistics, as well as other information.

Most banks and near banks have home pages on the Internet. You can access many of them through the Department of Finance at

http://www.fin.gc.ca/links/bankse.html#can

The Canadian Bankers Association provides information on banking, including the progress of various types of electronic banking and smart card banking. The CBA can be found at

http://www.cba.ca/

16

Money Creation and Deposit Insurance

Preview Questions

1. What is a fractional reserve banking system?

2. What happens to the total money supply when a person deposits in one depository institution a cheque drawn on another depository institution?

3. What happens to the overall money supply when a person who sells a Canadian government security to the Bank of Canada places the proceeds in a depository institution?

4. How does the existence of deposit insurance affect a financial institution's choice of risky versus nonrisky assets?

Life used to be simple for someone who wished to finance the purchase of a house, acquire stocks and bonds, take out insurance, or obtain a credit card. Each of those decisions involved going to any of a well-defined set of separate institutions. Insurance was always bought from an insurance company, for example; stocks and bonds were sold only by stock brokers; and money for a house was borrowed from a bank or credit union. Today, the choices are much more complicated and the distinctions between banks and "nonbanks" are becoming ever more blurred. All of this comes about in an era of deregulation of depository institutions. To understand the effects of deregulation, you need to learn about the regulation of such institutions and, before that, how money is created in our economy.

▶ **Money multiplier process**

The process by which an injection of new money into the banking system leads to a multiple expansion in the total money supply.

Did You Know That... virtually overnight, Nick Leeson, a 27-year-old manager in the Singapore branch of Barings Bank, was able to inflict losses of several billion dollars on the institution? Barings was founded in 1762. In 1803, it helped the United States purchase the Louisiana Territory from France. It provided credit to the British government during the Napoleonic Wars (1803–1815). During the 1850s, it financed the construction of Canada's Grand Trunk Railway. When Barings collapsed in 1995, it was bought by former competitors, thereby ending the life of one of the longest-running financial institutions in the world. Could the collapse of such an important bank lead to serious problems in the world's banking sector? A lot depends on whether the losses suffered by Barings' depositors would cause other depositors to lose confidence in other banks too. That, in turn, depends on the relationship between deposits at different banks.

If you were to attend a luncheon of local bankers and ask the question, "Do you as bankers create money?" you would get a uniformly negative response. Bankers are certain that they do not create money. Indeed, no individual bank can create money. But along with the Bank of Canada, depository institutions do create money; they determine the total deposits outstanding. In this chapter we will examine the **money multiplier process,** which explains how an injection of new money into the banking system leads to an eventual multiple expansion in the total money supply. We will also take a look at deposit insurance and its role in investment decisions made by financial institutions.

LINKS BETWEEN CHANGES IN THE MONEY SUPPLY AND OTHER ECONOMIC VARIABLES

How fast the money supply grows or does not grow is important because no matter what model of the economy is used, theories link the money supply growth rate to economic growth or to business fluctuations. There is in fact a long-standing relationship between changes in the money supply and changes in GDP. Some economists use this historical evidence to argue that money is an important determinant of the level of economic activity in the economy.

Another key economic variable in our economy is the price level. At least one theory attributes changes in the rate of inflation to changes in the growth rate of money in circulation. Figure 16.1 shows the relationship between the rate of growth of the money supply and the inflation rate. There seems to be a loose, albeit consistent, direct relationship between changes in the money supply and changes in the rate of inflation. Increases in the money supply growth rate seem to lead to increases in the inflation rate, after a time lag.

Figure 16.1
Money Supply Growth Versus the Inflation Rate

These time-series curves indicate a loose correspondence between money supply growth and the inflation rate. Actually, closer inspection reveals a direct relationship between changes in the growth rate of money and changes in the inflation rate *in a later period*. Increases in the rate of growth of money seem to lead to subsequent increases in the inflation rate; decreases in the rate of money growth seem to lead to subsequent reductions in the inflation rate.

Sources: Statistics Canada, *Canadian Economic Observer*, and M.C. Urquhart and K.A.H. Buckley, *Historical Statistics of Canada*.

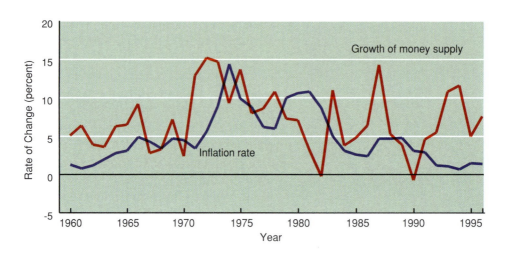

THE ORIGINS OF FRACTIONAL RESERVE BANKING

As early as 1000 BC, uncoined gold and silver were being used as money in Mesopotamia. Goldsmiths weighed and assessed the purity of those metals; later they started issuing paper notes indicating that the bearers held gold or silver of given weights and purity on deposit with the goldsmith. These notes could be transferred in exchange for goods and became the first paper currency. The gold and silver on deposit with the goldsmiths were the first bank deposits. Eventually, goldsmiths realized that the amount of gold and silver on deposit always exceeded the amount of gold and silver withdrawn—often by a predictable ratio. These goldsmiths started issuing to borrowers paper notes that exceeded in value the amount of gold and silver they actually kept on hand. They charged interest on these loans. This constituted the earliest form of what is now called **fractional reserve banking.** We know that goldsmiths operated this way in Delphi, Didyma, and Olympia in Greece as early as the seventh century BC. In Athens, fractional reserve banking was well developed by the sixth century BC.

In a fractional reserve banking system, banks do not keep sufficient reserves on hand to cover 100 percent of their depositors' accounts. And the reserves that are held by depository institutions in Canada are not kept in gold and silver, as they were with the early goldsmiths, but rather in vault cash, and in the case of the chartered banks, in the form of deposits on reserve with the Bank of Canada.

▶**Fractional reserve banking**

A system in which depository institutions hold reserves that are less than the amount of total deposits.

Try Preview Question 1:

What is a fractional reserve banking system?

RESERVES

▶ **Reserves**

In the Canadian banking system, deposits held by the chartered banks at the Bank of Canada, and vault cash.

▶ **Desired reserves**

The value of reserves that a depository institution wishes to hold in the form of vault cash or other deposits, or, in the case of the chartered banks, in the form of deposits with the Bank of Canada.

▶ **Desired reserve ratio**

The percentage of total deposits that depository institutions hold in the form of desired reserves.

▶ **Excess reserves**

The difference between actual reserves and desired reserves.

Depository institutions maintain some percentage of their customer deposits as **reserves.** Different types of depository institutions hold different percentages of reserves. Normally, the larger the institution, the larger the desired reserves. On chequing accounts, most depository institutions will keep 10 percent as reserves.

Take a hypothetical example. If the desired level of reserves is 10 percent and the bank[1] has $1 billion in customer chequing deposits, it will hold at least $100 million as reserves. These can be either deposits with the Bank of Canada or vault cash. Credit unions and trust companies, because they cannot hold reserves in the Bank of Canada, usually maintain accounts with the chartered banks that can act as reserves. The following discussion will focus on the chartered banks, but could be broadened to include the near banks as well. There are two distinguishable types of reserves: desired and excess.

1. *Desired reserves.* **Desired reserves** are the *minimum* amount of reserves—vault cash plus deposits with the Bank of Canada—that a depository institution wishes to hold to back its chequable deposits. They are expressed as a ratio of desired reserves to total chequable deposits (banks do not necessarily hold reserves on nonchequable deposits). The **desired reserve ratio** tends to be about 10 percent.

2. *Excess reserves.* Banks often hold reserves in excess of what they wish to hold. This difference between actual reserves and desired reserves is called **excess reserves.** Excess reserves can be negative, but they rarely are. (Negative excess reserves indicate that banks do not have sufficient reserves to meet their desired level. When this happens, they borrow from the Bank of Canada, sell assets such as securities, or call in loans.) Excess reserves are an important potential determinant of the rate of growth of the money supply, for as we shall see, it is only to the extent that banks have excess reserves that they can make new loans. Because reserves produce no income, profit-seeking financial institutions have an incentive to minimize excess reserves. They use them either to purchase income-producing securities or to make loans with which they earn income through interest payments received. In equation form, we can define excess reserves in this way:

$$\text{Excess reserves} = \text{actual reserves} - \text{desired reserves}$$

In the analysis that follows, we examine the relationship between the level of reserves and the size of the money supply. This analysis implies that factors influencing the level of the reserves of the banking system as a whole will ultimately affect the level of the money supply, other things held constant. We show first that when someone deposits in one depository institution a cheque that is written on another depository institution, the two banks involved are individually affected, but the overall money supply does not change. Then we show that when someone

---

[1] The term *bank* is used interchangeably with the term *depository institution* in this chapter because distinctions among financial institutions are becoming less and less meaningful. However, only the chartered banks keep reserves at the Bank of Canada, so the Bank of Canada only directly affects money creation at chartered banks.

deposits in a depository institution a cheque written on the Bank of Canada, a multiple expansion in the money supply results.

Concepts in Brief

- Ours is a fractional reserve banking system in which depository institutions hold only a percentage of their deposits as reserves, either as vault cash or, in the case of the chartered banks, on deposit with the Bank of Canada.
- Desired reserves are usually expressed as a ratio, in percentage terms, of desired reserves to total deposits.

THE RELATIONSHIP BETWEEN RESERVES AND TOTAL DEPOSITS

To show the relationship between reserves and depository institution deposits, we first analyse a single bank (existing alongside many others). A single bank is able to make new loans to its customers only to the extent that it has reserves above the desired level for covering the new deposits. When an individual bank has no excess reserves, it cannot make loans.

How a Single Bank Reacts to an Increase in Reserves

▶ **Balance sheet**

A statement of the assets and liabilities of any business entity, including financial institutions and the Bank of Canada. Assets are what is owned; liabilities are what is owed.

To examine the **balance sheet** of a single bank after its reserves are increased, the following assumptions are made:

1. The desired reserve ratio is 10 percent for all chequable deposits; that is, the bank holds an amount equal to 10 percent of all chequable deposits in reserve at the Bank of Canada or in vault cash.
2. Chequable deposits are the bank's only liabilities; reserves at the Bank of Canada and loans are the bank's only assets. Loans are promises made by customers to repay some amount in the future; that is, they are IOUs and as such are assets of the bank.
3. An individual bank can lend all it wants at current market interest rates.
4. Every time a loan is made to an individual (consumer or business), all the proceeds from the loan are put into a chequing account; no cash (currency or coins) is withdrawn.
5. Chartered banks seek to keep their excess reserves at a zero level because reserves at the Bank of Canada do not earn interest. (Chartered banks and near banks are run to make profits; we assume that all depository institutions wish to convert excess reserves that do not pay interest into interest-bearing loans.)

Look at the simplified initial position of the bank in Balance Sheet 16.1. Liabilities consist of $1 million in chequable deposits. Assets consist of $100,000 in reserves, which you can see are the desired reserves in the form of vault cash or deposits in the institution's reserve account at the Bank of Canada, and $900,000 in loans to customers. Total assets of $1 million equal total liabilities of $1 million. With a 10 percent reserve and $1 million in chequable deposits, the bank has the actual desired level of reserves of $100,000 and no excess reserves. The simplifying assumption here is that the bank has a zero net worth. A depository institution rarely has a **net worth** of more than a small percentage of its total assets.

▶ **Net worth**
The difference between assets and liabilities.

Balance Sheet 16.1 **Bank 1**	Assets			Liabilities	
	Total reserves		$100,000	Chequable deposits	$1,000,000
	Desired reserves	$100,000			
	Excess reserves	0			
	Loans		900,000		
	Total		$1,000,000	Total	$1,000,000

Assume that a *new* depositor writes a $100,000 cheque drawn on another depository institution and deposits it in Bank 1. Chequing deposits in Bank 1 immediately increase by $100,000, bringing the total to $1.1 million. Once the cheque clears, total reserves of Bank 1 increase to $200,000. A $1.1 million total in chequing deposits means that desired reserves will have to be 10 percent of $1.1 million, or $110,000. Bank 1 now has excess reserves equal to $200,000 minus $110,000, or $90,000. This is shown in Balance Sheet 16.2.

Balance Sheet 16.2 **Bank 1**	Assets			Liabilities	
	Total reserves		$200,000	Chequable deposits	$1,100,000
	Desired reserves	$110,000			
	Excess reserves	90,000			
	Loans		900,000		
	Total		$1,100,000	Total	$1,100,000

Look at excess reserves in Balance Sheet 16.2. Excess reserves were zero before the $100,000 deposit, and now they are $90,000—that's $90,000 worth of assets not earning any income. By assumption, Bank 1 will now lend out this entire $90,000 in excess reserves in order to obtain interest income. Loans will increase to $990,000. The borrowers who receive the new loans will not leave them on deposit in Bank 1. After all, they borrow money to spend it. As they spend it by writing cheques that are deposited in other banks, actual reserves will fall to $110,000 (as planned), and excess reserves will again become zero, as indicated in Balance Sheet 16.3.

Balance Sheet 16.3
Bank 1

Assets			Liabilities	
Total reserves		$110,000	Chequable deposits	$1,100,000
Desired reserves	$110,000			
Excess reserves	0			
Loans		990,000		
Total		$1,100,000	Total	$1,100,000

In this example, a person deposited an additional $100,000 cheque drawn on another bank. That $100,000 became part of the reserves of Bank 1. Because that deposit immediately created excess reserves in Bank 1, further loans were possible for Bank 1. The excess reserves were loaned out to earn interest. A bank will not lend more than its excess reserves because prudent banking practice dictates that it hold a certain amount of reserves at all times.

The maximum amount of new deposits that any one bank can create is equal to its excess reserves.

Effect on the Money Supply.   A look at the balance sheets for Bank 1 might give the impression that the money supply increased because of the new customer's $100,000 deposit. Remember, though, that the deposit was a cheque written on *another* bank. Therefore, the other bank suffered a *decline* in its chequing deposits and its reserves. While total assets and liabilities in Bank 1 have increased by $100,000, they have *decreased* in the other bank by $100,000. The *total* amount of money and credit in the economy is unaffected by the transfer of funds from one bank to another.

To see what happens to the overall money supply when funds are transferred from one bank to another, look at Balance Sheet 16.4. Assume that the $100,000 cheque was written on Bank 2 and that before the cheque cleared Bank 2 had assets and liabilities the same as those in Balance Sheet 16.1. What does Bank 2's balance sheet look like after the cheque has cleared? Chequable deposits have decreased by the amount of the $100,000 cheque and reserves are the desired $90,000. However, when the cheque cleared, Bank 2 found itself with zero reserves and had to call in $90,000 in loans to make its actual reserves meet the desired level. Thus Bank 1's increase in chequable deposits is exactly offset by Bank 2's decrease, leaving the money supply unaffected.

Balance Sheet 16.4
Bank 2

Assets			Liabilities	
Total reserves		$90,000	Chequable deposits	$900,000
Desired reserves	$90,000			
Excess reserves	0			
Loans		810,000		
Total		$900,000	Total	$900,000

Try Preview Question 2:
What happens to the total money supply when a person deposits in one depository institution a cheque drawn on another depository institution?

The thing to remember is that new reserves are not created when cheques written on one bank are deposited in another bank. The Bank of Canada can, however, create new reserves; that is the subject of the next section.

THE BANK OF CANADA'S DIRECT EFFECT ON THE OVERALL LEVEL OF RESERVES

Now we examine the Bank of Canada's direct effect on the level of reserves. An explanation of how a change in the level of reserves causes a multiple change in the total money supply follows. The Bank of Canada essentially determines the level of reserves in the monetary system.

Open Market Operations

▶ **Open market operations**
The purchase and sale of existing Canadian government securities (such as bonds) in the open private market by the Bank of Canada.

Open market operations are the purchase and sale of *existing* government securities in the open market (the private secondary Canadian securities market) by the Bank of Canada in order to change the money supply.

A Sample Transaction

Assume that the Bank of Canada decides to purchase $100,000 worth of Canadian government securities. The Bank pays for these securities by writing a cheque on itself for $100,000. This cheque is given to the bond dealer in exchange for the $100,000 worth of bonds. The bond dealer deposits the $100,000 cheque in its chequing account at a bank, which then sends the $100,000 cheque back to the Bank of Canada. When the Bank of Canada receives the cheque, it adds $100,000 to the reserve account of the bank that sent it the cheque. The Bank of Canada has created $100,000 of reserves. It can create reserves because it has the ability to "write up" (add to) the reserve accounts of the chartered banks whenever it buys Canadian securities. When the Bank of Canada buys a government security in the open market, it initially expands total reserves and the money supply by the amount of the purchase.

Using Balance Sheets. Consider the balance sheets of the Bank of Canada and of a chartered bank receiving the cheque. Balance Sheet 16.5 shows the results for the Bank of Canada after the bond purchase and for the bank after the bond dealer deposits the $100,000 cheque. The Bank of Canada's balance sheet (which here reflects only account *changes*) shows that after the purchase, its assets have increased by $100,000 in the form of Canadian government securities. Liabilities have also increased by $100,000 in the form of an increase in the reserve account of the bank. The balance sheet for the chartered bank shows an increase in assets of $100,000 in the form of reserves with the Bank of Canada. The bank also has an increase in its liabilities in the form of $100,000 in the chequing account of the bond dealer; this is an immediate $100,000 increase in the money supply.

Balance Sheet 16.5
Balance sheets for the Bank of Canada and a chartered bank when a Canadian government security is purchased by the Bank of Canada, showing changes in assets and liabilities.

The Bank of Canada		Chartered Bank	
Assets	Liabilities	Assets	Liabilities
+$100,000 Canadian government securities	+$100,000 chartered bank's reserves	+$100,000 reserves	+$100,000 chequing deposit owned by bond dealer

Sale of a $100,000 Canadian Government Security by the Bank of Canada

The process is reversed when the Bank of Canada sells a Canadian government security from its portfolio. When the individual or institution buying the security from the Bank of Canada writes a cheque for $100,000, the Bank of Canada reduces the reserves of the chartered bank on which the cheque was written. The $100,000 sale of the Canadian government security leads to a reduction in reserves in the banking system.

Balance Sheet 16.6 shows the results for the sale of a Canadian government security by the Bank of Canada. When the $100,000 cheque goes to the Bank of Canada, it reduces by $100,000 the reserve account of the chartered bank on which the cheque is written. The Bank of Canada's assets are also reduced by $100,000 because it no longer owns the Canadian government security. The bank's liabilities are reduced by $100,000 when that amount is deducted from the account of the bond purchaser, and the money supply is thereby reduced by that amount. The chartered bank's assets are also reduced by $100,000 because the Bank of Canada has reduced its reserves by that amount.

Balance Sheet 16.6
Balance sheets after the Bank of Canada has sold $100,000 of Canadian government securities, showing changes only.

The Bank of Canada		Chartered Bank	
Assets	Liabilities	Assets	Liabilities
−$100,000 Canadian government securities	−$100,000 chartered bank's reserves	−$100,000 reserves	−$100,000 chequing deposit owned by bond dealer

Concepts in Brief

- If a cheque is written on one depository institution and deposited in another, there is no change in total deposits or in the total money supply. No new reserves have been created.
- The Bank of Canada can directly increase chartered banks' reserves by purchasing Canadian government securities in the open market; it can decrease chartered banks' reserves by selling Canadian government securities in the open market.

MONEY EXPANSION BY THE BANKING SYSTEM

Consider now the entire banking system. For practical purposes, we can look at all depository institutions taken as a whole. To understand how money is created, we must understand how depository institutions respond to Bank of Canada actions that increase reserves in the entire system.

Bank of Canada Purchases of Canadian Government Securities

Assume that the Bank of Canada purchases a $100,000 Canadian government security from a bond dealer. The bond dealer deposits the $100,000 cheque in Bank 1 (which started out in the position depicted in Balance Sheet 16.1 on page 389). The cheque, however, is not written on another depository institution; rather, it is written on the Bank of Canada itself.

Look at the balance sheet for Bank 1 shown in Balance Sheet 16.7. It is the same as Balance Sheet 16.2. Reserves have been increased by $100,000 to $200,000, and chequable deposits have also been increased by $100,000. Because the desired reserves on $1.1 million of chequable deposits are only $110,000, there is $90,000 in excess reserves.

	Assets		Liabilities	
Balance Sheet 16.7 **Bank 1**				
	Total reserves	$200,000	Chequable deposits	$1,100,000
	Desired reserves	$110,000		
	Excess reserves	90,000		
	Loans	900,000		
	Total	$1,100,000	Total	$1,100,000

Effect on the Money Supply. The major difference between this example and the one given previously is that here the money supply has increased by $100,000 immediately. Why? Because chequing deposits held by the public—the bond dealers are members of the public—are part of the money supply, *and no other bank has lost reserves*. Thus the purchase of a $100,000 Canadian government security by the Bank of Canada from the public (a bond dealer or a bank) increases the money supply immediately by $100,000.

Not the End of the Process. The process of money creation does not stop here. Look again at Balance Sheet 16.7. Bank 1 has excess reserves of $90,000. No other depository institution (or combination of depository institutions) has negative excess reserves of $90,000 as a result of the Bank of Canada's bond purchase. (Remember, the Bank of Canada simply created the money to pay for the bond purchase.)

Bank 1 will not wish to hold non-interest-bearing excess reserves. It will expand its loans by creating deposits equal to $90,000. This is shown in Balance Sheet 16.8, which is exactly like Balance Sheet 16.3, except there has been no corresponding reduction in loans at any other depository institution.

Balance Sheet 16.8
Bank 1

Assets			Liabilities	
Total reserves		$110,000	Chequable deposits	$1,100,000
Desired reserves	$110,000			
Excess reserves	0			
Loans		990,000		
Total		$1,100,000	Total	$1,100,000

The individuals who have received the $90,000 of new loans will spend (write cheques on) these funds, which will then be deposited in other banks. To make this example simple, assume that the $90,000 in excess reserves was loaned to a single firm for the purpose of buying a Burger King franchise. After the firm buys the franchise, Burger King deposits the $90,000 cheque in its account at Bank 2. For the sake of simplicity, ignore the previous assets and liabilities in Bank 2 and concentrate only on the balance sheet *changes* resulting from this new deposit, as shown in Balance Sheet 16.9. A plus sign indicates that the entry has increased, and a minus sign indicates that the entry has decreased. For the depository institution, Bank 2, the $90,000 deposit, after the cheque has been sent to the Bank of Canada, becomes an increase in reserves (assets) as well as an increase in chequing deposits (liabilities) and hence the money supply. Because the desired reserve ratio is 10 percent, or $9,000, Bank 2 will have excess reserves of $81,000. But, of course, excess reserves are not income-producing, so Bank 2 will reduce them to zero by making loans of $81,000 (which will earn interest income) by creating deposits for borrowers equal to $81,000. This is shown in Balance Sheet 16.10.

Balance Sheet 16.9
Bank 2 (changes only)

Assets			Liabilities	
Total reserves		+$90,000	New chequable deposits	+$90,000
Desired reserves	$9,000			
Excess reserves	+81,000			
Total		+$90,000	Total	+$90,000

Balance Sheet 16.10
Bank 2 (changes only)

Assets			Liabilities	
Total reserves		$9,000	Chequable deposits	$90,000
Desired reserves	$9,000			
Excess reserves	0			
Loans		+81,000		
Total		$90,000	Total	$90,000

Remember that in this example, the original $100,000 deposit was a cheque issued by the Bank of Canada to the bond dealer. That $100,000 constituted an immediate increase in the money supply of $100,000 when deposited in the bond dealer's chequing account. The deposit creation process (in addition to the original $100,000) occurs because of the fractional reserve banking system, coupled with the desire of depository institutions to maintain a minimum level of excess reserves.

Continuation of the Deposit Creation Process. Assume that the company that has received the $81,000 loan from Bank 2 wants to buy into an oil-drilling firm. This oil-drilling firm has an account at Bank 3. Look at Bank 3's simplified account in Balance Sheet 16.11, where, again, only changes in the assets and liabilities are shown. When the firm borrowing from Bank 2 pays the $81,000 to the oil-drilling firm's owner, the owner deposits the cheque in Bank 3; chequable deposits and the money supply increase by $81,000. Total reserves of Bank 3 rise by that amount when the cheque is sent to the Bank of Canada.

Balance Sheet 16.11
Bank 3 (changes only)

Assets			Liabilities	
Total reserves		+$81,000	New chequable deposits	+$81,000
Desired reserves	$8,100			
Excess reserves	+72,900			
Total		+$81,000	Total	+$81,000

Because the desired reserve ratio is 10 percent, desired reserves rise by $8,100, and excess reserves are therefore $72,900. Bank 3 will want to lend those non-interest-earning assets (excess reserves). When it does, loans (in the form of created chequing deposits) will increase by $72,900. This bank's total reserves will fall to $8,100, and excess reserves become zero as the oil-drilling firm's manager writes cheques on the new deposit. This is shown in Balance Sheet 16.12.

Balance Sheet 16.12
Bank 3 (changes only)

Assets			Liabilities	
Total reserves		$8,100	Chequable deposits	$81,000
Desired reserves	$8,100			
Excess reserves	0			
Loans		+72,900		
Total		$81,000	Total	$81,000

Progression to Other Banks.   This process continues to Banks 4, 5, 6, and so on. Each bank obtains smaller and smaller increases in deposits because 10 percent of each deposit is held in reserves; therefore, each succeeding depository institution makes correspondingly smaller loans. Table 16.1 shows the new deposits, possible loans, and desired reserves for the remaining depository institutions in the system.

Effect on Total Deposits.   In this simple example, deposits increased initially by the $100,000 that the Bank of Canada paid the bond dealer in exchange for a bond. They were further increased by a $90,000 deposit in Bank 2, and they were again increased by an $81,000 deposit in Bank 3. Eventually, total deposits will increase by $1 million, as shown in Table 16.1. The money multiplier process is portrayed graphically in Figure 16.2.

Figure 16.2
The Multiple Expansion in the Money Supply Due to $100,000 in New Reserves When the Desired Reserve Ratio Is 10 Percent

The banks are all aligned in decreasing order of new deposits created. Bank 1 receives the $100,000 in new reserves and lends out $90,000. Bank 2 receives the $90,000 and lends out $81,000. The process continues through Banks 3 to 19 and then the rest of the banking system. Ultimately, assuming no leakages, the $100,000 of new reserves results in an increase in the money supply of $1,000,000, or 10 times the new reserves, because the desired reserve ratio is 10 percent.

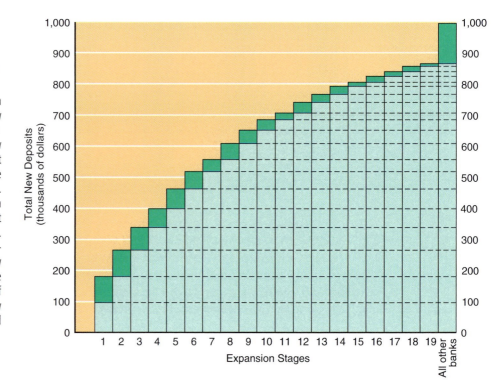

Table 16.1
Maximum Money Creation with 10 Percent Desired Reserves

This table shows the maximum new loans plus investments that banks can make, given the Bank of Canada's deposit of a $100,000 cheque in Bank 1. The desired reserve ratio is 10 percent. We assume that all excess reserves in each bank are used for new loans or investments.

Bank	New Deposits (new reserves)	New Desired Reserves	Maximum New Loans plus Investments (excess reserves)
1	$100,000 (from the Bank of Canada)	$10,000	$90,000
2	90,000	9,000	81,000
3	81,000	8,100	72,900
4	72,900	7,290	65,610
.	.	.	.
.	.	.	.
.	.	.	.
All other banks	656,100	65,610	590,490
	Totals $1,000,000	$100,000	$900,000

Increase in Overall Reserves

Even with fractional reserve banking, if there are zero excess reserves, deposits cannot expand unless overall reserves are increased. The original new deposit in Bank 1, in our example, was in the form of a cheque written on the Bank of Canada. It therefore represented new reserves to the banking system. Had that cheque been written on Bank 3, by contrast, nothing would have happened to the total amount of chequable deposits; there would have been no change in the total money supply. To repeat: Cheques written on banks within the system represent assets and liabilities that simply cancel each other out. Only when excess reserves are created by the Bank of Canada, or when new deposits from outside Canada are made, can the money supply increase.

In our example, the depository institutions use their excess reserves to make loans. It is not important how they put the money back into the system. If they bought certificates of deposit or any other security, the analysis would be the same because the party they bought those securities from would receive a cheque from the purchasing depository institution. The recipient of the cheque would then deposit it into its own depository institution. The deposit expansion process would be the same as we have already outlined.

You should be able to work through the foregoing example to show the reverse process when there is a decrease in reserves because the Bank of Canada sells a $100,000 government security. The result is a multiple contraction of deposits and therefore of the total money supply in circulation.

Try Preview Question 3:

What happens to the overall money supply when a person who sells a Canadian government security to the Bank of Canada places the proceeds in a depository institution?

Concepts in Brief

- When reserves are increased by the Bank of Canada through a purchase of Canadian government securities, the result is a multiple expansion of deposits and therefore of the money supply.
- When the Bank of Canada reduces the banking system's reserves by selling government securities, the result is a multiple contraction of deposits and therefore of the money supply.

THE MONEY MULTIPLIER

In the example just given, a $100,000 increase in reserves generated by the Bank of Canada's purchase of a security yielded a $1 million increase in total deposits; deposits increased by a multiple of 10 times the initial $100,000 increase in overall reserves. Conversely, a $100,000 decrease in reserves generated by the Bank of Canada's sale of a security will yield a $1 million decrease in total deposits; they will decrease by a multiple of 10 times the initial $100,000 decrease in overall reserves. We can now make a generalization about the extent to which the money supply will change when the banking system's reserves are increased or decreased. The maximum amount of new deposits that the banking system can create is equal to a multiple of its excess reserves. If we assume that no excess reserves are kept and that all loan proceeds are deposited in depository institutions in the system, the following equation applies:

$$\text{Potential money multiplier} = \frac{1}{\text{desired reserve ratio}}$$

▶ **Money multiplier**

The reciprocal of the desired reserve ratio, assuming no leakages into currency and no excess reserves. It is equal to 1 divided by the desired reserve ratio.

The **money multiplier** gives the *maximum* potential change in the money supply due to a change in reserves. The actual change in the money supply—currency plus chequable account balances—will be less than the potential multiplier because of leakages from the money creation process.

Forces That Reduce the Money Multiplier

We made a number of simplifying assumptions to come up with the potential money multiplier. In the real world, the actual money multiplier is considerably smaller. Several factors account for this.

Leakages.   The entire loan (cheque) from one bank is not always deposited in another bank. At least two leakages can occur:

- *Currency drains.* When deposits increase, the public may want to hold more currency. Currency that is kept in a person's wallet remains outside the banking system and cannot be held by banks as reserves from which to make loans. The greater the amount of cash leakage, the smaller the actual money multiplier.
- *Excess reserves.* Depository institutions may wish to maintain excess reserves. Depository institutions do not, in fact, always keep excess reserves at zero. To the extent that they want to keep positive excess reserves, the money multiplier will be smaller. A bank receiving $1 million in new deposits might, in our example with the 10 percent desired reserve ratio, keep more than $100,000 as reserves. The greater the excess reserves, the smaller the actual money multiplier. Empirically, the currency drain is more significant than the effect of excess reserves.

Real-World Money Multipliers.   The desired reserve ratio determines the maximum potential money multiplier because the reciprocal of the desired reserve ratio tells us what that is. The maximum is never attained for the money supply as a whole because of currency drains and excess reserves. Also, each definition of the money supply, M1 or M2, will yield different results for money multipliers. For several decades, the M1 multiplier has varied between 1.5 and 2.5. The M2 multiplier, however, has shown a trend upward, ranging from 2.25 at the beginning of the 1960s, to over 12.5 in the 1990s.

WAYS IN WHICH THE BANK OF CANADA CHANGES THE MONEY SUPPLY

As we have just seen, the Bank of Canada can change the money supply by directly changing reserves available to the banking system. One way it does this is by engaging in open market operations. To repeat: The purchase of a Canadian government security by the Bank of Canada results in an increase in reserves and leads to a multiple expansion in the money supply. A sale of a Canadian government security by the Bank of Canada results in a decrease in reserves and leads to a multiple contraction in the money supply.

However, the primary method the Bank of Canada uses to change the money supply is through directly increasing or decreasing reserves held by financial institutions.

▶ Redeposits
A way to increase the money supply. The Bank of Canada transfers some of its Government of Canada deposits to the reserve deposits of the chartered banks, thus increasing the available reserves at the chartered banks.

Drawdowns and Redeposits.   If the Bank of Canada wants to increase the money supply, it transfers Government of Canada deposits from its own holdings to the chartered banks (and other financial institutions). This technique, called **redepositing**, increases available reserves and allows the banks to increase their loans, and consequently, the money supply.

Conversely, if the Bank of Canada wants to decrease the money supply, it undertakes a **drawdown**, whereby it transfers Government of Canada deposits from the banks to itself, thus reducing available reserves in the banking system. Banks with no excess reserves prior to the drawdown will call in loans, thus decreasing the money supply.

▶ Drawdowns
A way to decrease the money supply. The Bank of Canada transfers some of the Government of Canada deposits at the chartered banks to its own Government of Canada deposits, thus decreasing available reserves at the chartered banks.

The Bank of Canada uses drawdowns and redeposits most frequently in its daily operations.

▶ Moral suasion
A request from the Governor of the Bank of Canada to the chartered banks to increase or decrease the amount of credit they grant in order to help the central bank increase or decrease the money supply.

Moral Suasion.   A third way the Bank of Canada can change the money supply is through **moral suasion**. If the central bank wanted to slow the money supply creation process, it could ask the CEOs of the chartered banks to limit the amount of credit they extend. The Bank of Canada has used moral suasion many times since its founding in 1936, but in general it is not a very reliable tool. It requires the chartered banks to hold more than their desired level of reserves, which constrains their ability to make profits.

Moral suasion works best when there are relatively few institutions in the financial system. This was the case earlier this century when there were only five large chartered banks. With the proliferation of credit unions, *caisses populaires* and trust companies, and with the blurring of the lines between them, moral suasion is losing its effectiveness as a technique for managing the money supply.

POLICY EXAMPLE   The Changing Determination of the Bank Rate

From its inception, the Bank of Canada has used the bank rate as a tool of monetary policy. In the early years, it would set the bank rate—the rate of interest charged on overnight loans to chartered banks—independently of market-determined rates of interest. The purpose of setting the bank rate was to indicate to financial markets the direction that the Bank of Canada wanted rates across the economy to move. If the Bank set the rate lower than market-determined rates, then it was taken as a signal that overall interest rates should move down.

The overnight loan rate used to be important for chartered banks. Until the early 1990s, the Bank of Canada determined legal reserve requirements for the banks rather than allowing them to keep a self-determined level of reserves. Consequently, if a bank on occasion found its reserves lower than required, it would have to borrow from the central bank until it could call in short-term demand loans and replenish its reserves. The rate of interest charged the chartered banks was the prevailing bank rate.

In March 1980, the Bank of Canada changed its method of setting the bank rate. Now, the rate would be set at one-quarter of one per cent above the rate determined in the weekly auction of Government of Canada three-month Treasury bills. Setting the bank rate slightly higher than prevailing short-term interest rates acted as a disincentive to the chartered banks to let their reserves fall below the legal requirement.

The 1991 *Bank Act* dispensed with legal reserve requirements. Instead, banks now hold whatever level of reserves they wish with the following exception. Banks are required to hold a minimum zero balance for cheque-clearing purposes—called a settlement balance—with the Bank of Canada. If a bank's daily cheque-clearing tally results in a negative balance, it must borrow from the Bank of Canada, at the bank rate, to bring that balance up to zero. Over the course of a month, if that bank's net settlement balance (the sum of all the surplus and deficit balances that month) is negative, then the bank must *again* borrow from the Bank of Canada to bring its monthly average to zero. If a bank incurs a negative daily settlement balance, then there exists a strong incentive to hold a surplus shortly thereafter to avoid having to borrow from the central bank *twice*. The opportunity cost of holding excess reserve balances in their settlement accounts acts as an incentive to the banks to minimize their excess reserve balances. However, the opportunity cost of incurring negative settlement balances—i.e., the bank rate—is usually enough for the banks to ensure they do not frequently fall into this situation.

In mid-1994, the Bank of Canada again made a change: the bank rate would be set within one-half of one per cent of the weekly rate charged on overnight loans. The Bank thought this to be a better determination than using the three-month rate, since the loans it makes to financial market players are very short-term, mostly just overnight.

Early in 1996, the Bank of Canada discontinued the practice of setting the rate one-half of one per cent above the market-determined overnight loan rate, and now keeps its bank rate within one-half of one percent of an announced interest rate. Any banks or other financial institutions which borrow overnight funds pay the upper limit of this operating band. Once again, these announcements are serving mainly as a signal to financial markets of central bank intentions regarding interest rate trends.

For critical analysis: Why did the Bank of Canada insist that chartered banks keep their reserves at required levels by borrowing to cover shortfalls?

Concepts in Brief

- The maximum money multiplier is equal to the reciprocal of the desired reserve ratio.
- The actual multiplier is much less than the maximum money multiplier because of currency drains and excess reserves voluntarily held by banks.
- The Bank of Canada changes the money supply in three ways: (1) It can change reserves and hence the money supply through open market operations in which it buys and sells existing Canadian government securities. (2) It can conduct drawdowns and redeposits. (3) It can use moral suasion on the chartered banks.

DEPOSIT INSURANCE AND FLAWED BANK REGULATION

When businesses fail, they create hardships for creditors, owners, workers, and customers. But when a depository institution fails, an even greater hardship results because many individuals and businesses depend on the safety and security of banks. While Canada has a history of relatively few bank failures, we are not immune to them. Between 1967 and 1989 there were 23 failures, and there have been a further 22 failures since then. However, when compared to the American experience of 1,065 failures between 1985 and 1993, the Canadian record looks quite good.

▶ **Canadian Deposit Insurance Corporation (CDIC)**

A government agency that insures the deposits held in federally incorporated financial institutions.

Nevertheless, in 1967 the federal government set up the **Canadian Deposit Insurance Corporation (CDIC)** to protect small investors who do not have the resources to accurately assess the soundness of federally incorporated financial institutions. Credit unions now have similar deposit insurance through their own institutions.

The Need for Deposit Insurance

▶ **Bank runs**

Attempts by many of a bank's depositors to convert chequing and time deposits into currency out of fear for the bank's solvency.

The CDIC was established to mitigate the primary cause of bank failures, **bank runs**—the simultaneous rush of depositors to convert their demand deposits or time deposits into currency.

Consider the following scenario. A bank begins to look shaky; its assets may not seem sufficient to cover its liabilities. If the bank has no deposit insurance, depositors in this bank (and any banks associated with it) will all want to withdraw their money from the bank at the same time. Their concern is that this shaky bank will not have enough money to return their deposits to them in the form of currency. Indeed, this is what happens in a bank failure when insurance doesn't exist. Just as with the failure of a regular business, the creditors of the bank may not all get paid, or if they do, they will get paid less than 100 percent of what they are owed. Depositors are creditors of a bank because their funds are on loan to the bank. In a fractional reserve banking system, banks do not hold 100 percent of their depositors' money in the form of reserves. Consequently, all depositors cannot withdraw all their money at the same time. It would be desirable to assure depositors that they can have their deposits converted into cash when they wish, no matter how serious the financial situation of the bank.

The CDIC provides this assurance. By insuring deposits, the CDIC bolsters trust in the banking system and provides depositors with the incentive to leave their deposits with the bank, even in the face of rumours of bank failures. In 1967, it was sufficient for the CDIC to cover each account up to $20,000. The current maximum is $60,000.

All financial institutions insured by the CDIC pay the same premium—one-sixth of one percent of insured deposits. The Canadian Bankers' Association opposes this method of determining premiums as it claims that the large chartered banks are at much less risk of failing than smaller financial institutions. If, for example, economic conditions led to widespread loan defaults in British Columbia, the chartered banks could rely on their more profitable operations in the rest of the country to keep them solvent. Smaller trust and mortgage loan companies do not have that option and consequently are at greater risk of failing. The CBA believes that those smaller companies should pay higher premiums to match their higher risk.

A Flaw in the Deposit Insurance Scheme

Because deposit insurance premiums are not based on the degree of risk of the depository institution's investments, there is no reward for investing in relatively non-risky assets. The result is that bankers have an incentive to invest in more high-yield assets, which carry more risk, than they would if there were no deposit insurance. Thus the premium rate is artificially low, permitting institution managers to obtain deposits at less than market price (because depositors will accept a lower interest payment on insured deposits); and even if the institution's portfolio becomes riskier, its deposit insurance premium does not rise. Consequently, depository institution managers can increase their net interest margin by using lower-cost insured deposits to purchase higher-yield, higher-risk assets. The gains to risk taking accrue to the managers and stockholders of the depository institutions; the losses go to the deposit insurer (and, as we will see, ultimately to taxpayers).

To combat the inherent flaws in the financial institution industry and in the deposit insurance system, a vast regulatory apparatus was installed. The CDIC was given regulatory powers to offset the risk-taking temptations to depository institution managers; those powers included the ability to require sound business practices by the insured institutions.

Deposit Insurance, Adverse Selection, and Moral Hazard

▶ **Asymmetric information**
Information possessed by one side of a transaction but not the other. The side with more information will be at an advantage.

When financial transactions take place, one party often does not have all the knowledge needed about the other party to make correct decisions. This is known as the problem of **asymmetric information**. For example, borrowers generally know more than lenders about the returns and risks associated with the investment projects they intend to undertake.

▶ **Adverse selection**

A problem created by asymmetric information prior to a transaction. Individuals who are the most undesirable from the other party's point of view end up being the ones who are most likely to want to engage in a particular financial transaction, such as borrowing.

Adverse Selection.   **Adverse selection** arises when there is asymmetric information before a transaction takes place. In financial markets, it often occurs because individuals and firms that are worse credit risks than they appear to be are the ones most willing to borrow at any given interest rate. This willingness makes them likely to be selected by lenders, yet their inferior ability to repay (relative to the interest rate being charged) means that loans to them more often yield adverse outcomes for lenders (default). The potential risks of adverse selection make lenders less likely to lend to anyone, and more inclined to charge higher interest rates when they do lend.

Adverse selection is often a problem when insurance is involved because people or firms that are relatively poor risks are sometimes able to disguise that fact from insurers. It is instructive to examine the way this works with the deposit insurance provided by the CDIC. Deposit insurance shields depositors from the potential adverse effects of risky decisions and so makes depositors willing to accept riskier investment strategies by their banks. Clearly, this encourages more high-flying, risk-loving entrepreneurs to become managers of banks. The consequences for the CDIC—and often for the taxpayer—are larger losses.

▶ **Moral hazard**

A situation in which, after a transaction has taken place, one of the parties to the transaction has an incentive to engage in behaviour that will be undesirable from the other party's point of view.

Moral Hazard.   **Moral hazard** arises as the result of information asymmetry after a transaction has occurred. In financial markets, lenders face the hazard that borrowers may engage in activities that are contrary to the lender's interest and thus might be said to be immoral from the lender's perspective. For example, because lenders do not share in the profits of business ventures, they generally want borrowers to agree to invest prudently. Yet once the loan has been made, borrower-investors have an incentive to invest in high-risk, high-return projects because they are able to keep all of the extra profits if the projects succeed. Such behaviour subjects the lender to greater hazards than are being compensated for under the terms of the loan agreement.

Moral hazard is also an important phenomenon in the presence of insurance contracts, such as the deposit insurance provided by the CDIC. Insured depositors know that they will not suffer losses if their bank fails. Hence they have little incentive to monitor their bank's investment activities or to punish their bank by withdrawing their funds if the bank assumes too much risk. Thus insured banks have incentives to take on more risks than they otherwise would—and with those risks come higher losses for the CDIC and for taxpayers.

Try Preview Question 4:
How does the existence of deposit insurance affect a financial institution's choice of risky versus nonrisky assets?

Thinking Critically About the Media   Bailouts That Cost Taxpayers Millions

When the Canadian Commercial Bank failed in 1985, the media alarmed us with inflated figures of how much the Canadian taxpayer was paying to bail out this bank. The same sorts of numbers are being bandied about for the potential bailout of banks in Japan. Although technically not inaccurate, such stories fail to point out that such bailouts always occur *after the fact*. The billion or so dollars lost by the Canadian Commercial Bank had already been lost by the time of the bailout. That is to say, the economy had already seen a $1 bil-

lion reduction in its wealth because of bad investments by the Canadian Commercial Bank. The same is now true for the Japanese economy. The investments made by Japanese banks that turned sour will not magically increase in value if the Japanese government decides to use taxpayers' money to bail out the banks. Banking rescue plans as such are simply a determination of who will bear losses that have already occurred.

INTERNATIONAL POLICY EXAMPLE
Will the Japanese Bail Out Their Banks?

Japan is facing a banking crisis that makes recent bank failures in Canada look like child's play. The policy question is how the Japanese government is going to bail out the banking system there. The Japanese banks in the mid-1990s held problem loans equal to about $1 trillion, or a quarter of Japan's GDP. Japanese authorities continued to allow banks to lend problem debtors enough money to cover unpaid interest. If the Japanese government chooses to bail out its banking system, the estimated cost will be close to $400 billion. Alternatively, the Japanese government could simply let the weakest banks go bankrupt. Some observers believe that a third solution will eventually come about: The Japanese government will pour in enough reserves to shore up the banking system in exchange for the nation's banks' agreeing to use all of their profits for the foreseeable future to write off bad debts. In the fall of 1995, the largest credit union in Japan, Cosmo Credit Corporation, failed. The Bank of Japan (Japan's central bank) stepped in and prevented a panic. By the time you read this, many more such interventions by the Bank of Japan will almost certainly have occurred.

For critical analysis: Who pays for the Japanese banking bailout if the "third way" is chosen?

Concepts in Brief

- Federal deposit insurance was created in 1967 when the Canadian Deposit Insurance Corporation (CDIC) was founded to insure deposits in federally incorporated depository institutions.
- Credit unions and *caisses populaires* have their own deposit insurance schemes.
- Deposit insurance was designed to prevent bank runs in which individual demand deposit and savings deposit holders attempt to turn their deposits into currency.
- Because of the way deposit insurance is set up in Canada, it encourages bank managers to invest in riskier assets to make higher rates of returns.

Issues and Applications

Deregulating the Financial Services Industry

Concepts Applied: Regulation, deregulation

Deregulation of the financial services industry is paving the way for new kinds of banks in Canada. Here, Bob Quart, CEO of Vancity Credit Union, shows off the control centre for its "virtual bank's" computer system.

Over the early years of this century, Canada created an array of regulations which constrained the behaviour of the financial services industry. Only banks could grant commercial mortgages, only licensed brokerage firms could sell stocks, only insurance companies could sell life insurance. But recently, the trend has been towards deregulation resulting in "one-stop shopping" for financial services.

Deregulation Step-by-Step

The first of a series of moves towards blurring the lines between financial intermediaries came in 1987 when chartered banks were given permission to acquire investment dealers. While the banks themselves could not sell stocks and bonds, their wholly-owned subsidiaries could.

In 1992, the insurance business was deregulated. Banks and trust and insurance companies are now allowed to carry out most of each other's business functions. For the banks, which previously could sell only mortgage insurance, this was a big step. They could now sell life insurance, property and accident insurance, and travel insurance, again through subsidiaries.

Consequently, in 1996, National Bank, which operates primarily in Quebec, joined forces with New York-based Metropolitan Life Insurance Co. to form National Bank Financial Services. Former bank employees now also sell insurance, while former insurance salespeople have added mortgages to their product lines.

Also in 1996, the Royal Bank of Canada teamed up with IBM and 60 US banks to offer its services via the Internet. This electronic network allows Royal Bank customers to transfer money, pay bills, purchase airline tickets, and trade stocks by computer from their homes.

In a futuristic application of electronic technology to banking, Vancouver City Savings Credit Union, one of Canada's largest, purchased Citizens Trust which it converted to a bank. However, this bank has no branches where customers talk over financial matters with their bankers. All business—from depositing and withdrawing money to applying for mortgages—is conducted electronically through the Internet or at ATMs.

More Changes to Come

A review of the Bank Act occurred in 1997. Prior to the review, the financial services industry lobbied the government for changes it wanted to see. The chartered banks hoped to get into the highly profitable business of automobile leasing, currently dominated by General Motors Acceptance Corporation and General Electric Capital Leasing. They also wanted to sell insurance at the branch level.

Independent investment dealers for their part wanted to expand the services they could offer investors by offering chequable deposit accounts with ATM cards for increased access. Investment brokers claimed it would simplify the brokerage business if clients could keep sums of money in accounts with the firms, and dealers could simply transfer the funds between clients' accounts.

Deregulation must be good for business at the Big Six chartered banks. In recent years their profits have been in the billions of dollars each.

For Critical Analysis

1. The term "nonbank bank" has been used a lot recently. What do you think it means?

2. Would there be an increased moral hazard problem associated with deposit insurance if banks were allowed to do everything—sell insurance, stocks and bonds, and airline tickets, plus everything else a bank does?

CHAPTER SUMMARY

1. Chartered banks maintain reserves, which consist of deposits in the Bank of Canada plus vault cash. Other financial institutions maintain reserves of deposits, sometimes in the chartered banks, and vault cash.

2. When depository institutions have more reserves than are desired, they are said to have excess reserves.

3. The Bank of Canada can control the money supply through open market operations—by buying and selling Canadian government securities.

4. When the Bank of Canada buys a bond, it pays for the bond by writing a cheque on itself. This creates additional reserves for the banking system. The result will be an increase in the money supply that is a multiple of the value of the bond purchased. If the Bank of Canada sells a bond, it reduces reserves in the banking system. The result will be a decrease in the money supply that is a multiple of the value of the bond sold.

5. Single depository institutions that have no excess reserves cannot alter the money supply.

6. The banking system as a whole can change the money supply pursuant to a change in reserves brought about by a Bank of Canada purchase or sale of government bonds. The Bank of Canada can also change the money supply by undertaking drawdowns or redeposits, or by using moral suasion.

7. The maximum money multiplier is equal to the reciprocal of the desired reserve ratio.

8. The actual money multiplier will be less than the maximum because of leakages—currency drains and excess reserve holdings of some banks.

9. The Canadian Deposit Insurance Corporation was created in 1967 to insure deposits in federally incorporated depository institutions. Credit unions and *caisses populaires* have their own system of deposit insurance. Because of the existence of deposit insurance, the probability of a run on the banking system, even if a significant number of depository institutions were to fail, is quite small.

10. A major flaw in the deposit insurance system has been the relatively low price for the insurance irrespective of risk. Moral hazard under the current deposit insurance system has led to overly risky and fraudulent behaviour on the part of some depository institution managers.

DISCUSSION OF PREVIEW QUESTIONS

1. **What is a fractional reserve banking system?**
   A fractional reserve banking system is one in which the reserves kept by the depository institutions are only a fraction of total deposits owned by the public. In general, depository institutions accept funds from the public and offer their depositors interest or other services. In turn the depository institutions lend out some of these deposits and earn interest. Because at any given time new deposits are coming in while people are drawing down on old deposits, prudent banking does not require a 100 percent reserve-deposit ratio. Because Canadian depository institutions keep less than 100 percent of their total deposits in the form of reserves, we refer to our banking structure as a *fractional* reserve system.

2. **What happens to the total money supply when a person deposits in one depository institution a cheque drawn on another depository institution?**
   Nothing; the total money supply is unaffected. A transfer of cheques from one depository institution to another does not generate any excess reserves in the banking system; hence there will be no overall deposit (and therefore money) creation.

Suppose that Gerald Wong deposits in Bank A a $1,000 cheque that he received for services rendered to Lisa Romano, who deals with Bank B. Wong deposits a $1,000 cheque in Bank A, drawn on Bank B. Note that Bank A experiences an increase in total deposits and reserves and can increase its lending. However, just the opposite happens to Bank B: It experiences a reduction in deposits and reserves and must curtail its lending. There will be no net change in excess reserves; hence no net change in deposit creation and therefore no net change in the money supply occurs.

3. **What happens to the overall money supply when a person who sells a Canadian government security to the Bank of Canada places the proceeds in a depository institution?**

Assume that Wong now sells a $1,000 bond to the Bank of Canada and in exchange receives a cheque for $1,000, which he deposits in Bank A. Wong has received a $1,000 chequable deposit (which is money) in exchange for a $1,000 bond (which is not money); the money supply has just increased by $1,000. Furthermore, Bank A has now increased its reserves by $1,000; of this, $900 is excess reserves (assuming a 10 percent desired reserve ratio). We stress that this increase in excess reserves for Bank A is *not* offset elsewhere in the banking institution; hence a net increase in excess reserves has occurred. Bank A may well lend all $900 (create $900 in chequable deposits for borrowers), thereby increasing the overall money supply by another $900; the total change so far is $1,900. There is no need for the process to end here, because the people who borrowed $900 from Bank A will now spend this $900 on goods or services provided by people who may

well deal with Bank B—which receives $900 in deposits and reserves and now has $720 in excess reserves that it can lend. And so the process of deposit and money creation continues.

4. **How does the existence of deposit insurance affect a financial institution's choice of risky versus nonrisky assets?**

The best way to answer this question is with an analogy. Assume that you are given $10,000 to gamble at the Windsor Casino. In situation 1, you share equally with your benefactor in losses and in gains. In situation 2, your benefactor lets you share in the gains (at less than 100 percent) but incurs all losses. Will your behaviour be any different in situation 1 than in situation 2 while you are gambling? The answer is, of course, yes. In situation 1, you will be much more careful—you will choose games of chance that offer less risk but lower potential payoffs. In situation 2, you might as well try to break the bank. At the roulette wheel, rather than going for odd or even or red or black, you might as well bet your benefactor's money on single numbers or groups of numbers or zero or double zero because if you hit it, you stand to gain a lot, but if you don't, you stand to lose nothing. Situation 2 is analogous to that of today's managers in depository institutions—it is a situation that involves moral hazard. When times get tough and business is bad, they have had a tendency to "go for broke." They bought risky but high-yielding assets, such as dubious real estate loans, loans at high interest rates to developing countries, and oil development loans. For those whose bets don't pay off, the federal government may bail out all the depositors. The few whose bets do pay off look like heroes.

PROBLEMS

(Answers to the odd-numbered problems appear at the back of the book.)

16-1. Bank 1 has received a deposit of $1 million. Assuming that the banks retain no excess reserves, answer the following questions.
    a. The desired reserve ratio is 25 percent.

Fill in the blanks in the table on the following page. What is the money multiplier?
    b. Now the desired reserve ratio is 5 percent. Fill in the blanks in a similar table. What is the money multiplier?

Multiple Deposit Creation			
Bank	Deposits	Reserves	Loans
Bank 1	$1,000,000	$_____	$_____
Bank 2	_____	_____	_____
Bank 3	_____	_____	_____
Bank 4	_____	_____	_____
Bank 5	_____	_____	_____
All other banks	_____	_____	_____
Totals	_____	_____	_____

16-2. Arrange the following items on the proper side of a bank's balance sheet.
   a. Chequing deposits
   b. Vault cash
   c. Time deposits
   d. Deposits with the Bank of Canada
   e. Loans to private businesses
   f. Loans to households
   g. Holdings of Canadian government, provincial, and municipal bonds
   h. Borrowings from other banks

Assets	Liabilities

16-3. If the desired reserve ratio is 10 percent, what will be the maximum change in the money supply in each of the following situations?
   a. Theola Smith deposits in Bank 2 a cheque drawn on Bank 3.
   b. Smith buys a $5,000 government bond from the Bank of Canada by drawing down on her chequing account.
   c. Smith sells a $10,000 government bond to the Bank of Canada and deposits the $10,000 in Bank 3.
   d. Smith finds $1,000 in coins and paper currency buried in her backyard and deposits it in her chequing account.
   e. Smith writes a $1,000 cheque on her own account and takes $1,000 in currency and buries it in her backyard.

16-4. The Bank of Canada purchases a $1 million government security from Gulwinder Mann, who deposits the proceeds in Bank 1. Use balance sheets to show the immediate effects of this transaction on the Bank of Canada and on Bank 1.

16-5. Continuing the example from Problem 16-4:
   a. Indicate Bank 1's position more precisely if desired reserves equal 5 percent of chequable deposits.
   b. By how much can Bank 1 increase its lending?

16-6. Assume a desired reserve ratio of 8 percent. A cheque for $60,000 is drawn on an account in Bank B and deposited in a chequable deposit in Bank A.
   a. How much have the excess reserves of Bank A increased?
   b. How much in the form of new loans is Bank A now able to extend to borrowers?
   c. By how much have reserves of Bank B decreased?
   d. By how much have excess reserves of Bank B decreased?
   e. The money supply has increased by how much?

16-7. Assume that the desired reserve ratio is 15 percent and that the Bank of Canada sells $3 million worth of government securities to a customer who pays with a cheque drawn on the Toronto-Dominion Bank.
   a. The excess reserves of the Toronto-Dominion Bank have changed by how much?
   b. By how much has the money supply changed?
   c. What is the maximum change in the money supply that can result from this sale?

16-8. Examine the following balance sheet of B Bank.

B Bank			
Assets		**Liabilities**	
Total reserves	$ 50	Chequable deposits	$200
Loans	100	Capital stock	200
Government securities	50		
Property	200		

Assume that the desired reserve ratio is 10 percent.

a. Calculate the excess reserves of B Bank.

b. How much money can B Bank lend out?

c. If B Bank lends the money in part (b) of this problem, what are the new values for total reserves? For chequable deposits? For loans?

d. What is the maximum expansion of the money supply if B Bank lends the amount suggested in part (b) of this problem?

16-9. Assume a 5 percent desired reserve ratio, zero excess reserves, no currency leakage, and a ready loan demand. The Bank of Canada buys a $1 million Treasury bill from a depository institution.

a. What is the maximum money multiplier?

b. By how much will total deposits rise?

16-10. It is the year 2310. Residents of an earth colony on Titan, the largest moon of the planet Saturn, use chequable deposits at financial institutions as the only form of money. Depository institutions on Titan wish to hold 10 percent of deposits as excess reserves at all times. There are no other deposits in the banking system. If the banking system on Titan has $300 million in reserves and the total quantity of money is $1.5 billion, what is the desired reserve ratio?

16-11. Take the CDIC Challenge which you will find at the Canadian Deposit Insurance Corporation Web site at http://www.cdic.ca/english/challenge/challenge.htm.

INTERACTING WITH THE INTERNET

Material on the CDIC, for depositors and for others interested in the system, can be found at

http://www.cdic.ca/

17

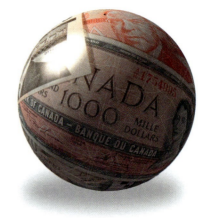

Monetary Policy

If you follow any of the news stories about the economic policies being made in Ottawa, you cannot fail to learn about what this nation's central bank, the Bank of Canada, is doing to stop a recession, cool down an overheated economy, or something else of that nature. Whatever the Bank of Canada does, some part of the press or the academic world is apt to "bash" it for doing the wrong thing. Whenever a vacancy occurs on its Board of Governors, speculation about the political leaning of the next appointee is rampant. Some analysts argue that even though the Bank of Canada is only a quasi-government agency, it is not really independent of the government's wishes. These commentators go further and argue that the Bank of Canada should become completely independent of the government. Is the Bank of Canada already independent? And if not, does it matter? To answer these questions, you need to know more about how monetary policy works.

Did You Know That... the Governor of the Bank of Canada is often considered the second most important person politically and economically in the country after the prime minister? Why is the head of the Bank of Canada considered so important? Because the Governor of the Bank of Canada and the rest of the Bank's Governors determine monetary policy in Canada. A strongly worded public statement by the Governor of the Bank of Canada can cause instant reaction in our financial markets and sometimes in those in the rest of the world.

This chapter deals with monetary policy—the Bank of Canada's altering interest rates or changing the supply of money (or the rate at which it grows) in order to achieve national economic goals. When you were introduced to aggregate demand in Chapter 10, you discovered that the position of the aggregate demand curve is determined by the willingness of firms, individuals, governments, and foreigners to purchase domestically produced goods and services. Monetary policy works in a variety of ways to change this willingness, both directly and indirectly.

Think about monetary policy in an intuitive way: An increase in the money supply adds to the amount of money that firms and individuals have on hand and so increases the amount that they wish to spend. The result is an increase in aggregate demand. A decrease in the money supply reduces the amount of money that people have on hand to spend and so decreases aggregate demand.

WHAT'S SO SPECIAL ABOUT MONEY?

By definition, monetary policy has to do, in the main, with money. But what is so special about money? Money is the product of a "social contract" in which we all agree to do two things:

1. Express all prices in terms of a common unit of account, which in Canada we call the dollar
2. Use a specific medium of exchange for market transactions

These two features of money distinguish it from all other goods in the economy. As a practical matter, money is involved on one side of every nonbarter transaction in the economy—and trillions of them occur every year. What this means is that something that changes the amount of money in circulation will have some effect on many transactions and thus on elements of GDP. If something affects the number of snowmobiles in existence, probably only the snowmobile market will be altered. But something that affects the amount of money in existence is going to affect *all* markets.

Holding Money

All of us engage in a flow of transactions. We buy and sell things all of our lives. But because we use money—dollars—as our medium of exchange, all *flows* of nonbarter transactions involve a *stock* of money. We can restate this as follows:

> To use money, one must hold money.

Given that everybody must hold money, we can now talk about the *demand* to hold it. People do not demand to hold money just to look at pictures of past prime ministers. They hold it to be able to use it to buy goods and services.

The Demand for Money: What People Wish to Hold

People have a certain motivation that makes them want to hold money balances. Individuals and firms could try to have zero non-interest-bearing money balances. But life is inconvenient without a ready supply of money balances. There is a demand for money by the public, motivated by several factors.

The Transactions Demand. The main reason people hold money is that money can be used to purchase goods and services. People are paid at specific intervals (once a week, once a month, and so on), but they wish to make purchases more or less continuously. To free themselves from making expenditures on goods and services only on payday, people find it beneficial to hold money. The benefit they receive is convenience: They willingly forgo interest earnings in order to avoid the inconvenience and expense of cashing in such nonmoney assets as bonds every time they wish to make a purchase.

▶ **Transactions demand**

Holding money as a medium of exchange to make payments. The level varies directly with nominal national income.

Thus people hold money to make regular, *expected* expenditures under the **transactions demand.** As national income rises, the community will want to hold more money. Suppose that national income rises due exclusively to price level increases. If people are making the same volume of physical purchases but the goods and services cost more due to higher prices, people will want to hold more money.

The Precautionary Demand. The transactions demand involves money held to make *expected* expenditures; people hold money for the **precautionary demand** to make *unexpected* purchases or to meet emergencies. It is not unreasonable to maintain that as the price level or real national income rises, people will want to hold more money. In effect, when people hold money for the precautionary demand, they incur a cost in forgone interest earnings that is offset by the benefit that the precautionary balance provides. Nonetheless, the higher the rate of interest, the lower the money balances people wish to hold for the precautionary demand.

▶ **Precautionary demand**

Holding money to meet unplanned expenditures and emergencies.

The Asset Demand. Remember that one of the functions of money is a store of value. People can hold money balances as a store of value, or they can hold bonds or stocks or other interest-earning assets. The desire to hold money as a store of value leads to the **asset demand** for money. People choose to hold money rather than other assets for two reasons: its liquidity and the lack of risk. Moreover, if deflation is expected, holding money balances makes sense.

▶ **Asset demand**

Holding money as a store of value, instead of other assets such as certificates of deposit, corporate bonds, and stocks.

The disadvantage of holding money balances as an asset, of course, is the interest earnings forgone. Each individual or business decides how much money to hold as an asset by looking at the opportunity cost of holding money. The higher the interest rate—which is our proxy for the opportunity cost of holding money—the lower the money balances people will want to hold as assets. Conversely, the lower the interest rate offered on alternative assets, the higher the money balances people will want to hold as assets.

The Demand for Money Curve

Assume that the transactions demand for money is fixed, given a certain level of income. That leaves the precautionary and asset demands for money, both determined by the opportunity cost of holding money. If we assume that the interest rate represents the cost of holding money balances, we can graph the relationship between the interest rate and the quantity of money demanded. In Figure 17.1, the demand for money curve shows a familiar downward slope. The horizontal axis measures the quantity of money demanded, and the vertical axis is the interest rate. In this sense, the interest rate is the price of holding money. At a higher price, a lower quantity of money is demanded, and vice versa.

Imagine two scenarios. In the first one, you can earn 20 percent a year if you put your cash into purchases of government securities. In the other scenario, you can earn 1 percent if you put your cash into purchases of government securities. If you have $1,000 average cash balances in a non-interest-bearing chequing account, in the second scenario over a one-year period, your opportunity cost would be 1 percent of $1,000, or $10. In the first scenario, your opportunity cost would be 20 percent of $1,000, or $200. Under which scenario would you hold more cash?

Try Preview Question 1:

What is the demand for money curve, and how is it related to the interest rate?

Figure 17.1

The Demand for Money Curve

If we use the interest rate as a proxy for the opportunity cost of holding money balances, the demand for money curve, M_{d}, is downward-sloping, similar to other demand curves.

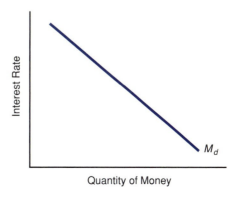

INTERNATIONAL EXAMPLE
The Choice Between Cash and Savings Accounts in Colombia

In countries with high inflation rates, nominal interest rates are also high. Remember from Chapter 7 that the nominal interest rate equals the real interest rate plus the expected rate of inflation. Colombia is one country that has consistently high rates of inflation. Consequently, its depository institutions usually offer high nominal interest rates to attract people's cash. In Ciudad, Bolívar, about an hour from Bogotá, the *Caja Social de Ahorros* (Social Savings Bank) services a low-income area of about a million people. This depository institution was started by a Jesuit priest and continues to be overseen by a board of directors appointed by the Jesuits. On passbook savings accounts, it pays 19 percent. This sounds high, but not compared to Colombia's 22 percent annual inflation. Thus its 10,000 depositors are willing to accept a *negative* real rate of interest of 3 percent. Why? In the first place, if they kept their cash as cash, they would suffer a 22 percent reduction in purchasing power every year. In the second place, the *Caja Social* keeps its low-income clients' money safe in a high-crime area.

For critical analysis: Why are nominal interest rates higher when a country experiences inflation?

Concepts in Brief

- To use money, people must hold money. Therefore, they have a demand for money balances.
- The determinants of the demand for money balances are the transactions demand, the precautionary demand, and the asset demand.
- Because holding money carries with it an opportunity cost—the interest income forgone—the demand for money curve showing the relationship between money balances and the interest rate slopes downward.

EFFECTS OF AN INCREASE IN THE MONEY SUPPLY

To understand how monetary policy works in its simplest form, we are going to run an experiment in which you increase the money supply in a very direct way. Assume that the government has given you hundreds of millions of dollars in just-printed bills that you load into a helicopter. You then go around the country, dropping the money out of the window. People pick it up and put it in their wallets. Some deposit the money in their chequing accounts. The first thing that happens is that they have too much money—not in the sense that they want to throw it away but rather in relation to other things that they own. There are a variety of ways to dispose of this "new" money.

Direct Effect

The simplest thing that people can do when they have excess money balances is to go out and spend it on goods and services. Here we have a direct impact on aggregate demand. Aggregate demand rises because with an increase in the money supply at any given price level, people now want to purchase more output of real goods and services.

Indirect Effect

Not everybody will necessarily spend the newfound money on real output. Some people may wish to deposit some or all of this excess cash in banks. The recipient banks now discover that they have higher reserves than they need to hold. As you learned in Chapter 16, one thing that banks can do to get interest-earning assets is to lend out the excess reserves. But banks cannot induce people to borrow more money than they were borrowing before unless the banks lower the interest rate that they charge on loans. This lower interest rate encourages people to take out those loans. Businesses will therefore engage in new investment with the money loaned. Individuals will engage in more consumption of such durable goods as housing, automobiles, and home entertainment centres. Either way, the increased loans have created a rise in aggregate demand. More people will be involved in more spending, even those who did not pick up any of the money that was originally dropped out of your helicopter.

Graphing the Effects of an Expansionary Monetary Policy

We have now established the existence of both the direct and indirect effects on aggregate demand when there is an expansion in the money supply. Look at Figure 17.2 (page 416). We start out in long-run and short-run equilibrium with long-run aggregate supply at $LRAS$, short-run aggregate supply at $SRAS_1$, and aggregate demand at AD_1. All three intersect at $700 billion of real GDP at a price level of 120, at point E_1. Because of the direct and indirect effects of the increase in the money supply, aggregate demand shifts outward to the right to AD_2. At price level 120, there is an excess demand for real goods and services equal to the horizontal distance between E_1 and A. This horizontal distance shown here is $50 billion. The excess demand for goods and services must be matched, dollar for dollar, by the corresponding excess supply of money (excess liquidity). It is this excess supply of money that has caused the aggregate demand curve to shift outward to AD_2.

In the short run, something has to give. Here the excess demand for real output induces a move to point E_2. The price level rises to 130 at an output rate of $725 billion per year. In the long run, though, expectations are revised upward, and input prices are revised accordingly. Therefore, the short-run aggregate supply curve, $SRAS_1$, begins to shift upward vertically to $SRAS_2$. Long-run equilibrium occurs at E_3, and the ultimate effect is a rise in the price level.

Figure 17.2
The Effects of Expansionary Monetary Policy

If we start with equilibrium at E_1, an increase in the money supply will cause the aggregate demand curve to shift to AD_2. There is an excess quantity of real goods and services demanded. The price level increases so that we move to E_2 at an output rate of $725 billion per year and a price level of 130. But input owners revise their expectations of prices upward, and $SRAS_1$ shifts to $SRAS_2$. The new long-run equilibrium is at E_3 at the long-run aggregate supply of $700 billion of real GDP per year and a price level of 135.

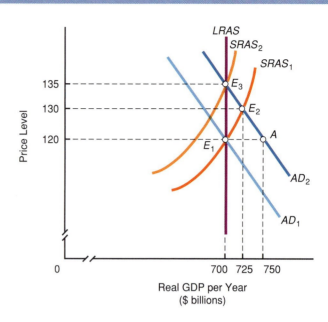

Concepts in Brief

- The direct effect of an increase in the money supply arises because people desire to spend more on real goods and services when they have excess money balances.
- The indirect effect of an increase in the money supply works through a lowering of the interest rates, which encourages businesses to make new investments with the money loaned to them. Individuals will also engage in more consumption (on consumer durables) because of lower interest rates.

▶ **Drawdown**

A movement of Government of Canada deposits from deposits of the chartered banks into the Bank of Canada's own government accounts.

▶ **Redeposit**

A movement of Government of Canada deposits from the Bank of Canada's own government accounts to the accounts of the chartered banks.

MONETARY POLICY IN THE REAL WORLD

Of course, monetary policy does not consist of dropping dollar bills from a helicopter. Nonetheless, it is true that the Bank of Canada seeks to alter consumption, investment, and aggregate demand as a whole by altering the rate of growth of the money supply. The Bank of Canada uses three tools as part of its policymaking action: drawdowns and redeposits, open market operations, and moral suasion.

Drawdowns and Redeposits

The Bank of Canada changes the amount of reserves in the system through the use of **drawdowns** and **redeposits**. When the Bank of Canada conducts a drawdown, it moves Government of Canada deposits from the accounts of the chartered banks held at the Bank of Canada, into the Bank's own government accounts. This has the effect of reducing the chartered banks' reserves, which induces the banks to call in loans to replenish their reserves. A drawdown has a contractionary effect on the money supply.

A redeposit occurs when the Bank of Canada moves government deposits into the accounts of the chartered banks, thus increasing their reserves. The banks then lend out their excess reserves thereby increasing the money supply.

Contractionary Monetary Policy: Effects on Aggregate Demand, the Price Level, and Real GDP.

When the Bank of Canada engages in contractionary monetary policy, it conducts drawdowns. Remember that when it does so, the chartered banks will call in loans. There will be fewer reserves available for the chartered banks to lend out. The way they ration available money among potential borrowers is by raising the rate of interest they charge on loans. Some borrowers, deeming the new rate too high, will eliminate themselves from the market. Consequently, some borrowers who otherwise would have borrowed in order to spend no longer will do so at the higher rate of interest. The aggregate demand curve shifts from AD_1 to AD_2 in Figure 17.3 (page 418). The initial equilibrium was at point E_1 with a price level of 120 and real GDP of $700 billion per year. AD_1, $SRAS_1$, and $LRAS$ all intersect at point E_1. Now that the Bank of Canada has conducted a drawdown, the aggregate demand curve shifts to AD_2. In the short run, we move along $SRAS_1$ to point E_2, at which point the price level has dropped to 110 and real GDP has decreased to $650 billion per year.

In the long run, in a fully adjusting economy, expectations adjust and so do factor (input) prices. All of the shock is absorbed in a lower price level as $SRAS_1$ moves to $SRAS_2$. The new equilibrium is at E_3, again at $700 billion real GDP per year but at a lower price level of 100.

Expansionary Monetary Policy: Effect of a Redeposit.

The Bank of Canada engages in expansionary monetary policy by conducting redeposits. Remember that a redeposit transfers Government of Canada deposits to the accounts of the chartered banks at the Bank of Canada. The chartered banks now have more reserves. Flush with excess reserves, the banks seek ways to lend them out. To induce customers to borrow more, the banks will cut interest rates even further. People who thought they were not going to be able to buy a new car, house, or whatever now find themselves able to do so. Their spending rises.

The graph of expansionary monetary policy was presented in Figure 17.2; it is the opposite case to Figure 17.3.

Open Market Operations

The Bank of Canada occasionally changes the amount of reserves in the system by its purchases and sales of Canadian government bonds. To understand how the Bank of Canada does so, you must first start out in an equilibrium in which everybody, including the holders of bonds, is satisfied with the current situation. There is some equilibrium level of interest rate (and bond prices) outstanding. Now if the Bank of

Figure 17.3
**Contractionary Monetary
Policy via Drawdowns**

If we start out in long-run and short-run equilibrium at point E_1, contractionary monetary policy using drawdowns will shift aggregate demand to AD_2. The new short-run equilibrium will be at E_2. This is at a lower price level, however. Input owners will revise their expectations downward, and $SRAS_1$ will shift to $SRAS_2$. The new long-run equilibrium will be at E_3.

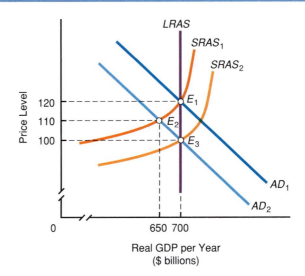

Canada wants to conduct open market operations, it must somehow induce individuals, businesses, and foreigners to hold more or fewer Canadian government bonds. The inducement must be in the form of making people better off. So if the Bank of Canada wants to buy bonds, it is going to have to offer to buy them at a higher price than exists in the marketplace. If it wants to sell bonds, it is going to have to offer them at a lower price than exists in the marketplace. Thus an open market operation must cause a change in the price of bonds.

Graphing the Sale of Bonds. The Bank of Canada sells some of the bonds in its portfolio. This is shown in part (a) of Figure 17.4. Notice that the supply of bonds is shown here as a vertical line with respect to price. The demand for bonds is downward-sloping. If the Bank of Canada offers more bonds for sale, it shifts the supply curve from S_1 to S_2. It cannot induce people to buy the extra bonds at the original price of P_1, so it must lower the price to P_2.

The Bank of Canada's Purchase of Bonds. The opposite occurs when the Bank of Canada purchases bonds. In part (b) of Figure 17.4, the original supply curve is S_1. The new supply curve of outstanding bonds will end up being S_3 because of the Bank of Canada's purchases of bonds. You can view this purchase of bonds as a reduction in the stock of bonds available for private investors to hold. To get people to give up these bonds, it must offer them a more attractive price. The price will rise from P_1 to P_3.

Relationship Between the Price of Existing Bonds and the Rate of Interest. There is an inverse relationship between the price of existing bonds and the rate of interest. Assume that the average yield on bonds is 5 percent. You decide to purchase a bond. A local corporation agrees to sell you a bond that will pay you $50 a year forever. What is the price you are willing to pay for it? $1,000. Why? Because $50 divided by $1,000 equals 5 percent. You purchase the bond. The next year something happens in the economy. For whatever reason, you can go out and obtain bonds that have effective yields of 10 percent. That is to say, the prevailing interest rate in the economy is now 10 percent. What has happened to the market price of the existing bond that you own, the one you purchased the year before? It will have fallen. If you try to sell it for $1,000, you will discover that no investors will buy it from you. Why should they when they can obtain $50 a year from someone else by paying only $500? Indeed, unless you offer your bond for sale at a price of $500, no buyers will be forthcoming. Hence an increase in the prevailing interest rate in the economy has caused the market value of your existing bond to fall.

The important point to understand is this:

Try Preview Question 2:

Why is the price of existing bonds inversely related to the interest rate?

The market price of existing bonds (and all fixed-income assets) is inversely related to the rate of interest prevailing in the economy.

Using Open Market Operations to Affect Aggregate Demand

When the Bank of Canada engages in contractionary monetary policy, it increases its sales of Canadian government bonds. Remember that when it does so, bond prices will fall. But lowering the price of bonds is the same thing as raising the interest rate on existing bonds. In any event, let's assume that the Bank of Canada sells bonds exclusively to banks. (This is not quite accurate because it actually deals with a small number of bond dealers.) The banks that purchase the bonds from the Bank of Canada do so with reserves. This puts banks too close to being unable to meet their reserve requirements, thus they reduce lending. Bond purchases cause a contraction in the economy as shown in Figure 17.3.

The Bank of Canada engages in expansionary monetary policy by purchasing bonds. Remember that for the Bank of Canada to purchase bonds, it must bid up the price it pays for bonds. That means that the interest rate on existing bonds will go down. In any event, the Bank of Canada buys the bonds from banks, which now have more reserves. The chartered banks reduce interest rates, which stimulates aggregate demand as shown in Figure 17.2.

Figure 17.4
Determining the Price of Bonds

In part (a), the Bank of Canada offers more bonds for sale. The price drops from P_1 to P_2. In part (b), the Bank of Canada purchases bonds. This is the equivalent of a reduction in the supply of bonds available for private investors to hold. The price of bonds must rise from P_1 to P_3 to clear the market.

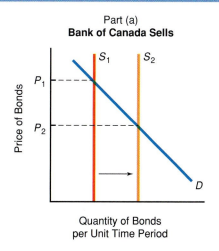

Part (a)
Bank of Canada Sells

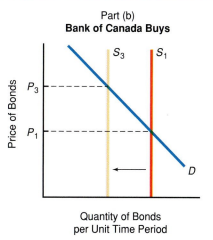

Part (b)
Bank of Canada Buys

A Real-World Caveat. Contractionary monetary policy has involved a reduction in the money supply with a consequent decline in the price level (deflation). In the real world of policymaking, contractionary monetary policy normally involves reducing the *rate of growth* of the money supply, thereby reducing the rate of increase in the price level (inflation). Similarly, real-world expansionary monetary policy typically involves increasing the rate of growth of the money supply. To show this in our diagrams, we would have to change them from static to dynamic, with a considerable amount of increased complexity.

Moral Suasion

▶ **Moral suasion**

A formal or informal request by the Governor of the Bank of Canada to the CEOs of the chartered banks to voluntarily restrict or expand credit or other loans, in an effort to control the money supply.

When the Bank of Canada wants to restrict the money supply, but doesn't want to conduct open market operations or drawdowns, another tool it can use is **moral suasion**. The Governor of the Bank of Canada might ask the presidents of the "Big Six" chartered banks for their assistance in tightening credit, for example. The banks are not commanded to do so, but to blatantly disobey could cause negative repercussions—such as fewer government deposits—for them.

Earlier in this century, this was a fairly effective and commonly used tool since there were only about 10 banks in Canada. However with the proliferation of other financial intermediaries who are all offering credit, this tool has lost much of its effectiveness. Even if the "Big Six" chartered banks cooperated with the Bank of Canada, credit unions, *caisses populaires*, trust companies, and insurance companies might well refuse to do so, thinking that their relative smallness would not affect the overall success of the plan.

Concepts in Brief

- Monetary policy consists of drawdowns and redeposits, open market operations, and moral suasion.
- When the Bank of Canada sells bonds, it must offer them at a lower price. When the Bank of Canada buys bonds, it must pay a higher price.
- There is an inverse relationship between the prevailing rate of interest in the economy and the market price of existing bonds.
- If we start out in long-run and short-run equilibrium, contractionary monetary policy first leads to a decrease in aggregate demand, resulting in a reduction in real GDP and in the price level. Eventually, though, the short-run aggregate supply curve shifts downward, and the new equilibrium is at *LRAS* but at an even lower price level. Expansionary monetary policy works the opposite way.

OPEN ECONOMY TRANSMISSION OF MONETARY POLICY

So far we have discussed monetary policy in a closed economy. When we move to an open economy, in which there is international trade and the international purchase and sale of all assets including dollars and other currencies, monetary policy becomes more complex. Consider first the effect on exports of any type of monetary policy.

The Net Export Effect

When we examined fiscal policy, we pointed out that deficit financing can lead to higher interest rates. Higher (real, after-tax) interest rates do something in the foreign sector—they attract foreign financial investment. More people want to purchase Canadian government securities, for example. But to purchase Canadian assets, people first have to obtain Canadian dollars. This means that the demand for dollars goes up in foreign exchange markets. The international price of the dollar therefore rises. This is called an *appreciation* of the dollar, and it tends to reduce net exports because it makes our exports more expensive in terms of foreign currency and imports cheaper in terms of dollars. Foreigners demand fewer of our goods and services, and we demand more of theirs. In this way, expansionary fiscal policy that creates deficit spending financed by government borrowing can lead to a reduction in net exports.

But what about expansionary monetary policy? If expansionary monetary policy reduces real, after-tax Canadian interest rates, there will be a positive net export effect because foreigners will want fewer Canadian financial instruments, demanding fewer dollars and thereby causing the international price of the dollar to fall. This makes our exports cheaper for the rest of the world, which then demands a larger quantity of our exports. It also means that foreign goods and services are more expensive in Canada, so we therefore demand fewer imports. We come up with two conclusions:

1. Expansionary fiscal policy may cause international flows of financial capital (responding to interest rate *increases*) to offset its effectiveness to some extent. The net export effect is in the opposite direction of fiscal policy.
2. Expansionary monetary policy may cause interest rates to fall. Such a fall will induce international outflows of financial capital, thereby lowering the value of the dollar and making Canadian goods more attractive. The net export effect of expansionary monetary policy will be in the same direction as the monetary policy effect.

Contractionary Monetary Policy

Now assume that the economy is experiencing inflation and the Bank of Canada wants to use contractionary monetary policy. In so doing, it may cause interest rates to rise. Rising interest rates will cause financial capital to flow into Canada. The demand for dollars will increase, and their international price will go up. Foreign goods will now look cheaper to Canadians, and imports will rise. Foreigners will not want our exports as much, and exports will fall. The result will be a deterioration in our international trade balance. Again, the international consequences reinforce the domestic consequences of monetary policy.

Globalization of International Money Markets

On a broader level, the Bank of Canada's ability to control the rate of growth of the money supply may be hampered as Canadian money markets become less isolated. With the push of a computer button, millions or even billions of dollars can change hands halfway around the world. In the world dollar market, the Bank of Canada finds an increasing number of dollars coming from *private* institutions. If the Bank of Canada reduces the growth of the money supply, individuals and firms in Canada can increasingly obtain dollars from other sources. People in Canada who want more liquidity can obtain their dollars from foreigners, or can even obtain foreign currencies and convert them into dollars in the world dollar market. Indeed, it is possible that as world markets become increasingly integrated, Canadian residents may someday conduct domestic transactions in *foreign* currencies.

MONETARY POLICY DURING PERIODS OF UNDERUTILIZED RESOURCES

If the economy is operating at an equilibrium output level that is below that given by the long-run aggregate supply curve, monetary policy (like fiscal policy) can generate increases in the equilibrium level of real GDP per year up to a long-run equilibrium on *LRAS*. In Figure 17.5, you see initial aggregate demand as AD_1. It inter-

Figure 17.5
Expansionary Monetary Policy with Underutilized Resources

If we start out with equilibrium at E_1, expansionary monetary policy will shift AD_1 to AD_2. The new equilibrium will be at E_2.

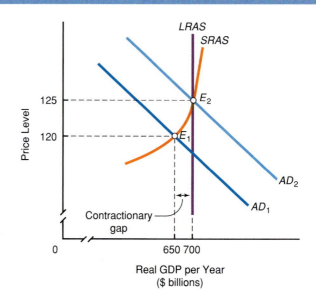

sects *SRAS* at E_1, at an output rate of $650 billion of real GDP per year and a price level of 120. There is a contractionary gap of $50 billion. That is the difference between *LRAS* and the current equilibrium. The Bank of Canada can engage in expansionary monetary policy, the direct and indirect effects of which will cause AD_1 to shift to AD_2. The new equilibrium is at E_2, at an output rate of $700 billion of real GDP per year and a price level of 125. Note that expansionary monetary policy gets the economy to its *LRAS* sooner than otherwise.

Concepts in Brief

- Monetary policy in an open economy has repercussions for net exports.
- If expansionary monetary policy reduces Canadian interest rates, there is a positive net export effect because foreigners will demand fewer Canadian financial instruments, thereby demanding fewer dollars and hence causing the international price of the dollar to fall. This makes our exports cheaper for the rest of the world.
- Expansionary monetary policy during periods of underutilized resources can cause the equilibrium level of real GDP to increase (sooner than it otherwise would) to the rate of real output consistent with the vertical long-run aggregate supply curve.

MONETARY POLICY AND INFLATION

Most theories of inflation relate to the short run. The price index in the short run can fluctuate because of events such as oil price shocks, labour union strikes, or discoveries of large amounts of new natural resources. In the long run, however, empirical studies show a relatively stable relationship between excessive growth in the money supply and inflation.

Simple supply and demand can explain why the price level rises when the money supply is increased. Suppose that a major oil discovery is made, and the supply of oil increases dramatically relative to the demand for oil. The relative price of oil will fall; now it will take more units of oil to exchange for specific quantities of non-oil products. Similarly, if the supply of money rises relative to the demand for money, it will take more units of money to purchase specific quantities of goods and services. That is merely another way of stating that the price level has increased or that the purchasing power of money has fallen. In fact, the classical economists referred to inflation as a situation in which more money is chasing the same quantity of goods and services.

▶ **Equation of exchange**

The formula indicating that the number of monetary units times the number of times each unit is spent on final goods and services is identical to the price level times output (or nominal national income).

The Equation of Exchange and the Quantity Theory

A simple way to show the relationship between changes in the quantity of money in circulation and the price level is through the **equation of exchange**, developed by

Irving Fisher:

$$M_sV \equiv PQ$$

where

▶ **Income velocity of money**

The number of times per year a dollar is spent on final goods and services; equal to GDP divided by the money supply.

$M_s =$ actual money balances held by the nonbanking public

$V =$ **income velocity of money**, or the number of times, on average, each monetary unit is spent on final goods and services

$P =$ price level or price index

$Q =$ real national output (real GDP)

Consider a numerical example involving a one-commodity economy. Assume that in this economy the total money supply, M_s, is \$100; the quantity of output, Q, is 50 units of a good; and the average price, P, of this output is \$10 per unit. Using the equation of exchange,

$$M_sV \equiv PQ$$
$$\$100V \equiv \$10 \times 50$$
$$\$100V \equiv \$500$$
$$V \equiv 5$$

Thus each dollar is spent an average of five times a year.

The Equation of Exchange as an Identity.

The equation of exchange must always be true—it is an *accounting identity*. The equation of exchange states that the total amount of money spent on final output, M_sV, is equal to the total amount of money *received* for final output, PQ. Thus a given flow of money can be seen from either the buyers' side or the producers' side. The value of goods purchased is equal to the value of goods sold.

If Q represents real national output and P is the price level, PQ equals the dollar value of national output, or nominal national income. Thus

$$M_sV \equiv PQ \equiv Y$$

The Crude Quantity Theory of Money and Prices.

▶ **Crude quantity theory of money and prices**

The belief that changes in the money supply lead to proportional changes in the price level.

If we now make some assumptions about different variables in the equation of exchange, we come up with the simplified theory of why prices change, called the **crude quantity theory of money and prices**. If you assume that the velocity of money, V, is constant and that real national output, Q, is basically stable, the simple equation of exchange tells you that a change in the money supply can lead only to a proportionate change in the price level. Continue with our numerical example. Q is 50 units of the good. V equals 5. If the money supply increases to 200, the only thing that can happen is that the price index, P, has to go up from 10 to 20. Otherwise the equation is no longer in balance.

Thinking Critically About the Media | Pity Those Poor Printing Presses

An examination of stories about hyperinflation throughout the world over the past several decades yields one common media statement: "Prices are increasing so fast that the money printing presses can't keep up with the inflation." What is wrong with this statement is that the order of causation is reversed. Hyperinflation is caused by an excessive growth in the money supply—hyperactive money print-ing presses, if you will. Countries that have experienced hyperinflation have typically had governments that resorted to printing excessive amounts of currency. Indeed, economists have hundreds of years of empirical evidence to validate such a statement, the media notwith-standing.

INTERNATIONAL EXAMPLE
Inflation and Money Growth Throughout the World

Is there much evidence that the rate of inflation is closely linked to the rate of monetary growth? The answer seems to be that in the long run there is a clear correlation between the two. Look at Figure 17.6. On the horizontal axis, in ratio form, is the rate of growth of the money supply. On the vertical axis is the annu-al rate of inflation (again, based on a ratio scale). As you can see, if you were to draw a line through the average of the points, it would slope upward: Faster monetary growth leads to a higher rate of inflation throughout different coun-tries. This relationship appears to hold in Canada also. Decades of relatively high money supply growth are consistent with relatively higher rates of inflation and vice versa in Canada.

Figure 17.6
International Relationship Between Money Supply Growth Rates and Rates of Inflation

If we plot rates of inflation and rates of monetary growth for different countries, we come up with a scatter diagram that shows an obvious direct rela-tionship. If you were to draw a line through the "average" of the points in this figure, it would be upward-sloping, showing that an increase in the rate of growth of the money supply leads to an increase in the rate of inflation.

Source: International Monetary Fund. Data are for latest available periods.

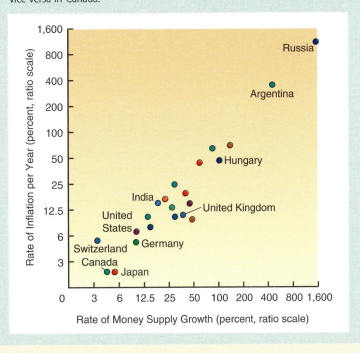

For critical analysis: Do the data shown in Figure 17.6 "prove" the crude quantity theory of money and prices?

Empirical Verification.   There is considerable evidence of the empirical validity of the relationship between excessive monetary growth and high rates of inflation. Look back at Figure 16.1 on page 386. There you see the loose correspondence between money supply growth and the rate of inflation in Canada from 1960 to the present.

Concepts in Brief

- The equation of exchange states that the expenditures by some people will equal income receipts by others, or $M_s V \equiv PQ$ (money supply times velocity equals nominal national income).
- Viewed as an accounting identity, the equation of exchange is always correct, because the amount of money spent on final output must equal the total amount of money received for final output.
- The crude quantity theory of money and prices states that a change in the money supply will bring about an equi-proportional change in the price level.

MONETARY POLICY IN ACTION: THE TRANSMISSION MECHANISM

At the start of this chapter, we talked about the direct and indirect effects of monetary policy. The direct effect is simply that an increase in the money supply causes people to have excess money balances. To get rid of these excess money balances, they increase their expenditures. The indirect effect occurs because some people have decided to purchase interest-bearing assets with their excess money balances. This causes the price of such assets—bonds—to go up. Because of the inverse relationship between the price of existing bonds and the interest rate, the interest rate in the economy falls. This lower interest rate induces people and businesses to spend more than they otherwise would have spent.

The Keynesian Transmission Mechanism

One school of economists believes that the indirect effect of monetary policy is the more important. This group, typically called Keynesian because of its belief in Keynes' work, asserts that the main effect of monetary policy occurs through changes in the interest rate. The Keynesian money transmission mechanism is shown in Figure 17.7. There you see that the money supply changes the interest rate, which in turn changes the desired rate of investment. This transmission mechanism can be seen explicitly in Figure 17.8. In part (a), you see that an increase in the money supply reduces the interest rate. This reduction in the interest rate causes desired investment expenditures to increase from I_1 to I_2 in part (b). This increase in investment shifts aggregate demand outward from AD_1 to AD_2 in part (c).

Figure 17.7
The Keynesian Money Transmission Mechanism

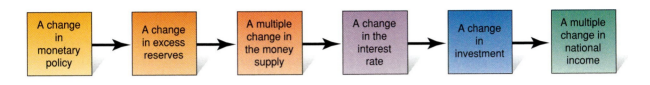

Figure 17.8
Adding Monetary Policy to the Keynesian Model

In part (a), we show a demand for money function, M_d. It slopes downward to show that at lower rates of interest, a larger quantity of money will be demanded. The money supply is given initially as M_s, so the equilibrium rate of interest will be r_1. At this rate of interest, we see from the planned investment schedule given in part (b) that the quantity of planned investment demanded per year will be I_1. After the shift in the money supply to M'_s, the resulting increase in investment from I_1 to I_2 shifts the aggregate demand curve in part (c) outward from AD_1 to AD_2. Equilibrium moves from E_1 to E_2, at $700 billion real GDP per year.

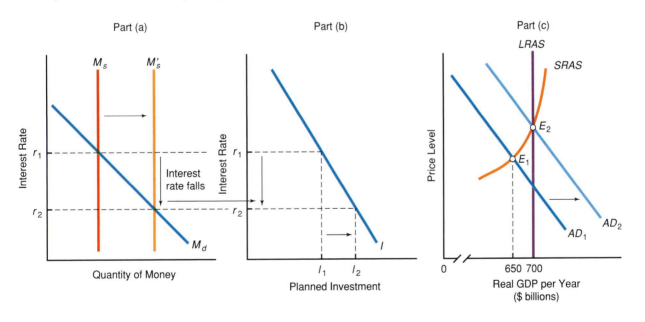

▶ **Monetarists**

Macroeconomists who believe that inflation is always caused by excessive monetary growth and that changes in the money supply affect aggregate demand both directly and indirectly.

The Monetarists' View of Money Supply Changes.   **Monetarists**, economists who believe in a modern quantity theory of money and prices, contend that monetary policy works its way more directly into the economy. They believe that changes in the money supply lead to changes in nominal GDP in the same direction. An increase in the money supply because of expansionary open market operations (purchases of bonds) by the Bank of Canada, for example, leads the public to have larger money holdings than desired. This excess quantity of money demanded induces the public to buy more of everything, especially more durable goods such as cars, stereos, and houses. If the economy is starting out at its long-run equilibrium rate of output, there can only be a short-run increase in real GDP. Ultimately, though, the public cannot buy more of everything; it simply bids up prices so that the price level rises.

Monetarists' Criticism of Monetary Policy.

The monetarists' belief that monetary policy works through changes in desired spending does not mean that they consider such policy an appropriate government stabilization tool. According to the monetarists, although monetary policy can affect real GDP (and employment) in the short run, the length of time required before money supply changes take effect is so long and variable that such policy is difficult to conduct. For example, an expansionary monetary policy to counteract a contractionary gap may not take effect for a year and a half, by which time inflation may be a problem. At that point, the expansionary monetary policy will end up making current inflation worse. Monetarists therefore see monetary policy as a *destabilizing* force in the economy.

▶ **Monetary rule**

A monetary policy that incorporates a rule specifying the annual rate of growth of some monetary aggregate.

According to the monetarists, therefore, policymakers should follow a **monetary rule:** Increase the money supply *smoothly* at a rate consistent with the economy's long-run average growth rate. *Smoothly* is an important word here. Increasing the money supply at 20 percent per year half the time and decreasing it at 17 percent per year the other half of the time would average out to about a 3 percent increase, but the results would be disastrous, say the monetarists. Instead of permitting the Bank of Canada to use its discretion in setting monetary policy, monetarists would force it to follow a rule such as "Increase the money supply smoothly at 3.5 percent per year" or "Abolish the Bank of Canada and replace it with a computer program allowing for a steady rise in the money supply."

Try Preview Question 3:

What is a monetarist?

BANK OF CANADA TARGET CHOICE: INTEREST RATES OR MONEY SUPPLY?

Money supply and interest rate targets cannot be pursued simultaneously. Interest rate targets force the Bank of Canada to abandon control over the money supply; money stock growth targets force it to allow interest rates to fluctuate.

Figure 17.9 shows the relationship between the total demand for money and the supply of money. Note that in the short run (in the sense that nominal national income is fixed), the demand for money is constant; short-run money supply changes leave the demand for money curve unaltered. In the short run, the Bank of Canada can choose either a particular interest rate (r_e or r_1) or a particular money supply (M_s or M'_s).

If the Bank of Canada wants interest rate r_e, it must select money supply M_s; if it desires a lower interest rate in the short run, it must increase the money supply. Thus by targeting an interest rate, the Bank of Canada must relinquish control of the money supply. Conversely, if it wants to target the money supply at, say, M'_s, it must allow the interest rate to fall to r_1.

Consider now the case in which the Bank of Canada wants to maintain the present level of interest rates. If actual market interest rates in the future rise persistently above the present (desired) rates, it will be continuously forced to increase the money supply. The initial increase in the money supply will only temporarily lower interest rates. The increased money stock eventually will induce inflation, and inflationary

Figure 17.9
Choosing a Monetary Policy Target

The Bank of Canada, in the short run, can select an interest rate or a money supply target, but not both. It cannot, for example, choose r_e and M'_s; if it selects r_e, it must accept M_s; if it selects M'_s, it must allow the interest rate to fall to r_1. The Bank of Canada can obtain point A or B. It cannot get to point C or D. It must therefore choose one target or the other.

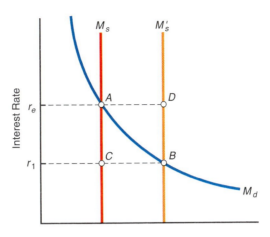

Quantity of Money Supplied and Demanded

premiums will be included in nominal interest rates. To pursue its low-interest-rate policy, the Bank of Canada must *again* increase the money stock because interest rates are still rising. Note that to attempt to maintain an interest rate target (stable interest rates), the Bank of Canada must abandon an independent money stock target. Symmetrical reasoning indicates that by setting growth rate targets at M_s or M'_s, the Bank of Canada must allow short-run fluctuations in interest rates when the economy experiences a contraction or an expansion.

But which should the Bank of Canada target, interest rates or monetary aggregates? (And which interest rate or which money stock?) It is generally agreed that the answer depends on the source of instability in the economy. If the source of instability is variations in private or public spending, monetary aggregate (money supply) targets should be set and pursued. However, if the source of instability is an unstable demand for (or perhaps supply of) money, interest rate targets are preferred.

The Monetary Conditions Index

From the early 1990s, the Bank of Canada has used the Monetary Conditions Index (MCI) as a rough measure of how tight monetary conditions in the economy are. The MCI is a weighted index made up of changes in short-term interest rates and changes in the foreign exchange value of the Canadian dollar.

The stated aim of the Bank of Canada is price stability. To this end, the Bank has promised to keep inflation between 1 percent and 3 percent through to the year 2002. We have seen that a decrease in interest rates or the exchange rate of the dollar will stimulate aggregate demand, leading to possible price increases although these increases take some time to occur due to lags in the economy. The Bank, however, can forecast future price increases through movements in the MCI.

For example, if the foreign exchange rate of the Canadian dollar fell consistently over a number of weeks, dragging the MCI down, there might be a risk of inflation recurring due to the net export effect. The Bank would estimate the seriousness of the risk, and act either to raise interest rates or to support the dollar to keep the

MCI in the target range (currently –4.5 to –5.5), which should ensure price stability. Conversely, if the exchange rate of the dollar were climbing, pulling the MCI up out of the target range, this could lead to a dampening of aggregate demand and falling prices. The Bank could intervene to ease monetary conditions by increasing the money supply, thus reducing interest rates. This would result in a fall of the MCI back into the Bank's target range.

To add to the complexity of choosing a target, other events in the Canadian (or world) economy may force the Bank of Canada to pursue a policy it doesn't necessarily like, as shown in the example which follows.

Try Preview Question 4:

How do the supply of, and demand for, money determine the interest rate?

POLICY EXAMPLE
Political Uncertainty and Monetary Targeting

In November 1995, the government of Quebec held a referendum asking Quebeckers if they wished to separate from Canada, thus creating their own nation. Leading up to the referendum there was much speculation about how the vote would turn out, and what the consequences of a "Yes" vote would be.

At the same time, Canada's economy was not growing quickly, inflation was relatively low, and unemployment was relatively high. The preferred monetary policy would be one of interest rate reductions, to allow spending to pick up.

However, with the uncertainty in Quebec the Bank of Canada held interest rates high to keep foreign capital from leaving Canada. What was happening, in fact, was that the Bank of Canada was forced to add a risk premium to its bank rate due to the political uncertainty.

But Quebeckers voted "No." The "No" vote allowed the Bank of Canada to reduce interest rates over the course of 1996, which in turn led to some easing of the unemployment rate.

For critical analysis: What would have happened to interest rates if Quebeckers had voted "Yes"?

Concepts in Brief

- In the Keynesian model, monetary transmission operates through a change in the interest rates, which changes investment, causing a multiple change in the equilibrium level of national income.
- Monetarists believe that changes in the money supply lead to changes in nominal GDP in the same direction. The effect is both direct and indirect, however, as individuals spend their excess money balances on cars, stereos, houses, and a variety of many other things.
- Monetarists, among others, argue in favour of a monetary rule—increasing the money supply smoothly at a rate consistent with the economy's long-run average growth rate. Monetarists do not believe in discretionary monetary (or fiscal) policy.
- The Bank of Canada can choose to stabilize interest rates or to change the money supply, but not both.

Issues and Applications

Is the Bank of Canada Independent, and If Not, Does It Matter?

Concepts Applied: Monetary policy, inflation, money supply, central banking

The Bank of Canada manipulates the money supply as a way to control inflation. Evidence shows that central banks that are free of political pressure have more success in preventing inflation.

In principle, the Bank of Canada, although "owned" by the federal government, is an independent agency. Nonetheless, the prime minister appoints the Directors for three-year terms, subject to cabinet approval. The prime minister also appoints the Governor of the Bank of Canada, again with cabinet approval, for a seven-year term. Given the obvious relationship between the government of the day and the Bank of Canada, is the Bank of Canada really an independent policy-making body?

What Does the Evidence Show?

The Bank of Canada was created with a view to keeping it free both of private interference and political pressure. Over the early years, it was understood that the Bank would conduct day-to-day monetary policy, but ultimately the federal government would bear responsibility for its actions.

During the late 1950s, the then-governor of the Bank of Canada was pursuing restrictive monetary policy in spite of relatively high unemployment and slow growth. The Minister of Finance of first one government, and then of a newly elected government, declared that they would not take responsibility for the consequences of the Bank's policies. Academics also began to criticize the Bank, but its Governor, James Coyne, was resolute and did not change his course. Finally, the government moved to fire Coyne by introducing legislation in Parliament declaring a less restrictive monetary policy and a vacancy in the position of the Governor of the Bank of Canada. While Parliament passed the legislation, the Senate defeated it. Eventually pressure was such that Coyne resigned. This event is now known as the *Coyne Affair*.

On taking office, the new Governor of the Bank of Canada, Louis Rasminsky, issued a statement that the Bank would be responsible for day-to-day conduct of monetary policy, but that if the government issued a written directive for a change in course and if the Governor could not agree, the Governor would have to resign. To this day, no such directive has been issued.

Does Independence Matter?

Whether the Bank of Canada is more or less independent of the government is not just an academic issue. Rather, there is now evidence to show that a central bank's degree of independence over time influences a country's long-term rate of inflation. The evidence indicates that at least since the 1950s, greater central bank independence tends to lessen a nation's inflation rate during periods of high worldwide inflation.

A Case in Point: New Zealand

The government in New Zealand decided to give its central bank one job: keeping the price level stable. It passed the Reserve Bank Act of 1989, setting desired price stability at inflation rates of zero to 2 percent. Only if New Zealand's central bank fails to achieve these goals can its governor be fired. Consequently, New Zealand's central bank no longer has to concern itself with short-term ups and downs in GDP growth rates. So far, its new independence and explicit mission have seemed to work: In 1989, the CPI increased by 5.7 percent; today, that increase is running at less than 1.5 percent per year.

For Critical Analysis

1. Since the government is ultimately responsible for the conduct of monetary policy, is the Bank of Canada really independent?

2. What would you expect to see happen to New Zealand's net exports after enactment of the Reserve Bank Act of 1989?

CHAPTER SUMMARY

1. The determinants of the demand for money balances are the transactions demand, the precautionary demand, and the asset demand.

2. Because holding money carries an opportunity cost—the interest income forgone—the demand for money curve showing the relationship between money balances and the interest rate slopes downward.

3. The direct effect of an increase in the money supply occurs through people desiring to spend more on real goods and services when they have excess money balances. The indirect effect of an increase in the money supply works through a lowering of the interest rate, thereby encouraging businesses to make new investments with the money loaned to them. Individuals will also engage in more consumption because of lower interest rates.

4. When the Bank of Canada sells bonds, it must offer them at a lower price. When it buys bonds, it must pay a higher price. There is an inverse relationship between the prevailing rate of interest in the economy and the market price of existing bonds.

5. If we start out in long-run and short-run equilibrium, contractionary monetary policy initially leads to a decrease in aggregate demand, resulting in a reduction in real GDP and in the price level. Eventually, though, the short-run aggregate supply curve shifts downward, and the new equilibrium is at *LRAS* but at an even lower price level. Expansionary monetary policy works the opposite way if we are starting out in both long-run and short-run equilibrium. The end result is simply a higher price level rather than a change in the equilibrium level of real GDP per year.

6. If expansionary monetary policy reduces Canadian interest rates, there is a positive net export effect because foreigners will demand fewer Canadian financial instruments, thereby demanding fewer dollars, causing the international price of the dollar to fall. This makes our exports cheaper for the rest of the world.

7. Expansionary monetary policy during periods of underutilized resources can cause the equilibrium level of real GDP to increase up to that rate of real output consistent with the vertical long-run aggregate supply curve.

8. The equation of exchange states that the expenditures by some people will equal income receipts by others: $M_sV \equiv PQ$ (money supply times velocity equals nominal national income). Viewed as an accounting identity, the equation of exchange is always correct because the amount of money spent on final output must equal the total amount of money received for final output.

9. The crude quantity theory of money and prices states that a change in the money supply will bring about a proportional change in the price level.

10. In the Keynesian model, monetary transmission operates through a change in the interest rates, which changes investment, causing a multiple change in national income.

11. Monetarists believe that changes in the money supply lead to changes in nominal GDP in the same direction. The effect is direct and indirect because individuals have excess money balances that they spend on cars, stereos, houses, and other things. Monetarists, among others, argue in favour of a monetary rule—increasing the money supply smoothly at a rate consistent with the economy's long-run growth rate. Monetarists do not believe in discretionary monetary (or fiscal) policy.

DISCUSSION OF PREVIEW QUESTIONS

1. **What is the demand for money curve, and how is it related to the interest rate?**

Three types of demands—transactions, precautionary, and asset—motivate people to hold money, and each type provides benefits to money holders. Because people get paid at discrete intervals but want to make expenditures more or less continuously, they find it convenient to hold a stock of money (transactions demand); the benefit they receive is convenience. People also desire a pool of readily available purchasing power in order to meet emergencies (precautionary demand); the benefit is a measure of security. Finally, money is an asset; it is a means of storing value or wealth. At certain times money becomes a superior form of wealth—superior to other asset forms (bonds, stocks, real estate, and the like) that are risky. Asset demand money holders receive the benefit of liquidity. There is an opportunity cost to holding money (especially the narrow form of money, M1). The opportunity cost is forgone interest. The demand for money curve shows an inverse relationship between the interest rate and desired money holdings. As the interest rate falls, the opportunity cost of holding money falls concomitantly; people are more and more disposed to avail themselves of the benefits of holding money as the cost of doing so falls.

2. **Why is the price of existing bonds inversely related to the interest rate?**

Suppose that you know nothing about some far-away planet except that a bond (or an investment project) there yields $100 per year forever. Can you determine whether that bond or investment project will have a high price; that is, will it be "valuable"? No, you can't; you would have to know what the interest rate was on that planet. If interest rates are very, very low, say, one-thousandth of 1 percent, that bond or investment would be very valuable indeed. This is because the interest rate summarizes the opportunity cost for investment projects or bonds; if interest rates are very low, a given amount of money can earn very little annually, but if interest rates are very high, a given amount of money can earn a great deal annually. Thus $100 per year looks good (high) or bad (low) depending on whether prevailing interest rates are low or high, respectively. The nature of a bond is such that it yields a given and known stream of revenues (nominal dollar amounts) over time. This given revenue stream will be priced relatively high if interest rates are relatively low and will command a low price if interest rates are high. In short, an inverse relationship exists between the price (market value) of an existing bond and the prevailing economy-wide interest rate.

3. **What is a monetarist?**

Monetarists are economists who maintain that changes in the money supply are the primary influence on the levels of employment, output, and prices. They maintain that there is little theoretical or empirical evidence to indicate the effectiveness of fiscal policy. Moreover, they maintain that monetary policy is not desirable either. This is because the time lag between changes in the money supply and changes in these macroeconomic variables is too long and imprecise, and that control of the money supply is not independent of politics. Consequently, present-day monetarists suggest that the government get out of the stabilization business; governments should use neither fiscal nor monetary policy. Instead, monetarists say governments should raise taxes and make expenditures only for pressing social matters (national defence, welfare, and so on), and monetary authorities should be commanded to increase the money supply at some constant and predetermined rate.

4. **How do the supply of, and demand for, money determine the interest rate?**

The accompanying graph depicts the total supply of and demand for money in an economy. To demonstrate that given these supply and demand schedules for money, the equilibrium interest rate will eventually be established at i_e,

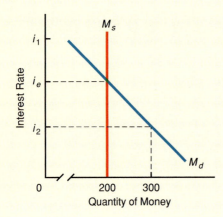

we must rule out all other possible interest rates. Thus let i_2 represent any interest rates below i_e. At i_2, the group wants to hold more money than is actually available ($M_d = 300 > M_s = 200$), and a shortage of liquidity exists. People become more liquid (hold more cash) by selling bonds (converting bonds, which are nonmoney, into money). As many people try to become more liquid, they attempt to sell many bonds. This forces bond prices down and interest rates up. These same conditions exist at all interest rates below i_e. Similarly, at all interest rates above i_e (i_1 in particular), $M_s > M_d$, and the group will be holding more money than it wants to hold to meet the three money-holding motives demands. Hence many people will buy bonds (to rid themselves of the opportunity cost of holding money), forcing bond prices up—and interest rates down towards i_e. At i_e, $M_d = M_s = 200$, and the group is voluntarily holding the available money supply.

PROBLEMS

(Answers to the odd-numbered problems appear at the back of the book.)

17-1. Briefly outline the Keynesian monetary transmission mechanism.

17-2. The equation that indicates the value (price) right now of a nonmaturing bond (called a consol) is $V = R/i$, where V is the present value, R is the annual net income generated from the bond, and i is the going interest rate.

   a. Assume that a bond promises the holder $1,000 per year forever. If the interest rate is 10 percent, what is the bond worth now (V)?

   b. Continuing part (a), what happens to the value of the bond (V) if interest rates rise to 20 percent? What if they fall to 5 percent?

   c. Suppose that there were an indestructible machine that was expected to generate $2,000 per year in revenues but costs $1,000 per year to maintain—forever. How would that machine be priced relative to the bond described in part (a)?

17-3. Show in the form of a chart the processes by which the Bank of Canada can reduce inflationary pressures by conducting drawdowns.

17-4. Assume that $M = \$30$ billion, $P = \$1.72$, and $Q = 90$ billion units per year. What is the income velocity of money?

17-5. Briefly outline expansionary monetary policy according to a monetarist.

MONETARY POLICY:
A KEYNESIAN PERSPECTIVE

According to the traditional Keynesian approach to monetary policy, changes in the money supply can affect the level of aggregate demand only through their effect on interest rates. Moreover, interest rate changes act on aggregate demand solely by changing the level of investment spending. Finally, the traditional Keynesian approach argues that there exist plausible circumstances under which monetary policy may have little or no effect on aggregate demand.

Figure D-1 measures real national income along the horizontal axis and total planned expenditures (aggregate demand) along the vertical axis. The components of aggregate demand are consumption (C), investment (I), government spending (G), and net exports (X). The height of the schedule labelled $C + I + G + X$ shows total planned expenditures (aggregate demand) as a function of income. This schedule slopes upward because consumption depends positively on income. Everywhere along the line labelled $Y = C + I + G + X$, planned spending equals income. At point Y^*, where the $C + I + G + X$ line intersects this 45-degree reference line, planned spending is consistent with income. At any income less than Y^*, spending exceeds income, so income and thus spending will tend to rise. At any level of income greater than Y^*, planned spending is less than income, so income and thus spending will tend to decline. Given the determinants of C, I, G, and X, total spending (aggregate demand) will be Y^*.

INCREASING THE MONEY SUPPLY

According to the Keynesian approach, an increase in the money supply pushes interest rates down. This reduces the cost of borrowing and thus induces firms to increase the level of investment spending from I to I'. As a result, the $C + I + G + X$ line shifts upward in Figure D-1 by the full amount of the rise in investment spending, thus yielding the line $C + I' + G + X$. The rise in investment spending causes income to rise, which in turn causes consumption spending to rise, which further

Figure D-1
An Increase in the Money Supply

An increase in the money supply increases income by lowering interest rates and thus increasing investment from I to I'.

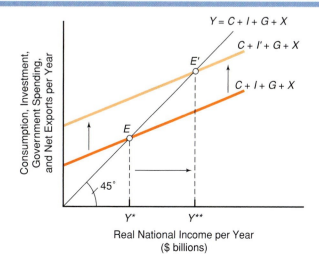

Real National Income per Year
($ billions)

increases income. Ultimately, aggregate demand rises to Y^{**}, where spending again equals income. A key conclusion of the Keynesian analysis is that total spending rises by *more* than the original rise in investment spending because consumption spending depends positively on income.

DECREASING THE MONEY SUPPLY

Not surprisingly, contractionary monetary policy works in exactly the reverse manner. A reduction in the money supply pushes interest rates up, which increases the cost of borrowing. Firms respond by reducing their investment spending, and this starts income downward. Consumers react to the lower income by scaling back on their consumption spending, which further depresses income. Thus the ultimate decline in income is larger than the initial drop in investment spending. Indeed, because the change in income is a multiple of the change in investment, Keynesians note that changes in investment spending (similar to changes in government spending) have a *multiplier* effect on the economy.

ARGUMENTS AGAINST MONETARY POLICY

It might be thought that this multiplier effect would make monetary policy a potent tool in the Keynesian arsenal, particularly when it comes to getting the economy out of a recession. In fact, however, many traditional Keynesians argue that monetary policy is likely to be relatively ineffective as a recession fighter. According to their line of reasoning, although monetary policy has the potential to reduce interest rates, changes in the money supply have little actual impact on interest rates. Instead, during recessions, people try to build up as much as they can in liquid assets to protect themselves from risks of unemployment and other losses of income. When the monetary authorities increase the money supply, individuals are willing to allow most of it to accumulate in their bank accounts. This desire for increased liquidity thus prevents interest rates from falling very much, which in turn means that there will be virtually no change in investment spending and thus little change in aggregate demand.

PROBLEMS

D-1. Assume that the following conditions exist:
a. All banks are fully loaned up—there are no excess reserves, and desired excess reserves are always zero.
b. The money multiplier is 3.
c. The planned investment schedule is such that at a 10 percent rate of interest, investment is $200 billion; at 9 percent, investment is $225 billion.
d. The investment multiplier is 3.
e. The initial equilibrium level of national income is $2 billion.

f. The equilibrium rate of interest is 10 percent.

Now the Bank of Canada engages in expansionary monetary policy. It buys $1 million worth of bonds, which increases the money supply, which in turn lowers the market rate of interest by 1 percent. Indicate by how much the money supply increased, and then trace out the numerical consequences of the associated reduction in interest rates on all the other variables mentioned.

Issues in Stabilization Policy

The 1970s and 1980s were hard years for many Canadians, as both inflation and unemployment continued to grow. We had increasing government deficits as unemployment reduced tax revenues, and inflation added to the cost of maintaining programs for the unemployed. Clearly the government needed to implement a focused economic policy to turn this trend around. So, it charged the Bank of Canada with the responsibility of using contractionary monetary policy to beat inflation. Was this the best policy the government could have chosen? To answer this question, you need to know more about certain issues pertaining to stabilization policies.

18

Preview Questions

1. What does the rational expectations hypothesis say about people's forecasting errors?

2. How do the new classical economists view economic policy?

3. What does the real business cycle theory say about the causes of recession?

4. How does the new Keynesian economics explain the stickiness of wages and prices?

▶ **Active (discretionary) policymaking**

All actions on the part of monetary and fiscal policymakers that are undertaken in response to or in anticipation of some change in the overall economy.

▶ **Passive (nondiscretionary) policymaking**

Policymaking that is carried out in response to a rule. It is therefore not in response to an actual or potential change in overall economic activity.

Did You Know That... since the Great Depression of the 1930s until today, the federal government has passed dozens of bills aimed at fighting recession by means of fiscal policy? In the mid-1990s, in one 17-month period, the Bank of Canada decreased short-term interest rates 20 times. And over a longer period, the Bank of Canada has even changed its basic operating targets.

ACTIVE VERSUS PASSIVE POLICYMAKING

All of these actions constitute part of what is called **active (discretionary) policymaking.** At the other extreme is **passive (nondiscretionary) policymaking,** in which there is no deliberate stabilization policy at all. You have already been introduced to one nondiscretionary policymaking idea in Chapter 17—the *monetary rule,* by which the money supply is allowed to increase at a fixed rate per year. In the fiscal arena, passive (nondiscretionary) policy might simply consist of balancing the federal budget over the business cycle. Recall from Chapter 13 that there are numerous time lags between the time that the economy enters a recession or a boom and when that event becomes known, acted on, and sensed by the economy. Proponents of passive policy argue strongly that such time lags often render short-term stabilization policy ineffective, or worse, procyclical.

To take a stand on this debate concerning active versus passive policymaking, you first need to know the potential trade-offs that policymakers believe they face. Then you need to see what the data actually show. The most important policy trade-off appears to be between price stability and unemployment. Before exploring that trade-off, we need first to look at the economy's natural, or long-run, rate of unemployment.

THE NATURAL RATE OF UNEMPLOYMENT

Recall from Chapter 7 that there are different types of unemployment: frictional, cyclical, seasonal, and structural. Frictional unemployment arises because individuals take the time to search for the best job opportunities. Except when the economy is in a recession or a depression, much unemployment is of this type.

Note that we did not say that frictional unemployment was the *sole* form of unemployment during normal times. There is also *wait unemployment,* caused by a variety of "rigidities" throughout the economy. Wait unemployment results from factors such as these:

1. Union activity that sets wages above the equilibrium level and also restricts the mobility of labour

2. Government-imposed licensing arrangements that restrict entry into specific occupations or professions

3. Government-imposed minimum wage laws and other laws that require all workers to be paid union wage rates on government contract jobs
4. Welfare and Employment Insurance benefits that reduce incentives to work
5. Changes in technology that make current workers' skills obsolete

In each case, these factors reduce individuals' abilities or incentives to choose employment rather than unemployment.

As an example, consider the effect of Employment Insurance benefits on the probability of an unemployed person finding a job. When unemployment benefits run out, according to economists Lawrence Katz and Bruce Meyer, the probability of an unemployed person finding a job doubles. The conclusion is that unemployed workers are more serious about finding a job when they are no longer receiving such benefits.

Frictional and wait unemployment both exist even when the economy is in long-run equilibrium—they are a natural consequence of costly information (the need to conduct a job search) and the existence of rigidities such as those noted. Because these two types of unemployment are a natural consequence of imperfect informa-

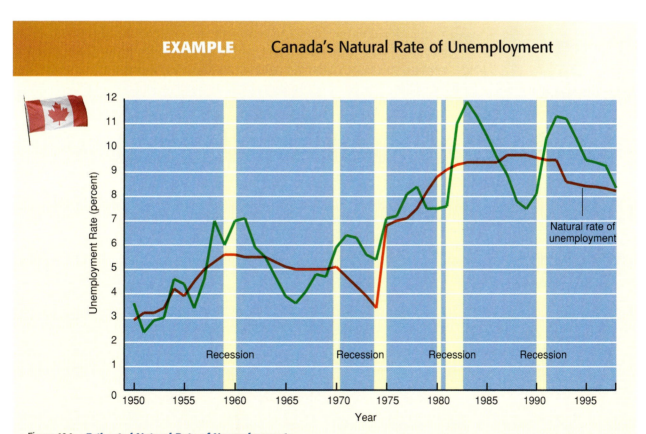

EXAMPLE   Canada's Natural Rate of Unemployment

Figure 18.1 **Estimated Natural Rate of Unemployment**

As you can see in this figure, the actual rate of unemployment has varied widely in Canada in the second half of the twentieth century. If we estimate the natural rate of unemployment by averaging unemployment rates from five years earlier to five years later at each point in time, we get the heavy solid line so labelled. It rose from the 1950s until the early 1990s and seems to have levelled off since then. (Post-1991 natural rate is approximated.)

Sources: Statistics Canada, CANSIM University Base, Series D76783, and M.C. Urquhart and K.A.H. Buckley, *Historical Statistics of Canada*.

In 1945, at the end of World War II, the unemployment rate was below 4 percent. By the early 1990s, it was above 10 percent. These two endpoints for half a century of unemployment rates prove nothing by themselves. But look at Figure 18.1 (page 439). There you see not only what has happened to the unemployment rate over that same time period, but also an estimate of the natural rate of unemployment. The solid line labelled "Natural rate of unemployment" is estimated by averaging unemployment rates from five years earlier to five years later at each point in time. This computation reveals that until about 1990, the natural rate of unemployment was rising. But since then, the natural rate of unemployment has held steady.

For critical analysis:
Of the factors listed on pages 438–39 that create wait unemployment, which do you think may explain the trend upward in the natural rate of unemployment since World War II?

▶ **Natural rate of unemployment**

The rate of unemployment that is estimated to prevail in long-run macroeconomic equilibrium, when all workers and employers have fully adjusted to any changes in the economy.

tion and rigidities, they are related to what economists call the **natural rate of unemployment.** It is defined as the rate of unemployment that would exist in the long run after everyone in the economy fully adjusted to any changes that have occurred. Recall that national output tends to return to the level implied by the long-run aggregate supply curve (*LRAS*). Thus whatever rate of unemployment the economy tends to return to can be called the natural rate of unemployment.

Departures from the Natural Rate of Unemployment

Even though the unemployment rate has a strong tendency to stay at and return to the natural rate, it is possible for fiscal and monetary policy to move the actual unemployment rate away from the natural rate, at least in the short run. Deviations

Figure 18.2
Impact of an Increase in Aggregate Demand on Output and Unemployment

If the economy is operating at E, it is in both short-run and long-run equilibrium. Here the actual rate of unemployment is equal to the natural rate of unemployment. Subsequent to expansionary monetary or fiscal policy, the aggregate demand curve shifts outward to AD_2. The price level rises to P_2; real GDP per year increases to Q_2. The unemployment rate will fall to below the natural rate of unemployment.

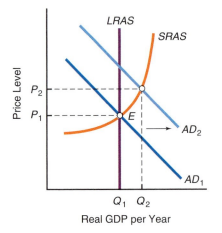

of the actual unemployment rate from the natural rate are called *cyclical unemployment* because they are observed over the course of nationwide business fluctuations. During recessions, the overall unemployment rate exceeds the natural rate; cyclical unemployment is positive. During periods of economic booms, the overall unemployment rate can go below the natural rate; at such times, cyclical unemployment is in essence negative.

To see how departures from the natural rate of unemployment can occur, let's consider two examples. Referring to Figure 18.2, we begin in equilibrium at point E, with the associated price level P_1 and real GDP per year of level Q_1.

The Impact of Expansionary Policy.   Now imagine that the government decides to use fiscal or monetary policy to stimulate the economy. Further suppose that this policy surprises decision makers throughout the economy in the sense that they did not anticipate that the policy would occur. The aggregate demand curve shifts from AD_1 to AD_2 in Figure 18.2, so both the price level and real GDP rise to P_2 and Q_2, respectively. In the labour market, individuals will find that conditions have improved markedly relative to what they expected. Firms seeking to expand output will want to hire more workers. To accomplish this, they will recruit more actively and possibly ask workers to work overtime, so that individuals in the labour market will find more job openings and more possible hours they can work. Consequently, as you learned in Chapter 7, the average duration of unemployment will fall so that the unemployment rate falls. This unexpected increase in aggregate demand simultaneously causes the price level to rise to P_2 and the unemployment rate to fall.

The Consequences of Contractionary Policy.   Instead of expansionary policy, the government could have decided to engage in contractionary (or deflationary) policy. As shown in Figure 18.3, the sequence of events would have been in the opposite direction of those in Figure 18.2. Again, beginning from an initial equilib-

Figure 18.3
Impact of a Decline in Aggregate Demand on Output and Unemployment

Starting from equilibrium at E, a decline in aggregate demand to AD_2 leads to a lower price level, P_2, and real GDP declines to Q_2. The unemployment rate will rise above the natural rate of unemployment.

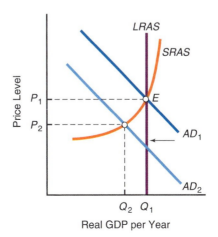

rium E, an unanticipated reduction in aggregate demand puts downward pressure on both prices and real GDP; the price level falls to P_2, and real GDP declines to Q_2. Fewer firms will be hiring, and those that are hiring will offer fewer overtime possibilities. Individuals looking for jobs will find that it takes longer than predicted. As a result, unemployed individuals will remain unemployed longer. The average duration of unemployment will rise, and so, too, will the rate of unemployment. The unexpected decrease in aggregate demand simultaneously causes the price level to fall to P_2 and the unemployment rate to rise.

The Phillips Curve: The Trade-Off?

Let's recap what we have just observed. An *unexpected* increase in aggregate demand causes the price level to rise and the unemployment rate to fall. Conversely, an *unexpected* decrease in aggregate demand causes the price level to fall and the unemployment rate to rise. Moreover, although not shown explicitly in either diagram, two additional points are true:

1. The greater the unexpected increase in aggregate demand, the greater the amount of inflation that results, and the lower the unemployment rate.
2. The greater the unexpected decrease in aggregate demand, the greater the deflation that results, and the higher the unemployment rate.

The Negative Relationship Between Inflation and Unemployment.
Figure 18.4 summarizes these findings. The inflation rate (*not* the price level) is measured along the vertical axis, and the unemployment rate is measured along the horizontal axis. Point A shows an initial starting point, with the unemployment rate at the natural rate, U^*. Note that as a matter of convenience, we are starting from an equilibrium in which the price level is stable (the inflation rate is zero). Unexpected

Figure 18.4
The Phillips Curve

Unanticipated changes in aggregate demand produce a negative relationship between the inflation rate and unemployment rate. U^* is the natural rate of unemployment.

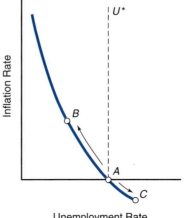

increases in aggregate demand cause the price level to rise—the inflation rate becomes positive—and cause the unemployment rate to fall. Thus the economy moves up to the left from *A* to *B*. Conversely, unexpected decreases in aggregate demand cause the price level to fall and the unemployment rate to rise above the natural rate—the economy moves from point *A* to point *C*. If we look at both increases and decreases in aggregate demand, we see that high inflation rates tend to be associated with low unemployment rates (as at *B*) and that low (or negative) inflation rates tend to be accompanied by high unemployment rates (as at *C*).

Is There a Trade-Off? The apparent negative relationship between the inflation rate and the unemployment rate shown in Figure 18.4 has come to be called the **Phillips curve**, after A. W. Phillips, who discovered that a similar relationship existed historically in the United Kingdom. Although Phillips presented his findings only as an empirical regularity, economists quickly came to view the relationship as representing a *trade-off* between inflation and unemployment. In particular, policymakers believed they could choose alternative combinations of unemployment and inflation (or worse, that the trade-off was inevitable because you could not get more of one without giving up the other). Thus it seemed that a government which disliked unemployment could select a point like *B* in Figure 18.4, with a positive inflation rate but a relatively low unemployment rate. Conversely, a government that feared inflation could choose a stable price level at *A*, but only at the expense of a higher associated unemployment rate. Indeed, the Phillips curve seemed to suggest that it was possible for policymakers to fine-tune the economy by selecting the policies that would produce the exact mix of unemployment and inflation that suited current government objectives. As it turned out, matters are not so simple.

The NAIRU. If we accept that a trade-off exists between the rate of inflation and the rate of unemployment, then the notion of "noninflationary" rates of unemployment seems appropriate. In fact, some economists have proposed what they call the **nonaccelerating inflation rate of unemployment (NAIRU)**. If the Phillips curve trade-off exists and if the NAIRU can be estimated, that estimate will define the short-run trade-off between the rate of unemployment and the rate of inflation. Economists who have estimated the NAIRU for the world's 24 richest industrial countries claim that it has been steadily rising since the 1960s. Critics of the NAIRU concept argue that inflationary expectations must be taken into account.

The Importance of Expectations

The reduction in unemployment that takes place as the economy moves from *A* to *B* in Figure 18.4 occurs because the wage offers encountered by unemployed workers are unexpectedly high. As far as the workers are concerned, these higher *nominal* wages appear, at least initially, to be increases in *real* wages; it is this fact that induces them to reduce their duration of search. This is a sensible way for the workers to view the world if aggregate demand fluctuates up and down at random, with no systematic or predictable variation one way or another. But if policymakers attempt to exploit the apparent trade-off in the Phillips curve, according to some macroeconomists, aggregate demand will no longer move up and down in an *unpredictable* way.

▶ **Phillips curve**

A curve showing the relationship between unemployment and changes in wages or prices. It was long thought to reflect a trade-off between unemployment and inflation.

▶ **Nonaccelerating inflation rate of unemployment (NAIRU)**

The rate of unemployment below which the rate of inflation tends to rise and above which the rate of inflation tends to fall.

Figure 18.5

A Shift in the Phillips Curve

When there is a change in the expected inflation rate, the Phillips curve (PC) shifts to incorporate the new expectations. PC_0 shows expectations of zero inflation; PC_5 reflects an expected inflation rate of 5 percent.

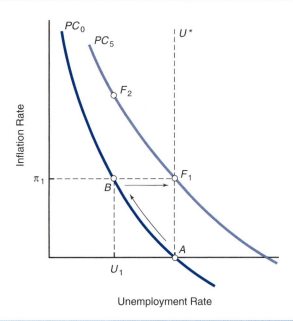

The Effects of an Unanticipated Policy.

Consider Figure 18.5, for example. If the Bank of Canada attempts to reduce the unemployment rate to U_1, it must increase the money supply enough to produce an inflation rate of π_1. If this is a one-shot affair in which the money supply is first increased and then held constant, the inflation rate will temporarily rise to π_1 and the unemployment rate will temporarily fall to U_1; but as soon as the money supply stops growing, the inflation rate will return to zero and unemployment will return to U^*, its natural rate. Thus a one-shot increase in the money supply will move the economy from point A to point B, and the economy will move of its own accord back to A.

If the authorities wish to prevent the unemployment rate from returning to U^*, some macroeconomists argue that the Bank of Canada must keep the money supply growing fast enough to keep the inflation rate up at π_1. But if the Bank of Canada does this, all of the economic participants in the economy—workers and job seekers included—will come to *expect* that inflation rate to continue. This, in turn, will change their expectations about wages. For example, suppose that π_1 equals 5 percent per year. When the expected inflation rate was zero, a 5 percent rise in nominal wages meant a 5 percent expected rise in real wages, and this was sufficient to induce some individuals to take jobs rather than remain unemployed. It was this perception of a rise in real wages that reduced search duration and caused the unemployment rate to drop from U^* to U_1. But if the expected inflation rate becomes 5 percent, a 5 percent rise in nominal wages means *no* rise in *real* wages. Once workers come to expect the higher inflation rate, rising nominal wages will no longer be sufficient to entice them out of unemployment. As a result, as the *expected* inflation rate moves up from 0 percent to 5 percent, the unemployment rate will move up also.

The Role of Expected Inflation.   In terms of Figure 18.5, as authorities initially increase aggregate demand, the economy moves from point A to point B. If the authorities continue the stimulus in an effort to keep the unemployment rate down, workers' expectations will adjust, causing the unemployment rate to rise. In this second stage, the economy moves from B to point F_1: The unemployment rate returns to the natural rate, U^*, but the inflation rate is now π_1 instead of zero. Once the adjustment of expectations has taken place, any further changes in policy will have to take place along a curve such as PC_5, say, a movement from F_1 to F_2. This new schedule is also a Phillips curve, differing from the first, PC_0, in that the actual inflation rate consistent with any given unemployment rate is higher because the expected inflation rate is higher.

Not surprisingly, when economic policymakers found that economic participants engaged in such adjustment behaviour, they were both surprised and dismayed. If decision makers can adjust their expectations to conform with fiscal and monetary policies, then policymakers cannot choose a permanently lower unemployment rate of U_1, even if they are willing to tolerate an inflation rate of π_1. Instead, the policymakers would end up with an unchanged unemployment rate in the long run, at the expense of a permanently higher inflation rate.

Initially, however, there did seem to be a small consolation, for it appeared that in the short run—before expectations adjusted—the unemployment rate could be *temporarily* reduced from U^* to U_1, even though eventually it would return to the natural rate. If an important federal election were approaching, it might be possible to stimulate the economy long enough to get the unemployment rate low enough to assure re-election. However, policymakers came to learn that not even this was likely to be a sure thing.

The Canadian Experience with the Phillips Curve

In separate articles in 1968, economists Milton Friedman and E. S. Phelps published pioneering studies suggesting that the apparent trade-off suggested by the Phillips curve could not be exploited by policymakers. Friedman and Phelps both argued that any attempt to reduce unemployment by inflating the economy would soon be thwarted by economic participants' incorporating the new higher inflation rate into their expectations. The Friedman-Phelps research thus implies that for any given unemployment rate, any inflation rate is possible, depending on the actions of policymakers. As reflected in Figure 18.6 (page 446), the propositions of Friedman and Phelps were to prove remarkably accurate.

When we examine the data for unemployment and inflation in Canada over the past half century, we see virtually no clear relationship between them. Although there seemed to have been a Phillips curve trade-off between unemployment and inflation from the mid-1950s to the mid-1960s, apparently once people in the economy realized what was happening, they started revising their forecasts accordingly. So, once policymakers attempted to exploit the Phillips curve, the apparent trade-off between unemployment and inflation disappeared.

Figure 18.6

The Phillips Curve: Theory Versus Data

If you plot points representing the rate of inflation and the rate of unemployment for Canada from 1950 to the present, there does not appear to be any Phillips curve trade-off between the two variables.

Sources: Statistics Canada, CANSIM University Base, Series D76783; *Canadian Economic Observer;* and M.C. Urquhart and K.A.H. Buckley, *Historical Statistics of Canada.*

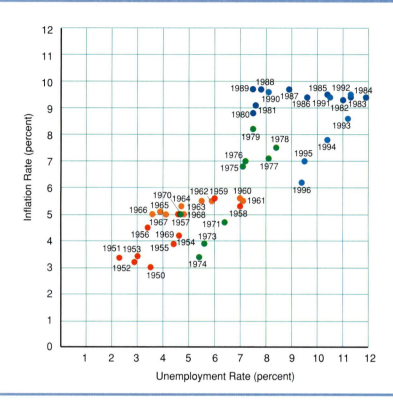

INTERNATIONAL EXAMPLE

Can European Policymakers Exploit the Phillips Curve?

Figure 18.7

Relationship Between Inflation and Unemployment in Europe

If we examine the so-called Phillips curve trade-off in Europe since 1967, there does not appear to be any long-run stable relationship between the rate of inflation and the rate of unemployment.

Source: David Blanchflower and Andrew Oswald.

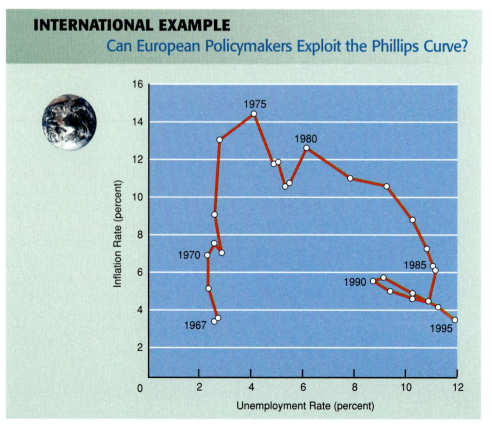

Although the data for Canada seem clear—policymakers cannot exploit the Phillips curve trade-off—is the same true in Europe? It appears that European policymakers cannot exploit the trade-off either. As Figure 18.7 shows, the unemployment rate in Europe remained almost constant from 1967 to 1974 in spite of a skyrocketing inflation rate.

If one believes in the Phillips curve analysis, there seems to be little hope today for European policymakers to reduce their double-digit unemployment rates. More complete research was conducted in 1994 by two British economists, David Blanchflower and Andrew Oswald, who spent five years analysing numerous data points across 12 countries. Their conclusion was that there is no relationship between inflation and unemployment.

For critical analysis: How do the data in Figure 18.6 and Figure 18.7 support the proponents of a monetary rule?

Concepts in Brief

- The natural rate of unemployment is the rate that exists in long-run equilibrium, when workers' expectations are consistent with actual conditions.
- Departures from the natural rate of unemployment can occur when individuals encounter unanticipated changes in fiscal or monetary policy; an unexpected rise in aggregate demand will reduce unemployment below the natural rate, whereas an unanticipated decrease in aggregate demand will push unemployment above the natural rate.
- The Phillips curve exhibits a negative relationship between the inflation rate and the unemployment rate that can be observed when there are *unanticipated* changes in aggregate demand.
- It was originally believed that the Phillips curve represented a trade-off between inflation and unemployment. In fact, no trade-off exists because workers' expectations adjust to any systematic attempts to reduce unemployment below the natural rate.

RATIONAL EXPECTATIONS AND THE NEW CLASSICAL MODEL

You already know that economists assume that economic participants act *as though* they were rational and calculating. We think of firms that rationally maximize profits when they choose today's rate of output, and consumers who rationally maximize utility when they choose how much of what goods to consume today. One of the pivotal features of current macro policy research is the assumption that rationality also applies to the way that economic participants think about the future as well as the present. This relationship was developed by Robert Lucas, who won the Nobel Prize in 1995 for his work. In particular, there is widespread agreement among a growing

▶ **Rational expectations hypothesis**

A theory stating that people combine the effects of past policy changes on important economic variables with their own judgment about the future effects of current and future policy changes.

▶ **New classical model**

A modern version of the classical model in which wages and prices are flexible, there is pure competition in all markets, and the rational expectations hypothesis is assumed to be working.

Try Preview Question 1:

What does the rational expectations hypothesis say about people's forecasting errors?

group of macroeconomics researchers that the **rational expectations hypothesis** extends our understanding of the behaviour of the macroeconomy. There are two key elements to this hypothesis:

1. Individuals base their forecasts (or expectations) about the future values of economic variables on all available past and current information.
2. These expectations incorporate individuals' understanding about how the economy operates, including the operation of monetary and fiscal policy.

In essence, the rational expectations hypothesis assumes the old saying is correct: "It is true that you may fool all the people some of the time; you can even fool some of the people all of the time; but you can't fool *all* of the people *all* of the time."

If we further assume that there is pure competition in all markets and that all prices and wages are flexible, we obtain the **new classical model** (referred to in Chapter 13 when discussing the Ricardian equivalence theorem). To see how rational expectations operate within the context of this model, let's take a simple example of the economy's response to a change in monetary policy.

The New Classical Model

Consider Figure 18.8, which shows the long-run aggregate supply curve ($LRAS$) for the economy, as well as the initial aggregate demand curve (AD_1) and the short-run aggregate supply curve ($SRAS_1$). The money supply is initially given by $M = M_1$, and the price level and real GDP are shown by P_1 and Q_1, respectively. Thus point A represents the initial equilibrium.

Suppose now that the money supply is unexpectedly increased to M_2, thereby causing the aggregate demand curve to shift outward to AD_2. Given the location of the short-run aggregate supply curve, this increase in aggregate demand will cause

Figure 18.8
Response to an Unanticipated Rise in Aggregate Demand

Unanticipated changes in aggregate demand have real effects. In this case, the rise in demand causes real output to rise from Q_1 to Q_2.

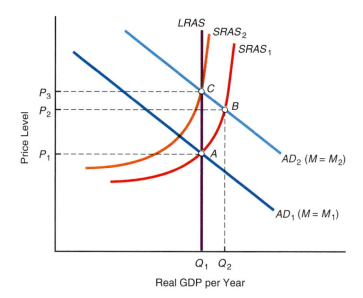

output and the price level to rise to Q_2 and P_2, respectively. The new short-run equilibrium is at B. Because output is *above* the long-run equilibrium level of Q_1, unemployment must be below long-run levels (the natural rate), and so workers will soon respond to the higher price level by demanding higher nominal wages. This will cause the short-run aggregate supply curve to shift upward vertically, moving the economy to the new long-run equilibrium at C. The price level thus continues its rise to P_3, even as real GDP declines back down to Q_1 (and unemployment returns to the natural rate). So as we have seen before, even though an increase in the money supply can raise output and lower unemployment in the short run, it has no effect on either variable in the long run.

The Response to Anticipated Policy. Now let's look at this disturbance with the perspective given by the rational expectations hypothesis, as it is embedded in the new classical model. Suppose that workers (and other input owners) know ahead of time that this increase in the money supply is about to take place. Assume also that they know when it is going to occur and understand that its ultimate effect will be to push the price level from P_1 to P_3. Will workers wait until after the price level has increased to insist that their nominal wages go up? The rational expectations hypothesis says that they will not. Instead, they will go to employers and insist on nominal wages that move upward in step with the higher prices. From the workers' perspective, this is the only way to protect their real wages from declining due to the anticipated increase in the money supply.

The Policy Irrelevance Proposition. As long as economic participants behave in this manner, when we draw the *SRAS* curve, we must be explicit about the nature of their expectations. This we have done in Figure 18.9. In the initial equi-

Figure 18.9
Effects of an Anticipated Rise in Aggregate Demand

When policy is fully anticipated, a rise in the money supply causes a rise in the price level from P_1 to P_3, with no change in real output.

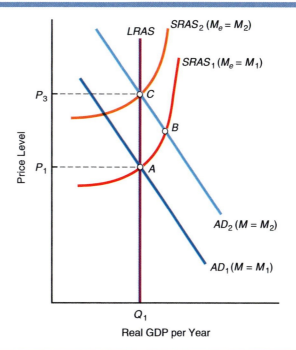

librium, the short-run aggregate supply curve is labelled to show that the expected money supply (M_e) and the actual money supply (M_1) are equal ($Me = M_1$). Similarly, when the money supply changes in a way that is anticipated by economic participants, the aggregate supply curve shifts to reflect this expected change in the money supply. The new short-run aggregate supply curve is labelled ($Me = M_2$) to reveal this. According to the rational expectations hypothesis, the short-run aggregate supply will shift upward *simultaneously* with the rise in aggregate demand. As a result, the economy will move directly from point *A* to point *C* in Figure 18.9 without passing through *B*: The *only* response to the rise in the money supply is a rise in the price level from P_1 to P_3; neither output nor unemployment changes at all. This conclusion—that fully anticipated monetary policy is irrelevant in determining the levels of real variables—is called the **policy irrelevance proposition**:

▶ **Policy irrelevance proposition**

The new classical and rational expectations conclusion that policy actions have no real effects in the short run if the policy actions are anticipated and none in the long run even if the policy actions are unanticipated.

> Under the assumption of rational expectations on the part of decision makers in the economy, anticipated monetary policy cannot alter either the rate of unemployment or the level of real GDP. Regardless of the nature of the anticipated policy, the unemployment rate will equal the natural rate, and real GDP will be determined solely by the economy's long-run aggregate supply curve.

Thinking Critically About the Media   Higher Interest Rates and "Tight" Monetary Policy

The media often report changes in interest rates to indicate changes in monetary policy, whether they are referring to Canada or any other country. The problem with such analyses is that they fail to distinguish between real and nominal interest rates. Normally, a high interest rate is evidence that a country's central bank has been pursuing *loose* monetary policy in the past rather than tight monetary policy now. Why? Because in the long run, consistent increases in the rate of growth of the money supply lead to a higher rate of inflation. A higher rate of inflation normally leads to expectations of inflation and therefore higher *nominal* interest rates. After all, the nominal interest rate is equal to the real rate of interest plus the expected rate of inflation. In the long run, evidence shows that monetary authorities have little effect on an economy's real rate of interest.

What Must People Know?   There are two important matters to keep in mind when considering this proposition. First, our discussion has assumed that economic participants know in advance exactly what the change in monetary policy is going to be and precisely when it is going to occur. In fact, the Bank of Canada does not announce exactly what the future course of monetary policy (down to the last dollar) is going to be. Instead, the Bank of Canada announces only in general terms what policy actions are intended for the future. It is tempting to conclude that because the Bank of Canada's intended policies are not freely available, they are not available at all. But such a conclusion is wrong. Economic participants have great incentives to learn how to predict the future behaviour of the monetary authorities, just as businesses try to forecast consumer behaviour and college students do their best to forecast what their next economics exam will look like. Even if the economic participants are not perfect at forecasting the course of policy, they are likely to come a lot closer than they would in total ignorance. The policy irrelevance proposition really assumes only that *people don't persistently make the same mistakes in forecasting the future.*

Figure 18.10
Effects of an Unanticipated Rise in Aggregate Demand
Even with rational expectations, an unanticipated change in demand can affect output in the short run.

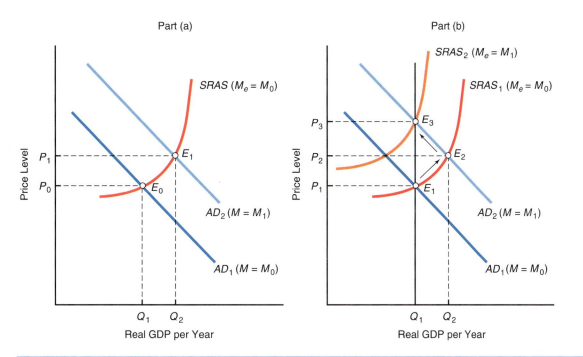

What Happens If People Don't Know Everything?   This brings us to our second point. Once we accept the fact that people are not perfect in their ability to predict the future, the possibility emerges that some policy actions will have systematic effects that look much like the movements A to B to C in Figure 18.8. For example, just as other economic participants sometimes make mistakes, it is likely that the Bank of Canada sometimes makes mistakes—meaning that the money supply may change in ways that even the Bank of Canada does not predict. And even if the Bank of Canada always accomplished every policy action it intended, there is no guarantee that other economic participants would fully forecast those actions. What happens if the Bank of Canada makes a mistake or if firms and workers misjudge the future course of policy? Matters will look much as they do in part (a) of Figure 18.10, which shows the effects of an unanticipated increase in the money supply. Economic participants expect the money supply to be M_0, but the actual money supply turns out to be M_1. Because $M_1 > M_0$, aggregate demand shifts relative to aggregate supply. The result is a rise in real output (real GDP) in the short run from Q_1 to Q_2; corresponding to this rise in real output will be an increase in employment and hence a fall in the unemployment rate. So even under the rational expectations hypothesis, monetary policy can have an effect on real variables in the short run, but only if the policy is unsystematic and therefore unanticipated.

Try Preview Question 2:
How do the new classical economists view economic policy?

In the long run, this effect on real variables will disappear because people will figure out that the Bank of Canada either accidentally increased the money supply or intentionally increased it in a way that somehow fooled individuals. Either way, people's expectations will soon be revised so that the short-run aggregate supply curve will shift upward. As shown in part (b) of Figure 18.10, real GDP will return to long-run levels, meaning that so will the employment and unemployment rates.

The Policy Dilemma

Perhaps the most striking and disturbing feature of the new classical model is that it seems to suggest that only mistakes can have real effects. If the Bank of Canada always does what it intends to do, and if other economic participants always correctly anticipate the Bank of Canada's actions, monetary policy will affect only the price level and nominal input prices. It appears that only if the Bank of Canada makes a mistake in executing monetary policy or people err in anticipating that policy will changes in the money supply cause fluctuations in real output and employment. If this reasoning is correct, the Bank of Canada is effectively precluded from using monetary policy in any rational way to lower the unemployment rate or to raise the level of real GDP. This is because fully anticipated changes in the money supply will lead to exactly offsetting changes in prices and hence no real effects. Many economists were disturbed at the prospect that if the economy happened to enter a recessionary period, policymakers would be powerless to push real GDP and unemployment back to long-run levels. As a result, they asked the question, "In light of the rational expectations hypothesis, is it ever possible for systematic policy to have predictable real effects on the economy?" The answer has led to even more developments in the way we think about macroeconomics.

Concepts in Brief

- The rational expectations hypothesis assumes that individuals' forecasts incorporate all available information, including an understanding of government policy and its effects on the economy.
- The new classical economics assumes that the rational expectations hypothesis is valid, and also that there is pure competition and that all prices and wages are flexible.
- The policy irrelevance proposition says that under the assumptions of the new classical model, fully anticipated monetary policy cannot alter either the rate of unemployment or the level of real GDP.
- The new classical model implies that policies can alter real economic variables only if the policies are unsystematic and therefore unanticipated, otherwise people learn and defeat the desired policy goals.

REAL BUSINESS CYCLE THEORY

The modern extension of new classical theory involves re-examining the first principles that assume fully flexible prices.

The Distinction Between Real and Monetary Shocks

▶ **Real business cycle theory**
An extension and modification of the theories of the new classical economists of the 1970s and 1980s, in which money is neutral and only real, supply-side factors matter in influencing labour employment and real output.

The research of the new business cycle theorists differs importantly from that of new classical theorists in that business cycle theorists seek to determine whether real, as opposed to purely monetary, forces might help explain aggregate economic fluctuations. An important stimulus for the development of **real business cycle theory**, as it has come to be known, was the economic turmoil of the 1970s. During that decade, world economies were staggered by two major disruptions to the supply of oil. The first occurred in 1973, the second in 1979. In both episodes, members of the Organization of Petroleum Exporting Countries (OPEC) reduced the amount of oil they were willing to supply and raised the price at which they offered it for sale. Each time, the price level rose sharply in Canada, and real GDP declined. Thus each episode produced a period of "stagflation"—real economic stagnation combined with high inflation. Figure 18.11 illustrates the pattern of events.

We begin at point E_1 with the economy in both short- and long-run equilibrium, with the associated supply curves, $SRAS_1$ and $LRAS_1$. Initially, the level of real GDP is Q_1, and the price level is P_1. Because the economy is in long-run equilibrium, the unemployment rate must be at the natural rate.

A reduction in the supply of oil, as occurred in 1973 and 1979, causes the $SRAS$ curve to shift to the left to $SRAS_2$ because fewer goods will be available for sale due

Figure 18.11
Effects of a Reduction in the Supply of Resources

The position of the *LRAS* depends on our endowments of all types of resources. Hence a reduction in the supply of one of those resources, such as oil, causes a reduction—an inward shift—in the aggregate supply curve. In addition, there is a rise in the equilibrium price level and a fall in the equilibrium rate of real GDP per year (output).

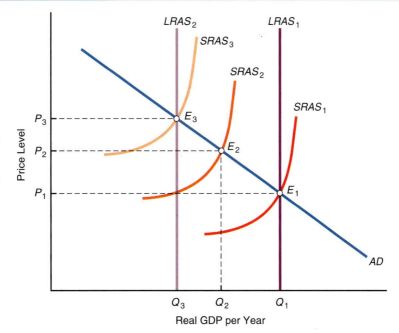

to the reduced supplies. If the reduction in oil supplies is (or is believed to be) permanent, the *LRAS* shifts to the left also. This assumption is reflected in Figure 18.11, where $LRAS_2$ shows the new long-run aggregate supply curve associated with the lowered output of oil.

In the short run, two adjustments begin to occur simultaneously. First, the prices of oil and petroleum-based products begin to rise, so that the overall price level rises to P_2. Second, the higher costs of production occasioned by the rise in oil prices induce firms to cut back production, so total output falls to Q_2 in the short run. The new temporary short-run equilibrium occurs at E_2, with a higher price level (P_2) and a lower level of real GDP (Q_2).

Impact on the Labour Market

If we were to focus on the labour market while this adjustment from E_1 to E_2 was taking place, we would find two developments occurring. The rise in the price level pushes the real wage rate downward, even as the scaled-back production plans of firms induce them to reduce the amount of labour inputs they are using. So not only does the real wage rate fall, but the level of employment declines as well. On both counts, workers are made worse off due to the reduction in the supply of oil.

Now this is not the full story, because owners of non-oil inputs (such as labour) who are willing to put up with reduced real payments in the short run simply will not tolerate them in the long run. Thus, for example, some workers who were willing to continue working at lower wages in the short run will eventually decide to retire, switch from full-time to part-time employment, or drop out of the labour force altogether. In effect, there is a reduction in the supply of non-oil inputs, reflected in an upward shift in the *SRAS* from $SRAS_2$ to $SRAS_3$. This puts additional upward pressure on the price level and exerts a downward force on real GDP. The final long-run equilibrium thus occurs at point E_3, with the price level at P_3 and real GDP at Q_3. (In principle, because the oil supply shock has had no long-term effect on labour markets, the natural rate of unemployment does not change when equilibrium moves from E_1 to E_3.)

Generalizing the Theory

Naturally, the focus of real business cycle theory goes well beyond the simple "oil shock" that we have discussed here, for it encompasses all types of real disturbances, including technological changes and shifts in the composition of the labour force. Moreover, a complete treatment of real shocks to the economy is typically much more complex than we have allowed for in our discussion. For example, an oil shock such as is shown in Figure 18.11 would likely also have effects on the real wealth of Canadians, causing a reduction in aggregate demand as well as aggregate supply. Nevertheless, our simple example still manages to capture the flavour of the theory.

It is clear that real business cycle theory has improved our understanding of the economy's behaviour, but there is also agreement among economists that it alone is incapable of explaining all of the facets of business cycles that we observe. For example, it is difficult to imagine a real disturbance that could possibly account for the Great Depression in this country, when real income fell 30 percent and the unem-

Try Preview Question 3:
What does the real business cycle theory say about the causes of recession?

ployment rate rose to 20 percent. Moreover, real business cycle theory continues to assume that prices are perfectly flexible and so fails to explain a great deal of the apparent rigidity of prices throughout the economy.

NEW KEYNESIAN ECONOMICS

▶ **New Keynesian econom-ics**

Economic models based on the idea that demand creates its own supply as a result of various possible government fiscal and monetary coordination failures.

Although the new classical and real business cycle theories both incorporate pure competition and flexible prices, a body of research called the **new Keynesian economics** drops both of these assumptions. The new Keynesian economists do not believe that market-clearing models of the economy can explain business cycles. Consequently, they argue that macroeconomics models must contain the "sticky" wages and prices assumption that Keynes outlined in his major work. Thus the new Keynesian research has as its goal a refinement of the theory of aggregate supply that explains how wages and prices behave in the short run. There are several such theories. The first one relates to the cost of changing prices.

Small-Menu Cost Theory

▶ **Small-menu cost theory**

A hypothesis that it is costly for firms to change prices in response to demand changes because of the cost of renegotiating contracts, printing price lists, and so on.

If prices do not respond to demand changes, two conditions must be true: Someone must be consciously deciding not to change prices, and that decision must be in the decision maker's self-interest. One combination of facts that is consistent with this scenario is the **small-menu cost theory**, which supposes that much of the economy is characterized by imperfect competition and that it is costly for firms to change their prices in response to changes in demand. The costs associated with changing prices are called *menu costs*, and they include the costs of renegotiating contracts, printing price lists (such as menus), and informing customers of price changes.

Many such costs may not be very large in magnitude; that is why they are called *small-menu costs*. Some of the costs of changing prices, however, such as those incurred in bringing together business managers from points around the country or the world for meetings on price changes, or renegotiating deals with customers, may be significant.

Firms in different industries have different cost structures. Such differences explain diverse small-menu costs. Therefore, the extent to which firms hold their prices constant in the face of changes in demand for their products will vary across industries. Not all prices will be rigid. Nonetheless, new Keynesian theorists argue that many—even most—firms' prices are sticky for relatively long time intervals. As a result, the aggregate level of prices could be very nearly rigid because of small-menu costs.

Although most economists agree that such costs exist, there is considerably less agreement on whether they are sufficient to explain the extent of price rigidity that is observed.

Efficiency Wage Theory

▶ **Efficiency wage theory**

The hypothesis that the productivity of workers depends on the level of the real wage rate.

An alternative approach within the new Keynesian framework is called the **efficiency wage theory**. It proposes that worker productivity actually *depends on* the wages that workers are paid, rather than being independent of wages, as is assumed in other theories. According to this theory, higher real wages encourage workers to work harder, improve their efficiency, increase morale, and raise their loyalty to the firm. Across the board, then, higher wages tend to increase workers' productivity, which in turn discourages firms from cutting real wages because of the damaging effect that such an action would have on productivity and profitability. Under highly competitive conditions, there will generally be an optimal wage—called the *efficiency wage*—that the firm should continue paying, even in the face of large fluctuations in the demand for its output.

The efficiency wage theory model is a rather simple idea, but it is somewhat revolutionary. All of the models of the labour market adopted by traditional classical, traditional Keynesian, monetarist, new classical, and new Keynesian theorists alike do not consider such real-wage effects on worker productivity.

There are significant, valid elements in the efficiency wage theory, but its importance in understanding national business fluctuations remains uncertain. For example, although the theory explains rigid real wages, it does not explain rigid prices. Moreover, the theory ignores the fact that firms can (and apparently do) rely on a host of incentives other than wages to encourage their workers to be loyal, efficient, and productive.

Try Preview Question 4:

How does the new Keynesian economics explain the stickiness of wages and prices?

INTERNATIONAL EXAMPLE
Henry Ford and the Efficiency Wage Model

One of the most clear-cut examples of the efficiency wage model involved the Ford Motor Company in the United States. When nominal wage rates were about US$2 to US$3 a day in 1914 (about US$30 in today's dollars and with no benefits such as health insurance), Henry Ford ordered his managers to start paying workers US$5 a day. Ford later argued that the increase in wages was a "cost-cutting" move. The evidence bears him out. Absenteeism dropped by over 70 percent. Moreover, labour turnover virtually disappeared. Consequently, Ford's managers had to spend less time training new workers.

For critical analysis: What alternative ways do managers have to provide incentives to their workers to become more efficient?

Effect of Aggregate Demand Changes on Output and Employment in the Long Run

Some new Keynesian economists argue that a reduction in aggregate demand that causes a recession may affect output and employment even in the long run. They point out that workers who are fired or laid off may lose job skills during their period of unemployment. Consequently, they will have a more difficult time finding new employment later. Furthermore, those who remain unemployed over long periods of time may change their attitudes towards work. They may even have a reduced desire to find employment later on. For these reasons and others, a recession could permanently raise the amount of frictional unemployment.

As yet, little research has been done to quantify this theory.

MACROECONOMIC MODELS AND THEIR IMPLICATIONS FOR STABILIZATION POLICY

Although it is impossible to compare accurately and completely every single detail of the various macroeconomic approaches we have examined, it is useful to summarize and contrast some of their key aspects. Table 18.1 presents features of our five key models: traditional classical, traditional Keynesian, new (modern) classical, new (modern) Keynesian, and modern monetarist. Realize when examining the table that we are painting with a broad brush.

Table 18.1

A Comparison of Macroeconomic Models

	Macroeconomic Model				
Issue	Traditional Classical	Traditional Keynesian	New Classical	New Keynesian	Modern Monetarist
Stability of capitalism	Yes	No	Yes	Yes, but can be enhanced by policy	Yes
Price-wage flexibility	Yes	No	Yes	Yes, but imperfect	Yes, but some restraints
Belief in natural rate of employment hypothesis	Yes	No	Yes	Yes	Yes
Factors sensitive to interest rate	Saving, consumption, investment	Demand for money	Saving, consumption, investment	Saving, consumption, investment	Saving, consumption, investment
View of the velocity of money	Stable	Unstable	No consensus	No consensus	Stable
Effect of changes in money supply on economy	Changes aggregate demand	Changes interest rates, which change investment and real output	No effect on real variables if anticipated	Changes aggregate demand	Directly changes aggregate demand
Effects of fiscal policy on the economy	Not applicable	Multiplier changes in aggregate demand and output	Generally ineffective*	Changes aggregate demand	Ineffective unless money supply changes also
Causes of inflation	Excess money growth	Excess real aggregate demand	Excess money growth	Excess money growth	Excess money growth
Stabilization policy	Unnecessary	Fiscal policy necessary and effective; monetary policy ineffective	Too difficult to conduct	Both fiscal and monetary policy may be useful	Too difficult to conduct

*Some fiscal policies affect relative prices (interest rates) and so many have real effects on economy.

STABILIZATION POLICY AND THE NEW GROWTH THEORISTS

Recall from Chapter 9 that there is a group of economists who support what is now called new growth theory. In this theory, real wealth creation comes from innovation, which is part of new technology. New growth theorists repeatedly point out that small differences in annual rates of growth over a few decades make a tremendous difference in the standard of living of each individual. Indeed, they argue that short-run monetary and fiscal stabilization policies are in fact beside the point. To them, the Keynesian emphasis on the business cycle appears to be a strange fixation.

If what really matters is the underlying growth rate rather than the business cycle around it, then any efforts to fine-tune the economy are perhaps misguided. Actually, according to the new growth theorists, one of the processes underlying the business cycle is that of discovery and innovation. This process generates long-run improvements in the standard of living. It determines in large part how steep the slope is over a long-run upward trend. The little wiggles—business cycles—take on less importance. The federal government should not be concerned with them.

Does that mean that government policy has no place in our economy? The answer from the new growth theorists is that the government does have a place, but it has little to do with discretionary changes in taxes or spending or monetary growth rates. Rather, it has to do with speeding up the pace of innovation. It also has to do with government's devising policies that promote new technology. One of these policies might be to strengthen patent protection. In any event, the new growth theorists would probably agree with economists who argue in favour of passive nondiscretionary stabilization policy.

In sum, stabilization policy analysis is really about the costs and benefits of getting the economy to where it *eventually* will go anyway—to its long-run aggregate supply curve (*LRAS*). According to the new growth theorists, the costs outweigh the benefits so that short-run stabilization policy should not be the main macroeconomic activity of the federal government. It is economic growth that shifts *LRAS* rightward. Government macroeconomic policy should focus, according to the new growth theorists, solely on this issue.

Concepts in Brief

- Real business cycle theory holds that even if all prices and wages are perfectly flexible, real shocks to the economy (such as technological change and changes in the supplies of factors of production) can cause national business fluctuations.
- The new Keynesian economics explains why various features of the economy, such as small-menu costs and wage rates that affect productivity, make it possible for monetary shocks to cause real effects.
- Although there remain significant differences between the classical and Keynesian branches of macroeconomics, the rivalry between them is an important source of innovation that helps improve our understanding of the economy.
- New growth theorists in general reject the effectiveness of short-run discretionary stabilization policies and argue, in contrast, that the federal government should focus its policy efforts on fostering a climate that will generate higher economic growth rates.

Issues and Applications

The Bank of Canada's High Interest Rate Policy

Concepts Applied: Nominal and real interest rates, unemployment, economic growth

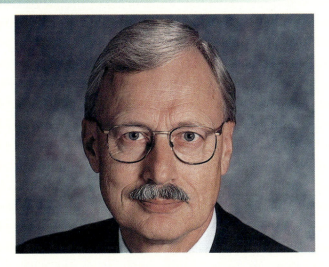

Gordon Thiessen, the Governor of the Bank of Canada, supports the use of relatively high interest rates to dampen inflation and stabilize the economy. Critics claim his plan keeps real interest rates high and encourages financial rather than productive investment in Canada.

A debate rages among economists about whether the Bank of Canada's interest rate policy is helping or harming the economy. In 1991, the Bank of Canada made a formal commitment to the federal government to keep inflation between 1 and 3 percent through to 1998. The Bank has used high interest rates as its policy tool in pursuit of this goal. High interest rates discourage consumer and business spending, dampen aggregate demand, and thus keep prices from rising.

The Governor of the Bank of Canada, Gordon Thiessen, asserts that his high interest rate policy allows businesses to make "smarter" decisions since they can plan on a relatively stable price level into the future. This in turn makes Canada more conducive to expanding business activity. Further, low inflation rates contribute to lower nominal interest payments on the federal debt since nominal interest rates are the sum of real rates plus a premium for expected inflation. The combination of low debt service payments and expanding business activity will result in a lower debt-to-GDP ratio. A lower debt-to-GDP ratio makes Canada a more attractive place for investment, which will induce economic growth. Overall, Mr. Thiessen's plan is one of short-term pain—continuing high unemployment—for long-term gain—economic growth which will lead to job creation in the future.

Critics of Mr. Thiessen's plan argue that the Bank of Canada has more than one mandate: the 1934 charter of the Bank also included a directive that it should promote trade, production, and employment in Canada. By following a high interest rate policy, the Bank of Canada has kept real interest rates high. Inflation has indeed been falling, but nominal interest rates are lagging. See Figure 18.12 for a history of real interest rates. High real interest

Figure 18.12
Real Interest Rates Since World War II

Real interest rates in Canada have varied from a low of minus one-half of 1 percent just after World War II to a high of 10 percent in 1980, in the wake of the OPEC oil price hikes. Real interest rates peaked again in 1990.

Source: CANSIM University Base, series B14006.

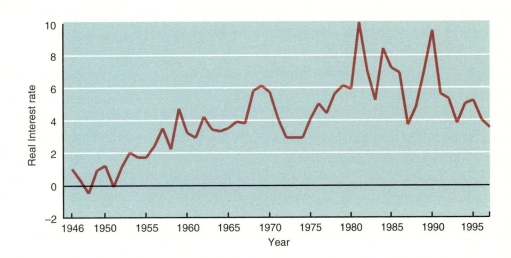

rates, argue the Bank of Canada's critics, encourage passive invest-ment—the purchase of financial instruments in order to earn a hefty return. Low real interest rates encourage active investment—invest-ment in capital equipment and job-creating businesses because the cost of borrowing is low. With active investment the tax base increases, raising government revenues and reducing the need for costly social programs, thus making a reduction of the debt-to-GDP ratio possible.

What should students of economics make of this debate? Is it time to turn from fighting inflation to job creation? The natural rate of unemployment in Canada is thought to be about 8.5 percent (look back at Figure 18.1). The unemployment rate in 1998 was 8.3

percent, with inflation at about 1.5 percent. Has the natural rate fall-en, suggesting that unemployment could be further reduced with-out risking renewed inflation?

For Critical Analysis

1. What different effects do you think passive and active invest-ment have on the Canadian economy?

2. According to the policy irrelevance proposition, will unem-ployment be affected by Mr. Thiessen's high interest rate pol-icy?

CHAPTER SUMMARY

1. The natural rate of unemployment is the rate that exists in long-run equilibrium, when work-ers' expectations are consistent with actual con-ditions. Departures from the natural rate of unemployment can occur when individuals are surprised by unanticipated changes in fiscal or monetary policy.

2. The Phillips curve shows a negative relationship between the inflation rate and the unemploy-ment rate that can be observed when there are unanticipated changes in aggregate demand. It was originally believed that the Phillips curve represented a trade-off between inflation and unemployment. In fact, no trade-off exists because workers' expectations adjust to system-atic attempts to reduce unemployment below its natural rate.

3. The rational expectations hypothesis assumes that individuals' forecasts incorporate all avail-able information, including an understanding of government policy and its effects on the econo-my. The new classical economics assumes that the rational expectations hypothesis is valid and

also that there is pure competition and that all prices and wages are flexible.

4. The policy irrelevance proposition says that under the assumptions of the new classical model, anticipated monetary policy cannot alter either the rate of unemployment or the level of real GDP. Thus according to the new classical model, policies can alter real economic variables only if the policies are unsystematic and there-fore unanticipated; such policies cannot affect output and employment systematically.

5. Real business cycle theory holds that even if all prices and wages are perfectly flexible, real shocks to the economy (such as technological change and changes in the supplies of factors of production) can cause national business fluctua-tions.

6. The new Keynesian economics explains why various features of the economy, such as small-menu costs and wage rates that affect productiv-ity, make it possible for monetary shocks to cause real effects.

DISCUSSION OF PREVIEW QUESTIONS

1. **What does the rational expectations hypothesis say about people's forecasting errors?**

   The simplest version of the rational expectations hypothesis says that people do not persistently make the same mistakes in forecasting the future. More generally, the hypothesis says that individuals base their forecasts about the future values of economic variables on the basis of all available past and current information and that these forecasts incorporate individuals' understanding about how the economy operates, including the operation of monetary and fiscal policy. As a result, people's forecasting errors are completely unpredictable over time and thus cannot be used by policymakers in formulating policy.

2. **How do the new classical economists view economic policy?**

   The new classical economists assume that the rational expectations hypothesis is valid and also that there is pure competition and that all prices and wages are flexible. As a result, they say, anticipated monetary policy cannot alter either the rate of unemployment or the level of real GDP. Regardless of the nature of the anticipated policy, the unemployment rate will equal the natural rate, and real GDP will be determined solely by the economy's long-run aggregate supply curve. This conclusion is called the policy irrelevance theorem.

3. **What does the real business cycle theory say about the causes of recession?**

   Real business cycle theory shows that even if all prices and wages are perfectly flexible, real shocks to the economy (such as technological change and changes in the supplies of factors of production) can cause national business fluctuations. One example of such real shocks is the type of oil shock that hit Canada's economy during the 1970s.

4. **How does the new Keynesian economics explain the stickiness of wages and prices?**

   Generally, a combination of factors is cited, including the existence of contracts, small-menu costs, and efficiency wages. The key point is that there are a variety of rational reasons that economic participants have for entering into agreements that fix either nominal or real relative prices (including wages). Given the existence of such agreements, as well as the existence of costs of changing prices of all types, monetary policy can have real effects on the economy by changing aggregate demand.

PROBLEMS

(Answers to the odd-numbered problems appear at the back of the book.)

18-1. Answer the following questions based on the accompanying graph.

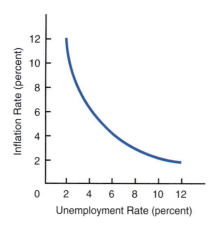

a. If we regard this curve as showing a trade-off between inflation and unemployment, how much unemployment will it "cost" to reduce inflation to 2 percent per year?

b. What might cause this curve to shift upward?

c. Why do economists argue that there is generally no useable trade-off between unemployment and inflation?

18-2. The natural rate of unemployment is a function of a variety of factors, including wage and price rigidities and interferences with labour mobility. Give some examples of such rigidities and interferences.

18-3. How does the existence of contracts, small-menu costs, and efficiency wages affect the amount of discretion available to policymakers?

18-4. Explain how the average duration of unemployment may be different for a given rate of unemployment.

18-5. What effect does the average duration of unemployment have on the rate of unemployment if we hold constant the variables you used to explain Problem 18-4?

18-6. What is meant by an optimal duration of unemployment? What may affect such an optimal duration of unemployment?

18-7. If both employers and workers incorrectly perceive the rate of inflation to the same extent, would the Phillips curve still be expected to be negatively sloped?

18-8. Unemployment is arbitrarily defined. What differences do different definitions have with respect to policy?

PART 6

Global Economics

Chapter 19

Comparative Advantage and the Open Economy

Chapter 20

Exchange Rates and the Balance of Payments

Chapter 21

Development: Economic Growth Around the World

Comparative Advantage and the Open Economy

If you are a consumer of milk, chicken, and eggs, then you are almost certainly consuming Canadian products. You are also almost certainly paying twice the world price for milk, and at least 20 percent more than the world price for the chicken and eggs. Yet, just across the border in the United States, consumers pay prices which are much closer to world prices. Why do Canadians have to pay high prices while Americans do not? In order to understand this issue, you have to know about international trade, comparative advantage, and protectionism.

Preview Questions

1. Is international trade important to Canada?

2. What is the relationship between imports and exports?

3. What are some arguments against free trade?

4. What is the ultimate effect of a restriction on imports?

Did You Know That... Bombardier Inc.'s Global Express, a long-range, high-speed business jet, is made near Toronto, but many of its parts come from other countries including Japan, Germany, the United States, and the United Kingdom?

The story of the Global Express is repeated in the automobile industry. Parts from literally all over the world end up in cars that are "made in Canada." The running shoes you buy, the sheets you sleep on, and the clothes you put on your back are often wholly or partly produced outside Canada. Clearly, international trade today affects you whether you are aware of it or not. We are entering an age of a truly global economy. Learning about international trade is simply learning about everyday life.

THE WORLDWIDE IMPORTANCE OF INTERNATIONAL TRADE

Look at part (a) of Figure 19.1. Since the end of World War II, world output of goods and services (world gross domestic product, or GDP) has increased almost every year until the present, when it is almost six times what it used to be. Look at the top line in part (a). World trade has increased to almost 13 times what it was in 1950.

Figure 19.1 **The Growth of World Trade**

In part (a), you can see the growth in world trade in relative terms because we use an index of 100 to represent real world trade in 1950. By the mid-1990s, that index had increased to over 1,300. At the same time, the index of world GDP (annual world income) had gone up to only around 600. World trade is clearly on the rise: Both imports and exports,

expressed as a percentage of annual national income (GDP) in part (b), have been rising.

Sources: Part (a) Steven Husted and Michael Melvin, *International Economics,* 3d ed. (New York: HarperCollins, 1995), p. 11, used with permission; Part (b) Statistics Canada.

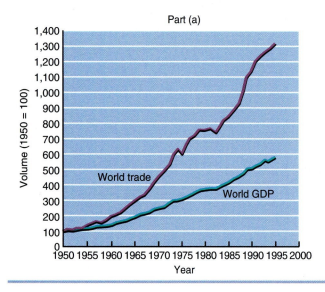

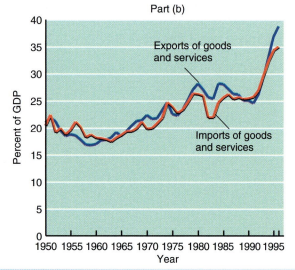

Try Preview Question 1:
Is international trade important to Canada?

Canada figured prominently in this expansion of world trade. In part (b) of Figure 19.1, you see imports and exports expressed as a percentage of total annual yearly income (GDP). While international trade was always important to Canada, with imports plus exports adding up to almost 50 percent of annual national income in 1950, today it accounts for over 71 percent of GDP.

INTERNATIONAL EXAMPLE
The Importance of International Trade in Various Countries

Table 19.1
Importance of Imports in Selected Countries

Country	Imports as a Percentage of Annual National Income
Luxembourg	95.0
Netherlands	58.0
Canada	35.0
Norway	30.0
Germany	23.0
United Kingdom	21.0
China	19.0
France	18.4
United States	12.8
Japan	6.8

Source: International Monetary Fund.

Figure 19.2
World Trade Flows

International merchandise trade amounts to over US$3 trillion worldwide. The percentage figures show the proportion of trade flowing in the various directions.

Source: World Trade Organization (data are for 1995).

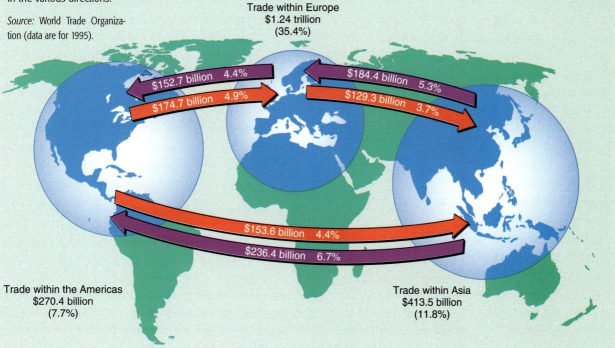

Trade within Europe
$1.24 trillion
(35.4%)

$152.7 billion 4.4%
$174.7 billion 4.9%
$184.4 billion 5.3%
$129.3 billion 3.7%
$153.6 billion 4.4%
$236.4 billion 6.7%

Trade within the Americas
$270.4 billion
(7.7%)

Trade within Asia
$413.5 billion
(11.8%)

While imports and exports in Canada each account for more than 30 percent of total annual national income, in some countries the figure is much higher. In others it is much less, as you can see in Table 19.1. Another way to understand the worldwide importance of international trade is to look at trade flows on the world map in Figure 19.2.

For critical analysis: The yearly volume of imports in Hong Kong is almost twice Hong Kong's total national income. How is that possible? (Hint: Is there another reason to import a good besides wanting to consume it?)

WHY WE TRADE: COMPARATIVE ADVANTAGE AND EXHAUSTING MUTUAL GAINS FROM EXCHANGE

You have already been introduced to the concepts of specialization and mutual gains from trade in Chapter 2. These ideas are worth repeating because they are essential to understanding why the world is better off because of more international trade. The best way to understand the gains from trade among nations is first to understand the output gains from specialization between individuals.

The Output Gains from Specialization

Suppose that a creative advertising specialist can generate two pages of ad copy (written words) or one computerized art rendering per hour. At the same time, a computer artist can write one page of ad copy or complete one computerized art rendering per hour. Here the ad specialist can come up with more pages of ad copy per hour than the computer specialist, and seemingly is just as good as the computer specialist at computerized art renderings. Is there any reason for the creative specialist and the computer specialist to "trade"? The answer is yes, because such trading will lead to higher output.

Consider the scenario of no trading. Assume that during each eight-hour day, the ad specialist and the computer whiz devote half of their day to writing ad copy and half to computerized art rendering. The ad specialist would create eight pages of ad copy (4 hours × 2) and four computerized art renderings (4 × 1). During that same period, the computer specialist would create four pages of ad copy (4 × 1) and four computerized art renderings (4 × 1). Each day, the combined output for the ad specialist and the computer specialist would be 12 pages of ad copy and eight computerized art renderings.

If the ad specialist specialized only in writing ad copy and the computer artist specialized only in creating computerized art renderings, their combined output would rise to 16 pages of ad copy (8 × 2) and eight computerized art renderings (8 × 1). Overall, production would increase by four pages of ad copy per day.

▶ **Comparative advantage**
The ability to produce a good or service at a lower opportunity cost compared to other producers.

The creative advertising employee has a comparative advantage in writing ad copy, and the computer specialist has a comparative advantage in doing computerized art renderings. **Comparative advantage** involves the ability to produce something at a lower opportunity cost compared to other producers, as we pointed out in Chapter 2.

Specialization Among Nations

To demonstrate the concept of comparative advantage for nations, let's take the example of France and Canada. In Table 19.2, we show the comparative costs of production of wine and beer in terms of worker-days. This is a simple two-country, two-commodity world in which we assume that labour is the only factor of production. As you can see from the table, in Canada, it takes one worker-day to produce 1 litre of wine, and the same is true for 1 litre of beer. In France, it takes one worker-day to produce 1 litre of wine but two worker-days for 1 litre of beer. In this sense, Canadians appear to be just as good at producing wine as the French and actually have an **absolute advantage** in producing beer.

▶ **Absolute advantage**
The ability to produce more output from given inputs of resources than other producers can.

Table 19.2
Comparative Costs of Production

Product	Canada	France
Wine (1 litre)	1 worker-day	1 worker-day
Beer (1 litre)	1 worker-day	2 worker-days

Trade will still take place, however, which may seem paradoxical. How can trade take place if Canada is able to produce both goods at least as cheaply as the French can? Why don't we just produce both ourselves? To understand why, let's assume first that there is no trade and no specialization and that the workforce in each country consists of 200 workers. These 200 workers are divided equally in the production of wine and beer. We see in Table 19.3 that 100 litres of wine and 100 litres of beer are produced per day in Canada. In France, 100 litres of wine and 50 litres of beer are produced per day. The total daily world production in our two-country world is 200 litres of wine and 150 litres of beer.

Table 19.3
Daily World Output Before Specialization

It is assumed that 200 workers are available in each country.

	Canada		France		
Product	Workers	Output (litres)	Workers	Output (litres)	World Output (litres)
Wine	100	100	100	100	200
Beer	100	100	100	50	150

Now the countries specialize. What can France produce more cheaply? Look at the comparative costs of production expressed in worker-days in Table 19.2. What is the cost of producing 1 litre more of wine? One worker-day. What is the cost of producing 1 litre more of beer? Two worker-days. We can say, then, that in France the opportunity cost of producing wine is less than that of producing beer. France will specialize in the activity that has the lower opportunity cost. In other words, France will specialize in its comparative advantage, which is the production of wine.

Table 19.4	Canada			France		
Daily World Output After Specialization						World Output
	Product	Workers	Output (litres)	Workers	Output (litres)	(litres)
It is assumed that 200 workers are available in each country.	Wine	---	---	200	200	200
	Beer	200	200	---	---	200

According to Table 19.4, after specialization, Canada produces 200 litres of beer and France produces 200 litres of wine. Notice that the total world production per day has gone up from 200 litres of wine and 150 litres of beer to 200 litres of wine and 200 litres of beer per day. This was done without any increased use of resources. The gain, 50 "free" litres of beer, results from a more efficient allocation of resources worldwide. World output is greater when countries specialize in producing the goods in which they have a comparative advantage and then engage in foreign trade. Another way of looking at this is to consider the choice between two ways of producing a good. Obviously, each country would choose the less costly production process. One way of "producing" a good is to import it, so if in fact the imported good is cheaper than the domestically produced good, we will "produce" it by importing it. Not everybody, of course, is better off when free trade occurs. In our example, Canadian wine makers and French beer makers are worse off because those two *domestic* industries have disappeared.

Some people are worried that Canada (or any country, for that matter) might someday "run out of exports" because of overaggressive foreign competition. The analysis of comparative advantage tells us the opposite. No matter how much other countries compete for our business, Canada (or any other country) will always have a comparative advantage in something that it can export. In 10 or 20 years, that something may not be what we export today, but it will be exportable nonetheless because we will have a comparative advantage in producing it.

Other Benefits from International Trade: The Transmission of Ideas

Beyond the fact that comparative advantage generally results in an overall increase in the output of goods produced and consumed, there is another benefit to international trade—the international transmission of ideas. According to economic historians, international trade has been the principal means by which new goods, services, and processes have spread around the world. For example, coffee was initially grown in Arabia near the Red Sea. Around 675 AD, it began to be roasted and consumed as a beverage. Eventually, it was exported to other parts of the world, and the Dutch started cultivating it in their colonies during the seventeenth century and the French in the eighteenth century. The lowly potato is native to the Peruvian Andes. In the sixteenth century, it was brought to Europe by Spanish explorers. Thereafter, its cultivation and consumption spread rapidly.

All of the *intellectual property* that has been introduced throughout the world is a result of international trade. This includes new music, such as rock and roll in the

1950s and hip-hop and grunge in the 1990s. It includes the software applications that are common for computer users everywhere.

New processes have been transmitted through international trade. One of those involves the Japanese manufacturing innovation which emphasized redesigning the system rather than running the existing system in the best possible way. Inventories were reduced to just-in-time levels by re-engineering machine setup methods. Just-in-time inventory control is now common in Canadian factories.

THE RELATIONSHIP BETWEEN IMPORTS AND EXPORTS

The basic proposition in understanding all of international trade is this:

> In the long run, imports are paid for by exports.[1]

The reason that imports are ultimately paid for by exports is that foreigners want something in exchange for the goods that are shipped to Canada. For the most part, they want goods made in Canada. From this truism comes a remarkable corollary:

> Any restriction of imports ultimately reduces exports.

This is a shocking revelation to many people who want to restrict foreign competition in order to protect domestic jobs. Although it is possible to protect certain Canadian jobs by restricting foreign competition, it is impossible to make *everyone* better off by imposing import restrictions. Why? Because ultimately such restrictions lead to a reduction in employment in the export industries of the nation.

Think of exports as simply another way of producing goods. International trade is merely an economic activity like all others; it is a production process that transforms exports into imports.

Try Preview Question 2:
What is the relationship between imports and exports?

INTERNATIONAL EXAMPLE
The Importation of Priests into Spain

Imports affect not only goods but also services and the movement of labour. In Spain, some 3,000 priests retire each year, but barely 250 young men are ordained to replace them. Over 70 percent of the priests in Spain are now over the age of 50. The Spanish church estimates that by 2005, the number of priests will have fallen to half the 20,441 who were active in Spain in 1990. The Spanish church has had to seek young seminarians from Latin America under what it calls "Operation Moses." It is currently subsidizing the travel and training of an increasing number of young Latin Americans to take over where native Spaniards have been before.

For critical analysis: How might the Spanish church induce more native Spaniards to become priests?

---

[1] We have to modify this rule by adding that in the short run, imports can also be paid for by the sale (or export) of real and financial assets, such as land, stocks, and bonds, or through an extension of credit from other countries.

INTERNATIONAL COMPETITIVENESS

"Canada is falling behind." "We need to stay competitive internationally." These and similar statements are often heard in government circles when the subject of international trade comes up. There are two problems with this issue. The first has to do with a simple definition. What does "global competitiveness" really mean? When one company competes against another, it is in competition. Is Canada like one big corporation, in competition with other countries? Certainly not. The standard of living in each country is almost solely a function of how well the economy functions within that *country*, not how it functions relative to other countries.

Another problem arises with respect to the real world. According to the International Institute for Management Development in Lausanne, Switzerland, Canada has been *improving* its world competitive position. In 1994, Canada was ranked 20th in the world; by 1997, Canada was ranked 10th. According to the report, Canada's improved ranking is due to better government, improving technology and a highly productive labour force. Other factors include Canada's sophisticated financial system and better management of the private sector.

Concepts in Brief

- Countries can be better off materially if they specialize in producing goods for which they have a comparative advantage.
- It is important to distinguish between absolute and comparative advantage; the former refers to the ability to produce a unit of output with fewer physical units of input; the latter refers to producing output that has the lowest opportunity cost for a nation.
- Different nations will always have different comparative advantages because of differing opportunity costs due to different resource mixes.

ARGUMENTS AGAINST FREE TRADE

Numerous arguments are raised against free trade. They mainly point out the costs of trade; they do not consider the benefits, or the possible alternatives for reducing the costs of free trade while still reaping benefits.

The Infant Industry Argument

▶ **Infant industry argument**
The contention that tariffs should be imposed to protect from import competition an industry that is trying to get started. Presumably, after the industry becomes technologically efficient, the tariff can be lifted.

A country may feel that if a particular industry were allowed to develop domestically, it could eventually become efficient enough to compete effectively in the world market. Therefore, if some restrictions were placed on imports, domestic producers would be given the time needed to develop their efficiency to the point where they would be able to compete in the domestic market without any restrictions on imports. In graphic terminology, we would expect that if the protected industry truly does experience improvements in production techniques or technological breakthroughs towards greater efficiency in the future, the supply curve will shift outward to the right so that the domestic industry can produce larger quantities at each and every price. This **infant industry argument** has some merit in the short run and has been used to protect a number of industries in their infancy around the world. Such a policy can be abused, however. Often the protective import-restricting arrangements remain even after the infant has matured. If other countries can still produce more cheaply, the people who benefit from this type of situation are obviously the shareholders (and specialized factors of production that will earn economic rents) in the industry that is still being protected from world competition. The people who lose out are the consumers, who must pay a price higher than the world price for the product in question. In any event, it is very difficult to know beforehand which industries will eventually survive. In other words, we cannot predict very well the specific infant industries that should be protected. Note that when we talk about which industry "should be" protected, we are in the realm of normative economics. We are making a value judgment, a subjective statement of what *ought to be*.

Countering Foreign Subsidies and Dumping

Another strong argument against unrestricted foreign trade concerns countering other nations' subsidies to their own producers. When a foreign government subsidizes its producers, our producers claim that they cannot compete fairly with these subsidized foreigners. To the extent that such subsidies fluctuate, it can be argued that unrestricted free trade will seriously disrupt domestic producers. They will not know when foreign governments are going to subsidize their producers and when they are not. Our competing industries will be expanding and contracting too frequently.

▶ **Dumping**
Selling a good or a service abroad at a price below its cost of production or below the price charged in the home market.

The phenomenon called *dumping* is also used as an argument against unrestricted trade. **Dumping** occurs when a producer sells its products abroad at a price below its cost of production or below the price that is charged in the home market. Although cries of dumping are often heard against foreign producers, they typically occur only when the foreign nation is in the throes of a serious recession. The foreign producer does not want to slow down its production at home. Because it anticipates an end to the recession and doesn't want to hold large inventories, it dumps its products abroad at prices below its costs. This does, in fact, disrupt international trade. It also creates instability in domestic production and therefore may impair commercial well-being at home.

EXAMPLE   **Dumping Chinese Garlic**

In 1996, Canadian garlic growers complained to the Canadian International Trade Tribunal (CITT) that, between 1992 and 1996, growers from mainland China had been dumping fresh garlic on the Canadian market, thus suppressing price and causing profits to decline. The domestic producers claimed that over this period Canadian demand for garlic had increased by 8 million kilograms, and at the same time the market share filled by Chinese garlic had grown from 29 percent to 68 percent.

The CITT investigated the garlic growers' complaint. It determined that the "normal" price of garlic in China, that is the price which reflects the producers' costs, would be $1.91 per kilogram. (Since China does not have a free market in garlic, the CITT determined this price by looking at prices in other garlic-growing countries such as Mexico.) However, Chinese garlic was selling in Canada for 58 cents per kilogram, a price reduction of 70 percent.

The CITT concluded that Chinese garlic growers had dumped 6 million kilograms of garlic on the Canadian market between 1992 and 1996. As a result, importers of Chinese garlic must pay a countervailing duty sufficient to bring its selling price to $1.91 per kilogram, in line with Canadian prices.

For critical analysis: Since consumers benefit from the low prices of dumping, why might they be in favour of countervailing duties?

Protecting Canadian Jobs

Perhaps the argument used most often against free trade is that unrestrained competition from other countries will eliminate Canadian jobs because other countries have lower-cost labour than we do. (Less restrictive environmental standards in other countries might also lower their costs relative to ours.) This is a compelling argument, particularly for politicians from areas that might be threatened by foreign competition. For example, a Member of Parliament from an area with shoe factories would certainly be upset about the possibility of constituents' losing their jobs because of competition from lower-priced shoe manufacturers in Brazil and Italy. But of course this argument against free trade is equally applicable to trade between the provinces.

Economists David Gould, G. L. Woodbridge, and Roy Ruffin examined the data on the relationship between increases in imports and the rate of unemployment. Their conclusion was that there is no causal link between the two. Indeed, in half the cases they studied, when imports increased, unemployment fell.

Another issue has to do with the cost of protecting Canadian jobs by restricting international trade. Several years ago, the North-South Institute examined the cost of protection in the Canadian textile and clothing industries. It found that consumers were paying about $36,000 per year in taxes and higher prices to protect each textile and clothing industry job which at the time paid about $10,000 per year to the average worker.

In the long run, the industries that have had the most protection—textiles, clothing, and iron and steel—have seen the most dramatic reductions in employment in Canada.

Try Preview Question 3:
What are some arguments against free trade?

Thinking Critically About the Media   **Unfair Competition from Low-Wage Countries**

Protectionists are able to get the media to carry stories about how low-wage countries are stealing Canadian jobs. The facts are exactly the opposite. The highest-labour-cost country in the world is Germany, and it is also the largest exporter in the world. The United States, Japan, France, and the United Kingdom also have relatively high labour costs, and they, too, are some of the world's biggest exporters. If the low-wage myth were true, Canada would never be able to compete with, say, Mexican labour. Yet the reality is that Canada exports much more to Mexico than it imports. Finally, both the World Bank and the Organisation for Economic Cooperation and Development (OECD) have done exhaustive studies on the issue. Their conclusion is that there is no evidence that trade with low-wage countries results in large-scale job losses to industrial countries. The real competition for Canadian manufacturing comes from high-wage countries, such as the United States, Germany and Japan.

Concepts in Brief

- The infant industry argument against free trade contends that new industries should be protected against world competition so that they can become technologically efficient in the long run.
- Unrestricted foreign trade may allow foreign governments to subsidize exports or foreign producers to engage in dumping—selling products in other countries below their cost of production. To the extent that foreign export subsidies and dumping create more instability in domestic production, they may impair our well-being.

WAYS TO RESTRICT FOREIGN TRADE

There are many ways in which international trade can be stopped or at least stifled. These include quotas and taxes (the latter are usually called *tariffs* when applied to internationally traded items). Let's talk first about quotas.

▶ **Quota system**

A government-imposed restriction on the quantity of a specific good that another country is allowed to sell in Canada. In other words, quotas are restrictions on imports. These restrictions are usually applied to one or several specific countries.

Quotas

Under the **quota system**, individual countries or groups of foreign producers are restricted to a certain amount of trade. An import quota specifies the maximum amount of a commodity that may be imported during a specified period of time. For

Figure 19.3
The Effect of Quotas on Textile Imports

Without restrictions, 90 million metres of textiles would be imported each year into Canada at the world price of $1.00 per metre. If the federal government imposes a quota of only 80 million metres, the effective supply curve becomes vertical at that quantity. It intersects the demand curve at the new equilibrium price of $1.50 per metre.

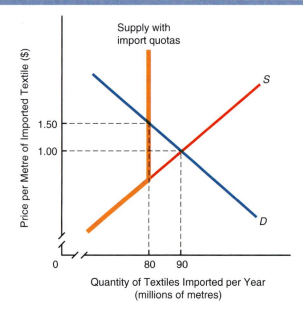

example, the government might not allow more than 50 million barrels of foreign crude oil to enter Canada in a particular year.

Consider the example of quotas on textiles. Figure 19.3 presents the demand and the supply curves for imported textiles. In an unrestricted import market, the equilibrium quantity imported is 90 million metres at a price of $1 per metre (expressed in constant-quality units). When an import quota is imposed, the supply curve is no longer *S*. Rather, the supply curve becomes vertical at some amount less than the equilibrium quantity—here, 80 million metres per year. The price to the Canadian consumer increases from $1.00 to $1.50. The domestic suppliers of textiles obviously benefit by an increase in revenues because they can now charge a higher price.

Voluntary Quotas. Quotas do not have to be explicit and defined by law. They can be "voluntary." Such a quota is called a **voluntary export restraint agreement (VER).** In the early 1980s, the Canadian government asked Japan voluntarily to restrain its automobile exports to Canada for a period of three years. The Japanese government did so, and even now continues to limit its automobile exports to the west.

▶ **Voluntary export restraint agreement (VER)**

An official agreement with another country that "voluntarily" restricts the quantity of its exports to Canada.

Tariffs

We can analyse tariffs by using standard supply and demand diagrams. Let's use as our example computer software, some of which is made in the United States and some of which is made domestically. In part (a) of Figure 19.4, you see the demand and supply of US software. The equilibrium price is $100 per constant-quality unit, and the equilibrium quantity is 10 million per year. In part (b), you see the same

Figure 19.4

The Effect of a Tariff on American-Made Computer Software

Without a tariff, Canada buys units of American software per year at an average price of $100, as shown in part (a). Canadian producers sell 5 million units of domestically made software, also at $100 each, as shown in part (b). A $50-per-unit tariff will shift the American import supply curve to S_2 in part (a), so that the new equilibrium is at E_2, with price $125 and quantity sold reduced to 8 million per year. The demand curve for Canadian-made software (for which there is no tariff) shifts to D_2 in part (b). Sales increase to 6.5 million per year.

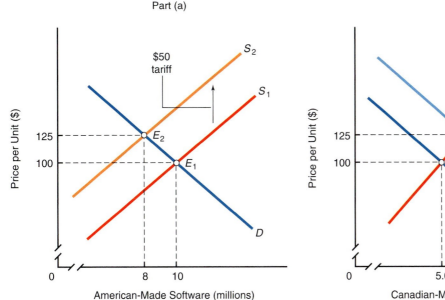

Part (a)

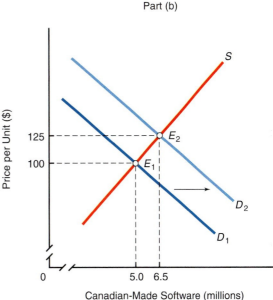

Part (b)

equilibrium price of $100, and the *domestic* equilibrium quantity is 5 million units per year.

Now a tariff of $50 is imposed on all imported American software. The supply curve shifts upward by $50 to S_2. For purchasers of American software, the price increases to $125. The quantity demanded falls to 8 million per year. In part (b), you see that at the higher price of imported American software, the demand curve for Canadian-made software shifts outward to the right to D_2. The equilibrium price increases to $125, and the equilibrium quantity increases to 6.5 million units per year. So the tariff benefits domestic software producers because it increases the demand for their products due to the higher price of a close substitute, American software. This causes a redistribution of income from Canadian consumers of software to Canadian producers of software.

Try Preview Question 4:
What is the ultimate effect of a restriction on imports

Tariffs in Canada. In Figure 19.5 (page 478) we see that tariffs on all imported goods have varied widely, but in general have been falling since the mid-1930s. The highest rates since Confederation occurred as part of Sir John A. Macdonald's National Policy of 1879.

Current Tariff Laws. Canada has always depended to a large extent on trade, first with England and now with the United States. About one in three jobs in

Figure 19.5
Tariff Rates in Canada Since 1867

Tariff rates in Canada have varied widely; indeed, in Parliament, tariffs are a political football. Import-competing industries prefer high tariffs. In the twentieth century, the highest single tariff we had was the Bennett Retaliatory Tariff (1933), which was imposed in retaliation against the United States' Smoot-Hawley Tariff of 1930.
Source: Statistics Canada.

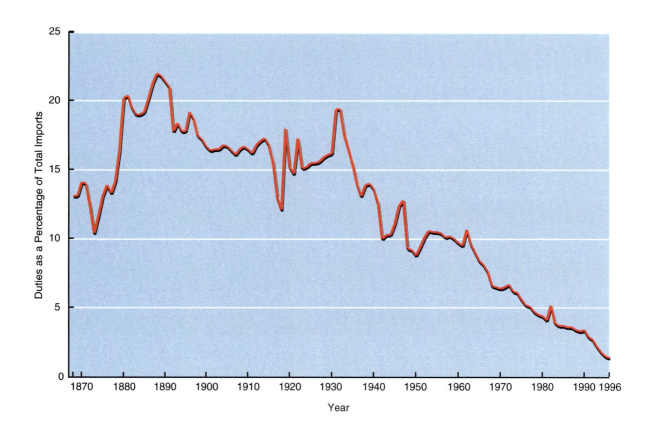

Canada depends on our exports; about 11,000 jobs are either created or sustained by each $1 billion in new exports.

Not surprisingly, the federal government in recent years has emphasized the importance of expanded trade for Canada. In 1985, Canada signed a free trade agreement with the United States; in 1994, Canada and the United States included Mexico in the **North American Free Trade Agreement (NAFTA)**. This remains Canada's most significant trade agreement, covering more than 80 percent of our exports. In 1997, Canada signed a separate free trade agreement with Chile, which will come into effect possibly as early as 1999.

Canada was also a signatory of the **General Agreement on Tariffs and Trade (GATT)** which was signed in 1947. The 127 member nations of GATT account for more than 85 percent of world trade. As you can see in Figure 19.5, there have been a number of rounds of negotiations to reduce tariffs since the early 1960s. The latest round was called the "Uruguay Round" because that is where the meetings were held.

▶ **North American Free Trade Agreement (NAFTA)**
A free trade agreement between Canada, the United States, and Mexico, which covers about 80 percent of our exports.

▶ **General Agreement on Tariffs and Trade (GATT)**
An international agreement established in 1947 to further world trade by reducing barriers and tariffs.

The World Trade Organization (WTO)

▶ **World Trade Organization (WTO)**

The successor organization to GATT, it handles all trade disputes among its 117 member nations.

The Uruguay Round of the General Agreement on Tariffs and Trade (GATT) was ratified by 117 nations at the end of 1993. A year later the entire treaty was ratified. As of January 1, 1995, the new **World Trade Organization (WTO)** replaced GATT.

The ratification of GATT will result in a cut of roughly 40 percent in tariffs worldwide. Agricultural subsidies will be reduced and perhaps eventually eliminated. Protection for patents will be extended worldwide. The WTO will have arbitration boards to settle international disputes over trade issues. No country has a veto. A country that loses a WTO ruling has to comply or face trade sanctions by the country that wins arbitration.

In short, the passage of GATT and the creation of the WTO constitute the furthest-reaching global trade agreement in history. Advanced technologies in particular will benefit from the worldwide extension of the protection of patents. Copyrights on books and recordings will be protected from piracy better than ever before. Protectionist rules, such as "local content" requirements that force foreign firms to use locally produced inputs, will be eliminated. Also, other countries will have to treat Canadian service suppliers no less favourably than they treat their own service suppliers.

POLICY EXAMPLE   **Should Culture Be Excluded from Free Trade Agreements?**

Figure 19.6
The Health of the Canadian Magazine Industry

Since 1990, the number of different Canadian magazines has risen and fallen with the amount of advertising revenue available to the Canadian magazine publishing industry.

Source: Maclean's, June 2, 1997.

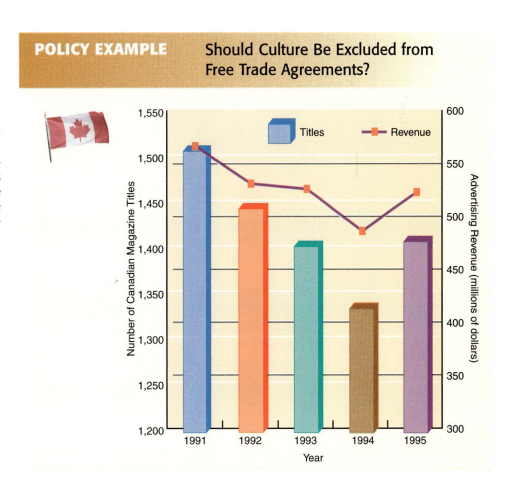

For the past 60 years, Canada has aggressively protected its magazine industry by placing tariffs on imported American magazines, by not allowing foreign-controlled magazines produced in Canada to claim advertising as a tax-deductible cost, and by giving postal subsidies to all-Canadian magazines. The federal government went further in 1995, putting an 80 percent tariff on "split-run" editions of magazines such as *Time* and *Sports Illustrated*—those magazines with American content financed by Canadian advertising. The federal government was trying to direct Canadian advertising revenue to Canadian publications so that our 1,400 consumer and trade magazines can preserve Canadian culture.

In 1997, the WTO ruled against three of the four protective measures, allowing for the time being only the postal subsidies for Canadian magazines to continue. The publishing industry fears that with no protection, Canadian titles will start to die off within a few months, down to perhaps two or three survivors within five years. As Figure 19.6 on the previous page shows, the health of the Canadian magazine industry is directly related to the amount of available advertising revenue.

American magazine publishers claim the publishing business is just another business. The Canadian position is that Canadian magazines preserve our culture against the already large onslaught of American media today. Whether culture should be protected from free trade, and whether the WTO is the appropriate body to make that decision is still a matter for debate.

For critical analysis: Why do Canadian magazines need government protection to ensure they attract Canadian advertising revenue?

Concepts in Brief

- One means of restricting foreign trade is a quota system. Beneficiaries of quotas are the importers who get the quota rights and the domestic producers of the restricted good.
- Another means of restricting imports is a tariff, which is a tax on imports only. An import tariff benefits import-competing industries and harms consumers by raising prices.
- Canada's most significant trade agreement is the North American Free Trade Agreement between Canada, the United States, and Mexico.
- The other important international institution created to improve trade among nations is the General Agreement on Tariffs and Trade (GATT). The latest round of trade talks under GATT, the Uruguay Round, led to the creation of the World Trade Organization (WTO).

Issues and Applications

Playing Chicken with the United States

Concepts Applied: Comparative advantage, competitiveness, quotas, tariffs, benefits from trade

Canadian chicken and dairy farmers claim that the cost of farming in Canada is higher than in the US because of our more severe climate. They welcome high import duties to protect them from lower-cost US imports, but these high duties raise the cost of their products to Canadian consumers.

Canada's dairy, egg, and poultry producers won a major battle with their American counterparts in 1996. In spite of our free trade agreement with the Americans, which prohibits any new tariffs between Canada and the US, a NAFTA dispute settlement board declared that Canada could retain its tariff rate quotas (TRQs) placed on dairy and poultry products under WTO auspices. But have consumers also won this war?

Supply-Management at Work

In the late 1960s, dairy and poultry farmers opted to take part in a supply-management system designed to smooth the often wild fluctuations in farm prices and farm incomes. The supply-management system consists of production quotas which restrict output and keep prices stable and high enough for farmers to make a living. Since imports of competing products increase supply and reduce market price, the Canadian government also devised a system of import quotas on American dairy and poultry products.

In 1995, member countries of the WTO (which includes Canada and the United States) removed agricultural import quotas and replaced them with tariffs offering equivalent protection. It was agreed that these tariffs will be substantially reduced over the next 10 years. Table 19.5 shows some of the Canadian TRQs on dairy and poultry products which the United States complained were unduly high.

The United States appealed under the NAFTA, but because the US had not voiced concerns during the WTO talks, the dispute settlement board ruled in favour of Canada.

Winners and Losers with Restricted Trade

Dairy and poultry farmers and the federal and provincial governments were indeed pleased. As a 1996 *Informetrica* study showed, they had a lot to lose with completely open borders: over the period 1996 to 2000, farmers could have lost up to $16 billion in income, and the federal and provincial governments up to $18.1 billion in revenues if the TRQs were declared illegal. Canadian farm workers could have lost upwards of 28,000 person-hours of employment.

Canadian consumers, however, would have gained from open borders. With the removal of the TRQs, the Consumer Price Index could have dropped about 1.5 percent. Americans could have gained from open borders too. One estimate predicts that US exports to Canada of dairy products alone would rise from under $100 million to $1 billion.

Table 19.5 — **Canadian Duties on Imports of Selected American Products**		
Product	1993 Duty (%)	1995 Duty (%)
Frozen whole chicken	6.2	273.4
Fluid milk (1%–6% butter fat)	8.7	276.7
Ice cream and ice milk	7.7	307.2
Yoghurt	7.5	272.5

The 1993 duty was in effect prior to the WTO agreement to remove import quotas.

Source: The Financial Post, August 22, 1996.

What's the Problem?

Why can't Canada's 36,000 dairy and poultry producers compete with their American counterparts without government protection? Are they so inefficient that they need both production quotas and TRQs to survive?

Supporters of the supply-management system have answers to these questions. They say that the Americans have a comparative advantage in producing dairy and poultry products. The costs of doing business in Canada are high, they suggest, because of our difficult weather. Americans don't have to heat their barns and hen-houses to protect their animals and, in addition, they have access to cheaper feed, so their overall costs are lower. Supporters also point out that, especially in poultry, Americans experience large economies of scale as huge "agribusinesses" operate giant farms. By contrast, the supply-management system has allowed Canada to retain the family farm, which typically is smaller and less cost-efficient. But proponents are also quick to mention that the supply-management system is justified not only because of maintenance of the family farm, but also because the output of the family farm is more wholesome than that of an agribusiness.

However, Canadian beef farmers disagree. Back in the 1960s, they decided not to take part in a supply-management system. Since that time they have become very competitive, exporting almost half of their production in spite of Canada's position as one of the world's largest importers of beef.

For Critical Analysis

1. If the TRQs on dairy and poultry are eventually removed, but Canada's supply-management system is not dismantled, what will be the effect on Canadian dairy and poultry farmers?

2. Can you think of any reason that Canadian beef farmers can be competitive in a world market but dairy and poultry farmers cannot?

CHAPTER SUMMARY

1. It is important to distinguish between absolute and comparative advantage. A person or country that can do everything "better" (with higher labour productivity) than every other person or country has an absolute advantage in everything. Nevertheless, trade will still be advantageous if people specialize in the things that they do *relatively* best, exploiting their respective comparative advantage.

2. Along with the gains, there are costs from trade. Certain industries and their employees may be hurt if trade is opened up.

3. An import quota restricts the quantity of imports coming into the country. It therefore raises the price. Consumers always lose.

4. When governments impose "voluntary" quotas, they are called voluntary export restraints (VERs).

5. An import tariff raises the domestic price of foreign produced goods. It therefore allows domestic producers to raise their own prices. The result is a higher price to consumers, a lower quantity of imports, and a lower volume of international trade.

6. Canada's most important trade agreement is the North American Free Trade Agreement (NAFTA), signed by Canada, the United States, and Mexico. The NAFTA covers about 80 percent of Canada's exports.

7. The other main international institution created to improve trade among nations was the General Agreement on Tariffs and Trade (GATT), replaced in 1995 by the World Trade Organization (WTO).

DISCUSSION OF PREVIEW QUESTIONS

1. Is international trade important to Canada?

The direct impact of international trade on Canada, as measured by the ratio of exports to GDP, is relatively large compared with many other nations. It is hard to imagine what life would be like without international trade. Initially, many prices would rise rapidly, but eventually domestic production would begin on many goods we presently import. However, consider life without imports of coffee, tea, bananas, and foreign wines, motorcycles, automobiles, televisions, VCRs, and hundreds of other goods from food and clothing to electronics—not to mention vital imports such as bauxite, chromium, cobalt, nickel, platinum, and tin.

2. What is the relationship between imports and exports?

Because foreigners eventually want real goods and services as payment for the real goods and services they export to other countries, ultimately each country pays for its imports with its exports. Hence on a worldwide basis, the value of imports must equal the value of exports.

3. What are some arguments against free trade?

The infant industry argument maintains that new industries developing domestically need protection from foreign competitors until they are mature enough themselves to compete with foreigners, at which time protection will be removed. One problem with this argument is that it is difficult to tell when maturity has been reached, and domestic industries will fight against weaning. Moreover, this argument is hardly relevant to most Canadian industries. It is also alleged (and is true to a large extent) that free trade leads to instability for specific domestic industries as comparative advantage changes in a dynamic world. Countries that have traditionally held a comparative advantage in the production of some goods occasionally lose that advantage (while gaining others). Regional hardships are a result, and protection of domestic jobs is demanded.

4. What is the ultimate effect of a restriction on imports?

Because each country must pay for its imports with its exports, any restriction on imports must ultimately lead to a reduction in exports. So even though restrictions on imports because of tariffs or quotas may benefit workers and business owners in the protected domestic industry, such protection will harm workers and business owners in the export sector in general.

PROBLEMS

(Answers to the odd-numbered problems appear at the back of the book.)

19-1. Examine the hypothetical table of worker-hours required to produce caviar and wheat in Canada and in Russia.

Product	Canada	Russia
Caviar (kilogram)	6 worker-hours	9 worker-hours
Wheat (bushel)	3 worker-hours	6 worker-hours

a. What is the opportunity cost to Canada of producing one kilogram of caviar per time period? What is the opportunity cost to Canada of producing one bushel of wheat?

b. What is the opportunity cost to Russia of producing one kilogram of caviar per time period? What is the opportunity cost to Russia of producing one bushel of wheat?

c. Canada has a comparative advantage in what? Russia has a comparative advantage in what?

19-2. Study the hypothetical table of worker-hours required to produce coffee and beans in Colombia and Turkey.

Product	Colombia	Turkey
Coffee (kilogram)	2 worker-hours	1 worker-hour
Beans (kilogram)	6 worker-hours	2 worker-hours

a. What is the opportunity cost to Colombia of producing one kilogram of coffee? One kilogram of beans?
b. What is the opportunity cost to Turkey of producing one kilogram of coffee? One kilogram of beans?
c. Colombia has a comparative advantage in what? Turkey has a comparative advantage in what?

19-3. Assume that Canada can produce *everything* with fewer worker-hours than any other country on earth. Even under this extreme assumption, why would Canada still trade with other countries?

19-4. Examine the hypothetical table of worker-hours required to produce cheese and cloth in two countries, A and B.

Product	Country A	Country B
Cheese (kilogram)	$2/3$ worker-hours	2 worker-hours
Cloth (metre)	$1/2$ worker-hours	1 worker-hour

a. What is the opportunity cost to country A of producing one kilogram of cheese? One metre of cloth?
b. What is the opportunity cost to country B of producing one kilogram of cheese? One metre of cloth?
c. Country A has a comparative advantage in what?
d. Country B has a comparative advantage in what?

19-5. The use of tariffs and quotas to restrict imports results in higher prices and is successful in reducing imports. In what way is using a tariff different from using a quota?

19-6. Two countries, Austral Land and Boreal Land, have the following production opportunities shown in the graphs.

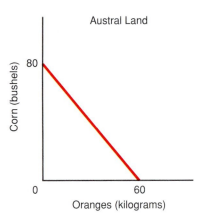

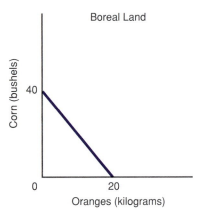

a. Who has an absolute advantage in corn? In oranges?
b. Who has a comparative advantage in corn? In oranges?
c. Should Boreal Land export at all? If so, which good should it export?
d. What is Austral Land's opportunity cost of oranges in terms of corn? What is Boreal Land's opportunity cost of corn in terms of oranges?

19-7. The accompanying graph gives the supply and demand for peaches. *S* and *D* are Canada's supply and demand curves, respectively. Assume that the world price of peaches is 50 cents per kilogram.

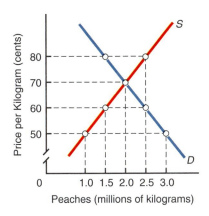

a. How many kilograms are produced domestically? How many kilograms are imported?

b. Suppose that Canada imposes a 10-cent-per-kilogram tariff. How many kilograms would now be produced domestically? How many kilograms would be imported? What are the federal government's revenues?

c. Suppose now that the government imposes a 20-cent-per-kilogram tariff. What price can domestic growers now receive for their peaches? How many kilograms will domestic growers produce? How many kilograms will be imported? What are government revenues?

19-8. Explain why an increase in taxes on imports (tariffs) will reduce exports.

19-9. Assume that a country with whom Canada is trading imposes restrictions on Canadian-made imports into that country. Will Canada be better off by simultaneously imposing restrictions on the other country's imports into Canada? Why or why not?

19-10. Look at the *Canadian Trade Review* on the Department of Foreign Affairs and International Trade Web site at: http://www.infoexport.gc.ca/section4/revue-e.asp

a. What three types of products does Canada export the most?

b. What three countries does Canada sell the most goods and services to?

c. Which trade agreement—the GATT or the NAFTA—would be most important for Canada? Why? (Hint: Think about your answer to part b.)

INTERACTING WITH THE INTERNET

File Edit View Go Favorites Help

Back Forward Stop Refresh Home Search Favorites History Channels Fullscreen Mail Print Edit

Check out Canada's yearly volume of exports at

      http://www.infoexport.gc.ca/section4/clock-e.asp

The text of the NAFTA can be found at

      http://uls.tradecompass.com/ecs/demo/ftas/nafta/

The World Trade Organization Web site is at

      http://www.wto.org/

A very good source for general information on the nations of the world is the CIA's *World Factbook* at

      http://www.odci.gov/cia/publications/factbook/index.html

Exchange Rates and the Balance of Payments

Preview Questions

1. What is the difference between the balance of trade and the balance of payments?

2. What is a foreign exchange rate?

3. What is a flexible exchange rate system?

4. What is the gold standard?

If you talk to Canadians who travelled to Europe in the mid-1980s, they will probably tell you how cheap their trip was. If you go to Europe today, the stories will be quite different. What difference does a decade make? Well, when you are talking about the dollar, a lot. Today, in some countries such as Germany and Japan the dollar buys barely half what it did in 1985. Should we be worrying about a weaker dollar? To answer this question, you need to know about international financial transactions and the determinants of foreign exchange rates.

Did You Know That... every day, around the clock, over $1 trillion of foreign currencies are traded? Along with that trading come news headlines, such as "The dollar weakened today," "The dollar under attack," and "The Bank of Canada intervened in money markets today to halt the dollar's slide." If you are confused by such newspaper headlines, join the crowd. Surprisingly, though, if you regard the dollar, the pound sterling, the deutsche mark, the yen, and the franc as assets that are subject to the laws of supply and demand, the world of international finance becomes much clearer. Perhaps the first step is to examine the meaning of the terms used with respect to Canada's international financial transactions during any one-year period.

THE BALANCE OF PAYMENTS AND INTERNATIONAL CAPITAL MOVEMENTS

Governments typically keep track of each year's economic activities by calculating the gross domestic product—the total of expenditures on all newly produced final domestic goods and services—and its components. In the world of international trade also, a summary information system has been developed. It relates to the balance of trade and the balance of payments. The **balance of trade** refers specifically to exports and imports of *goods and services* as discussed in Chapter 19. When international trade is in balance, the value of exports equals the value of imports.

▶ **Balance of trade**

The value of goods and services bought and sold in the world market.

The **balance of payments** is a more general concept that expresses the total of all economic transactions between two countries, usually for a period of one year. Each country's balance of payments summarizes information about that country's exports, imports, earnings by domestic residents on assets located abroad, earnings on domestic assets owned by foreign residents, international capital movements, and official transactions by central banks and governments. In essence, then, the balance

▶ **Balance of payments**

A summary record of a country's economic transactions with foreign residents and governments over a year.

Table 20.1
Surplus (+) and Deficit (−) Items on the International Accounts

Surplus Items (+)	Deficit Items (−)
Exports of merchandise	Imports of merchandise
Private and governmental gifts from foreigners	Private and governmental gifts to foreigners
Foreign use of domestically owned transportation	Use of foreign-owned transportation
Foreign tourists' expenditures in this country	Tourism expenditures abroad
Foreign military spending in this country	Military spending abroad
Interest and dividend receipts from foreigners	Interest and dividends paid to foreigners
Sales of domestic assets to foreigners	Purchases of foreign assets
Funds deposited in this country by foreigners	Funds placed in foreign depository institutions
Sales of gold to foreigners	Purchases of gold from foreigners
Sales of domestic currency to foreigners	Purchases of foreign currency

of payments is a record of all the transactions between households, firms, and government of one country and the rest of the world. Any transaction that leads to a *payment* by a country's residents (or government) is a deficit item, identified by a negative sign (–) when we examine the actual numbers that might be in Table 20.1. Any transaction that leads to a *receipt* by a country's residents (or government) is a surplus item and is identified by a plus sign (+) when actual numbers are considered. Table 20.1 gives a listing of the surplus and deficit items on international accounts.

Accounting Identities

▶ **Accounting identities**
Statements that certain numerical measurements are equal by accepted definition (for example, "assets equal liabilities plus stockholders' equity").

Accounting identities—definitions of equivalent values—exist for financial institutions and other businesses. We begin with simple accounting identities that must hold for families, and then go on to describe international accounting identities.

If a family unit is spending more than its current income, such a situation necessarily implies that the family unit must be doing one of the following:

1. Drawing down its wealth. The family must reduce its money holdings, or it must sell stocks, bonds, or other assets.
2. Borrowing.
3. Receiving gifts from friends or relatives.
4. Receiving public transfers from a government, which obtained the funds by taxing others. (A transfer is a payment, in money or in goods or services, made without receiving goods or services in return.)

In effect, we can use this information to derive an identity: If a family unit is currently spending more than it is earning, it must draw on previously acquired wealth, borrow, or receive either private or public aid. Similarly, an identity exists for a family unit that is currently spending less than it is earning: It must increase its wealth by increasing its money holdings or by lending and acquiring other financial assets, or it must pay taxes or bestow gifts on others. When we consider businesses and governments, each unit in each group faces its own identities or constraints; thus, net lending by households must equal net borrowing by businesses and governments.

Even though our individual family unit's accounts must balance, in the sense that the identity discussed previously must hold, sometimes the item that brings about the balance cannot continue indefinitely. *If family expenditures exceed family income and this situation is financed by borrowing, the household may be considered to be in disequilibrium because such a situation cannot continue indefinitely.* If such a deficit is financed by drawing on previously accumulated assets, the family may also be in disequilibrium because it cannot continue indefinitely to draw on its wealth; eventually, it will become impossible for that family to continue such a lifestyle. (Of course, if the family members are retired, they may well be in equilibrium by drawing on previously acquired assets to finance current deficits; this example illustrates that it is necessary to understand circumstances fully before pronouncing an economic unit in disequilibrium.)

Individual households, businesses, and governments, as well as the entire group of households, businesses, and governments, must eventually reach equilibrium. Certain economic adjustment mechanisms have evolved to ensure equilibrium. Deficit households must eventually increase their incomes or decrease their expenditures. They will find that they have to pay higher interest rates if they wish to borrow to finance their deficits. Eventually their credit sources will dry up, and they will be forced into equilibrium. Businesses, on occasion, must lower costs and/or prices—or go bankrupt—to reach equilibrium.

When countries trade or interact, certain identities or constraints must also hold. Countries buy goods from people in other countries; they also lend to and present gifts to people in other countries. If a country interacts with others, an accounting identity ensures a balance (but not an equilibrium, as will soon become clear). Let's look at the three categories of balance of payments transactions: current account transactions, capital account transactions, and official settlements account transactions.

Current Account Transactions

During any designated period, all payments and gifts that are related to the purchase or sale of both goods and services constitute the current account in international trade. The three major types of current account transactions are the exchange of merchandise goods, the exchange of services, and transfers.

Table 20.2
Canadian Balance of Payments Account, 1996 (in Billions of Dollars)

Current Account			
(1)	Exports of goods	+280.5	
(2)	Imports of goods	−239.6	
(3)	Balance of trade		+40.9
(4)	Exports of services	+38.9	
(5)	Imports of services	−48.8	
(6)	Balance of services		−9.9
(7)	Balance on goods and services [(3) + (6)]		+31.0
(8)	Net investment income	−27.7	
(9)	Net transfers	+0.3	
(10)	Balance on current account		+3.6

Capital Account			
(11)	Canadian capital going abroad	−63.5	
(12)	Foreign capital coming into Canada	+56.6[a]	
(13)	Balance on capital account [(11)+(12)]		−6.9
(14)	Balance on current account plus balance on capital account [(10) + (13)]		−3.3
(15)	Official transactions		+3.3
(16)	Total (balance)		$0.00

Source: Bank of Canada Review.

[a] Includes a $3.2 billion statistical discrepancy, probably unaccounted capital outflows, many of which relate to the underground economy.

Merchandise Trade Transactions.   The largest portion of any country's balance of payments current account is typically the importing and exporting of merchandise goods. During 1996, for example, as can be seen in lines 1 and 2 of Table 20.2 on the previous page, Canada exported $280.5 billion of merchandise and imported $239.6 billion. The balance of merchandise trade is defined as the difference between the value of merchandise exports and the value of merchandise imports. For 1996, Canada had a balance of merchandise trade surplus because the value of its merchandise exports exceeded the value of its merchandise imports. This surplus amounted to $40.9 billion (line 3).

Thinking Critically About the Media   Perhaps the Trade Situation Isn't So Bad After All

Virtually every month, there appears a spate of articles and TV sound bites about Canada's current account deficit. The official numbers may be in error, however, for they ignore the multinational nature of modern firms. Canadian international trade figures exclude sales in other countries for subsidiaries of Canadian-owned companies. Because of a host of other problems, some government economists believe that they are underestimating the value of Canadian exports by as much as 10 percent. Economist Paul Krugman agrees. When he added up the value of world exports and compared it with the value of world imports, he found that the planet Earth had a trade deficit of $100 billion! Perhaps we are trading with aliens and don't know it.

Service Exports and Imports.   The balance of (merchandise) trade has to do with tangible items—you can feel them, touch them, and see them. Service exports and imports have to do with invisible or intangible items that are bought and sold, such as shipping, insurance, tourist expenditures, and banking services. As can be seen in lines 4 and 5 of Table 20.2, in 1996, service exports were $38.9 billion and service imports were $48.8 billion. Thus the balance of services was in deficit about $9.9 billion in 1996 (line 6). Exports constitute receipts or inflows into Canada and are positive; imports constitute payments abroad or outflows of money and are negative.

When we combine the balance of merchandise trade with the balance of services, we obtain a balance on goods and services equal to $31.0 billion in 1996 (line 7).

Investment Income.   Canadians earn investment income on assets they own in foreign countries. These earnings represent an inflow into Canada. Conversely, when Canadians pay income to foreigners who own assets in Canada, those earnings represent an outflow from Canada. On line (8) you can see that net investment income for 1996 was −$27.7 billion. The fact that there is a negative sign before the number for investment income means that Canadians paid out more earnings on domestic assets owned by foreigners than they earned on assets owned in other countries.

Transfers.   Canadians give gifts to relatives and others abroad. The federal government grants gifts to foreign countries. Foreigners give gifts to Canadians, and some foreign governments have granted money to the Canadian government. In the current account, we see that net transfers—the total amount of gifts given by Canadians minus the total amount received by Canadians from abroad—came to $0.3 billion in 1996 (line 9).

Balancing the Current Account.   The balance on current account tracks the value of a country's exports of goods and services, earnings on investments abroad and transfer payments (private and government) relative to the value of that country's import of goods and services, earnings on investments in Canada, and transfer payments (private and government). In 1996, it was a $3.6 billion.

If exports exceed imports, a current account surplus is said to exist; if imports exceed exports, a current account deficit is said to exist. A current account surplus means that we are exporting more than we are importing. Such a surplus must be offset by the import of money or money equivalent, which means (in the absence of central bank intervention) a capital account deficit.

Capital Account Transactions

In world markets, it is possible to buy and sell not only goods and services but also real and financial assets. This is what the capital accounts are concerned with in international transactions. Capital account transactions occur because of foreign investments—either foreigners investing in Canada or Canadians investing in other countries. The purchase of shares of stock on the London stock exchange by a Canadian causes an outflow of funds. The building of a Japanese automobile factory in Canada causes an inflow of funds. Any time foreigners buy Canadian government securities, that is an inflow of funds. Any time Canadians buy foreign government securities, there is an outflow of funds. Loans to and from foreigners cause outflows and inflows.

Line 11 of Table 20.2 indicates that in 1996, the value of private and government capital going out of Canada was −$63.5 billion, and line 12 shows that the value of private and government capital coming into Canada (including a statistical discrepancy) was +$56.6 billion. Canadian capital going abroad constitutes payments or outflows and is therefore negative. Foreign capital coming into Canada constitutes receipts or inflows and is therefore positive. Thus there was a negative net capital movement of −$6.9 billion out of Canada (line 13). This is also called the balance on capital account.

There is a relationship between the current account and the capital account, assuming no interventions by the central banks of countries. *The current account and the capital account must sum to zero. In other words, the current account deficit equals the capital account surplus. Any country experiencing a current account surplus, such as Canada, should also be running a capital account deficit.*

Does Canada's Frequent Current Account Deficit Mean It Has a Weak Economy?

Figure 20.1

The Relationship Between the Current Account and the Capital Account

To some extent, the capital account is the mirror image of the current account. We can see this in the years since 1976. When the current account was in surplus, the capital account was in deficit. When the current account was in deficit, the capital account was in surplus. Indeed, virtually the only time foreigners can invest in Canada is when the current account is in deficit.

Source: Bank of Canada Review.

In recent years, the current account in Canada has been in deficit more than it has been in surplus. This is not something new. During the second half of the nineteenth century, Canada had many years of current account deficits. They were equally matched by capital account surpluses, as the rest of the world sent capital to Canada to finance the building of the railroads and the development of Canada's industrial economy. By the end of World War I, Canadians had repaid all their external debt and had become a net creditor. However, this condition was short-lived, and by 1950 Canada was once again experiencing current account deficits. This can be seen in Figure 20.1. Whenever Canada is in deficit in its current account, it is in surplus in its capital account.

Contrary to popular belief, Canada does not necessarily have a current account deficit because it is a weak economy and cannot compete in world markets. Rather, Canada appears to be a good place to invest capital because there are strong prospects for growth and investment opportunities. So long as foreigners wish to invest more in Canada than Canadians wish to invest abroad, there will always be a deficit in our current account balance. Canadians are the beneficiaries of international capital flows.

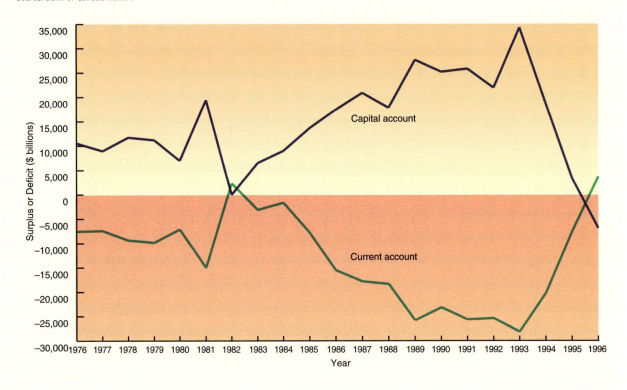

For critical analysis: Why are politicians, nonetheless, so worried about the current account deficit?

Official Settlement Account Transactions

The third type of balance of payments transaction concerns official reserve assets, which consist of the following:

1. Foreign currencies
2. Gold
3. **Special drawing rights (SDRs)**, which are reserve assets that the International Monetary Fund created to be used by countries to settle international payment obligations
4. The reserve position in the International Monetary Fund
5. Financial assets held by an official agency, such as the Bank of Canada.

> ▶ **Special drawing rights (SDRs)**
>
> Reserve assets created by the International Monetary Fund that countries can use to settle international payments.

To consider how official settlement account transactions occur, look again at Table 20.2. The deficit in our capital account was −$6.9 billion. And the surplus in our current account was +$3.6 billion, so we had a deficit on the combined accounts (line 14) of −$3.3 billion. In other words, Canada obtained less in foreign money in all its international transactions than it used. How is this deficiency made up? By our central bank drawing down its existing balances of foreign monies, or the +$3.3 billion in official transactions shown on line 15 in Table 20.2. You might ask why there is a positive sign on line 15. The answer is because this represents a *supply* (an inflow) of foreign exchange into our international transactions.

> **Try Preview Question 1**:
>
> What is the difference between the balance of trade and the balance of payments?

The balance (line 16) in Table 20.2 is zero, as it must be with double-entry bookkeeping. Our balance of payments surplus is measured by the official transactions figure on line 15. (This does not mean we are in equilibrium, though.)

Thinking Critically About the Media   Developing Countries Are Getting All the Capital

Many developing countries are growing more rapidly than the developed countries. Several reports have been commented on by the media in recent years in which it is argued that developing economies are "sucking up" all the world's capital. Let's put the numbers in context. About US$60 billion a year of capital moves from advanced to developing countries. All of the countries in the world, in contrast, invest over US$4 trillion a year. So such capital flows represent only 1.5 percent of total world investment. What's to worry?

What Affects the Balance of Payments?

A major factor affecting our balance of payments is our rate of inflation relative to that of our trading partners. Assume that the rates of inflation in Canada and in the United States are equal. All of a sudden, our inflation rate increases. The Americans will find that Canadian products are becoming more expensive, and we will export fewer of them to the United States. Canadians will find American products relatively cheaper, and we will import more. The converse will occur if our rate of inflation suddenly falls relative to that of the United States. All other things held constant, whenever our rate of inflation exceeds that of our trading partners, we expect to see a "worsening" of our balance of trade and payments. Conversely, when our rate of inflation is less than that of our trading partners, other things being constant, we expect to see an "improvement" in our balance of trade and payments.

Another important factor that sometimes influences our balance of payments is our relative political stability. Political instability causes *capital flight:* Owners of capital in countries anticipating or experiencing political instability will often move assets to countries that are politically stable, such as Canada. Hence our balance of payments is likely to worsen whenever the threat of separation looms in Quebec.

Concepts in Brief

- The balance of payments reflects the value of all transactions in international trade, including goods, services, financial assets, and gifts.
- The merchandise trade balance gives us the difference between exports and imports of tangible items. Merchandise trade transactions are represented by exports and imports of tangible items.
- Service exports and imports relate to the trade of intangible items, such as shipping, insurance, and tourist expenditures.
- Investment income includes income earned by foreigners on Canadian investments and income earned by Canadians on foreign investments.
- Transfers involve international private gifts and federal government grants or gifts to foreign nations.
- When we add the balance of merchandise trade plus the balance of services and take account of net transfers, we come up with the balance on current account, which is a summary statistic taking into account the three transactions that form the current account transactions.
- There are also capital account transactions that relate to the buying and selling of financial and real assets. Foreign capital is always entering Canada, and Canadian capital is always flowing abroad. The difference is called the balance on capital account.
- Another type of balance of payments transaction concerns the official settlement assets of individual countries, or what is often simply called official transactions. By standard accounting convention, official transactions are exactly equal, but opposite in sign, to the balance of payments of Canada.
- Our balance of trade can be affected by our relative rate of inflation and by political instability elsewhere compared to the stability that exists in Canada.

DETERMINING FOREIGN EXCHANGE RATES

▶ **Foreign exchange market**
The market for buying and selling foreign currencies.

When you buy foreign products, such as French wine, you have dollars with which to pay the French winemaker. The French winemaker, however, cannot pay workers in dollars. The workers are French, they live in France, and they must have francs to buy goods and services in that country. There must therefore be some way of exchanging dollars for the francs that the winemaker will accept. That exchange occurs in a **foreign exchange market**, which in this case specializes in exchanging francs and dollars. (When you obtain foreign currencies at a bank or an airport currency exchange, you are participating in the foreign exchange market.)

The particular exchange rate between francs and dollars that would prevail depends on the current demand for and supply of francs and dollars. In a sense, then, our analysis of the exchange rate between dollars and francs will be familiar, for we have used supply and demand throughout this book. If it costs you 20 cents to buy one franc, that is the **foreign exchange rate** determined by the current demand for and supply of francs in the foreign exchange market. The French person going to the foreign exchange market would need five francs to buy one dollar. (Our numbers are, of course, hypothetical.)

We will continue our example in which the only two countries in the world are France and Canada. Now let's consider what determines the demand for and supply of foreign currency in the foreign exchange market.

▶ **Foreign exchange rate**
The price of one currency in terms of another.

Try Preview Question 2:
What is a foreign exchange rate?

Demand for and Supply of Foreign Currency

You wish to buy some French Bordeaux wine. To do so, you must have French francs. You go to the foreign exchange market (or your Canadian bank). Your desire to buy the French wine therefore causes you to offer (supply) dollars to the foreign exchange market. Your demand for French francs is equivalent to your supply of Canadian dollars to the foreign exchange market. Indeed:

> Every Canadian transaction concerning the importation of foreign goods constitutes a supply of dollars and a demand for some foreign currency, and the opposite is true for export transactions.

In this case, this import transaction constitutes a demand for French francs.

In our example, we will assume that only two goods are being traded, French wine and Canadian jeans. The Canadian demand for French wine creates a supply of dollars and a demand for francs in the foreign exchange market. Similarly, the French demand for Canadian jeans creates a supply of francs and a demand for dollars in the foreign exchange market. In the situation of **flexible exchange rates**, the supply of and demand for dollars and francs in the foreign exchange market will determine the equilibrium foreign exchange rate. The equilibrium exchange rate will tell us how many francs a dollar can be exchanged for—that is, the dollar price of francs—or how many dollars (or fractions of a dollar) a franc can be exchanged for—the franc price of dollars.

▶ **Flexible exchange rates**
Exchange rates that are allowed to fluctuate in the open market in response to changes in supply and demand. Sometimes called *floating exchange rates.*

The Equilibrium Foreign Exchange Rate

To determine the equilibrium foreign exchange rate, we have to find out what determines the demand for and supply of foreign exchange. We will ignore for the moment any speculative aspect of buying foreign exchange; that is, we assume that there are no individuals who wish to buy francs simply because they think that their price will go up in the future.

The idea of an exchange rate is no different from the idea of paying a certain price for something you want to buy. If you like coffee, you know you have to pay about $1.00 a cup. If the price went up to $2.50, you would probably buy fewer cups. If the

Part (a)
Demand Schedule for French Wine in Canada per Week

Price per Litre	Quantity Demanded (litres)
$10	1
8	2
6	3
4	4

Part (b)
Canadian Demand Curve for French Wine

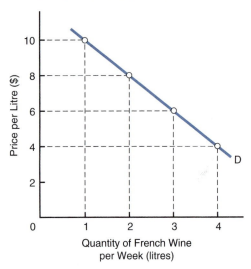

Part (c)
Francs Required to Purchase Quantity Demanded (at $P = 20$ francs per litre)

Quantity Demanded (litres)	Francs Required
1	20
2	40
3	60
4	80

Part (d)
Derived Demand Schedule for Francs in Canada with Which to Pay for Imports of Wine

Dollar Price of One Franc	Dollar Price of Wine	Quantity of Wine Demanded (litres)	Quantity of Francs Demanded per Week
$ .50	$10	1	20
.40	8	2	40
.30	6	3	60
.20	4	4	80

Part (e)
Canadian Derived Demand for Francs

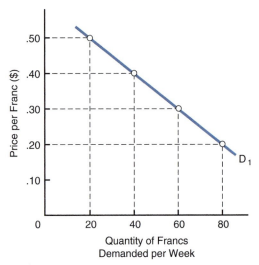

Figure 20.2
Deriving the Demand for French Francs

In part (a), we show the demand schedule for French wine in Canada, expressed in terms of dollars per litre. In part (b), we show the demand curve, D, which slopes downward. In part (c), we show the number of francs required to purchase up to four litres of wine. If the price per litre of wine in France is 20 francs, we can now find the quantity of francs needed to pay for the various quantities demanded. In part (d), we see the derived demand for francs in Canada in order to purchase the various quantities of wine given in part (a). The resultant demand curve, D_1, is shown in part (e). It is the Canadian derived demand for francs.

price went down to 5 cents, you might buy more. In other words, the demand curve for cups of coffee, expressed in terms of dollars, slopes downward following the law of demand. The demand curve for francs slopes downward also, and we will see why.

Demand Schedule for French Francs. Let's think more closely about the demand schedule for francs. Let's say that it costs you 20 cents to purchase one franc; that is the exchange rate between dollars and francs. If tomorrow you had to pay 25 cents for the same franc, the exchange rate would have changed. Looking at such an increase with respect to the franc, we would say that there has been an **appreciation** in the value of the franc in the foreign exchange market. But this increase in the value of the franc means that there has been a **depreciation** in the value of the dollar in the foreign exchange market. The dollar used to buy five francs; tomorrow, the dollar will be able to buy only four francs at a price of 25 cents per franc. If the dollar price of francs rises, you will probably demand fewer francs. Why? The answer lies in looking at the reason you demand francs in the first place.

You demand francs in order to buy French wine. Your demand curve for French wine, we will assume, follows the law of demand and therefore slopes downward. If it costs you more Canadian dollars to buy the same quantity of French wine, presumably you will not buy the same quantity; your quantity demanded will be less. We say that your demand for French francs is *derived* from your demand for French wine. In part (a) of Figure 20.2, we present the hypothetical demand schedule for French wine in Canada by a representative wine drinker. In part (b), we show graphically the Canadian demand curve for French wine in terms of Canadian dollars taken from part (a).

Let us assume that the price per litre of French wine in France is 20 francs. Given that price, we can find the number of francs required to purchase up to four litres of French wine. That information is given in part (c) of Figure 20.2. If one litre requires 20 francs, four litres require 80 francs. Now we have enough information to determine the derived demand curve for French francs. If one franc costs 20 cents, a bottle of wine would cost $4 (20 francs per bottle × 20 cents per franc = $4 per bottle). At $4 per bottle, the typical representative Canadian wine drinker would, we see from part (a) of Figure 20.2, demand four litres. From part (c) we see that 80 francs would be demanded to buy the four litres of wine. We show this quantity demanded in part (d). In part (e), we draw the derived demand curve for francs. Now consider what happens if the price of francs goes up to 30 cents. A bottle of French wine costing 20 francs in France would now cost $6. From part (a) we see that at $6 per litre, three litres will be imported from France into Canada by our representative domestic wine drinker. From part (c) we see that three litres would require 60 francs to be purchased; thus in parts (d) and (e) we see that at a price of one franc per 30 cents, the quantity demanded will be 60 francs. We continue similar calculations all the way up to a price of 50 cents per franc. At that price a bottle of French wine costing 20 francs in France would cost $10, and our representative wine drinker would import only one bottle.

Downward-Sloping Derived Demand. As can be expected, as the price of francs falls, the quantity demanded will rise. The only difference here from the standard demand analysis developed in Chapter 3 and used throughout this text is that

---

▶ **Appreciation**

An increase in the value of a currency in terms of other currencies.

▶ **Depreciation**

A decrease in the value of a currency in terms of other currencies.

the demand for francs is derived from the demand for a final product—French wine in our example.

Supply of French Francs. The supply of French francs is a derived supply in that it is derived from a French person's demand for Canadian jeans. We could go through an example similar to the one for wine to come up with a supply schedule of French francs in France. It slopes upward. Obviously, the French want dollars in order to purchase Canadian goods. In principle, the French will be willing to supply more francs when the dollar price of francs goes up because they can then buy more Canadian goods with the same quantity of francs; that is, the franc would be worth more in exchange for Canadian goods than when the dollar price for francs was lower. Let's take an example. Suppose a pair of jeans in Canada costs $10. If the exchange rate is 25 cents for one franc, the French have to come up with 40 francs ($10 at 25 cents per franc) to buy one pair of jeans. If, however, the exchange rate goes up to 50 cents for one franc, the French must come up with only 20 francs ($10 at 50 cents per franc) to buy a pair of Canadian jeans. At a lower price (in francs) of Canadian jeans, the French will demand a larger quantity. In other words, as the price of French francs goes up in terms of dollars, the quantity of Canadian jeans demanded will go up, and hence the quantity of French francs supplied will go up. Therefore, the supply schedule of foreign currency (francs) will slope upward.[1]

We could easily work through a detailed numerical example to show that the supply curve of French francs slopes upward. Rather than do that, we will simply draw it as upward-sloping in Figure 20.3. In our hypothetical example, assuming that there

---

[1] Actually, the supply schedule of foreign currency will be upward-sloping if we assume that the demand for Canadian imported jeans on the part of the French is price-elastic. If the demand schedule for jeans is price-inelastic, the supply schedule will be negatively sloped. In the case of unit elasticity of demand, the supply schedule for francs will be a vertical line. Throughout the rest of this chapter, we will assume that demand is price-elastic. Remember that the price elasticity of demand tells us whether or not total expenditures by jeans purchasers in France will rise or fall when the French franc drops in value. In the long run, it is quite realistic to think that the price elasticity of demand for imports is numerically greater than 1 anyway.

Figure 20.3
The Equilibrium Exchange Rate for Two Individuals

The derived demand curve for French francs is taken from part (e) of Figure 20.2. The derived supply curve, S, results from the representative French purchaser of Canadian jeans, who supplies francs to the foreign exchange market when demanding Canadian dollars in order to buy Canadian jeans. D_1 and S intersect at E. The equilibrium exchange rate is 20 cents per franc.

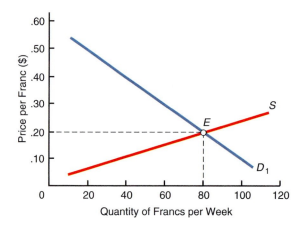

Figure 20.4
Aggregate Demand for and Supply of French Francs

The aggregate supply curve for French francs results from the total French demand for Canadian jeans. The demand curve, *D*, slopes downward like most demand curves, and the supply curve, *S*, slopes upward. The foreign exchange price, or the Canadian dollar price of francs, is given on the vertical axis. The number of francs, in millions, is represented on the horizontal axis. If the foreign exchange rate is 25 cents—that is, if it takes 25 cents to buy one franc—Canadians will demand 80 million francs. The equilibrium exchange rate is at the intersection of *D* and *S*. The equilibrium exchange rate is 20 cents. At this point, 100 million French francs are both demanded and supplied each year.

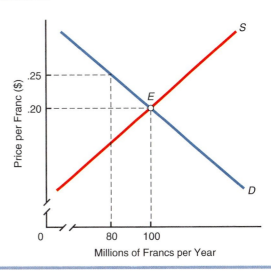

is only one wine drinker in Canada and one demander of jeans in France, the equilibrium exchange rate will be set at 20 cents per franc, or five francs to one dollar. Let us now look at the aggregate demand for and supply of French francs. We take all demanders of French wine and all demanders of Canadian jeans and put their demands for and supplies of francs together into one diagram. Thus we are showing an aggregate version of the demand for and supply of French francs. The horizontal axis in Figure 20.4 represents a quantity of foreign exchange—the number of francs per year. The vertical axis represents the exchange rate—the price of foreign currency (francs) expressed in dollars (per franc). Thus at the foreign currency price of 25 cents per franc, you know that it will cost you 25 cents to buy one franc. At the foreign currency price of 20 cents per franc, you know that it will cost you 20 cents to buy one franc. The equilibrium is again established at 20 cents for one franc. This equilibrium is not established because Canadians like to buy francs or because the French like to buy dollars. Rather, the equilibrium exchange rate depends on how many pairs of jeans the French want and how much French wine the Canadians want (given their respective incomes, their tastes, and the relative price of wine and jeans).[2]

A Shift in Demand. Assume that a successful advertising campaign by Canadian wine importers has caused the Canadian demand (curve) for French wine to double. Canadians demand twice as much wine at all prices. Their demand curve for French wine has shifted outward to the right.

The increased demand for French wine can be translated into an increased demand for francs. All Canadians clamouring for bottles of French wine will supply more dollars to the foreign exchange market while demanding more French francs to pay for the wine. Figure 20.5 presents a new demand schedule, D_2, for French

---

[2] Remember that we are dealing with a two-country world in which we are considering only the exchange of Canadian jeans and French wine. In the real world, more than just goods and services are exchanged among countries. Some Canadians buy French financial assets; some French buy Canadian financial assets. We are ignoring such transactions for the moment.

Figure 20.5
A Shift in the Demand Schedule

The demand schedule for French wine shifts to the right, causing the derived demand schedule for francs to shift to the right also. We have shown this as a shift from D_1 to D_2. We have assumed that the French supply schedule for francs has remained stable—that is, French demand for Canadian jeans has remained constant. The old equilibrium foreign exchange rate was 20 cents. The new equilibrium exchange rate will be E_2; it will now cost 30 cents to buy one franc. The higher price of francs will be translated into a higher Canadian dollar price for French wine and a lower French franc price for Canadian jeans.

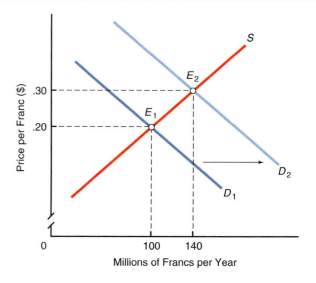

francs; this demand schedule is to the right of and outward from the original demand schedule. If the French do not change their desire for Canadian jeans, the supply schedule for French francs will remain stable. A new equilibrium will be established at a higher exchange rate. In our particular example, the new equilibrium is established at an exchange rate of 30 cents per franc. It now takes 30 cents to buy one French franc, whereas it took 20 cents before. This is translated as an increase in the price of French wine to Canadians and as a decrease in the price of Canadian jeans to the French. (Otherwise stated, there has been a decline in the foreign exchange value of the dollar.)

A Shift in Supply.   We just assumed that Canadians' preference for French wine had shifted. Because the demand for French francs is a derived demand by Canadians for French wine, it has caused a shift in the demand curve for francs. Alternatively, assume that the supply curve of French francs shifts outward to the right. This may occur for many reasons, the most probable one being a relative rise in the French price level. For example, if the price of all French-made clothes went up 100 percent in francs, Canadian jeans would become relatively cheaper. That would mean that French people would want to buy more Canadian jeans. But remember that when they want to buy more Canadian jeans, they supply more francs to the foreign exchange market. Thus we see in Figure 20.6 that the supply curve of French francs moves from S to S_1. In the absence of restrictions—that is, in a system of flexible exchange rates—the new equilibrium exchange rate will be one franc equals 10 cents, or $1 equals 10 francs. The quantity of francs demanded and supplied will increase from 100 million per year to 200 million per year. We say, then, that in a flexible international exchange rate system, shifts in the demand for and supply of foreign currencies will cause changes in the equilibrium foreign exchange rates. Those rates will remain in effect until supply or demand shifts.

Figure 20.6
A Shift in the Supply of French Francs

There has been a shift in the supply curve for French francs. The new equilibrium will occur at E_1, meaning that 10 cents, rather than 20 cents, will now buy one franc. After the exchange rate adjustment, the amount of francs demanded and supplied will increase to 200 million per year.

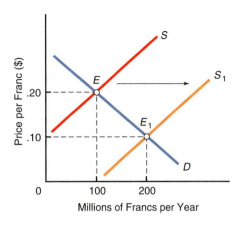

Market Determinants of Exchange Rates

The foreign exchange market is affected by many other changes in market variables in addition to changes in relative price levels, including these:

1. *Changes in real interest rates.* If Canada's interest rate, corrected for people's expectations of inflation, abruptly increases relative to the rest of the world, international investors elsewhere will increase their demand for dollar-denominated assets, thereby increasing the demand for dollars in foreign exchange markets. An increased demand for dollars in foreign exchange markets, other things held constant, will cause the dollar to appreciate and other currencies to depreciate.

2. *Changes in productivity.* Whenever one country's productivity increases relative to another's, the former country will become more price competitive in world markets. The demand for its exports will increase, and so, too, will the demand for its currency.

3. *Changes in product preferences.* If Germany's citizens suddenly develop a taste for Canadian-made automobiles, this will increase the derived demand for Canadian dollars in foreign exchange markets.

4. *Perceptions of economic stability.* As already mentioned, if Canada looks economically and politically more stable relative to other countries, more foreigners will want to put their savings into Canadian assets than into their own domestic assets. This will increase the demand for dollars.

Try Preview Question 3:

What is a flexible exchange rate system?

Concepts in Brief

- The foreign exchange rate is the rate at which one country's currency can be exchanged for another's.
- The demand for foreign exchange is a derived demand; it is derived from the demand for foreign goods and services (and financial assets). The supply of

foreign exchange is derived from foreigners' demands for our goods and services.

- In general, the demand curve of foreign exchange slopes downward and the supply curve of foreign exchange slopes upward. The equilibrium foreign exchange rate occurs at the intersection of the demand and supply curves for a currency.
- A shift in the demand for foreign goods will result in a shift in the demand for foreign exchange. The equilibrium foreign exchange rate will change. A shift in the supply of foreign currency will also cause a change in the equilibrium exchange rate.

THE GOLD STANDARD AND THE INTERNATIONAL MONETARY FUND

The current system of more or less freely floating exchange rates is a recent development. We have had, in the past, periods of a gold standard, fixed exchange rates under the International Monetary Fund, and variants of these two.

The Gold Standard

▶ **Gold standard**

An international monetary system in which countries fix their exchange rates in terms of gold. All currencies are fixed in terms of all others, and any balance of payments deficits or surpluses can be made up by shipments of gold.

Until the 1930s, many countries were on a **gold standard**. The values of their currencies were tied directly to gold.[3] Countries operating under this gold standard agreed to redeem their currencies for a fixed amount of gold at the request of any holder of that currency. Although gold was not necessarily the means of exchange for world trade, it was the unit to which all currencies under the gold standard were pegged. And because all currencies in the system were linked to gold, exchange rates between those currencies were fixed. Indeed, the gold standard has been offered as the prototype of a fixed exchange rate system. The heyday of the gold standard was from about 1870 to 1914. England had been on such a standard as far back as the 1820s.

There turns out to be a relationship between the balance of payments and changes in domestic money supplies throughout the world. Under a gold standard, the international financial market reached equilibrium through the effect of gold flows on each country's money supply. When a country suffered a deficit in its balance of payments, more gold would flow out than in. Because the domestic money supply was based on gold, an outflow of gold to foreigners caused an automatic reduction in the domestic money supply. This caused several things to happen. Interest rates rose, thereby attracting foreign capital and improving the balance of payments. At the same time, the reduction in the money supply was equivalent to a restrictive monetary policy, which caused national output and prices to fall. Imports

---

[3] This is a simplification. Most countries were on a *specie metal standard* using gold, silver, copper, and other precious metals as money. Countries operating under this standard agreed to redeem their currencies for a fixed exchange rate.

were discouraged and exports were encouraged, thereby again improving the balance of payments.

Two problems that plagued the gold standard were that no country had control of its domestic monetary policy and that the world's commerce was at the mercy of gold discoveries.

Try Preview Question 4:
What is the gold standard?

POLICY EXAMPLE — Should We Go Back to the Gold Standard?

In the past several decades, Canada has regularly run a current account deficit. The dollar has become weaker. We have had inflation. We have had recessions. Some economists and politicians argue that we should return to the gold standard. Canada operated under a gold standard from 1879 to 1931, except for a period during World War I. During this time, the dollar was defined as 23.22 grains of gold. During that time period, general prices more than doubled during World War I, there was a major recession in 1920–1921, and the Great Depression occurred.

Clearly, a gold standard guarantees neither stable prices nor economic stability.

For critical analysis: Why does no country today operate on a gold standard?

Bretton Woods and the International Monetary Fund

In 1944, as World War II was ending, representatives from the world's capitalist countries met in Bretton Woods, New Hampshire, to create a new international payment system to replace the gold standard, which had collapsed during the 1930s. The Bretton Woods agreement created the **International Monetary Fund (IMF)**, to administer the agreement and to lend to member countries in balance of payments deficit. The arrangements thus provided are now called the old IMF system or the Bretton Woods system.

Each member country was assigned an IMF contribution quota determined by its international trade volume and national income. Twenty-five percent of the quota was contributed in gold or US dollars and 75 percent in its own currency. At the time, the IMF therefore consisted of a pool of gold, dollars, and other major currencies.

Member governments were then obligated to intervene to maintain the values of their currencies in foreign exchange markets within 1 percent of the declared **par value**—the officially determined value. Except for a transitional arrangement permitting a one-time adjustment of up to 10 percent in par value, members could alter exchange rates thereafter only with the approval of the IMF. The agreement stated that such approval would be given only if the country's balance of payments was in *fundamental disequilibrium*, a term that has never been officially defined.

▶ **International Monetary Fund (IMF)**
An institution set up, in 1945, under the Bretton Woods agreement to manage the international monetary system. It established fixed exchange rates for the world's currencies.

▶ **Par value**
The legally established value of the monetary unit of one country in terms of that of another.

Special Drawing Rights.   In 1967, the IMF created a new type of international money, *special drawing rights (SDRs)*. SDRs are exchanged only between monetary authorities (central banks). Their existence temporarily changed the IMF into a world central bank. The IMF creates SDRs the same way that the Bank of Canada can create dollars. The IMF allocates SDRs to member countries in accordance with their quotas. Currently, the SDR's value is determined by making one SDR equal to a bundle of currencies. In reality, the SDR rises or falls in terms of the American dollar.

End of the Old IMF.   In 1970, Canada moved away from the IMF peg and allowed the dollar to float. In 1971, the United States' government suspended the convertibility of the US dollar into gold. Finally, in March 1973, the finance ministers of the European Economic Community (now the European Union, or EU) announced that they would let their currencies float against the US dollar, something Japan had already begun doing with its yen. Since 1973, Canada and most other trading countries have had either freely floating exchange rates or managed ("dirty") floating exchange rates.

THE DIRTY FLOAT AND MANAGED EXCHANGE RATES

▶ **Dirty float**

A system between flexible and fixed exchange rates in which central banks occasionally enter foreign exchange markets to influence rates.

Canada went off the Bretton Woods system in 1970, but it has nonetheless tried to keep certain elements of that system in play. We have occasionally engaged in what is called a **dirty float**, or management of flexible exchange rates. The management of flexible exchange rates has usually come about through international policy cooperation. For example, the Group of Seven (G-7) nations—Canada, France, Germany, Italy, Japan, the United Kingdom, and the United States—have for some time shared information on their policy objectives and procedures. They do this through regular meetings between economic policy secretaries, ministers, and staff members. One of their principal objectives has been to "smooth out" foreign exchange rates.

Is it possible for these groups to "manage" foreign exchange rates? Some economists do not think so. For example, economists Michael Bordo and Anna Schwartz studied the foreign exchange intervention actions coordinated by the Federal Reserve and the United States' Treasury for the second half of the 1980s. Besides showing that such interventions were sporadic and variable, Bordo and Schwartz came to an even more compelling conclusion: Exchange rate interventions were trivial relative to the total trading of foreign exchange on a daily basis. Thus their conclusion is that neither the Canadian central bank nor the central banks of the other G-7 nations can influence exchange rates in the long run.

Concepts in Brief

- The International Monetary Fund was developed after World War II as an institution to maintain fixed exchange rates in the world. Since 1970, however, fixed exchange rates have disappeared in most major trading countries.
- A dirty float occurs in a flexible exchange rate system whenever central banks intervene to influence exchange rates.

Issues and Applications

Should We Worry About the Weak Dollar?

Concepts Applied: Flexible exchange rates, current account deficit, depreciation

The dollar became relatively weaker against the yen and deutsche mark in 1984. However, the dollar has held its value when weighted against the currencies of all Canadian trading partners.

The course of history has seen various countries emerge at different times to dominate world trade. Rome's currency was the world's strongest for a period of 400 years, but then it lost its attractiveness in world trade. The United Kingdom saw its currency, the pound sterling, lose its world dominance over a period of 50 years. Now the United States' currency is on top. Do we need to worry because not only has Canada's currency never dominated world currency markets, it now also seems to be becoming weaker relative to those of our major trading partners?

The Dwindling Value of the Dollar

The dollar definitely does not seem to buy as much as it used to. Figure 20.7 shows what has happened to dollar exchange rates with respect to the yen and the deutsche mark. The value of the dollar against those two currencies has been falling steadily since 1984. There are several reasons the yen and the mark have become so strong and the dollar so weak. Until 1997, both Japan and Germany had lower rates of inflation than Canada. Also, at least in Germany, investors have earned higher rates of return.

Who Is Hurt by the Falling Dollar?

Besides the outraged Canadian tourist in Germany, France, Switzerland, and Japan, who else is hurt by the weak dollar? The weaker dollar translates into higher prices for imported goods, such

---

Figure 20.7
The Dollar Relative to the Deutsche Mark and the Yen

From the mid-1980s to the late 1990s, the value of the Canadian dollar in terms of the German (deutsche) mark and the Japanese yen tended to decline.

Source: Bank of Canada Review.

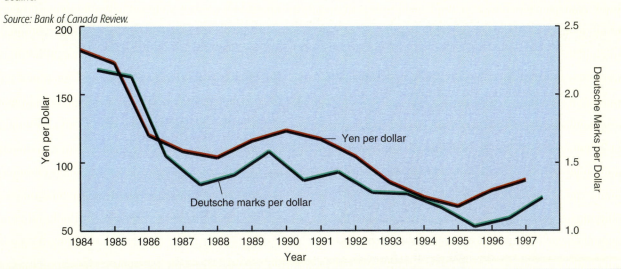

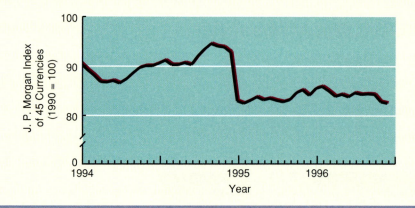

Figure 20.8
The Dollar Relative to an Index of 45 Currencies

If we look at the dollar relative to a basket of 45 of the world's currencies, it has held more or less firm since 1994.

Source: J. P. Morgan Company.

as BMWs, Mercedes, Toyotas, NEC computers, and Nintendo videogames. So Canadians who purchase imported goods from countries whose currencies are stronger relative to the dollar must now pay more than they did before. But there is a flip side to this equation. Foreigners now find our products cheaper, so employees and shareholders in Canadian companies that export find themselves better off.

Is the Dollar Really So Weak?

The dollar is indisputably changing relative to the yen, the deutsche mark, the Swiss franc, the French franc, the American dollar, and a few other currencies. But as you can see in Figure 20.8, the dollar has actually held its own since early 1995. Weighted against the currencies of all of Canada's trading partners, the dollar has been relatively stable since 1990.

The Dollar Is Still in Demand

Even though our dollar does not dominate money markets, millions of dollars of Canadian currency are held overseas. To obtain these dollar bills, foreigners have had to give up something of value, such as oil, computers, and tomatoes. In return, we were kind enough to give them pieces of paper money that cost us virtually nothing to produce. As long as they hold on to those pieces of paper, we are obtaining an interest-free loan which is repaid when foreigners buy goods and services from us.

For Critical Analysis

1. Why would a lower rate of inflation in Germany lead to a weaker dollar?

2. Why would foreigners agree to hold dollar bills instead of their own currencies?

CHAPTER SUMMARY

1. The balance of merchandise trade is defined as the value of goods bought and sold in the world market, usually during the period of one year. The balance of payments is a more inclusive concept that includes the value of all transactions in the world market.

2. Canadians purchase financial assets in other countries, and foreigners purchase Canadian financial assets, such as stocks or bonds. The buying and selling of foreign financial assets has the same effect on the balance of payments as the buying and selling of goods and services.

3. Our balance of trade and payments can be affected by our relative rate of inflation and by political instability elsewhere compared to the stability that exists in Canada.

4. Market determinants of exchange rates are changes in real interest rates (interest rates corrected for inflation), changes in productivity, changes in product preferences, and perceptions of economic stability.

5. To transact business internationally, it is necessary to convert domestic currencies into other currencies. This is done via the foreign exchange market. If we were trading with France only, French producers would want to be paid in francs because they must pay their workers in francs. Canadian producers would want to be paid in dollars because Canadian workers are paid in dollars.

6. A Canadian's desire for French wine is expressed in terms of a supply of dollars, which is in turn a demand for French francs in the foreign exchange market. The opposite situation arises when the French wish to buy Canadian jeans. Their demand for jeans creates a demand for Canadian dollars and a supply of French francs. We put the demand and supply schedules together to find the equilibrium foreign exchange rate. The demand schedule for foreign exchange is a derived demand—it is derived from Canadians' demand for foreign products.

7. With no government intervention, a market-clearing equilibrium foreign exchange rate will emerge. After a shift in demand or supply, the exchange rate will change so that it will again clear the market.

8. If Canadians increase their demand for French wine, the demand curve for French wine shifts to the right. The derived demand for francs also shifts to the right. The supply schedule of francs, however, remains stable because the French demand for Canadian jeans has remained constant. The shifted demand schedule intersects the stable supply schedule at a higher price (the foreign exchange rate increases). This is an appreciation of the value of the French franc (a depreciation of the value of the dollar against the franc).

9. In a managed exchange rate system (a "dirty float"), central banks occasionally intervene in foreign exchange markets to influence exchange rates.

10. Under a gold standard, movement of gold across countries changes domestic money supplies, causing price levels to change and to correct balance of payments imbalances.

11. In 1945, the International Monetary Fund (IMF) was created to maintain fixed exchange rates throughout the world. This system was abandoned in 1970.

DISCUSSION OF PREVIEW QUESTIONS

1. **What is the difference between the balance of trade and the balance of payments?**
The balance of trade is defined as the difference between the value of exports and the value of imports. If the value of exports exceeds the value of imports, a trade surplus exists; if the value of exports is less than the value of imports, a trade deficit exists; if export and import values are equal, we refer to this situation as a trade balance. The balance of payments is more general and takes into account the value of *all* international transactions. Thus the balance of payments identifies not only goods and services transactions among countries but also investments (financial and nonfinancial) and gifts (private and public). When the value of all these transactions is such that one country is sending more to other countries than it is receiving in return, a balance of payments deficit exists. A payments surplus and payments balance are self-explanatory.

2. **What is a foreign exchange rate?**
We know that countries trade with one another; they buy and sell goods, make and receive financial and nonfinancial investments, and give and receive gifts. However, countries have different currencies. People who sell to, invest in, or receive gifts from Canada ultimately want their own currency so that they can use the money domestically. Similarly, Canadian residents who

sell to, invest in, or receive gifts from people in other countries ultimately want Canadian dollars to spend in Canada. Because most people want to end up with their own currencies, foreign exchange markets have evolved to enable people to sell one currency for other currencies. A foreign exchange rate, then, is the rate at which one country's currency can be exchanged for another's. For example, the exchange rate between the United Kingdom (UK) and Canada might dictate that one pound sterling is equivalent to $2.50; alternately stated, the Canadian dollar is worth 0.40 pounds sterling.

3. **What is a flexible exchange rate system?**

A flexible exchange rate system is an international monetary system in which foreign exchange rates are allowed to fluctuate to reflect changes in the supply of and demand for international currencies. Say that Canada and the UK are in payments balance at the exchange rate of one pound sterling to Canadian $2.50. The Canadian demand for sterling is derived from private and government desires to buy British goods, to invest in the UK, or to send gifts to the British people and is *inversely* related to the number of dollars it takes to buy one pound. Conversely, the supply of sterling is derived from the UK's private and governmental desires to buy Canadian goods and services, to invest in Canada, and to send gifts to Canadian residents. The supply of sterling is *directly* related to the number of dollars one pound is worth. The intersection of the supply and demand curves for sterling determines the market foreign exchange rate of dollars per pound. In a system of flexible exchange rates, shifts in the supply or demand curves will lead to changes in the foreign exchange rates between countries.

4. **What is the gold standard?**

The gold standard is an international monetary system in which each country values its currency unit at a specific quantity of gold. Under such a standard, exchange rates are fixed in terms of each other. For example, the Canadian dollar was originally backed by one-twenty-eighth of an ounce of gold, and the British valued their pound sterling (or paper backed by gold) at one-quarter of an ounce of gold; the British monetary unit was therefore worth seven times the Canadian monetary unit. The resulting exchange rate was that one pound sterling was worth $7. The gold standard was, in matters of exchange rates, similar to the fixed exchange rate system. However, payment imbalances were automatically corrected by gold flows. For instance, if Canada had a payment deficit with the UK (which therefore had a payment surplus with Canada), gold would flow from Canada to the UK. The result of these gold flows (which, in effect, are equivalent to money movements) would be to raise the price level in the UK and lower it in Canada. This would lead to an increase in Canadian exports and a decrease in Canadian imports and a corresponding increase in British imports and decrease in British exports. Thus, in the past, the gold standard brought countries into payment balance by altering price *levels* in each country. The current system of flexible exchange rates corrects payment imbalances leaving price levels unaltered; it changes *one* price—the exchange rate.

PROBLEMS

(Answers to the odd-numbered problems appear at the back of the book.)

20-1. In the graph, what can be said about the shift from D to D_1?

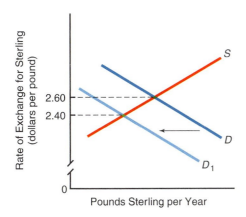

a. It could be caused by the British demanding fewer Canadian products.
b. It is a result of increased Canadian demand for British goods.
c. It causes an appreciation of the dollar relative to the pound.
d. It causes an appreciation of the pound relative to the dollar.

20-2. If the rate of exchange between the pound and the dollar is $2.00 for one pound, and Canada then experiences severe inflation, we would expect the exchange rate (under a flexible rate system) to change. What would be the new rate?

a. More than $2.00 for one pound
b. Less than $2.00 for one pound
c. More than one pound for $2.00
d. None of the above

20-3. The dollar, the pound sterling, and the deutsche mark are the currency units of Canada, the United Kingdom, and Germany, respectively. Suppose that these countries decide to go on a gold standard and define the value of their currencies in terms of gold as follows: $400 = 1 ounce of

gold; 160 pounds sterling = 1 ounce of gold; and 475 marks = 1 ounce of gold. What would the exchange rate be between the dollar and the pound? Between the dollar and the mark? Between the mark and the pound?

20-4. Examine the following hypothetical data for Canadian international transactions, in billions of dollars.

Exports: goods, 165.8; services, 130.5
Imports: goods, −250.7; services, −99.3
Net investment: −20.0
Net transfers: −20.0

a. What is the balance of trade?
b. What is the balance on goods and services?
c. What is the balance on current account?

20-5. Maintenance of a fixed exchange rate system requires government intervention to keep exchange rates stable. What is the policy implication of this fact? (Hint: Think in terms of the money supply.)

20-6. Suppose that we have the following demand schedule for German beer in Canada per week:

Price per Case	Quantity Demanded (cases)
$40	2
32	4
24	6
16	8
8	10

a. If the price is 30 deutsche marks per case, how many marks are required to purchase each quantity demanded?
b. Now derive the demand schedule for marks per week in Canada to pay for German beer.
c. At a price of 80 cents per mark, how many cases of beer would be imported from Germany per week?

20-7. The accompanying graph shows the supply of and demand for pounds sterling.

  a.   Assuming that the demand for sterling is represented by *D*, what is the dollar price of pounds? What is the equilibrium quantity?

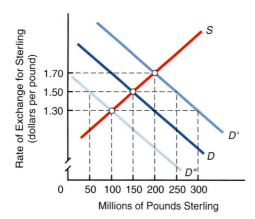

  b.   Suppose that there is general inflation in Canada. Starting at *D*, which demand curve could represent this situation? If exchange rates are allowed to float freely, what would be the new dollar price of one pound sterling? What would be the equilibrium quantity?

  c.   Suppose that the inflation in part (b) occurs and Canada has the dollar price of one pound sterling fixed at $1.50. How would the Bank of Canada be able to accomplish this?

  d.   Now suppose that instead of inflation, there was general deflation in Canada. Which demand curve could represent this situation? How could Canada maintain a fixed price of $1.50 per pound sterling in this situation?

20-8. Which of the following will cause the yen to appreciate? Explain.

  a.   Canadian real incomes increase relative to Japanese real incomes.

  b.   It is expected that in the future the yen will depreciate relative to the dollar.

  c.   The Canadian inflation rate rises relative to the Japanese inflation rate.

  d.   The after-tax, risk-adjusted real interest rate in Canada rises relative to that in Japan.

  e.   Canadian tastes change in favour of Japanese-made goods.

20-9. Visit the Bank of Canada's exchange rate Web site at: http://www.bank-banque-canada.ca/english/exchange.htm.

  a.   Over the four days of exchange rates listed, has the Canadian dollar appreciated or depreciated against the US dollar? the pound sterling? the Japanese yen? the Hong Kong dollar?

  b.   Using the most current rates, calculate the exchange rate between the US dollar and the pound sterling; the pound sterling and the Japanese yen; the Japanese yen and the Hong Kong dollar.

File   Edit   View   Go   Favorites   Help

← → Back Forward Stop Refresh Home Search Favorites History Channels Fullscreen Mail Print Edit

INTERACTING WITH THE INTERNET

The International Monetary Fund publishes current exchange rates for a number of countries. These can be found at

   http://www.imf.org/external/np/tre/sdr/drates/8101.htm

These rates are updated twice a day from Monday to Friday. Current rates quoted in Canadian dollars on a few countries can be found at the Bank of Canada's Web site

   http://www/bank-banque-canada.ca/english/exchange.htm

Development:
Economic Growth
Around the World

Many Canadians do not yet use a home-banking program on their computer in order to make transactions with their local bank. But if you live in Brazil, one of the world's developing countries, you can use a system developed by *União de Bancos Brasileiros.* How is it possible that such a technological advancement can take place more rapidly in a less developed country than in one of the most developed countries in the world? The answer lies in understanding what causes economic development and why there may be a bright future for the world's developing economies.

Preview Questions

1. **What is a developing country?**

2. **Must developing countries develop by industrializing?**

3. **Can developing countries create their own capital stock?**

4. **Does a lack of protected property rights hinder a developing country's development?**

Did You Know That... a 1967 best-selling business book called *The American Challenge* predicted that by 1985, the world's economies would be owned and run by a dozen huge American multinationals, producing over 90 percent of the world's manufactured goods? Of course, nothing could be further from the truth today. American companies remain important in the world economy, but they do not dominate. Since that prediction was made, Germany, Japan, South Korea, Hong Kong, Singapore, and Taiwan grew to become economic powerhouses. Today, there are indeed many "rich" countries, including, of course, Canada. But this country was not always rich. In fact, it was quite poor 200 years ago. If you go back far enough, every country was poor and undeveloped. Why do some countries develop faster than others? In other words, what causes economic development? Although there are no easy answers to this important question, economists now have enough data to know what conditions favour economic growth in the developing world.

PUTTING WORLD POVERTY IN PERSPECTIVE

It is difficult to comprehend the reality of poverty in the world today. At least one-half, if not two-thirds, of the world's population lives at subsistence level, with just enough to eat for survival. The official poverty level in Canada exceeds the average income in at least half the world. That is not to say that we should ignore problems at home with the poor and homeless simply because they are living better than many people elsewhere in the world. Rather, it is necessary for Canadians to keep their perspective on what are considered problems for this country relative to what are considered problems elsewhere.

WHAT IS DEVELOPMENT ECONOMICS?

How did developed countries travel the path from extreme poverty to relative riches? That is the essential issue of development economics. It is the study of why some countries develop and others do not. Further, it is the study of changes in policies that might help developing countries get richer. It is not good enough simply to say that people in diverse countries are different and therefore that is why some countries are rich while some are poor. Economists do not deny that different cultures create different work ethics, but they are unwilling to accept such a pat and fatalistic answer.

Look at any world map. About four-fifths of the countries you will see on that map are considered relatively poor. The goal of students of development economics is to help the more than four billion people with low living standards today join the billion or so who have relatively high living standards.

INDUSTRIALLY ADVANCED ECONOMIES

► **Industrially advanced countries (IACs)**

Canada, Japan, the United States, and the countries of Western Europe, all of which have market economies based on a large skilled labour force and a large technically advanced stock of capital goods.

Any system of defining poor countries and rich countries, developing countries and developed countries, is, of course, arbitrary. Nonetheless, it is instructive to examine some figures on the difference between **industrially advanced countries (IACs)** and so-called developing countries. There are 19 IACs. (Excluded from this classification are countries whose economies are based on a single resource, such as oil, but whose industrial development in other fields is minimal.) The latest data available on the IACs (1995) show an estimated per capita income of $16,341, an annual growth rate of about 2.2 percent, and a population growth of about 0.6 percent. At the other end of the scale, the more than 100 developing countries have a per capita income of $980, an annual growth rate of almost 3 percent, and a population growth rate of 2 percent per year, more than three times that of the IACs.

To be sure, we must be careful about accepting such data at face value. There is a tremendous disparity in incomes among the developing countries, and the data are notoriously inaccurate. Nonetheless, it is certain that a tremendous gap exists between average incomes in the IACs and in the developing countries.

Thinking Critically About the Media   The Gap Between the Rich and the Poor

Contrary to what we are often told by the media, government statisticians, and politicians, the rich countries are not leaving the poor countries in the dust. The International Monetary Fund revised its estimates of relative size of economies a few years ago and came up with this startling conclusion: The share of world output produced by the rich industrial economies is only 54 percent rather than the 75 percent formerly reported. Because the majority of countries in the developing world are growing faster than those in the developed world, the world's rich countries will dominate the world economy less and less in the future.

Newly Industrialized Economies

Not all developing countries are stuck in abject poverty. The developing countries vary greatly in their ability to experience economic growth, but one group of recently industrialized economies achieved annual growth rates two and three times that of Canada. These newly industrialized economies are the so-called Four Tigers—Singapore, Hong Kong, Taiwan, and South Korea—all on the Pacific Rim. From 1960 to 1995, per capita income in these economies grew sixfold. One of the reasons the newly industrialized countries have grown so rapidly is that a huge increase in world trade and in international communications has allowed technology to be disseminated much more quickly today than in the past. Indeed, these countries have advanced so quickly that three of the four now have a higher per capita income than Spain, the United Kingdom, and Italy. Yet during the same 35-year period, a number of sub-Saharan African countries experienced a *fall* in real per capita income.

Try Preview Question 1:
What is a developing country?

Concepts in Brief

- Any definition of developing countries or industrially advanced countries (IACs) is arbitrary. Nonetheless, we have identified 19 IACs and over 100 developing countries.
- The IACs have per capita incomes that are roughly 17 times the per capita incomes in the developing countries. Population in developing countries is growing more than three times as fast as in the IACs.
- Four newly industrialized countries on the Pacific Rim—Singapore, Taiwan, South Korea, and Hong Kong—have increased their real per capita incomes sixfold since 1960.

ECONOMIC DEVELOPMENT: INDUSTRY VERSUS AGRICULTURE

One of the most widely discussed theories of development concerns the need for balanced growth, with industry and agriculture given equal importance. One characteristic of many developed countries is their high degree of industrialization, although there are clearly exceptions—Hong Kong, for example. In general, countries with relatively high standards of living are more industrialized than countries with low standards of living. The policy prescription then seems obvious: Less developed countries in which a large percentage of the total resources are devoted to agricultural pursuits should attempt to obtain more balanced growth by industrializing.

Although the theory is fairly acceptable at first glance, it leads to some absurd results. We find in many developing countries with steel factories and automobile plants that the people are actually worse off because of this attempted industrialization. Most developing countries currently cannot profitably produce steel or automobiles because they lack the necessary domestic human and physical capital. They can engage in such industrial activities only with heavy government subsidization of the industry itself. Import restrictions abound, preventing the purchase of foreign, mostly cheaper substitutes for the industrial products that the country itself produces. Also, in general, the existence of subsidies leads to a misallocation of resources and a lower economic welfare for the country as a whole.

INTERNATIONAL EXAMPLE
Industrialized Poverty

Amazingly, some of the poorest countries in the world today have some of the highest rates of industrialization. Industry's share of gross output is greater in sub-Saharan Africa than in Denmark, is greater in Zimbabwe, Botswana, and Trinidad and Tobago than in Japan, and is greater in Argentina than in every country in the European Union!

Agriculture represents a relatively low share of gross output in some of the world's poorest countries. For example, agriculture represents a greater share of national output in Denmark than it does in Trinidad and Tobago. The same is true in Spain relative to Botswana, and in Portugal relative to Gabon. It is clear that industrialization does not necessarily lead to high standards of living.

For critical analysis: If industry represents a large share of gross output in extremely poor countries, what does this tell you about the rate of return on investment in industry in those countries?

The Stages of Development: Agriculture to Industry to Services

If we analyse the development of modern rich countries, we find that they went through three stages. First is the agricultural stage, when most of the population is involved in agriculture. Then comes the manufacturing stage, when much of the population becomes involved in the industrialized sector of the economy. And finally there is a shift towards services. That is exactly what happened in Canada: The so-called tertiary, or service, sector of the economy continues to grow, whereas the manufacturing sector (and its share of employment) is declining in relative importance.

However, it is important to understand the need for early specialization in a country's comparative advantage. We have repeatedly referred to the doctrine of comparative advantage, and it is even more appropriate for the developing countries of the world. If trading is allowed among countries, a country is normally best off if it produces what it has a comparative advantage at producing and imports the rest (see Chapter 19). This means that many developing countries should continue to specialize in agricultural production or in labour-intensive manufactured goods.

Try Preview Question 2: Must developing countries develop by industrializing?

How Subsidized Agriculture Affects Developing Countries

Modern Western countries have continually subsidized their own agricultural sectors to allow them to compete more easily with the developing countries in this area. If we lived in a world of no subsidization, we would probably see less food being produced in the highly developed Western world (except for Canada, the United States, and Australia) and much more being produced in the developing countries of the rest of the world. They would trade food for manufactured goods. It would seem, then, that one of the most detrimental aspects of our economic policy for the developing countries has been the continued subsidization of the Canadian farmer. Canada, of course, is not alone; virtually the entire European Union does exactly the same thing.

Even with this situation, however, a policy of using higher taxes on imported goods or domestic manufacturing subsidies in order to increase industrialization in the developing countries may do more harm than good. Industrialization is generally beneficial only if it comes about naturally, when the market conditions are such that the countries' entrepreneurs freely decide to build factories instead of increasing farm output because it is profitable to do so.

> ### Concepts in Brief
>
> - A balanced-growth theory predicts that industry and agriculture must grow together in order for a country to experience growth.
> - For many developing countries, balanced growth requires subsidization of manufacturing firms.
> - Historically, there are three stages of economic development: the agricultural stage, the manufacturing stage, and the service-sector stage, when a large part of the workforce is employed in providing services.

NATURAL RESOURCES AND ECONOMIC DEVELOPMENT

One theory of development states that for a country to develop, it must have a large natural resource base. The theory continues to assert that much of the world is running out of natural resources, thereby limiting economic growth and development. We must point out that only the narrowest definition of a natural resource could lead to such an opinion. In broader terms, a natural resource is something scarce occurring in nature that we can use for our own purposes. Natural resources therefore include knowledge of the use of something. The natural resources that we could define several hundred years ago did not, for example, include hydroelectric power—no one knew that such a natural resource existed or, indeed, how to make it exist.

In any event, it is difficult to find a strong correlation between the natural resources of a country and its stage of development. Japan has virtually no crude oil and must import most of the natural resources that it uses as inputs for its industrial production. Brazil has huge amounts of natural resources, including fertile soil and abundant minerals, yet Brazil has a much lower per capita income than Japan. Only when we include the human element of natural resources can we say that natural resources determine economic development.

Natural resources by themselves are not particularly useful for economic development. They must be transformed into something usable for either investment or consumption. This leads us to another aspect of development, the trade-off between investment and consumption. The normal way this subject is analysed is by dealing with investment simply as capital accumulation.

CAPITAL ACCUMULATION

It is often asserted that a necessary prerequisite for economic development is a large capital stock—machines and other durable goods that can be used to aid in the production of consumption goods and more capital goods in the future. It is true that industrially advanced countries indeed have larger capital stocks per capita than developing countries. It is also true that the larger the capital stock for any given population, the higher the possible rate of economic growth (assuming that the population makes good use of the capital goods). This is basically one of the foundations for many of the foreign aid programs in which Canada and other countries have engaged. We and other countries have attempted to give developing countries capital so that they, too, might grow. However, the amount of capital that we have actually given to other countries is quite small: a hydroelectric dam here, a factory there.

Thinking Critically About the Media — The Dark Side of the PC Revolution

According to more than a handful of articles, the "PC revolution" will increase the gap between the rich and the poor. According to one "expert," technology can only be afforded by the rich, and furthermore, computers displace "hordes of workers." Nothing could be further from the truth. The country that has the most computers in place per capita is the United States, and its unemployment rate has not varied much in the past two decades. Moreover, even if computers are essential to the success of a business, their prices are dropping every month. And what is to prevent several businesses in less developed countries from sharing a PC if the price is too high?

Domestic Capital Formation

How does a developing country accumulate capital? The answer is that it must save, and invest those accumulated savings profitably. Saving, of course, means not consuming. Resources must be released from consumer goods production in order to be used for investment.

Saving and the Poor.
It is often stated that people in developing countries cannot save because they are barely subsisting. This is not actually true. Many anthropological studies—of villages in India, for example—have revealed that saving is in fact going on, but it takes forms that we don't recognize in our money economy; for example, saving may involve storing dried onions that can later be traded for other goods. Some researchers speculate that much saving in developing countries takes the form of rearing children who then feel a moral obligation to support their parents during the latter's retirement. In any event, saving does take place even in the most poverty-stricken areas. In general, there is no pronounced relationship between the *percentage* of income saved and the level of income (over the long run).

Basically, then, saving is a method by which individuals can realize an optimal consumption stream throughout their expected lifetimes. The word *optimal* here does not mean adequate or necessary or decent; it means most desirable from the individual's point of view (given that individual's resources).

Evidence of Saving in Developing Countries.
Savings in developing countries do not necessarily flow into what we might consider productive capital formation projects. We do see the results of literally centuries of saving in the form of religious monuments such as cathedrals, and in government buildings. Indeed, one major problem in developing countries is that much of the saving that occurs does not get channelled into productive capital formation. This is also true of much of the foreign aid that has been sent to developing countries. These countries could productively use more factories and a better infrastructure—roads and communications—rather than more government buildings and fancy stadiums built exclusively for merrymaking and sports.

Try Preview Question 3:
Can developing countries create their own capital stock?

Property Rights and Economic Development

If you were in a country in which bank accounts and businesses were periodically expropriated by the government, how willing would you be to leave your money in a savings account or to invest in a business? Certainly, you would be less willing than if such things never occurred. Periodic expropriation of private property rarely occurs in developed countries. It *has* occurred in numerous developing countries, however. For example, private property was once nationalized in Chile and still is in Cuba. In some cases, former owners are compensated, but rarely for the full value of the property taken over by the state.

Empirically, we have seen that, other things being equal, the more certain private property rights are, the more private capital accumulation there will be. People are more willing to invest their savings in endeavours that will increase their wealth in future years. They have property rights in their wealth that are sanctioned and enforced by the government. In fact, some economic historians have attempted to show that it was the development of well-defined private property rights that allowed Western Europe to increase its growth rate after many centuries of stagnation. The degree of certainty with which one can reap the gains from investing also determines the extent to which businesspeople in *other* countries will invest capital in developing countries. The threat of nationalization in some countries may scare away foreign investment that would allow these countries to become more developed.

In a sentence, economic development depends more on individuals who are able to perceive opportunities and then take advantage of those opportunities than it does on capital or natural resources.[1] Risks will not be taken, though, if the risk takers cannot expect a reward. The political institutions must be such that risk takers are rewarded. That requires well-established property rights, lack of the threat of expropriation of profits, and no fear of government nationalization of businesses.

Try Preview Question 4:

Does a lack of protected property rights hinder a developing country's development?

Concepts in Brief

- Some policymakers believe that a large capital stock is a prerequisite for economic growth and development. They therefore suggest that developing countries need more capital.
- The human element, however, is vital; the labour force must be capable of using any capital that the developing country acquires. This requires training and education.
- Saving is a prerequisite for capital formation.
- Saving goes on even in poor developing countries, although not necessarily in the same form as in rich developed countries.
- Saving and individual capital accumulation will be greater the more certain individuals are about the safety of their wealth.

---

[1] The member countries of OPEC might be considered exceptions to this generalization.

THE IMPORTANCE OF AN OPEN ECONOMY

The data are conclusive: Open economies experience faster economic development than economies closed to international trade. That is to say, the less government protects the domestic economy by imposing trade barriers, the faster that economy will experience economic development. According to a study by economists Nouriel Roubini and Xavier Sala-i-Martin, when a country goes from being relatively open to relatively closed via government-enacted trade barriers, it will have a 2.5 percentage point decrease in its growth rate.

Open economies accomplish several things. For one, individuals and businesses end up specializing in those endeavours in which they have a comparative advantage. International trade encourages individuals and businesses to discover ways to specialize so that they can become more productive and earn higher incomes. Increased productivity and the subsequent increase in the rate of economic development are the results. Open economies also allow the importation of already developed technology. For instance, no developing country today needs to spend years to figure out how to make computers or how to use them; that has already been done elsewhere.

The True Cost of Protectionism

A statistical study of the cost of trade barriers might give the impression that taxes on imported goods simply raise their price to domestic consumers. But there is another cost that is normally hidden. Statisticians call it a *Type II error*—the cost of omission. It is the cost of what would have been had there not been tariff barriers. The best example of a Type II error is the cost of overregulating the pharmaceutical industry. If it causes fewer lifesaving drugs to be introduced, it is a Type II error. When trade is restricted in a developing country, that country's people are deprived of a potential larger range of new goods and production processes. Such new foreign products could spur local support businesses, which in turn would cause other businesses to be created. Developing countries that have restricted the entry of computer products have clearly slowed down the development of their own software industry. Trade barriers sometimes guarantee that new goods and services never appear in protected countries. According to economist Paul Romer, because of protectionism, many developing countries do not simply cut back on their consumption of the entire range of goods available to rich countries; rather, they use a smaller quantity of a much smaller range of goods. He calculates that the cumulative forgone benefits from new economic activity blocked by an across-the-board 10 percent tariff in a developing country might be as high as 20 percent of annual national income.

THE IMPORTANCE OF AN EDUCATED POPULATION

Both theoretically and empirically, we know that a more educated workforce aids economic development because it allows individuals to build on the ideas of others. According to economists David Gould and Roy Ruffin, increasing the rate of enrolment in secondary schools by only two percentage points, from eight to 10 percent, raises the average rate of economic growth by half a percent per year. Thus we must conclude that developing countries can advance more rapidly if they invest more heavily in secondary education. Or stated in the negative, economic development cannot be sustained if a country allows a sizable portion of its population to avoid education. After all, education allows young people who grew up poor to acquire skills that enable them to avoid poverty as adults.

Some of the fastest-growing countries in the world, including the Four Tigers, virtually eliminated illiteracy very early on.

INTERNATIONAL POLICY EXAMPLE
Should School Tuition Vouchers Be Used in Developing Countries?

Nobel Prize–winning economist Gary Becker has argued in favour of a school voucher system in developing countries. According to his scheme, low-income parents would receive the vouchers, which could then be used at any approved school in their country. The participating schools would also have to provide meals for their students. According to Becker, such vouchers would stimulate competition among private and public schools in developing countries. There is a problem for very poor families, however. They want their children to work to provide income. Becker suggests that such families be given a bonus that offsets the income loss while their children are going to school.

For critical analysis: Do parents in developed countries have to be compensated for sending their children to school? Explain.

LETTING COMPANIES DISAPPEAR: CREATIVE DESTRUCTION

Economist Joseph Schumpeter (1883–1950) championed the concept of *creative destruction*. He pointed out that new technologies and successful new businesses end up destroying old jobs, old companies, and old industries. Change is painful and costly, but it is necessary for economic advancement. Nowhere is this more important than in developing countries, where the principle is often ignored.

Developing countries have had a history of supporting current companies and industries by preventing new technologies and new companies from entering the marketplace. The process of creative destruction has not been allowed to work its magic.

One key element in providing the most favourable condition for economic development is allowing businesses to fail. A corollary to this principle is that governments should not consistently use their taxpayers' money to subsidize or even own businesses. It does little good (and normally a lot of harm) for governments in developing countries to own banks, phone companies, electric companies, car companies, or airlines. There are few historical examples of state-owned companies doing other than one thing—draining the public coffers.

Do not get the impression that government-owned and -operated businesses are run by individuals who are somehow less competent than those in the private sector. Rather, the incentive structure for managers in private businesses is different from that for managers in state-owned businesses.

THE RELATIONSHIP BETWEEN POPULATION GROWTH AND ECONOMIC DEVELOPMENT

World population is growing at the rate of 2.8 people each and every second. That turns out to be 242,000 a day, or 88.3 million a year. Today, there are about 5.8 billion people on earth. By the year 2030, according to the United Nations, there will be 8.5 billion. Look at Figure 21.1 to see which countries are growing the most.

Now look at Figure 21.2 (page 522). There you see that virtually all of the growth in population comes from developing countries. Some countries, such as Germany, are expected to lose population over the next several decades.

Figure 21.1
Expected Growth in World Population by 2030

Asia and Africa are expected to gain the most in population by the year 2030.

Source: United Nations.

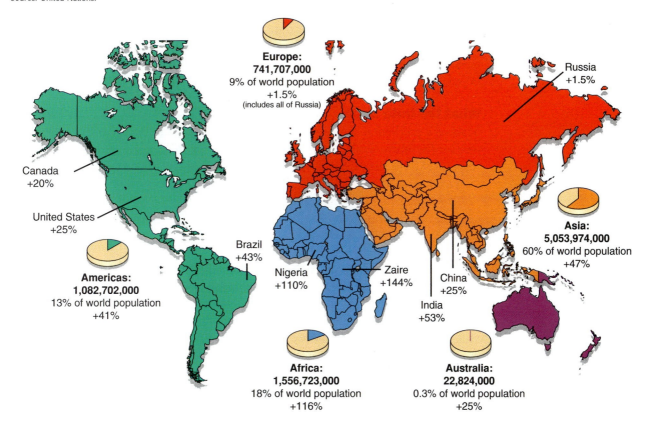

Figure 21.2
Population Growth by 2050

Population will increase dramatically in the developing countries. The industrially advanced countries will grow very little in population over the next half century.

Source: United States Population Reference Bureau.

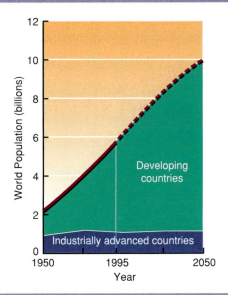

The Conventional Wisdom

Ever since the Reverend Thomas Robert Malthus wrote his essay *The Principle of Population* in 1798, excessive population growth has been a concern. Modern-day Malthusians are able to generate just as much enthusiasm for the concept that population growth is bad. We are told that rapid population growth threatens economic development and the quality of life. This message was made loud and clear by numerous participants in the United Nations' International Conference on Population and Development held in Cairo, Egypt, in the fall of 1994.

What the Data Show.   First of all, according to economist Nicholas Eberstadt, Malthus's prediction that population would outstrip food supplies has never held true for the entire world. Figure 21.3 shows how population has grown over the past 35 years. At the same time, the food supply, measured by calories per person, has also increased somewhat steadily.

Also, the price of food, corrected for inflation, has been falling steadily for over a century. That means that the supply of food is expanding faster than the demand caused by increased population.

Population Density and Economic Development.   There is no consistent relationship between population density and economic development. Japan, for example, has a higher per capita income than many Western European countries, yet it has more people per square kilometre than India, one of the poorest countries. Hong Kong is the most densely populated country. Fifty years ago it was one of the poorest, but today its per capita income exceeds that in France and the United Kingdom. (Hong Kong has almost no natural resources either—it has to import even its drinking water.) As a general proposition, some of the richest countries in the world today are the most densely populated—South Korea, Taiwan, Belgium, the Netherlands, England, Germany, and Japan.

Figure 21.3
Population and Food Supplies

Malthus has been proved wrong: Population has not outstripped the world's food supply. In fact, for at least the past half century, calories consumed per person have been increasing at a rate even faster than the increase in population.

Source: United States Department of Agriculture.

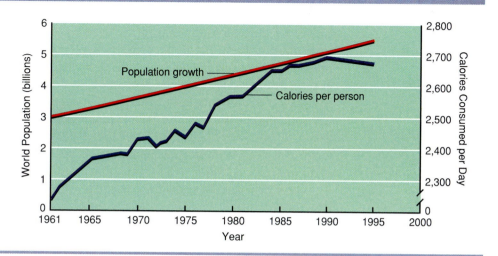

The Relationship Between Population Growth Rates and Economic Development.

Again there seems to be little relationship between economic development and rapid population growth. Consider Malaysia, which grew from a sparsely populated country of villages in the 1890s to a country of cities in the 1930s. During this period, its population increased from 1.5 million to 6 million, but its standard of living also increased, by about 140 percent. Historically, the largest increases in Western living standards took place during the period when the Western population was growing faster than it is in today's developing countries. Also, in spite of relatively high population growth rates, per capita incomes in many, if not most, developing countries are much higher today than they were four decades ago. Much of the population growth in developing countries has occurred because both adults and children live longer than they used to, not necessarily because families are having more children. There are just fewer deaths caused by malnutrition and contagious diseases than there used to be.

The Relationship Between Average Family Income and Size

One thing that economists know for sure is that over the past century, as countries became richer, the average family size fell. Otherwise stated, the more economic development occurs, the slower the population growth rate. Predictions of birthrates in developing countries have often turned out to be overstated if those countries experience rapid economic growth. This was the case in Hong Kong, Mexico, Taiwan, and Colombia.

Recent research on population and economic development has revealed that social and economic modernization has been accompanied by what might be called a fertility revolution—the spread of deliberate family size limitation within marriage and a decline in childbearing. Modernization reduces infant mortality, which in turn reduces the incentive for couples to have many children to make sure that enough will survive to satisfy each couple's demand. Also, modernization lowers the demand for children for a variety of reasons, not least being that couples in more developed countries do not need to rely on their children to take care of them in old age.

Population and Productivity

Recall the discussion of comparative advantage and specialization in Chapter 19. Specialization turns out to be a function of the size of the market, which is, of course, a function of population. Thus a growing population can help improve the quality of life because it allows individuals to devote their talents to what they are best suited to do—whatever their comparative advantage is. Individuals don't "exhaust" the earth's resources. People create wealth through imagination and innovation. It was not all that long ago that oil was considered useless. So was sand; today, it is used to make silicone and glass from which computer chips and fibre optics are manufactured.

Three hundred years ago, there were one-tenth the number of humans who now live. Yet the world is incredibly more wealthy than it was three centuries ago. Today, there are six times as many Canadians as there were 100 years ago. Yet today we live longer and are about seven times richer per capita.

FOREIGN AID

Many countries, including Canada, extend assistance to developing countries. A number of reasons are given to justify this assistance, which can be in the form of grants, low-interest loans, food, or technical expertise. Although the humanitarian argument in support of foreign aid is often given, security and economics also enter into the discussion. During the Cold War, many Western nations gave foreign aid to developing countries in order to support noncommunist régimes or to prevent communist takeovers. Canada also extends foreign aid to help develop foreign markets for the output of Canadian firms. This is particularly true when foreign aid is tied to the purchase of Canadian products. Tied foreign aid requires that the recipient spend all or part of the sum extended as foreign aid on Canadian-produced goods.

The Results of Foreign Aid

Since the end of World War II, the developed world has transferred about $2.4 trillion (in today's dollars) to developing countries. The results have been mixed. According to one study by economist Peter Bauer, there is little correlation between the level of foreign aid received and changes in living standards. He also found that foreign aid did not necessarily reduce infant mortality rates. His conclusion was that foreign aid simply raised the standard of living of the recipient countries' richest people.

Consider Tanzania. Between 1970 and 1988, this African country received $8.6 billion in aid, four times that country's 1988 gross domestic product. This is the equivalent of someone giving Canada around $3 trillion. During the same period, Sudan was given $9.6 billion, an amount equal to one year's output. Zaire, Togo, Zambia, Mozambique, and Niger each received around $6 billion during the same period. What happened to these billions of dollars? In all of these countries, gross output actually fell. Critics of foreign aid point out that much of the money went into new government centres, showy airports, and grand conference halls. Some of it also went into government officials' Swiss bank accounts. According to economist George Ayittey, Zaire ex-president Mobutu Sese Seko was worth $10 billion at his death, and Zambia's Kenneth Kaunda is currently worth $6 billion.

INTERNATIONAL EXAMPLE
The World Bank and the Development of Poor Countries (or Lack Thereof)

The International Bank for Reconstruction and Development, known as the World Bank, was established in 1944. To date it has lent over $300 billion, mostly to poor countries. However, its accomplishments have recently been questioned. For example, since 1951, India has received $55 billion—more foreign aid than any other country on earth—yet over 40 percent of India's population still lives in poverty. In sub-Saharan Africa, massive amounts of money have gone into development planning, yet that region has a lower per capita income than it did before it received aid.

Another criticism of the World Bank is that its lending policies during the 1970s encouraged large-scale, capital-intensive technology, which helped governments in less developed countries to plunder their natural resources. These large-scale projects displaced millions of poor and tribal peoples. In India, World Bank development projects uprooted over 20 million people. Throughout the world, dam projects have altered natural ecologies. Indeed, a mid-1990's internal review of the bank's lending portfolio found that almost 40 percent of recently evaluated projects did not adhere to established environmental and social policies.

The major problem with the World Bank's lending activities is that they help government bureaucracies flourish with funds that could be used to help individuals in the host countries.

For critical analysis: How does lending to governments in less developed countries hinder market reforms?

Concepts in Brief

- The openness of an economy can determine its rate, or lack thereof, of economic development. Open economies allow, among other things, the importation of technology from the rest of the world.
- The more educated the workforce, the greater the chance of successful economic development, so enrolment in secondary schools is a key determinant of economic growth.
- While many believe population growth hinders economic development, there is little historic relationship between either population density or growth rates and economic growth rates.
- Critics of foreign aid point out that foreign aid will not increase the rate of economic growth unless a well-functioning capital base and infrastructure are in place.

Issues and Applications

Can PCs Bridge the Gap Between Less Advanced and More Advanced Economies?

Concepts Applied: International trade, technology, open economies

The PC revolution allows less advanced economies to benefit from new technology at a low investment cost and at a faster rate than in already developed countries.

The PC revolution is showing up in the world's developing countries, sometimes at a faster pace than in Canada. In its wake is a quickly narrowing competitive gap between the more advanced and the less advanced economies. There are several reasons the PC may be at the heart of improved economies in developing countries.

Low-Price Accessibility

Even in the developed countries, the PC revolution would never have happened without dramatic improvements in microprocessors, memory chips, and software, all occurring while prices continue to drop. Computer technology is now economically viable for most businesses except in the extremely poor countries, according to Eduardo Talero, information technology specialist at the World Bank.

"Necessity: The Mother of Invention"

Another reason PC technology has taken off in some countries is simply that it was needed. The advanced home-banking system in Brazil referred to at the beginning of this chapter did depend on cheap technology and software. Also, high inflation rates in Brazil have meant that people who did not deposit their earnings immediately would see the real value of their wealth drop through inflation. Home banking allows for instantaneous transfers of earnings. Necessity is the mother of invention.

The Benefit of Being a Latecomer

Perhaps just as important for developing countries, the fact that they are latecomers has helped them tremendously. Developing countries by definition have had low levels of technology in their business infrastructure. Consequently, they have not invested large amounts in old systems, such as IBM mainframe computers. When the PC revolution came along, they were able to take advantage of it without waiting for their old equipment to wear out. Economic theory predicts that late starters—developing countries—can benefit from new technology at a much faster rate than the already developed countries. And that is what has been happening.

Bringing Down the Trade Barriers

The developing countries that have reduced their trade barriers fastest have seen technology circulate the most freely and have experienced the greatest benefits. Many Latin American countries are leading the way by allowing unfettered imports of computer equipment and software. The PC market in Latin America is growing at a rate of almost 25 percent a year. Sales in Eastern Europe are growing at 15 percent a year. Software sales are growing even faster.

For Critical Analysis

1. Why do latecomers adopt technology faster than already established economies?
2. Why is an open economy necessary for technological innovation to spread rapidly?

CHAPTER SUMMARY

1. The 19 industrially advanced countries (IACs)— Canada, the United States, Japan, and the countries of Western Europe—have market economies based on a large skilled labour force and a large technically advanced stock of capital goods.

2. One of the major characteristics of developing countries is a high rate of population growth. However, high population growth does not necessarily prevent or retard economic development.

3. Some authorities contend that balanced development of industry and agriculture is necessary for growth in the developing countries. There are, however, exceptions to this rule; Hong Kong is one.

4. Industrialization in many developing countries has involved subsidization of manufacturing. Such subsidization leads to a misallocation of resources and to a lower per capita standard of living for the population even though the country may become more highly industrialized.

5. Capital accumulation is an important determinant of economic development. However, massive transfers of capital to developing countries do not guarantee economic development. Appropriately trained personnel must be available to use the capital given to these countries.

6. Domestic capital formation requires saving— nonconsumption of current income. Even the poorest countries' citizens do some saving. In fact, there is no pronounced relationship between percentage of income saved and level of income.

7. Saving in the developing countries may take on different forms than in more developed countries. For example, having children is a form of saving if those children feel an obligation to support their parents during retirement.

8. The more certain private property rights are, the more private capital accumulation there will be, other things being equal.

DISCUSSION OF PREVIEW QUESTIONS

1. **What is a developing country?**
   Developing countries are arbitrarily defined as those with very low per capita incomes. Relative to developed countries, people in developing countries have lower incomes, life expectancies, literacy rates, and daily caloric intake, and higher infant mortality rates.

2. **Must developing countries develop by industrializing?**
   Proponents of the balanced-growth theory point out that the industrially advanced countries (IACs) are highly industrialized and the developing countries are mostly agrarian. They feel that balanced growth requires that the developing countries expand the manufacturing sector; labourers and other resources should be reallo-

   cated to promote industrialization. It is often suggested that the developing countries restrict imports of nonagricultural goods to help industrialization. It is alleged that these countries must industrialize even if their comparative advantage lies in the production of agricultural goods because they can't compete with the subsidized agricultural sectors of the IACs. Yet it is easy to oversell the pro-industrialization balanced-growth approach. Numerous examples of gross inefficiency can be cited when the developing countries attempted to develop steel and automobile industries. Moreover, when the developing countries restrict the imports of manufactured goods, they lower living standards and promote inefficiency. It would seem that the time to develop the industrial sector would be when it is profitable for businesses to do so.

3. Can developing countries create their own capital stock?

It is often asserted that a large capital stock is necessary for economic development, the developing countries are too poor to save sufficient amounts to develop domestic capital formation, and the IACs should therefore give capital to the developing countries. Experts disagree about the validity of each contention. The question under discussion here deals with the second proposition. A good deal of evidence exists to support the notion that the developing countries do save—although in forms that are not easily observed or cannot be readily converted into capital. Even people with extremely low incomes are forced by economic circumstances to provide for future consumption; they often store dried or cured food. On a nationwide scale, much evidence of capital formation exists: cathedrals, pyramids, great walls, fortresses, government buildings, and so on. Of course, the problem is to get savings into forms that can be used to produce goods or services.

4. Does a lack of protected property rights hinder a developing country's development?

Yes. When individuals fear that their property rights will not be protected, they invest in ways that reflect this risk. Thus people in politically and economically unstable countries prefer to accumulate diamonds, gold, silver, and currency in foreign banks rather than invest in factories, equipment, and savings in domestic bank accounts. Similarly, a country that expropriates property or nationalizes industry discourages investment by foreign businesses. Many developing countries could be aided to a great extent by attracting foreign investment—but foreign investors will require property rights guarantees.

PROBLEMS

(Answers to the odd-numbered problems appear at the back of the book.)

21-1. List five developing countries and five industrially advanced countries.

21-2. What problems are associated with advancements in medicine and health that are made available to developing countries?

21-3. Outline a typical pattern of economic development.

21-4. Suppose that you are shown the following data for two countries, known only as country X and country Z:

Country	GDP	Population
X	$ 81 billion	9 million
Z	$135 billion	90 million

a. From this information, which country would you expect to be classified as a developing country? Why?

b. Now suppose that you were also given the following data:

Country	Life Expectancy at Birth (years)	Infant Mortality per 1,000 Live Births	Literacy (%)
X	70	15	60
Z	58	50	70

Are these figures consistent with your answer to part (a)?

c. Should we expect the developing country identified in part (a) to have a much greater population density than the other country?

21-5. Would unrestricted labour immigration end up helping or hurting developing countries? Explain.

21-6. Many countries in Africa have extremely large potential stocks of natural resources. Nonetheless, those natural resources often remain unexploited. Give reasons why this situation continues to exist.

21-7. Sketch a scenario in which population growth causes an increase in income per capita.

21-8. Visit the Organisation for Economic Cooperation and Development (OECD) development indicators Web site at http://www.oecd.org/dac/Indicators/htm/list.htm.

    a.   What indicators of general development does the OECD use?

    b.   Now open the general development indicators table. List four of the poorest countries according to per capita GDP. (For example, countries with per capita GDP less than US$500.) What is the life expectancy in these countries?

    c.   List four of the richer countries according to per capita GDP. (Countries with per capita GDP greater than US$10,000.) What is the life expectancy in these countries?

    d.   What conclusions can you draw about life expectancy and economic wealth as represented by per capita GDP? Which set of countries would you expect to experience more rapid economic development? Why?

INTERACTING WITH THE INTERNET

File Edit View Go Favorites Help

Back Forward Stop Refresh Home Search Favorites History Channels Fullscreen Mail Print Edit

Summary macroeconomic data on most countries of the world, including developing ones, can be found in the Penn World Tables at

http://www.nber.org/pwt56.html

If the release number of the data changes, it might be necessary to search from

http://www.nber.org

The World Bank maintains two sites with valuable information on economic development. Perhaps the more important is "Social Indicators of Development," which covers a wide variety of health, demographic, and economic information. It is found at

http://www.ciesin.org/IC/wbank/sid-home.html

Brief reports on countries that borrow from the World Bank are contained in "Trends in Developing Economies," which is located at

http://www.ciesin.org/IC/wbank/tde-home.html

ANSWERS TO ODD-NUMBERED PROBLEMS

Chapter 1
The Nature of Economics

1-1.   A large number of possible factors might affect the probability of death, including age, occupation, diet, and current health. Thus one model would show that the older someone is, the greater is the probability of dying within the next five years; another would show that the riskier the occupation, other things being equal, the greater the probability of dying within five years; and so forth.

1-3.   a.   We should observe younger drivers to be more frequently involved in traffic accidents than older persons.

       b.   Slower monetary expansion should be associated with less inflation.

       c.   Professional basketball players receiving smaller salaries should be observed to have done less well in their high school studies.

       d.   Employees being promoted rapidly should have lower rates of absenteeism than those being promoted more slowly.

1-5.   The decreasing relative attractiveness of mail communication has no doubt decreased students' demand for writing skills. Whether the influence has been a significant one is a subject for empirical research. As for the direction of causation, it may well be running both ways. Cheaper non-written forms of communication may decrease the demand for writing skills. Lower levels of writing skills probably further increase the demand for audio and video communications media.

1-7.   a.   Normative, involving a value judgment about what should be

       b.   Positive, for it is a statement of what has actually occurred

       c.   Positive, for it is a statement of what actually is

       d.   Normative, involving a value judgment about what should be

Chapter 2
Scarcity and the World of Trade-Offs

2-1.   The law of increasing relative cost does seem to hold because of the principle that some resources may be more suited to one productive use than to another. In moving from cheese to apples, the economy will first transfer those resources most easily sacrificed by the cheese sector, holding on to the very specialized (to cheese) factors until the last. Thus different factor intensities will lead to increasing relative costs.

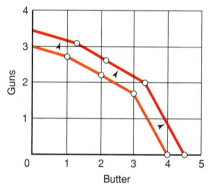

Production Possibilities Curve
for Guns and Butter
(before and after 10 percent growth)

2-3.   a.   Neither, because each can produce the same total number of jackets per time period (2 jackets per hour)

       b.   Neither, because each has the same cost of producing ties ($\frac{2}{3}$ jacket per tie)

       c.   No, because with equal costs of production, there are no gains from specialization

       d.   Output will be the same as if they did not specialize (16 jackets per day and 24 ties per day)

2-5.   a.   Only the extra expense of lunch in a restaurant, above what lunch at home would have cost, is part of the cost of going to the game.

       b.   This is part of the cost of going to the game because you would not have incurred it if you had watched the game on TV at home.

       c.   This is part of the cost of going to the game because you would not have incurred it if you had watched the game on TV at home.

2-7. For most people, air is probably not an economic good because most of us would not pay simply to have a larger volume of the air we are currently breathing. But for almost everyone, clean air is an economic good because most of us would be willing to give something up to have cleaner air.

Appendix A
Reading and Working with Graphs

A-1.

y	x
12	4
9	3
6	2
3	1
0	0
−3	−1
−6	−2
−9	−3
−12	−4

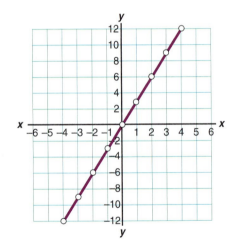

Chapter 3
Demand and Supply

3-1. The equilibrium price is $30. The quantity supplied and demanded is about 1,050 thousand skateboards per year.

3-3.
a. The demand curve for vitamin C will shift outward to the right because the product has taken on a desirable new quality. (Change in tastes and preferences)

b. The demand curve for teachers will shift inward to the left because the substitute good, the interactive educational CD-

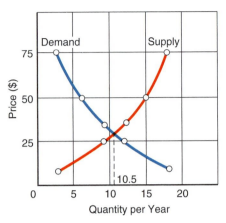

ROM, is now a lower-cost alternative. (Change in the price of a substitute)

c. The demand curve for beer will shift outward to the right because the price of a complementary good—pretzels—has decreased. Is it any wonder that pub owners often give pretzels away? (Change in the price of a complement)

3-5. As the graph indicates, demand doesn't change, supply decreases, the equilibrium price of oranges rises, and the equilibrium quantity falls.

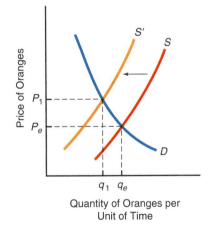

3-7. The speaker has learned well the definition of a surplus but has overlooked one point. The "surpluses" that result from the above-equilibrium minimum prices don't go begging; the excess quantities supplied are in effect purchased by government agencies. In that sense, they are not surpluses at all. When one includes the quantity that is demanded by the government agencies, along with the quantities being bought by private purchasers at the support price, the quantity demanded will equal the quantity supplied, and there will be an equilibrium of sorts.

3-9. As the graph illustrates, rain consumers are not willing to pay a positive price to have nature's bounty increased. Thus the equilibrium quantity is 200 centimetres per year (the amount supplied freely by nature), and the equilibrium price is zero (the amount that consumers will pay for an additional unit, given that nature is already producing 200 centimetres per year).

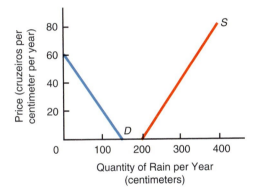

Chapter 4
Extensions of Demand and Supply Analysis

4-1. a. The demand curve will shift to the right (increase).
      b. The supply curve will shift to the right (increase).
      c. Because the price floor, or minimum price, is below the equilibrium price of 50 cents, there will be no effect on price or quantity.
      d. Because the price floor is now greater than the equilibrium price, there will be a surplus at the new price of 75 cents.
      e. Assuming that grapefruits are a substitute for oranges, the demand curve for oranges will shift to the right (increase).
      f. Assuming that oranges are a normal good, the demand curve will shift to the left (decrease).

4-3. The "equilibrium" price is $40 per calculator, and the equilibrium quantity is zero calculators per year. This is so because at a price of $40, the quantity demanded—zero—is equal to the quantity supplied—also zero. None will be produced or bought because the highest price that

any consumer is willing to pay for even a single calculator ($30) is below the lowest price at which any producer is willing to produce even one calculator ($50).

4-5. The equilibrium price is $4 per crate, and the equilibrium quantity is 5 million crates per year. At $2 per crate, the quantity demanded is 9 million crates per year and the quantity supplied is 1 million. This is called a shortage, or excess quantity demanded. The excess quantity demanded is 8 million crates per year. At $5 per crate, the quantity demanded is 2 million crates per year and the quantity supplied is 8 million crates. This is called a surplus, or excess quantity supplied. The excess quantity supplied is 6 million crates per year.

4-7. As shown in the graph, if the equilibrium price of apples is 10 cents, a price floor of 15 cents will result in a surplus equal to $Q_s - Q_d$. A price floor of 5 cents per apple will have no effect, however, because it is below the equilibrium price and thus does not prevent suppliers and demanders from doing what they want to do—produce and consume Q_e apples at 10 cents each.

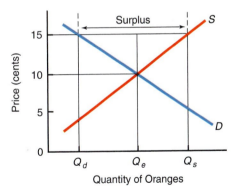

Chapter 5
The Public Sector

5-1. The marginal tax rate on the first $3,000 of taxable income is 0 percent because no taxes are imposed until $5,000 is earned. The marginal rate on $10,000 is 20 percent, as it is on $100,000 and all other amounts above the $5,000 level, because for each additional dollar earned after $5,000, 20 cents will be taxed away. The average tax rate, which is the tax amount divided by the pretax income, is 0 for $3,000, 10 percent for $10,000, and 19 percent for

$100,000. The average tax rate will approach a maximum of 20 percent as income increases. It cannot reach exactly 20 percent because of the untaxed $5,000 at the beginning. Such is the nature of a degressive tax system.

5-3. Mr. Smith pays nothing on his first $1,500 of income, 14 percent ($70) on the $500 of earnings between $1,500 and $2,000, and 20 percent ($100) on the $500 that he earns above $2,000. Thus Mr. Smith has a total tax bill of $170 on an income of $2,500; his average tax rate is 6.8 percent, and his marginal tax rate is 20 percent.

5-5. Market failure means that the unrestrained operation of a market leads to either too few or too many resources being used in that activity.

5-7. a. If you give and everyone else does also, you account for 1 percent. If you are the only one who gives, you account for 100 percent. If you give nothing, you account for 0 percent, regardless of what others give.

   b. In principle, your contribution matters whatever the level of participation. But as a practical matter, if participation is near 100 percent, the absence of your contribution may have little effect.

   c. There is no free ride. If you do not make your contribution, total contributions will be lower, and the quality of the services provided will be lower.

5-9. The existence of these costs implies the notion of rational ignorance, so that individuals choose not to be informed about certain issues because the cost of being informed is high relative to any benefit forthcoming from the state of the issue. This also contributes to the growth of special-interest groups because individuals have no strong economic incentive to act against them.

Chapter 6
Economies in Transition

6-1. On the supply side, all of the industries responsible for automobile inputs would have to be considered. This would include steel (and coke and coal), glass, tires (and rubber), plastics, railroads (and thus steel again), aluminum (and electricity), and manufacturers of stereos, hubcaps, and air conditioners, to name a few. On the demand side, you would have to take into account industries involving complements (such as oil, gasoline, concrete, and asphalt) and substitutes (including bicycles, motorcycles, buses, and walking shoes). Moreover, resource allocation decisions regarding labour and the other inputs, complements, and substitutes for these goods must also be made.

6-3. a. Profit equals total revenue minus total cost. Because revenue is fixed (at $172), if the firm wishes to maximize profit, this is equivalent to minimizing costs. To find total costs, simply multiply the price of each input by the amount of the input that must be used for each technique.

Costs of A = ($10)(7) + ($2)(6) + ($15)(2) + ($8)(1) = $120
Costs of B = ($10)(4) + ($2)(7) + ($15)(6) + ($8)(3) = $168
Costs of C = ($10)(1) + ($2)(18) + ($15)(3) + ($8)(2) = $107

Because C has the lowest costs, it yields the highest profits, and thus it will be used.

   b. Profit equals $172 - $107 = $65.

   c. Each technique's costs rise by the increase in the price of labour multiplied by the amount of labour used by that technique. Because technique A uses the least amount of labour, its costs rise the least, and it thus becomes the lowest-cost technique at $132. (The new cost of B is $182, and the new cost of C is $143.) Hence technique A will be used, resulting in profits of $172 - $132 = $40.

6-5. a. In the market system, the techniques that yield the highest (positive) profits will be used.

   b. Profit equals total revenue minus total cost. Because revenue from 100 units is fixed (at $100), if the firm wishes to maximize profit, this is equivalent to minimizing costs. To find total costs, simply multiply the price of each input by the amount of the input that must be used for each technique.

Costs of A = ($10)(6) + ($8)(5) = $100
Costs of B = ($10)(5) + ($8)(6) = $98
Costs of C = ($10)(4) + ($8)(7) = $96

Because technique C has the lowest costs, it

also yields the highest profits ($100 - $96 = $4).

c. Following the same methods yields these costs: A = $98, B = $100, and C = $102. Technique A will be used because it is the most profitable.

d. The profits from using technique A to produce 100 units of X are $100 - $98 = $2.

Chapter 7
The Macroeconomy: Unemployment and Inflation

7-1. Although your boss gave you a raise of $1,200 ($30,000 × 0.04), you are not $1,200 better off after taxes. You are now in the 26 percent marginal tax bracket. You must pay 0.26 × $1,200 in additional taxes, or $312. That leaves you with an additional $888 in take-home pay. That is how much better off you are because of the raise.

7-3. a. 5 percent
b. One month
c. 5 percent
d. 10 percent
e. In this example, the unemployment rate doubled, but it is not obvious that the economy has become sicker or that workers are worse off.

7-5. a. The nominal rate of interest is composed of the real rate of interest plus the anticipated rate of inflation. If the current rate of inflation is zero and people anticipate that there will continue to be no inflation, the real rate of interest equals the nominal rate of interest—in this example, 12 percent.

b. If the nominal rate of interest stays at 12 percent while the rate of inflation goes to 13 percent, and if that rate is anticipated to last, the real rate of interest drops to a *negative* 1 percent! Lending money at 12 percent would not normally be advisable in such a situation.

7-7. a. 10, 9, 8, 7, 6, 5, 4, 3
b. 8.0, 8.3, 9.4, 10.9, 12.0, 13.8, 16.0

Chapter 8
Measuring the Economy's Performance

8-1. a. GDP = $950; NDP = $900; NI = $875

b. GDP = $825
c. The value of depreciation exceeding gross private investment implies that the total capital stock of the country is declining. This would likely decrease future productivity because capital is a productive resource.

8-3. a. Coal; $2
b. $3. Auto manufacturers took something worth $5 and transformed it into an auto that they sold for $8.
c. $9, because intermediate goods are not counted.
d. $9, resulting from adding the value added at each stage. Note that in this economy, which produces only autos, the earnings and the income approaches both yield a GDP estimate of $9.

8-5. a. It falls.
b. It is unchanged because illegal transactions are not measured anyway.
c. It rises.

8-7. a. Nominal GDP for 1992 = ($4)(10) + ($12)(20) + ($6)(5) + ($25)(10) = $560. Nominal GDP for 1997 = ($8)(12) + ($36)(15) + ($10)(15) + ($30)(12) = $1,146.
b. Real GDP for 1992 = $560. Real GDP for 1997 = ($4)(12) + ($12)(15) + ($6)(15) + ($25)(12) = $618.

Chapter 9
Economic Growth: Technology, Research and Development, and Knowledge

9-1. Point B is associated with the highest feasible growth rate. Capital goods implicitly represent future consumption, and point B has the highest feasible ratio of capital goods to current consumption (and thus the highest ratio of future consumption to current consumption).

9-3. a. M
b. K

Chapter 10
Micro Foundations: Aggregate Demand and Aggregate Supply

10-1. At P_1, the quantity of *AS* exceeds the quantity of *AD*; therefore, a surplus of real national income (output) exists. At that price level, suppliers are willing to produce more than buyers want to purchase; in this surplus situation, producers find their inventories rising involuntarily, and they find it profitable to reduce prices and output. At P_2, the quantity of AD exceeds the quantity of AS, and a shortage exists. At that price level, buyers want more than producers are willing to produce, and buyers, competing for goods and services, will bid the price level upward. A higher price level induces an increase in the quantity of AS and a decrease in the quantity of AD. Only at P_e does the quantity of AS equal the quantity of AD; at P_e, equilibrium exists.

10-3. The long-run aggregate supply curve is vertical at the point representing the maximum potential output possible. Prices can vary, but output cannot. In the short run, some increase in the level of output is possible with prices rising. This is possible because of the existence of some excess capacity, as well as flexibility in the nature and intensity of work. Therefore, the positively sloped portion of the aggregate supply curve constitutes the short-run aggregate supply curve.

10-5. a. The price level increases.
       b. National output decreases.

Chapter 11
Classical and Keynesian Macro Analyses

11-1. If the interest rate is higher than equilibrium, desired saving exceeds desired investment. Those who desire investment funds from savers will offer to pay lower rates of interest. Savers, in competition with each other, will be willing to accept lower rates of interest. The interest rate will be bid down, which will simultaneously decrease the quantity of saving desired and increase the quantity of investment desired.

11-3. Equilibrium starts out at E_1 with the price level at 100 and equilibrium real GDP at Q_0. When AD_1 shifts to AD_2, the end result is that the equilibrium is at E_1 with the same equilibrium level of real GDP per year but a price level of only 90. The equilibrium level of real GDP is supply-determined.

Chapter 12
Consumption, Income, and the Multiplier

12-1.

Disposable Income	Consumption	Saving
$ 500	$510	$−10
600	600	0
700	690	10
800	780	20
900	870	30
1,000	960	40

a.

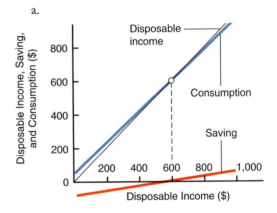

b. The marginal propensity to consume is 0.9; the marginal propensity to save is 0.1.

c.

Disposable Income	Average Propensity to Consume	Average Propensity to Save
$ 500	1.0200	−.0200
600	1.0000	0
700	.9857	.0142
800	.9750	.0250
900	.9667	.0333
1,000	.9600	.0400

12-3. Stock: a, c; Flow: b, d, e, f, g

Real National Income	Consumption Expenditures	Saving	Investment	APC	APS	MPC	MPS
$1,000	$1,100	$−100	$100	1.1	−.1	.9	.1
2,000	2,000	0	100	1.0	.0	.9	.1
3,000	2,900	100	100	.967	.033	.9	.1
4,000	3,800	200	100	.950	.050	.9	.1
5,000	4,700	300	100	.940	.060	.9	.1
6,000	5,600	400	100	.933	.067	.9	.1

12-5.

a.

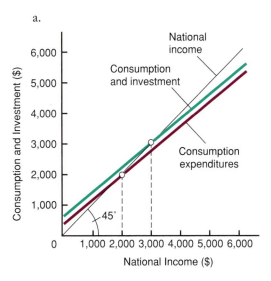

b.

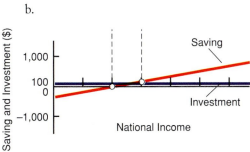

c. The multiplier effect from the inclusion of investment is to raise equilibrium national income by $1,000 over the equilibrium level it would otherwise have reached.

d. The value of the multiplier is 10.

e. The equilibrium level of national income without investment is $2,000; with investment, it is $3,000.

f. Equilibrium income will rise by $1,000.

g. Equilibrium income will again rise by $1,000 to $4,000.

12-7.
a. Multiplier = 10
b. Multiplier = 3.33
c. Multiplier = 6.67
d. Multiplier = 2.86

Chapter 13
Fiscal Policy

13-1. Discretionary fiscal policy is policy in which the levels of government spending and taxes change as a result of a deliberate decision by the government. *Example:* A change in the structure of tax rates, a change in government expenditures not associated with a change in government revenues. Automatic stabilizers cause the level of government spending or taxes to change as a result of endogenous changes in a variable such as income, other than changes due to deliberate decisions of the government. *Example:* Government revenues increasing from taxes during an economic expansion.

13-3. Consumers must not regard current budget deficits as equivalent to higher future taxes and current budget surpluses as equivalent to lower future taxes. For example, if consumers regard a $1 million deficit as imposing an equivalent amount of new taxes on them in the future, they will increase current saving so as to be in a position to pay the higher future taxes. As a result, current consumption will decline, and at least some, and possibly all, of the stabilizing effect of the deficit will be wiped out.

Appendix C
Fiscal Policy: A Keynesian Perspective

C-1. a. The marginal propensity to consume is equal to $1 - MPS$, or $\frac{6}{7}$.

  b. Investment or government spending must increase by $20 billion.

  c. The government would have to cut taxes by $23.33 billion.

C-3. a. Aggregate demand will shift downward by $500; therefore, national income will fall by $5,000.

  b. Aggregate demand will shift upward by $0.9(\$500) = \$450$; therefore, national income will rise by $4,500.

Chapter 14
Deficit Spending and the Public Debt

14-1. The federal budget deficit is the difference between federal spending and federal taxes—in this case, $30 billion.

14-3. Ultimately, all government debt must be repaid by means of taxation. (The government cannot forever "repay" its debt by issuing more debt because ultimately the public debt would exceed the wealth of the entire country!) Thus when the government adds to the debt, it is simultaneously adding to future taxes that must be equivalent in present value to the added debt.

14-5. Some observers say that the true burden of government is the real value of the resources it uses. Changing the way the books are kept leaves this burden unchanged. Moreover, neither current nor future taxes would be affected by this accounting change, so no one's tax liability would be altered. In brief, the change will have no real consequences. The net public debt equals the gross public debt minus the portion held by government agencies (what the government owes to itself).

Chapter 15
Money and the Banking System

15-1. a. The painting by Renoir would have the greatest advantage as a store of value, for works of art have generally appreciated over time. As a medium of exchange or a unit of account, it would be deficient because of its high, and sometimes variable, value and the limited market for its exchange.

  b. A 90-day treasury bill also has a good store of value; it is guaranteed by the government and it will pay some interest. Of course, to the extent that the money to be returned for the matured bill is an imperfect store of value, so will be the bill. A 90-day bill will not vary much in value over its life because the redemption date is not far off and there is a ready market for its exchange; thus it is a serviceable medium of exchange and unit of account. But the large denominations in which these bills are issued detract from the latter functions.

  c. It is important to distinguish between the balances in a notice deposit account and the account itself. The account is a relationship between depositor and bank. The money in the account will have the attributes of money, qualified by the increased return that interest pays, the "notice" risk of withdrawal, and the solvency of the trust company in St. John's.

  d. There are significant transactions costs in exchanging one share of IBM stock, and its value can be volatile in the short run, making it an imperfect medium of exchange and unit of account. Its qualities as a store of value depend on the health of the company and the economy in which it operates.

  e. A $50 Bank of Canada note is cash, and its qualities will correspond accordingly. Of course, its denomination is a multiple of the common unit of our account, which is $1.

  f. A MasterCard, like the notice account, indicates the existence of a relationship. Its transferability is severely limited, and its value depends on the terms of the credit agreement. (There is probably an illegal market for MasterCards, in which they assume an independent value for exchange, although they probably lack most of the advantages of a store of value or unit of account.)

  g. Because it is negotiable, a chequing account could be a useful medium of exchange, as long as its size does not restrict the available market too strongly. The only limits on its qualities as a store of value are the reliability of the credit union and the value of the money into which it can be converted. Because the value is determined by the size of an anticipated transaction, there is no real independent unit of account to be measured by the chequing account.

h. Assuming that the pass is for the lifetime of the Expos and not for an owner who could not trade the pass, the ticket would be like many other nonmoney goods. Its money qualities would depend on the market available for its exchange and the value taken on by the good in the market. The fortunes of the Expos, the Montreal consumers' taste for baseball, and other demand determinants would affect the three monetary qualities of a lifetime pass.

15-3. M2 consists of the values of M1 plus balances in personal savings accounts and non-personal notice deposits.

15-5. a. V
b. A
c. V
d. E

15-7. If there are n goods, the number of exchange rates will be $n(n - 1)/2$. In this case, $n = 10$, so the number of exchange rates will be $10(10 - 1)/2 = 90/2 = 45$.

Chapter 16
Money Creation and Deposit Insurance

16-1. a. Multiple Deposit Creation

Bank	Deposits	Reserves	Loans
Bank 1	$1,000,000	$ 250,000	$ 750,000
Bank 2	750,000	187,500	562,500
Bank 3	562,500	140,625	421,875
Bank 4	421,875	105,469	316,406
Bank 5	316,406	79,102	237,304
All other banks	949,219	237,304	711,915
Totals	4,000,000	1,000,000	3,000,000

The money multiplier is 4.

b. Multiple Deposit Creation

Bank	Deposits	Reserves	Loans
Bank 1	$ 1,000,000	$ 50,000	$ 950,000
Bank 2	950,000	47,500	902,500
Bank 3	902,500	45,125	857,375
Bank 4	857,375	42,869	814,506
Bank 5	814,506	40,725	773,781
All other banks	15,475,619	773,781	14,701,838
Totals	20,000,000	1,000,000	19,000,000

The money multiplier is 20.

16-3. a. No change.
b. The money supply decreases by $50,000.
c. The money supply rises by $100,000.
d. This is a little tricky. If the Bank of Canada had been "keeping track" of currency, the $1,000 currency buried in Smith's backyard is accounted for; therefore, the money supply will rise by $9,000 because the Bank of Canada did not have to "create" the $1,000 already in existence.
e. The money supply will decrease by $9,000; see (d).

16-5. a.

ASSETS		LIABILITIES	
Total reserves	+$1,000,000	Demand deposits	+$1,000,000
Required reserves ($50,000) + excess reserves ($950,000)			
Total	+$1,000,000	Total	+$1,000,000

b. Bank 1 can increase its lending by $950,000.

16-7. a. The bank's excess reserves have decreased by $2,550,000.
b. The money supply has decreased by $3 million.
c. The money supply can decrease by as much as $20 million.

16-9. a. The maximum money multiplier will be $1/r$ where r = desired reserve ratio. In this case, $r = 0.05$, so the multiplier is $1/0.05 = 20$.
b. Deposits will rise by an amount equal to the multiplier times the initial change in reserves. In this case, the rise will be equal to $1 million $\times$ 20 = $20 million.

Chapter 17
Monetary Policy

17-1. A change in monetary policy leads to a change in interest rates, which leads to a change in investment. This, then, through the multiplier process, leads to a change in income.

17.3

17-5. An expansionary open market operation (purchase of bonds), for example, means that the public has larger money holdings than desired. This excess quantity of money demanded induces the public to buy more of everything, especially more durable goods. So if the economy is starting out at its long-run equilibrium rate of output, there can only be a short-run increase in real GDP. Ultimately, the public cannot buy more of everything, so it simply bids up prices, such that the price level rises.

Appendix D
Monetary Policy: A Keynesian Perspective

D-1. By its purchase of $100 million in bonds, the Bank of Canada increased excess reserves by $100 million. This ultimately caused a $300 million increase in the money supply after full multiple expansion. The 1 percent drop in the interest rate, from 10 to 9 percent, caused investment to rise by $2.5 billion, from $20 billion to $22.5 billion. An investment multiplier of 3 indicates that equilibrium national income rose by $7.5 billion to $207.5 billion.

Chapter 18
Issues in Stabilization Policy

18-1. a. 10 percent
       b. A rise in the expected rate of inflation will cause the curve to shift upward by the amount of the rise.
       c. They argue thus because the systematic policies that attempt to exploit the seeming trade-off will be incorporated into workers' and firms' expectations. As a result, the expected inflation rate will move in lockstep with the actual rate (excepting random errors), so that the unemployment rate will not change when the inflation rate changes.

18-3. The existence of contracts, small-menu costs, and efficiency wages will increase the amount of discretion available to policymakers because all of these will tend to slow the adjustment of wages to changes in expectations.

18-5. A rise in the duration of unemployment will tend to raise the average unemployment rate because each unemployed person will be counted as unemployed more times over any given time period.

18-7. Yes. It is precisely the fact that both employers and workers incorrectly perceive a change in nominal demand as a change in real demand which generates the negatively sloping Phillips curve.

Chapter 19
Comparative Advantage and the Open Economy

19-1. a. The opportunity cost to Canada of producing one kilogram of caviar is two bushels of wheat. The six hours that were needed to make the caviar could have been used to grow two bushels. The opportunity cost of producing one bushel of wheat is 0.5 kilogram of caviar.

 b. The opportunity cost to Russia of producing one kilogram of caviar is 0.67 bushels of wheat. The opportunity cost of producing a bushel of wheat in Russia is 1.5 kilograms of caviar.

 c. Canada has a comparative advantage in wheat because it has a lower opportunity cost in terms of caviar. Russia has a comparative advantage in caviar. Less wheat is forgone to produce a kilogram of caviar in Russia.

19-3. The assumption given in the question is equivalent to Canada's having an absolute advantage in the production of all goods and services. But the basis of world trade lies in differences in comparative advantage. As long as other countries have a lower opportunity cost in producing some goods and services, Canada will benefit from international trade.

19-5. Tariffs yield government revenues; quotas do not.

19-7. a. One million kilograms are produced and 2 million kilograms are imported.

 b. With a 10 cent tariff, 1.5 million kilograms would be produced and 1 million kilograms would be imported. Government revenues would amount to ($2.5 million − $1.5 million) × $.10 = $100,000.

 c. With a 20 cent tariff, domestic growers can receive 70 cents per kilogram. They will produce 2 million kilograms, and no peaches will be imported, in which case government revenues are zero.

19-9. In general, trade restrictions are harmful both to a nation's trading partners and to the nation itself. There may, however, be an exception. If Canada were to impose a tariff in response to other countries' restrictions, that may discourage other countries from imposing restrictions as often as they otherwise would.

Chapter 20
Exchange Rates and the Balance of Payments

20-1. The answer is (c). A declining dollar price of the pound implies an increasing pound price of the dollar—appreciation of the dollar. (a) is incorrect because an increase in demand for Canadian products would affect the supply of pounds and the demand for dollars, whereas here we are dealing with the demand for pounds. (b) explains a phenomenon that would have just the opposite result as that shown in the graph: An increased Canadian demand for British goods would lead to an increase in the demand for the pound, not a decrease as shown. (d) is incorrect because the pound depreciates.

20-3. One pound equals $3.50; $1 equals 0.2857 pound. One mark equals 35 cents; $1 equals 2.857 marks. One mark equals 0.1 pound; one pound equals 10 marks.

20-5. To maintain the exchange rate, domestic policy variables such as the money supply are also affected. Suppose that the government plans an expansive monetary policy to encourage output growth. A balance of payments deficit leads the government to buy up dollars, which in turn leads to a contraction in the domestic money supply. Therefore, in order to maintain the expansionary monetary policy, the government would have to expand the money supply in larger magnitudes than it would without the balance of payments deficits with a fixed exchange rate system.

20-7. a. The dollar price of pounds is $1.50. The equilibrium quantity is 150 million pounds.

 b. Curve D' describes this situation. The new dollar price of pounds would be $1.70, and the equilibrium quantity would be 200 million.

 c. At a price of $1.50 per pound, 250 million pounds sterling would be demanded and only 150 million would be supplied, so the Bank of Canada would have to supply an extra 100 million pounds to Canadian buyers of British goods or British exporters.

d. Curve D'' describes this situation. 150 million pounds sterling would be supplied at a price of $1.50, but only 50 million pounds would be demanded. Therefore, the Bank of Canada would have to buy up 100 million pounds sterling.

Chapter 21
Development: Economic Growth Around the World

21-1. The following countries may be considered developing countries: Burkina Faso, Bangladesh, Afghanistan, India, and China; there are many others. The following are considered industrially advanced countries: Canada, Australia, Germany, France, and the United States; there are many others.

21-3. Initially, there is an agricultural stage where most of the population is involved in agriculture. Many developing countries are still in this stage. Then comes the manufacturing stage. Industry dominates the economy, and gains from the division of labour lead to rapid increases in output. In the final stage, the service sector becomes prominent in the economy. Canada and other industrially advanced countries are in this stage.

21-5. Economic development depends greatly on individuals who are able to perceive and take advantage of opportunities. Immigrants who possessed attributes such as these started Canada on the road to our present affluence. In general, voluntary exchange is mutually beneficial. If the potential immigrants are willing and able to offer their services at prices (wages) that existing residents are willing to pay, and to purchase the goods and services offered for sale by existing residents, the immigrants' arrival is likely to benefit existing residents as well as themselves.

21-7. It is important to remember that all resources are owned by human beings, and that in general there is an optimal (wealth-maximizing) mix of land, labour, and capital. So even though population growth (relative to growth in capital or land) would be expected to lower wages, it would also be expected to raise the earnings of capital and land. On balance, if the population growth moved the country closer to the optimal mix of land, labour, and capital, the added income accruing to the owners of land and capital would more than offset the reduced earnings of labour, producing an overall rise in per capita income.

ANSWERS TO CRITICAL ANALYSIS QUESTIONS

Chapter 1
The Nature of Economics

Issues and Applications: How Relevant Is Love in a Marriage Contract?

1. There is no difference between what economists and most people would predict about a good marriage. Economists assume that people act rationally, that is, they will not make decisions which leave them worse off. Marriage to a partner one does not love will probably not make a person happy. Therefore economists would expect to see marriage between people who love each other. Most people would expect to see the same.

2. If divorce is impossible, then people will spend a very long time (relative to the time spent when divorce is possible) looking for a spouse. Since the marriage is to last forever, the potential benefit is large. Thus people will incur relatively large "courting" costs looking for a mate before committing to marriage.

Chapter 2
Scarcity and the World of Trade-Offs

Issues and Applications: The Cost of Crime

1. Opportunity cost is such an important concept in analysing government programs to prevent crime because it highlights the trade-offs involved in crime prevention. A sum like $1 billion may not seem too much to eradicate crime in Toronto or Montreal, for example. But because our resources are limited, when that billion is converted into the hospitals and colleges and art galleries that would now be out of our reach, the trade-off becomes clear. It is not necessarily the dollars we spend on crime prevention that we need to count; we need to count the alternatives which we cannot now afford.

2. The opportunity cost of policing would rise as we added more resources to crime prevention. Picture a production possibilities curve representing all government services on the one hand and policing on the other. It would have the typical bowed out shape of the PPC in Figure 2.2 as we transferred less suitable

resources out of other government services and into policing. Not everyone would be able to do such a physical, dangerous job efficiently!

Chapter 3
Demand and Supply

Issues and Applications: How the Prices of Hockey Cards Have Responded to Changes in Supply and Demand

1. If the hockey players' lockout had actually dampened demand for hockey cards, the 1996 demand would have been weaker, and the demand curve would have shifted out less than shown in both parts of Figure 3.13. Prices for typical cards would be lower than P_2 in part (a) and P_4 in part (b).

2. The expansion of the National Hockey League into more American cities provides hockey card producers with new opportunities for producing hockey cards today. *Ceteris paribus*, the supply curve for 1998-99 hockey cards in a graph similar to part (b) would be further to the right, reflecting a greater supply of cards of the now larger number of players. However, the number of hockey cards produced in the 1979-80 and 1989-90 seasons would not change, and the supply of those cards would remain as pictured.

Chapter 4
Extensions of Demand and Supply Analysis

Issues and Applications: Grunge Meets Greed

1. Ticketmaster would not require a service charge as high as $50 because there would probably be little demand for tickets at that inflated price. A firm can only ask for a price as high as demanders will bear and, as we know, the quantity demanded of any good decreases as the price rises. Even if some fans would be willing to pay an additional $50 for a Pearl Jam ticket, it is unlikely that Ticketmaster could fill a venue with fans. In that case, Ticketmaster's revenues would be less than if it charged a lower service fee.

2. If the government restricted Ticketmaster to a $2 service charge on a $50 ticket, for example, the price to the customer would be $52 rather than the $60 it would be with a $10 charge. Look at Figure 4.4. At a price of $52, the demand for tickets would exceed the supply as it does at price P_1 and a shortage of tickets would occur. Some fans might purchase $52 tickets, and sell them to more devoted fans for $60 or even more. Without more information on the demand for rock concert tickets, we cannot say exactly how high a price, like P_2, scalpers would get.

Chapter 5
The Public Sector

Issues and Applications: Should We Switch to a Flat Tax?

1. Employees at Revenue Canada might well be against a flat-tax system. Advocates of a flat tax claim that one of the benefits would be a significantly downsized Revenue Canada, implying that many Revenue Canada employees might lose their jobs. We know from Chapter 1 that the rationality assumption tells us that people usually don't make decisions that reduce their well-being. It is likely that Revenue Canada employees would want to keep their jobs to maintain their well-being, and would thus oppose a flat-tax system.

2. A flat-tax system is more efficient than a progressive tax system because the method of calculation of tax owing is much simpler: there is only one calculation to make, rather than the many calculations required in a progressive system. There would be efficiencies realized by taxpayers who could complete their tax returns easily, and by Revenue Canada employees who could check the calculation as simply. The opportunity cost of the yearly tax return would fall, leaving resources free to pursue more productive activities.

Chapter 6
Economies in Transition

Issues and Applications: The Peruvian Transition from No Ownership to Clear Title

1. If suitcase farmers were given clear ownership rights to their land, they would have an incentive to settle down and produce a legal crop. With private owner-

ship comes the incentive to improve the land, since the profits from tilling it clearly belong to the owner.

2. It is not really possible to have wealth without property rights. If there are no property rights, who owns the wealth? What barriers are there to prohibit others from seizing your wealth, if it is not clearly defined as your property? Property rights—that is the right to own something exclusively—are necessary for the collection and retention of articles that make up wealth.

Chapter 7
The Macroeconomy: Unemployment and Inflation

Issues and Applications: The Policy Effects of Changes in the CPI

1. An incorrect measure of the CPI may not have an effect on losers and gainers from unanticipated inflation so long as the CPI measurement is consistent in its under- or overestimation. Lenders who lose, and debtors who gain, from inflation do so because they cannot predict the rate of inflation. If unanticipated inflation changes the CPI to reflect a higher price level, the losers will still lose and the gainers will still gain.

2. Pensioners and workers with COLA clauses would benefit from an improved measure of the CPI. An undercalculation of inflation causes increases in their incomes to be smaller than they would otherwise be, and this results in a decrease in their real incomes.

Chapter 8
Measuring the Economy's Performance

Issues and Applications: The Worldwide Underground Economy

1. Revenue Canada is overestimating the lost tax revenue because its estimate of "off-the-books" income is too high. If all underground activities were declared, those relating to drug trafficking, illegal gambling, and prostitution would decrease as authorities put an end to them. The size of the underground economy would shrink, and the lost tax revenue would decline as well.

2. If the government declared many transactions which are now part of the underground economy free of tax,

the incentive to avoid federal and sales tax would disappear. For example, if street vendors did not have to pay sales tax on their sales, there would be no reason for them not to declare their income.

Chapter 9
Economic Growth: Technology, Research and Development, and Growth

Issues and Applications: Democracy and Prosperity: Cause or Effect?

1. More democracy typically promotes property rights which are more clearly defined and consistently enforced. As we learned in Chapter 6, property rights are essential for the accumulation of wealth or savings. And as we learned in this chapter, saving tends to lead to economic growth. If more democracy leads to lower rates of growth in the short term, it is likely that it will lead to higher rates of growth in the long term.

2. Robert Barro's research shows that countries which achieve high standards of living through economic growth tend to become more democratic over time. The question here is whether this process can be reversed: that is, do countries whose standards of living stagnate become less democratic over time. Consider the example of Russia. Since the breakup of the Soviet Union which was slowly becoming more democratic, Russia has experienced severe economic troubles— massive inflation, a dramatic decline in GDP, and an increasing underground economy. Many politicians and citizens are calling for a return to the old system of communism that guaranteed employment and housing for all. The statement probably has merit.

Chapter 10
Micro Foundations: Aggregate Demand and Aggregate Supply

Issues and Applications: The Ultimate Aggregate Supply Shock—The Kobe Earthquake

1. Table 10.2 sets out several things that the Japanese government could do to shift its *LRAS* to the right. Finding new deposits of natural resources is not always possible, but Japan could reduce trade barriers and regulatory impediments to business. It could also reduce marginal tax rates, so that businesses have an incentive to expand.

2. A natural disaster is usually not good for an economy for it shifts the *LRAS* curve to the left. You can also picture it as a shift inward of the production possibilities frontier discussed in Chapters 2 and 9. Since the natural disaster destroys wealth, the only way it could be good for an economy is if it led to the accumulation of relatively more wealth in the long run. For example, if an earthquake destroyed a block of abandoned derelict buildings, then the reconstruction process would add more to the wealth of the economy that the natural disaster destroyed.

Chapter 11
Classical and Keynesian Macro Analyses

Issues and Applications: High European Unemployment, or Keynes Revisited?

1. It might be difficult for European politicians to dismantle programs that result in large amounts of wait unemployment because of the basic assumption that underlies all economics: people are motivated by self-interest. While businesses might be pleased to see the end of costly employment charges, prospective workers would likely object to removal of generous unemployment benefits. And there are many more voters in the form of unemployed workers than there are businesses, so the pressure on politicians to support social programs would probably outweigh requests to eliminate them.

2. Persistent high levels of unemployment will slow economic growth in any country. Resources are lying idle in the form of potential workers, and possibly in the form of idle capital equipment. Programs which provide incentives for workers to perform "on-the-books" labour will foster long-term economic growth.

Chapter 12
Consumption, Income, and the Multiplier

Issues and Applications: Can Native Land Claims Settlements Have a Multiplier Effect?

1. For British Columbia's economy to benefit from the $6 billion settlement to the aboriginal bands, that money would have to be spent in BC, or spent in another territory which trades with BC. For the benefit to return to the British Columbia economy, spending at some point of the multiplier process must occur in that province.

2. The multiplier is an estimate subject to many errors: greater savings rates than anticipated, and more spending in non-BC jurisdictions than anticipated, to name but two. If the multiplier is very small, then the BC economy may not benefit, that is, the $6 billion payout may exceed the returns from the multiplier process.

Chapter 13
Fiscal Policy

Issues and Applications: The Real-World Political Constraints on Fiscal Policy

1. Critics of the plan to automate lighthouses would say the opportunity cost of the program will be the lives lost at sea which could have been saved by the intervention of lighthouse keepers. Proponents of the program would say the opportunity cost is the goods and services the government could have provided with the funds used to modernize the lighthouses.

2. The immediate effect of raising taxes is usually a decrease in aggregate demand, and a fall or slowdown in economic growth. To the extent that the lighthouse keepers would continue to be employed, pay taxes, and consume in the economy, the decrease in aggregate demand would be reduced. The net effect of the negative pressure of the tax multiplier and the positive influence of the income multiplier cannot be determined here without more information about the relative sizes of the multipliers.

Chapter 14
Deficit Spending and the Public Debt

Issues and Applications: Employment Insurance and the Deficit

1. The underlying trade-off facing the government is whether to eliminate the federal deficit now or to reduce unemployment now. In choosing to eliminate the federal deficit, the government has left payroll taxes at their current level and has avoided spending on job creation projects. Nevertheless, in the latter part of 1998, the unemployment rate started to creep down. It appears that the trade-off may have been relatively short term in nature.

2. If the employee's share of the EI payroll tax were reduced, employees would have more disposable income. With more disposable income, consumption (and saving) would increase. Businesses would experience inventory decreases and would increase their rate of production, employing more workers in the process. With more people employed, unemployment would fall, tax revenues would increase, and payments out of the EI fund would decrease. The deficit would fall.

Chapter 15
Money and the Banking System

Issues and Applications: Watch Out for E-Cash

1. The Bank of Canada may have difficulty measuring the size of e-cash in the money supply. Currently, the Bank counts currency in chartered bank vaults, and balances in chequing accounts. Once you have converted the money in your chequing account into cash which you carry with you, it is no longer officially part of the money supply. If balances in demand deposits are transferred into e-cash controlled by non-bank businesses, the Bank of Canada will not be able to count or to control that part of the money supply. Indeed, e-cash will not be part of the money supply.

2. E-cash is a form of money if it serves the three functions of money. It will act as a medium of exchange, perhaps even better than real cash where electronic commerce is involved. It will act as a store of value, retaining its purchasing power (in the absence of inflation) until used. And e-cash will also act as a unit of account the same way that cash does now. E-cash would appear to be yet another form of money in our history of evolving currencies.

Chapter 16
Money Creation and Deposit Insurance

Issues and Applications: Deregulating the Financial Services Industry

1. A bank is a business that holds funds for customers and grants loans to customers who qualify. A non-bank bank is a business that does the above but is not a bank. An example of a nonbank bank would be an insurance company, or a trust company such as Canada Trust.

2. There could be an increased moral hazard problem as

banks diversify their services. With deposit insurance, banks already have an incentive to take on riskier investments than may be prudent. The additional profits the bank could earn from the sale of insurance or airline tickets would act as an increased incentive to sell to high-risk customers, or to grant credit to less-than-creditworthy customers for air travel. Because of the existence of deposit insurance, customers would still lack the incentive to monitor the bank's decisions closely.

Chapter 17
Monetary Policy

Issues and Applications: Is the Bank of Canada Independent, and If Not, Does It Matter?

1. Keynesians would be likely to oppose an act like New Zealand's Reserve Bank Act of 1989. Keynesians believe that the government should intervene to smooth and encourage the workings of the economy. If the Bank of Canada were given the one job of keeping the price level stable, it would eliminate the use of monetary policy as an expansionary policy instrument, as it frequently results in inflation.

2. "The Bank of Canada can never be truly independent of the federal government as long as the government has the power to appoint and dismiss the Governors. The Bank, however, operates as though it were independent. A recent example is the Bank's announcement that its goal is to keep inflation between 1 and 3 percent regardless of its effect on unemployment. The Liberal government may wish to focus on reducing unemployment, but will have to do so within the economic environment created by the Bank's low inflation policies."

Chapter 18
Issues in Stabilization Policy

Issues and Applications: The Bank of Canada's High Interest Rate Policy

1. Passive investment in financial instruments to earn a hefty return will result in a reduction in interest rates. As we learned in Chapter 17, as bond prices rise, interest rates fall. With lower interest rates, investors will be tempted to turn to active investing in technology and businesses. Active investment in businesses and technology will stimulate aggregate demand.

Depending on the output gap, the result in the economy will be inflation if the economy is at full employment, or economic growth if the economy is not.

2. The policy irrelevance proposition states that no real variables can be affected by anticipated policy. Since Mr. Theissen announced his plan to keep interest rates relatively high to combat inflation, players in the economy are informed, and will not act to decrease unemployment.

Chapter 19
Comparative Advantage and the Open Economy

Issues and Applications: Playing Chicken with the United States

1. If the TRQs on dairy and poultry are eventually removed, imports from the United States will be much cheaper in Canadian markets. Canadian dairy and poultry farmers will have to compete with the imports—which means working to reduce their costs. Some producers will probably go out of business, but, as the beef producers have shown, others should be able to become competitive with US producers.

2. Canada has a comparative advantage in producing beef, but not dairy products or poultry. Dairy and poultry farmers argue that the Canadian climate drives up their costs. Beef farmers do not face those same costs, as beef cattle remain outside in all but the most inclement weather. Also, beef cattle can graze on open fields in the summer, while dairy cows must be milked, and poultry fed purchased feed. Since comparative advantage derives from having a lower cost of production that other countries, Canadian beef farmers have an advantage over dairy and poultry producers.

Chapter 20
Exchange Rates and the Balance of Payments

Issues and Applications: Should We Worry About the Weak Dollar?

1. A lower rate of inflation in Germany would lead to a weaker Canadian dollar because of the change in relative prices. Lower inflation in Germany means that

German goods and services will now be relatively less expensive. Consumers will substitute the relatively cheaper German products for Canadian products. The demand for the Deutsche mark will increase, the Deutsche mark will appreciate, and the Canadian dollar will depreciate. Figure 20-5 depicts this scenario.

2. Foreigners will agree to hold Canadian dollars instead of their own currencies if they anticipate consuming Canadian goods and services. Everything from clothing and produce, to Canadian stocks and bonds, to tourism, must be paid for in Canadian dollars—which foreigners must obtain somehow. Another reason foreigners might hold Canadian dollars is for speculative purposes. In 1998 the Canadian dollar reached all-time lows vis-à-vis the US dollar. A speculator may purchase Canadian dollars when the value is low, hold them until the value rises in the currency market, and then sell them to make a capital gain.

Chapter 21
Development: Economic Growth Around the World

Issues and Applications: Can PCs Bridge the Gap Between Less Advanced and More Advanced Economies?

1. Latecomers adopt new technology more quickly than established economies because they have fewer resources invested in old technology. Businesses and governments in established economies which have invested millions of dollars in a computer system are reluctant to invest more millions every time innovation produces a better product—even though the relative price of the new system is falling. However, when businesses and governments in developing economies invest in new technology they are more likely to be adding to, rather than replacing, their existing technology.

2. For technological innovation to spread rapidly in a country, businesses and consumers must have quick and inexpensive access to the technology. An economy which is closed typically applies either import quotas or high import tariffs to products entering the country. If these trade barriers apply to new technology, then businesses and consumers have neither quick nor inexpensive access to it, and the innovations will not spread

GLOSSARY

Absolute advantage The ability to produce a good or service at an "absolutely" lower cost, usually measured in units of labour or resource input required to produce one unit of the good or service.

Accounting identities Statements that certain numerical measurements are equal by accepted definition (for example, "assets equal liabilities plus stockholders' equity").

Action time lag The time required between recognizing an economic problem and putting policy into effect. The action time lag is short for monetary policy but quite long for fiscal policy, which requires legislative approval.

Active (discretionary) policymaking All actions on the part of monetary and fiscal policymakers that are undertaken in response to or in anticipation of some change in the overall economy.

Adverse selection A problem created by asymmetric information prior to a transaction. Individuals who are the most undesirable from the other party's point of view end up being the ones who are most likely to want to engage in a particular financial transaction, such as borrowing.

Aggregate demand The total of all planned expenditures for the entire economy.

Aggregate demand curve A curve showing planned purchase rates for all goods and services in the economy at various price levels, all other things held constant.

Aggregate demand shock Any shock that causes the aggregate demand curve to shift inward or outward.

Aggregate supply The total of all planned production for the entire economy.

Aggregate supply shock Any shock that causes the aggregate supply curve to shift inward or outward.

Aggregates Total amounts or quantities; aggregate demand, for example, is total planned expenditures throughout a nation.

Anticipated inflation The inflation rate that we believe will occur; when it does, we are in a situation of fully anticipated inflation.

Anticombines legislation Laws that restrict the formation of monopolies and regulate certain anti-competitive business practices.

Appreciation An increase in the value of a currency in terms of other currencies.

Asset demand Holding money as a store of value, instead of other assets such as certificates of deposit, corporate bonds, and stocks.

Assets Amounts owned; all items to which a business or household holds legal claim.

Asymmetric information Information possessed by one side of a transaction but not the other. The side with more information will be at an advantage.

Automatic, or built-in, stabilizers Special provisions of the tax law that cause changes in the economy without the direct action of the government. Examples are the progressive income tax system and Employment Insurance.

Autonomous consumption The part of consumption that is independent of (does not depend on) the level of disposable income. Changes in autonomous consumption shift the consumption function.

Average propensity to consume (APC) Consumption divided by disposable income; for any given level of income, the proportion of total disposable income that is consumed.

Average propensity to save (APS) Saving divided by disposable income; for any given level of income, the proportion of total disposable income that is saved.

Average tax rate The total tax payment divided by total income. It is the proportion of total income paid in taxes.

Balance of payments A summary record of a country's economic transactions with foreign residents and governments over a year.

Balance of trade The value of goods and services bought and sold in the world market.

Balance sheet A statement of the assets and liabilities of any business entity, including financial institutions and the Bank of Canada. Assets are what is owned; liabilities are what is owed.

The Bank of Canada Canada's central bank.

Bank runs Attempts by many of a bank's depositors to convert chequing and time deposits into currency out of fear for the bank's solvency.

Barter The direct exchange of goods and services for other goods and services without the use of money.

Base year The year that is chosen as the point of reference for comparison of prices in other years.

Black market A market in which goods are traded at prices above their legal maximum prices or in which illegal goods are sold.

Bureaucrats Nonelected government officials who are responsible for the day-to-day operation of government and the observance of its regulations and laws.

Business fluctuations The ups and downs in overall business activity, as evidenced by changes in national income, employment, and the price level.

Canadian Deposit Insurance Corporation (CDIC) A government agency that insures the deposits held in federally incorporated financial institutions.

Canadian Payments Association (CPA) A regulated organization which operates a national cheque-clearing and settlements system.

Capital consumption allowance Another name for depreciation, the amount that businesses would have to save in order to take care of the deterioration of machines and other equipment.

Capital gain The positive difference between the purchase price and the sale price of an asset. If a share of stock is bought for $5 and then sold for $15, the capital gain is $10.

Capital goods Producer durables; nonconsumable goods that firms use to make other goods.

Capital loss The negative difference between the purchase price and the sale price of an asset.

Capitalism An economic system in which

individuals own productive resources; these individuals can use the resources in whatever manner they choose, subject to common protective legal restrictions.

Central bank A banker's bank, usually an official institution that also serves as a country's treasury's bank. Central banks normally regulate commercial banks.

Ceteris paribus **assumption** The assumption that nothing changes except the factor or factors being studied.

Chequable deposits Any deposits in a near bank or a commercial bank on which a cheque may be written.

Collective decision making How voters, politicians, and other interested parties act and how these actions influence nonmarket decisions.

Communism In its purest form, an economic system in which the state has disappeared and individuals contribute to the economy according to their productivity and are given income according to their needs.

Comparative advantage The ability to produce a good or service at a lower opportunity cost compared to other producers.

Complements Two goods are complements if both are used together for consumption or enjoyment—for example, coffee and cream. The more you buy of one, the more you buy of the other. For complements, a change in the price of one causes an opposite shift in the demand for the other.

Constant dollars Dollars expressed in terms of real purchasing power using a particular year as the base or standard of comparison, in contrast to current dollars.

Consumer Price Index (CPI) A statistical measure of a weighted average of prices of a specified set of goods and services purchased by wage earners in urban areas.

Consumption Spending on new goods and services out of a household's current income. Whatever is not consumed is saved. Consumption includes such things as buying food and going to a concert.

Consumption function The relationship between amount consumed and disposable income. A consumption function tells us how much people plan to consume at various levels of disposable income.

Consumption goods Goods bought by households to use up, such as food, clothing, and movies.

Contraction A business fluctuation during which the pace of national economic activity is slowing down.

Contractionary gap The gap that exists whenever the equilibrium level of real national income per year is less than the full-employment level as shown by the position of the long-run aggregate supply curve.

Cost-of-living adjustments (COLAs) Clauses in contracts that allow for increases in specified nominal values to take account of changes in the cost of living.

Cost-push inflation Inflation caused by a continually decreasing short-run aggregate supply curve.

Crowding-out effect The tendency of expansionary fiscal policy to cause a decrease in planned investment or planned consumption in the private sector; this decrease normally results from the rise in interest rates.

Crude quantity theory of money and prices The belief that changes in the money supply lead to proportional changes in the price level.

Cyclical unemployment Unemployment resulting from business recessions that occur when aggregate (total) demand is insufficient to create full employment.

Deflation The situation in which the average of all prices of goods and services in an economy is falling.

Demand A schedule of how much of a good or service people will purchase at any price during a specified time period, other things being constant.

Demand curve A graphical representation of the demand schedule; a negatively sloped line showing the inverse relationship between the price and the quantity demanded (other things being equal).

Demand deposits Chequing account balances in commercial banks and other types of financial institutions, such as credit unions and trust companies; any accounts in financial institutions on which you can easily write cheques without many restrictions.

Demand-pull inflation Inflation caused by increases in aggregate demand not matched by increases in aggregate supply.

Demerit good A good that has been deemed socially undesirable through the political process. Cigarettes are an example.

Depreciation A decrease in the value of a currency in terms of other currencies. Reduction in the value of capital goods over a one-year period due to physical wear and tear and also to obsolescence; also called *capital consumption allowance.*

Depression An extremely severe recession.

Desired reserve ratio The percentage of total deposits that depository institutions hold in the form of desired reserves.

Desired reserves The value of reserves that a depository institution wishes to hold in the form of vault cash or other deposits, or, in the case of the chartered banks, in the form of deposits with the Bank of Canada.

Direct expenditure offsets Actions on the part of the private sector in spending money that offset government fiscal policy actions. Any increase in government spending in an area that competes with the private sector will have some direct expenditure offset.

Dirty float A system between flexible and fixed exchange rates in which central banks occasionally enter foreign exchange markets to influence rates.

Discouraged workers Individuals who have stopped looking for a job because they are convinced that they will not find a suitable one. Typically, they become convinced after unsuccessfully searching for a job.

Disposable personal income (DPI) Personal income after personal income taxes have been paid.

Dissaving Negative saving; a situation in which spending exceeds income. Dissaving can occur when a household is able to borrow or use up existing owned assets.

Division of labour The segregation of a resource into different specific tasks; for example, one automobile worker puts on bumpers, another doors, and so on.

Drawdowns A way to decrease the money supply. The Bank of Canada transfers some of the Government of Canada deposits at the chartered banks to its own Government of Canada deposits, thus decreasing available reserves at the chartered banks.

Dumping Selling a good or a service abroad at a price below its cost of production or below the price charged in the home market.

Durable consumer goods Consumer

goods that have a life span of more than three years.

Economic goods Goods that are scarce.

Economic growth Increases in per capita real GDP measured by its rate of change per year.

Economic system The institutional means through which resources are used to satisfy human wants.

Economics The study of how people allocate their limited resources to satisfy their unlimited wants.

Effect time lag The time that elapses between the onset of policy and the results of that policy.

Efficiency The case in which a given level of inputs is used to produce the maximum output possible. Alternatively, the situation in which a given output is produced at minimum cost.

Efficiency wage theory The hypothesis that the productivity of workers depends on the level of the real wage rate.

Effluent fee A charge to a polluter that gives the right to discharge into the air or water a certain amount of pollution. Also called a *pollution tax*.

Empirical Relying on real-world data in evaluating the usefulness of a model.

Endowments The various resources in an economy, including both physical resources and such human resources as ingenuity and management skills.

Entrepreneurship The factor of production involving human resources that perform the functions of raising capital, organizing, managing, assembling other factors of production, and making basic business policy decisions. The entrepreneur is a risk taker.

Equation of exchange The formula indicating that the number of monetary units times the number of times each unit is spent on final goods and services is identical to the price level times output (or nominal national income).

Equilibrium The situation when quantity supplied equals quantity demanded at a particular price.

Excess reserves The difference between actual reserves and desired reserves.

Exclusion principle The principle that no one can be excluded from the benefits of a public good, even if that person hasn't paid for it.

Expansion A business fluctuation in which overall business activity is rising at a more rapid rate than previously, or at a more rapid rate than the overall historical trend for the nation.

Expansionary gap The gap that exists whenever the equilibrium level of real national income per year is greater than the full-employment level as shown by the position of the long-run aggregate supply curve.

Expenditure approach A way of computing national income by adding up the dollar value at current market prices of all final goods and services.

Externality A consequence of an economic activity that spills over to affect third parties. Pollution is an externality.

Fiduciary monetary system A system in which currency is issued by the government and its value is based uniquely on the public's faith that the currency represents command over goods and services.

Final goods and services Goods and services that are at their final stage of production and will not be transformed into yet other goods or services. For example, wheat is normally not a final good because usually it is used to make bread, which is a final good.

Financial intermediaries Institutions that transfer funds between ultimate lenders (savers) and ultimate borrowers.

Financial intermediation The process by which financial institutions accept savings from businesses, households, and governments and lend the savings to other businesses, households, and governments.

Fiscal policy The discretionary changing of government expenditures and/or taxes in order to achieve national economic goals, such as high employment with price stability.

Fixed investment Purchases by businesses of newly produced producer durables, or capital goods, such as production machinery and office equipment.

Flexible exchange rates Exchange rates that are allowed to fluctuate in the open market in response to changes in supply and demand. Sometimes called *floating exchange rates*.

Flow A quantity measured per unit of time; something that occurs over time, such as the income you make per week or per year, or the number of individuals who

are fired every month.

Foreign exchange market The market for buying and selling foreign currencies.

Foreign exchange rate The price of one currency in terms of another.

45-degree reference line The line along which planned real expenditures equal real national income per year.

Fractional reserve banking A system in which depository institutions hold reserves that are less than the amount of total deposits.

Free-rider problem A problem that arises when individuals presume that others will pay for public goods so that, individually, they can escape paying for their portion without causing a reduction in production.

Frictional unemployment Unemployment due to the fact that workers must search for appropriate job offers. This takes time, and so they remain temporarily ("frictionally") unemployed.

Full employment An arbitrary level of unemployment that corresponds to "normal" friction in the labour market. Today, it is estimated to be around 8 percent.

GDP deflator A price index measuring the changes in prices of all new goods and services produced in the economy.

General Agreement on Tariffs and Trade (GATT) An international agreement established in 1947 to further world trade by reducing barriers and tariffs.

Gold standard An international monetary system in which countries fix their exchange rates in terms of gold. All currencies are fixed in terms of all others, and any balance of payments deficits or surpluses can be made up by shipments of gold.

Goods All things from which individuals derive satisfaction or happiness.

Government, or political, goods Goods (and services) provided by the public sector; they can be either private or public goods.

Gross domestic income (GDI) The sum of all income—wages, corporate profits before taxes, interest, farm and non-incorporated nonfarm income, and inventory valuation adjustment—paid to the four factors of production.

Gross domestic product (GDP) The total market value of all final goods and services produced by factors of production located within a nation's borders.

Gross private domestic investment The creation of capital goods, such as factories and machines, that can yield production and hence consumption in the future. Also included in this definition are changes in business inventories and repairs made to machines or buildings.

Gross public debt All federal government debt irrespective of who owns it.

Human capital The accumulated training and education of workers.

Hyperinflation Extremely rapid rise of the average of all prices in an economy.

Import quota A physical supply restriction on imports of a particular good, such as sugar. Foreign exporters are unable to sell in Canada more than the quantity specified in the import quota.

Incentive structure The motivational rewards and costs that individuals face in any given situation. Each economic system has its own incentive structure. The incentive structure is different under a system of private property than under a system of government-owned property, for example.

Incentives Things that encourage us to engage in a particular activity.

Income approach A way of measuring national income by adding up all components of national income, including wages, interest, rent, and profits.

Income velocity of money The number of times per year a dollar is spent on final goods and services; equal to GDP divided by the money supply.

Indirect business taxes less subsidies All business taxes except the tax on corporate profits. Indirect business taxes include sales and business property taxes. Subsidies to business from government are subtracted because they represent a flow of taxes back to business.

Industrially advanced countries (IACs) Canada, Japan, the United States, and the countries of Western Europe, all of which have market economies based on a large skilled labour force and a large technically advanced stock of capital goods.

Inefficient point Any point below the production possibilities curve at which resources are being used inefficiently.

Infant industry argument The contention that tariffs should be imposed to protect from import competition an indus-

try that is trying to get started. Presumably, after the industry becomes technologically efficient, the tariff can be lifted.

Inferior goods Goods for which demand falls as income rises.

Inflation The situation in which the average of all prices of goods and services in an economy is rising.

Innovation Transforming an invention into something that is useful to humans.

Interest rate effect One of the reasons that the aggregate demand curve slopes downward is because higher price levels indirectly increase the interest rate, which in turn causes businesses and consumers to reduce desired spending due to the higher cost of borrowing.

Intermediate goods Goods used up entirely in the production of final goods.

International Monetary Fund (IMF) An institution set up in 1945 under the Bretton Woods agreement to manage the international monetary system. It established fixed exchange rates for the world's currencies.

Inventory investment Changes in the stocks of finished goods and goods in process, as well as changes in the raw materials that businesses keep on hand. Whenever inventories are decreasing, inventory investment is negative; whenever they are increasing, inventory investment is positive.

Investment The spending by businesses on things such as machines and buildings, which can be used to produce goods and services in the future. The investment part of total income is the portion that will be used in the process of producing goods in the future.

Keynesian short-run aggregate supply curve The horizontal portion of the aggregate supply curve in which there is unemployment and unused capacity in the economy.

Labour Productive contributions of humans who work, involving both mental and physical activities.

Labour force Individuals aged 15 years or older who either have jobs or are looking and available for jobs; the number of employed plus the number of unemployed.

Labour force participation rate The percentage of working-age individuals who are not living on a reservation, or in the military, or resident in an institution for

the incapacitated, and who are employed or seeking employment.

Labour productivity Total real domestic output (real GDP) divided by the number of workers (output per worker).

Laissez-faire French for "leave [it] alone"; applied to an economic system in which the government minimizes its interference with the economy.

Land The natural resources that are available from nature. Land as a resource includes location, original fertility and mineral deposits, topography, climate, water, and vegetation.

Law of demand The observation that there is a negative, or inverse, relationship between the price of any good or service and the quantity demanded, holding other factors constant.

Law of increasing relative cost The observation that the opportunity cost of additional units of a good generally increases as society attempts to produce more of that good. This accounts for the bowed-out shape of the production possibilities curve.

Law of supply The observation that the higher the price of a good, the more of that good sellers will make available over a specified time period, other things being equal.

Least-cost combination The level of input use that produces a given level of output at minimum cost.

Liabilities Amounts owed; the legal claims against a business or household by nonowners.

Liquidity The degree to which an asset can be acquired or disposed of without much danger of any intervening loss in *nominal* value and with small transaction costs. Money is the most liquid asset.

Long-run aggregate supply curve A vertical line representing real output of goods and services based on full information and after full adjustment has occurred. Can also be viewed as representing the real output of the economy under conditions of full employment—the full-employment level of real GDP.

Lump-sum tax A tax that does not depend on income or the circumstances of the taxpayer. An example is a $1,000 tax that every family must pay, irrespective of its economic situation.

M1 The money supply, taken as the total

value of currency plus demand deposits in chartered banks.

M2 M1 plus (1) personal savings and (2) non-personal notice deposits.

Macroeconomics The study of the behaviour of the economy as a whole, including such economy-wide phenomena as changes in unemployment, the general price level, and national income.

Majority rule A collective decision-making system in which group decisions are made on the basis of 50.1 percent of the vote. In other words, whatever more than half of the electorate votes for, the entire electorate has to accept.

Marginal propensity to consume (MPC) The ratio of the change in consumption to the change in disposable income. A marginal propensity to consume of 0.8 tells us that an additional $100 in take-home pay will lead to an additional $80 consumed.

Marginal propensity to save (MPS) The ratio of the change in saving to the change in disposable income. A marginal propensity to save of 0.2 indicates that out of an additional $100 in take-home pay, $20 will be saved. Whatever is not saved is consumed. The marginal propensity to save plus the marginal propensity to consume must always equal 1, by definition.

Marginal tax rate The change in the tax payment divided by the change in income, or the percentage of additional dollars that must be paid in taxes. The marginal tax rate is applied to the highest tax bracket of taxable income reached.

Market All of the arrangements that individuals have for exchanging with one another. Thus we can speak of the labour market, the automobile market, and the credit market.

Market clearing, or equilibrium, price The price that clears the market, at which quantity demanded equals quantity supplied; the price where the demand curve intersects the supply curve.

Market demand The demand of all consumers in the marketplace for a particular good or service. The summing at each price of the quantity demanded by each individual.

Market failure A situation in which an unrestrained market economy leads to too few or too many resources going to a specific economic activity.

Medium of exchange Any asset that sellers will accept as payment.

Merit good A good that has been deemed socially desirable through the political process. Museums are an example.

Microeconomics The study of decision making undertaken by individuals (or households) and by firms.

Minimum wage A wage floor, legislated by government, setting the lowest hourly rate that firms may legally pay workers.

Mixed economy An economic system in which decisions about how resources should be used are made partly by the private sector and partly by the government, or the public sector.

Models, or theories Simplified representations of the real world used as the basis for predictions or explanations.

Monetarists Macroeconomists who believe that inflation is always caused by excessive monetary growth and that changes in the money supply affect aggregate demand both directly and indirectly.

Monetary rule A monetary policy that incorporates a rule specifying the annual rate of growth of some monetary aggregate.

Money Any medium that is universally accepted in an economy both by sellers of goods and services as payment for those goods and services and by creditors as payment for debts.

Money illusion Reacting to changes in money prices rather than relative prices. If workers whose wages double when the price level also doubles think they are better off, the workers are suffering from money illusion.

Money multiplier The reciprocal of the desired reserve ratio, assuming no leakages into currency and no excess reserves. It is equal to 1 divided by the desired reserve ratio.

Money multiplier process The process by which an injection of new money into the banking system leads to a multiple expansion in the total money supply.

Money price The price that we observe today, expressed in today's dollars. Also called the *absolute, nominal,* or *current price.*

Money supply The amount of money in circulation.

Monopoly A firm that has great control over the price of a good. In the extreme case, a monopoly is the only seller of a good or service.

Moral hazard A situation in which, after a transaction has taken place, one of the parties to the transaction has an incentive to engage in behaviour that will be undesirable from the other party's point of view.

Moral suasion A formal or informal request by the governor of the Bank of Canada to the CEOs of the chartered banks to voluntarily restrict or expand credit or other loans, in an effort to control the money supply.

Multiplier The ratio of the change in the equilibrium level of real national income to the change in autonomous expenditures; the number by which a change in autonomous investment or autonomous consumption, for example, is multiplied to get the change in the equilibrium level of real national income.

National income (NI) The total of all factor payments to resource owners. It can be obtained by subtracting indirect business taxes less subsidies from NDP.

National income accounting A measurement system used to estimate national income and its components; one approach to measuring an economy's aggregate performance.

Natural rate of unemployment The rate of unemployment that is estimated to prevail in long-run macroeconomic equilibrium, when all workers and employers have fully adjusted to any changes in the economy.

Near bank Financial institutions such as trust companies, credit unions and *caisses populaires* that offer most of the same services as commercial banks.

Net domestic product (NDP) GDP minus depreciation.

Net investment Gross private domestic investment minus an estimate of the wear and tear on the existing capital stock. Net investment therefore measures the change in capital stock over a one-year period.

Net public debt Gross public debt minus the value of financial assets held by government agencies.

Net worth The difference between assets and liabilities.

New classical model A modern version of the classical model in which wages and prices are flexible, there is pure competition in all markets, and the rational expectations hypothesis is assumed to be working.

New growth theory A relatively modern theory of economic growth which examines the factors that determine why technology, research, innovation, and the like are undertaken and how they interact.

New Keynesian economics Economic models based on the idea that demand creates its own supply as a result of various possible government fiscal and monetary coordination failures.

Nominal rate of interest The market rate of interest expressed in today's dollars.

Nominal values The values of variables such as GDP and investment expressed in current dollars, also called *money values;* measurement in terms of the actual market prices at which goods are sold.

Nonaccelerating inflation rate of unemployment (NAIRU) The rate of unemployment below which the rate of inflation tends to rise and above which the rate of inflation tends to fall.

Nondurable consumer goods Consumer goods that are used up within three years.

Nonincome expense items The total of indirect business taxes less subsidies and depreciation.

Non-personal notice deposits Interest-earning funds deposited by firms at chartered banks which can in practice be withdrawn at any time without payment of a penalty.

Nonprice rationing devices All methods used to ration scarce goods that are price-controlled. Whenever the price system is not allowed to work, nonprice rationing devices will evolve to ration the affected goods and services.

Normal goods Goods for which demand rises as income rises. Most goods are considered normal.

Normative economics Analysis involving value judgments about economic policies; relates to whether things are good or bad. A statement of *what ought to be.*

North American Free Trade Agreement (NAFTA) A free trade agreement between Canada, the United States, and Mexico which covers about 80 percent of our exports.

Open economy effect One of the reasons that the aggregate demand curve slopes downward is because higher price levels result in foreigners' desiring to buy fewer Canadian-made goods while Canadians now desire more foreign-made goods, thereby reducing net exports, which is equivalent to a reduction in the amount of real goods and services purchased in Canada.

Open market operations The purchase and sale of existing Canadian government securities (such as bonds) in the open private market by the Bank of Canada.

Opportunity cost The highest-valued, next-best alternative that must be sacrificed to attain something or to satisfy a want.

Par value The legally established value of the monetary unit of one country in terms of that of another.

Passive (nondiscretionary) policymaking Policymaking that is carried out in response to a rule. It is therefore not in response to an actual or potential change in overall economic activity.

Patent A government protection that gives an inventor the exclusive right to make, use, or sell an invention for a limited period of time (currently, 20 years in Canada).

Personal income (PI) The amount of income that households actually receive before they pay personal income taxes.

Phillips curve A curve showing the relationship between unemployment and changes in wages or prices. It was long thought to reflect a trade-off between unemployment and inflation.

Physical capital All manufactured resources, including buildings, equipment, machines, and improvements to land that is used for production.

Policy irrelevance proposition The new classical and rational expectations conclusion that policy actions have no real effects in the short run if the policy actions are anticipated and none in the long run even if the policy actions are unanticipated.

Positive economics Analysis that is strictly limited to making either purely descriptive statements or scientific predictions; for example, "If *A*, then *B*." A statement of *what is.*

Precautionary demand Holding money to meet unplanned expenditures and emergencies.

Price ceiling A legal maximum price that may be charged for a particular good or service.

Price controls Government-mandated minimum or maximum prices that may be charged for goods and services.

Price floor A legal minimum price below which a good or service may not be sold. Legal minimum wages are an example.

Price index The cost of today's market basket of goods expressed as a percentage of the cost of the same market basket during a base year.

Price system An economic system in which relative prices are constantly changing to reflect changes in supply and demand for different commodities. The prices of those commodities are signals to everyone within the system as to what is relatively scarce and what is relatively abundant.

Principle of rival consumption The recognition that individuals are rivals in consuming private goods because one person's consumption reduces the amount available for others to consume.

Private goods Goods that can be consumed by only one individual at a time. Private goods are subject to the principle of rival consumption.

Privatization The sale or transfer of state-owned property and businesses to the private sector, in part or in whole. Also refers to *contracting out*—letting private business take over government-provided services such as garbage collection.

Producer durables, or capital goods Durable goods having an expected service life of more than three years that are used by businesses to produce other goods and services.

Producer Price Index (PPI) A statistical measure of a weighted average of prices of commodities that firms purchase from other firms.

Production Any activity that results in the conversion of resources into products that can be used in consumption.

Production possibilities curve (PPC) A curve representing all possible combinations of total output that could be produced assuming (1) a fixed amount of productive resources of a given quality, and (2) the efficient use of those resources.

Progressive taxation A tax system in which as income increases, a higher percentage of the additional income is taxed. The marginal tax rate exceeds the average tax rate as income rises.

Property rights The rights of an owner to use and to exchange property.

Proportional rule A decision-making system in which actions are based on the proportion of the "votes" cast and are in proportion to them. In a market system, if 10 percent of the "dollar votes" are cast for blue cars, 10 percent of the output will be blue cars.

Proportional taxation A tax system in which regardless of an individual's income, the tax bill comprises exactly the same proportion. Also called a *flat-rate tax.*

Public debt The total value of all outstanding federal government securities.

Public goods Goods to which the principle of rival consumption does not apply; they can be jointly consumed by many individuals simultaneously at no additional cost and with no reduction in quality or quantity.

Purchasing power The value of money for buying goods and services. If your money income stays the same but the price of one good that you are buying goes up, your effective purchasing power falls, and vice versa.

Purchasing power parity Adjustment in exchange rate conversions that takes into account differences in the true cost of living across countries.

Quota A set amount of output (less than the equilibrium amount) which farmers can supply to marketing boards for sale.

Quota system A government-imposed restriction on the quantity of a specific good that another country is allowed to sell in Canada. In other words, quotas are restrictions on imports. These restrictions are usually applied to one or several specific countries.

Rational expectations hypothesis A theory stating that people combine the effects of past policy changes on important economic variables with their own judgment about the future effects of current and future policy changes.

Rationality assumption The assumption that people do not intentionally make decisions that would leave them worse off.

Real-balance effect The change in the real value of money balances when the price level changes, all other things held constant. Also called the *wealth effect.*

Real business cycle theory An extension and modification of the theories of the new classical economists of the 1970s and 1980s, in which money is neutral and only real, supply-side factors matter in influencing labour employment and real output.

Real rate of interest The nominal rate of interest minus the anticipated rate of inflation.

Real values Measurement of economic values after adjustments have been made for changes in the average of prices between years.

Recession A period of time during which the rate of growth of business activity is consistently less than its long-term trend, or is negative.

Recognition time lag The time required to gather information about the current state of the economy.

Redeposits A way to increase the money supply. The Bank of Canada transfers some of its Government of Canada deposits to the reserve deposits of the chartered banks, thus increasing the available reserves at the chartered banks.

Regressive taxation A tax system in which as more dollars are earned, the percentage of tax paid on them falls. The marginal tax rate is less than the average tax rate as income rises.

Relative price The price of a commodity expressed in terms of another commodity.

Rent control The placement of price ceilings on rents.

Repricing, or menu, cost of inflation The cost associated with recalculating prices and printing new price lists when there is inflation.

Reserves In the Canadian banking system, deposits held by the chartered banks at the Bank of Canada, and vault cash.

Resource allocation The assignment of resources to specific uses by determining what will be produced, how it will be produced, and for whom it will be produced.

Resources Things used to produce other things to satisfy people's wants.

Retained earnings Earnings that a corporation saves, or retains, for investment in other productive activities; earnings that are not distributed to stockholders.

Ricardian equivalence theorem The proposition that an increase in the government budget deficit has no effect on aggregate demand.

Saving The act of not consuming all of one's current income. Whatever is not consumed out of spendable income is, by definition, saved. *Saving* is an action measured over time (a flow), whereas *savings* are a stock, an accumulation resulting from the act of saving in the past.

Savings deposits Interest-earning funds at chartered banks that can be withdrawn at any time without payment of a penalty.

Say's law A dictum of economist J. B. Say that supply creates its own demand; producing goods and services generates the means and the willingness to purchase other goods and services.

Scarcity A situation in which the ingredients for producing the things that people desire are insufficient to satisfy all wants.

Seasonal unemployment Unemployment resulting from the seasonal pattern of work in specific industries. It is usually due to seasonal fluctuations in demand or to changing weather conditions, rendering work difficult, if not impossible, as in the agriculture, construction, and tourist industries.

Services Mental or physical labour or help purchased by consumers. Examples are the assistance of doctors, lawyers, dentists, repair personnel, housecleaners, educators, retailers, and wholesalers; things purchased or used by consumers that do not have physical characteristics.

Shortage A situation in which quantity demanded is greater than quantity supplied at a price below the market clearing price.

Short-run aggregate supply curve The relationship between aggregate supply and the price level in the short run, all other things held constant; the curve is normally positively sloped.

Small-menu cost theory A hypothesis that it is costly for firms to change prices in response to demand changes because of the cost of renegotiating contracts, printing price lists, and so on.

Socialism An economic system in which the state owns the major share of productive resources except labour. Socialism also usually involves the redistribution of income.

Special drawing rights (SDRs) Reserve assets created by the International Monetary Fund that countries can use to settle international payments.

Specialization The division of productive activities among persons and regions so that no one individual or area is totally self-sufficient. An individual may specialize, for example, in law or medicine. A nation may specialize in the production of lobsters, computers, or cameras.

Stock The quantity of something, measured at a given point in time—for example, an inventory of goods or a bank account. Stocks are defined independently of time, although they are assessed at a point in time.

Store of value The ability to hold value over time; a necessary property of money.

Structural unemployment Unemployment resulting from fundamental changes in the structure of the economy. It occurs, for example, when the demand for a product falls drastically so that workers specializing in the production of that product find themselves out of work.

Subsidy A negative tax; a payment to a producer from the government, usually in the form of a cash grant.

Substitutes Two goods are substitutes when either one can be used to satisfy a similar want—for example, coffee and tea. The more you buy of one, the less you buy of the other. For substitutes, the change in the price of one causes demand for the other to shift in the same direction as the price change.

Supply A schedule showing the relationship between price and quantity supplied for a specified period of time, other things being equal.

Supply curve The graphical representation of the supply schedule; a line (curve) showing the supply schedule, which generally slopes upward (has a positive slope), other things being equal.

Supply-side economics The notion that creating incentives for individuals and firms to increase productivity will cause the aggregate supply curve to shift outward.

Surplus A situation in which quantity supplied is greater than quantity demanded at a price above the market clearing price.

Tax bracket A specified interval of income to which a specific and unique marginal tax rate is applied.

Tax incidence The distribution of tax burdens among various groups in society.

Technology Society's pool of applied knowledge concerning how goods and services can be produced.

Terms of exchange The terms under which trading takes place. Usually the terms of exchange are equal to the price at which a good is traded.

Theory of public choice The study of collective decision making.

Third parties Parties who are not directly involved in a given activity or transaction.

Total income The yearly amount earned by the nation's resources (factors of production). Total income therefore includes wages, rents, interest, and profits that are received, respectively, by workers, landowners, capital owners, and entrepreneurs.

Transaction costs All of the costs associated with exchanging, including the informational costs of finding out price and quality, service record, and durability of a product, plus the cost of contracting and enforcing that contract.

Transactions demand Holding money as a medium of exchange to make payments. The level varies directly with nominal national income.

Transfer payments Money payments made by governments to individuals for which in return no services or goods are concurrently rendered. Examples are welfare, old age security payments, and Employment Insurance benefits.

Transfers in kind Payments that are in the form of actual goods and services, such as public education, low-cost public housing, and health care, and for which in return no goods or services are rendered concurrently.

Unanticipated inflation Inflation at a rate that comes as a surprise, either higher or lower than the rate anticipated.

Unemployment The total number of adults aged 15 years or older who are willing and able to work, and who are actively looking for work but have not found a job.

Unit of account A measure by which prices are expressed; the common denominator of the price system; a central property of money.

Value added The dollar value of an industry's sales minus the value of intermediate goods (for example, raw materials and parts) used in production.

Voluntary exchange An act of trading, done on a voluntary basis, in which both parties to the trade are subjectively better off after the exchange.

Voluntary export restraint (VER) An official agreement with another country that "voluntarily" restricts the quantity of its exports to Canada.

Wait unemployment Unemployment that is caused by wage rigidities resulting from minimum wages, unions, and other factors.

Wants What people would buy if their incomes were unlimited.

Wealth The stock of assets owned by a person, household, firm, or country. For a household, wealth can consist of a house, cars, personal belongings, bank accounts, and cash.

World Trade Organization (WTO) The successor organization to GATT, it handles all trade disputes among its 117 member nations.

INDEX